Automating Software Design

Automating Software Design

*Edited by Michael R. Lowry
and Robert D. McCartney*

Menlo Park / Cambridge / London

AAAI Press / The MIT Press

Research for the following chapters of this book was sponsored by a number of government and sponsoring agencies. The views, opinions, and conclusions contained in
this book are the authors' and should not be interpreted as representing the official
opinion or policy of any granting agency including the U.S. Government or any agency thereof.

The research in chapter 4 by W. Lewis Johnson and Martin S. Feather was sponsored in part by the Air Force
Systems Command, Rome Air Development Center, under contracts F30602-85-C-0221 and F30602-89-C-
0103. It was also sponsored in part by the Defense Advanced Research Projects Agency under contract no.
NCC-2-520.

The research reported in chapter 10 by Jack Mostow, was supported in part by the Defense Advanced Re-
search Projects Agency (DARPA) under Contract Number N00014-85-K-0116, in part by the National Sci-
ence Foundation (NSF) under Grant Number DMC-8610507, and in part by the Center for Computer Aids to
Industrial Productivity (CAIP), Rutgers University, with funds provided by the New Jersey Commission on
Science and Technology and by CAIP's industrial members. Portions of this chapter appeared in *Research on
Engineering Design*, 1(3): 167–186, © 1989, Springer-Verlag. Reprinted with permission.

The research reported in chapter 11 by Christopher Tong was supported in part by the Defense Advanced Research Projects Agency (DARPA) under Contract Number N00014-85-K-0116, in part by the National Science Foundation (NSF) under Grant Number DMC-8610507, and in part by the Center for Computer Aids to Industrial Productivity (CAIP), Rutgers University, with funds provided by the New Jersey Commission on Science and Technology and by CAIP's industrial members.

The research reported in chapter 12 by Wesley Braudaway, was supported in part by the Defense Advanced Research Projects Agency (DARPA) under Contract Number N00014-85-K-0116, in part by the National Science Foundation (NSF) under Grant Number DMC-8610507, and in part by the Center for Computer Aids to Industrial Productivity (CAIP), Rutgers University, with funds provided by the New Jersey Commission on Science and Technology and by CAIP's industrial members. The first author has also received support from IBM. Portions of this chapter are based on "Constraint Incorporation and the Structure Mismatch Problem." In Benjamin, Paul (ed.) *Change of Representation and Inductive Bias.* Kluwer Academic Publishers, © 1990. Reprinted with permission.

The research reported in chapter 13 by Robert McCartney has been supported in part by the Office of Naval Research Grant N00014-79-C-0529, and by the University of Connecticut Research Foundation Grant 1171-000-22-0506-35-046.

The research reported in chapter 14 by Jan Komorowski was supported by the FINSOFT III program sponsored by the Technology Development Center of Finland, the Finnish Academy, and a grant from the Norwegian Institute of Technology.

The research reported in chapter 15 by Robert J. Hall was conducted at the Artificial Intelligence Laboratory of the Massachusetts Institute of Technology. The lab's AI research is supported in part by the National Science Foundation under grant IRI-8616644, the Defense Advanced Research Projects Agency of the Department of Defense under naval research contract N00014-88-K-0487, IBM Corporation, NYNEX Corporation, and Siemens Corporation.

The research reported in chapter 16 was partially presented in an invited address at CSCSI'88 as well as at the IFIP TC10/WG10.1 Workshop on Concepts and Characteristics of Declarative Systems. This research was partially supported by NSERC grant OGP0036903.

The research reported in chapter 17 by Jeremy Wertheimer was conducted at the Artificial Intelligence Laboratory of the Massachusetts Institute of Technology. Support for the laboratory's AI research has been provided in part by the following organizations: National Science Foundation under grant IRI-8616644, Defense Advanced Research Projects Agency of the Department of Defense under Naval research contract N00014-88-K-0487, IBM Corporation, NYNEX Corporation, and Siemens Corporation. The author was supported by a National Science Foundation graduate fellowship. Support for this research during a visit by the author to Kestrel Institute was provided by the Air Force Office of Scientific Research under contract F49620-88-C-0033.

The research presented in chapter 18 by Uday Reddy was supported by National Aeronautics and Space Administration grant NAG-1-613, National Science Foundation grant CCR-87-00098, and a grant from Motorola Corporation.

The research presented in chapter 19 by Douglas R. Smith was supported in part by the Office of Naval Research under contract N00014-87-K-0550, the Rome Air Development Center under contracts F30602-86-C-0026 and F30602-88-C-0127, and the Air Force Office of Scientific Research under contract F49620-88-C-0033.

The research presented in chapter 20 by Michael Lowry was supported in part by the Office of Naval Research under contract N00014-87-K-0550.

The research presented in chapter 22 by David Steier sponsored in part by a Schlumberger Graduate Fellowship and the Defense Advanced Research Projects Agency (DARPA) and was monitored by the Air Force Avionics Laboratory under contracts F33615-81-K-1539 and F33615-87-C-1499 and the National Science Foundation (NSF) under grant DCR-84 12139. Preparation of this chapter was supported by the Engineering Design Research Center at Carnegie-Mellon University, an NSF-sponsored engineering research center.

Acknowledgments

The editors would like to thank the authors of the chapters in this book for putting in much more work than is expected from contributors to an edited collection. Their careful reviews of each other's chapters not only raised the quality of the material but also created a cohesion for the book as a whole.

Contents

Section One

Knowledge-Based Tools for Large Software Systems

Much of current software engineering research is driven by the development of large-scale embedded software systems. In contrast, our research is driven by a type of system known as very large information systems (VLISs), which are characterized by massive size and constant evolution rather than computational complexity and real-time performance requirements. In many real-world situations, reengineering is the only way to evolve VLIS. This chapter discusses the need for the renovation of information systems, the re-engineering strategy of system renovation, and the role of system specifications in the process of system re-engineering.

The difficulty of constructing and maintaining large software systems based on existing technology has become widely recognized. A primary challenge is the need to access up-to-date information about a complex and evolving system. Our research is in applying explicit knowledge representation and reasoning to the management of information about large systems. The LaSSIE system is a prototype that uses a frame-based description language and makes inferences based on its classification hierarchy.

Section Four

Knowledge Compilation

This chapter presents the techniques implemented in the RICK compiler, a refinement-based constraint incorporator for compiling knowledge. RICK is a prototype program that constructs constrained generators using least commitment, top-down refinement of the solution representation. RICK avoids the structure mismatch problem for local constraints by using an abstract solution representation rather than prematurely committing to an inadequate parameter representation.

This chapter examines the role of sibling independence in algorithm synthesis in the context of the MEDUSA system. The author defines functional dependence, looks at the associated problems, considers restricted alternatives to complete independence, and discusses the effects of these alternatives on the control of an algorithm synthesizer.

This chapter discusses a restricted form of function sharing—a redistribution of intermediate results—in the domain of program optimization. Redistributions are studied that can be implemented by the introduction of new local variables, additional function arguments, and additional function return values. Examples are given showing that these optimizations can capture many well-known types of optimizations.

Section Five

Formal Derivation Systems

The work presented in this chapter aims at narrowing the gap between declarative and procedural knowledge in a systematic and correct way. A refinement calculus based on a simple but powerful principle of partial deduction is defined. An environment that was implemented providing an experimental test bed is presented.

The paradigm of predicative programming sets a long-range goal for a way to produce software. The program synthesis project LOPS, which has realized a strategic and knowledge-based approach to software design, is a step toward this goal. This chapter discusses the paradigm and briefly reviews the project.

Section Six

Cognitive and Planning Approaches to Software Design

Conclusion

Foreword

Cordell Green

The field of knowledge-based software engineering (KBSE) is maturing and producing a steady flow of results. Progress is being made, not only in the laboratory but also in practice. The number of industrial applications is growing, with several successes in both software development and maintenance reported in this book. Many researchers world-wide are codifying software knowledge and experimenting with technology that will allow us to create and shape software much more quickly and surely.

This book presents selected articles from the proceedings of two workshops on "Automating Software Design" held at AAAI in 1988 and IJCAI in 1989. Each workshop was attended by over 60 researchers working in the field. During the summer of 1990 each article was carefully updated, reviewed by both the editors and other authors, and then revised. Overall the book provides a broad picture of the state of the art in KBSE. The variety and scope of the work reported here is impressive and is representative of the field, but is by no means exhaustive. References are included to guide the interested reader into the literature.

This book is intended for practitioners, graduate students, and researchers from the fields of artificial intelligence, software engineering, and formal methods. Much of the content addresses the application of artificial intelligence techniques and formal methods to software engineering. The field of programming languages also plays a key role in these inter-relationships. The exposition of the commonality between these fields should be of value to people working in all these fields, which are of necessity interdisciplinary.

Advances in Theory

My first experience in the field of automatic program synthesis was in 1967 when I started using theorem provers for program synthesis and plan synthesis. I worked out how to incrementally construct programs from proofs, and how to fit situation calculus into logic. This was adequate formally, but was missing the knowledge base needed to provide enough power. At that time, very few researchers were pursuing the field, and more research was needed to develop the knowledge bases.

Since then, the field has broadened to include other aspects of KBSE, and has and progressed. On the research front, there have been considerable advances in knowledge bases as well as in research frameworks, specification methods, program synthesis, and program analysis. Recent work in program synthesis, like earlier work, has also been applied to plan synthesis by exploiting the natural analogy between programs and plans.

Research frameworks were explored in the 1970s and further refined in the 1980s. Large, coherent national projects such as the US Air Force's Knowledge-based Software Assistant project are developing frameworks for the integration of the work of several research groups into systems aimed at the entire software life cycle. Not only have frameworks for the whole life cycle been developed, but also significant emphasis has been placed on program synthesis. Here two formalisms have been explored — predicate calculus and transformations, both reviewed in the introduction.

The content of the knowledge bases has been the focus of important research. Formalized knowledge has been developed for such important general design methods as divide and conquer, finite difference, local search, and global search. Formalized domain-specific knowledge has also been developed to complement the general design theories. Together, these knowledge bases and the accompanying tools allow higher-level starting points to specify problems as well as a more natural style of derivations of more optimized implementations. The higher-level starting point for automated program synthesis is a very high-level specification language. Very high-level specifications are closer to application domain requirements and are simpler than the software they specify. Such languages have evolved to a point where they are quite adequate to specify many, if not most, applications.

The most costly part of the software life cycle is the maintenance phase. This includes enhancement, porting to new platforms, bug fixes, change management and many associated activities. Such changes are also referred to as software re-engineering. Two aspects discussed in this book that yield to knowledge-based technology are the continued evolution of software specifications, and the re-engineering of existing bodies of code. The re-engineering aspect is especially important economically since most software costs deal with re-engineering the vast amount of software already in existence.

Significant economy and reliability will be obtained by maintaining and evolving software at the specification level. By having the capability for automatic generation of code from specifications, only the simpler specifications need be maintained and evolved. Specification evolution is a new and very interesting subfield of software maintenance and design. It consists of the theory and practice of modifying specifications via appropriate transformation rules. These transformations typically preserve key invariants in the requirements while introducing desired changes. These rules work at the specification level and incorporate ancillary changes that are known to be necessary to avoid modification errors. The research challenge is to find a coherent and useful transformation knowledge base for such design modifications.

What about re-engineering? It appears that re-engineering will be the first practical application of KBSE technology. Detailed formal representations of software objects, including requirements, specifications, code, and project management knowledge have been worked out and have been represented in knowledge bases. These representations enable not only knowledge-based synthesis, but also more intelligent analysis and other assistance. Better analysis lays the groundwork for better reverse engineering and re-engineering. Reverse engineering is the process of analyzing, documenting and abstracting existing code. Reverse engineering is the first step in re-engineering. Much can be done here with current technology, although the difficult task of automatically abstracting very high-level specifications from code remains a challenge.

Knowledge-based technology is compatible with conventional software engineering techniques for scaling up to large applications, such as modularization and abstraction. Furthermore, it can augment these conventional techniques with intelligent project management, configuration management, testing and other intelligent assistance in the software life cycle.

Scaling up: From Theory to Practice

The technology reported here is of great value to real world software engineering. Many aspects of the software development process can benefit from techniques reported in this book. One obvious benefit is the combination of rapid prototyping and automated derivation of efficient implementations, but there are more benefits and some may have a major effect on practicing software engineers sooner.

Is it really possible for this technology to enter the software mainstream? Yes, it is happening. The availability of workstations with large address spaces and other suitable tools has been a major enabling technology. Another factor is that barriers to acceptance are being lowered as a result of specialization of the technology to particular areas. The technology has been specialized not only to particular applications, but also to particular languages and particular phases of the software life cycle. This book presents contributions in all these areas.

If the transition path to knowledge-based technology is painless and unobtrusive, timely market acceptance is possible. One such path is to allow developers to continue to work on the same code, and in the same language they have used in the past. For instance, packages of knowledge-based utilities for reverse engineering and re-engineering existing software can minimally perturb the typical organization's current software maintenance methods. Developers and maintainers can continue to work in their preferred language with their favorite tools, but can use new, unobtrusive analysis packages that help them understand their existing software.

Dozens of industrial pilot applications are already in existence. The technology has been shown to scale up to large applications. For instance, there are currently knowledge-based reverse engineering tools that analyze software systems containing several million lines of code. The complexity of the analysis remains near linear in the size of the software being analyzed. In these early practical successes, very large bodies of code are transformed by modest-sized rule bases. The short development times to develop such rule bases for the automation of large tasks has attractive economics.

I anticipate accelerated progress in the 1990s. The combined capabilities of transformation rule systems, knowledge bases for representing software, and other technologies have matured enough so that these knowledge-based methods now have an advantage over more conventional technology in large software engineering applications. Successful industrial pilot applications, advances in workstations, and the number of people working in the field, all point to significant advances in both applications and research in the coming decade.

Note to Readers

I recommend reading McCartney's rational introduction to the terrain and then selected papers of interest. The papers are grouped into sections with introductions that overview each section. Lowry's concluding chapter includes future projections which may help guide the reader on the impact and future evolution of the field.

Knowledge-Based Software Engineering: Where We Are and Where We Are Going

Robert McCartney

The first disappointment for most users of computers is that real computers are not like those in science fiction stories—rather than responding to simple requests, they demand textual input in some arcane language. Even an expert user ultimately faces this problem: Computers are not easy to program. Software design automation is an attempt to deal with this fundamental problem. The approach examined in this book integrates methods from AI with those from software engineering; we refer to this approach as *knowledge-based software engineering* (KBSE). Research in this area will contribute not only to the efficient design of software but also to both AI and software engineering in general.

Developing a software system is a creative task, requiring intelligence, expertise, and discipline in the designers. The underlying goal of software engineering is to make software production more efficient by managing the complexity of software design and maintenance. Software engineering has improved programming (primarily) in two ways: by raising the level of the source code (originally using assemblers, now using increasingly more sophisticated compilers) and by using techniques that impose discipline on the structure of the design, such as well-described modules with defined interfaces. Overall, the goal is software that can be understood; if the code is understandable, then it is easier to test, debug, verify, and maintain.

The Software Crisis

Over the last few years, advances in hardware performance (and price) have far outpaced gains in software productivity, to the point that the limiting factor in computerization is software. This limitation should be no surprise: The improvements in hardware technology have not only been of unprecedented scale, but they were largely based on improving existing features—faster processors, larger and faster memory. In software development, a few limiting features can be identified, but the process is generally not well understood, especially as projects scale up to large groups of programmers.

Brooks (1987) argues that software is fundamentally more complex than other human artifacts. First, software systems have fewer repeated elements for their size than other products (above the level of source statements) because of the use of subroutines. Contrast this condition with the structural regularity of memory chips, for example. Second, scaling up software systems has a nonlinear effect on complexity; a larger system includes a larger number of potentially interacting parts. This complexity has management, as well as technical, effects because the increased complexity makes it more difficult to maintain an overview of the system under development and avoid interactions between parts of the system being developed by different people or groups. Third, software is constantly being modified after development. Multiple versions produced by field changes are either absent or extremely rare in most products but are the rule in software systems.

The development and maintenance of software is a labor-intensive task. It is limited by the supply and quality of software professionals as well how effectively they are used. The demand for large, complex computer systems has risen faster than the capacity for producing them; as a result, large projects are typically late and over budget. A particularly severe problem is maintenance. To maintain a system requires understanding, and systems are harder to understand, in part because of their size and complexity but also because their function and execution environments change over time. A structure and algorithms that made sense under an old environment might be completely opaque in the current one, adding to the confusion of the typically junior people whose job it is to keep the programs running. Current estimates put maintenance at 80 percent of the life-cycle cost of the average software system, and indications are that this cost will increase.

Knowledge Is Power

In all phases of software development, having access to the appropriate knowledge can lead to success. Most of the problems incurred in software development can be traced to the lack of (or incorrect) knowledge: The specification is not well understood by the programmer, the desired behavior is not well understood by the requirement analyst or the user, the programmers of one subsystem do not understand the effects their code has on overall system performance, and so on. Moreover, when code is written, a lot of information is simply lost; the code is a distillation of many design decisions from requirement specifications down. Some of these decisions might be available for examination at the end of the process and later usable during maintenance, but these decisions are exceptions. Typically, little (if any) of the decision history is explicit. For example, the documentation rarely includes information about approaches that were considered and rejected for some reason. Even if such information were explicitly available, its volume could make it impossible to use.

In a practical sense, the focus of AI is dealing with knowledge: how to represent it, how to reason with it, and how to extract useful information from large amounts of it. Purely from an information-handling standpoint, AI techniques should be able to improve the software engineering process if the knowledge used is explicitly represented. However, AI has a purpose other than simply dealing with knowledge, that is, to reproduce cognitive processes, to be able to exhibit intelligent behavior. Although the long-term goal of general-purpose intelligence will not likely be reached soon, real progress is possible in restricted domains. Specifically, people in the KBSE community are working on systems that perform tasks that are now performed by human programmers and designers, such as decomposing a task into subtasks or performing nonlocal optimizations on source code. The goal is to automate much of the process; the approach is to automate different parts of the process, learning what techniques and tools are effective for the ultimate goal while providing increased productivity.

Knowledge-Based Software Engineering and Computer-Aided Software Engineering

A number of tools are commercially available that are classed as computer-aided software-engineering (CASE) tools. These tools, which provide a step toward software automation, fall into three categories. *Code generators* are programs that can be used to generate special-purpose (routine) software, such as reports and graphic interfaces, which are often interactively specified by filling in templates on a display. *Analysis and design aids* track systems at the intermodule level, checking for overall consistency of the module hierarchy and data-structure use, for example. *Project management tools* help managers lay out a project in terms of dependencies, plan the project, and monitor its progress. The ultimate goal in CASE is integrated tools that support all phases of the software process, allowing information from one phase to be used in another. This information sharing typically involves the use of databases to store and access information from the various tools.

The capabilities of CASE tools can be extended in two ways by the application of AI techniques. At the simplest level,the evolutionary approach involves replacing the databases currently used in CASE tools with knowledge bases. *Knowledge bases* are augmentations of databases. In addition to facts, they contain rules and inference mechanisms, which allow new facts to be inferred from combinations of other facts, and often include other specialized mechanisms such as support for objects and feature inheritance. Knowledge bases, therefore, can support reasoning; rather than simply storing facts, a user can generally specify (using rules) how facts can be used to infer other facts, and the mechanisms provided will perform these inferences. The increased reasoning ability can be used to improve the performance and range of current CASE tools, not by fundamentally changing the process but by increasing the quality of the information available. This approach is being explored in the CASE research community (Chen, Nunamaker, and Weber 1989).

As an alternative, the application of AI techniques can be used to fundamentally change the notion of CASE. If we really want to provide life-cycle support to software systems, we need to provide more than is offered by the previous CASE view. First, we can formalize the knowledge used in the development process. This formalization means having a defined specification language and an explicit set of operators (refinements) that can be applied to the specification or the code at the various stages of development. Second, we can develop and use formal domain models. Software cannot be understood in a vacuum; it is necessary to also understand the application domain. Having the domain knowledge separate from the programming knowledge will facilitate the transfer of tools from one domain to another. Third, we can change the software process so that verification and maintenance are done on the specification rather than the source code. One of our goals is to make the process of going from specification to code as easy as possible—when it becomes easy enough, it will be feasible to make any changes on the specification and use the design system to reimplement from there.

Producing fully automated systems that develop code from the specification is one way to make the desired process change, but there are more easily attained alternatives. Suppose our systems are not fully automated but remember all the decisions made during development. If the decision information is sufficiently detailed (and accessible), then it could be useful in understanding the software, particularly during maintenance. Furthermore, it should be possible to make changes to the specification and then replay the decision sequence, only altering from the first design where changes make it necessary. Reusing this sequence demands that we are able to reason about the system throughout the design. It is not enough to know what the decisions were; it is necessary to understand the rationale behind the decisions—what goals were being met, what conditions led us to this choice, and so forth. Reasoning at this level of sophistication is not trivial and demands the level of understanding that the aforementioned formalization can provide.

Some Context for This Book

One way to provide a context for the chapters in this book would be to present a survey of the previous work. I chose not to however; the interested reader is encouraged to read any of a number of published surveys and collections (Balzer 1985; Barr and Feigenbaum 1982; Lowry and Duran 1989; Rich and Waters 1986). Instead, in the next two sections, I look at some techniques that are commonly used in KBSE and then examine the software life cycle, characterizing different phases and the corresponding KBSE issues. Finally, I give an overview of the contents of the book.

Fundamental Techniques

Early work in KBSE was primarily concerned with the problem of *program synthesis*, the process of going from a formal specification to executable code. It is in this context that I briefly examine three approaches to this problem: theorem proving, transformational implementation, and interactive programming environments. These approaches can be (and have been) applied to all phases of the software development cycle; combinations and variants of these approaches appear in every chapter of this collection.

Theorem Proving

The theorem-proving approach to programming was based on the observation (Floyd 1967) that a program could be derived from a formal specification and the use of techniques such as the resolution method (Robinson 1965) for automating proofs in first-order logic. In particular, suppose I specify a program with input x and output y by a set of conditions that must hold on the input, $P(x)$, and a set of conditions that must hold on the input and output of the program after it is executed, $Q(x,y)$. I attempt to prove the statement

$$\forall x \, \exists y \, [P(x) \rightarrow Q(x,y)] \, .$$

I perform this proof by attempting to construct the program f such that

$$\forall x \, [P(x) \rightarrow Q(x,f(x))] \, .$$

If I succeed, then f is the desired program. In the late 1960s, Green (1969) and Waldinger and Lee (1969) showed how programs could be built as a side effect to a resolution proof and successfully demonstrated the approach. In later work, Manna and Waldinger (1980) developed the *nonclausal resolution rule,* which leads to proofs that are shorter and easier to follow.

There are two fundamental difficulties with a purely deductive approach. First, the proof procedures are computationally very expensive. Both resolution and nonclausal resolution are sound and complete inference mechanisms for which programs can be written, but neither efficiently constructs proofs. The computational constraints preclude the synthesis of all but short programs. Second, the use of these techniques demands that the user provide a formal domain theory and specification. This approach is expensive and demands different skills than those possessed by most programmers.

Transformational Approaches

Another approach to software development involves the use of transformation rules. The object is to start with a specification that corresponds to an implementation of the desired program (but one that is inefficient or includes constructs that are not directly executable), then perform incremental changes on this specification. After some number of these changes, the program is executable and functionally equivalent to the specification. Each incremental change is implemented by a transformation: A construct in the program is replaced by a new one. If all the individual transformations preserver correctness, then a transformed program will satisfy the specification of the program that was transformed.

The allowable transformations can be specified as rules; either simple rewrite rules of the form $a \rightarrow b$, where a is a pattern matching something in the program, and b is the pattern replacing a, or as conditional rewrite rules of the form *if c then a $\rightarrow$ b,* where the transformation of a to b is only permitted if condition c holds. As an example, consider the following: To test whether a predicate P holds for all elements of a non-empty list, I can test whether it is true for the first element and all the tail elements. Given first and rest functions to decompose a list, this list can be expressed as the transform *if l is a non-empty list, then P(all (l)) $\rightarrow$ P(first (l)) and P(all(rest (l))).*

The fundamental difficulty with transformational systems is search control: (1) at any point in the synthesis, there are a number of possible transformations to apply; (2) a derivation can require thousands of transformations to reach its solution; and (3)the application order of the transformations need not correspond to the focused approach that a human designer would use, making the process difficult to monitor and evaluate.

Controlling search remains a fundamental research problem; various approaches have included large grain rules corresponding to programmer expertise, which lead to shorter (and more understandable) derivations (Barstow 1979), and using efficiency or other structural information to guide search (Kant 1979; McCartney 1987).

Interactive Tools

One way of dealing with the search problems inherent in the theorem-proving and transformational approaches is to make the system interactive—let the user supply the intuition and intelligence during synthesis by making the choices, and let the system track the results and the process where no decisions are needed. There are two difficulties that need to be addressed in moving to an interactive system: Both theorem proving and transformation can involve a huge number of small steps in the derivation, and the steps available do not necessarily correspond well with the primitives that a programmer might use in writing a program. These two difficulties mean that adding interaction at each choice point is not sufficient in developing a usable interactive system.

One response, exemplified by the Programmer's Apprentice and related projects (Rich and Waters 1988), could be termed *schema-based programming*. This approach is based on having a library of programming schemas (referred to as cliches by the Programmer's Apprentice researchers)—standard ways that programmers perform tasks—available in an editing environment. These schemas are represented as templates corresponding to programming tasks; when a task is recognized (by the user) in a specification, s/he chooses a schema to perform it, and the system instantiates it in place. Schemas correspond to large-scale transformation rules that add a lot of structure, leading therefore to relatively short derivations. Of equal importance, if these schemas correspond to structures natural to programmers, the programming process using one of these tools is similar to the one that programmers already use.

The use of schemas is not restricted to interactive systems, but well-chosen schemas are of great importance in making interactive environments useful. A side benefit of schemas is that they provide a method for *reverse engineering:* If you can recognize the schemas in the source code, the reverse transformations should provide assistance in inferring a specification from the implementation.

Another way of dealing with the large number (and difficulty) of steps taken in an interactive development is to provide a replay mechanism. The idea is that the first time a program is developed, it will require interaction for every step in the derivation. Suppose, however, we modify the program by modifying the specification: When the new program is derived, the steps will be the same as before except where the code reflects the changed specification. Because programs are typically modified a large number of times over their lifetime, the amortized interaction cost is low.

To make replay possible, the derivation must be augmented with its internal structure; the transformation process can be viewed as a top-down design tree, with the overall system goals and constraints at the root, intermediate goals and constraints at internal nodes, and transformation steps at the leaves. The PADDLE language (Wile 1983), which was designed to represent transformational derivations, made much of this information explicit. Other possible state information includes the rationale for decisions made, the conditions that allowed such decisions, and what overall system considerations influenced certain decisions. What information to store from the internal states in a derivation and how to reuse this information has remained an active area of research (Mostow 1989).

Knowledge-Based Software Engineering and the Software Life Cycle

Although researchers disagree on technique, they agree on a fundamental goal: integrated tools that operate over the entire software life cycle. The goal is a set of tools that operate from specification acquisition to code generation, tools that allow information from any phase of the development process to be available (and usable) at any other phase in the process. The extended automatic programming paradigm presented by Balzer (1985) exemplifies this view; it differs from the *waterfall model* currently in vogue at the Department of Defense (DOD Standard 2167A) primarily in the addition of feedback from later to earlier phases. This approach provides information on how decisions made at one stage are reflected later in the design and, therefore, can be used to incrementally improve the earlier phase. The *spiral model* of software development (Boehm 1986) involves repetition of the specify-design-code-validate cycle, starting with an easily specified and implemented prototype, then extending it on each repetition of the cycle. The common feature of these models is their lack of linearity; software development is not restricted to being a linear process from specification to implementation. Taken to their logical conclusions (correctness preserved from phase to phase, ability to remember, and reuse efforts), models of this sort have a great impact on maintenance and verification:

First, because correctness is preserved, and the ability to reuse implementations exists, maintenance (enhancing or changing system function) can be performed at a higher level than traditional source code—at the specification level for changed function and at the algorithm design level for a changed hardware-software environment. These changes are then percolated forward using replay to reuse the parts of the design that are unaffected by the changes. Second, understanding is enhanced by offering the user views at multiple levels of abstraction, everything from the specification to the output code. For example, optimization can obscure the original (clear) structure of a piece of code; having the intermediate-level designs available can solve this difficulty. Third, a feedback mechanism allows the user to evaluate a decision made at one phase with the effects it causes in later phases. Given an undesirable result, the user can identify and reevaluate the design decisions leading to this result. To reach the goal of an integrated software development environment, progress must be made on the individual phases of the process as well as on the questions involving replay and the use of information between phases.

One Phase or Many?

Current research can be characterized in part by the methods employed and in part by what phase of the software process it addresses. Some projects attempt integration over all phases—the development of representations, tools, and techniques that lead to systems that work, from requirements to implementation to maintenance. Dealing with global issues and interphase communication, these systems naturally use a top-down approach. Many current projects have taken the other tack: The bottom-up approach of focusing on one phase for now, deemphasizing the integration problems for the moment. This approach can be justified in part because some of the problems to be overcome are specific to a particular phase and in part because the success gained by concentration in one area will transfer to the others. Four phases that have separately been considered are specification acquisition, high-level design, implementation, and optimization.

Specification acquisition is the process of going from what a user wants—an informal description of the proposed system behavior—to a formal, unambiguous description of what the system will do. The specification does not describe the internal system structure but how the system responds to its input. Specification acquisition is complicated by the fact that users typically do not know exactly what they want, or they do not necessarily know the ramifications of what they want. The process requires a lot of domain information and is, by its nature, iterative.

High-level design, or algorithm synthesis, is the process of going from a functional specification of what a system does to an operational one. The output describes the structure of the solution in terms of algorithm structure, control, and data flow among modules whose description is independent of a particular implementation language. Among the issues being examined are how do we decompose a system into modules without performing unbounded search in the space of decompositions, what are (and how do we represent) the necessary set of decompositions, and what is the role of both general and domain knowledge in this process.

Implementation, the process of going from an operational specification to code in some language, is a relatively well-studied area. Current work is dominated by work on domain-specific systems. An early result (Barstow 1979) was that knowledge can effectively substitute for reasoning ability in writing programs; current work in a number of domains bears out this finding. Research in the area is often concerned with what information in a domain is useful, how this information can be represented, and how the information can be used by a system during the implementation process.

Optimization is the process by which working code is made more efficient. It is also the reason why a lot of code is difficult to understand. The idea of producing an understandable system and then optimizing it is compelling; the unoptimized system can be used for verification (and maintenance), and the optimized version has good performance. Research has concerned both local and global optimization techniques; although both techniques require an understanding of the semantics of the program, the problem is most critical for the global optimization techniques.

Overview of the Book

This book is a collection of edited papers that reflect current work as of 1990. The authors were chosen from participants in two workshops on automating software design, one held in Minneapolis in 1988 and the other in Detroit in 1989; most of the chapters are edited (and updated) versions of papers given at these workshops. The book does not present a unified front of what KBSE is or should be; rather, it presents the status of ongoing work by a number of different researchers. The work varies widely, not only in terms of approach but also in terms of practical applicability. Some of these projects are currently usable or reflected in commercial products; their technology is reasonably well understood and can lead to more efficient software design now. Other projects are of a more speculative nature, involving both problems that are beyond current capabilities and technologies that are as yet untested. The book contains 23 chapters, organized by topic into sections, as follows.

Large System Applications

In section 1, authors examine applications of KBSE for large systems. As a result of their size, these systems are particularly difficult to manage over time. Both of the articles in this section address the need to extract information from large, existing systems.

Devanbu, Ballard, Brachman, and Selfridge present the LASSIE system, which provides support for understanding and maintaining large software systems. It uses sophisticated knowledge representation and reasoning techniques to provide access to large systems, including multiple views of the system, the methods for browsing through the code, and retrieval of parts of a system for possible reuse in another application.

Alagappan and Kozacynski look at software design issues in the context of very large information systems. Although these systems do not involve a great deal of computational complexity, they are extremely large and are constantly being modified. The approach proposed for such systems is *re-en-*

gineering, a combination of recovering specifications from implementations and elaborating specifications to implementations.

Knowledge-Based Specification Tools

Section 2 deals primarily with specification acquisition tools. These tools provide interactive support for developing and modifying formal specifications.

Kelly and Nonnenmann present WATSON, a system that allows users to acquire formal specifications in the telephone configuration domain from informal traces of proposed behavior. This system inductively generates finite-state machines that produce the desired behavior, using domain knowledge to constrain the space of automata considered. An interesting feature of this work is the explicit partitioning of the knowledge to address different design concerns.

Johnson and Feather discuss ongoing work with ARIES, a tool designed to support requirements analysis and specification development. Their approach to specification development is evolutionary—a specification is evolved by applying meaning-changing transformations to a formal specification. To support this approach, they developed a library of such transformations. They discuss how their categorization supports both the use of the transformations and the assessment of the library containing them.

Lubars examines design reuse for software designed by refinement, including the interaction between requirements specification and design. He examines strategies for supporting reuse and shows how these ideas are developed and implemented in the ROSE-2 software reuse system, including mechanisms for dependency-directed backtracking and multiple design views.

Domain-Specific Program Synthesis

Section 3 presents work in domain-specific program synthesis—systems that are capable of generating sophisticated programs within a single domain.

Barstow discusses ΦNIX, which produces device-control software used in oil well logging. Device control is done in real time and involves the interaction of one or more devices with their environment over time. The ΦNIX, system uses streams to model this temporal interaction and supports both applicative and imperative programming constructs.

Kant examines how detailed data-attribute information considered from a number of viewpoints can be used to control synthesis, using examples from the mathematical modeling domain. She examines techniques for representing, propagating, and acquiring data attributes and relations and shows how such information can be used to guide automated software design.

Kant, Daube, MacGregor, and Wald discuss their work with the SINAPSE system, which generates finite-difference programs based on mathematical models described by partial differential equations. The system is implemented on top of a symbolic manipulation language, making the mathematical specification easier, and generates programs in Fortran, Connection Machine Fortran, and C.

Setliff presents results from ELF, a system that generates very large scale integration (VLSI) routing programs for different technologies based on user requirements. Knowledge about the particular technology and technology-independent program synthesis knowledge are used to design component algorithms and compatible data structures at an abstract level. A code-generation phase then takes this design information and generates executable router code. She presents experimental results of synthesizing routers and their performance on a number of benchmarks.

Knowledge Compilation

Section 4 addresses the need to design efficient algorithms. These chapters look at ways to integrate knowledge, and perform optimizations to meet this need without resorting to exhaustive search.

Mostow discusses a transformational model of *knowledge compilation,* the approach of integrating domain information into the synthesis of efficient algorithms. He illustrates this approach with an example of gear train design from the DIOGENES project. He evaluates what the potential is for improving computer-aided design using knowledge compilation and where progress needs to be made to achieve these improvements.

Tong presents results from the KBSDE project and discusses knowledge compilation as a classification process, assigning specification components to search algorithm components. This divide-and-conquer technique of partitioning the specification into separate components addresses the control problems inherent in transformational implementations.

Braudaway examines the refinement of generate-and-test programs, which are easy to describe and implement but typically too inefficient to practically use. By incorporating some or all of the test constraints in the generator, this inefficiency can be overcome; however, the choice of representation chosen for the solution can preclude this incorporation. He presents an approach (and examples) from the RICK program, which takes a least commitment approach to solution representation while it constructs constrained generators.

McCartney examines the effects of subtask independence on the search costs in algorithm design. He examines the search effects of functional dependence and considers implementations to support a restricted case of functional dependence. He also considers cost dependence and discusses the effects of using different cost metrics.

Hall looks at optimizing by redistributing intermediate results, a restricted form of function sharing. Although these optimizations are restricted, they are general enough to encompass a number of well-known optimization types. He presents what the correctness conditions are for using such optimizations and how his system can automatically derive and use approximations of these conditions to evaluate the correctness of potential redistributions.

Formal Program Derivation

Section 5 looks at a number of systems and topics in formal program derivation. Common threads include the development and implementation of tactics for search control.

Komorowski looks at the use of partial deduction in optimizing logic programs. *Partial deduction* can increase the efficiency of a logic program but can lead to an exponentially larger program. He presents tactics that are designed to allow the efficiency improvements without the exponential size increase. The tactics that rely on human expertise to target where optimizations are appropriate.

Bibel discusses concurrent software production (over the various phases) in light of his work with LOPS. He examines current software production practice and suggests ways to eliminate many of the problems inherent in the current approach.

Wertheimer gives a formal derivation of the RETE algorithm, which is used to incrementally keep partial match information for the preconditions of rules. The significance of this work is that it shows that a highly specific (and complex) algorithm can be derived from a specification using formal methods.

Reddy discusses FOCUS, a program design system that emphasizes human-oriented deductive techniques, a small search space, and a tree-based organization of program derivations. The system is flexible in regard to development strategies, and its storage of dependencies between parts of the derivation promotes the replay of derivations.

Smith describes the KIDS system, which can interactively be used to produce efficient software from a formal specification. He presents an example of deriving an algorithm that illustrates the use of algorithm design tactics, generalized deductive inference, program simplification, finite-differencing optimizations, and partial evaluation.

Lowry describes an algorithm design tactic for local search algorithms, based on formalizing the structure common to hill-climbing algorithms. An algorithm design tactic restricts search by guiding the derivation of algorithms in its class. He illustrates this process by showing how the STRATA system uses this tactic to derive the simplex algorithm from the specification of the linear optimization problem.

Heisel, Reif, and Stephan present results from the KIV system, a formal, interactive system that supports reasoning about imperative programs. Its flexibility allows its use in both program development and verification. They present examples illustrating how this system can be used to implement two program development methods found in the literature. Their system is sufficiently flexible to support both program development and program verification.

Cognitive and Planning Approaches to Software Design

Section 6 examines the applications of two AI technologies—learning and planning—to software design.

Steier presents results from DESIGNER-SOAR, an algorithm design system built on the SOAR problem-solving and learning architecture. In his theory of algorithm design, design is performed in multiple problem spaces (chosen opportunistically), means-end analysis on the desired results drives the design, and all the knowledge necessary for design can be acquired by learning.

Linden examines relationships between planning and software design. Recent research on incremental and reactive plan modification has shown the advantages gained from having highly detailed plan representations. He shows how these results can be transferred to software design, in particular with representations that encode the design process into the software.

Finally...

The book concludes with a vision of the future evolution of knowledge-based software engineering. Lowry examines how KBSE techniques promote additive programming methods and how they can be developed and introduced in an evolutionary way. He predicts that in the 1990s, significant commercial applications of KBSE are likely in software maintenance and domain-specific program synthesis. He explains how, in the next century, software engineering will be elevated to the discipline of capturing and automating currently undocumented domain and design knowledge.

Acknowledgements

The author gratefully acknowledges the help of Michael Lowry in the structure and content of this presentation. Thanks to Steve Demurjian at the University of Connecticut for engaging in discussions about the current direction of CASE from the software engineering perspective. Finally, I wish to thank Elaine Kant and Christopher Tong for their useful reviews.

References

Balzer, R. 1985. A 15-Year perspective on Automatic Programming. *IEEE Transactions on Software Engineering* SE-11:1257–1267.

Barr, A., and Feigenbaum, E., eds. 1982. *Handbook of Artificial Intelligence*, volume 2. Reading, Mass.: Addison-Wesley.

Barstow, D. R. 1979. An Experiment in Knowledge-Based Automatic Programming. *Artificial Intelligence* 12:73–119.

Boehm, B. W. 1986. A Spiral Model of Software Development and Enhancement. *ACM SIGSOFT Software Engineering Notes* 11(4): 22–42.

Brooks, F. P. , Jr. 1987. No Silver Bullet: Essence and Accidents of Software Engineering. *IEEE Computer* 20(4): 10-19.

Chen, M.; Nunamaker, J. F., Jr.; and Weber, E. S. 1989. Computer-Aided Software Engineering:

Present Status and Future Directions. *Data Base* 20(1): 7–13.

Floyd, R. W. 1967. Assigning Meaning to Programs. In Proceedings of the Symposia in Applied Mathematics 19:19–32.

Green, C. 1969. Application of Theorem Proving to Problem Solving. In Proceedings of the First International Joint Conference on Artificial Intelligence, 219–239. Menlo Park, Calif.: International Joint Conferences on Artificial Intelligence.

Kant, E. 1979. A Knowledge-Based Approach to Using Efficiency Estimation in Program Synthesis. In Proceedings of the Sixth International Joint Conference on Artificial Intelligence, 457–462. Menlo Park, Calif.: International Joint Conferences on Artificial Intelligence.

Lowry, M. R., and Duran, R. 1989. Knowledge-Based Software Engineering. In The Handbook of Artificial Intelligence, eds. A. Barr and P. Cohen. Reading, Mass.: Addison-Wesley.

McCartney, R. 1987. Synthesizing algorithms with Performance Constraints. In Proceedings of the Sixth National Conference on Artificial Intelligence, 149–154. Menlo Park, Calif.: American Association for Artificial Intelligence.

Manna, Z., and Waldinger, R. J. 1980. A Deductive Approach to Program Synthesis. *ACM Transactions on Programming Languages and Systems* 2(1): 90–121.

Mostow, J. 1989. Design by Derivational Analogy: Issues in the Automated Replay of Design Plans. Artificial Intelligence 40(1–3): 119–184.

Rich, C., and Waters, R. C. 1988. The Programmer's Apprentice: A Research Overview. *IEEE Computer* 21(11): 10–25.

Rich, C., and Waters, R. C. , eds. 1986. *Readings in Artificial Intelligence and Software Engineering*. San Mateo, Calif.: Morgan-Kaufmann.

Robinson, J. A. 1965. A Machine-Oriented Logic Based on the Resolution Principle. *Journal of the ACM* 12(1): 23–41.

Waldinger, R. J., and Lee, R. C. 1969. Prow: A Step toward Automatic Program Writing. In Proceedings of the First International Joint Conference on Artificial Intelligence, 241–252. Menlo Park, Calif.: International Joint Conferences on Artificial Intelligence.

Wile, D. S. 1983. Program Developments: Formal Explanations of Implementations. *Communications of the ACM* 26(11): 902–911.

Knowledge-Based Tools for Large Software Systems

Once confined to the research laboratory, knowledge-based software engineering has advanced to the stage of industrial pilot projects in certain areas. This section describes two projects applying knowledge-based techniques to the maintenance of large software systems. Software maintenance refers to the work done on a software system after it becomes operational. Studies consistently find that over half of the software-engineering resources are devoted to software maintenance. Thus, the potential impact of knowledge-based support for software maintenance is considerable.

The authors of the first chapter are members of a research laboratory at Andersen Consulting, one of the largest business software developers and system integrators in the world. Their experience gives them a practical perspective on the problems of maintaining very large information systems. A fundamental problem is that as a software system evolves to incorporate new requirements, it loses its coherency, and further modifications become increasingly difficult. Software ages because modifications are currently done as patches to source code rather than as changes to the specification followed by reimplementation. A side effect of this aging process is that the design documentation becomes outdated, and the source code becomes the only reliable information about the system. Thus, when extensive renovation is necessary, the design documentation is no longer a valid source of information. Re-engineering is necessary to recover the design of the existing system from the source code to reuse it in a new version of the system.

A difficult re-engineering task occurs in the renovation of older systems written in assembler language. The authors describe a working system that helps a programmer recover the logic of an assembler program and work in progress on recovering data-structure design. The system combines conventional code analysis techniques with knowledge-based methods for recognizing patterns and abstracting code. The result of the abstraction process is a design specification that can be merged using a computer-aided software engineering (CASE) tool with new requirements.

The first chapter concludes with a vision of the future of knowledge-based re-engi-neering. An integral component of this vision is the work on knowledge-based specification acquisition reported in the next section of this book. The later sections on program synthesis are also relevant to the goal of elevating system evolution from the code level to the specification level by enabling efficient programs to be automati-cally rederived from modified specifications.

The second chapter describes work done at AT&T Bell Laboratories by authors well known for their research on knowledge representation and natural language un-derstanding. They have applied this research to the development of LaSSIE, a knowl-edge-based software understanding system. LaSSIE helps programmers modify and maintain complicated telephone switching software by answering queries about the existing system. Software maintainers spend at least half their time trying to under-stand the system code, system documentation, and requests from users. Software un-derstanding can be so difficult that the authors call it the "discovery problem." Soft-ware understanding is a prerequisite to other maintenance activities such as bug-fixing or modification. Software understanding is also a prerequisite to retrieving existing code for reuse.

Because LaSSIE uses knowledge-based inference, it provides significant advan-tages over conventional bottom-up cross-referencing tools and database retrieval methods based on key words. The approach is to construct knowledge-based descrip-tions of different views of a software system and then to use formal inference methods to build taxonomic hierarchies. Some of these descriptions can automatically be gen-erated from source files, thus keeping these descriptions consistent with the latest version of the system. A user queries LaSSIE through a natural language front-end. Semantic processing techniques resolve ambiguities in queries and help the user browse through the knowledge base.

1

The Evolution of Very Large Information Systems

V. Alagappan and W. Kozaczynski

The understanding of software engineering problems and their appropriate solutions is derived from the target application systems, which for our clients are very large information systems (VLISs). *Information systems* are large integrated human-machine systems that provide information to support the operational, managerial, analytic, and decision-making functions of an organization. Information systems use computer hardware and software, models for analysis and planning, models for control and decision making, databases, and manual procedures. An information system is not a monolithic structure. Rather, it is a federation of subsystems that is developed according to a systemwide design plan. These subsystems are integrated and evolve over time to support the business functions.

Typically, the operational scope of an information system spans different levels of business activities and is characterized as a pyramid structure (figure 1). Each layer of the pyramid represents a class of information-processing activities and provides a processing foundation for levels above it. In general, as one ascends the layers of the pyramid: (1) the complexity of the

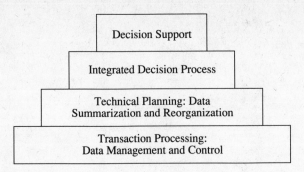

Figure 1. Pyramid Structure of Business Activities.

business problem being addressed increases; (2) the additional use of business-specific knowledge is required; (3) the degree of integration across activities increases; (4) the amount of information increases; and (5) the form of the information being processed becomes more complex.

The information system activities shown in figure 1 apply to all the important management responsibilities associated with normal business functions (for example, accounting, finance, production, operations, marketing, and sales). Information systems that support the business functions are often referred to as the "heart of the business" or the "business lifeline." Such information systems are totally ingrained in a business endeavor and generally function on a continuous basis. A loss of performance at any activity level in the pyramid would ultimately have an adverse effect on the organization's operations.

Information systems differ from real-time embedded control systems such as those used for missiles, manufacturing processes, and elevators. As is the case with embedded systems, information system development is concerned with the functional adequacy and performance of the software. However, information systems are more strongly characterized by relatively simple functional demands, massive size, enormous volumes of data, continuous use, and constant evolution. For example, consider the demands on the information system of a large credit card company with worldwide operations. Although the function of the business problem is relatively simple (transaction processing), the volume of data, the growth of the customer base, the geographic constraints of the market, the need to continually offer better services, and the need to operate the system on a continuous basis represent a dimension of complexity beyond that of the algorithmic requirements of the basic business function. In essence, the complexity of VLIS is rooted in the size of the system and the demographic complexity of the application environment rather than the algorithmic complexity of the business functions.

The system design process is often thought of as involving the creating, generating, or enumerating of design artifacts and, subsequently, the evaluating, detailing, refining, integrating, manipulating, and modifying of these artifacts until the result satisfactorily covers the requirements of the problem definition. This formulation is clearly forward oriented and pays little attention to the problem of system evolution. The ability to continually evolve is crucial for VLIS.

Information systems must constantly adapt to the changing business strategies and needs of a company. Change is a norm rather than an exception for these systems. Unless systems can effectively adapt to the needs of the company, the company's stability and competitive position will be jeopardized. Customer billing systems, for example, are the lifeline for many companies. Many cases exist today where the new services that a company can offer its clients are constrained by the billing system's capability to charge the customer for these services.

Because of constant evolution, VLIS comes to age and requires periodic renovation. This renovation usually takes place under critical operability constraints; that is, the system must continuously operate, even while it is being renovated. Imagine, for example, a state government's department of motor vehicles and its driver and vehicle registration systems. These systems must continuously be available to the state and federal law enforcement agencies. These agencies place a few hundred requests for information each hour, generating thousands of transactions. In numerous real-world situations, the only practical way to renovate and maintain such VLIS is through re-engineering. *Re-engineering* is the process of recovering the design and the code of the existing system version to reuse it in the new system version (Chikofsky and Cross 1990).

This chapter discusses the issues of system specifications in the context of re-engineering VLIS. In the first section, The VLIS Re-engineering Context, we establish a context within which re-engineering of VLIS is necessary. The second section, Current Work, discusses current work pertaining to low-level re-engineering. In the third section, Future Re-engineering Tools, we discuss issues relevant to high-level re-engineering and applicable existing work.

The Very Large Information System Re-engineering Context

In this section, we discuss information system characteristics, system specifications, the system renovation process, and the acquisition of system specifications through software analysis.

Information System Characteristics

Let us make a distinction between system requirements and system characteristics. A *system requirement* is a statement of what is needed or desired in a system, and a *system characteristic* is a current trait of a system. For example, an airline reservation system requirement might be to handle 500,000 reservations a day. A characteristic of the system, however, might be that it can handle only 350,000 reservations a day at its peak. This limit might be the result of operating constraints. During the renovation of the system, this performance characteristic must be modified to handle an additional 150,000 reservations a day, as required.

To maintain or renovate an existing information system, one must identify and specify the characteristics that can be controlled through the design process. We divide information system characteristics into two types: functional and nonfunctional.

Functional characteristics describe the functions offered to the users of the system (that is, they describe what the information system does) and are a reflection of the system's business functions. Functional characteristics can further be classified according to business and control.

Nonfunctional characteristics describe the quality features of an information system (that is, how well the system performs different functions) and other factors (for example, modifiability) that are important for the developers-maintainers of the information systems.

As previously discussed, the ability of VLIS to evolve is critical. The ease with which a system can change or evolve is directly related to its functional complexity. A system's ability to evolve also depends on the following nonfunctional characteristics: First is *system reusability*, that is, the extent to which system components can be reused. This reusability, in turn, depends on the generality of system solutions, the system software and hardware, and the system structure and modularity. The second characteristic is *system modifiability,* that is, the extent to which a system can incorporate changes. Third is *system testability,* or the extent to which a system helps in establishing test criteria and evaluating other system characteristics. Fourth is the operational complexity of data and algorithms.

System Specification

A *system specification* is an expression of information system characteristics and the relationships between the system and its environment. Formal system specifications are computer-manipulable representations that have well-defined semantics. System specifications can aid in the process of system evolution because they provide the semantics for representing and rationalizing system evolution. Specifications of nonfunctional system characteristics are as important as the functional characteristics because they effectively constrain the system design.

The System Renovation Process

An information system lives in, and is part of, an encompassing organizational system, which, in turn, is part of a broader business context. Both the organizational system and its business context undergo continuous change. Because an organization's fundamental business does not change rapidly, we work with evolutionary, not revolutionary, transformations of the organization. The information system plays an important part in the scope, rate, and cost of organizational system evolution. In particular, the ability of an organization to change can be limited by the rigidity of the existing information systems.

As a general rule, organizations start considering a serious system renovation only when an existing system begins to show signs of age such as inflexibility, inability to incorporate new requirements, restricted capacity, and performance degradation. The problem with extensive renovation is that it must not negatively affect the organization's operations. Imagine, for example, a bank that cannot access its customer accounts for a few days or a worldwide delivery service that cannot locate customer packages. Renovating systems under such operational constraints is like attempting to replace the engine of a moving automobile. The need for periodic system renovation and the constraints under which the system replacement must occur are characteristic of the VLIS domain.

Acquisition of System Specifications through Software Analysis

We find that the average VLIS is built to last a long time (10 to 15 years). However, once the system is built, it is modified to handle the effects of changes in the organization or encompassing business environment. These modifications to the information system make the system design documents less valid. As a result, the system's code becomes the only source of reliable information about the system's characteristics.

A practical way to develop or renovate and maintain VLIS is through re-engineering. Re-engineering is a combination of reverse and forward engineering. *Reverse engineering* is the process of recovering the system design and specifications from an existing system. *Forward engineering* is the process of constructing system specifications and developing a system from these specifications. System specifications are constructed by integrating specifications derived from new system requirements with the desirable system specifications of the old system. Figure 2 shows a simplified view of the re-engineering process. Although, it might seem that the whole system is renovated at once, a system is actually renovated in portions. That is, a segment (or subsystem) of the system is first identified, then a new version of the segment is produced using the re-engineering approach. This version replaces the old version of the segment. After an integration period, a new segment of the system is identified for renovation.

The re-engineering approach is appropriate when the following conditions are met: First, the time required to re-engineer the core (sub)system is short compared to the system's life expectancy. Second, the core function makes

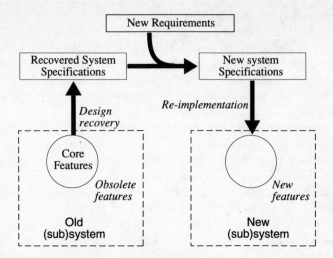

Figure 2. Simplified View of Re-engineering Process

up the dominant portion of the (sub)system. Third, the (sub)system core function will not dramatically change while the system is being re-engineered. The re-engineering approach also depends on available expertise, system information availability and quality, the cost of re-engineering versus the cost of complete system redevelopment in terms of human and monetary resources, and the amount of risk reduced by using re-engineering.

Current Work

Most work in reverse engineering to date has focused on the analysis of functional system characteristics (system logic), which in the case of VLIS is captured in program logic and the design of persistent data.

Automatic Program Understanding

Analyzing a program to understand its logic and design is a difficult and time-consuming process that depends on the programming language and the complexity of the system task performed by the program. The process of program understanding involves both top-down and bottom-up approaches (Rich and Waters 1989). A large body of research exists on the subject of automatic program analysis, which concentrates on dependency analysis and plan analysis.

The main objective of program *dependency analysis* (Biggerstaff, Hoskins, and Webster 1989; Cleveland 1989; Wilde and Nejmeh 1987) is to automatically identify program components such as functions, source blocks, libraries, and data items and discover the relationships between them in a large software artifact. *Plan analysis* is a transformational process that attempts to identify language-independent programming plans (Waters 1978; Wills 1987) from programs written in a variety of high-level languages. *Transformational analysis* uses plan analysis and attempts to gradually reduce a program from the bottom up. The reduction is achieved through the identification of low-level structural plans and then higher-level functional plans. The usefulness of the approach depends on the availability of an extensive library of standard plans and domain-specific plans (Hartman 1989; Letovsky 1988; Ning and Harandi 1989; Wills 1987).

Program Analysis Support—An Example of Assembler Analysis Work

Large transaction systems have several million lines of code and several hundred programs. Most systems that are 15 years old or older were originally written in assembler languages. Many of these systems are still in use, and companies using such systems are finding it prohibitively expensive to maintain them. The dilemma posed by assembler-based systems is twofold. Because most automatic program analysis techniques have not been developed for high-level languages, the re-engineering of low-level assemblers is done by hand or with inadequate tools. Also, it is increasingly difficult for companies to hire, train, or retain software professionals to maintain their assembler code. For these reasons, we began an effort to build tools supporting design recovery of large assembler-based systems.

Our objective was not to automatically transform the code into a different form but to provide the engineers with tools that could assist them in the process of uncovering and documenting the assembler program logic. The initial requirements for the workbench were determined based on previous work on PUNS (Cleveland 1989) and the results of a protocol analysis (Sasso 1989). The subsequent requirements were determined by our client partners, who worked with us for several months critiquing the intermediate prototype systems we developed.

We developed a knowledge-based interactive Basic Assembler Language Software Re-engineering Workbench (BAL-SRW) that assists the user in using reverse engineering to reduce assembler programs to their design specifications. This reduction is achieved through a series of abstractions, which effectively collapse program function into progressively higher-level concepts. The output of the process is a program design constructed by the analyst in a graphically oriented language such as structure charts or Jackson (1983) diagrams. The extracted information can be merged with the specification derived from the new requirements using a CASE tool. This combined information contributes to the renovation of the existing system.

The workbench provides the following facilities to aid the analyst in the program design recovery process: (1) initial program and subsystem analysis; (2) program navigation; (3) structural and lexical simplification; (4) logical focusing; and (5) annotation and design construction.

Initial program and subsystem analysis is a one-time pass of the assembler program that provides the analyst with information about the overall program complexity, the context in which the program executes, and its relationship to other system modules. The information about program complexity facilitates estimation of the effort required to re-engineer the program.

Program module dependency information is filed and then analyzed for a number of modules that are part of the same system logical unit. The module dependency analysis is a weak form of subsystem analysis. Further work in subsystem analysis is required to assist the technical experts in identifying a strategy to re-engineer the programs.

Program navigation consists of features that allow the analyst to explore the existing program's structure. In BAL-SRW, the source browse facility and the control-flow graph facility can be used for navigation. The *source browse facility* is used to browse the source of the assembled listing as well as any annotations the analyst makes. It also determines where symbols are referenced and declared. This facility is useful because in data-intensive systems as much as 70 percent of the code is made up of data declarations. The *control-flow graph facility* is used to browse the control-flow graph (Aho, Sethi, and Ullman 1987). It allows the analyst to view (1) source code from a basic block, (2) parent and child relationships between basic blocks when the blocks are grouped together, (3) basic blocks from which control is received and to which control is passed, and (4) all modified data fields within a basic block.

A sample screen of BAL-SRW is shown in figure 3. The upper-left window on the screen is the source code browser. The bottom window presents a part of a program design represented in the form of a structure chart. The window in the upper-right corner contains a program flow graph.

Our experience with two very large systems suggests that the average size of an assembler program is about 10,000 lines of code after assembly, and the average size of a basic block is 4 instructions (on the average, every fourth instruction is a branch). Even if 70 percent of the code represents data definitions, for a 10,000-line program we get flow graphs with more than 700 nodes. We have seen cases where programs have 3,000 nodes in their flow graphs. Because graphs with over 200 nodes become incomprehensible, we had to develop methods to automatically reduce their size.

Structural simplification identifies those structures in the control-flow diagram that can logically be reduced to one block. The workbench supports automatic and semiautomatic identification and substitution of hammocks and other proper control structures and subroutines.

Hammocks are subgraphs of the flow graph, with one entry point and all external outflows converging on one node (Ferrante, Ottenstain, and Warren 1987). An example of a hammock is shown in figure 4. In this example, if the control is passed to the topmost block, it can only leave the hammock through

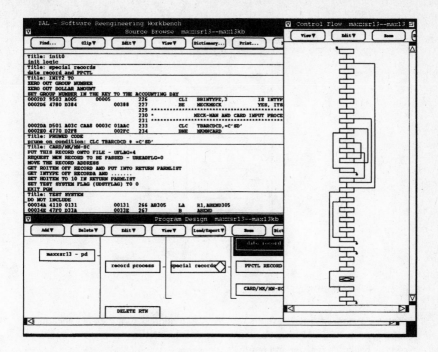

Figure 3. Sample BAL-SRW Screen.

the block at the bottom. Hammocks are difficult to identify because they can have a complex internal structure and can be nested within each other (Hopcroft and Tarjan 1973). Once identified, however, hammocks can be reduced to a single nested block on the surface layer of the flow graph because they form a unit of work. We developed a method to identify nested hammocks composed of lexically consecutive blocks of code. Other flow structures, such as while-do loops and logical-or, are also simplified.

We usually think of a subroutine as a segment of code that has one entry point and one exit point. This definition is not always true in assembler language, which is not based on call routines but go-to routines. In many cases, especially in routines that handle errors, subroutines have multiple exit points. However, not all subroutines must be hammocks. In this case, the workbench must use a combination of formal and heuristic-based methods to identify subroutines. Two commonly used heuristics follow:

A subroutine is called using a BAL Rx,<address> or a BALR Rx,Ry instruction, and it returns to the caller using a BR Rx (an unconditional branch on register x) instruction, and the value of Rx is not changed between the entry and the exit points.

A subroutine is called as in the first example, but the first line of the subroutine

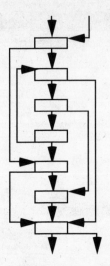

Figure 4. An Example of a Hammock.

contains a store instruction that saves the return address to a memory location. After processing and before the return to the caller, the routine loads the return address back to a register and returns to the caller using BR Rx.

The following example illustrates a mixture of heuristics and formal methods:

First, we remove all edges that represent potential calls to subroutines (the BAL and BALR instructions) from the control-flow graph. At this point, the subroutine bodies should become unreachable and disconnected subgraphs of the flow graph. We know the potential entry points to the subroutines that are the targets of the removed edges. All we have to do now is find out if the subroutines return properly. To make this discovery, we construct spanning trees of the unreachable subgraphs rooted at the entry points. If the subroutines are well behaved, all the leaves of these trees should end with branching instructions to the callers; that is, they should branch to the addresses just below the instructions implementing the subroutine calls.

Our experiments show that not all programs simplify equally well. For example, we performed an experiment with four small (by assembler standards) programs: two performing numeric calculations in a financial system and the other two performing data reformatting and packaging in the same system. We limited the size of the programs to manually verify the results. The programs implementing business logic have frequently been modified during their lives. Their structure and readability have significantly deteriorated since they were created. The data-reformatting programs have been changed only a few times. This different exposure to change showed in the results of our experiment. The business-oriented programs simplified to 66 percent of their original size, which means that only 34 percent of the code was recognized as subroutines or hammocks.

However, the data-formatting programs simplified to only 17 percent and 28 percent of their initial size. This result means that almost 80 percent of their code was still well structured according to BAL-SRW. These results indicate how the progressive change in the functional scope increases the logical complexity and decreases the structure of the application-oriented programs. Similar results were observed for large programs.

Another way to reduce the size of the analyzed program is to recognize and substitute programming patterns. The workbench contains an assembler code pattern understanding (ACPU) system that identifies functionally related pieces of code and replaces them with sentences in a natural or formal language to make the code more understandable. The program information and the pattern-recognition knowledge are captured in a plan library that the user can edit.

Figure 5 shows a few simple plans that were placed in the library and used in processing real-world programs. The ZERO_OUT_ADDRESSED_FIELD plan requires the recognition of two CLEAR_REGISTER patterns in any order before recognizing a MVCL instruction. The recognition of the CLEAR_REGISTER pattern must be triggered by other plans. Because the clearing of a register can be implemented in a number of ways, several CLEAR_REGISTER plans can exist. In the figure we only show two such plans. These sample plans show how several plans can be defined (when one plan is not sufficient) to recognize patterns in the same pattern class. The plans in figure 5 recognize the following or similar sequences of assembler instructions:

```
SR R1,R1       XR R3,R3
XR R2,R2       XR R4,R4
MVCL X,R1      MVCL X,
```

ACPU derives new patterns from the existing patterns using plans. A plan is triggered (to generate a new pattern) if all its components have been recognized and satisfied; that is, all the pattern expressions in the path expression (see the plans in figure 5) are successfully matched with the existing patterns, and the matched patterns meet the sequencing requirements of the path expression.

ACPU reduces the search space by focusing only on patterns that are formed by adjacent instructions. Based on this simplifying (yet reasonable) assumption, ACPU achieves acceptable performance. For example, ACPU matches over 100 plans against a 24,000-line program in 15 minutes. identifying over 2,000 plans. In the experiment, two-thirds of the ACPU processing time was spent on *plan conflict resolution* (when two plans compete for the same section of code).

```
the-plan ZERO_OUT_ADDRESSED_FIELD
     args: ?X
     path: (seq-op
               (arb-op
          (the-pattern CLEAR_REGISTER has-operands ?R0)
               (the-pattern CLEAR_REGISTER has-operands ?R1))
          (the-pattern MVCL has-operands ?X, ?R0))
     spec: zero out field pointed to by ?X


     the-plan CLEAR_REGISTER
          args: ?R
          spec: (the-pattern SR has-operands ?R, ?R)
```

Figure 5. A Few Plans from the Plan Library.

Logical focusing is achieved through the processes of identifying unreach-able code and pruning. *Program pruning* involves removing a line of logic that can only be reached under certain user-supplied conditions (for example, transaction code is equal to a particular value). Pruning has proven effective in isolating parts of application logic. The analyst can interactively apply and undo pruning.

Annotation and design construction are primarily accomplished by using the BAL-SRW source browse facility and program design editor. *Clip notes* are pieces of explanatory replacement text that are substituted for regions of source code lines to simplify a program. Clip notes can also contain a combi-nation of clip notes and source code lines. When a clip note represents a logi-cal function unit that the analyst wants to carry forward, it is placed in the program design editor. This tool allows the analyst to document the logical design of the program. A program design is shown as a graphic, hierarchical representation of the logical flow of program steps. When the design is fully recovered, the results can be exported to a forward CASE tool.

Data-Design Recovery Work

The logic of VLIS relies heavily on its persistent data structures. The logical design of a transaction system is made up of hundreds or thousands of pro-grams. Even if the programs' functions were clear, the interactions between them might not be obvious because they communicate through a large pool of persistent files and databases. For example, one state's driver and motor vehicle registration systems are composed of 7000 program units. The systems store over 2500 bytes of the basic driver information and support over 200 different transaction types.

The current state of a transaction system represents a snapshot of the business activities at the time of the last transaction. This state is stored in the system's data files. Transaction systems maintain the integrity of their data. A system will not allow certain transactions to commit if they violate this integrity. For example, a banking system will not allow a customer to withdraw more money from an account than is shown in the account's current balance.

As the system evolves, the original system data designs age. Symptoms of this process are as follows: First, special files are created that replicate data in existing files. Second, data items become obsolete and are no longer collected or validated. Third, data items are reused for purposes different from those for which they were originally designed. Fourth, data naming conventions disappear. Fifth, programs reinterpret or restrict data items for internal purposes, thus imposing implicit limitations on other programs.

The problem of the data-design recovery was recognized as critical to system re-engineering. It can be discussed on three different conceptual levels: (1) data rationalization, (2) program and system data model recovery, and (3) identification of domain-specific data patterns and constraints.

Data rationalization is a process by which system programs are changed so that all of them refer to the same data definitions. Data rationalization is mainly performed to improve system maintainability. In large systems, it is not uncommon for the same file and record to have different definitions in different programs. For example, the following two Cobol data declarations can refer to the same customer address field:

```
02 CUSTOMER-ADDRESS PIC X(40).    02 CUSTADR.
                                      03 STREET   PIC X(34).
                                      03 ZIP          PIC 9(5).
```

The variety of naming and structuring conventions for the same data element across a system seriously obscures the system logic. Current data-rationalization tools perform a shallow analysis of the data (record) declarations in the system programs and produce discrepancy reports. The process of unifying inconsistent data views is primarily manual; that is, in the previous example, the user would have to decide which data declaration should be used in the system.

The recovery of the system data model is the next level of data analysis. It is a prerequisite for system data renovation or redesign. The objective of this recovery process is to produce a normalized view or schema of the system data. The process is composed of two major steps.

The first step is the identification of the individual program data models. This task involves the analysis not only of the program data declarations but also the program data flow. For example, a Cobol programmer is not forced to declare input-output record structures at all. The language treats all structures as sequences of characters or bytes and, therefore, allows arbitrary assignments between them. A programmer can impose a certain structure on a sequence of bytes by assigning them to a memory region with this structure. For example, the CUSTOMER-ADDRESS field in the previous example can be moved into an array of 40 bytes to allow the programmer access to the individual bytes in the address.

The second step is the reconciliation of a number of program data models into a single system data model. For systems without an integrated database, the task is particularly difficult; all definition-usage discrepancy must automatically be resolved. As indicated, programmers are free to express program views of the model through a variety of language-specific features. Therefore, it must be recognized that programs read from, or write into, the same file and the same records. Different record definitions must then be rationalized automatically. Finally, the relationships between records in the system must be discovered. For example, if a program matches records from two files, the system should be able to conclude that there is a dependency between these records and infer its cardinality.

There are no tools performing system data model recovery. However, tools and techniques exist that produce data model abstractions for systems using integrated databases for which a database schema is available (Bachman 1988).

The final level of the data analysis should lead to the identification of domain-specific data patterns and constraints. For example, a group of fields can be recognized as collectively representing an address (an instance of the address concepts). Recognition of the domain-specific data patterns is similar to the recognition of programming patterns. It is based on the assumption that a library of data plans exists describing (1) component data elements with types, (2) group composition rules, (3) data naming conventions (and, possibly, key words in the comments associated with the data definitions), (4) data usage-processing patterns and the conditions under which this processing can occur, and (5) strategies for recognizing all these elements.

The first three elements describe the structure of a data pattern and help the recognition system perform initial matching on data names and natural language descriptions (comments). The fourth plan component is used to identify data constraints. For example, if an instance of the address is recognized, a constraint can also be recognized in that the system accepts only addresses in a particular zip code.

Currently, we are developing knowledge-based tools to derive a canonical program data model that describes a program's expectations about the system's persistent data. At this point, we are concentrating on the structural and simple use properties of the data. We are also working on reconciling data views between programs. This effort means that if two or more programs use the same file, our system should be able to determine that the programs process instances of the same data or record type, propose a unified data definition of this type, and apply program changes to implement the new definition. Our long-term plan includes tools for identifying the domain-specific data plans.

Future Re-engineering Tools

Tools to support the re-engineering process can be divided into three general categories: (1) system analysis and design recovery tools, which support analysis and extraction of the existing system design; (2) specification capturing tools, which support construction, design and integration, maintenance, verification, and validation of system specifications for both the old and the new systems; and (3) software development tools, which are used for the synthesis of system software from the system specifications.

Our objective is to build a VLIS re-engineering environment that will be capable of supporting re-engineering on the level of system specifications. However, progress in this area is critically dependent on the progress in the area of system specification languages (the major component of the specification capturing tools). These specifications, after all, are paradigms into which the existing systems must be reverse engineered. In effect, the progress of re-engineering as a viable strategy for VLIS will equally be determined by the parallel development of the system design recovery tools and the system specification formalisms.

System Design Specification Capture and Verification

In the context of VLIS re-engineering, a specification formalism or language should meet the following requirements: (1) address both functional and nonfunctional system characteristics; (2) allow for the refinement of system-level concepts into lower-level design constraints; (3) allow for formal verification of the logical consistency of a specification; and (4) permit semantic validation of a system specification by the users, which, in turn, implies the high readability of the specifications and the prototyping capability of system logic and user interfaces.

The first two requirements are interrelated. The current specification formalisms concentrate on the functional (logical) aspects of the specified system. Understanding the nonfunctional system characteristics (Shwanke, Altucher, and Platoff 1989) is especially important in our environment. Some of the nonfunctional characteristics can be thought of as being implicitly addressed. For example, systems with a high percentage of reusable code and high testability should be easier to modify. As the higher-level concepts are refined into more concrete designs, the quality of operational characteristics such as performance and resource use gains importance.

Applicability of Knowledge-Based Software Assistant Work

Ideas and tools developed on the Knowledge-based Software Assistant (KBSA) project are applicable to design recovery. Projects such as the Knowledge-Based Specification Assistant (KBSpecA) (chapter 4) and the Knowledge-Based Software Assistant Concept Demonstration (DeBellis 1990) provide insight into features that will be useful in future tools that assist in system evolution. In this subsection, we give a simple example of a re-engineering scenario. Using this example, we illustrate how the work being done in KBSA is applicable to re-engineering.

Consider a scenario where a manufacturing company needs to merge its existing corporate headquarters and factory payroll systems. Assume that these systems have existed for a long time and have not been well maintained. For example, as federal regulations and employment policies change, the old policies and regulations remain in the system and are either commented out or branched around. However, because maintenance programmers often do not have sufficient time to make changes, or they expect old policies and regulations to be reinstated, they leave the logic in the system and simply never call it. In our example, we show that with re-engineering, relevant data and accurate business rules that should persist in the new system are recovered.

The areas of interest from KBSA work generally include the gathering and organization of requirements and specifications. Here we specifically discuss the applicability of evolution transformations, the history mechanism, the hypertext mechanism, the analysis and evaluation mechanism, and the paraphraser.

Evolution transformations are a means of making global changes to the design knowledge base. They help an analyst incrementally develop (in the forward fashion) a specification. They allow the analyst to gradually refine, synthesize and elaborate the specification until the analyst is confident of the system's behavior.

Although the evolution transformations were developed for forward development, the technology itself is equally applicable to design recovery. Correctness-preserving transformations were used in a similar vein for design recovery (Letovsky 1988). In SpecA and ARIES (chapter 4), many of the transformations have corresponding inverse transformations. We would expect a re-engineering tool to have a full complement of such inverse transformations for reconstructing high-level specifications.

In a re-engineering context, a new evolution transformation that automatically recognizes the record format of data and transforms it into a design knowledge base object would be useful. Let us call this transformation Recognize_Class. In our example, we would use Recognize_Class as depicted in figure 6. The Company_Officer record definition becomes the officer knowledge base object class, and the Company_Worker record becomes the worker

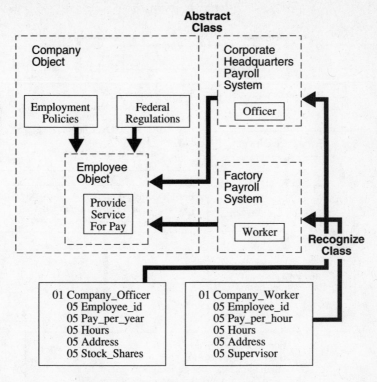

Figure 6. Evolution Transformations Recognize Class and Abstract Class.

knowledge base class. Once these new classes are created, we can use an evolution transformation that already exists, namely, Abstract_Class. We can use Abstract_Class to abstract both officer and worker to an employee knowledge base class. Abstract class takes a group of existing classes and creates a common superclass to those classes by moving slots that are common to both to the new superclass.

For example, in the process of abstraction, the employee object will have the following slots: Employee-id, Hours, and Address. The officer will inherit the employee attributes and also have the pay-per-year attribute. The worker will inherit the employee attributes and have the pay-per-hour attribute. The analyst might decide the hours attribute is not explicit enough and change it to hours-this-period.

The history mechanism is used to both record and reuse changes to the knowledge base. This facility would be most useful for testing and verifying hypotheses of how a specification can be elaborated further. In the design recovery process, this facility is valuable for hypothesizing about a recovered design and replaying selective development histories.

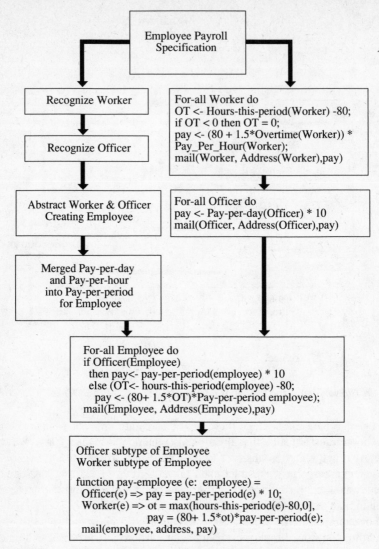

Figure 7. Recovering the Employee Class Definition (left) and Recovering the Control Specification (right).

It is impractical to think that one person could recover the design of the entire VLIS. Therefore, it is expected that any suite of re-engineering tools must lend itself to a multiuser environment. The history mechanism can be used to track the stages that have been passed through in specification recovery. If the analysts have different agendas (for example, one concentrates on recovering data and another on control), they can work in parallel and create (temporarily) inconsistent versions of a specification. When they reach stable points in their development, the design histories of each developer can be merged using techniques described in Feather (1988, 1989) to create a consistent specification.

In our example, one analyst might recover the control specification, as shown on the right side of figure 7. Informal specifications of pay are recovered for the worker first and then the officer. The left side of figure 7 represents the history of recovering the employee class definition, as previously described. These development histories are then merged. The final steps in figure 7 show the more formal specification that can now be added to the system specification repository.

The *hypertext mechanism* allows the analyst to define links between certain specification objects and informal requirements. The system further extends these links to allow the analyst greater ease of navigation through the system information.

A hypertext facility could help the analyst use the notes made during design recovery. For example, at the point at which the analyst decides to merge development histories, the analyst could verify notes connected through the hypertext links to terms relevant to the merge (for example, worker, employee, officer, pay). Easy access to this information would give the analyst more insight into understanding the existing system and allow for more formal specification of the design being recovered.

Analysis and evaluation mechanisms provide feedback to the developer on the current state of the requirements and specifications. This feedback can be based on the syntactic or semantic correctness of the specification entered by the analyst. Feedback is collected on an agenda mechanism. A model of how the agenda items interact is being developed to proactively suggest what actions the analyst should take to resolve the most important outstanding issues. This approach expedites the development of a complete and correct specification.

The agenda mechanism is relevant to design recovery as well. While recovering a design, an analyst might take several actions. With a model showing how the design recovery agenda items interacted, the analyst could be guided in what steps to take to best recover the system specifications.

In our example, assume that the analyst determined that company workers not only get paid overtime when they work over 80 hours a week but also accrue vacation time. Using the specification language described in DeBellis (1990), we could specify this example as follows:

Demon Extra-Vacation-Demon (w: Worker)
    When Hours-this-period(w) > 80 do accrue-vacation(w)

When the analyst tries to abstract the worker and officer classes into employee, the agenda mechanism brings this invariant to the attention of the analyst. The decision to be made is whether to generalize this invariant to include officers:

Demon Extra-Vacation-Demon(e: Employee)
When Hours-worked(e) > 80 do accrue-vacation(e)

If the new system assumes that the policy for vacation accrual only applies to workers and not to officers, the analyst would decide not to generalize this invariant.

The paraphraser clarifies formal requirements to be understandable from the context of either the application domain or the system. *Paraphrasing* is important for getting a textual description of what has been recovered so far. Aspects of the paraphraser that are particularly interesting include the abilities to hide detail and to generate specifications from a particular view. Hiding detail is essential in the process of VLIS design recovery.

Using particular views is important to see the system from the perspective of one of the system components, for example, the database. In design recovery, one must understand the interaction between system components. This interaction could be supported by the paraphraser. Given the current specification in our example, the paraphraser could establish the following two descriptions:

Employee is the name of an object class. Officer is a sub-type of Employee. Worker is a sub-type of Employee. Each Employee has an Employee-Id, Pay-per-period, Hours-this-period which are numbers. Each employee has an Address which is alphanumeric. Each Worker has a supervisor who is an Employee. Each Officer has Stock-shares which is a number.

An employee is paid. If the Employee is an Officer the pay is the pay-per-period multiplied by 10. The pay period for an Officer is 1 day. If the Employee is a Worker, the pay is calculated as follows: overtime is hours-this-period minus 80. Pay is calculated by (80+1.5*overtime)*pay-per-period of a worker. The pay period for a worker is 1 hour. The pay is mailed to the employee's address. Each Worker accrues vacation if hours worked is greater than 80.

Paraphrasing becomes important when specifications are being reviewed. It allows people who cannot read formal representations an opportunity to review specifications. Although not yet ready for commercial use, the ideas and tools being developed for the KBSA projects have a natural overlap with the types of aids required in the design recovery process and VLIS evolution.

Conclusion

The intent of this chapter was to discuss the implications of VLIS evolution on the process of VLIS design and specification maintenance. It is our position that the software development and maintenance process is a function of the domain in which the software operates. The software engineering problem takes on a unique set of constraints when it is considered in the context of developing and maintaining VLISs. Specifically, the issues associated with system evolution place a distinctive set of constraints on the software renovation process of large commercial information systems.

We tried to show the importance of reverse engineering as a viable approach to system renovation. We argued that system specifications should be constructed not only prospectively but also retrospectively. Given a system, we should be able to recover a specification that would lead to system development. This specification should be consistent with our understanding of the problem domain. We have introduced the notion of nonfunctional characteristics and explained the important role it plays in constraining system design. We tried to illustrate the current re-engineering practice with examples of the work done at our center. We also discussed some of the theoretical work applicable to the analysis of existing system code. In the final part of the chapter, we showed the applicability of the KBSA work to the recovery of system specifications and, more generally, to the evolution of VLISs. This discussion illustrates another point of view on the software engineering domain. We believe that the re-engineering and forward-engineering tools must be integrated into holistic system development and evolution environments.

The need for intensive work in the area of VLIS evolution support is not disputed. We believe that significant efforts need to be focused on system design representations, design evaluation, design recovery, and design integration.

Acknowledgments

We would like to thank our colleagues Mike DeBellis, Jim Ning, Edy Liongosari, Bill Sasso, and Gerry Williams for their research contributions and helpful comments that have helped make this chapter possible. We also thank the reviewers for their help in putting the final version of this chapter together.

References

Aho, A. V.; Sethi, R.; and Ullman, J. D. 1987. *Compilers: Principles, Techniques, and Tools.* Reading, Mass.: Addison-Wesley.

Bachman, C. 1988. A Case for Reverse Engineering (Software Tools). *Datamation* 34(13): 49–56.

Biggerstaff, T. J.; Hoskins, J.; and Webster, D. 1989. Desire: A System for Design Recovery, Technical Report STP-081-89, MCC Corp., Austin, Texas.

Chikofsky, E. J., and Cross, J. H., II. 1990. Reverse Engineering and Design Recovery: A Taxonomy. *IEEE Software* 7 (1) (January 1990): 13–17.

Cleveland, L. 1989. A Program Understanding Support Environment. *IBM Systems Journal* 28(2): 324-344.

DeBellis, M. 1990. The Concept Demonstration Rapid Prototype System. In Proceedings of the Fifth Knowledge-Based Software Assistant Conference. Syracuse, NY: Rome Air Development Center.

Feather, M. 1989. Detecting Interference When Merging Specification Evolutions. In Proceedings of the Fifth International Workshop on Software Specification and Design. Detroit, Mich.:

International Joint Conference on Artificial Intelligence.

Feather, M. 1988. Constructing Specifications by Combining Parallel Elaborations, Technical Report ISI/RS-88-216, USC/Information Sciences Institute, Marina del Rey, California.

Ferrante, J.; Ottenstain, K. J.; and Warren, J. D. 1987. The Program Dependency Graph and Its Use in Optimization. *ACM Transactions on Programming Languages and Systems* 9(3): 319–349.

Hartman, J. E. 1989. Automatic Control Understanding for Natural Programs. Ph.D. diss., Dept. of Computer Sciences, Univ. of Texas at Austin.

Hopcroft, J. E., and Tarjan, R. E. 1973. Dividing a Graph into Triconnected Components, *Society of Industrial and Applied Mathematics Journal on Computing* 2(3): 135-158.

Jackson, M. A. 1983. *System Development.* London: Prentice/Hall International, Inc.

Johnson, L.; Cohen, D.; Feather, M.; Kogan, D.; Myers, J.; Yue, K.; and Balzer, R. 1988. The Knowledge-Based Specification Assistant—Final Report, USC/Information Sciences Institute, Marina del Rey, California.

Letovsky, S. I. 1988. Plan Analysis of Programs. Ph.D. diss., Dept. of Computer Science, Yale Univ.

Ning, J. Q., and Harandi, M. T. 1988. Automating the Function-Level Understanding of Programs. In Proceedings of the Second International Conference on Industrial & Engineering Applications of Artificial Intelligence and Expert Systems, Vol. 2: 631-636. New York: Association for Computing Machinery.

Reubenstein, H. B., and Waters, R. C. 1988. The Requirements Apprentice: An Initial Scenario. In Proceedings of the Fifth International Workshop on Software Specification and Design. Detroit, Mich.: International Joint Conference on Artificial Intelligence.

Rich, C., and Waters, R. C. 1989. Intelligent Assistance for Program Recognition, Design, Optimization, and Debugging. AI Memo, 1100, AI Laboratory, Massachusetts Institute of Technology.

Rich, C.; Waters, R. C.; and Reubenstein, H. B. 1988. The Programmer's Apprentice: A Research Overview. *Computer.* 21(11): 10-25.

Sasso, W. C. 1989. Empirical Study of Re-Engineering Behavior: Design Recovery by Experienced Professionals. *Software Engineering: Tools, Practices, Techniques.* 1(1) (May-June 1990): 13-20.

Schwanke, R. W.; Altucher, G.; and Platoff, M. A. 1989. Discovering, Visualizing, and Controlling Software Structure. In Proceedings of the Fifth IEEE International Workshop on Software Specification and Design. Detroit, Mich: International Joint Conference on Artificial Intelligence.

Waters, R. C. 1978. A Method for Automatically Analyzing Logical Structure of Programs. Ph.D. diss., Dept. of Computer Science, Massachusetts Institute of Technology.

Wilde, N., and Nejmeh, B. 1987. Dependency Analysis: An Aid for Software Maintenance, Technical Report, SERC-TR-13-F, Software Engineering Research Center, Univ. of Florida.

Wills, L. M. 1987. Automated Program Recognition, Technical Report, 904, AI Laboratory, Massachusetts Institute of Technology.

2

LaSSIE: A Knowledge-Based Software Information System

*Premkumar Devanbu, Bruce W. Ballard,
Ronald J. Brachman, and Peter G. Selfridge*

The problems that arise with large, complex software systems include producing the code, managing a multiperson enterprise, testing the system, and assuring its integrity with respect to various specifications and other design documents. In many ways, the most difficult problem involves maintenance, which includes fixing bugs and, more importantly, upgrading the system to add new features or adapting the system for slightly different purposes. Some software systems, including those that control the space shuttle, nuclear power plants, and communication networks, have become so large and complex that no one person—or even a small set of people—understands them. This lack of a reliable knowledge source is exacerbated by people moving within an organization or leaving it altogether.

One common aspect of maintenance and other problems with large software is the *discovery problem*, that is, the process of learning about an existing system to use or modify it. A developer must spend a great deal of time discovering aspects of an existing system, ranging from the overall software organization and the conceptual framework that drove this organization to the location and details of specific functions and data structures. This discovery is prerequisite to implementing the actual modification for which the developer is responsible. Discovery also has much in common with the problem of re-trieving code for reuse. One could imagine, for example, a system that could retrieve an existing piece of code that implements a specified function. The discovery process then becomes a process of formulating a series of queries to retrieve information, including actual code, about the system.

We undertook the task of building an information system to aid in the dis-covery process. This chapter first examines the problem of developing such an information system in detail. An existing large software system is used as a test case in this work, and four specific discovery queries are examined to further motivate our approach. Next, the core system we developed, called LaSSIE, is described in detail. Two extensions to LaSSIE are then described: the addition of low-level code knowledge and the integration of a natural language front end. Finally, we put this effort into perspective by examining the queries that LaSSIE now handles, comparing our effort to previous work on software re-trieval and related systems and outlining directions for future work.

The Problem in More Detail

The AT&T Definity 75/85 (AT&T 1985) is a private branch exchange (PBX) that can handle as many as 1600 telephone lines. As a modern digital switch, it is controlled by a large and complicated software system that enables it to perform the basic switching functions as well as implement a sizable collec-tion of features that can be customized. This software is complex in several ways. It contains about a million lines of C code; it consists of multiple ver-sions, the latest of which is always in a state of flux; and, most importantly, it is a manifestation of a complex conceptual model of the switch architecture and its function. Because of this complexity, the code can be understood only with reference to a framework that exists apart from it—a framework that reflects the hardware and software architecture as well as the various resource and real-time response constraints that the system is designed to satisfy.

The kinds of questions asked by Definity developers give us some insight into the conceptual model(s) of a large switch. Consider these queries, typi-cal of the ones elicited in extensive discussions with developers:

Question 1: How do I allocate an international toll trunk?

Question 2: What messages are sent by a process in the network layer when an attendant pushes a button to activate the hold feature?

Question 3: What C functions enable the call forwarding feature at a tele-phone?

Question 4: What functions in the line manager process access global variables defined in /usr/pgs/gp/tgpall/profum.h?

These queries require different kinds of answers, which depend on knowledge associated with at least four different views of the system:

A Functional View: What is the code doing relative to the switching function? Our information system should know how internal operations, or actions, relate to external events such as a user picking up a telephone. For question 1, some code might be described as allocating a trunk, which is an operation internal to the switch.

An Architectural View: What is the hardware and software configuration? Definity 75/85 has a number of layers in its software architecture, each of which presents a conceptual base for the layers above it. For question 2, one needs to know what processes are in the network layer.

A Feature View: How are basic system functions associated with features such as call forwarding? For question 3, we must capture the way in which a feature cuts across a number of basic functions and has ramifications on all layers.

A Code View: How do the code-level components (source files, header files, functions, declarations, and so on) relate to each other? Functions call functions, source files include header files, functions and declarations are defined in source files, and so on. For question 4, these relationships need to be represented.

In addition to these somewhat independent views, some additional issues must be addressed in a software information system capable of handling queries such as these. The views must be integrated to answer queries such as question 2 that combine them. The system must also allow queries about the structure of the knowledge base itself in addition to individual facts in the domain. How the queries are asked is important if the system is going to be useful; using a formal query language will be much less effective than being able to query in a subset of English. Finally, the role of classification (discussed later) will enable the system to outperform a static key-word approach.

The LaSSIE System

LaSSIE is an experimental knowledge-based information system running on a Symbolics 3600 under ZetaLisp/Flavors, portions of which have been ported to run on the Sun workstation. It consists of a knowledge base, a window interface based on ARGON (Patel-Schneider 1984), a graphic browsing tool based on the ISI-GRAPHER (Robins 1988), and a customized version of the TELI natural language interface (Ballard and Stumberger 1986). The system is designed to be used in a formulate-retrieve-reformulate cycle. If the answer to an initial query is unsatisfactory, the user can reformulate the query in a variety of ways and try again. The reformulation step can be carried out by using descriptions of retrieved individuals or exploring the knowledge base for related concepts. Natural language can be used to formulate a query or reformulate part of a previous query.

In all modes of querying, the knowledge base plays a key role in processing queries and in assisting the user in reformulating a query when necessary. Therefore, the design of this knowledge base is crucial. We now describe the perspective from which the knowledge base was constructed. The LaSSIE knowledge base primarily captures the functioning of the system from a conceptual viewpoint, with some information about its architectural aspects.

Functional Knowledge

Most of the functions of Definity 75/85 can be described in terms of the operations that it performs. Some examples are (1) connect a user to a call, (2) initialize a call-control process, (3) audit the digit translation database, (4) release buffer space to free some memory, (5) light a light emitting diode when a call is terminated at a station, and (6) allocate a touch tone recognizer because of a pickup by a user.

Corresponding to each of these actions are segments of code and the files that contain them. Notice also that these actions can be cast into the general form Actor does Action on Object to Recipient using Agent because-of Action. This general form was used to formulate descriptions of a wide range of actions in the call-processing area of Definity 75/85. It also motivated the design of LaSSIE's natural language interface. We then coded these descriptions in the KANDOR knowledge representation system (Patel-Schneider 1984), which classifies them into a conceptual hierarchy using a formally defined subsumption inference operation. This hierarchical knowledge base is the core of LaSSIE, consisting of about 200 frames and 3800 individuals that describe Definity 75/85 using functional, architectural, and code-level concepts and their interrelationships.

The Knowledge Base

As shown in figure 1, the four principal object types of concern in our domain are OBJECT, ACTION, DOER, and STATE. The edges of the taxonomy have their common is-a meaning. In particular, a TRUNK is-a RESOURCE-OBJECT, a COMMUNICATIONS-DEVICE, and a DOER. DOER represents those THINGs in the system that are capable of performing actions. Nodes below DOER and OBJECT represent the architectural component of the system, that is, its hardware and software components. Nodes below ACTION represent the system's functional component, that is, the operations that are performed to or by the system. The relationship between the two system components is captured by various slot-filler relationships between ACTIONs, OBJECTs and DOERs. Each action description combines the top-level concepts in various ways using KANDOR descriptions. A typical one follows:

```
1        (knd-de frame USER-CONNECT-ACTION
2               NETWORK-ACTION CALL-CONTROL-ACTION
3               defined
4               (exists has-actor (generic PROCESS))
5               (exists has-agent (value Bus-Controller))
6               (all has-operand (generic USER))
7               (exists has-environment (generic CALL-STATE))
8               (exists has-result (value Talking-State)))
```

In other words, USER-CONNECT-ACTION (1) is by definition (3) a network action (2) and a call-control action (2), which is done by a process (4) using the bus controller (5) on a user (6), which takes the user from some call state (7) to the talking state (8). LaSSIE's knowledge base contains 102 action concept descriptions of this type, which are classified into a tangled hierarchy. Farther down in the hierarchy, the action concepts become specific.

The most specific action types, each of which correspond to a particular function/source file, are coded as individuals (Definity 75/85 has only one function for each source file); for example:

```
1     (knd-de individual ADD-USER-ACTION
2        (ACTION)
3        (has-actor Call-Control-Process)
4        (has-agent Bus-Controller)
5        (has-operand Generic-User)
6        (has-recipient Generic-Call)
7        (has-environment Generic-Call-State)
8        (has-result Talking-State)
9        (implemented-by /usr/pgs/gp/tgpall/profum.c))
```

In other words, ADD-USER-ACTION (1) is an action (2) that is performed by the call-control process (3) using the bus controller (4); its operand is any user (5), and its recipient is a call (6); it takes its operand from any call state (7) to the talking state (8); and it is implemented by the source file /usr/pgs/gp/tgpall/profum.c (9). It should be noted here that the KANDOR classification algorithm will ensure that this individual gets classified under the frame USER-CONNECT-ACTION mentioned previously. It is this kind of classification that organizes the large number of frames and individuals in LaSSIE into a usable form.

Why Classification Is Essential

In a large software system, it is difficult to know how one part of the system relates to another. Our approach is to build explicit descriptions of the actions performed by different parts of the system, then use formal inference to build a taxonomic hierarchy, where all is-a links are derived from the de-

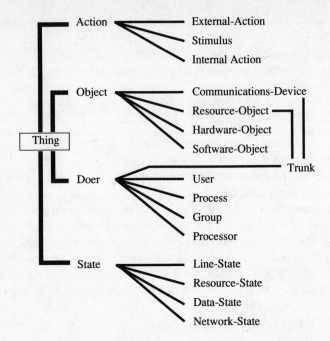

Figure 1. The Top Three Levels of the Lassie Knowledge Base

scriptions themselves. The formal, logical nature of the inference, which is based on an intuitive set-theoretic semantics, ensures that actions are classified where one would expect to find them. The inference procedure that accomplishes this classification is described in Patel-Schneider, Brachman, and Levesque (1984). Thus, programmers working on distinct components of the system can describe the operations performed by their specific components and be sure that their work is properly organized and categorized with other components for retrieval and reuse by later programmers.

The taxonomy can also be useful in query formulation and reformulation. When querying the database, if there are no answers or if there are too many answers, a tool such as ARGON (Patel-Schneider, Brachman, and Levesque 1984) can be used to specialize, generalize, or look for alternatives for an appropriate portion of the query; modify this portion; and retry the query. For example, a programmer might query the system for an action that reinitializes a trunk. This query can be stated as "a process-operation whose operand is a trunk and whose result is the initialized-state". If no such action exists, the user can use the taxonomy to generalize either TRUNK, INITIALIZED-STATE or PROCESS-OPERATION to see whether any matching instances are retrieved.

Large AT&T switches such as Definity 75/85 and 5ESS are actually structured to support reuse. The layered architecture is intended to promote the reuse of primitives from lower levels to construct higher-level operations. Although this architecture type is intended to simplify construction and maintenance, identifying the appropriate primitives when they are needed can be difficult. When primitives are not used as they were intended, the original simplicity of the system is lost; in addition to needless recoding, the system becomes harder to maintain and understand. It is dangerous for the same operation to be reimplemented several times by different programmers in different subsystems; besides the wasted work, when a bug develops in this operation, every single implementation must be found and fixed. The LaSSIE knowledge base helps prevent this loss of architecture by explicitly codifying the primitives supported by the architecture into a formal, taxonomic knowledge base and making it available for browsing and querying with a powerful user interface.

Incorporating the Code View

Representing the code view of Definity 75/85 means developing a general representation of code objects and their interrelationships, then populating this generic taxonomy with instances from the system. The goal is to facilitate answering queries that contain requests for general information about file structure (What extensions do source files have?), general information about Definity 75/85 software (Where are Definity 75/85 header files located?), and information about specific code objects (What functions call apost and include errproc.h?).

We have designed a taxonomic and relational model of the C language and C programming conventions and implemented most of this model in the KANDOR knowledge base. This knowledge base, which is integrated with the functional and architectural knowledge described in the previous section, represents the Unix file structure, including directories, C source files, header files, object files, make files, and their interrelationships, and cross-reference information, including source files and functions, header files, macro definitions, and type (struct) declarations. The relationship knowledge includes both *defined-in* (as in what function is defined in what source file or what macro is defined in what header file) and *referenced-in* (as in what functions reference [call] what other functions) *relationships*.

We added information specific to Definity 75/85 and its own software methodology to this generic knowledge base. This information includes directory and file naming conventions as well as conventions about the file structure itself.

This conceptual framework of about 40 frames has been populated with individuals automatically generated from 310 Definity 75/85 source and header files. This generation was done in a three-stage process starting with

the data file created by CSCOPE (Steffen 1985), which is then further analyzed to generate two-place relations between code objects, which are then
grouped together and used to generate legal KANDOR definitions. Besides the
310 files, the resulting knowledge base includes 27 directories, 433 functions, 39 structure definitions, and 1416 #define statements (macros). These
objects are richly interconnected; a fairly typical function will call a dozen
others and use several dozen #define statements.

Adding a Natural Language Interface

To provide a natural language interface for LaSSIE, we customized the TELI
system, which maintains data structures for each of several types of knowledge about the domain it is being applied to (Ballard and Stumberger 1986;
Ballard 1988). This information includes (1) a taxonomy of the domain,
which enables the parser to perform various types of disambiguation; (2) a
lexicon, which lists each word known to the system along with information
about it; and (3) a list of compatibility tuples, which indicate plausible associations among objects and, thus, reflect the semantics of the domain at hand.
For example, an agent can perform an action on a resource, but actions cannot be performed on agents, resources cannot perform actions, and so on.

In LaSSIE, KANDOR individuals generally correspond to proper nouns (that
is, names), and a frame can correspond to either a verb or a common noun.
Generally, frames under ACTION correspond to verbs describing actions,
and nodes under OBJECT or DOER correspond to nouns. For example, the
frame ALLOCATE-ACTION maps to the verbs allocate, reserve, and grab,
and PROCESS maps to the noun process. Individuals are usually associated
with one or more proper nouns in an obvious way. For example, the individual process Bus-Controller is named bus controller.

As previously explained, action frames include slot restrictions corresponding to case roles, including the actor, the operand, the recipient, and the
cause of the action. One or more English prepositions naturally correspond to
each of these. Thus, each slot associated with an action frame gives rise to
compatibility tuples, as previously described. As an example, consider the
following frame definition with its associated verb connect (actually, the
form shown generates a table entry for the action, associating it with a verb
name, and generates a standard KND-DE call to define a KANDOR frame):

```
1    (verbframe CALL-CONNECT-TRUNK-ACTION
2        (connect) (ACTION)
3        (exists has-operand (generic TRUNK))
4        (exists has-recipient (generic CALL))
5        (exists has-actor (value Call-Control-Process)))
```

For this frame and its slots, the following compatibility tuples are generated:

```
<Call-Control-Process connect TRUNK>
<Call-Control-Process connect to CALL>
```

The annotation of the knowledge base was manually done, after which the conversion to the TELI data structures is automatic. The resulting compatibility tuples for LaSSIE include 167 verb case frames, corresponding to a total of 40 verbs. The lexicon contains 882 entries, including 193 common nouns and 260 proper nouns.

To process a query such as "What actions by the line controller are caused by an action by an attendant?" TELI parses the input, making intimate use of the compatibility tuples and the taxonomy to ensure globally consistent case bindings. The final parse tree is then converted into a semantic structure resembling a first-order logical form, which is sent to a LaSSIE-specific filter to strip out quantifiers associated with words such as a and the. The resulting structure is then passed back to LaSSIE for translation into a query that is executed (thus performing a retrieval) but that also provides an editable ARGON expression. For example, TELI's output for the query is:

```
(set A1 (ACTION A1)
    ((ACTION BY AGENT) A1 Line-Controller)
    ((ACTION CAUSE ACTION) A2 A1)
    ((ACTION BY AGENT) A2 P1)
    (ATTENDANT P1))
```

This output is then translated into the following editable ARGON query:

```
ACTION
    HAS-ACTOR   Line-Controller
    HAS-CAUSE   ACTION
                    HAS-ACTOR     ATTENDANT
```

Note that the user of LaSSIE need not know the details of the underlying knowledge base to pose questions in English but, by seeing the associated ARGON query, can learn about the knowledge base when the input is processed. For example, the query "What actions by a process reserve a touch tone recognizer because of a pickup by a user?" would translate to

```
ALLOCATE-ACTION
    HAS-ACTOR   PROCESS
    HAS-CAUSE   OFF-HOOK-ACTION
                    HAS-ACTOR      USER
```

In this case, the user would learn that the action verb "reserve" corresponds to ALLOCATE-ACTION and pickup to OFF-HOOK-ACTION and that actors of, and causes of, ACTIONs are specified by using the HAS-ACTOR and HAS-CAUSE slots, respectively.

Discussion

The overall goal of the LaSSIE project is to build an information system that represents a significant amount of knowledge of a large software system. Our motivating problem was discovery: the need by developers to be able to access existing system knowledge prior to modifying or extending it. As we built LaSSIE, we were forced to elucidate the kinds of knowledge that we needed to represent as well as how it was to be represented. LaSSIE represents hundreds of interrelated facts about the call-processing part of Definity 75/85, including a taxonomic breakdown of high-level actions that drive the system and low-level knowledge about the code structure. The knowledge of the code structure was automatically generated from source files. We added a natural language interface that allows many queries to be formulated in English and uses the underlying knowledge base to help resolve lexical and syntactic ambiguities. The use of the existing ARGON system allows a powerful form of exploration.

Results

LaSSIE can answer hundreds of queries about Definity 75/85, including queries about actions, architecture, code, and combinations of these three elements. ARGON or TELI is used to formulate these queries, which are answered by showing a list of matching instances. These instances can be used to generalize or specialize the query, and the process continues. With regard to the discovery queries presented in The Problem in Detail, which illustrate some important classes of queries, the current version of LaSSIE successfully answers questions 1, 3, and 4 exactly as stated.

Question 2 is an interesting case: Although it cannot be handled exactly as stated, LaSSIE can be used to home in on the answer. Question 2 is "What messages are sent by a process in the network layer when an attendant pushes a button to achieve the hold feature? The problem is that the sending of a message is not represented at a fine enough grain, so that "message sent when an attendant pushes a button" cannot directly be retrieved. (To precisely answer this question, the actual code would have to be run or simulated, which means that computing a correct answer would be undecidable.) However, LaSSIE can be used to answer the related query, "What functions are called when an attendant pushes a button to activate the hold feature. At this point, the user can manually inspect the functions' source code to determine which messages could be sent under actual running conditions. Even for queries that cannot be handled exactly, LaSSIE's mode of interaction is rich enough to provide at least a partial answer.

To date, LaSSIE provides only limited help when a user attempts to retrieve an inconsistent or otherwise inappropriate query. In situations where a nonnull response to a query would violate the structure of the knowledge base (for example, asking for a button push by a button), the input is rejected by the natural language interface. However, well-formed but logically inconsistent queries are not caught (for example, an action whose actor is not a doer). When a user asks a legitimate query that simply has no satisfying instances in the existing knowledge base, the user is expected to edit the query to weaken the request. A possible example is "a communications device that is not a hardware object," which has no satisfying instances in the current LaSSIE knowledge base but is a legitimate query because the concept it asks about could be made to have instances without changing the domain structure or introducing inconsistencies into the system.

Current Work

This chapter discussed the initial implementation of LaSSIE that runs on the Symbolics Lisp machine. A partial port to the Sun workstation was completed and forms one of the main areas for current work with LaSSIE. The new knowledge base is based on the CLASSIC knowledge representation system discussed in Borgida et al. (1989), which is a direct successor to the KANDOR system used for LaSSIE's implementation on the Symbolics machine. The new knowledge base is identical to, or directly correlated with, the one discussed here. One difference is that most uses of the exists construct in the KANDOR knowledge base result in a pair of clauses in CLASSIC; for example:

> KANDOR
> > (exists has-operand (generic TRUNK))
> CLASSIC
> > (exists has-operand)
> > (all has-operand (generic TRUNK))

Note that the KANDOR version (has an operand which is a trunk) is logically weaker than the CLASSIC version (which has an operand and all of whose operands are trunks). A feature of CLASSIC without counterpart in KANDOR that might be useful for a future LaSSIE knowledge base is its provision for rules, that is, necessary but insufficient conditions for an individual being an instance of an object.

Related Work

Traditional approaches to software retrieval fall into two complementary categories: *high-level classification techniques*, which emphasize retrieval by software category, and *low-level cross-reference tools*, which facilitate various kinds of browsing at the code level.

The goal of high-level classification techniques is usually to create a database of programs and program parts that can be retrieved for reuse. Two methods of indexing are normally used. In the first, key words are used to describe and classify software components, and key words are used for retrieval in the traditional fashion: A user will list a set of uninterpreted terms that describe the desired component, and the system will retrieve all components that are close in some multidimensional space defined by the key words. The CATALOG system (Frakes and Nejmeh 1987) is of this type. Clearly, the utility of a key-word system depends on how well the key words describe the components and how well they match those key words normally thought of by a user. The additional issue of generating the database arises here, as it does with any such database.

Prieto-Diaz (1987) expanded the notion of strict key-word retrieval by forming a static taxonomy of concepts or facets that impose an organization on the set of key words. For example, the facet Function includes the terms add, append, create, and evaluate, and the facet Objects includes the terms arrays, expressions, files, and functions. The system is queried much like a key-word system but might be more amenable to a query-modify retrieval cycle than pure key-word description. Once designed, however, this classification scheme is static and fixed.

At the low level, a number of tools are derived from the notion of a cross-reference listing, which indexes two code components with each other, for example, files and function calls. MASTERSCOPE (Teitelman 1974) was one of the earliest such tools; it was integrated with the InterLisp environment. CSCOPE (Steffen 1985) and CIA(Chen and Ramamoorthy 1986) are tools that run in the C environment; they both automatically generate a database of two-place relations (essentially, the defined-in and the referenced-in relations) and allow a user to query or browse the relationships of a large software system. CIA the more comprehensive of the two, is based on the relationships between five code objects—files, functions, global variables, type definitions, and macro definitions (#define statements)—and it allows limited two-place queries. For example, one can ask for all functions that call a given function or all macros used in a given file. The current implementation is unable to handle queries with conjunctions, negation, or quantification.

Neither of these approaches—software classification techniques and cross-reference tools—comes close to achieving the power of LaSSIE, in part because they do not provide inference capabilities. They could not handle the classes of queries illustrated by questions 1 through 4. They do not address the issue of integrating high-level functional knowledge and code knowledge, attempt to model the underlying domain, or capture more than a single view of software.

Directions for Future Research

LaSSIE has reached a plateau of accomplishment, but there is a long way to go before it is the ideal software information system. For example, we need to incorporate more of the architectural view of Definity 75/85. This process involves a detailed examination of the process-level functioning of the system, including details on the purpose of specific processes, the messages they send, and the meanings of these messages.

On a practical level, we are redesigning LaSSIE to use the CLASSIC knowledge representation language (Borgida et al. 1989). Current plans also include porting the system from the Symbolics machine to run on Sun worksta-.

tions and other Common Lisp environments. This move involves redesigning the ARGON interface.

We must also continue to address the problem of knowledge acquisition. Constructing a knowledge base is labor intensive, and we need to examine the possibility of doing some of the construction automatically. The acquisition of the code knowledge in the current version of LaSSIE was done automatically; acquiring other kinds of knowledge in a similar manner is a research project in itself. There is reason to believe that some large software systems include enough highly standardized comments that this knowledge acquisition can be done. Recently, there has been some promising research in the area. Biggerstaff (1988) proposes an approach to reconstructing the lost design of software from a variety of sources, including source code, design documents, and a domain model; mimicking the process by which an expert who is well acquainted with, for example, windowing systems in general, might reconstruct the design of a new windowing system using his(her) knowledge of the general structure of such systems. On a more formal (and somewhat closer to the code) level, Letovsky (1988) and Wills (1988) use formal methods to discover algorithmic patterns (loops, tests, accumulations, and so on) in programs.

Summary

Our approach to the problem of maintaining and extending large software systems is to use explicit knowledge representation and reasoning technology. This approach has led us to formulate complementary models of a software system in terms of its function, architecture, features, and code. To this end, we constructed a knowledge base that captures critical aspects of three of these four views of the Definity 75/85 switching system. We also customized and incorporated a natural language component to be used either alone or in conjunction with the ARGON interface.

As a result of these efforts, LaSSIE is the first information system to incorporate multiple views of a large software system embedded in an environment that lets a user query the system and explore the knowledge base. Although much remains to be done, LaSSIE can successfully handle many classes of queries about a large software system.

References

AT&T. 1985. *AT&T Technical Journal:* Special Issue on the System 75 Digital Communications System 64(1).

Ballard, B. W. 1986. User Specification of Syntactic Case Frames in TELI: A Transportable, User-Customized Natural Language Processor. In Proceedings of the Eleventh International Conference on Computational Linguistics, 454–460.

Ballard, B. W. 1988. A Lexical, Syntactic, and Semantic Framework for a User-Customized

Natural Language Question-Answering System. In *Lexical-Semantic Relational Models,* ed. Martha Evens, 211–236. Cambridge: Cambridge University Press.

Ballard, B. W., and Stumberger, D. E. 1986. Semantic Acquisition in TELI: A Transportable, User-Customized Natural Language Processor. In Proceedings of the Twenty-Fourth Annual Meeting of the ACL, 20–28. Cambridge, Mass.: Association of Computational Linguistics.

Biggerstaff, T. J. 1988. Design Recovery for Maintenance, Technical Report STP-378-88, MCC Corp., Austin, Texas.

Borgida, A.; Brachman, R. J.; McGuinness, D.; and Resnick, L. A. 1989. CLASSIC: A Structural Data Model for Objects. In Proceedings of the Association of Computing Machinery SIGMOD-89, 58-67. New York: Association of Computing Machinery.

Chen, Y. F., and Ramamoorthy, C. V. 1986. The C Information Abstractor. Presented at COMP-SAC, Chicago, October.

Frakes, W. B., and Nejmeh, B. A. 1987. An Information System for Software Reuse. In Proceedings of the Tenth Minnowbrook Workshop on Software Reuse, 142–151.

Letovsky, S. I. 1988. Plan Analysis of Programs. Ph.D. thesis, Yale Univ.

Patel-Schneider, P. F. 1984. Small Can Be Beautiful in Knowledge Representation. In Proceedings of the IEEE Workshop on Principles of Knowledge-Based Systems, 11-16. Washington, D.C.: IEEE Computer Society.

Patel-Schneider, P. F.; Brachman, R. J.; and Levesque, H. J. 1984. ARGON: Knowledge Representation Meets Information Retrieval. In Proceedings of the First Conference on Artificial Intelligence Applications, 280–286.

Prieto-Diaz, R., and Freeman, P. 1987. Classifying Software for Reusability. IEEE Software 4:6–16.

Robins, G. 1988. The ISI Grapher Manual, Technical Manual ISI/TM-88-197, USC/Information Sciences Institute, Marina del Rey, California.

Steffen, J. 1985. The CScope Program, Berkeley Unix Release 3.2, originally written by Joe Steffen.

Teitelman, W., 1974. *The Interlisp Reference Manual,* Boston, Mass.: Bolt, Beranek and Neuman.

Wills, L. 1974. Automated Program Recognition, Technical Report, 904, AI Laboratory, Massachusetts Institute of Technology.

❧ SECTION TWO ❧

Knowledge-Based Specification Acquisition

There are two stages in knowledge-based software engineering: problem formalization and program synthesis. Problem formalization corresponds to the traditional software engineering activities of requirement and specification acquisition and certain aspects of high-level design. Problem formalization cannot entirely be automated because it involves developing a consistent and complete problem specification from a user's vague, inconsistent, and incomplete statement of needs. However, as the chapters in this section show, knowledge-based tools can assist the process of problem formalization. The chapters in subsequent sections address automating program synthesis.

The first chapter describes the WATSON system developed by Van Kelly and Uwe Nonnenmann at AT&T Bell Laboratories. WATSON derives formal specifications of telephone features, such as call waiting, from informal natural language scenarios presented by telephone feature designers. WATSON addresses one central difficulty in formal specification development: Most people do not have the background necessary to write precise specifications in mathematically oriented specification languages. Even those who do have sufficient training have difficulty ensuring that their specifications are internally consistent, complete, and externally consistent with domain constraints.

Less sophisticated users should be shielded from the complexities of formal specifications, but more advanced users should be provided tools for validating and evolving their specifications. The WATSON system addresses the needs of less advanced users through domain knowledge encoded in temporal logic and through advanced AI reasoning methods. Domain knowledge enables WATSON to communicate with a user in natural, domain-oriented terms; fill semantic gaps in a scenario using domain constraints; and detect inconsistencies and incompleteness in a scenario. When WATSON needs additional information, it asks the telephone feature designer using the context of the scenario.

As knowledge-based software engineering advances to commercial reality, a new software engineering activity will be born: domain analysis. A domain analyst formalizes do-

main knowledge for use in both specification acquisition tools such as WATSON and program synthesis tools. WATSON provides limited support for domain analysis through a set of tools for accessing and modifying WATSON's formal theories of the telephone domain.

The Knowledge-Based Specification Assistant described in the chapter by Johnson and Feather is part of the U.S. Air Force's knowledge-based software assistant (KBSA) project. The KBSA project, started in 1985, is a 15-year, 3-phase research program. The goal is to develop the technology for formally based, computer-mediated specification, development, evolution, and long-term maintenance of computer software. The Knowledge-Based Specification Assistant was developed during the first phase of the KBSA project. It supports the incremental development and evolution of formal specifications. The successor in the second phase is the ARIES project, which is intended to support both requirements acquisition and specification evolution.

In contrast to WATSON, the Specification Assistant is targeted at helping system analysts and is concerned with larger, less constrained design problems. The Specification Assistant enables an analyst to develop a specification by applying a sequence of evolution transformations. Evolution transformations use the same framework as meaning-preserving transformations for program synthesis but perform specification-level, meaningful changes such as revising the type hierarchy or changing data-flow and control-flow paths. This framework includes building macrotransformations as compositions of basic evolution transformations, replaying transformation histories to retrace a development, and supporting the retrieval of appropriate transformations. In contrast to current computer-aided software-engineering (CASE) tools for editing diagrams, the Specification Assistant operates on the underlying specification and, therefore, can change many semantic dimensions at once. The Specification Assistant could provide part of the technology for the next generation of upper CASE tools. Upper CASE refers to tools that support requirement and specification acquisition.

The successor project ARIES uses a more sophisticated specification language that subsumes the constructs used in current CASE tools and AI knowledge representation languages. ARIES can translate a specification into several different representations, including LOOM, which is a proposed standard for knowledge representation languages; standard CASE diagrams; and English. ARIES also supports rapid prototyping by translating a specification into a default implementation in Lisp.

The third chapter describes a line of research by Mitchell Lubars, currently a research scientist at MCC. The objective is to support high-level design reuse and exploration through several knowledge-based representations and automated reasoning tools. The representations include abstract design schemas; design records that encapsulate requirements and design decisions; and multiple views of an evolving design specification, including standard CASE diagrams. The automated reasoning tools include a truth maintenance system that manipulates the design records during design exploration and knowledge-based refinement that enables a user to customize an abstract design schema to his/her particular requirements. Rapid prototyping is also supported. Lubars's chapter is in part a historical review of the lessons learned from his previous research on the IDeA and ROSE-1 systems. His chapter supports the argument that current CASE tools need to evolve in the direction of knowledge-based tools to provide better support for software design.

CHAPTER

3

Reducing the Complexity of Formal Specification Acquisition

Van E. Kelly and Uwe Nonnenmann

More than in the United States, software engineering in Europe emphasizes preimplementation formal specifications of software systems. *Formal specifications* are abstract system descriptions written in a mathematically precise specification language, such as VDM, Z, LOTOS, or a temporal logic dialect (Wing 1990). Depending on the language chosen, formal specifications can be analyzed for functional correctness or performance estimation using either static (proof-based) or dynamic (simulation-based) techniques. These specifications can serve as a common source for both coding guidance and deriving test data needed for later system maintenance. In some cases, they can also be used as rapid prototypes to allow early end user acceptance testing. Anecdotal comparisons of formal specifications with older informal techniques point to a significantly higher final product quality, with earlier defect removal, for roughly comparable levels of total development cost (Nix and Collins 1988), even without much automated support for specification acquisition or analysis.

In mainstream U.S. software engineering, the trend has been to provide automated support for less formal specification techniques through CASE tools. By providing an interface emphasizing graphic diagramming, menu selections, and fill-in-the-blank interactions, CASE tools insulate the programmer or analyst from the need to read or write a specification language as such. They also demand less mathematical sophistication from their users than formal techniques. However, their accessibility comes at a cost: Because they lack support for making precise yet abstract definitions of system function, they do not offer as many side benefits in early defect removal, coding guidance, and derivation of test data as the more formal techniques.

Automating Formal Specifications

Our research goal is to support formal specifications with an automated acquisition and analysis environment. Our prototype environment, WATSON, reads and interprets informal natural language *scenarios,* or abridged traces, of desired system behavior. It induces a plausible formal specification for a system capable of producing these behaviors and then tests and refines the conjecture by posing extended behavior scenarios, also in natural language, to a human developer functioning as an oracle. Like a CASE tool, WATSON shields the system specifier from the need to read or write a specification language; however, its methods are different.

A domain-independent environment for specifying arbitrary software systems is still years away. WATSON operates in a more tractable yet nontrivial application domain of finite-state *reactive systems:* those whose most important behavior requirements are associations of particular sequences of input stimuli with corresponding sequences of output responses. Examples of reactive systems abound in industrial process control, data communications, aerospace, robotics, and medical electronics. Focusing on reactive systems (or, somewhat more precisely, on specifications covering only reactive behavioral properties of software systems) enables us to avoid many sources of computational explosion in reasoning about general software systems.

WATSON uses first-order temporal logic (Galton 1987) as its core specification language and automatic theorem proving as its main inference tool. *Temporal logic* is an extension of classical logic that permits each assertion in a logical theory to be associated with a temporal context, such as now, henceforth, immediately, or eventually. Temporal logic is extremely flexible, supporting several styles of formal specification. WATSON specializes in one of these, a variant of Lamport's (1989) *transition axiom method,* which easily generalizes beyond the finite-state case and, thus, facilitates our eventual goal of specifying reactive properties of arbitrary systems. This style also lends itself well to fairly simple static and dynamic analysis.

WATSON augments its temporal logic specifications using two other AI knowledge representation techniques: *goal-directed plans,* which generalize and categorize the informal scenarios of system behavior; and *model-based reasoning,* which constructs and examines fragmentary finite-state implementations of a formal specification. The relationships among the three major knowledge representations within WATSON are a major theme of this chapter.

An important effect of using logic as a central knowledge representation is an enhanced ability to separate general knowledge about an application domain from specific knowledge about a particular system being designed. The presence of this general domain knowledge at the beginning of a specification process is the key to WATSON's apparent intelligence. *Domain knowledge* is used to correct routine omissions and errors in scenarios, constrain the space of possible scenario generalizations, shape the structure of models used in model-based reasoning, and plan queries posed to its human oracles. Being purely declarative, domain knowledge can be reused completely and verbatim for specifying multiple systems within the same general domain. Our experience with WATSON reinforces the growing recognition of domain analysis as a separate and necessary activity of software engineering.

Another major theme of this chapter is WATSON's user interface, which takes over much of the initiative for planning and managing the specification design process. This approach turns out to be essential for preserving an example-based style of human-machine dialog, insulating a system specifier from raw temporal logic notation. A human specification writer working with WATSON performs only two major functions: providing an original set of natural language scenarios and serving as an oracle to answer yes-no questions about variant scenarios proposed by WATSON. Thus, WATSON must occupy a little-explored region of the user interface spectrum between completely automated systems (such as compilers) and the current crop of passive, user-driven CASE environments. The use of AI-based natural language interpretation and generation techniques is critical to this aspect of WATSON.

In the remainder of this chapter, we first characterize WATSON's application domain and describe how WATSON is used. Next, we present WATSON's knowledge representation structures in detail, followed by a similar discussion of its user interface philosophy. We then discuss related research and the implementation status before drawing our final conclusions.

WATSON's Prototype Application Domain

In telephony, call-control features are embedded software modules within telephone switches that modify switch behavior toward telephones and other connected terminals. Examples include features to forward telephone calls from one station to another or notify users of incoming calls during a conversation. A feature is typically designed as a finite-state machine control skeleton decorated with subroutine calls to handle errors or query or update databases (for

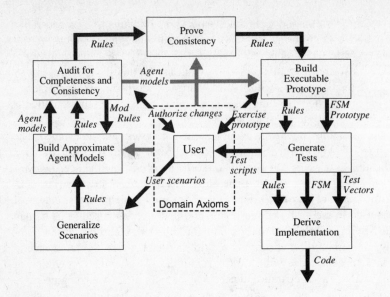

Figure 1. Watson Schematic Overview.

example, to look up or change a call forwarding number). Even though feature skeleta can appear simple in isolation, designing them is difficult, in part because of the possibility of pathological n-way interactions among the hundreds or even thousands of features cohabiting in any particular switch.

Engineers are currently trained to specify new features using informal scenarios of a feature's input-output behavior. If these scenarios could be converted to executable formal specifications, bad interactions with existing features could be detected early, before expending major human programming effort to develop them as products. WATSON generates formal specifications for feature control skeleta together with verification conditions for some of their attached code, producing executable prototypes (through simulation) and test data as a side effect of its operation.

Using WATSON: A Software Process View

An overview of WATSON's operation during the evolution of a formal specification is shown in figure 1. The human feature specifier is pictured in the center of the diagram surrounded by a moat of telephony domain knowledge, suggesting WATSON's view of humans as knowledge sources of last resort, to be bothered only for issues that formalized domain knowledge cannot resolve. Processing proceeds clockwise around the circle, beginning with constructing an initial interpretation of a scenario and conjecturing a rough finite-state design of the feature-control skeleton. Next in sequence, WATSON's understanding is refined in an interactive audit step, followed by a fine-grained consistency test using brute force automatic theorem proving. Following this test, various postprocessing steps can produce executable prototypes, high-level code designs, or test data from the final constructed specification. Each of these process steps is elaborated in the following paragraphs.

A Priori Domain Knowledge

The telephony domain knowledge needed for WATSON in this application includes knowledge about telephone hardware, network protocols, expected end user etiquette, exception handling, time-outs, and preferred styles of control skeleton design. Fortunately, in the case of telephony, a great deal of requisite knowledge was codified and is amenable to straightforward representation in temporal logic.

A well-developed domain theory is especially important to WATSON because finite-state machine induction from examples is an extremely under-constrained problem, even in the case of exhaustive traces; it is easy to find formally correct machines, but most of these are unacceptable in some way. For example, the absolutely smallest deterministic finite-state machine (fewest states) covering a set of scenarios often has unintended infinite looping behaviors that are catastrophic for system robustness in the presence of faults. However, placing each scenario in its own disjoint region of state space senselessly replicates similar functions. Extensive domain knowledge focuses WATSON's attention on the most practical and robust regions in the space of possible designs.

Formalizing and Generalizing Scenarios

Figure 2 describes ordinary point-to-point telephone calling in an informal scenario form accepted by WATSON. Various examples of incompleteness exist in this scenario: It does not mention that a telephone never stops ringing or getting a dial-tone, nor does it tell what happens to poor Mary at the end of the scenario, who is left off the hook waiting for something to happen.

WATSON first converts each such scenario into temporal logic notation. For English-language scenarios (as in figure 2), this conversion is accomplished using a broad-coverage natural language front end (Ballard and Stumberger 1986). Alternatively, WATSON accepts pictorial scenarios created by two proprietary graphic animation tools. These scenarios are already written in a formal notation and only need a simple translation.

Each scenario, now expressed in logic, is converted into a goal-directed plan, where each individual plan step, or *episode,* corresponds to a single stimulus-response cycle in the external behavior of the feature. For the example scenario, there are four episodes, one for each of the four paragraphs. Each episode involves three types of logical assertions: *antecedents* that describe constraints on the state of each agent or process in the world when the

First Joe is on-hook
and Joe picks up the handset,
then Joe starts getting dial-tone.

Next Joe dials Mary,
then Mary starts ringing
and Joe starts hearing ringback.

Next Mary goes off-hook
then Joe gets connected to Mary.

Next Joe hangs up
then Joe gets disconnected from Mary.

Figure 2. Simple Telephony Scenario.

episode begins, an externally provided *stimulus* that triggers state changes (for example, someone dials a number), and *consequents* that partially specify a change in world state after the stimulus. At this stage, the plan can be incomplete because of the human omission of details noted earlier.

The next step is to generalize each consequent of every episode into a special temporal logic axiom, called a *transition rule,* guessing sufficient conditions for this consequent to become asserted. These sufficient conditions are, in general, derived from the episode antecedents and stimulus but can often be weakened. As a simple example, from the first episode in figure 2, WATSON (incorrectly as it turns out) induces a general rule:

All phones going off-hook must immediately start to get dial-tone."

When in doubt, WATSON tends to overgeneralize rather than undergeneralize because the inconsistencies and nondeterminism created by overgeneralizations are somewhat easier to detect and correct than the coverage gaps caused by undergeneralizations. In later stages, WATSON will correct overgeneralizations by strengthening the sufficient conditions in the transition rules.

Model-Based Reasoning

Before refining its understanding of the scenarios, WATSON constructs its first crude approximation of a feature-control skeleton, based on its highly tentative conclusions from the previous step. The form of this approximate model lies midway between a single global finite-state machine for the entire feature and a separate machine for each agent's view of the feature's operation. The world in which the feature operates is divided into a set of local agents, or processes, each of which is assigned a private view of the feature.

Several sorts of agents cooperate in the operation of a feature, such as terminals, calls, and trunk lines. All agents of a given type possess separate but isomorphic slices of a global state machine, and all slices can freely examine (but not modify) each other's state. Because of the flaws (for example, overgeneralizations) in WATSON's understanding at this point, the attempt to build this model usually fails initially, but this failure generates useful data for pinpointing WATSON's misunderstandings. For example, the faultily generalized rule previously mentioned results in a readily detectable case of nondeterminism when trying to construct the model slice for a telephone terminal; specifically, an off-hook stimulus can bring a terminal into either a state receiving a dial-tone or a connected (talking) state. In later analysis steps, both the transition rules and these models are corrected and updated in tandem.

Note that these local agent models, even when fully refined into deterministic finite-state machines, are still not detailed enough to serve as an adequate operational specification for a feature. Any formal feature specification that WATSON finally produces is based on the transition rules, not on the local agent models. The value of the local models is that they make explicit (at a coarse-grained level) some graph-theoretic properties of the specifications that are only implicit in the domain knowledge and the transition rules, such as the overall connectedness of the global-state space. During WATSON's later phases, checking the local models for such properties can be faster than trying to directly prove them using the theorem prover.

Interactive Audit for Completeness and Correctness

The bugs in WATSON's plans, models, and transition rules at this stage are repaired in an audit phase in which WATSON proposes corrected and expanded scenarios to its human partner. WATSON performs four major types of correction at this stage:

First is interpolating routine omissions in the plan representation of the scenario. In the example in figure 2, this interpolation includes determining when tones stop being heard and postulating the existence of a (never-mentioned) connection request from Joe to Mary, something that is a prerequisite to establishing a connection according to the background knowledge for telephony.

Second is eliminating inconsistencies and nondeterminism in the local agent models caused by overgeneralization of one or more transition rules. For instance, WATSON notices its earlier blunder in concluding "all phones going off-hook must immediately start to get dial-tone" by comparing the episode where Joe went off-hook and got a dial-tone with the later episode where Mary went off-hook and was connected to Joe. After weighing several alternative solutions to find the simplest solution for this inconsistency, WATSON specializes the offending rule to only apply to nonringing phones.

Third is detecting dead or unreachable sections of the local agent models' state space and adjusting the sufficient conditions of rules to make them live and reachable. For example, even though it is possible for a telephone to have a connection request to another telephone that can never be fulfilled (such as when calling a busy or non-existent telephone), this experience didn't occur in the example scenario. WATSON uses the fact that Mary's telephone begins ringing when Joe calls to conjecture that this unreachable portion of the state graph might be reachable if Mary's telephone were somehow unable to begin ringing, that is, if she were either off-hook or already ringing when Joe called.

Fourth is extending the coverage of the current scenario set by varying the scenario endings. For example, Joe might hang up at any time before the call to Mary completes. In all such cases, WATSON concludes that all tones should be removed from Joe, and Joe's connection request(s), if any, should be aborted.

Figure 3 shows WATSON's enhanced understanding of the original scenario after the interactive audit stage. Interpolations to correct routine omissions are shown in italics, and changes to eliminate inconsistencies and unreachable states are in boldface.

The alternate scenario endings cannot be shown here because of the linear view of time taken within a single scenario. The endings would be represented as separate scenarios/plans but are fully integrated into a single set of local agent models and transition rules.

Final Consistency Test and Postprocessing. By the time WATSON finishes its interactive audit, all its local agent models are internally consistent and deterministic, and the transition rules, under a special consequent completion interpretation described in Transition Rules and Nonmonotonicity, are a formal specification for a class of computations that will correctly implement the behavior of all the scenarios. However, because of incompleteness in WATSON's model-based reasoning, rigor demands an additional theorem-proving step, reverifying that these transition rules do not violate any of the temporal constraints in our body of domain knowledge.

This step is accomplished in a separate consistency test, which can require minutes or even hours of noninteractive automated theorem proving. Compared with the earlier model-based audit stage, this step gives extremely limited help in diagnosing specific problems, but it is much more sensitive as a go-no-go verification. Because it decomposes most proofs by cases, WATSON collects some information about near misses, but more work remains to be done to exploit these near misses.

Assuming that the transition rules (the final WATSON specification) for a new feature pass this consistency test, there are several subsequent uses for them. First, they can be executed as a system prototype on a special simulation test bed as an early customer acceptance test for the feature. A prototype of such a test bed was developed in 1984 for a precursor of WATSON (DeTreville 1984). Second, and more ambitiously, the rules can be used to derive test

First Joe is on-hook
but Joe is not ringing
and Joe picks up the handset,
then Joe is now off-hook
and Joe starts getting dial-tone.

Next Joe dials Mary,
then, assuming Mary is on-hook
and Mary isn't already ringing,
Mary starts ringing,
and Joe stops getting dial-tone,
and Joe has a connection request to Mary,
and Joe starts hearing ringback.

Next Mary goes off-hook
then Joe stops hearing ringback
and Mary stops ringing
and Joe's connection request to Mary is fulfilled
and Joe gets connected to Mary.

Next Joe hangs up
then Joe is now on-hook
and Joe gets disconnected from Mary.

Next Mary hangs up.

Figure 3. Expanded and Corrected Telephony Scenario.

data for acceptance tests for (conventionally produced) implementations of the feature. We are currently implementing such a capability. In the future, a third use would be as input for a transformational derivation of a feature implementation, but we have not yet pursued work in this difficult application.

Knowledge Structures

The information captured in each of WATSON's three declarative knowledge representations—scenarios/plans, temporal logic axioms, and local agent models—partially overlaps, but no two of the three representations subsume the other. Each knowledge structure is critical to the efficient computation of at least one important property of the target specification.

Where the knowledge content of the three representations overlaps, well-understood theories govern their mutual consistency, as diagrammed in figure 4. A set of temporal logic axioms is related to a class of finite-state machines by the Kripke model semantics of modal logics (Galton 1987), in which the states of the machines correspond to possible worlds in which the axioms might be evaluated, and temporal operators in the axioms describe sets of possible paths in the state-transition graphs of the machines. Even WATSON's extremely incomplete local agent models are true Kripke models in this sense.

Possibly more familiar to most software engineers is *trace theory,* a framework that interrelates equivalence classes of finite-state machines, such as WATSON's local agent models, with sets of their execution-trace scenarios (Rem, van de Snepscheut, and Udding 1983). Somewhat more heuristically, results from justified generalization in program induction and machine learning (Andraea 1985) constrain the sort of temporal generalizations one might make when generating transition rules from scenarios. We now consider each knowledge source individually and in detail.

Scenarios/Plans

After being translated from English to an internal logic form, narrative scenarios provided by human engineers are analyzed as a chain of individual stimulus-response episodes in the operation of a telephone system. As previously mentioned, each episode records three kinds of information: (1) antecedents, assertions known to be true before the episode; (2) a stimulus, which can also have implicit, persistent side effects (for example, a telephone off-hook remains so until it is hung up); and (3) explicit consequents, assertions known to be true (either momentarily or persistently) at the end of the episode that were not true at the beginning.

Some of the antecedents are explicitly given in the scenario, and others default from persistent consequents of previous scenario episodes or from background knowledge about the circumstances in which a particular stimulus is relevant. Likewise, some consequents are explicitly given, and others are inferred from the side effects of stimuli. Where explicit and inferred antecedents or consequents clash, WATSON can infer an omission of some sort in the scenario.

Each scenario presented by the user is further analyzed as an instance of a plan whose goal is either delivering a billable service (such as connecting Joe and Mary in figure 2) or causing a side effect such as an incremental change in the long-term operating parameters of the system (such as changing Joe's call forwarding number). When WATSON encounters a scenario in which no recognizable goal is achieved (for example, Joe dials Mary, receives a busy signal, and hangs up again), it classifies this plan as a failed variant of another, successful plan. For each successful plan, there must be several ways to fail. In successful plans, episodes leading to the goal are assumed to be a purposeful, maximally efficient means of achieving the goal, and hence, each action taken is a necessary goal prerequisite. Furthermore, with the exception

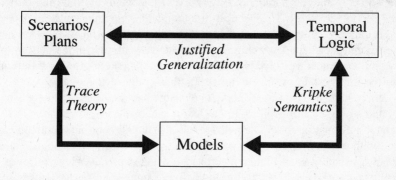

Figure 4. Three Interacting Knowledge Sources.

of persistent side effects (such as writing changes to a database during a scenario), each scenario is assumed to represent a cycle through the state-transition graph of each agent mentioned, with no internal subcycles. WATSON allows humans to violate this principle (for example, Mary is left hanging off-hook at the end) as long as it can figure a way to extend the scenario and complete the cycle (postulate that Mary can hang up the telephone) or hypothesize a distinction among two or more seemingly identical states during the sequence.

Scenarios have six different purposes within WATSON: First, individual episodes are generalized into state-transition constraints, as previously mentioned. Second, differences between successful and failed versions of a scenario can be generalized into templates for hypothesizing unanticipated but analogous failure modes for future successful scenarios. Third, scenarios are directly used to constrain the topology of the local agent models that WATSON is allowed to construct. Each agent active in a scenario (ignoring side effects) is assumed to execute a state-transition cycle beginning and ending in an idle state, with no embedded subcycles. Fourth, scenarios are used for setting the contexts for all user interactions, as explained later. Fifth, scenarios are used as a relevance filter for the set of concepts in the temporal knowledge base. For example, even though WATSON can have information about an audio tone called a busy signal, it tries to ignore this information if the current set of scenarios never mentions a telephone receiving a busy signal. Sixth, initialization conditions for new telephone features are deduced from the scenarios.

Temporal Logic Axioms

By far the most complex and diverse knowledge source used in WATSON is its axiom knowledge base written in a dialect of first-order temporal logic with equality. This knowledge base includes both transition rules generalized from particular feature scenarios, and its application-domain background knowledge about telephony. The richness of a temporal logic representation makes it an attractive intermediate language, linking English with WATSON's other two more specialized knowledge representations. With careful restrictions on certain constructs, reasonably efficient automatic theorem proving based on off-the-shelf resolution technology is possible within such a logic.

Direct human access to the logic knowledge base is difficult. Whereas the meaning of a scenario is likely to be clear to a human user, much of the background information in this knowledge base is subtle, requiring a domain expert with an intuition for temporal logic to write it down and a sophisticated English paraphraser to explain its effects to a non-expert user in terms of hypothetical scenarios. Thus, in the following examples, no reader knowledge of temporal logic is assumed, and all logic axioms are paraphrased in an English form that suggests their practical effect on the operation of WATSON.

Knowledge Taxonomy. Although arbitrary temporal logic formulas could be stored in WATSON's knowledge base, in practice, four major categories of assertions predominate: (1) *state invariants,* which must be true for all agents in all states of the world (for example, "No phone should ever be considered on-hook and off-hook at the same time"); (2) *sensitivity conditions,* which describe when external stimuli can be presented to the telephone network (for example, "Dialing is ignored unless the dialing phone is connected to a dialing decoder unit"); (3) *arity constraints,* which restrict how many individuals can be related to other individuals in particular ways (for example, "By no single stimulus can a phone request connections to two or more other phones at the same time"); and (4) *transition constraints,* which are duals of state invariants, describing before-and-after conditions that all state transitions must obey (for example, "Any phone connected to another phone when it goes on-hook immediately becomes disconnected"). Transition constraints include but are not limited to the rules generalized from scenarios.

This regularity of form within the domain knowledge eases the task of translating between temporal logic and English. We developed a prototype of an English paraphraser for WATSON's domain knowledge, but to date, it only works well for short formulas involving less than a half dozen literals.

Uses of Theorem Proving. Besides temporal logic's utility as an intermediate language for background knowledge, WATSON uses direct theorem proving in temporal logic for several purposes, for example, calculating initial values for local agent models, analyzing similarities (for example, subsumption or disjointedness) between episodes from the same or different scenarios, detecting harmful interactions among features, and guaranteeing that certain properties of a specification must hold over all possible implementations.

This last point deserves elaboration for readers unfamiliar with the model theory of formal logics. Often, we want to guarantee that a certain desirable behavioral property (call it P) of a feature must be guaranteed by a specification S of this feature independent of how it is implemented. The only effective way to demonstrate this guarantee is to show that P logically follows from S by creating a formal proof of P.

Sometimes we cannot make this guarantee. The next best thing is to show that some possible implementations of the feature exist that obey P. We can show these implementations using two effective methods. One way is to prove that P logically follows from an augmented specification S' consisting of S and additional logical axioms that constrain the style of implementation. Another way is to produce some Kripke model for S, such as one of WAT-SON's local agent models, and verify that this model obeys P using a fast model-checking procedure instead of a proof. WATSON uses both techniques at different times. The next paragraph describes how WATSON creates an augmented specification for its final consistency test. The constructions used in WATSON's model-based reasoning are described in the following section.

Transition Rules and Nonmonotonicity. The final specification WATSON produces is based on a set of transition rules but includes a few miscellaneous domain axioms plus a set of closed-world axioms derived from the transition rules. A set of transition rules expresses knowledge only about necessary state transitions to cover a set of scenarios. As an open-ended specification, it does not rule out other arbitrary state changes caused by as-yet-unspecified transition rules. WATSON uses a *consequent completion* operation to construct a theory that includes a given set of transition rules but only permits state transitions explicitly sanctioned by these rules. Consequent completion is an extended temporal version of *predicate completion* (Clarke 1978) used in formalizing database semantics. It drastically prunes the set of (Kripke) models that satisfy the transition rules and corresponds to a shift of view from regarding a specification as partial to treating it as exhaustive.

For example, consider the following two transition rules: "If a ringing phone goes off-hook, it must stop ringing" and "If a ringing phone Y is being called by X and X hangs up, then Y stops ringing." With these two rules, if no other transition rules contained a consequent about phones ceasing to ring, then computing a consequent completion with respect to these two rules results in an additional closed-world axiom: "If a phone stops ringing, then it must be the case that either it just went off-hook or someone who was calling it just hung up."

If a certain desirable behavioral property (that is, a temporal logic theorem) logically follows from a completed set of rules but not from the uncompleted version, then this property might not continue to hold when these rules (that is, a telephone feature specification) are combined with rules derived from other scenarios—a potential weak spot or nonmonotonicity. Such properties require constant reverification whenever rules are combined. Unfortunately, WATSON's local agent models are based on just such properties and, thus, must frequently be recomputed.

WATSON also contains other sources of potential nonmonotonicity besides consequent completion, for example, the revision of transition rules during the interactive audit phase. Choosing an appropriate level of generality for a transition rule involves two different considerations: how much to generalize the sort (type) of each agent in the episode (for example, what kinds of phones might "Joe" represent?) and which episode antecedents should be filtered from a rule's sufficient conditions (for example, those involving only agents not mentioned in the rule's consequent). Even without consequent completion, revising transition rules, especially in the direction of less generality, can cause specification properties that were previously provable to become false.

The amount of reverification necessitated by rule revisions can be reduced (but not eliminated) by careful static ordering of process steps in WATSON's interactive audit phase, exploiting metaknowledge about when various aspects of a specification gain stability. For instance, once WATSON eliminates all unreachable regions of the state space of its local agent models, it knows that no subsequent steps will ever cause a currently reachable known state to become unreachable. Another technique to reduce the recomputation effort involves batching several unrelated rule changes rather than reverifying each potentially nonmonotonic property after each change. The scenario in figure 2, for example, can be processed in only 4 update-reverify cycles, even though 11 rule modifications occur.

Local Agent Models

The last of WATSON's declarative knowledge structures is the set of incomplete models maintained for each agent's or process's local view of the system state. We previously described these knowledge structures as a collection of deterministic finite-state machines, one for each distinct type of agent or process in the system. More precisely, these models are general graph constructions capable of representing both well-formed and ill-formed state-transition graphs (for example, overspecified, underspecified, nondeterministic, or disconnected transition graphs). During its heuristic audits, WATSON analyzes how these graphs deviate from well-formed graphs and adjusts its scenario interpretations so that these graphs will converge to well-formed state-transition graphs. This construction involves three parts:

State Partition: WATSON allocates the information content in the global system state into the local states of a (potentially infinite) set of agents or processes in the world, such as telephones, telephone switchboards, and calls in progress. Temporal logic predicates used to describe conditions on the global state in the domain knowledge are reexpressed in terms of local state functions, as described in Lamport 1989.

State Equivalence Class Lattice: For each type of agent, WATSON computes a lattice structure that estimates the minimum set of states induced by the local state functions. The lattice is induced by enumerating all compatible combinations of values for the local state functions taken singly, pairwise, in triples, and so on. Only state functions related to assertions or events encountered in the current set of scenarios need be considered. Each state in the lattice is, thus, an equivalence class of all states that can be distinguished based on a particular set of predicates, and some such classes might in practice be nonsingletons or might even be empty in an actual implementation. This encoding of possible states is more compact than a flat enumeration and resembles the hierarchical graph structure used in state charts (Harel et al. 1990).

Prestates and Poststates: For each episode in the current scenarios, WATSON determines which states (that is, state equivalence classes) are possible for each agent mentioned in the episode, both before the episode and immediately afterward. This relation approximates the state-transition function of the final desired automaton.

As mentioned earlier, the major benefit from constructing these models is speed. When the domain axioms and the models contain similar information, interrogating the models is typically about 100 times faster than proving a theorem. Even though building and updating these models accounts for over 70 percent of WATSON's central processing (CPU) use in our case studies to date, it is still roughly 6 times more costly not to use them. Using model-based reasoning for accelerating an automated logical reasoning system is an old but underused idea dating back at least to Gelernter's (1959) geometry theorem prover, which exhibited speedups similar to WATSON's.

Constructing local agent models is clearly not the same or as difficult as decomposing the world into separate communicating automata. As previously mentioned, each local agent model can freely refer to the internal states of other agents when computing its state transitions. Note also that some information in the global state is redundantly stored among agents, and some might not be stored at all, leaving the local agent models incomplete. For the example scenario, the local model for each telephone (for example, Joe) does not store the destination of outstanding connection requests, merely one bit telling whether any such requests exist. This loss of information is far from catastrophic. At worst, it means that verifying certain properties of feature behavior (for example, that Joe gets connected to the same phone for which he has an outstanding connection request) requires the theorem prover.

Human Interface Design

WATSON is designed to serve two different classes of users: numerous telephone feature designers and a few telephony domain experts who maintain its internal knowledge base. The feature designers are at least marginally computer literate but are novices in formal specification methodologies. The rarer domain experts must have strong intuitions about how temporal logic works and understand the layout of WATSON's knowledge bases, even if they don't want to read and write a formal notation. The human interfaces for both these groups share common technology, especially in natural language input-output, but the face WATSON presents to telephony engineers is much less formal and much more assertive—controlling the flow of a conversation by posing specific but informally phrased questions and slipping mathematical rigor through the back door. In this subsection, we first describe the common natural language technology, then the reasoning capabilities useful to each type of prospective user.

Natural Language Facilities

To date, WATSON's natural language input capabilities have been based on TELI, an English case-frame parser with some capabilities for customization by nonlinguists and a retargetable English-to-logic translator back end. Previous users of TELI include database query generators, a frame-based knowledge base update tool, and a software cross-reference browser. WATSON's output facilities are cruder: a home brew paraphraser consisting of a library of about a dozen simple, somewhat ad hoc strategies for expressing the intent of various logic formulas as fragments of hypothetical scenarios. The paraphraser is still in its infancy.

TELI's added value for WATSON is making a logiclike domain description and scenario language appear to be a colloquial English subset, automatically tolerating minor variations in linguistic use. This approach makes the input process much less brittle for new users. TELI handles many common sorts of pronoun-antecedent correspondence; variations in verb tense, voice, and modals; elision; synonyms; and slang. It passes to WATSON not only a best-guess translation of an English utterance into a logic notation but also a detailed English parse so that WATSON can second-guess.

Another advantage of using a natural language front end is facilitating unsolicited input from the user (even a naive feature designer) at any interaction point. In contexts where a yes-no answer is being solicited, an optional yes-because explanation might be appropriate if the justification contains additional domain knowledge that can prevent WATSON from chasing future red herrings. This option can reduce frustration on the part of experienced users.

Obviously, numerous unsolved theoretical problems with natural language interpretation affect even a small telephony sublanguage. One can easily produce legal sentences that confuse TELI, and even if TELI produces a translation, other ambiguities can be lurking. WATSON relies heavily on two techniques for such situations:

The first technique is *generalization:* When a concept is too complex for TELI, users can instead give an example of the concept and let WATSON's scenario-understanding mechanism perform the appropriate generalizations. For example, when interpreting the sentence "Joe should not be calling Mary while Joe is calling Sue," WATSON can be told to treat "Joe-Mary-Sue" as shorthand for the concept of three arbitrary but distinct telephones, and it will generalize whatever TELI asserts to be true of Joe-Mary-Sue as true of all telephone trios. This verbal subterfuge avoids some problems in quantifier scoping and pronoun resolution in complicated utterances.

The second technique is the *paraphrase*. When an utterance is judged ambiguous, user feedback can be solicited using a paraphrase of a possible interpretation. For example, in the utterance "An off-hook phone should not ring," WATSON notes a likely ambiguity regarding whether a telephone should be allowed to begin ringing at the same moment that it goes back on the hook or whether it must already be on the hook before ringing can begin. It can then ask the domain expert for further clarification: "Suppose Joe is off-hook and hangs up. Can Joe hanging up ever trigger Joe starting to ring?"

These two techniques are clearly limited and are not a panacea. However, such problems most frequently affect only the domain expert user, who might well have enough familiarity with temporal logic concepts to directly encode knowledge in logic in an emergency. Input problems are much less frequent in the more constrained world of feature scenario traces.

Interface for Feature Designers

To a feature designer, the notion of formal feature specification can be new and threatening. Temporal logic is almost certainly a mysterious "black art." Thus, WATSON must take charge of the design process, obtaining the information needed to refine its model approximations by asking intelligible questions of a feature designer. The art lies in picking the right questions and the right time to ask them.

The limitations of the designer force WATSON to severely censor the types of questions that might be asked. Questions too logically subtle for a simple English paraphrase must be simplified, even if this simplification results in learning less useful information. Questions beyond a designer's assumed area of competence are categorically rejected, especially questions that would require the user to envision variations in system behavior over multiple features or a variety of scenarios. WATSON demands that all queries be couched in the context of episodes within a scenario previously input by the user or a trivially modified hypothetical variant. The following question illustrates an information-rich question related to the example scenario that WATSON must reject because of its generality and its subtlety (beyond the scope of WATSON's simple paraphraser):

> Is it true that whenever some phone (call it Joe) goes off-hook, Joe should start getting dial-tone unless it is the case that Joe is ringing and/or there is some other phone requesting a connection to Joe which is getting a ringback tone?

A suboptimal but permissible question that WATSON might ask instead is

> At the beginning of the scenario, if Joe were ringing, would Joe start to get the dial-tone?

Each WATSON query to humans can be answered yes, no, or don't know using a mouse-click pop-up menu, but the user can add an English explanation. A designer's explanation should be a new scenario that covers this question (and presumably some others like it) when adequately generalized. If a feature designer tries to directly enter new background knowledge (instead of a scenario), WATSON accepts the input but restricts the use of this knowledge to the current feature being designed.

Because all questions relate to specific scenario episodes, WATSON can minimize discontinuities in focus by grouping the questions it intends to ask according to specific episodes. This discourse plan (unrelated to the plans used to generalize scenarios) is currently nothing more than a simple agenda of pending questions. It is initially computed when a scenario is first entered and is updated after each user response, because one answer can resolve multiple issues (because of possible generalizations) or permit additional questions to be asked.

Tool Kit for Domain Experts

In contrast to the naive feature designer, people actively maintaining WATSON's background knowledge base will need additional capabilities to change and analyze WATSON's domain knowledge. They need natural language capabilities for paraphrasing, stating, and retracting domain knowledge, as previously described. They also need to compare different knowledge base configurations using benchmark scenarios, which have either proved difficult in the past or whose interpretation is especially critical to numerous features (for example, scenarios giving the major test cases for critical telephone user interaction protocols). To perform this analysis, maintainers might want to install new types of interactive audits or different consistency tests. Thus, these users need additional knowledge base audit tools beyond those used by feature designers.

In its current state, the user interface for domain experts is not nearly as polished as that for feature designers. All we provide is a tool kit of high-level knowledge base operators that can be hooked together using Lisp. Most of these operators work on whole logical theories (sets of logic axioms) at a time, not on individual formulas. Besides WATSON's theorem prover, these operations include (1) filters that extract subsets of domain knowledge based on the form or content of logical axioms; (2) consequent completion operations that augment a partial theory with closed-world axioms, causing WATSON to treat it as a complete, stand-alone system specification; (3) query reformulators to permit complex theorems to be decomposed by cases or converted into mathematical induction arguments, both of which can greatly speed proofs; (4) a theory librarian to track various augmented, filtered, and combined axiom sets, preprocessing them on demand for the theorem prover; and (5) paraphrasers and generalizers for constructing new user interaction dialogs.

Complex consistency and completeness checks can be constructed in just a few lines of code using the knowledge tool kit. The original implementation of WATSON's final consistency test required about 15 pages of fairly dense Lisp source code. We recently used the tool kit to reimplement and extend the consistency test, requiring less than a page of Lisp code (besides the tool kit itself). However, we still consider the tool kit a stop-gap, demanding too much expertise in Lisp programming from knowledge maintainers. An extensive library of prefabricated knowledge base audits is needed, but additional experimental work is required to decide the most useful ones.

Related Research

As an interdisciplinary effort, WATSON draws inspiration from five different computer-science disciplines.

Programming from Informal Specifications

The general goals of WATSON recall the SAFE project at USC/Information Sciences Institute (Balzer, Goldman, and Wile 1977; Goldman, Balzer, and Wile 1977). SAFE attempted to understand an English prose description of a process, inferring the relevant entities mentioned in the process and their key relationships. It then generated an algorithm to implement the process. Of the 6 types of specification ambiguities corrected by SAFE, 4 of them, accounting for 88 percent of these corrections, were artifacts from using fairly unconstrained natural language input. Conversely, the scenario ambiguities corrected by WATSON did not arise in the SAFE case studies because SAFE's initial specifications were more expansive (100 to 200 words).

Formalizing Domain Knowledge

Three separate groups of software engineers recently focused attention on the desirability of collecting and preserving formal representations of domain knowledge. Arango (1989) surveys the rise of domain analysis within the context of efforts to maximize and measure software reuse. Another group of researchers works on generalizing database modeling techniques into requirement modeling for information systems (for example, RML [Greenspan, Borgida, and Mylopoulos 1986]). A third segment is working on domain analysis as a methodology for building better automatic programming systems (Barstow 1985). Largely unknown among software engineers, a fourth research community is working on advanced domain analysis techniques, the AI "commonsense reasoning" effort (Davis 1990).

Although there is talk of converging domain analysis efforts into a coherent engineering discipline, there is still wide divergence among researchers about the proper degree of generality for representing domain knowledge. WATSON and RML both emphasize declarative, logic-based representations in which facts about the domain intuitively correspond to individual assertions in the domain theory. Such systems attempt to optimize incremental knowledge acquisition and knowledge reuse, but applying knowledge to any specific problem requires (at the least) an expensive general deductive procedure such as theorem proving. At the other pole, Barstow's domain theory is predigested by humans into program-transformation rules—extremely specific coding techniques for programming in narrow application fields. These rules can be applied in cookbook fashion without requiring much inference beyond simple pattern matching. Arango notes other, even more predigested representations for domain knowledge, including libraries of software modules and their interface definitions.

Acquiring Programs from Examples

Several approaches have been used to learn programs based on sample traces: the pattern-matching approaches of Biermann and Krishnawamy (1976) and Bauer (1979), the language-recognizer generators of Angluin (1978) and Berwick (1986), Shavlik's (1989) trace-induction system PLEESE, and Andreae's NODDY system. Of these approaches, those of Andreae and Shavlik are the closest to the spirit of WATSON with their encoding of explicit domain knowledge. The other approaches attempt domain independence, requiring that their input examples be either numerous or meticulously annotated.

Andreae's NODDY, like WATSON, uses domain knowledge to constrain the generality of the programs it writes, much like the function of negative examples in an example-based learning system. NODDY writes robot programs, and its domain knowledge involves analytic geometry and bounds on the degrees of freedom in its solution space.

Shavlik's PLEESE does not work in a domain of reactive systems. However, it uses domain knowledge in an interesting way not paralleled by either WATSON or NODDY. In PLEESE, the form in which domain knowledge is expressed provides part of its inductive bias; that is, the form partially constrains the structure of the final programs PLEESE generalizes from its examples. For example, recursive definitions of domain concepts lead to explicit recurrences in PLEESE's final solution. Although this double use for domain knowledge seems benign and economical in Shavlik's example domains, we deliberately decouple WATSON's domain knowledge from its inductive bias. We consider it difficult enough to get a large domain theory logically correct without having to also worry about how its form of expression might affect some other part of the system.

Automated Protocol Synthesis

Some systems for automated synthesis and verification of communication protocols among finite-state machines use knowledge representations (for example, some version of temporal logic) and inference procedures similar to those of WATSON (Clarke 1985), but the goals of protocol synthesis are almost orthogonal to ours. Protocol synthesis typically begins with a given *service specification,* which is a finite-state system defining acceptable system behavior. The goal of protocol synthesis is to decompose this machine into a network of more primitive, completely separate but communicating finite-state machines whose composite behavior implements the desired service specification. For WATSON, however, a service specification is not the beginning but the final goal. WATSON's decomposition of system behavior into local agent models superficially resembles the derivation of a protocol implementation, but the local agent models are not truly separate machines. In its current form, WATSON is quite disconnected from the core issues of protocol synthesis and analysis.

Automated Temporal Logic Theorem Proving

General-purpose automatic theorem provers divide into two types. The first type relies on a self-contained, complete inference algorithm such as resolution-paramodulation for ordinary clausal first-order logic with equality. The other type uses (at least conceptually) a weaker inference method, such as term rewriting, plus an encoding of stronger inference rules as axioms or meta-axioms. These meta-axioms must be combined with a logical theory before theorem proving can begin. Usually, the first type of prover is faster because less time is spent deciding which inference rule to apply, but it has been restricted to nonmodal logics. The second approach is more general and offers a finer-grained way to tailor inference procedures for nonstandard logics.

WATSON's prover evolved pragmatically as a novel sort of hybrid. It is based on a resolution-paramodulation first-order prover for speed, but it implements temporal reasoning with a combination of nonstandard clause-normalization procedures (a kind of theory pre-conditioning) and explicit temporal metaaxioms. To date, this compromise approach has been satisfactory, even though it has entailed incomplete temporal reasoning to maintain tractability.

An alternative approach was proposed (Ohlbach 1988) that extends resolution-paramodulation into a temporal reasoning procedure. This approach uses a novel encoding of nested temporal operators (or other modal operators) into world path expressions attached to each atom in a logical formula. We recognize the potential superiority of this method over our current approach in both speed and completeness of reasoning and are investigating how to apply Ohlbach's results to the next version of our theorem prover.

Implementation Status

WATSON's precursor was PHOAN (DeTreville 1984), which implemented a weaker form of WATSON's domain consistency test for hand-generated transition rules. A research prototype of WATSON has existed since 1987 and successfully synthesized a few simple features. This prototype handled a few scenarios of the complexity of figure 2, requiring from 40 seconds to 7 minutes of CPU time for each scenario on a Sun4/110 running under KCL to perform a complete specification synthesis through the consistency test stage. For these examples, the number of distinct states required for a telephone station model ranged from 7 to 33.

WATSON is currently being enhanced and utilized to analyze existing features of two different products, a PBX (mid-sized private telephone switch) and a smaller key-telephone system. For the PBX, WATSON generates detailed system tests from scenarios, sharing a large domain knowledge base with several other AI-based tools. The other project involves techniques for combining a WATSON specification with other kinds of formal specifications of nonreactive system properties.

Despite the declarative nature of its domain theory, WATSON still includes a few heuristic procedures that were hand coded with telephony in mind, giving us concern when we contemplate applying it in other domains. The reasoning used in partitioning global state among local state functions is not general enough. We have also not adequately formalized the space of possible generalizations of transition rules. The heuristics for recognizing plan goals within scenarios are crude. WATSON's internal representation of its own process steps needs to be made more explicit, so that its own process programming can be more flexible and abstract. These topics are all for future research.

Conclusions

WATSON exemplifies the practical value of AI techniques for software engineering. Not only are many of the ideas in WATSON directly borrowed from AI (for example, goal-directed plans, model-based reasoning, predicate completion, natural language parsing), but its development was expedited by mature, stable, interworkable software available from our local AI community, most notably TELI and the CLASSIC knowledge base infrastructure (Brachman et al. 1990). Furthermore, exploratory programming disciplines practiced widely (but rarely documented) within the AI field enabled us to optimize WATSON for modifiability. WATSON is not a finely honed application of a few crisp theoretical insights for solving an abstract problem. Its ill-structured and changing application domain demands an eclectic, evolutionary approach, a forte of AI technology.

If there is one unifying theme in our research to date, it lies in leveraging existing human expertise in novel ways, helping ordinary people (that is, conventionally trained telephony engineers) achieve extraordinary results (mathematically precise specifications). Designing WATSON has been a series of straightforward but unconventional engineering compromises in the design of a human-machine partnership: trading off what particular kinds of people can do well against what machines can do passably well. First, restricting WATSON's scope to reactive specifications makes automated verification at least marginally tractable for an interactive design environment. Second, adopting general logical inference as our computational paradigm simplifies domain knowledge acquisition and maintenance but at the cost (affordable so far) of needing automatic theorem-proving technology to apply domain knowledge. Third, machine mediating the task of generalizing from examples buys a separation of concerns between the particular scenarios envisioned by human engineers and the integrated models and logical theories required in the final specification. The hidden cost is handling non-monotonicities caused by flawed generalizations. Fourth, shifting the human engineer's role from architect to oracle smooths and speeds the specification design process, especially for less experienced engineers. The down side is managing a necessary evolution of WATSON's audits and consistency tests to accommodate wider classes of applications. If we had but one piece of advice for other researchers in specification techniques, it would be to precisely determine who their end users are to be and to pay more attention to opportunities for shifting the human-machine boundary.

References

Andreae, P. 1985. Justified Generalization: Acquiring Procedures from Examples, Technical Report, 834, AI Laboratory, Massachusetts Institute of Technology.

Angluin, D. 1978. Inductive Inference of Formal Languages from Positive Data. *Information and Control* 45:117–135.

Arango, G. 1989. Domain Analysis—From Art Form to Engineering Discipline. In Proceedings of the Fifth International Workshop on Software Specification and Design, *ACM SIGSOFT Engineering Notes* 14(3): 152–159.

Ballard, B., and Stumberger, D. 1986. Semantic Acquisition in TELI: A Transportable, User-Customizable Natural Language Processor. In ACL-24 Proceedings, 20–29. Cambridge, Mass.: Association for Computational Linguistics.

Balzer, R.; Goldman, N.; and Wile, D. 1977. Informality in Program Specifications. In Proceedings of the Fifth International Joint Conference on Artificial Intelligence, 389–397. Menlo Park, Calif.: International Joint Conferences on Artificial Intelligence.

Barstow, D. 1985. Specific Automatic Programming. *IEEE Transactions on Software Engineering* volume SE-11(11): 1321-1336.

Bauer, M. A. 1979. Programming by Examples. *Artificial Intelligence 12* (1): 1–21.

Berwick, R. 1986. Learning from Positive-Only Examples: The Subset Principle and Three Case Studies, in *Machine Learning: An Artificial Intelligence Approach,* volume 2, eds. *R.* Michalski,

J. Carbonell, and T. Mitchell, 625-646. San Mateo, Calif.: Morgan Kaufmann.

Biermann, A., and Krishnawamy, R. 1976. Constructing Programs from Example Computations. *IEEE Transactions on Software Engineering* 2(3): 141–153.

Brachman, R. J.; McGuinness, D. L.; Patel-Schneider, P. F.; Resnick, L. A.; and Bordiga, A. 1990. Living with Classic: When and How to Use a KL-One–Like Language. In *Principles of Semantic Networks,* ed. L. Sowa. San Mateo, Calif.: Morgan Kaufmann.

Clarke, E. M.; Browne M. C.; Emerson, E. A.; and Sistla, A. P. 1985. Using Temporal Logic for Automatic Verification of Finite-State Systems. In *Logics and Models of Concurrent Systems,* ed. K. R. Apt. NATO AIS Series, volume F13, 3-26. New York: Springer Verlag.

Clarke, K. L. 1978. Negation as Failure. In *Logic and Databases,*eds. *H.* Gallaire and J. Minker, 293–322. New York: Plenum.

Davis, E. 1990. *Representations of Commonsense Knowledge.* San Mateo, Calif.: Morgan Kaufmann.

DeTreville, J. 1984. Phoan: An Intelligent System for Distributed Control Synthesis. In ACM SIGSOFT/SIGPLAN Software Engineering Symposium on Practical Software Development Environments, ed. P. Henderson, 96–103. New York: Association for Computing Machinery.

Galton, A., ed. 1987. *Temporal Logics and Their Applications.* London: Academic.

Gelernter, H. 1959. The Realization of a Geometry-Theorem Proving Machine. In *Automation of Reasoning,* eds. J. Siekmann and G. Wrightson, G., 99–117. New York: Springer Verlag.

Goldman, N.; Balzer, R.; and Wile, D. 1977. The Inference of Domain Structure from Informal Process Descriptions, Research Report 77-64, USC/Information Sciences Institute, Marina del Rey, Calif.

Greenspan, S. J.; Borgida, A.; and Mylopoulos, J. 1986. A Requirements Modeling Language and Its Logic. *Information Systems* 11(1): 9–23.

Harel, D.; Lachover, H.; Naamad, A.; et. al. 1990. Statemate: A Working Environment for the Development of Complex Reactive Systems. *IEEE Transactions of Software Engineering* 16(4): 403–414.

Kelly, V.E., and Nonnenmann, U. 1987. Inferring Formal Software Specifications from Episodic Descriptions. In Proceedings of the National Conference on Artificial Intelligence, 127–132. Menlo Park, Calif.: American Association for Artificial Intelligence.

Lamport, L. 1989. A Simple Approach to Specifying Concurrent Systems. *CACM* 32(1): 32–47.

Nix, C. J., and Collins, B. P. 1988. The Use of Software Engineering, Including the Z Notation, in the Development of CICS. *Quality Assurance* 14(3): 103–110.

Ohlbach, H. J. 1988. A Resolution Calculus for Modal Logics. In *Ninth International Conference on Automated Deduction,* 500–516. New York: Springer Verlag.

Rem, M.; van de Snepscheut, J. L. A.; and Udding, J. T. 1983. Trace Theory and the Definition of Hierarchical Components. In *Third Caltech Conference on Very Large Scale Integration,* 225–239. New York: Computer Science Press.

Wing, J.1990. A Specifier's Introduction to Formal Methods. *IEEE Computer* 23(9): 8–24.

4

Using Evolution Transformations to Construct Specifications

W. Lewis Johnson and Martin S. Feather

The Knowledge-based Software Assistant, as proposed in Green et al. (1986), was conceived as an integrated knowledge-based system to support all aspects of the software life cycle. Such an assistant would support specification-based software development: Programs would be written in an executable specification language from which efficient implementations would mechanically be derived. A number of systems have since been developed, each providing assistance for individual software activities. This chapter describes research conducted in the course of developing two of these systems. The first, the Knowledge-based Specification Assistant (KBSA Project 1988; Johnson 1988), was specifically aimed at supporting the evolutionary development of specifications. The second project, ARIES (acquisition of requirements and incremental evolution into specifications), is currently under way. It provides integrated support for both requirement analysis and specification development. ARIES is jointly being developed with Lockheed Sanders.

The original project report anticipated that specifications would evolve but did not describe the mechanism for such evolution. In part as a result of the work on the Specification Assistant, the current vision of an ultimate Knowl-edge-based Software Assistant embraces the notion of a formalized specification development process (Elefante 1989). In our approach, a de-scription of the system to be built is created in a machine-processable form from the early stages of a software development project and is gradually refined and evolved to produce a formal specification together with support-ing documentation. During this process, changes to requirements and specifications frequently occur and must be supported and managed. This chapter presents the mechanism that we have developed to support the pro-cess called *evolution transformations*. The chapter describes how evolution transformations can be employed in developing specifications, and compares this approach to other incremental specification techniques. We provide a de-tailed description of our representation of transformations and of our mecha-nisms for retrieving and applying them. Our current efforts at reorganizing the transformation library into basic operators and macrooperators are sum-marized. The chapter concludes with a discussion of how evolution transfor-mation technology can be applied to other software development tasks.

Evolution Transformation

During the specification development process, a system description under-goes well-defined semantic changes (Goldman 1983). New details are added, revisions are made to resolve conflicts between definitions, and high-level re-quirements on overall behavior are transformed into requirements on the be-havior of individual system components. Evolution of the system description continues as a system is maintained. To support evolution, we have con-structed a library of transformations for modifying specifications. This li-brary consists primarily of so-called evolution transformations, that is, trans-formations whose purpose is to elaborate and change specifications in specific ways. Like conventional correctness-preserving transformations (also called meaning-preserving transformations), they can be invoked by the user or by other transformations, and they are executed by a mechanical transformation system to cause changes to a specification. Correctness-pre-serving transformations are generally applied to derive efficient implementa-tions from specifications, keeping the meaning of the specification un-changed; in contrast, our evolution transformations deliberately change the meaning of specifications. We do, in fact, include some meaning-preserving transformations in our library, but instead of deriving efficient implementa-tions, their purpose is to reorder specifications (for better presentations), rewrite specifications into equivalent forms using different language con-structs, eliminate redundancies, or make explicit some otherwise implicit specification features. Some of these transformations can also appear in a transformational implementation system, to be used to replace high-level specification constructs with low-level implementation ones.

Our evolution transformations perform semantic changes, such as revising the type hierarchy defined in a specification, changing data-flow and control-flow paths, and introducing processes to satisfy requirements. A single transformation can perform a number of individual changes to a specification; for example, if a definition is changed, all references to this definition throughout the specification can be changed in a corresponding manner to retain semantic consistency.

Advantages of Transformational Evolution

The evolutionary development of specifications by transformation has several advantages. First, because the transformations mechanically take care of low-level editing details, changes can be succinctly directed and reliably performed. This result is analogous to the advantage of using conventional correctness-preserving transformations for deriving efficient implementations from specifications, cogent arguments for which can be found in Balzer, Goldman, and Wile (1976) and Bauer (1976).

Second, the transformational development of specifications facilitates the separation of concerns during the analysis process. The initial analysis of requirements can focus on modeling the system environment and describing the effects that the intended system will have on this environment. These effects can be stated with little regard for the particular design that will achieve them. As a separate activity, the analyst can then propose a design and transform the requirement statements into constraints on the design. Evolution transformations have two distinct roles in this process: to aid in constructing the initial model of environment and requirements and to transform the requirements into specifications in a way that preserves the meaning of the requirements as much as possible.

Third, the record of transformation steps preserves the history of how high-level requirements are developed into lower-level specifications. This approach provides traceability, which is helpful for understanding the resulting specifications and assuring that all the original requirements have suitably been incorporated.

Fourth, the transformation record can be undone and replayed, permitting the exploration of different specification choices. This approach permits a developer to explore several (relatively) unrelated evolutions to the same specification, with the resulting separation of concerns and its attendant benefits. To do this exploration, the same starting specification is separately evolved into several specifications, and the transformational record is kept in each case; the resulting (multiple) specifications can then be combined by serially replaying all of the transformations on the initial specification (Feather 1989a). The same method also permits multiple developers to independently make changes to a common specification, combining their changes later. Where the separate evolutions are not, in fact, independent, comparison of the transformations can reveal the interference (Feather 1989b). This development model was extended to the case in which the separate evolutions describe different users' conflicting requirements, and negotiation techniques are utilized to resolve the conflicts (Robinson 1989).

Last, when a specification has been transformed into an efficient implementation and is later to be changed, conducting the change through the use of evolution transformations can facilitate the replay of the original transformational development on the changed specification (Feather 1990).

Developing a Library of Transformations

We began our exploration of evolution transformations by concentrating on two problems, a patient monitoring system and an air traffic control system, and manually worked out development scenarios to discover what transformations were necessary. We then implemented general-purpose versions of these transformations, which could be applied to mechanically achieve these developments. The result of this exploration was a sizable library containing about 100 transformations of a wide variety of types. This library is significantly more extensive than similar libraries developed by Balzer (1985) and Fickas (1987). In addition, although other researchers have studied evolution steps similar to those captured by our transformations (Narayanaswamy 1988; Johnson 1989), they have not developed transformations to enact these steps.

The ARIES system expands on this work; we are developing a transformation library that is extensive enough and powerful enough to apply to a wide range of specifications. Two issues have been of particular concern in the current work. First, a method is needed for characterizing the effects of evolution transformations. This method is necessary to ensure the coverage provided by the library (that is, to determine what range of transformations is required in the library for it to support a wide range of analyst activities) and to retrieve from the library (that is, retrieve the appropriate transformation to make the desired specification change). Second, we need to be able to apply transformations to specifications expressed in a variety of notations. Whereas the Specification Assistant operated only on specifications expressed in the specification language GIST (Goldman et al. 1988), ARIES supports a wide spectrum of other notations, including hypertext, flow diagrams, state-transition diagrams, and domain-specific notations. We needed a common internal representation capturing the semantics of all these notations. By applying the transformations to the internal representation, the same transformation library can be applied to specifications expressed in a variety of notations.

The solution to both problems required identifying the different semantic dimensions embodied in a specification. The ARIES system internally represents specifications as descriptions along each of these dimensions. These descriptions are relatively independent of any particular notation that might be used to express these semantics. This arrangement provides a means of characterizing the effects of transformations: Each transformation performs specific changes to one or more semantic dimensions of the specification. Adequate library coverage can then be achieved by making sure that all possible changes along each semantic dimension are supported. Notation independence makes it possible for analysts to use the same transformations to edit different notations. When an analyst proposes a change to a particular view of a specification, this change can be along one or more semantic dimensions, which, in turn, can suggest appropriate transformations to apply.

Related Work

Burstall and Goguen (1977) argue that complex specifications should be put together from simple ones and developed their language CLEAR to provide a mathematical foundation for this construction process. They recognize that the construction process itself has structure, employs a number of repeatedly used operations, and is worthy of explicit formalization and support—a position that we agree with.

Goldman (1983) observes that natural language descriptions of complex tasks often incorporate an evolutionary vein: The final description can be viewed as an elaboration of some simpler description, itself the elaboration of a yet simpler description, and so on, back to some description deemed sufficiently simple to be comprehended from a non-evolutionary description. He identifies three dimensions of change between successive descriptions: *structural,* concerning the amount of detail the specification reveals about each individual state of the process; *temporal,* concerning the amount of change between successive states revealed by the specification; and *coverage,* concerning the range of possible behaviors permitted by a specification. We were motivated by these observations about description to try to apply such an evolutionary approach to the construction of specifications.

Fickas (1986) suggests the application of an AI problem-solving approach to specification construction. Fundamental to his approach is the notion that the steps of the construction process can be viewed as the primitive operations of a more general problem-solving process and, hence, are ultimately mechanizable. Continuing work in this direction is reported in Robinson (1989) and Anderson and Fickas (1989). Fickas and his colleagues have concentrated on domain-specific goals arising in the course of specification development, whereas our efforts have concentrated on problem-independent goals.

In the Programmer's Apprentice project (Rich, Schrobe, and Waters 1979; Waters 1985), the aim—to build a tool that will act as an intelligent assistant to a skilled programmer—focuses on a different part of the software development activity than our work; however, much of what they have found has relevance to our enterprise. In their approach, programs are constructed by combining algorithmic fragments stored in a library. These algorithmic fragments are expressed using a sophisticated plan representation, with the resulting benefit of being readily combinable and identifiable. Their more recent project on supporting requirements acquisition, the Requirements Apprentice (Reubenstein and Waters 1989), addresses the early stages of the software development process and includes techniques that are similar to those of the Programmer's Apprentice but that operate on representations of requirements. The use of the Programmer's Apprentice is, thus, centered on the selection of the appropriate fragment and its composition with the growing program, with minor transformations to tailor these introduced fragments. In contrast, our approach centers on the selection of the appropriate evolution transformations and the reformulation of abstract descriptions of system behavior using such transformations. However, the two approaches are closely related. Many evolution transformations instantiate cliches as part of their function. We are currently exploring ways of making these cliches more explicit in our transformation system.

Karen Huff (Huff and Lesser 1987) developed a software process modeling and planning system that is in some ways similar to ours. Her GRAPPLE language for defining planning operators influenced our representation of evolution transformations. Conversely, her metaoperators applying to process plans were influenced by our work on evolution transformations.

Kelly and Nonnenmann's WATSON system (chapter 3) constructs formal specifications of telephone system behavior from informal scenarios expressed in natural language. Their system formalizes the scenarios and then attempts to incrementally generalize the scenarios to produce a finite-state machine. Their system is able to assume significant initiative in the formalization process because the domain of interest, namely, telephony, is highly constrained and because the programs being specified, call-control features, are relatively small. Our work is concerned with larger, less constrained design problems where greater analyst involvement is needed. It is also aimed toward the construction of specific behaviors that start from general requirements. Nevertheless, we have recognized for some time that acquisition from scenarios is a useful complement to the work we are doing in highly constrained design situations (Johnson 1986; Benner and Johnson 1989).

The PRISMA project (Niskier, Maibaum, and Schwabe 1989) is also a system for assisting in the construction of specifications from requirements. It has the following main characteristics: First are multiple views of the (emerging) specification, where the views that they explored are data flow diagrams, entity-relationship models, and Petri nets. Second, each view is represented in the same underlying semantic net formalism but represents a different aspect of the specification. This representation is suited to graphical presentation and admits to certain consistency and completeness heuristics whose semantics depend on the view being represented. For example, the lack of an input link has a different interpretation in each diagram. In a data flow diagram it indicates a process-lacking input; in an entity-relationship diagram it indicates an entity with no attributes; and in a Petri net diagram it indicates an event with no preconditions (prior events). Third, heuristics exist to compare the different views of (different aspects of) the same specification and aid in constructing new views or support checking for partial consistency between views. Fourth, errors detected by these heuristics are added to an agenda of tasks requiring resolution along with advice on how to accomplish this resolution. Fifth, a paraphraser produces natural language presentations of many of the kinds of information manipulated by the system (for example, of the requirement information represented in the different views, the agenda of tasks and advice for performing these tasks, the results of the heuristics that detect uses of requirement freedoms).

There is a striking similarity between the approach of the PRISMA project and ours—the use of multiple views, their presentations, and an underlying semantic net formalism. These researchers clearly thought about and developed heuristics to operate on or between views, an aspect that we only recently began to address. Conversely, we provided more support for evolution.

An Example of Transformational Specification Development

Our transformational approach to specification development is not specific to any particular domain. We examined several different domains, including hospital patient monitoring systems and library systems. However, to demonstrate the power and scalability of the approach, we devoted significant effort to a particular domain, namely air traffic control. We have been modeling requirements for the Berlin Air Route Traffic Control Center (BARTTC) for air traffic control in the airspace around Tempelhof Airport in Berlin. We also studied the requirements for U.S. domestic in-route air traffic control systems, that is, those systems responsible for the control of air traffic cruising at the high altitudes reserved for jet aircraft. These requirements are drawn from manuals on pilot and controller procedures (Aviation Supplies 1989; Air Traffic Operations 1989) and the experiences of the current Federal Aviation Administration Advanced Automation Program (Hunt and Zellweger 1987), whose goal is to develop the next generation of air traffic control systems.

In this chapter, we focus on a particular part of the air traffic control problem. One duty of an air traffic control system is to monitor the progress of controlled aircraft and ensure that they adhere to their planned courses. We examine how the process of monitoring aircraft flights is transformed during specification development.

Figure 1 shows an initial view of aircraft course monitoring. We use a *context diagram*, which shows the interactions between a system and its ex-

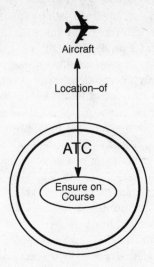

Figure 1. Initial Context Diagram of the Air Traffic Control System.

ternal environment and the information that flows between them. In these diagrams, ovals denote processes, boxes and miscellaneous icons denote objects, and double circles indicate system boundaries. The diagram distills course monitoring to its essential elements: the interaction between aircraft and the air traffic control system. The air traffic control system has a process called Ensure-On-Course as one of its subfunctions. It examines the location of the aircraft and compares it against the aircraft's expected location. If the two are sufficiently different, the air traffic control system attempts to affect a course change, changing the location of the aircraft.

This abstracted view of the air traffic control system is useful as a basis for stating course monitoring requirements. It is a natural abstraction for the domain, corresponding to the way flight procedures are commonly described in flight manuals (Aviation Supplies 1989). We do not go into details here about how much the expected location and the actual location are permitted to differ. Instead, we discuss how any such requirements can be transformed into specifications of system function.

Figure 2 shows a detailed view of the air traffic control process: More of the agents of the proposed system are introduced, specifically, radars and controllers. The air traffic control system is no longer viewed as a single agent; instead, there are two classes of agents, the air traffic control computer system and the controllers. Determining the locations of the aircraft is performed as follows: The radar observes the aircraft and transmits a set of radar messages, indicating that targets have been observed at particular locations. A Track-Correlation function inputs these radar messages and process-

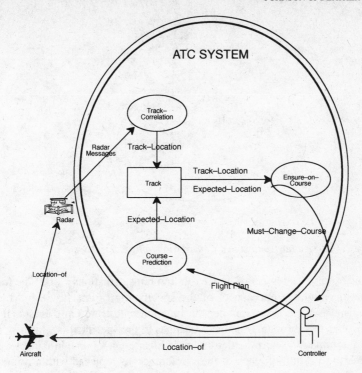

Figure 2. Detailed Context Diagram of the Air Traffic Control System.

es them to produce a set of tracks. Each track corresponds to a specific aircraft; the locations of the tracks are updated as the aircraft positions change. Meanwhile, expected aircraft locations are computed from the aircraft flight plans, which, in turn, are input by the controllers. The Ensure-On-Course process is modified so that it issues notifications to the controller (by signaling Must-Change-Course for an aircraft); the controller then issues commands to the aircraft over the radio.

To get to this detailed level of description, a number of transformations must be performed. Most of the transformations have to do with designing the pattern of data flow through the system. We implemented a number of the evolution transformations necessary to carry out this transformation process. The most important one is called Splice-Data-Accesses. Figure 3 shows the result of applying this transformation to the version in figure 1. It operates as follows: In the initial version, Ensure-On-Course directly accesses aircraft locations. Splice-Data-Accesses is used to introduce a new class of object, called Track, which has a location that matches the aircraft's location. The Ensure-On-Course process is modified in a corresponding way to refer to the track locations instead of the aircraft locations.

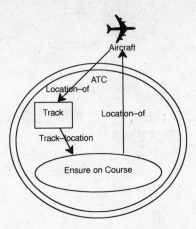

Figure 3. Intermediate Context Diagram of Air Traffic Control System.

This example is typical of how evolution transformations work. The transformation modifies one aspect of the specification (data flow) and keeps other aspects fixed (for example, the function of Ensure-On-Course). It accomplishes this through systematic changes to the specification. In this case, the transformation scans the definition of Ensure-On-Course looking for references to Location-of; each of these references is replaced with a reference to the Track-Location attribute of tracks.

Completing the derivation of this example requires further application of the following transformations: Splice-Data-Accesses is again applied to introduce the object Radar-Message, which is an intermediate object between Aircraft and Track. Maintain-Invariant-Reactively is invoked to construct processes for continuously updating the radar messages and the tracks. A transformation called Install-Protocol is used to introduce a notification protocol between the Ensure-On-Course process and the controller, so that Ensure-On-Course issues notifications to the controller whenever the location of the aircraft must be changed. A new process called Course-Prediction is added to compute expected locations from flight plans. Through this derivation, the specification is gradually refined into a version in which each system component interacts only with those data and agents that it will be able to interact with in the implemented system. The specification is now ready for detailed design and implementation.

Characterizing Transformations
Along Dimensions of Semantic Properties

The fundamental idea underlying our work is the ability to view a specification along a number of different semantic dimensions, for example,

a data flow dimension and an entity-relationship dimension. We then characterize our evolution transformations by the effects they induce along each dimension; for example, one transformation might add a new node to the entity-relationship dimension without changing the data flow. Network notations
such as entity-relationship diagrams and data-flow diagrams are commonly
used in describing systems; we take the logical progression of this idea and
describe each of our dimensions as a semantic network of nodes and links
(relations) connecting these nodes. Based on these descriptions, we characterize the effects of an evolution transformation in terms of generic network-
modification operators (for example, add a node; insert a link between two
nodes) applied to the various dimensions.

Given the right network abstraction and an appropriate notation for presenting it, transformations with complex effects can be viewed simply and
intuitively. However, our approach goes beyond simply providing editors for
particular diagrams, as is common in CASE tools. Additionally, we draw a
strong distinction between the representation of specifications, such as a semantic network, and the presentation of specifications. This idea was previously introduced in the Knowledge-Based Requirements Assistant and other
systems with advanced user interfaces. Because we define our transformations in terms of the representation rather than the presentation, the same
transformation can be applied to any presentation that depicts the affected semantic dimensions. Some transformations can simultaneously affect multiple
semantic dimensions, resulting in changes to an even broader range of presentations. Thus, for example, Splice-Data-Accesses changes both the information flow of a system (by rerouting data accesses) and the entity-relationship model of the system (by introducing new intermediate objects and
attributes). The system's information flow can be viewed using a context diagram or a more conventional data flow diagram; the system's entity-relationship model can be viewed using an entity-relationship diagram or an inheritance hierarchy diagram.

Background: An Outline of Our Specification Semantics

To understand the semantic dimensions and their effects, we must give an
overview of the semantic concerns that we attempt to represent and manipulate. Our goals have been to (1) represent semantic concerns that are commonly recognized as important in requirements engineering and AI, (2) support the
translation of commonly used notations into and out of our framework, and (3)
support our own research in requirements modeling and design. The result is a
semantic framework that supports many common notations.

The basic units of the ARIES system descriptions are types, instances, relations, events, and invariants. These units are grouped with a simple modularization mechanism called *folders*. The treatment of types, instances, and relations is compatible with most object-oriented approaches to requirements

engineering (for example, Hagelstein 1988). However, our entity-relationship model is more general and expressive than most in supporting a wide range of entity-relationship notations. For those readers who are familiar with such systems, the following list summarizes the specific features that our entity-relationship system supports: First, each type can have multiple subtypes and supertypes. Second, each instance can simultaneously belong to any number of types. Third, relations hold among any types of objects; there is no restriction that these types be primitive with respect to any particular machine representation. Fourth, relations need not be binary but can have arbitrary arity. Fifth, relations are fully associative; there is no need for separate relations to record the inverse of a given relation.

System descriptions can describe behavior over time, modeled as a linear sequence of states. Each state is fully described in terms of what instances exist, what relations hold between them, and what events are active.

Events subsume all system processes and external events described as part of a system description. Events have duration, possibly spanning multiple states in a behavior and involving multiple entities of the system. Events can have preconditions, postconditions, and methods consisting of procedural steps. They can explicitly be activated by other events or can spontaneously occur when their preconditions are met. They can have input and output.

Not all interactions with an event must occur through its input and output ports. It is often useful, particularly at the early stages of system specification, to describe events without concern for the specific input and output. For example, the early version of the Ensure-On-Course event described in An Example of Transformational Specification Development directly observed aircraft and modified their locations. An aircraft cannot be considered an input in the conventional sense here. Event declarations whose purpose is to describe activity, rather than specify particular artifacts, tend to have this flavor. Information flow here refers to any transfer of information between agents and their environment. The transformation example in An Example of Transformational Specification Development is aimed at transforming idealized information flows into concrete data flows.

Invariants are predicates that must hold during all states in the system. Invariants are divided into subclasses according to their intended function. Domain axioms are predicates about the environment that are assumed to hold, such as the configuration of airspaces. These invariants will hold regardless of what the system being specified might or might not do. Functional constraints are invariants that involve the system being specified or that are to be guaranteed by the system being specified. Thus, they are a kind of functional requirement and must explicitly be implemented or respected in the system being specified. An example of such a constraint is the requirement that aircraft not deviate from their designated courses by more than a set amount. Dependency links are established during the design process between such requirements and the events or other specification components (for example, Ensure-On-Course) that are intended to satisfy them.

Folders are used to organize specification information. Each folder contains a set of concept definitions. A folder can inherit from other folders, meaning that concepts within the folder can refer to concepts appearing in the inherited folders. A folder can also import specific concepts from other folders; for example, it can be used to select the correct concept if the inherited folders contain multiple concepts of the same name. It is also possible to give inherited concepts new names in the context of a folder, for example, renaming an inherited concept direction to heading. Folders are the principal mechanism for encapsulation and reuse. ARIES has an extensively populated library of generic and domain-specific folders.

As part of our current research, we are investigating the use of parameterized folders. *Parameterized folders* contain free variables, which must be bound when the folder is used. An example of such a folder is tracker-concepts, which defines concepts related to tracking, such as trajectories, location predication, and smoothing. This folder contains a free variable, tracked-object-type, which is the type of the object being tracked (for example, aircraft). Such folders are used by instantiating a copy of the folder with the variables bound, for example, specifying that the value of tracked-object-type is aircraft. The result is the definition of a tracker of aircraft positions. Such parameterized folders are an important mechanism for representing requirement cliches, as in the Requirements Apprentice (Reubenstein and Waters 1989). Many transformations introduce specification constructs having a stereotypic form; Splice-Data-Accesses is one such transformation. The form of the intermediate object created by this transformation can be stored in a folder and instantiated as needed. We expect to make increasing use of such parameterized folders in our transformation library.

Associated with specification components are a variety of attributes, including nonfunctional ones. We do not dwell on these details here (see Harris [1988]). The main conclusion that the reader should draw from this discussion is that most important requirement notations can be captured in this framework, particularly those employing diagrams. Likewise, knowledge representation schemes oriented toward concept modeling are readily accommodated in this scheme as well. The framework was partly implemented in two systems: ARIES and the KBSA Concept Demonstration system (DeBellis 1990). The following translators were implemented to translate several notations into or out of (or both) this ARIES framework (for translation out of ARIES, this function is only possible for those concepts for which a corresponding concept exists in the target): GIST (Balzer et al. 1983), (most of) the REFINE language (derived from the V language [Reasoning Systems 1986]), (most of) LOOM (MacGregor 1989), entity-relationship diagrams, concept hierarchies, and ENGLISH (Grove et al. 1971) (but only from ARIES into ENGLISH

[Swartout 1982]; we have not pursued natural language understanding as input). Translators for context diagrams, state-transition diagrams, and information flow diagrams are currently under development.

Dimensions of Semantic Properties

In our studies of specification evolution, we have found the following dimensions of semantic properties to be important for characterizing the changes that occur: (1) the modular organization of the specification, that is, which concepts are components of which folders and which folders inherit from which folders; (2) the entity-relationship model defined in the specification, that is, what relations might hold for each type, what attributes it can have, what generalizations and specializations are defined, and what instances are known; (3) information flow links, indicating for each process or event what external information it accesses, what facts about the world it can change, and what values are computed and supplied; (4) control-flow links, indicating what process steps must follow a given process step and what process steps are substeps of a given process step; and (5) state-description links, associating statements and events with preconditions and postconditions that must hold in the states before and after execution, respectively.

Each semantic dimension is modeled using a collection of relations, each representing one aspect of the dimension previously described. Thus, for example, the entity-relationship model is captured using the relations specialization-of, parameter-of, type-of, instance-of, and attribute-of. This model makes distinctions that are missing from many of the notations being supported. Thus, entity-relationship diagrams typically show specialization-of as just another relation in the application's data model. Here, it treated not as part of the application's data model but of ARIES's language for structuring data models.

This semantic model captures information beyond what conventional notations typically show; however, conventional diagrams can easily be generalized to capture such information. For example, entity-relationship diagrams are generally used only to show relationships among types, whereas our entity-relationship dimension also includes instances. However, entity-relationship style diagrams could also be used to describe instances. The information flow dimension generalizes conventional data flow; it captures the flow of information that is not mediated by conventional message passing. Thus, we can describe air traffic control as monitoring aircraft locations and changing them without implying that the aircraft are somehow sending location messages to the air traffic control system. Still, we can easily generalize conventional data flow diagrams to show such abstract information flow.

Generic Network-Modification Operations

Because we represent each semantic dimension as a semantic network of nodes and relations, we are able to identify a number of generic network-modification operations that apply to any semantic network and, thus, to each semantic dimension. The most primitive network-manipulation operations are insert and remove for adding and deleting links and create and destroy for creating and destroying objects. The meaning of an operation depends on the semantic dimension to which it is applied and the relation being affected; thus, for example, the operation of adding a link in the information flow dimension could mean making a process access information about an external object, whereas the same operation in the entity-relationship dimension could mean making one type become a specialization of another.

In addition to these primitive operations, we identified a number of frequently recurring complex operations:

- Update—Remove a link from one node, and add it to another node.
- Promote (a specialization of update)—if one of the linked nodes is part of an ordered lattice, then update the link so that it connects a higher node in the lattice.
- Demote (the opposite of promote)—move the link to a lower node in the lattice.
- Splice—Remove a link from between two nodes A and B, and reroute the connection through a third node, C, so that A is linked to C, and C is linked to B.
- Split—Replace a node A with two links B and C, linked in some fashion, where B and C divide the attributes of A.
- Join—Replace two nodes A and B with a node C, merging their attributes.

Examples of Dimensions of Semantic Properties and Changes within Them

We sketch some instances of semantic properties that arise in our specification of air traffic control. These examples show how information is actually captured along the different dimensions previously outlined and illustrate the semantic distinctions that are made along each dimension.

Modular Organization: The concepts of mass, direction, mobile object, and location are components of the physical-object folder. The concepts of aircraft, airport, control tower, and so on, are components of the atc-model folder. Three folders are inherited folders of the atc-system folder: (1) atc-model, containing objects and activities common to air traffic control; (2) system, containing definitions of various categories of systems, for example, signal-processing system; and (3) upper-model, a collection of generic concepts for modeling the semantics of natural language defined by the PENMAN project (Bateman 1990). The atc-model folder, in turn, has nine inherited folders, including physical-objects, vehicle, system, and upper-model. The concepts in a folder can be defined in terms of the concepts inherited from other folders, for example, the atc-model's air location is defined in terms of the physical object's location.

Entity-Relationship Model: The specialization relationship is used to express the type hierarchy; for example, aircraft is a specialization of vehicle, which, in turn, is a specialization of mobile-object. Similarly, the instance-of relationship is used to express which types an object belongs to, for example, the bartcc-facility is an instanceof the type atc-facility.

Information Flow: As discussed earlier, information flow involves the transfer of information (accesses to, and modifications of, information) between components. For example, the early versions of the Ensure-On-Course event access and modify aircraft locations; hence, both kinds of information flow links, accesses-fact and modifies-fact, hold between Ensure-On-Course and aircraft. Some of these information flows are later transformed into concrete data flows. The data flow relationship expresses the flow of data between components, for example, from the radar process to the Track-Correlation function and from the Track-Correlation function to the Ensure-On-Course process.

Control Flow: There are two kinds of control-flow links: control-substep and control-successor. Control-substep captures the flow of control when an event consists of a series of steps; the relationship holds between the event and its substeps. For example, Track-Correlation has the operation to update an individual track as a substep. Control-successor holds between actions that are in temporal sequence; for example, Ensure-On-Course is activated whenever Track-Correlation updates tracks. A third category of control link, describing causal relationships between events, will need to be included as well, along the lines that Yue (1989) developed for the Specification Assistant.

State Description: Links of this kind are between events and their preconditions and postconditions; for example, a precondition to Ensure-On-Course taking action is that an aircraft be off course, and its postcondition is that the aircraft be back on course (this postcondition is true at least in the early versions of the specification; in later versions, the postcondition is that it has triggered the activity of notifying the controller, which ultimately causes the aircraft to return to its course).

The meaning of a modification operation will depend on the semantic dimension to which it is applied: In the entity-relationship dimension, to insert a specialization-of link means to assert that one concept is a specialization of another, for example, that the type surveillance-aircraft is a specialization of the type aircraft. In the information flow dimension, to remove an accesses-fact link means to remove accesses to a category of external information from a component; for example, to remove access by atc-system to the aircraft location-of relation. For the specialization links of the entity-relationship dimension, to splice means to assert that some type is intermediary to two other types in the specialization hierarchy; for example, splicing military aircraft between aircraft and surveillance aircraft. In the information flow dimension, to splice means to reroute an information flow between two components through an intermediary; for example, our earlier splicing of track between aircraft and the air traffic control system. In the control-flow dimension, to splice means to reroute a direct control flow between two components through an intermediary; for example, in the early versions of the specification, there would be a direct control flow from an aircraft's Maneuver process to air traffic control Ensure-On-Course process, whereas in later versions, this direct link would have been spliced through the Track-Correlation process.

Transformation Details

We now look in detail at what evolution transformations do and discuss how they operate on the semantic network model of specifications. The discussion centers on a particular transformation, Splice-Data-Accesses.

Figure 4 shows offline documentation generated by the ARIES system for the Splice-Data-Accesses transformation. Both ARIES and the Specification Assistant can generate offline documentation of transformations (to be included in manuals and reports) and online help. In the Specification Assistant, the online help provided guidance for the user about what parameters must be supplied to the transformation, what types they should be, and how they should be input. In ARIES, this online help is being integrated into the ARIES diagram editing capability currently under development.

Transformations Operate on the Metamodel

As described in Background: An Outline of Our Specification Semantics, our systems support world modeling in terms of a semantic network of entities and relationships. Events perform actions that create or destroy entities and change relationships. At the same time, transformations are understood as operating on a semantic network of entities and relationships. Thus, the space of possible system descriptions is itself a domain that can be modeled in the ARIES framework. This model of specification objects and relationships is called the ARIES metamodel.

The ARIES metamodel is implemented as a set of types and relations in ARIES. The model is divided into two ARIES folders: the User-Metamodel, consisting of those types and relations that an ARIES user might need to be aware of, and the Lisp-Environment, consisting of those types and relations that are only used internally by ARIES. The user metamodel includes those concepts previously described: types, relations, events, invariants, folders, and so on. Outside evaluations of the Knowledge-Based Requirements Assistant and the Specification Assistant (Abbott 1989) indicated a need for Knowledge-based Software Assistant systems to have an understanding of their own system model; this approach provides such a model.

The ARIES system as a whole is implemented in AP5 (Cohen 1989), a set of database programming extensions to Lisp developed at USC/Information

Splice-Data-Accesses: Transformation
Concept description: Splice a data object into the information-access path from object to an agent or activity. The transformation can be applied when the agent or activity, called Accessor, accesses some relation Accessed-Relation, which is an attribute of some object Accessed-Object. The transformation modifies the definition of Accessor so that it does not access Accessed-Relation anymore. It performs this modification as follows. It creates a new type Intermediary-Object, with a new attribute Intermediary-Rel, which correspond to Accessed-Object and Accessed-Relation, respectively. Every reference to Accessed-Relation in Accessor is replaced with a reference to Intermediary-Rel. The result is a specification with the same behavior as before but with a different pattern of information flow.
Note: This transformation creates a new type and new relations. If you instead want to modify existing types or relations, you might want to use the more general transformation Generalized-Splice.
Input parameters:
   Accessor: Entity:
      Component currently accessing the relation
   Accessed-Relation: Entity: Relation currently being accessed directly
      Accessed-Object: Entity: Object type that Accessed-Relation is an attribute of
   Intermediary-Object-Type-Name: Entity:
      Name of type of intermediary object
   Intermediary-Rel-Name: Entity:
      Name of new object's relation, to be accessed instead of Accessed-Relation
   Correspondence-Rel-Name: Entity:
      Name of new relation mapping old object to new data object
Output parameters:
   Intermediary-Object:
      New object type, named Intermediary-Object-Type-Name
   Intermediary-Rel:
      New object's relation, to be accessed instead of Accessed-Relation
   Correspondence-Rel:
      New relation mapping old object to the intermediary object
Precondition: The Accessor must be an event or type declaration.
Goal: The Accessor does not access the Accessed-Relation.
Main effects:
   An Accesses-Fact relation between Accessor and Accessed-Relation is spliced .
   A Type-Declaration named Intermediary-Object is created.
   A Relation-Declaration named Intermediary-Rel is created.
   A Relation-Declaration named Correspondence-Rel is created.

Figure 4. Machine-Generated Documentation for Splice-Data-Accesses.

Sciences Institute. AP5 is the language that specifications are compiled into. That is, to test and simulate specifications, specifications are compiled into a prototype in AP5 and Lisp so that analysts can set up simulation scenarios and run them. In an analogous fashion, the ARIES metamodel is compiled into AP5 types and relations. Transformations operate by making queries and assertions to this database, just as a prototype of a user specification would.

One important advantage of AP5 in connection with this work is that it does not assume any particular internal data structure for storing relations. Programmers can select whichever data structure they see fit. In ARIES, it is convenient to use parse trees as the representation of some of the system description components because they contain program text. In ARIES, the POPART metaprogramming system is used for this purpose (Wile 1986; Johnson and Yue 1988). However, relations that are not directly part of the program text, such as data flow relations, can also be captured in the same database. The transformations need not be concerned with the particular implementation of the metamodel. Furthermore, an alternate data representation for the ARIES metamodel was also implemented in the REFINE programming environment. This implementation makes it possible for tools in the ARIES system to operate on specifications developed in the KNOWLEDGE-BASED SOFTWARE ASSISTANT Concept Demonstration system, which is primarily written in REFINE (Meyers and Williams 1990).

Transformations as Events

Continuing with the metamodel metaphor, transformations are modeled as events in the metamodel space. A special folder in ARIES called Transformation-Library contains specifications of all the transformations in the system. The same tools for viewing and validating specifications, such as the GIST paraphraser, can be applied to transformations. Likewise, transformations are compiled into Lisp and AP5 functions that operate on the database model of specifications. The explicit specification of transformations enables ARIES to help plan the application of transformations and determine their effects.

Like ordinary events, transformations have input, output, preconditions, goals, and methods. These features are illustrated in figure 4. The input are the accessed relation and the accessor as well as the names of the new types and relations that the transformation creates. These input are all typed; the types, such as relation-declaration, are all part of the ARIES metamodel. In general, preconditions and goals are used to determine the applicability and effectiveness of transformations; here, only a goal is defined. The goal in the case of Splice-Data-Accesses is that no information accesses to the spliced relation exist. The method of the transformation is not shown because it involves implementation details that are unlikely to interest an analyst.

Because transformations are specification objects, they can be described using a combination of formal descriptions and hypertext. Some of the textual descriptions shown in figure 4 are extracted from such hypertext descriptions; some are machine-generated natural language.

Effect Descriptions

The principal effects of each transformation are explicitly recorded as part of the transformation definition. Each effect is a generic operation applied to a combination of the transformation's input, output, and other related objects that are not directly input or output. In the case of Splice-Data-Accesses, one splice is performed, and three specification objects are created.

In general, transformations can have two possible effects: main effects and possible effects. *Main effects* are guaranteed to result from a transformation application (assuming that the goal of the transformation is not already satisfied). *Possible effects* might or might not result, depending on the particular situation in which the transformation is applied.

In principle, it should be possible to employ symbolic evaluation tools, such as those of the Specification Assistant, to analyze transformations and automatically determine their effects because the transformations are much like any other events. Currently, however, it is not possible, and the effect descriptions must be recorded separately by the transformation writer.

Retrieving and Using Transformations

When using a library of operators such as our evolution transformation library, a user must do the following: find an appropriate operator, understand what it does, and determine how to apply it to achieve the desired effect. These activities are seldom trivial, particularly if the population of the library is large, and the effects of the operators are potentially complex. Consequently, we have been concerned with providing automated support for these activities. Some new capabilities in these directions were recently developed, and further developments are anticipated.

Effect descriptions are used to assist the transformation retrieval process. The user can specify a desired effect in terms of the class of operation and the objects of interest. For each operand, an object class can be specified, or a particular specification component object can be referred to. Given this description, the retrieval mechanism retrieves three sets of transformations: those that are guaranteed to achieve the desired effect, those that might achieve the desired effect but only in restricted circumstances, and those that achieve part of the desired effect.

The next step is to integrate the retrieval mechanism with the presentation editors being developed for ARIES by Lockheed Sanders. Each presentation is directly manipulable; the user will be able to button on nodes and arcs in diagrams and perform generic operations such as Promote or Splice. The user's gesture will be used as a description of an appropriate transformation to apply. If the gesture unambiguously indicates a particular transformation, the transformation will directly be applied; if not, the user will be asked to disambiguate.

In another application mode, the user will perform a gesture and ask the system to find all transformations that include this gesture as a substep. This request allows the system to suggest macrotransformations that the user might be unfamiliar with. Thus, an ARIES user can start by using the basic gestures to edit a system description and gradually move to progressively more powerful and complex transformations.

It is important to note that the mapping between presentation gestures and modification operators on the internal representation might be indirect. Figures 4 and 5 show the effects of splicing in the radar track into the air traffic control system from both a presentation standpoint and a representation standpoint. Internally, an accesses-fact relationship holds between Ensure-On-Course and Location-Of. Externally, however, the individual accesses-fact relationships are not depicted. Instead, the label on the information flow arc indicates what relations are being accessed. It will be necessary for the presentation system to translate external operations on labels into internal operations on arcs. For beginning users to clearly understand the effects of Splice-Data-Accesses, we demonstrate the transformation on diagrams where each arc has a single label and a single direction. According to the semantics of context diagrams, an arc with multiple labels or directions can be transformed into an equivalent set of arcs with single labels and directions. In this simplified case, the splicing of data accesses directly corresponds to the splicing of information flow arcs.

We have been experimenting with various types of intelligent assistance for the process of applying transformations. In the Specification Assistant, a record was kept of each transformation that was applied and on what parameters. The analyst could undo a sequence of transformations at any time, perform additional changes, and then replay the transformations. The Specification Assistant automatically determined whether the transformations were still applicable and, if not, requested the developer supply new input for the transformations that could not be applied. This mechanism was intended as an aid for supporting the merger of parallel sequences of transformation applications. The ARIES system will build on this capability by using goals and effect descriptions to help suggest transformations to apply and further determine transformation applicability. It will be possible for the system to take design constraints, such as restrictions on allowed information flow, and automatically suggest transformations that repair constraint violations.

Assessing Library Completeness

The previous analysis gave us the means for determining what transformations to include in our library and the basis for assessing the library's completeness. We distinguish two categories of transformations: *basic transformations,* which perform some simple operation along one or more dimensions, and *macrotransformations,* which perform multiple operations. We have been extending the basic transformation set to cover all types of op-

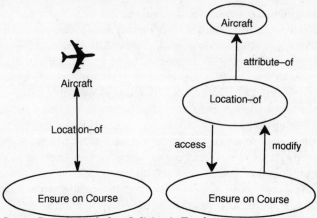

Figure 5. System Description before Splicing in Track.

erations along all dimensions. Macrotransformations are defined as compound transformations, achieving their effect by invoking a combination of the basic transformations.

Splice-Data-Accesses is an example of such a macrotransformation. Another is Add-Disjoint-Subtypes, first described by Balzer (1985). This transformation defines two disjoint subtypes of a specified type and revises the signatures of all relations over the type so that they are instead restricted to one subtype or the other. The operations of adding the subtypes and specializing the relations are distinct operations, which could be performed independent of each other. Therefore, we realized these individual operations in separate transformations, Add-Specialization and Specialize-Parameter. Add-Disjoint-Subtypes now invokes these other transformations as substeps. Users are free to either use the larger command or directly invoke the substeps for some other purpose.

Although the space of possible macrotransformations is unlimited, the space of basic transformations is limited, and we are attempting to achieve complete coverage of the space. At a minimum, we must ensure that each type of link operation can be performed on each type of link and each type of node.

In one sense, this degree of coverage is almost trivially achievable, given suitable general transformations. For example, there is a general Update-Attribute transformation that can update any attribute of any type; this transformation can be used to affect any update operation. There are three reasons why additional work is involved.

First, various types of nodes have necessary conditions associated with them. For example, every concept must have a name and must be part of a folder. Every node type that has distinct conditions should have an associated

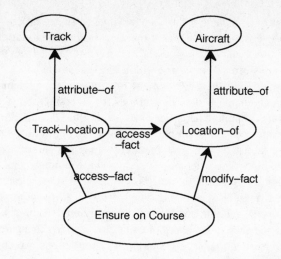

Figure 6. System Description after Splicing in Track.

transformation that can properly create instances of it.

Second, constraints exist among the possible relationships between nodes. Transformations must respect these constraints. For example, the accesses-fact relations on an event must be consistent with the procedural definition of the event. If the definition accesses some piece of information, then an accesses-fact relation must hold between the event and the accessed information. It is not good enough for a transformation to modify the accesses-fact relation by itself; it must also modify the parts of the definition that entail the accesses-fact relation (as is done by Splice-Data-Accesses).

Because our effect descriptions are partial characterizations, there can be more than one possible way to achieve the same effect. For example, there are many ways to split a node, depending on how the attributes of the split node are divided. Thus, it is not enough to require that every kind of node can be split; we must capture each method of node splitting that commonly occurs. We can discriminate among such methods in terms of the links that they affect.

This analysis provides solid guidelines for assessing transformation coverage. Once we provide transformations that perform each possible operation, obeying all constraints, and account for the different possible side effects that can occur, then we can be confident that the library will meet arbitrary user needs. There is still room for variation about how the transformations achieve their required effects, of course. For example, a transformation creating a concept can satisfy the well-formedness constraint that the type be named in several ways (for example, ask the user for a name, or construct a new name at random). We cannot guarantee that our approach to satisfying this constraint (asking the user) will satisfy all users. However, we can expect the basic function of the transformation to agree with user expectations.

Previous work in the development of reusable component libraries has generally been unable to provide methods for assessing library completeness along the lines identified here. For example, Prieto-Diaz and Freeman (1987) factor software component properties along a number of different dimensions but fail to establish a taxonomic hierarchy along any dimension. Thus, there is no way to determine whether one component is more general in applicability than another. Systems that rely on a classification hierarchy of objects (Allen and Lee 1989; see chapter 5) primarily classify on the basis of input and object types. Without a notion of generic operations, the classification of effect is ad hoc at best. By restricting our classification to a particular kind of software component, namely, evolution transformations, we are able to do a much better job of classifying our components.

Applicable Results and Future Challenges

Formalized evolution transformations are a potential benefit to all software-evolution activities, not just specification development. The analysis of transformations in this chapter provides a framework for applying evolution transformations to other languages. Any language that supports the mechanical derivation of semantic relations on software objects is a candidate for formalized evolution. Strongly typed languages such as Ada and Pascal fit in this category. In the case of languages with poor typing mechanisms, annotations introduced by designers can help. For example, Andersen Consulting's Basic Assembler Language Software Reengineering Workbench provides interactive tools for reengineering assembly language programs (chapter 1). Design information is captured through a combination of automatic tools and manual entry. Andersen is considering implementing evolution transformations that operate on such reengineered programs.

This chapter described the semantic basis for developing a reusable library of transformations. Work on extending the library coverage is ongoing. The main technical challenges that remain have to do with providing sufficient automated support for the transformation retrieval and application processes and for deriving effects and preconditions of transformations from their method bodies. Given the work accomplished to date, we believe that it will be straightforward to develop a system that retrieves transformations through the iterative reformulation of queries, as in BACKBORD (Yen, Neches, and DeBellis 1988) and that guides the user in applying the transformation to achieve the desired effect. We envision that the system will ultimately take an active role in the interactive planning of specification changes. Failed preconditions on transformations could then trigger a search of the transformation library for transformations that could make the preconditions true. The system could provide suggestions at each stage about what transformations would be appropriate to perform.

Acknowledgments

We wish to acknowledge the members of the Specification Assistant project at USC/Information Sciences Institute for their participation in this research, in particular, Jay Myers, Dan Kogan, Kai Yue, and Kevin Benner. Our colleagues at Lockheed Sanders, David Harris, Jay Runkel, and Paul Lakowski are responsible for many of the good ideas behind this work; the bad ideas are solely our responsibility. Charles Rich provided useful advice throughout the ARIES project. Vairam Alagappan, Van Kelly, Michael Lowry, Jay Myers, and K. Narayanaswamy reviewed earlier drafts of this chapter and made many helpful comments.

References

Abbott, D. A. 1989. KBSA's Requirements Assistant and Aerospace Needs. In Proceedings of the Fourth Annual KBSA Conference. Rome, N.Y.: Rome Laboratory.

Air Traffic Operations Service. 1989. 7110.65F: Air Traffic Control. Washington, D.C.: Government Printing Office.

Allen, B. P., and Lee, S. D. 1989. A Knowledge-Based Environment for the Development of Software Parts Composition Systems. In Proceedings of the Eleventh International Conference on Software Engineering, 104-112. Washington, D.C.: IEEE Computer Society Press.

Anderson, J. S., and Fickas, S. 1989. A Proposed Perspective Shift: Viewing Specification Design as a Planning Problem. In Proceedings of the Fifth International Workshop on Software Specification and Design, 177–184. Washington, D.C.: IEEE Computer Society Press.

ASA. 1989. *Airman's Information Manual*. Seattle, Wash.: Aviation Supplies and Academics, Inc.

Balzer, R. 1985. Automated Enhancement of Knowledge Representations. In Proceedings of the Ninth International Joint Conference on Artificial Intelligence, 203–207. Menlo Park, Calif.: American Association for Artificial Intelligence.

Balzer, R.; Goldman, N.; and D. S. Wile. 1976. On the Transformational Implementation Approach to Programming. In Proceedings of the Second International Conference on Software Engineering, 337–344. Washington, D.C.: IEEE Computer Society Press.

Balzer, R.; Cohen, D.; Feather, M. S.; Goldman, N. M.; Swartout, W., and Wile, D. S. 1983. Operational Specification as the Basis for Specification Validation. In *Theory and Practice of Software Technology,* eds. D. Ferrari, M. Bolognani, and J. Goguen, 21–49. Amsterdam: North-Holland.

Bateman, J. 1990. Upper Modeling: Organizing Knowledge for Natural Language Processing. In Proceedings of the Fourth International Natural Language Generation Workshop, 54-61. Pittsburgh, Penn.

Bauer, F. L. 1976. Programming as an Evolutionary Process. In Proceedings of the Second International Conference on Software Engineering, 223-234. Washington, D.C.: IEE Computer Society Press.

Benner, K., and Johnson, W. L. 1989. The Use of Scenarios for the Development and Validation of Specifications. In Proceedings of the Computers in Aerospace VII Conference. New York: AIAA.

Burstall, R. M., and Goguen, J. 1977. Putting Theories Together to Make Specifications. In Proceedings of the Fifth International Joint Conference on Artificial Intelligence, 1045–1058. Menlo Park, Calif.: International Joint Conferences on Artificial Intelligence.

Cohen, D. 1989. AP5 Manual, USC/Information Sciences Institute, Marina del Rey, California.

DeBellis, M. 1990. The KBSA Concept Demonstration Prototype. In Proceedings of the Fifth Annual RADC KNOWLEDGE-BASED SOFTWARE ASSISTANT (KBSA) Conference, 211-225. Rome, N.Y.: Rome Laboratory.

Elefante, D. 1989. Overview of the Knowledge-Based Specification Assistant. In Proceedings of the Computers in Aerospace VII Conference. New York: AIAA.

Feather, M. S. 1990. Specification Evolution and Program (Re)Transformation. In Proceedings of the Fifth Annual RADC KNOWLEDGE-BASED SOFTWARE ASSISTANT (KBSA) Conference, 403-417. Rome, N.Y.: Rome Laboratory.

Feather, M. S. 1989a. Constructing Specifications by Combining Parallel Elaborations. *IEEE Transactions on Software Engineering* 15(2): 198–208.

Feather, M. S. 1989b. Detecting Interference When Merging Specification Evolutions. In Proceedings of the Fifth International Workshop on Software Specification and Design, 169-176. Washington, D.C.: IEEE Computer Society Press.

Fickas, S. 1987. Automating the Specification Process, Technical. Report, CIS-TR-87-05, Dept. of Computer and Information Science, Univ. of Oregon.

Fickas, S. 1986. A Knowledge-Based Approach to Specification Acquisition and Construction, Technical Report, 86-1, Dept. of Computer and Information Science, Univ. of Oregon.

Goldman, N. M. 1983. Three Dimensions of Design Development, Technical Report RS-83-2, USC/Information Sciences Institute, Marina del Rey, Calif.

Goldman, N.; Wile, D.; Feather, M.; and Johnson, W. L. 1988. GIST Language Description, USC/Information Sciences Institute, Marina del Rey, Calif.

Green, C.; Luckham, D.; Balzer, R.; Cheatham, T.; and Rich, C. 1986. Report on a KNOWLEDGE-BASED SOFTWARE ASSISTANT. In *Readings in Artificial Intelligence and Software Engineering,* eds. C. Rich and R. C. Waters, 377-427. San Mateo, Calif.: Morgan Kaufmann.

Grove, P. B., and the Merriam-Webster Editorial Staff. 1971. *Webster's Third New International Dictionary.* Springfield, Mass.:G. & C. Merriam .

Hagelstein, J. 1988. Declarative Approach to Information System Requirements. *Journal of Knowledge-Based Systems* 1(4): 211–220.

Harris, D. 1988. The Knowledge-Based Requirements Assistant. *IEEE Expert* 3(4).

Huff, K. E., and Lesser, V. R. 1987. The GRAPPLE Plan Formalism, Technical Report, 87-08, Dept. of Computer and Information Science, Univ. of Massachusetts.

Hunt, V., and Zellweger, A. 1987. The FAA's Advanced Automation System: Strategies for Future Air Traffic Control Systems. *IEEE Computer* 20(2): 19-32.

Johnson, P. 1989. Structural Evolution in Exploratory Software Development. In Proceedings of the AAAI Spring Symposium on Software Engineering, 35-39. Menlo Park, Calif.: American Association for Artificial Intelligence.

Johnson, W. L. 1988. Deriving Specifications from Requirements. In Proceedings of the Tenth International Conference on Software Engineering, 428–437. Washington, D.C.: IEEE Computer Society Press.

Johnson, W. L. 1986. Specification via Scenarios and Views. In Proceedings of the Third International Software Process Workshop, 61-63. Washington, D.C.: IEEE Computer Society Press.

The KBSA Project. 1988. Knowledge-based Specification Assistant: Final Report. Marina del Rey, Calif.: USC/Information Sciences Institute.

Johnson, W. L., and Yue, K. 1988. An Integrated Specification Development Framework, Technical Report RS-88-215, USC/Information Sciences Institute, Marina del Rey, Calif.

MacGregor, R. 1989. Loom Users Manual. Marina del Rey, Calif.: USC/Information Sciences Institute.

Myers, J. J., and Williams, G. 1990. Exploiting Metamodel Correspondences to Provide Paraphrasing Capabilities for the Concept Demonstration. In Proceedings of the Fifth Annual RADC KNOWLEDGE-BASED SOFTWARE ASSISTANT (KBSA) Conference, 331-345. Rome, N.Y.: Rome Laboratory.

Narayanaswamy, K. 1988. Static Analysis-Based Program Evolution Support in the Common Lisp Framework, 222-230. In Proceedings of the Tenth International Software Engineering Conference. Washington, D.C.: IEEE Computer Society Press.

Niskier, C.; Maibaum, T.; and Schwabe, D. 1989. A Look through PRISMA: Towards Pluralistic Knowledge-Based Environments for Software Specification Acquisition. In Proceedings of the Fifth International Workshop on Software Specification and Design, 128–136. Washington, D.C.: IEEE Computer Society Press.

Prieto-Diaz, R., and Freeman, P. 1987. Classifying Software for Reusability. IEEE Software 5(1): 6-16.

Reasoning Systems. 1986. REFINE User's Guide. Reasoning Systems, Palo Alto, Calif.

Reubenstein, H. B., and Waters, R. C. 1989. The Requirements Apprentice: An Initial Scenario. In Proceedings of the Fifth International Workshop on Software Specification and Design, 211–218. Washington, D.C.: IEEE Computer Society Press.

Rich, C.; Schrobe, H. E.; and Waters, R. C. 1979. An Overview of the PROGRAMMER'S APPRENTICE. In Proceedings of the Sixth International Joint Conference on Artificial Intelligence, 827–828. Menlo Park, Calif.: International Joint Conferences on Artificial Intelligence.

Robinson, W. N. 1989. Integrating Multiple Specifications Using Domain Goals. In Proceedings of the Fifth International Workshop on Software Specification and Design, 219–226. Washington, D.C.: IEEE Computer Society Press.

Swartout, W. 1982. GIST English Generator. In Proceedings of the First National Conference on Artificial Intelligence, 404-409. Menlo Park, Calif.: American Association for Artificial Intelligence.

Waters, R. C. 1985. The Programmer's Apprentice: A Session with KBEmacs. IEEE Transactions on Software Engineering SE-11(11): 1296–1320.

Wile, D. S. 1983. Program Developments: Formal Explanations of Implementations. In New Paradigms for Software Development, ed. W. Agresti, 239–248. Washington, D.C.: IEEE Computer Society Press.

Yen, J.; Neches, R.; and DeBellis, M. 1988. Specification by Reformulation: A Paradigm for Building Integrated User Support Environments. In Proceedings of the Seventh National Conference on Artificial Intelligence, 814-819. Menlo Park, Calif.: American Association for Artificial Intelligence.

Yue, K. 1989. Representing First Order Logic-Based Specifications in Petri-Net–Like graphs. In Proceedings of the Fifth International Workshop on Software Specification and Design, 291–293. Washington, D.C.: IEEE Computer Society Press.

5

The ROSE-2 Strategies for Supporting High-Level Software Design Reuse

Mitchell D. Lubars

The software design process is a complex combination of activities that allows software designers to formulate solutions to existing problems and record the elements of these solutions in software designs. One way that designers can deal with the complexity of the process and achieve significant improvements in their productivity is to reuse past software requirements and designs and adapt them to solve their new problems.

Reusing high-level requirements and designs offers several advantages to system designers: It eliminates the need to reinvent system architectures, which tend to be stable within system families; it permits the reuse of past analyses and sets of requirements that can be pertinent to the new system development; it allows the reuse of key design decisions to avoid the costly analyses that led to these decisions in the original design; and it provides pointers to lower-level reusable components in the software development process such as low-level designs, algorithms, code, and test cases. Thus, reusing high-level designs can be useful in providing a wide-spectrum approach to software reusability (Lubars 1988b). As an example, consider the reuse of a factory automation software system. By reusing the high-level design and requirements, the user can focus on issues such as which components the factory should manufacture and where the processing capabilities should be allocated within the system. The reusable design can provide the lower-level design and implementation details and pull in the appropriate inventory control algorithms and the code to operate the factory machinery from the associated libraries.

The key to successful high-level design reuse is in providing reusable designs that are sufficiently abstract that they can be applied to a family of related design problems. In conjunction, they need to contain information that describes how the designs can be customized (specialized) to solve particular user problems. Ideally, this information includes requirement alternatives, so that sets of user requirements can be used to select a high-level design and then customize it to satisfy these requirements. With the proper automated support, this process can be taken one step further, and the user can be assisted in exploring different combinations of requirements by observing how these requirements cause refinements that lead to different design customizations. The user can then evaluate the designs to determine if they adequately solve his/her problems or whether he/she needs to adjust the requirements to produce different customizations.

The *knowledge-based refinement paradigm* is a software development process in which user-supplied requirements are used to select and customize a high-level design (Harandi and Lubars 1986). The paradigm is supported by a knowledge base of high-level design abstractions, called *design schemas* (Lubars 1987), and refinement rules (Barstow 1979). The schemas and rules are used to customize the user's designs to satisfy his/her requirements and design decisions. I am developing a system, ROSE-2 (reuse of software elements), that facilitates high-level design reuse by supporting the knowledge-based refinement paradigm.

The ROSE-2 user selects design schemas from a design library to include in new software designs. A design schema includes information about several important issues that need to be resolved to complete the design of a component. Such issues include questions about particular user requirements and choices between design alternatives; for example, What components should a factory manufacture? and How should processing resources be allocated? Such issues guide the user to specify how he/she wants ROSE-2 to customize the design. As the user resolves design issues, ROSE-2 applies refinement rules associated with the design schema to complete the desired customization. The user can then evaluate the resulting design and possibly change some of his/her requirements and design decisions. This process of resolving issues, evaluating the design, and changing the resolution of issues constitutes design exploration within the scope of the reused design abstraction.

To support the design exploration process, ROSE-2 records all the dependencies between the user's requirements and their consequences in the design, using an underlying truth maintenance system (Doyle 1979; McDermott and Doyle 1980). When the user changes his/her requirements, ROSE-2 performs dependency-directed backtracking to undo these consequences. To help the user evaluate the design, ROSE-2 maintains the design in a low-level general design representation (Lubars 1989a) and presents several different views of this design to the user. For example, the user might want to view the system's hierarchical structure, the data flow between a set of its components, its control flow, its state-oriented behavior, or its underlying requirements with their consequences. The low-level design representation has a semantic basis defined in terms of PETRI nets (Peterson 1977), and all design views are guaranteed to be kept consistent with each other.

Two systems were built before ROSE-2 that had a similar goal of assisting in high-level software design reuse using the knowledge-based refinement paradigm. These systems, IDeA (intelligent design aid) (Lubars 1986) and ROSE-1 (Lubars 1988b), were much less general in their support of design exploration and contained less expressive design representations. In particular, they exclusively represented designs as data flow diagrams and were unable to present the user with any other design views. However, they contained a broader spectrum of support than is yet available in ROSE-2, including a sophisticated strategy for selecting reusable design schemas from a library and code generation techniques for constructing rapid prototypes of the designed system. In this chapter, I first discuss some of the important strategies that can be used to support design reuse and briefly review IDeA and ROSE-1 as a background for ROSE-2. The remainder of the chapter focuses on details of ROSE-2 and future directions in the ROSE project.

Strategies for Supporting Software Design Reuse

The key objective in software design reuse is to provide mechanisms that help the user select and adapt design abstractions to solve software problems. In performing such reuse, the user should be presented with clear requirements and design alternatives that he/she can choose from to solve problems. The user's selection can guide a design reuse assistant in customizing the design to satisfy these requirements and design decisions. The design can then be presented to the user for evaluation. Our approach for supporting this objective is primarily based on five key strategies: (1) using design schemas to represent abstract reusable design solutions, (2) organizing requirements and design alternatives into issue-based structures, (3) developing and customizing designs using the knowledge-based refinement paradigm, (4) using dependency-directed backtracking to support design exploration, and (5) presenting multiple design views to enhance the reuse and evaluation of designs.

In this section, I explain the importance of these strategies using examples of how they support software design reuse.

Software Design Reuse and Design Schemas

Reusable high-level designs need to satisfy two important properties: They must be abstract enough so that they can be applied to solve a variety of design problems, and they must contain enough associated information so that the user can customize them to his/her particular problems without needing to understand all their low-level detail. Such reusable structures are called design schemas (Lubars and Harandi 1987) and have been the basic reusable components in IDeA, ROSE-1, and ROSE-2. Design schemas contain the following elements: First is the basic architecture for constructing systems of a general form. Second is a set of requirements and design alternatives that specify which customizations can be applied to the design. Third is a set of specialization rules that select among alternative design customizations. Fourth is a set of refinement rules that perform specific design customizations. Fifth is a set of constraints that enforce dependencies between different requirements and design decisions. For example, one user requirement or design decision can necessitate several other different design decisions, which can then customize many parts of the design. These constraints guarantee that users only need to specify requirements once, even though they might cause many different design customizations. Sixth is classification information to assist in selecting design schemas from a reuse library.

The schema-based process of reusing designs involves the following steps: First is choosing a design schema from a library that matches a given set of user requirements. This process is called *schema selection*. Second is creating an instance of a selected design schema based on the given user requirements. This causes some of the schema's refinement rules to fire, thus customizing the design to satisfy the user's initial requirements. This process is called *schema instantiation*. Third is supplying additional requirements and design decisions to further guide the refinement and customization of the design. This information is used to select and fire additional refinement rules. It can be elicited by the design reuse assistant based on needed information.

As an example, suppose the user wants to design a software system that will operate the machinery in a semiautomated factory. The user might begin by formulating some initial requirements such as develop a factory automation software system that performs the functions of operating the machinery and managing the factory inventory. This description would be used to select a factory automation software design schema from a reuse library and instantiate a copy of it. Some subset of the schema's refinement rules would fire to generate a partial version of the default design, perhaps decomposing the system into modules and adding control flow for the standard procedures. Based on information in the schema, the user might then be prompted to supply additional requirements that trigger more refinement rules to complete the design customization.

Issue-Based Information System Structures

An important strategy for facilitating the reuse of design schemas is to organize requirements and design alternatives as part of the design schema and to structure them in ways that help the user evaluate these alternatives and consider their implications for the resulting design. One way of organizing this information is to use the issue-based information system (IBIS) approach (Kunz and Rittel 1979; Conklin and Begeman 1988).

In the IBIS method, requirements and design questions are formulated as issues, and the alternatives for resolving the issues (specific requirements or design decisions) are formulated as positions. Each of these positions can be supported by, or objected to, by arguments. For example, in the factory automation system, three issues might ask the following questions: What should the factory be programmed to manufacture? What is the anticipated manufacturing capacity of the factory? Is extra processing capability required to operate the machinery? Possible positions to resolve these issues are that the factory should manufacture gears, bolts, sprockets, or pulleys; the anticipated manufacturing capacity will be high, moderate, or low; and extra processing capability will or will not be required. Arguments might also support or object to any of these positions, for example, the market for sprockets is currently weak, or high manufacturing capacity will require that the factory have additional processing capability to operate the machinery.

The IBIS method was shown to be useful in the manual design process for supporting design exploration and recording design history (Yakemovic and Conklin 1989). It was also advocated as a method for relating design decisions to the actual artifacts generated during the design process (Potts and Bruns 1988). One of the representational goals in design reuse is to incorporate the IBIS method into design schemas and the design reuse mechanisms so that the following requirements are met:

First, requirements and design alternatives are clearly presented to the user as he/she attempts to reuse and customize designs. For example, the previous issue structures can be presented to the user after he/she has selected the factory automation design schema to guide him/her in resolving these issues. Second, the user can examine the relative benefits and disadvantages of the various alternatives. For example, he/she might decide based on the previous arguments that the factory should not manufacture sprockets. Third, the design history can explicitly be recorded and examined as the user chooses alternatives, and the design is subsequently customized. For example, the user's chosen positions will be recorded, and the resulting design customizations will be justified by arguments based on these positions. The user can later examine parts of the design in terms of their rationale and examine which requirements were responsible for these design components.

The Knowledge-Based Refinement Paradigm

The selection of design schemas and the application of refinement rules to semiautomatically customize designs based on user requirements is a software development process called the *knowledge-based refinement paradigm* (Harandi and Lubars 1986). The paradigm is based on a philosophy that views the entire software development process as a succession of knowledge-based refinements made to an initial model of the desired system. Initially, the model contains only the high-level requirements of the desired system. The model is then successively refined until a detailed software design is generated. This process can be supported by selecting design schemas from a design reuse library based on user requirements. The schemas are then instantiated to construct an initial design model, and the schema's refinement rules are applied to the model to customize it and introduce the additional detail. Where additional user requirements are needed, the user is presented with relevant issues, positions, and arguments to help him/her make these decisions. The advantages of the knowledge-based refinement paradigm are that it helps to (1) reduce the size and complexity of user-supplied software requirements by supplementing them with detail from the design schemas, (2) assure that complete and consistent requirements are provided by checking them against constraints and issue structures in the design schema, (3) partially automate software design construction by applying the schema's refinement rules, (4) support software specification and design as parallel and complementary activities by refining designs in direct response to user-supplied requirements, and (5) support software design reuse as an integral part of the design process.

Again referring to our factory automation software example, we notice that the user initially selected the design schema based on a general description of the problem, and his/her initial requirements did not address what the factory was to manufacture or what its manufacturing capacity would be. Nevertheless, this information is sufficient to begin refining a solution to the general factory automation problem. However, before the design can be completed, the user needs to resolve the remaining issues. A design reuse assistant can prompt the user by presenting him/her with the issue structures and allow him/her to select the desired positions. In response, the reuse assistant can continue to refine the design to satisfy the additional requirements (for example, what the factory is to manufacture and what its anticipated capacity is).

Design Exploration and Dependency-Directed Backtracking

As part of the design process, the user might want to explore different design schema selections and customizations. The user must be able to supply and retract different requirements and design decisions and observe the effects as different sets of refinement rules are applied to customize the design. This process is called *design exploration*.

In the ideal mode of design exploration, a user provides some requirements and design decisions (positions in the IBIS sense) that resolve some design issues and then examines the design to see how it has subsequently been customized. To understand how the design reuse assistant performed these customizations, the user might examine some of the arguments that recorded the sequence of rule-based refinements. The user might also peruse other positions that he/she had not yet considered and the arguments that support them. S/he might then want to explore some of these alternatives instead and retract his/her earlier decisions. The design reuse assistant would then undo the earlier design customizations using dependency-directed backtracking (Doyle 1979; McDermott and Doyle 1980) and permit the user to incrementally provide some new positions (requirements and design decisions) that resolve the issues in other ways.

For example, suppose the user initially decides the factory should manufacture bolts and anticipates a moderate manufacturing capacity. As the user examines the effects of these decisions on the resulting design, he/she notices that there might be a bottleneck where the software operates the actual factory machinery. The user wonders why additional processing capabilities weren't introduced to alleviate this potential bottleneck, but when he/she examines the issue regarding extra processing capability, he/she observes (through the arguments) that the extra processing capability is only introduced if the anticipated factory capacity is high. Thus, the user decides to change his/her position and now asserts that the anticipated factory capacity will be high instead of moderate. As a consequence, several of the previous design refinements are undone, and additional refinement rules fire to introduce the additional processing capability. The user can verify this step by examining the design and the issue structures.

Multiple Design Views

The user needs to evaluate generated designs to verify that the designs meet their requirements. To accomplish this task, the user must to able to answer specific questions about the design; for example, what are the major subsystems? what information flows between some set of components? what are the important states and events that the system responds to? what are the sequence of activities the system performs? An important way to answer such questions is to present different views of the generated design. For example, state-transition diagrams and state charts (Harel 1987) are well suited to answering state- and event-oriented questions, real-time structured analysis representations (Ward and Mellor 1985; Hatley and Pirbhai 1987) are well suited to answering data-flow and control-flow oriented questions, and structural views are well suited to answering questions about the subsystems and lower-level system components. In the factory automation example, the user was able to examine a control-flow view to identify a potential bottleneck and observe that extra processing capabilities had not been introduced into the design.

To support multiple views, a system needs to have a canonical design representation that can record all the information presentable in any of its views and maintain this representation so that changes made to any of its views are kept mutually consistent. For example, deletions of components in a flow-oriented view might necessitate the deletion of components in structural and state-oriented views as well.

Another advantage of representing designs in a canonical representation is that it can enhance their reusability. Because some designers and organizations have preferences for how designs are represented, canonical representations with multiple views make it possible for individuals with different view preferences to share designs; otherwise, they might not. Multiple design views are an important aspect for promoting software design reuse and supporting user evaluation of generated designs.

IDeA and ROSE-1

IDeA was developed as an early prototypical design reuse assistant; its primary goal was to support software design reuse and development using the knowledge-based refinement paradigm (Harandi and Lubars 1986). IDeA represented designs as data flow diagrams. The user could specify desired systems in terms of input and output data flow types, classifying properties of the data flows (Prieto-Diaz and Freeman 1987), and a key-word based description of system function. IDeA then selected the design schema that best satisfied these specifications and applied refinement rules to add detail to the data flow designs. Figures 1 and 2 show examples of an initially selected design schema and its first level of refinement. In these figures, the top-right window shows the data flow diagram, the top-left window describes the data flows, and the bottom-left window describes the data flow transformations.

IDeA's schema-selection mechanisms provided considerable flexibility in locating design schemas. Selected design schemas might match only some of the user's specifications, or they might contain input and output data flows that the user did not specify. Any differences between the user's specifications and the selected schemas were added to a goal agenda so that the user could resolve them at a later time.

IDeA would often select design schemas that were more abstract than the user's specifications. In these cases, the specifications provided contextual information that helped IDeA to customize the schema and guide the selection of the appropriate refinement rules (Lubars and Harandi 1986). For example, in figure 1, the user's input specified that the design should process student records, but the selected schema processed achiever records (an abstraction of student records). This result directed IDeA to customize all the components of the design to deal with the scholastic achievement context.

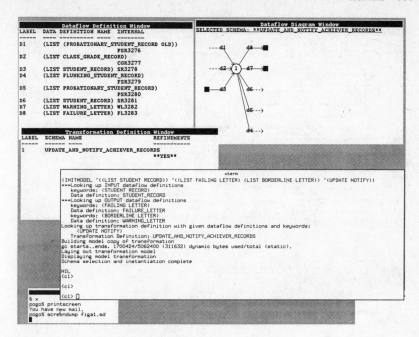

Figure 1. Selection of an Initial Design Schema in IDeA.

Another important feature of IDeA was the ability to generate executable design prototypes. IDeA accomplished this task by converting the data flow diagrams to process graph specifications using the POLYLITH (Purtilo 1985) module interconnection language. Each data flow transformation in the design described a separate reusable process that IDeA selected from a catalog. The data flows specified the interprocess connections and their data types. IDeA used the processes, connections, and type information to construct a POLYLITH specification, which the POLYLITH run-time system automatically instantiated and executed. Although the design simulations were slow, they provided important feedback enabling the user to evaluate his/her specifications and perhaps quickly change them and regenerate a new design.

ROSE-1 was constructed by combining the concepts of IDeA with the software template (STS) algorithm and data-type reuse system (Volpano and Kieburtz 1985). The IDeA-based component served as ROSE-1's front end, constructing high-level data flow designs of the desired system (Lubars 1988b). Once the designs were refined to sufficiently detailed levels, ROSE-1 converted them into series of functional expressions. The data flow transformations were then mapped to abstract algorithms in the STS back-end library, and abstract data types and implementations were inferred from the information in the data flow descriptions (Volpano 1988). The STS back end

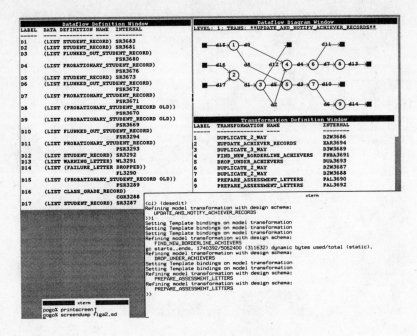

Figure 2. The First Level of Design Refinement in IDeA.

could then generate prototype code for the designs in either C, Pascal, or ADA. These prototypes were much more efficient than the POLYLITH design simulations generated by IDeA. In addition, this combination gave ROSE-1 a wide-spectrum approach to software design reuse (Lubars 1988b). By reusing high-level designs and refinement rules, ROSE-1 inferred pointers to lower-level reusable components and composed them into executable programs with minimum user interaction.

Experience with IDeA and ROSE-1 indicated that their techniques in supporting the knowledge-based refinement paradigm and software design reuse were generally good, but their representations were expressively weak and inflexible. For example, the data flow designs did not represent control-related information. Thus, the generation of prototypes from data flow diagrams was a fairly straightforward and naive translation and did not take advantage of any explicit patterns of control sequencing or potential optimizations. Another problem was that IDeA and ROSE-1 could not present the user with alternative views of the designs. Thus, designs that were not easily represented as data flow diagrams could not be reused in IDeA and ROSE-1. In addition, it was impossible to view these designs from other perspectives, such as state-oriented, control-oriented, or structure-oriented views.

IDeA and ROSE-1 also had a weak notion of design history and did not support dependency-directed backtracking. They also did not organize design alternatives in a style that helped the user consider alternatives during design exploration, although they did use design alternatives to discriminate between conflicting refinement rules. Because IDeA and ROSE-1 did not support dependency-directed backtracking, the user performed design exploration by changing his/her initial specifications and reapplying the refinement paradigm.

ROSE-2

ROSE-2 is currently being developed to correct several of the limitations in IDeA and ROSE-1. The ROSE-2 work to date has focused on improving the representation and viewing capabilities of ROSE-1 and incorporating much stronger support for design history and design exploration while still supporting the knowledge-based refinement paradigm.

The IBIS Approach and Issues in ROSE-2

An important aspect of ROSE-2 is its explicit use of the IBIS approach (Kunz and Rittel 1979; Conklin and Begeman 1988) to represent the structure of design issues, positions, and arguments.

The ROSE-2 design schemas use design issues to represent requirements and design questions and positions to represent the various alternatives for resolving these questions. ROSE-2 presents these issue structures to the user along with the arguments that suggest reasons for accepting or rejecting the various positions. In addition, ROSE-2 can show dependencies between different issues to the user. For example, choosing a particular position to resolve some issue can force the user to accept another position as the resolution of some other issue. Similarly, selecting position for an issue can preclude choosing some other positions to resolve another issue. ROSE-2 helps the user observe the consequences of decisions (Lubars 1989b). These dependency maintenance features are supported by the underlying PROTEUS rule-based and truth maintenance system (Petrie et. al. 1987). The information is graphically presented using a variation of the graphic IBIS notation (Conklin and Begeman 1988).

Figure 3 shows an example of the IBIS-style view in ROSE-2, depicting the design choices and dependencies in a truss design problem. In the figure, issues are indicated as I nodes, positions are indicated as P nodes, and arguments are indicated as A nodes. For example, the issue to determine the truss size (tsize-of-st) can be resolved in one of two ways (denoted by the 3- and 5-meter positions). Similarly, the truss can be installed (the installation-of-st issue) by being either deployed or erected. The link types between nodes are denoted with specific icons. For example, an argument that supports a position is denoted with a + symbol, and an argument that objects to a position is denoted with a − symbol. We can see in figure 3 that through arguments and

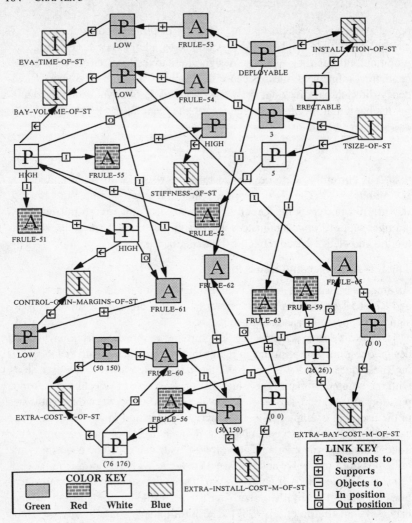

Figure 3. An Example IBIS-Style View in ROSE-2.

links, a truss size of 5 meters supports having a high bay volume, and a truss size of 3 supports having a low bay volume. The selection status of positions and arguments is indicated using color; selected nodes are shown in green, rejected nodes are shown in red, and uncommitted nodes are shown in white. In figure 3, the user selected the positions associated with a 3-meter truss, which is deployable. The ROSE-2 interface allows the user to select and unselect nodes, using a mouse-driven interface. As the user makes design choices, he/she can watch the colors of the nodes change as the consequences of the decision propagate through the IBIS-style network.

Design Schemas and Design Exploration in Rose-2

Rose-2 represents IBIS-style structures as an explicit part of the information contained in its reusable design schemas. Rose-2 schemas also include refinement rules that generate instances of designs to satisfy the various combinations of users' requirements and design decisions (positions). The rule invocations are recorded by the underlying PROTEUS truth maintenance system (Petrie et. al. 1987). This approach allows the components of Rose-2 designs to be directly traced to the user's resolution of issues. The user can change his/her selected positions during design exploration, and Rose-2 will use dependency-directed backtracking to undo the previous design refinements and then perform a new set of refinements that satisfy the user's revised positions. Thus, the user can quickly explore several different design variations of a single reusable design abstraction based on different sets of requirements and design decisions.

Design Representation and Multiple Views

Another area of improvement in Rose-2 is in the method of representing software designs and presenting design views to the user. IDeA and Rose-1 simply represented designs as data flow diagrams and directly displayed these diagrams to the user. Rose-2 designs are based on a much more expressive and general design representation (GDR), which allows Rose-2 to present several different design views to the user (Lubars 1989a).

GDR is an object-oriented representation consisting of a set of low-level object classes and properties. These components can be combined in complex ways to achieve a variety of design patterns. Designs represented in GDR can be viewed in several high-level design visualizations, such as reference views (Biggerstaff, Hoskins, and Webster 1989), data flow diagrams (deMarco 1978), structure charts (Yourdon and Constantine 1979), real-time structured analysis (Ward and Mellor 1985; Hatley and Pirbhai 1987), state-transition diagrams and statecharts (Harel 1987), Petri nets (Peterson 1977), and Verdi (Graf 1987). (Verdi is a visual language developed at MCC Corp. for constructing and simulating distributed system designs.)

The transition semantics of GDR are defined in terms of PETRI nets. This approach gives GDR designs a uniform and unambiguous interpretation. Furthermore, because of the uniform underlying representation, high-level design visualizations and methodologies can be mixed within a single software design. For example, part of a design can be developed using real-time structured analysis and another part might be developed using statecharts or Verdi.

Currently, Rose-2 represents designs in GDR and presents designs to the user using reference views, Verdi views, and a variety of flow-oriented views. Each of these views is a projection of the underlying design, represented in GDR. Future improvements to Rose-2 will allow it to support additional views as well.

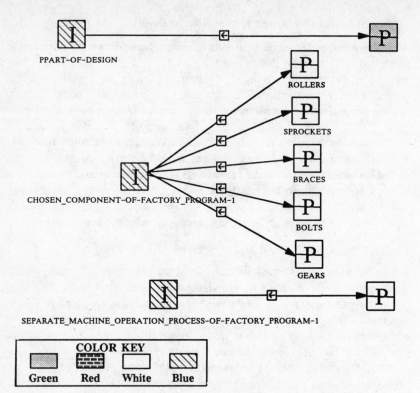

PPART-OF-DESIGN

ROLLERS

SPROCKETS

BRACES

CHOSEN_COMPONENT-OF-FACTORY_PROGRAM-1

BOLTS

GEARS

SEPARATE_MACHINE_OPERATION_PROCESS-OF-FACTORY_PROGRAM-1

COLOR KEY

Green   Red   White   Blue

*Figure 4. The IBIS-Style View of the Factory Automation Software Issues.
The user has decided to include this design schema.*

A ROSE-2 Example

As an example, consider ROSE-2's support for design derivation and exploration, reusing a factory automation software design schema. This example is
similar to the earlier examples but is a concrete application of ROSE-2's current
technology using a simplified version of the design schema. As shown in the
IBIS-style view in figure 4, three top-level issues pertain to this design schema.
The first issue is whether the schema is to be instantiated into the design, the
second issue concerns which components the factory is to be programmed to
manufacture, and the third issue concerns whether the factory's processing
load is high enough to necessitate the introduction of an additional process to
handle the machine operation software. Because there are no links between the
positions of the three issues, these issues are mutually independent.

In figure 4, the user has already made the decision to instantiate the factory
automation design schema into the design. This fact is indicated by its single
(yes-no) position node shown in green. However, the user has not yet

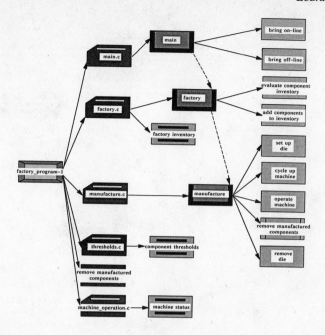

Figure 5. The Reference View of the Default Factory Automation Software Design.

specified any particular components to be manufactured by the factory, nor has he/she indicated that the extra machine operation process is required (indicated by the white position nodes). By default, the schema assumes that the extra processing capability is not required. ROSE-2 automatically refines the design to conform to the user's requirements; that is, instantiate the schema, nothing is specified to be manufactured, and extra processing is not requested.

The user now wants to examine various views of his/her generated design. First, the user chooses to generate a reference view of the current design, as shown in figure 5. This view shows the structural hierarchy of the program, including the program, its modules (files), procedures, global variables, and blocks. Different iconic forms and colors differentiate the structural entity types. Additional information that can be displayed in this view includes calling relationships (shown as dashed lines) between the program's procedures and references to the global variables. For example, in figure 5, the main procedure calls factory, and factory calls manufacture. References to global variables are not shown in this example.

Next, the user chooses to examine the control flow between the top-level design components. Figure 6 shows the design's modules and a multiparty interaction construct, the synchronization primitive in Verdi that permits several independent processes to temporarily synchronize and exchange data. In this

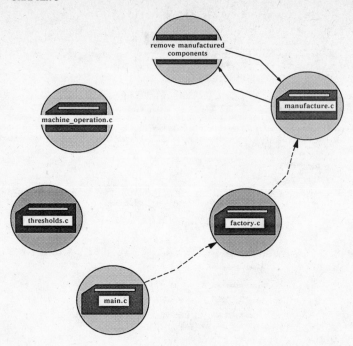

Figure 6. The Control Flow View of the Default Factory Automation Software Design.

view, the user can see calling relationships between the main, factory, and manufacture modules. In addition, the remove manufactured components interaction communicates with the manufacture module through two control flows.

The top-level control-flow view does not give the user enough design detail to see how the factory automation program will be implemented. Rather than looking at lower-level control-flow views of the individual modules, the user decides to pop up a Verdi (Graf 1987) view that shows the control flow within all the processes and procedures. Figure 7 shows the Verdi view. In this view, the user sees the individual blocks of the main, factory, and manufacture procedures and the control flow between them. The user notices that the design is incomplete because there are two threads of control flow in the manufacture procedure, that is, because the user has not yet specified that the factory be programmed to manufacture any components. The user also notices that the manufacture procedure has a comparatively large amount of work to do and might be a bottleneck if the factory contains a lot of machinery to operate.

The user returns to the IBIS-style view and chooses the positions that the factory will manufacture bolts and sprockets. In addition, the user decides that he/she will probably need to introduce additional processing to achieve acceptable factory throughput. Thus, he/she chooses this position as well. These changes are shown in figure 8, with the new positions now displayed

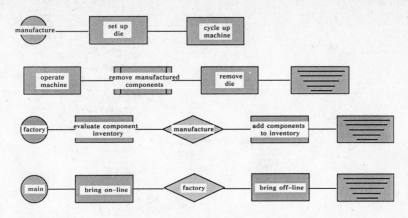

Figure 7. The Verdi View of the Default Factory Automation Software Design.

in green. In response to these changes, ROSE-2 performs dependency-directed backtracking to undo all the design refinements that were based on the assumption that the user did not want the separate machine operation process. ROSE-2 then performs additional refinements to introduce the machine operation process and to manufacture bolts and sprockets.

The user then examines how these new requirements affected the design. He/she begins by popping up another reference view and comparing it with the previous reference view. The new reference view (figure 9) shows the following changes made to the previous view (figure 5): (1) the introduction of new multiparty interactions for manufacture bolts and manufacture sprockets; (2) the introduction of a new process, machine_operation, in the machine_operation module; (3) the redistribution of the cycle-up machine and operate machine functions from the manufacture procedure to the machine_operation process to balance the processing requirements; and (4) the introduction of blocks (boxes in the Verdi terminology) for manufacture bolts and manufacture sprockets into the manufacture procedure and the machine_operation process (these two processes interact through these boxes to collectively accomplish the manufacturing function).

The user then wishes to examine the control-flow views to see how the new requirements affected the design derivation. The top-level control-flow view and the Verdi view can be seen in figures 10 and 11, respectively. In this case, there is so much control flow at the top level that the top-level control-flow view is almost useless; the newly introduced multiparty interactions share a lot of control flow with the machine_operation and manufacture modules. The Verdi view is much more informative and clearly shows the blocks and control flow in the main, manufacture, and factory procedures and the machine operation process. In addition, all threads of control are now

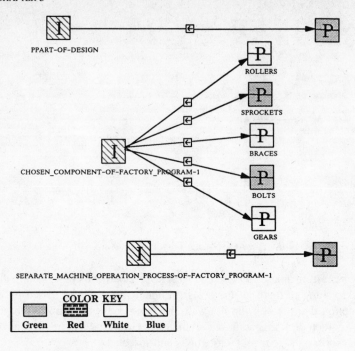

Figure 8. The IBIS-Style view of the Factory Automation Software Issues,
After the User Decides to Manufacture Sprockets and Bolts and
Introduces the Additional Machine Operation Process.

complete in this view, and it is easy to determine which procedures and processes share interactions to accomplish their function. At this point, the user has a complete high-level design and can either decide to construct its implementation or continue experimenting with other variations.

Future Work in ROSE-2

The work to date in ROSE-2 has focused on supporting the basic capabilities of the knowledge-based refinement paradigm, design exploration, improved design representations with multiple views, and the IBIS method for structuring software issues and recording design history. The information to support all these capabilities is recorded into reusable structures, called design schemas. ROSE-2 has not yet addressed two related key problems: (1) how to select design schemas from a reuse library based on user specifications and (2) how to assist in the construction of design schemas.

IDeA and ROSE-1 selected design schemas in two important ways: based on domain-oriented descriptions of the input and output data flows and based

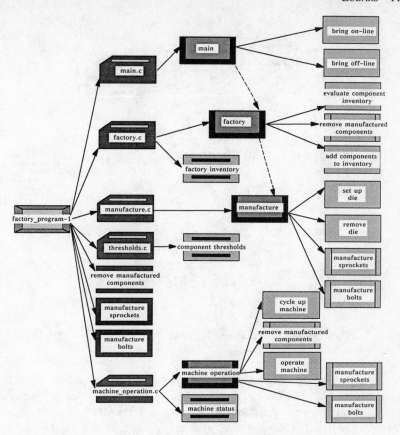

Figure 9. The New Reference View of the Factory Automation Software Design.

on a key-word match with a description of the desired function. The data flow descriptions were cataloged in a manner similar to faceted classification (Prieto-Diaz and Freeman 1987). These strategies were reasonably successful, and in general, the selection of reusable software components based on multiple selection criteria appears to be a powerful approach. In ROSE-2, I plan to introduce additional selection strategies to further increase the flexibility of selecting reusable components. Other possible selection strategies include selection by level of decomposition (for example, system, subsystem, module, unit) (Rossak and Mittermeir 1987), structure of the desired component, subcomponents of the desired component (for example, locate a design that includes an aircraft tracking component), historical information (for example, location based on author's name and authorship date, past usage), features of the reusable component (Prieto-Diaz and Freeman 1987).

A serious limitation in using IDeA, ROSE-1, and ROSE-2 is the problem of

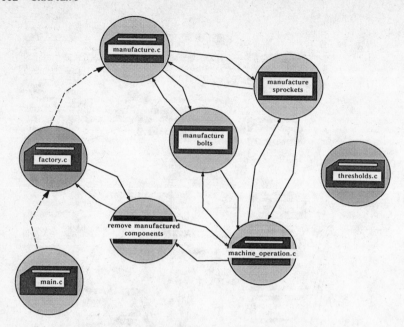

*Figure 10. The New Top-Level Control Flow View of the
Factory Automation Software Design.*

populating the reuse libraries with design schemas and refinement rules. To date, this analytic process has primarily been a manual one that is laborious and frequently error prone. Consequently, only a few small examples have been demonstrated in these systems to date.

Current work in two areas will eventually help in populating the ROSE-2 reuse libraries. These areas are *design recovery*, which is the process of acquiring design information from code and other existing artifacts (Biggerstaff 1989), and domain analysis (Arango 1987; Prieto-Diaz 1987; Lubars 1988b), which is the process of methodically analyzing information about an application domain and recording this information in a form that can easily be encoded into reuse libraries and rules, such as ROSE-2's design schemas.

Design recovery tools, such as DESIRE (Biggerstaff, Hoskins, and Webster 1989), currently include components to extract structural and analytic information from designs and represent this information in hypermedia representations (Webster 1989). This information can then be further annotated by a designer. The DESIRE project is also examining ways to use information about the application domain to assist in the recovery process. Some of the recovered information has also been mechanically translated into GDR designs and presented by ROSE-2's design-viewing capability.

MCC researchers have also been investigating domain analysis techniques and are exploring the possibility of building tools to assist in portions of the

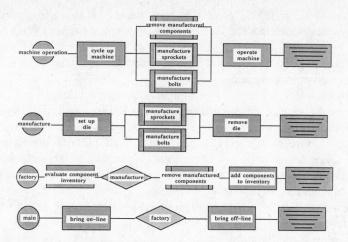

Figure 11. The New Verdi View of the Factory Automation Software Design.

domain analysis process. We have been working with two commercial organizations to gain additional experience in domain analysis and to gain some
intuition about what portions of the process might be automated. Researchers
plan to begin constructing such tools in the near future, believing that these
tools, in combination with the current and future capabilities of Desire, will
provide considerable assistance in constructing reuse libraries for ROSE-2.

Related Work

The PSIsystem (Barstow 1979) pioneered the use of refinement rules in program synthesis and provided much of the early inspiration for applying the
knowledge-based refinement paradigm (Kant and Barstow 1981) to the problem of high-level software design. DRACO (Neighbors 1984) addressed the
issue of software reuse through the application of domain-specific transformation rules, and indeed, most of the transformations were also of a refinement nature. A software maintenance paradigm based on the Draco approach, TMM (Arango et. al. 1986), was also proposed as a way to take
advantage of design histories and support re-engineering. Other transformational implementation systems of a more general nature include GLITTER
(Fickas 1985), TI (Balzer 1981), REFINE (Smith, Kotik, and Westfold 1986),
and PDS (Cheatham, Holloway, and Townley 1981). These systems differ
from ROSE-2 in that they primarily address lower-level design and program
synthesis, whereas ROSE-2 is oriented toward higher-level design and stresses
design representations and views to evaluate the designs.

   The Programmer's Apprentice (Rich and Waters 1988) allows users to
reuse program cliches during the development of new programs. This ap-

proach is similar to ROSE-2's use of design schemas, but is at a lower level of program development. The Requirements Apprentice (Rich, Waters, and Reubenstein 1987) uses a similar approach to support the reuse of requirements cliches but does not yet connect the reuse of requirement cliches with design or program generation.

Many CASE tools allow software designers to construct designs in a variety of different high-level representations (Lempp and Lauber 1988). However, these representations are generally not different views of a single design. Indeed, most current CASE tools do not have a single unifying representation with a strong semantic basis such as ROSE-2's GDR. One notable exception is STATEMATE, which is able to present three separate design views: structural, behavioral, and activity (Harel et. al. 1988).

A few representations have been proposed for representing design objects in underlying design models. The unified model approach (Black et. al. 1987) seems to be the most similar to GDR, with an underlying model constructed from frame instances connected by semantic primitives (Shank and Abelson 1977). Mappings have also been defined from this representation to several higher-level design representations. Another related approach, with fewer and less specialized object classes, is Mark and Rombach's (1987) software-engineering metamodel. This approach, however, is oriented toward larger-grained software artifacts than GDR. The plan calculus (Rich 1981) and semantic program graphs (Meyers and Reiss 1989) both contain similar goals and components to those in GDR but are oriented toward representing programming-level information.

Other work that is similar to ROSE-2 includes REMAP (Dhar and Jarke 1988), which uses a truth maintenance system to represent dependencies between design decisions and supports dependency-directed backtracking, and the support of multiple program views in PECAN (Reiss 1987).

Conclusions

A successful strategy for reusing high-level software designs requires that the user be able to select and customize designs based on his/her requirements and high-level design decisions without being concerned with the lower-level design and implementation details. The ROSE research has focused on merging five strategies to assist the user in design customization, design exploration, and design evaluation within the context of software design reuse. These strategies are using design schemas to represent abstract reusable design solutions, organizing requirements and design alternatives into issue-based structures, developing and customizing designs using the knowledge-based refinement paradigm, using dependency-directed backtracking to support design exploration, and presenting multiple design views to enhance the reuse and evaluation of designs.

ROSE-2 is currently being developed as a high-level software design reuse assistant that incorporates the five strategies. ROSE-2 was inspired by its two predecessors, IDeA and ROSE-1. These systems incorporated only two of the fundamental strategies, namely, representing abstract reusable designs as design schemas and supporting the knowledge-based refinement paradigm. Consequently, IDeA and ROSE-1 were not as flexible as ROSE-2 in helping the user to reason about design issues, perform design exploration, and view designs from multiple high-level visualizations. However, they provided better support for schema selection and design prototyping than has yet been provided in ROSE-2, and their approaches in these areas will continue to provide inspiration as ROSE-2 develops and matures.

ROSE-2's support for design traceability and reasoning about requirements and design alternatives is based on the IBIS style of representing issue structures. Supplemented with dependency-directed backtracking, the IBIS features facilitate design exploration. ROSE-2 represents the actual designs in GDR, which permits ROSE-2 to present the user with a variety of different views of the underlying design to assist in design evaluation.

Important work still remains to be done in ROSE-2, particularly in the areas of selecting design schemas from a reuse library and in providing techniques and tools to assist in populating ROSE-2's reuse libraries with design schemas and rules. In particular, researchers plan to generalize on the schema-selection successes in IDeA and ROSE-1 by allowing schema selection using multiple selection criteria in conjunction with a faceted classification approach.

To support the population of ROSE-2 libraries, researchers are constructing tools to support the recovery of design information from existing program code and artifacts and are investigating domain analysis methods and looking for opportunities to assist some of these methods with automated tools. The combination of the ROSE-2 support for the refinement paradigm, design exploration, design schema selection, and library population will create an integrated environment for supporting the software design process based on the refinement paradigm, with thorough support for reuse, design exploration, design history recording, and design evaluation.

References

Arango, G. 1987. Domain Engineering for Mechanical Reuse, ASE RTP 74, Dept. of Information and Computer Science, Univ. of California at Irvine.

Arango, G.; Baxter, I.; Freeman, P.; and Pidgeon, C. 1986. TMM: Software Maintenance by Transformation. *IEEE Software* 3(5): 27–39.

Balzer, R. 1981. Balzer. Transformational Implementation: An Example. *IEEE Transactions on Software Engineering* SE-7(1): 3–14.

Barstow, D. R. 1979. *Knowledge-Based Program Construction*. New York: Elsevier .

Biggerstaff, T. 1989. Design Recovery for Maintenance and Reuse. *IEEE Computer* 22(7): 36-49.

Biggerstaff, T.; Hoskins, J.; and Webster, D. 1989. Desire: A System for Design Recovery, Technical Report STP-081-89, MCC Corp., Austin, Texas.

Black, W. J.; Sutcliffe, A. G.; Loucopoulos, P.; and Layzell, P. J. 1987. Translation between Pragmatic Software Development Methods. In Proceedings of the First European Software Engineering Conference, 357–365.

Cheatham, T. E., Jr.; Holloway, G. H.; and Townley, J. A. 1981. Program Refinement by Transformation. In Proceedings of the Fifth International Conference on Software Engineering, 430–437. Washington, D.C.: IEEE Computer Society Press.

Conklin, J., and Begeman, M. L. 1988. IBIS: A Hypertext Tool for Exploratory Policy Discussion, Technical Report STP-082-88, MCC Corp., Austin, Texas.

deMarco, T. 1978. *Structured Analysis and System Specification*. New York: Yourdon.

Dhar, V., and Jarke, M. 1988. Dependency-Directed Reasoning and Learning in Systems Maintenance Support. *IEEE Transactions on Software Engineering* SE-14(2): 211–227.

Doyle, J. 1979. A Truth Maintenance System. *Artificial Intelligence* 12:231–272.

Fickas, S. F. 1985. Automating the Transformational Development of Software. *IEEE Transactions on Software Engineering* SE-11(11): 1268–1277.

Graf, M. 1987. Building a Visual Designer's Environment. Technical Report STP-318-87, MCC Corp., Austin, Texas.

Harandi, M. T., and Lubars, M. D. 1986. Knowledge-Based Software Development: A Paradigm and a Tool. In Proceedings of the 1986 National Computer Conference, 43–50. Reston, Va.: AFIPS Press.

Harel, D. 1987. Statecharts: A Visual Approach to Complex Systems. *Science of Computer Programming* 8:231–274.

Harel, D.; Lachover, H.; Naamad, A.; Pneuli, A.; Politi, M.; Sherman, R.; and ShtulTrauring, A. 1988. Statemate: A Working Environment for the Development of Reactive Systems. Presented at the Tenth International Conference on Software Engineering. Singapore, April 11–15, 1988.

Hatley, D. J., and Pirbhai, I. A. 1987. *Strategies for Real-Time System Specification*. New York: Dorset.

Kant, E., and Barstow, D. R. 1981. The Refinement Paradigm: The Interaction of Coding and Efficiency Knowledge in Program Synthesis. *IEEE Transactions on Software Engineering* SE-7(5): 458–471.

Kunz, W., and Rittel, H. 1979. Issues as Elements of Information Systems, Working Paper, 131, Institut fur Grundlagen der Planung, I.A. University of Stuttgart.

Lempp, and P., and Lauber, R. 1988. What Productivity to Expect from a CASE Environment: Results of a User Survey. In *Productivity: Progress, Prospects, and Payoff*, 13–19.

Lubars, M. D. 1989a. A General Design Representation, Technical Report STP-066-89, MCC Corp., Austin, Texas.

Lubars, M. D. 1989b. Representing Design Dependencies in the Issue-Based Information System Style, Technical Report STP-426-89, MCC Corp., Austin, Texas.

Lubars, M. D. 1988a. Domain Analysis and Domain Engineering in IDeA, Technical Report STP-295-88, MCC Corp., Austin, Texas.

Lubars, M. D. 1988b. Wide-Spectrum Support for Software Reusability. In IEEE Tutorial, Software Reuse: Emerging Technology, 275–281. Ed. W. Tracz. Washington, D.C.: IEEE Computer Society.

Lubars, M. D. 1987. Schematic Techniques for High-Level Support of Software Specification and Design. In Proceedings of the Fourth International Workshop on Software Specification and Design, 68–75. Washington, D.C.: IEEE Computer Society Press.

Lubars, M. D. 1986. A Knowledge-Based Design Aid for the Construction of Software Systems, UIUCDCS-R-86-1304, Dept. of Computer Science, Univ. of Illinois.

Lubars, M. D., and Harandi, M. T. 1987. Knowledge-Based Software Design Using Design Schemas. In Proceedings of the Ninth International Conference on Software Engineering, 253–262. Washington, D.C.: IEEE Computer Society Press.

Lubars, M. D., and Harandi, M. T. 1986. Intelligent Support for Software Specification and Design. *IEEE Expert* 1(4): 33–41

McDermott, D., and Doyle, J. 1980. Non-Monotonic Logic I. *Artificial Intelligence* 13:41–72.

Mark, L. and Rombach, H. D.. 1987. A Meta Information Base for Software Engineering, Technical Report, TR-1765, Dept. of Computer Science, Univ. of Maryland.

Meyers, S., and Reiss, S. P. 1989. Representing Programs in Multiparadigm Software Development Environments. In Proceedings of COMPSAC '89, 420–427. Washington, D.C.: IEEE Computer Society Press.

Neighbors, J. M. 1984. The Draco Approach to Constructing Software from Reusable Components. *IEEE Transactions on Software Engineering* SE-10(5): 564–574.

Peterson, J. L. 1977. Petri Nets. *ACM Computing Surveys* 9(3): 223–252.

Petrie, C. J.; Russinoff, D. M.; Steiner, D. D.; and Ballou, N. 1987. PROTEUS 2: System Description, Technical Report AI-136-87, MCC Corp., Austin, Texas.

Potts, C., and Bruns, G. 1988. Recording the Reasons for Design Decisions. Presented at the Tenth International Conference on Software Engineering. Singapore, April 11–15, 1988.

Prieto-Diaz, R. 1987. Domain Analysis for Reusability. In Proceedings of COMPSAC 87, 23–29. Washington, D.C.: IEEE Computer Society Press.

Prieto-Diaz, R., and Freeman, P. 1987. Classifying Software for Reusability. *IEEE Software* 4(1): 6–16. Washington, D.C.: IEEE Computer Society Press.

Purtilo, J. 1985. POLYLITH: An Environment to Support Management of Tool Interfaces. In Proceedings of the ACM SIGPLAN Symposium on Programming Issues in Programming Environments, 12–18. New York: Association of Computing Machinery.

Reiss, S. P. 1987. Pecan: Program Development systems That Support Multiple Views. IEEE Transactions on Software Engineering SE-11(3): 276–285.

Rich, C. 1981. A Formal Representation for Plans in the Programmer's Apprentice. In Proceedings of the Seventh International Joint Conference on Artificial Intelligence, 1044–1052. Menlo Park, Calif.: International Joint Conferences on Artificial Intelligence.

Rich, C., and Waters, R. C. 1988. Programmers Apprentice: A Research Overview. *IEEE Computer* 21(11): 10–25.

Rich, C.; Waters, R. C.; and Reubenstein, H. B.. Toward a Requirements Apprentice. In Proceedings of the Fourth International Workshop on Software Specification and Design, 79–86. Washington, D.C.: IEEE Computer Society Press.

Rossak, W., and Mittermeir, R. T. 1987. Structuring Software Archives for Reusability. In Applied Informatics, Proceedings of the IASTED International Symposium, 157–160.

Shank, R. C., and Abelson, A. P. 1977. *Scripts, Plans, Goals and Understanding.* New York: Lawrence Erlbaum.

Smith, D. R.; Kotik, G. B.; and Westfold, S. J. 1986. Research on Knowledge-Based Software Environments at Kestrel Institute. *IEEE Transactions on Software Engineering* SE-11(11): 1278–1295.

Volpano, D. 1988. STS—Software Templates System, Technical Report STP-257-87, MCC Corp., Austin, Texas.

Volpano, D. D., and Kieburtz, R. B. 1985. Software Templates. In Proceedings of the Eighth International Conference on Software Engineering, 55–60. Washington, D.C.: IEEE Computer Society Press.

Ward, P. T., and Mellor, S. J. 1985. *Structured Development for Real-Time Systems, Volume 1: Introduction and Tools*. Englewood Cliffs, N.J.: Yourdon.

Webster, D. 1989. Desire-88 Prototype Tools. Technical Report STP-069-89, MCC Corp., Austin, Texas.

Yakemovic, K. C., and Conklin, J. 1989. The Capture of Design Rationale on an Industrial Development Project: Preliminary Report. Technical Report STP-279-89, MCC Corp., Austin, Texas.

Yourdon, E., and Constantine, L. L. 1979. *Structured Design: Fundamentals of a Discipline of Computer and Systems Design*. Englewood Cliffs, N.J.: Prentice-Hall.

Domain-Specific
Program Synthesis

The chapters in the next three sections describe various approaches to knowledge-based program synthesis. All use some combination of inference and transformational implementation, both overviewed in the introduction to this book. However, these three sections vary in their research methodology. The chapters in this section emphasize power in a narrow domain, taking a vertical slice over the full spectrum of software development, from requirements acquisition to code optimization. The results are impressive: Programs consisting of thousands of lines of efficient code that would take weeks to manually generate are automatically generated in minutes. In contrast, the chapters in the next section on knowledge compilation emphasize domain-independent techniques based on AI methods. The chapters in the third section seek to automate or assist the formal development of programs from formal specifications. These chapters are more mathematical than the first two sections.

The research methodology of the chapters in this section is similar to that of early expert system research. The emphasis is on high-level performance through shallow reasoning. Domain knowledge is hard wired into rules, reducing both the number of inferences required and the range of applicability. The research objective is to understand the principles of high-performance program synthesis before generalizing to domain-independent techniques that can be combined with separately encoded domain knowledge. In contrast, the chapters in the next two sections use explicit, formalized domain knowledge. Because the domain knowledge is explicit, it can be interchanged, resulting in more generality but requiring deeper and more complex reasoning. Search control is a more difficult issue in these systems.

The systems presented in this section could also provide the technology for the next generation of application generators. Current application generators are limited to filling in code templates and, therefore, seldom generate efficient code. In contrast, the program synthesis systems presented here fill in abstract algorithm and data-structure templates that are then refined to efficient code in a target language through transformational implementation. These systems also do much more reasoning in selecting the abstract templates with knowledge-based representations and inference techniques. This approach means that the specification level for these program synthesis systems is at a higher level than for current application generators.

The first three chapters in this section were written by David Barstow, Elaine Kant, and their colleagues at Schlumberger Laboratory. While graduate students at Stanford University, Barstow and Kant developed the program synthesis component of the PSI system under the direction of Cordell Green. After working separately in academia for several years, they joined Schlumberger, whose primary business is providing equipment and expertise for oil well exploration. Schlumberger's scientists and engineers annually generate hundreds of thousands of lines of code for tasks as diverse as device-control software and mathematical modeling. This environment, with its ready access to domain experts, has been conducive to the development of the domain-specific paradigm. The fourth chapter was written by Dorothy Setliff, currently a professor at the University of Pittsburgh after recently graduating from Carnegie Mellon University. Setliff combined her knowledge of VLSI computer-aided design (CAD) software with program synthesis techniques to develop a system that automatically generates VLSI CAD software.

Barstow's chapter first reviews the basic ideas of transformational implementation, in which an abstract specification is transformed into a concrete implementation through the application of a body of transformation rules. The application domain for his ΦNIX system is device-control software for oil well exploration tools. From a technical viewpoint, an innovative aspect to ΦNIX is the integration of functional program constructs (side-effect free) with imperative program constructs (with side effects) through environments that encapsulate one type of construct for use in the other type of construct. Although Barstow believes that automatic programming is necessarily domain specific, he notes that most of his efforts to date have concentrated on the development of a domain-independent set of transformation rules. This suggests that a domain-independent kernel could be useful to domain-specific systems.

Kant and her colleagues present two chapters on the synthesis of mathematical modeling and data- interpretation software. The first chapter describes how a rich knowledge representation for data attributes enables the DAROS system to synthesize better programs faster. The program synthesis search space is reduced because detailed data descriptions enable consistency constraints to eliminate some search paths and better order the remaining search paths. These detailed data descriptions also help code optimization and generation of representation-intensive code, such as data-format conversion subroutines. DAROS's knowledge-based representations and inference methods are richer than conventional techniques for checking the consistency of data attributes, such as type checking algorithms. This chapter also discusses how sophisticated representations could help interactive knowledge acquisition.

Kant's second chapter presents more recent work on the SINAPSE system. SINAPSE synthesizes efficient finite-difference programs that implement mathematical models formulated as differential equations with initial boundary conditions. It provides in-

teractive, domain-oriented assistance to a user for specifying the requirements of a mathematical model. Domain-specific rules transform these high-level requirements into a formal mathematical model represented as a set of equations in MATHEMATICA. Alternatively, equation sets can directly be specified in MATHEMATICA. SINAPSE transforms these equations into efficient code through a combination of algorithm schema and refinement rules. Because SINAPSE is restricted to the narrow domain of finite-difference programs, the search space is relatively small, with only about four dozen decision points, and most of the design decisions are automatically made. This approach frees the user from needing to know the details of the low-level code or target architecture. Future plans for SINAPSE include adapting it to new domains and eventually providing tools that enable end users to extend the system themselves. The hypothesis is that a critical mass of domain knowledge will enable tools to interact with an end user to add new knowledge without the end user needing to know the internal details of SINAPSE.

Setliff's chapter begins with an observation shared by the earlier chapters on software maintenance: As a software system is modified to fit new requirements, it loses its coherency and eventually becomes unmaintainable. This is a particular problem for VLSI design tools because hardware technology is evolving so rapidly that the design software can't keep pace. A solution to this problem is program synthesis systems that generate new design tools given the specification of new hardware technologies. Setliff's ELF system generates one class of design tools: maze routers. The maze routers ELF automatically generates compare favorably with commercially available maze routers that are manually generated. ELF combines knowledge about the domain of maze routers with generic techniques for program synthesis. The domain knowledge is hard wired into rules, so that ELF needs many fewer decisions than if it was reasoning from more general principles. ELF uses constraint propagation to select appropriate abstract algorithms and data structures and then transformational implementation techniques to transform these into efficient code.

6

Automatic Programming for Device-Control Software

David Barstow

One strategy for solving the software problem is to try to remove it completely through automation, that is, to build an automatic programming system. The general idea is obviously attractive, but it is hard to give a precise definition of what it means. (In fact, the term automatic programming was first used in 1954 to refer to early Fortran compilers.) For the purposes of this discussion, I assume that an *automatic programming system* interacts with the user in natural terms, makes all the implementation decisions, and produces robust and efficient software. Note that this definition implies that an automatic programming system is domain specific, both to permit natural interaction and to support the decision-making process (Barstow 1984).

This chapter concerns an attempt to build a domain-specific automatic programming system for device-control software. In its current form, the system embodies many of the components necessary for one approach to building an automatic programming system; these components were tested on a small example, but the system falls short of my definition.

In the next section, the domain is discussed, including the application area and the computational framework for the target software. The following sections give an overview of the general approach, discussions of the components that were developed, and a scenario of the system implementing a small example. The concluding sections address several open and unresolved issues suggested by this work.

The Domain

This work is concerned with device-control software and a particular computational model designed for that domain.

Device-Control Software

In general, the characteristics of device-control software are as follows: First, it is both value and behavior oriented: It must record data values as well as control the device's behavior. Second, it must satisfy real-time constraints: It must record data when they are available and ensure that the device performs the right activities at the right times. Third, it involves both concurrency and distributed computation: Often, multiple devices must be controlled at the same time, and the devices are often physically distant from the computers. Fourth, it is only of moderate size: It is better characterized as programming in the small than as programming in the large.

The work described here has primarily focused on the software that controls and records data from oil well logging tools. An example of such a device is shown in figure 1. The device is referred to as SLT-L^{TM} (sonic logging tool, version L) and measures the speed of sound in the rock formation. Sonic measurements are made by triggering a sonic transmitter in the tool and detecting the arrival of the corresponding compressional sound wave at a receiver elsewhere in the tool. The SLT-L has two transmitters and four receivers that are coupled in a way that permits four distinct measurements to be made, corresponding to different directions and distances in the formation. A set of four measurements can be combined to eliminate effects of the bore hole itself and compute the speed of sound in the formation.

To maximize the quality of the data, each measurement is controlled by two parameters, one to adjust the gain on an analog-to-digital converter and the other to adjust the time at which the receiver begins to listen for the sound. These parameters must separately be adjusted for each of the four measurements. A second quality control technique involves comparing current measurements with earlier ones to ensure that there are no major discontinuities. This comparison must be made separately for each of the four measurements. Altogether, a program to control and record the data from SLT-L would be a few thousand lines long and might require a few months or a year to write manually. It is typical of the type of programming that researchers on this project hope to automate.

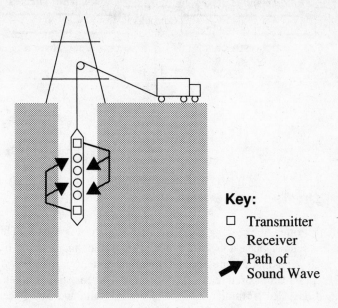

Figure 1. Sonic Logging Tool, Version L.

Stream Machine

As illustrated in figure 2, the interaction of a device-control program with its environment can be modeled in terms of temporally ordered sequences of values, often referred to as *streams*. That is, the software has a specific set of input and output streams on which it sends and receives signals. Abstractly, streams can be thought of as first-in–first-out buffers of unbounded length. Concretely, streams can be implemented in a variety of ways, including buffers, global variables, and registers. For example, the interaction of the SLT-L software with the SLT-L tool occurs by writing and reading registers; the input and output streams thus consist of the sequences of values stored in the registers.

In addition to modeling a program's external interaction, streams can also be used to model the internal interaction among its various components. Specifically, the work at Schlumberger is targeted at a coarse-grained data flow model of computation known as the Stream Machine (Barth, Guthery, and Barstow 1985). A complete description of the Stream Machine is beyond the scope of this chapter, but the model can be summarized as follows: First, a program consists of a fixed network of processes and communication streams; each stream can have only one writer but can have multiple readers. Second, processes normally read values from a stream in the order that they are written; when a process attempts to read a value from a stream before this

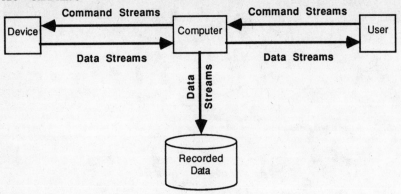

Figure 2. Device Control through Streams.

value is written, the reading process suspends until it is written. Third, under certain circumstances, a process can read from a stream in a time-based fashion, such as reading the most recently written value.

Except for time-based reads, the Stream Machine is similar to other coarse-grained data flow formulations (for example, Kahn and MacQueen [1977]) but differs from other approaches to distributed computation (for example, Hoare [1978]) in that communication does not require an explicit rendezvous between processes. Note also that Stream Machine programs without time-based reads are computationally equivalent to fine-grained data-flow programs without nondeterministic merge; therefore, they are deterministic in the values they produce, regardless of the relative rates of the processes.

ΦNIX

The overall framework for our work is shown in figure 3. The programming process is divided into two activities: *formalization*, during which the user and the system interactively develop a specification in formal computational terms, and *implementation*, during which the system produces a program that satisfies the specification and can be executed on the truck. To date, the primary focus of this effort has been on the implementation activity, which researchers are addressing with the transformational paradigm, with little effort directed toward interactive formalization.

To test this approach, researchers built an experimental system, called ΦNIX, that embodies much of the infrastructure required for a transformational implementation system. The infrastructure was tested by using it to implement a small part of the specification of the SLT-L tool described earlier.

Transformational Implementation

In the *transformational implementation paradigm* (Balzer 1985; Kant and

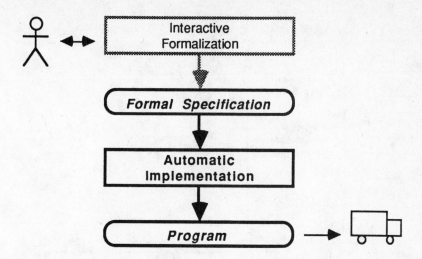

Figure 3. The ΦNIX Framework.

Barstow 1981; Smith, Kotik, and Westfold 1985), an abstract specification is repeatedly transformed through successively more concrete forms until a program in the target language is produced (figure 4a). Therefore, a transformation system includes a set of transformations and a mechanism for repeatedly applying transformations to the specification. Most systems assume that the individual transformations preserve correctness, so that the final implementation is a valid implementation of the initial specification.

Although transformation systems differ in this regard, a typical transformation only involves relatively small changes. Therefore, the sequence of transformations for even a small program can involve hundreds or thousands of steps. At any step in a transformation sequence, several transformations could be applied, each of which would lead to a different implementation. In other words, a set of transformations generates a set of implementations for any given specification. Generally, within this set of implementations, some will be preferred over others (for example, for efficiency reasons). Thus, the tree of possible transformation sequences can be viewed as a search space that can be explored to find the best implementation for a given specification; selection of one branch over another amounts to making an implementation decision (figure 4b).

In general, a transformation system consists of three major components: First is the *wide-spectrum language*, which is used to describe the program as it is being transformed. Such a language is termed wide spectrum because it must incorporate abstract concepts at the specification level as well as concrete concepts from the implementation level. In fact, the specification lan-

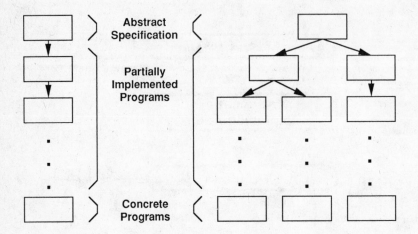

Figure 4. Transformational Implementation.

guage and the target language must be sublanguages of the wide-spectrum language. Second is the *body of transformations*. These transformations are a representation of knowledge about alternative programming techniques. Some transformations can describe techniques for refining or implementing abstract concepts; others can describe techniques for simplifying or reformulating an abstract program. Third is the *search-control mechanism*. The space generated by any realistic body of transformations is impossibly large to exhaustively explore. Thus, some mechanism for controlling the search is important. It is usually assumed that each of the transformations is correctness preserving. Thus, the major issue in search control involves finding efficient programs. The following sections of this chapter describe the components of the ΦNIX system in detail.

Example Program

The examples in the remainder of this chapter are taken from a program that ΦNIX successfully implemented. The program is a small part of the SLT-L software, namely, the routine to correct the output if a discontinuity is found in the measurements. The following is an English description of the program's specification:

> There are two input streams: DataIn is a stream of integers; Error is a stream of Booleans. If the *ith* element of Error is True, then the data in the *i+1st* element

of DataIn is invalid. There is one output stream: DataOut is a stream of integers. DataOut is a copy of the input stream except that if an element of DataIn is invalid, then the corresponding element of DataOut should be the preceding element of DataOut.

The resulting program is a single Stream Machine process whose body is about a dozen lines long.

Wide-Spectrum Language

ΦNIX uses a wide-spectrum language (called ΦANG) to describe the program as it is being transformed. ΦANG is wide along two dimensions: the degree of abstraction of the data types and operators, and the nature of the computational paradigms.

Abstraction Hierarchy of Data Types

All values in ΦANG are typed, and ΦANG includes a large collection of data types. The data types are organized in an abstraction hierarchy. For example, figure 5 shows part of the ΦANG data-type hierarchy for collections. The most abstract type, Collection, is at the top of the hierarchy. The most concrete types (for example, LinkedList) are at the bottom of the hierarchy. Generally, moving a step down in the hierarchy corresponds to adding some fundamental property. For example, Collection, is primarily concerned with membership—whether a specific value is an element of a collection. Multiset is concerned with cardinality as well as membership—how many times a value is an element of a collection. Sequence is concerned with ordering—whether a specific value precedes another value in a collection. Note that Stream is simply another kind of sequence.

Some types have associated definitions based on types elsewhere in the hierarchy. For example, abstract indexes are used to maintain the ordering in sequences. If the index set is a range of integers, then the sequence can be viewed as a Vector, which is at an intermediate level in the hierarchy for Mapping.

Each data type has associated operators. For example, the operators associated with Collection include Member, Union, and EnumerateElements. Concrete types inherit operators from more abstract types and can also have some operators of their own. For example, Sequence inherits Member from Collection but also has operators for finding successor and predecessor indices.

Computational Paradigms

ΦANG includes a variety of computational paradigms. One such paradigm involves *applicative expressions*, where an applicative operator takes input values and produces output values but has no side effects. Many of the operators associated with the data-type hierarchy are applicative. Some are pure func-

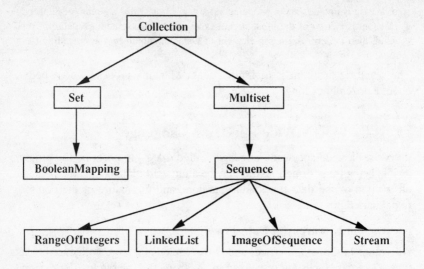

Figure 5. Partial Abstraction Hierarchy for Collections.

tions; others are *functionals* whose output values depend on component operators. An applicative expression is a graph of invocations of applicative operators with data links connecting the output of some invocations with the input of others. Cycles are permitted. Figure 6 shows an applicative expression that occurs at an intermediate step in the implementation of the example program. The StreamSplit operator takes one input (a stream) and produces two output (the first item and a stream of the remaining items). The StreamConstruct operator takes two input (an item and a stream) and produces one output (a new stream with the input item preceding the items of the input stream). The StreamApply:Fix operator takes three inputs (all streams) and produces a single output (a stream of the results of applying the user-defined Fix operator to successive sets of items from the input streams). Within the applicative paradigm, ΦANG also supports operators defined in terms of specifications, stated as preconditions and postconditions on the input and output values.

The second major computational paradigm involves *imperative expressions*. An imperative operator executes within a context, taking values from the context and having side effects on values in the context. The data types in the hierarchy have associated imperative procedures as well as *procedurals* (procedures whose behavior depends on component operators). An imperative expression is a graph of invocations of imperative operators with control links defining a partial ordering on the execution of the invocations. Cycles are not permitted; cyclic computations (such as control loops) are modeled by suitable procedurals. Figure 7 shows an imperative expression that implements the StreamSplit operator. The Consume operator stores the next value

Data Flow

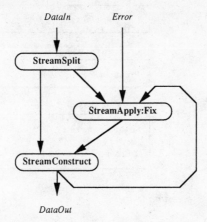

Figure 6. Applicative Expression.

from the DataIn stream in the variable X. The Produce operator writes the value of X onto stream Stream1. StreamEnumerate is a procedural that repeatedly consumes values from the DataIn stream, storing them in Y and executing the body of the procedural, namely, the Produce operator.

Concurrent execution of the components of an imperative expression is permitted. The only synchronization mechanism is based on streams: If an operator tries to consume an element from a stream at a certain index, and no element has yet been produced at this index, the consumer suspends execution until an element is produced.

ΦANG supports the mixture of computational paradigms through the use of environments. An *imperative environment* is an applicative operator defined in terms of imperative expressions. It consists of a local context and an imperative expression that operates in this context. The input values of the environment provide the initial values for the context, and the output values of the environment are taken from the context. Similarly, an *applicative environment* is an imperative operator defined in terms of applicative expressions. Input values for the applicative expression are taken from the context of the environment, and the output values of the environment provide new context values. Thus, an applicative environment is similar to a multiple assignment statement.

Body of Transformations

ΦNIX's body of transformations is organized in terms of a taxonomic hierarchy, as shown in figure 8. There are two broad classes of transformations,

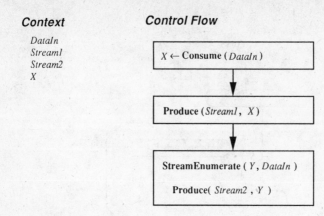

Figure 7. Imperative Expression.

those that bridge major computational paradigms (specification, applicative expression, and imperative expression) and those that transform an expression without changing paradigms. The latter group is further divided into refinements of abstract data types and operators into more concrete data types and operators, reformulations of composite expressions, and simplifications of composite expressions. For each subdivision, there are groupings for applicative and imperative expressions.

Currently, ΦNIX has 31 transformations. They were developed by focusing on the example error-correction program described earlier. The second column in figure 8 shows the total number of transformations in the various transformation classes.

Example Transformations

Examples of transformations from several of the classes are given below in the form of English paraphrases of the internal representation:

ApplicativeOperatorIntoImperativeEnvironment

The applicative operator **StreamSplit** can be replaced by an imperative environment whose body has the form

$X \leftarrow Consume(Input1);$
Produce($Output1,X$);
StreamEnumerate($Y,Input1$)
      Produce($Output,Y$)

ReformulateApplicativeExpression

Applicative subexpressions of the forms StreamElement$(X,1)$ and StreamShift$(X,1)$ can be replaced by a subexpression of the form StreamSplit(X).

Transformation Class	Number of Transformations
Transformation	
TransformationAcrossLevels	
SpecificationIntoApplicativeExpression	1
ApplicativeExpressionIntoImperativeEnvironment	3
ApplicativeOperatorIntoImperativeEnvironment	1
TransformationWithinLevel	
RefineDatatype	3
RefineOperator	
RefineApplicativeOperator	0
RefineImperativeOperator	1
ReformulateExpression	
ReformulateApplicativeExpression	4
ReformulateImperativeExpression	7
SimplifyExpression	
SimplifyApplicativeExpression	1
SimplifyImperativeExpression	10
Total	31

Figure 8. Taxonomic Hierarchy of Transformations.

ReformulateImperativeExpression

An imperative subexpression of the form $Y \leftarrow \text{Consume}(S)$ immediately preceded by a subexpression of the form $\text{Produce}(S,X)$ can be replaced by a subexpression of the form $Y \leftarrow X$.

SimplifyApplicativeExpression

An applicative operator with no output data links can be deleted.

Applying a Transformation

Each transformation describes a way that a composite expression can be changed and consists of a pattern and a replacement. For example, figure 9 shows the pattern and replacement for the StreamSplit transformation previously given.

Two primary activities are involved in applying a transformation. The first is to match the pattern against some expression in the program being transformed. Matching a pattern either fails or succeeds; if it succeeds, it can also identify specific parts of the expression for use when the transformation is applied. For example, when the pattern shown in figure 9 is matched, the variables X, Y, and Z are bound to a data flow source and two data flow sinks. The second activity is to replace the matched part of the subexpression with the replacement after making suitable substitutions for match variables. For example, the replacement shown in figure 9 would be attached to the data flow sources and sinks that are bound to X, Y, and Z.

Megatransformations

To simplify the development of a practical body of transformations, it is useful to have transformations that can apply other transformations, referred to as *megatransformations*. For example, to refine an applicative expression into an imperative expression, it is necessary to refine each of the applicative operators into its imperative definition. Given only the primitive transformations indicated in the hierarchy in figure 8, this refinement would require the application of a large number of transformations, a number roughly proportional to the number of operators in the applicative expression. To simplify the use of such common transformation sequences, ΦNIX's transformation language was extended to include simple actions, such as applying a specific transformation or applying any matching transformation in a group of transformations. The language was also extended to include rudimentary control structures, such as loops and conditionals, and constructs for changing the focus of attention to different parts of the program. While developing the transformations for the example program, 11 megatransformations were defined.

Search-Control Mechanism

As noted earlier, a specification and a body of transformations define a space of possible implementations that can be explored to find the best concrete program that satisfies the abstract specification. Even with a simple program, such as the error-correction example, the space is impossibly large to completely explore. Thus, some mechanism is required to reduce the space to a manageable size. Most transformation systems assume that all the transformations preserve correctness and, by transitivity, that any path that leads to a complete program leads to a correct program. Thus, the key issues for search-control mechanisms involve finding paths that lead to efficient implementations and avoiding paths that lead to dead ends.

Although some research has been done on automatic search-control mechanisms for program transformation systems, most current systems, including ΦNIX, avoid the issue by relying on the user to select which transformation to apply and where to apply it. Because this selection can involve a substantial amount of tedious work, ΦNIX includes a simple *script language* in which the user can describe a strategy for applying a set of transformations to a particular specification. (In fact, the language is exactly the same as that used for megatransformations.)

Some researchers have suggested that such scripts should even be viewed

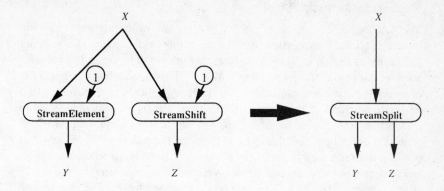

Figure 9. Pattern and Replacement.

as one of the results of writing a program (Wile 1983; chapter 18). In this view, writing a program consists of writing a specification and an implementation strategy. In the case of ΦNIX, researchers view the script language more as a temporary expedient to support the development of a comprehensive and useful set of transformations, with the hope of developing more automatic mechanisms in the future.

Scenario

As noted earlier, ΦNIX has successfully implemented the example error-correction program. In this section, the transformational sequence is summarized.

Specification

A formal statement of the specification gives the constraints that the output streams must satisfy with respect to the input streams: The first elements of the DataOut and DataIn streams are the same, and the stream of the remaining elements of DataOut is the same as the stream that results from applying the Fix function to the remaining elements of DataIn and the corresponding elements of Error and DataOut. In terms of ΦANG's operators, the specification is an applicative expression with a Boolean result, which can be stated as follows:

```
(And  (Equal  (StreamElement DataOut 1)
              (StreamElement DataIn 1))
      (Equal  (StreamShift DataOut 1)
              (StreamApply:Fix (StreamShift DataIn 1) Error DataOut)))
```

The corresponding data flow graph is shown in Figure 10a.

Major Transformation Steps

The first major step involves refining the constraint-oriented specification into an applicative expression that directly computes *DataOut*. The resulting expression is shown in figure 10b. Note that the graph in figure 10b includes a cycle. An applicative expression with a cycle is a well-formed ΦANG expression, but it is computationally effective only if the cycle does not depend on future elements of the output stream. Thus, a flow analysis is required to ensure that there are no harmful cycles. ΦNIX includes a minimal flow analyzer that determines that this cycle is harmless because the StreamConstruct operator does not need to know any elements of DataOut to produce the first.

The next major step involves refining the applicative expression into an imperative expression. This task is essentially accomplished by defining intermediate streams for each of the local data flow paths and replacing applicative operators with their imperative definitions. The resulting expression consists of three processes communicating through three local streams, as shown in figure 10c.

The third major step involves merging the processes into one. This task is essentially accomplished by collapsing producer-consumer pairs and results in the program shown in figure 10d.

The final major step involves simplifying the merged process. One simplification involves using a local variable instead of consuming a value from DataOut; the other involves refining a stream enumeration into a forever loop. The final program is shown in figure 10e.

Transformation Use

There are 84 steps in the transformation sequence that leads from the specification to the final program. Of these, 50 involve simplifications, 25 involve reformulations, and the remaining 9 involve refinements. The entire process is controlled by a single script. The script, in turn, calls both regular transformations and megatransformations. As initially developed, the script is about 40 lines long; more effective use of megatransformations would reduce the script to about 30 lines.

Discussion

In this section, I will discuss several issues, including larger target programs, automatic search control, and domain knowledge.

Larger Target Programs

Although the example program is small, ΦNIX embodies most of the infrastructure (specification language, wide-spectrum language, transformation and megatransformation languages, script mechanism) required for an interactive transformational implementation of a larger and more realistic program, such

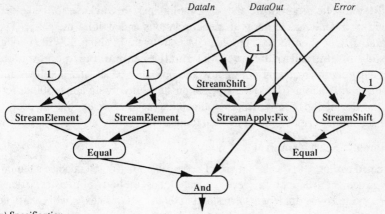

(a) Specification

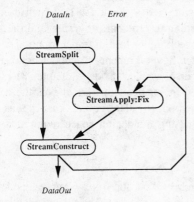

(b) Applicative Expression

$X \leftarrow$ **Consume**(*DataIn*);
Produce(*DataOut*,X);
StreamEnumerate
   (*X* ,*DataIn* ;*Y* ,*Error* ;*Z* ,*DataOut*)
   $W \leftarrow$ **Fix**(*X* ,*Y* ,*Z*);
   Produce(*DataOut*,W)

(d) Merged Process

$X \leftarrow$ **Consume**(*DataIn*);
Produce(*Stream1*,X);
StreamEnumerate(*Yë*,*DataIn*)
   Produce(*Stream2*,Y)

StreamEnumerate
   (*X* ,*DataIn* ;*Y* ,*Error* ;*Z* ,*DataOut*)
   $W \leftarrow$ **Fix**(*X* ,*Y* ,*Z*);
   Produce(*Stream3*,W)

$X \leftarrow$ **Consume**(*Stream1*);
Produce(*DataOut*,X);
StreamEnumerate(*Y* ,*Stream3*)
   Produce(*DataOut*,Y)

(c) Concurrent Processes

$W \leftarrow$ **Consume**(*DataIn*);
Produce(*DataOut*,W);
while True do
   $X \leftarrow$ **Consume**(*DataIn*);
   $X \leftarrow$ **Consume**(*Error*);
   $W \leftarrow$ **Fix**(*X* ,*Y* ,*W*);
   Produce(*DataOut*,W)

(e) Final Program

Figure 10. Major Steps in Scenario

as the complete program for the SLT-L tool. Thus, the major effort involved would be extending the body of transformations and writing the script. The formal specification of the complete SLT-L software is about 500 lines long. Based on similarities between the small example and the complete specification, the resulting program would probably be about 2,000 lines and would require about 10,000 transformation steps, involving about 500 different transformations. Script length is much harder to estimate, but the projection is that the script would be several thousand lines long.

Automatic Search Control

As noted earlier, ΦNIX's current use of scripts is primarily intended as a temporary expedient to support the development of a useful body of transformations. As suggested by script lengths measured in thousands of lines, it will clearly be important to provide a much more automatic form of search control.

There has been some research in this area in the context of earlier transformation systems. Two notable projects were LIBRA (Kant 1981), which used analytic techniques to identify paths leading to efficient programs, and GLITTER (Fickas 1985), which used heuristic techniques to find transformation sequences that satisfy goals stated by a user. Several recent projects have taken a mixed approach to search control. For example, SINAPSE (chapter 8) requires that the user make about a dozen major decisions but makes the remaining minor decisions itself. KIDS (chapter 19) also requires that the user make the major decisions, thereby restricting the search space required for other decisions.

Domain Knowledge

Despite the domain-oriented view researchers took, the ΦNIX components developed to date have been relatively domain independent. The major reflection of this domain is in the computational models embodied in the wide-spectrum language, and these models themselves are largely domain independent.

There are two areas in which Schlumberger researchers expect domain knowledge to play a more substantial role. One is related to search control and decision making. In their current form, scripts represent decisions that embody domain understanding but do not actually represent the domain understanding. Consider, for example, the decision to merge three processes into one in the scenario presented earlier. Implicit in this decision was an expectation that the resulting program would be more efficient. This expectation is true in the context of the current logging system, in which small processes can incur significant overhead for context switching but might not be true in a system with a large number of processors and fast communication channels.

The other role for domain knowledge is related to the interactive formalization activity of our automatic programming framework. Perhaps the most important observation to make about formalization is that it is largely a domain-specific activity: Interaction takes place in terms that are natural to the domain, and its purpose is primarily to translate these terms into computational terms. Thus, ΦNIX must have a substantial amount of domain knowledge to support the formalization process. For the domain of device-control software, much of this knowledge is about the device being controlled, and some preliminary studies have identified some techniques for representing knowledge about devices (Greenspan and Barstow 1986). For oil well logging devices, another important area of knowledge relates to the physics of the tool's sensors. Some research in this area has been done (for example, work on qualitative physics [Bobrow 1985]), but it is too early to know whether this work will apply to the formalization problem.

These expectations about the roles of domain knowledge are consistent with the experience of other automatic programming projects. For example, ELF (chapter 9), a domain-specific synthesizer of very large system integration routing algorithms, uses target domain knowledge to guide its search, corresponding to the role ΦNIX researchers foresee in decision making and search control. Also, users of KIDS (chapter 19), a general-purpose deductive transformation system, generally spend a significant fraction of their time defining domain-specific concepts and transformations that map these concepts into computational concepts. This approach closely corresponds to what researchers for this project have called formalization.

Conclusion

The goal of automatic programming is attractive, but it also elusive. Work on the ΦNIX project has also not yet achieved this goal, but there are some positive signs. In particular, if extensions to its base of transformations enable ΦNIX to transformationally implement the complete SLT-L software, then it will be a strong indication of the viability of the transformational implementation paradigm. If the issues of automated search control and interactive formalization can also successfully be resolved, then the prospects for automatic programming for device-control software will be good.

References

Balzer, R. 1985. A 15-Year Perspective on Automatic Programming. *IEEE Transactions on Software Engineering* 11(11): 1257–1268.

Barstow, D. 1986. A Perspective on Automatic Programming. *AI Magazine* 5(1): 5–28. Also in Rich, C., and Waters, R., eds. *Artificial Intelligence and Software Engineering*. San Mateo, Calif.: Morgan Kaufmann.

Barth, P.; Guthery, S.; and Barstow, D. 1985. The Stream Machine: A Data Flow Architecture for Real-Time Applications. In Proceedings of the Eighth International Conference on Software Engineering, 103–110. Washington, D.C.: IEEE Computer Society Press.

Bobrow, D., ed. 1985. *Qualitative Reasoning about Physical Systems*. Cambridge, Mass.: MIT Press.

Fickas, S. 1985. Automating the Transformational Development of Software. *IEEE Transactions on Software Engineering* 11(11): 1268–1277.

Greenspan, S., and Barstow, D. 1986. Using a Device Model as Domain Knowledge in the Automatic Programming of Software to Control Remote Devices, Technical Report SYS-86-7, Schlumberger-Doll Research, Ridgefield, Conn..

Hoare, C. A. R. 1978. Communicating Sequential Processes. *Communications of the ACM* 21(8): 666–677.

Kahn, G., and MacQueen, D. 1977. Coroutines and Networks of Parallel Processes. Information Processing 77, International Federation of Information Processing Societies.

Kant, E. 1981. *Efficiency in Program Synthesis*. Ann Arbor, Mich..: UMI Research .

Kant, E., and Barstow, D. 1981. The Refinement Paradigm: The Interaction of Coding and Efficiency Knowledge in Program Synthesis. *IEEE Transactions on Software Engineering* 7(5): 458–471.

Smith, D.; Kotik, G.; and Westfold, S. 1985. Research on knowledge-based software environments at Kestrel Institute. *IEEE Transactions on Software Engineering* 11(11): 1278–1295.

Wile, D. 1983. Program Developments: Formal Explanations of Implementations. *Communications of the ACM* 26(11): 902–911.

7

Data Relationships and Software Design

Elaine Kant

The topics of representing, monitoring, propagating, and acquiring data attributes and relationships are of particular interest in the domains of data interpretation and mathematical model design. However, data relationships appear in many other contexts: tracing requirements through design decisions, associating test data and results with programs, and accumulating assertions about data during symbolic evaluation to help in algorithm design.

My interest in data attributes and relationships arises from research on an integrated notebook and problem-solving environment for scientists. The goal of this system was to help scientists represent and reason about mathematical models of sensor tools for oil well logging and about inverse models, which infer geologic properties from measurements made by special instruments, called logging tools, that contain a variety of sensors. The tools are lowered into a bore hole, and measurements are recorded as the tools are raised to the surface. For example, the problems described in this chapter are based on nuclear logging tools that estimate porosity (important for figuring how much hydrocarbon can be in the pores of the rocks). Such tools emit neutron particles or gamma rays and then count the particles that bounce back from the rocks, oil, water, and other matter surrounding the bore hole.

These counts give a fairly direct measurement of density. The porosity estimates are based on the measured densities. However, it is not easy to figure out which parts of the surrounding material contribute to the count measure at a particular instant of time. Thus, the data-interpretation techniques are highly mathematical and involve approximating three-dimensional integral expressions with matrix operations such as deconvolutions. Because the problems are computationally intensive, efficient algorithms and problem reformulations are often needed. A comprehensive description of the kinds of domain knowledge and problem-solving strategies needed for solving problems in the domain of interpreting well logs is given in Barstow (1986).

Models should be described in a notation that is as mathematical as possible, then symbolically manipulated and transformed into efficient, executable code in a conventional language. This chapter describes the DAROS system, a prototype of a mathematical modeling assistant in which Data Attributes and Relationships help Organize Software models. The prototype was implemented in HYPERCLASS (which consists of components previously called STROBE (Smith and Carando 1986) and Impulse (Smith, Barth, and Young 1987). Research on this system showed the importance of tracking data relationships (for example, EstimateOf, InverseOf, FourierTransformOf) to understand the structure of specifications and automate program design. Although this project ended in 1988, related work on the synthesis of scientific programming continued in the SINAPSE system (see chapter 8).

Data descriptors (representations of the attributes and relationships of data) can have a rich structure. For example, the effective use of data descriptions for suggesting design steps requires that operations on data have input and output conditions expressed in terms of these descriptors. A given data descriptor, in isolation or as part of an operation description, serves not only as a constraint against which to check actual data but also as a pattern against which to match and evaluate a partial design.

Although all automated software design systems represent and modify data relationships, the topic of data relationships does not seem to be widely discussed in isolation. However, the desirability of domain modeling is noted (Greenspan, Borgida, and Mylopoulos 1986; Balzer 1985; Neighbors 1984), general knowledge representation techniques are of course relevant (Brachman and Schmolze 1985), and the benefits of including a database or object-oriented representation in the development environment are recognized (Smith, Kotik, and Westfold 1985; Balzer 1985). Similarly, much research that explores the use of rules and overlays for refining data representations touches on attributes of data (Kotik 1984; Rich 1981; Barstow 1986). This chapter does not present a finished theory but, rather, poses and addresses three specific questions about the role of data relationships in automating software design. The next three sections address these three questions in turn: What benefits arise from detailed data descriptions? Is there exploitable structure to the space of data attributes and relationships? What techniques are best for checking, propagating, and acquiring data descriptions? A detailed example is included in the first section. The final section of the chapter summarizes experience with DAROS.

Uses of Data Descriptors

Data attributes often guide software design in data-centered applications involving statistical analysis, business processing, or data interpretation. The next five subsections illustrate how detailed data descriptions can help automated systems (1) make basic refinement decisions with means-ends analysis, (2) optimize operation and representation implementation, (3) support data-centered process chain design, (4) automate data input and output, and (5) automate representation conversion. If the run-time environment does not share its data representation with a design environment, not all these techniques are applicable. Data and Operation Acquisition and Acquiring Data Descriptions discuss the uses of data descriptors for knowledge acquisition.

Refinement by Means-Ends Analysis

When input-output specifications are refined by backward-chaining means-ends analysis, data descriptors can control the search. The automated software design system inspects descriptions of each desired output to determine how it could be produced. The system searches its knowledge base for descriptions of operations that produce the right type of data, then applies preference rules or asks the user to narrow the choices. After selecting an operation whose output descriptions most closely match the desired output, the system tries to match this operation's input to data values that were previously computed or are input to the program. If appropriate data sources are not found, the system subgoals to build a new subconfiguration that computes the missing input. Once decisions are made about what operations to use, data description information is propagated as discussed in Propagating Data Descriptions. Information can be propagated forward or backward to operations that occur before or after the most recently refined program step. In this style of automated development, type information and other data descriptors provide feasibility tests when the system searches for operations with appropriate output or for sources of the input.

In mathematical modeling programs, data descriptor information typically includes annotations about the data types, domain attributes (for example, EstimateOf relationships between items), and data dimensions. Another type of useful attribute is the constraint between data input or between data input and output (for example, the inner dimensions in a matrix multiplication must be the same).

Design-time search control and inference are more efficient when data descriptions are more complete. Detailed descriptions restrict the set of operations that can produce and consume specified types of data. Detailed descriptions also filter the set of implementations suggested for data structures by reducing the number of representations that satisfy all the constraints of the set of operations that act on the data.

In addition to completely filtering some options, data description matches are used in operator preference rules (see Data Matching). To summarize, the choice is to prefer operations whose output data best match the descriptors. The preference takes into account the closeness of the data type, the number and values of data attributes (assuming an object-oriented representation), and the specificity of constraints or rule conditions. The quality of the match of the proposed operation input to existing data items is also factored into the heuristic rating. We are not concerned here with quantifying best operator match, just with which attributes of data descriptors help decide the quality of the match (Data Matching elaborates on the attributes used in data matching). Although the application domain is mathematical and, therefore, fairly precise, determining the intent and consequence of a concise problem specification for a specific operator internal to the derived program is not as well defined.

Consider an example in the domain of mathematical modeling (similar examples were implemented but not exactly as presented here). Some mathematical models define a mapping between sets of physical properties (such as material densities at specific spatial locations near the bore hole) and sets of measured responses (such as neutrons or gamma rays counted by a sensor on the logging tool). A *forward model* is a function or procedure that computes the measurements (counts) from the properties (density), whereas an *inverse model* predicts properties (density) from responses (counts). A common goal in mathematical modeling is an effectively computable approximation of an algebraic description of physical properties. The actual values of the physical property are not known and must be estimated from knowledge about how to solve the model expression for the property. My example is an instance of this problem; the goal is to produce a program that, given the responses and a forward model, computes an estimate of the properties and also evaluates the accuracy of the estimate. The next few subsections show how DAROS derives this program by means-ends analysis. The method for computing the properties from the responses is to apply an inverse model (multiply by an inverse matrix). This inverse model is computed by taking the inverse of a matrix that is the least squares fit between the responses and the properties. DAROS proposes each of these steps, in turn, based on matches between the desired output and the output of the available operators. Thus, the representations of data and their use to describe operator input and output are critical.

Representation of Background Knowledge. To understand how to use means-ends analysis and data attributes in this example, we need to examine some of the DAROS background knowledge. This knowledge includes representations for data items such as Matrix and (physical) Property, general mathematical operations such as MultiplyMatrix and InvertMatrix, and domain-specific operations such as ApplyInverseMatrixModel.

Representations of matrix operations include the constraints that the data type of any input or output must be a matrix and that the dimensions must match (as explained in Array Dimensions). The InvertMatrix operation that follows, shown as one example of these representations, actually performs an approximation operation, called a *pseudoinverse*, if the matrix is not square. A side effect of applying this operation is a record of the matrix being inverted in the InverseOf attribute in the output data object. The first level of indention in this representation identifies the attributes of the object. The second level shows attributes of the attributes, called *facets*. In the constraints, the notation TheInverse.InverseOf means the value of the attribute InverseOf of the value of attribute TheInverse. Constraints are discussed in more detail in Propagating Data Descriptions.

```
InvertMatrix
    TheMatrix:              <name>
        Data type:          Matrix
    Role:                   DataInput
    TheInverse:             <name>
        Data type:          Matrix
        Role:               DataOutput
    Operation:              CodeDetails
        Data type:          Lisp
    InvRec:
    Constraints:            TheInverse.InverseOf = TheMatrix
```

The FitLeastSquaresMatrix operation includes a FitEquation relationship between input and output matrixes. The matrix multiplication of A by B is indicated by the $A*B$ notation.

```
FitLeastSquaresMatrix
    ASpecializationOf:      FitLeastSquares
    GoalMatrix:             <name>
        Role:               DataInput
        OccurrenceNumber:   1
    DataMatrix:             <name>
        Role:               DataInput
        OccurrenceNumber:   2
    ParameterMatrix:        <name>
        Role:               DataOutput
    FitEquation:            GoalMatrix = ParameterMatrix * DataMatrix
```

The ForwardMatrixModel specifies a ModelExpression relationship between its components. The ModelExpression relationship expresses how the ModelTransform models the mapping of the StudiedObject to the Measurements. In this case, StudiedObjects is a property vector that contains values for a specific property (such as material density) at a set of points equally spaced down the bore hole. Measurements is a response vector containing the counts measured as the sensor passes locations equally spaced along the bore hole. TransformMatrix is a sensitivity matrix that expresses how sums of the different material densities produce different counts. Each row of the sensitivity matrix represents the linear coefficients of some response of a sensor tool to the vector of property values. The matrix multiplication operation sums the contributions of the properties at different points, weighted according to their distance. Many of the entries in the sensitivity matrix will be zero because the distance is too great for the property to contribute to the measured value. In the general case, the entries will each be vectors or matrixes of properties, responses, or sensitivities that sum over different properties as well as different locations.

ForwardMatrixModel
    ASpecializationOf: ForwardModel
    StudiedObjects: <namelist>
        Data type: PropertyMatrix
    Measurements: <namelist>
        Data type: ResponseMatrix
    ModelTransform: <name>
        Data type: SensitivityMatrix
    ModelExpression: Measurements = ModelTransform * StudiedObjects

The ApplyInverseMatrixModel operation has constraints beyond those for the data types of its arguments because it inherits constraints from its parent ApplyModel. This constraint says that the Response, Property, and InverseModel values must have InModel attributes whose values are the same model, some M, and that Property value should have its EstimateOf attribute filled with the same object as the StudiedObjects of this same model M.

ApplyModel
    ASpecializationOf: ModelOperation
    InverseModel: <name>
        Data type: Model
    Response: <name>
        Data type: Model
    Property: <name>
        Data type: Model
    Constraints: Property.InModel = Response.InModel
                           Inverse.InModel = Property.InModel
                           Property.EstimateOf = Property.InModel.StudiedObjects

```
ApplyInverseMatrixModel
  ASpecializationOf:    ApplyModel
  InverseModel:         <name>
    Data type:            InverseMatrix
  Response:             <name>
    Data type:            ResponseMatrix
  Property:             <name>
    Data type:            PropertyMatrix
  Operation:            MatrixMultiply
```

Thus far, we have seen several examples of representations of operations. An example of a representation for a data item that is useful in our example is EstimatedProperty, which is an estimate of the StudiedObjects of the model to which it belongs:

```
EstimatedProperty
  ASpecializationOf:    PropertyMatrix
  InModel:              <name>
  EstimateOf:           <name>
  EstRel:               <name>
  Constraints:          EstimateOf = InModel.StudiedObjects
```

Problem Specification and Instantiation. The problem specification for the inverse modeling program (figure 1) includes an instance Model-M1 of a ForwardMatrixModel and its named component input and output, X, Z, and S. The latter two are givens of the problem and will have specific data values. The first subgoal given to DAROS is Compute[EstimatedProperty[Model-M1]]. The object X' is instantiated to represent the estimated property.

Once the values of StudiedObjects, Measurements, and Transform are filled in for Model-M1, instantiation of other attribute values is automatic from inheritance. Examples of automatically instantiated attributes, shown by clear boxes, are the ModelExpression of Model-M1 and the ASpecializationOf and InModel values for S, Z, X, and X'. The next subsection explains how the shaded boxes are inferred.

Array Dimensions. Two attributes of interest for any array are the element type (real or complex, for example) and the array dimensions (for example, the rows and columns in a matrix, which is a two-dimensional array). In addition, DAROS extends the definitions of type and dimension to include more than just data-type or numeric information.

An element type might not just be real valued; it might also be defined to have units such as time in seconds or rate in feet each second. Thus, when multiplying two matrixes, we also do an analysis to ensure that it makes sense to multiply their elements, and we can infer the element type of the result.

Similarly, an array dimension has semantic content, representing not just the number of elements in a row but also the meaning of the row. For example, a response vector R3 can represent a specific sequence of counts taken at

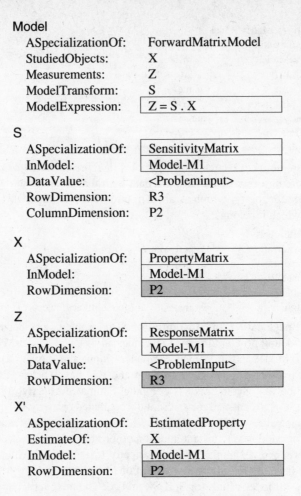

Model

ASpecializationOf:	ForwardMatrixModel
StudiedObjects:	X
Measurements:	Z
ModelTransform:	S
ModelExpression:	$Z = S \cdot X$

S

ASpecializationOf:	SensitivityMatrix
InModel:	Model-M1
DataValue:	\<Probleminput\>
RowDimension:	R3
ColumnDimension:	P2

X

ASpecializationOf:	PropertyMatrix
InModel:	Model-M1
RowDimension:	P2

Z

ASpecializationOf:	ResponseMatrix
InModel:	Model-M1
DataValue:	\<ProblemInput\>
RowDimension:	R3

X'

ASpecializationOf:	EstimatedProperty
EstimateOf:	X
InModel:	Model-M1
RowDimension:	P2

Figure 1. Model Specification Instantiation.

different sensors on the tool, or it can represent induction responses to materials at different distances in the formation. Similarly, a sensitivity matrix S1 with a set of responses R3 to a specific set of properties P2 does not have the same dimensions as another sensitivity matrix S2 with dimensions RA3 by P2 if R3 and RA3 represent different sequences of responses—even if both sets have the same number of responses.

When arrays are related to each other because they belong to the same model, are estimates of each other, or participate in the same instance of an operation such as matrix multiplication, then constraints on these objects will force the array dimensions to match. The shaded boxes in figure 1 indicate the dimension propagation that occurs when the dimensions of S are filled in for the example.

When an array such as S is created, numbered variables such as P2 and R3 are automatically generated on demand to represent the dimensions. However, automatically generated variables can be overridden. For example, the user might want to change R3 to the RA3 previously mentioned, a specific set of three responses to a sensor tool. Changing R3 in any data item causes all the values to be updated to match because of the constraints about matching dimensions in data objects in the same model.

Means-Ends Analysis Example. The initial goal in the problem specification is to compute the estimated property of a model. Thus, DAROS's first step is to look for operations whose output match the EstimatedProperty object. Many generic mathematical operations such as MultiplyMatrix match, but the ApplyInverseMatrixModel operation matches more closely. First, EstimatedProperty is closer in the taxonomic hierarchy to PropertyMatrix (its direct specialization) than it is to a generic data type such as Matrix (other objects such as MeasurementMatrix also lie along this path). Also, there are additional constraints inherited from the ApplyModel object. The constraints, which insist that all arguments belong to the same model, are satisfied because all are in Model-M1. Therefore, the ApplyInverseMatrix-Model operation is a better match because it has more satisfied constraints and has arguments closer in the hierarchy than MultiplyMatrix. The notion of moving constraints into the generator of possibilities, as discussed in chapter 12, takes the use of constraints a step further.

After DAROS selects and instantiates ApplyInverseMatrixModel and fills in X' as the Property value, it propagates constraint information (see Propagating Data Descriptions). This information includes constraints about dimensions inherited from the MultiplyMatrix operation and some others inherited from the ancestor operation concerned with finding the inverse of a transformation matrix. The result of the constraint propagation is descriptions of two new data objects that are the Response and InverseModelMatrix arguments to ApplyInverseMatrixModel.

DataObject-1
  ASpecializationOf: ResponseMatrix
  InModel: Model-M1
  RowDimension: R3

DataObject-2
  ASpecializationOf: InverseMatrix
  InModel: Model-M1
  ColumnDimension: R3
  RowDimension: P2
  InverseOf: S

Now DAROS must figure out if these objects are already known to the system or if they must, in turn, be generated. DataObject-1 exactly matches and, therefore, can be identified with program input Z. DataObject-2 does not match any known quantity but does nicely match the output of an InvertMatrix operation—better that it matches generic operations such as MultiplyMatrix—because of the presence of the InverseOf attribute on InvertMatrix's output. Because S is known to be the inverse of DataObject-2, the input to the InvertMatrix operation is directly available. However, although S is a named object, it is not an input to the program and must itself be computed.

A plausible match for computing S is the FitLeastSquaresMatrix operation. Although its output is simply a matrix, as InvertMatrix and MultiplyMatrix are, it is a better choice because its FitEquation relationship matches the ModelExpression when instantiated with S as the ParameterMatrix. When the dimensional relationships between S and the data and goal matrix are computed, they are consistent with Z and X, respectively, filling these roles. At this point, DAROS satisfies the initial goal of estimating the model property. The desired program is

(ApplyInverseMatrixModel
 (InvertMatrix (FitLeastSquaresMatrix Z X))
 Z)

Optimization

The optimizations considered here are special kinds of refinements that depend on exploiting explicit representations of the attributes of abstract data objects. Examples are decisions about how to represent abstract data types and how to implement operations on specialized data objects.

The desire for efficient implementation of the matrix inversion motivates one such set of optimizing transformations in a continuation of the example presented in Refinement by Means-End Analysis. This example was eventually implemented in the SINAPSE system. The system is described in chapter 8, and details of the example are given in Kant et al. (1990). In general, a large diagonal matrix can be inverted much faster—in time proportional to N, where N is the size of the (square) matrix—than the generic matrix inversion time, which is proportional to N^3. If the system can find a representation change that produces a diagonal matrix but is not itself too expensive, then it has found a good optimization. For a complete solution, all data involved must be transformed, then the whole problem solved in the transform space, and the answers inversely transformed back into the original space. This general algorithm schema applies to any similar problem, with the details of the transformation dependent on the solution space.

In the example, the domain knowledge that a transformation matrix represents the sensitivity of a moving sensor tool implies that the matrix to be inverted is a *circulant matrix*, in which each row contains the same elements as the preceding row but rotated one element to the right. A discrete Fourier transformation (DFT) operation, which takes time $N \log N$, converts a circulant matrix in the spatial domain to a diagonal matrix in the frequency domain. The diagonal matrix can then be inverted quickly with the specialized InvertDiagonalMatrix operation and converted back to the original domain (the inverse of DFT is similar to the DFT operation). The improved efficiency of all the operations in the transformed space (multiplication is similar to inversion) further indicates the benefit of the transformation. Thus, for large N, the total run time, including conversion, is much better. The DAROS system did not address the use of such efficiency information to make representation selections. Some obvious ideas are to associate primitive efficiency attributes with data objects and more complex efficiency computation rules with operation objects. For details on this topic, see Kant (1983, 1986) and chapter 13.

Achieving the optimization just described requires that abstract attributes (Circulant, Diagonal) of mathematical objects (Matrix) be propagated (or removed or added) by operations as appropriate. For example, the system must know that multiplication (or addition) of two matrixes yields a diagonal matrix if both input are diagonal and that the Fourier transform of a matrix is diagonal if the matrix is circulant. In the SINAPSE implementation, these facts are stored as backward-chaining rules that are executed whenever the properties of a data object are requested. In DAROS, they could have been implemented by testing whether the properties were true as constraints. Although an obvious location for the information that a circulant matrix becomes diagonal under the DFT operation is a rule that is part of the DFT operation itself, it is also useful to index the attribute transformation under the attribute types, such as Diagonal. This approach enables the system to consider optimizations during refinement. For example, when an expensive operation such as InvertMatrix is required, and the refinement system is permitted to think harder, it can look for more efficient specializations of the operation. It would then find the specialized operation, such as InvertDiagonalMatrix, and consider what additional attributes are required (such as the input matrix being diagonal). Next, the system could consider whether any representation changes would produce the desired attributes. The indexing of transformations under attribute types has not been implemented.

The system makes a related kind of efficiency decision during design—how to represent abstract data structures, which partially determine the implementation of the operations using this data structure. The decision depends in part on which operations create and use the data items. Knowing the uses and sizes of data sets often helps the system determine which operation implementations and data representations are most time and space efficient. In addition, data-use patterns can help in deleting obsolete data files and in programming storage control in the absence of automatic garbage collection. Rather than calling separate analysis procedures to determine data use and size, the system can treat this information as an attribute of the data and propagate it along with other attributes.

A knowledge representation scheme should associate data attributes with an abstract representation of the data separate from any detailed representation decision. For example, the Diagonal attribute on a matrix exists independently of the storage and access representations. Separate representations detail whether to store all array elements, including zero-valued elements, or only a vector of nonzero (diagonal) elements. In the latter case, specialized access operations produce the zero value for the implicitly represented (off-diagonal) elements. Similarly, the Circulant attribute is independent of the representation choice of storing only the first row and generating the other rows by rotation or index manipulation. Associating the attributes with the abstract description makes revising implementations easier and adds to the conceptual clarity.

Process Chains

Backward-chaining means-ends analysis of input-output data is not the only appropriate refinement technique for program synthesis. Some classes of software are better described with finite-state–machine or data flow paradigms. For example, data analysis and interpretation programs often have the flavor of being a chain of transformation processes connected by data flows (one such system is discussed in Kant [1988]). Even the process of software development itself, with programs considered as data, has this characteristic flow. We see how data attributes can also help in the synthesis of such process chains.

In the process chain paradigm, a data item goes through a known series of states, often with optional feedback loops. In software design, for example, states include problem description, preliminary design, detailed design, unit tested, and functionally tested. In data interpretation, states include raw, smoothed, environmentally corrected, modeled, and quality checked. In mathematical modeling, states include selection of design class, refinement of conceptual model, algorithmic implementation of model, application of model, and evaluation of model. These states can be considered as attributes of the program as data. After a processing step or a collection of steps, attributes can be added or removed, or states can be changed.

When a program is considered as data, the collection of attributes on the program suggest what to do next. Thus, another heuristic for choosing between refinement steps is whether the operation is a specialization of the expected stage of processing. Let's continue the design of a mathematical model started in Refinement by Means-End Analysis and suppose that the user specifies that a ProjectedResponse be computed next. Preliminary type filtering includes MultiplyMatrix and ApplyForwardMatrixModel among the alternative operations that generate this class of data. The decision heuristics already favor ApplyForwardMatrixModel for specificity in the operation hierarchy, but they also prefer it by a stage-of-processing argument: ApplyForwardMatrixModel is a kind of model evaluation stage of processing for an inverse modeling problem, and the previous operation, ApplyInverseMatrixModel, is a kind of model application stage.

This type of paradigm is especially useful when the user creates process chains at run time with an interpreter or programming environment. The process of deciding what to do next is interactive. DAROS filters the available options and makes suggestions based on what the user has done so far (a form of plan recognition), but the user has the final say about what to do. The system uses the state values to decide which operations are applicable and to do error checking. If a process does not correctly terminate, attributes are not added, and the expected next stage is not applicable; so, corrective action must be taken.

Data Input and Output

If data descriptions are a declarative part of a program specification, then interfaces for data input and output are easier to automatically design, especially if the final program executes in the same programming environment as the design system. On data input, DAROS checks the consistency of the user input with the expected values by inspecting the data types and constraints between data items. Outputs can be displayed, or monitored, by a simple user request. The constraint mechanism checks whether a data object has monitoring turned on whenever the data value is modified. If the output display depends on the input, then the data type determines the proper output format. Also, DAROS can automatically generate labels, background reference lines, and axis scaling on output plots with multiple components if it understands the relationships between curves and can obtain size information. For example, a concise specification for the user is a request to display a ProjectedResponse. DAROS infers that the user wants to graph the projected values (which are estimates of the measured responses) against the measured values to show the closeness of the estimate. Graphing a projected response of InductionResponses at a set of depths should, therefore, result in three pairs of curves. The three elements in the InductionResponses dimension have names corresponding to the distance from the sensor at which the materials are being measured (shallow, intermediate, deep). DAROS uses these names to label the curves: TrueResponse-shallow, TrueResponse-intermediate, . . . , ProjectedResponse-intermediate, ProjectedResponse-deep. The user can always specify other labels, but the default naming strategy is an easy way to refer to subcomponents.

Data-Format Conversion

In many problems, especially those in the data-interpretation domain, substantial programming effort is devoted to data-format conversion (Nestor et al. 1990). Data-representation formats vary along the dimensions of storage organization for uniform structures (lists or arrays, file-record indexing), physical quantity units, or interleaving of complex structures (different orders of storing multidimensional arrays). Conversion is needed to interface existing data files to programs to analyze or display the data or extract pieces of an existing data file. Within a single program, different representations of data can be more efficient for different purposes.

We can automate format conversion more easily if data descriptions are sufficiently detailed. Given a file-description language, for example, we can automatically convert a file with one descriptor into a file that fits another descriptor for the same values or a subset of these values. Similarly, if a program requires a subset of a file's data, then a simple read-from-named-file is a sufficient specification when the file has a descriptor because we can automate the process of extracting data from self-describing files.

Consider describing the storage format of array data for our example mathematical modeling program. The program or a standard library declares standard dimensions such as Point and InductionResponses (a set of three values). It also declares DEPTH, which is a vector of dimension Point that lists the depths at which measurements are taken, and RESP, which is a matrix of dimensions {InductionResponses, Point} that gives the value of each of the three responses at each measurement point. Data in a file can be stored in a variety of ways that we want to describe with a file format descriptor. The following examples assume that the input is an Ascii file that is read left to right and top to bottom, one token at a time. The *file descriptor* is a sequence of array descriptors. An *array descriptor* is a nested list of dimensions and array names. An open parenthesis immediately followed by a dimension name can be interpreted as the start of an enumeration of the dimension; it can be followed by an array name that contains this dimension or by another parenthesis and dimension name that is to be enumerated inside the outer loop. In other words, this listing gives the most slowly changing indexes first (for example, the row dimension for a matrix). The following examples give three different formats for ordering the same data:

1. ((Point DEPTH)
    (InductionResponses (Point RESP)))

D1	D2	D3	D4	D5
R11	R12	R13	R14	R15
R21	R22	R23	R24	R25
R31	R32	R33	R34	R35

This example describes four rows of numbers. The first row has, for each measurement in Point, the depth values from Depth. The second through fourth rows have, for each of the InductionResponses in turn, the values at each measurement point of RESP. In other words, this arrangement describes a list of the values in (Forall P in Point, (DEPTH[P])) followed by those in (Forall IR in InductionResponses, (Forall P in Point, (RESP[IR, P]))). The row division is conceptual: Both spaces and line terminators are token separators. The arrays will be stored out or read in, one token to each array value, according to the size of the dimensions, not the presence of line terminators.

2. (Point DEPTH (InductionResponses RESP))

D1	R11	R21	R31
D2	R12	R22	R32
D3	R13	R23	R33
D4	R14	R24	R34
D5	R15	R25	R35

This example describes four columns of numbers, each enumerating the values of all the measurement points in Point down the column but interleaved. The first column has depth values, the next column has values of the first induction response at each point, and the last two columns have the second and third induction responses. Alternatively, consider this list the list of the values (Forall P in Point, (DEPTH[P], (Forall IR in InductionResponses, RESP[IR, P]))).

3. ((Point DEPTH)
    (Point (InductionResponses RESP)))

D1	D2	D3	D4	D5
	R11	R21	R31	
	R12	R22	R32	
	R13	R23	R33	
	R14	R24	R34	
	R15	R25	R35	

This example describes a row of Depth measurements followed by three columns of numbers, each enumerating the values of all the measurement points in Point down the column but interleaved. This list can be interpreted as (Forall P in Point, (DEPTH[P])) followed by (Forall P in Point, (Forall IR in InductionResponses, (RESP[IR, P]))). The first column has values of the first induction response at each point, and the last two columns have the second and third induction responses.

The Structure of Data Attributes and Relationships

Thus far we have seen some examples of the possible benefits of using data attributes and relationships for making refinement decisions with means-ends analysis; optimizing operation and representation implementation; supporting data-centered process chain design; and automating data input, output, and representation conversion. This section considers the structure of the space of these data attributes and relationships and asks whether exploitable properties of the structure exist. Data Creation, Data Matching, and Data and Operation Acquisition discuss the benefits of structuring data attributes and relationships between data items. Explicit representations make it easier to create data descriptions during automated software design, evaluate the quality of matches between current and expected data descriptions, and acquire new data descriptions. A rich structure with various attributes representing different purposes is harder to construct and make consistent but is more likely to contain correct concepts that can be composed and reused. In addition, a richer representation structure enables the generation of better explanations.

The taxonomies presented in Some Taxonomies of Data Attributes and Relationships attempt to capture data attributes and relationships important to the domain of mathematical modeling and mathematical approximation and to separate domain-independent attributes and relationships. The taxonomies present examples of concepts rather than exhaustive lists.

A data item typically has many independent attributes. Some are part of the representational structure and are common to any data item (Brachman and Schmolze 1985), but most attributes shown are at a level above these representational properties and depend on the particular type of data item. Attribute types, as well as data items, can be represented as objects in an object-oriented language; specialization of attribute types corresponds to the role differentiation in Klone (Brachman and Schmolze 1985). Attributes of objects can themselves have attributes, called *facets*, when they are discussed relative to a data item.

Data Creation

An instance of a data description is usually a network of structure and attributes of the subdescriptions (back pointers, derived values) that is best created by the instantiation of generic descriptors. Generic attributes such as Role make it easier for the system to find and instantiate substructures without requiring a programmer to write different code to instantiate each new type of data item. New instantiation code would be needed because it would have to use the different names of attributes playing the same component roles. To avoid having the programmer write extra code, DAROS represents *structural descriptions*—conditions on the relationships between parts of data items—in a constraint language (see Propagating Data Descriptions). Specializations of the data items inherit the constraint descriptions. The system uses these constraint expressions when it creates data instances to compute derived attribute values and check that all the constraints imposed on data by the operations in which they participate are consistent.

Data Matching

In evaluating the quality of a match, the degree of similarity of the matched items, as well as the relative value of different types of attributes, is of interest. Thus, the system must be able to determine both a quality of match for each attribute-value pair and a weighting of attributes. Two criteria are the presence of matching attributes and the degree of similarity of the values that are filled in. One measure of match quality for a pair of attributes that are present is the number of specialization links that separate objects representing attribute values in a taxonomy.

Not all attributes are of equal interest in matching. For example, annotations about the editing date or the user who entered a definition might not be relevant. Also, required attributes count more heavily than optional attributes, and the values (but not the presence) of derived attributes are of interest. A Modality facet, described in some Taxonomies of Data Attributes and Relationships, indicates which of these possibilities is the case. Another weighting rule is to count domain attributes more heavily than pure mathematical attributes or programming attributes because they are usually more specific.

To weight matches of domain attributes more heavily, the representation must distinguish between domain, programming, and mathematical facts. Traditionally in program synthesis, the interesting data attributes are the programming implementations chosen for data objects (list, array, record, and so on). In addition to the implementation type, this description includes component relationships such as fields of records or pointers to descriptions of the elements of set types. The number of elements of a set type is also represented. At least three different kinds of information need to be represented: domain facts (is it property or response or sensitivity), mathematical facts (is it a function or a matrix or a vector), and programmatic facts (is the representation a list or array; what is the operation syntax).

The subclasses of structural relationships previously discussed also reflect this distinction. Each subclass has a Domain facet on the subclass object that specifies either an application domain, such as "SensorToolModeling," or the areas "Programming" or "Mathematics," so that the names of all the subclasses do not have to be known. (The edges of the Mathematics domain are, of course, rather fuzzy). Higher in the taxonomy, objects are purely in the application, mathematics, or programming world. However, before a concrete program is complete, a data object or operation must have attributes of all three worlds filled in; constraints can cross worlds.

Data and Operation Acquisition

Knowledge acquisition is simplified by the use of hierarchies (so only incremental changes need be noted) and facets (to indicate required or expected attributes on classes of objects). For example, when a new object is added, an automated knowledge-acquisition assistant (not implemented) could check that attributes are added at the right level (for example, objects in the application-domain taxonomy should not have constraints that refer to programming entities). The assistant can also check the descriptors of a new operation's input and output data types to see if they have domain attributes (such as Circulant or Symmetric on a Matrix) that need propagation rules. An assistant could also present the current set of propagation rules as candidates. Similarly, the assistance can suggest constraints on the relationship between dimensions of input and output of new (or sufficiently modified) operations.

Separating attributes by Domain—application, mathematics, or programming—should make it easier to add new concrete programming constructs that cross the boundaries. For example, if the knowledge base already contains an ApplyForwardModel object and a MultiplyMatrix object, then adding the concept of ApplyForwardMatrixModel is mostly a matter of role mapping. *Role mapping* is similar to the notion of overlays (Rich 1981). Here, the system or user must pair attributes in the operation (Sensor-ToolModeling domain), such as Property and ForwardModel, with the corresponding input (or output) arguments in the MultiplyMatrix object in the Mathematics domain; both sets of constraints about matching models and matrix dimensions can then be inherited and checked for consistency. A good design-time role-mapping facility reduces the necessity of explicitly entering all cross-product concepts into the knowledge base.

The knowledge base can also contain descriptions of the relationships between data and approximation techniques in the mathematical domain that are specialized in the application domain. For example, the approximation LinearizeFunction (figure 2) describes how any function can be linearized by a transformation matrix. Constraints indicate that the column (row) dimension of the matrix is the domain (range) of the original function. If the data concept ForwardModelFunction exists, when we add the concept Sensitivity-Matrix to the knowledge base and say that it is an estimate of ForwardModelFunction using the LinearizeFunction, then MathDataType, ColumnDimension, and RowDimension are automatically filled in.

Some Taxonomies of Data Attributes and Relationships

Four classes of data relationships are described here: attributes of data items (figure 3), structural relationships within data items (figure 4), transformation relationships between data items (figure 5), and comparative relationships between data items (figure 6). Links from left to right in the figures indicate a specialization relationship. Selected facets and values are indented underneath the attribute names.

The class objects for data attributes are called *descriptors*. The first level of descriptors shown in figure 3 is the subclassification, which does not appear on any actual data objects. The next level down shows some descriptors that we

```
Approximation
    Given:
    Approx:
    Constraints:
        (Approx.Value.MathDataType = Approx.DataType)

Linearize Function
    ASpecializationOf:       Approximation
    Given:
        Datatype:                Function
    Approx:
        Datatype:                Matrix
    Linearization:           <code>
    Constraints:
        (Given.Domain = Approx.ColumnDimension)
        (Given.Range   = Approx.RowDimension)

ForwardModelFunction
    DomainDataType:       ModelTransform
    MathDataType:         Function
    Domain:               Property
    Range:                Response

SensitivityMatrix
    EstimateOf:      ForwardModelfunction
    ApproxTechnique:       LinearizeFunction
    MathDataType:         Matrix
    ColumnDimension:      Property
    RowDimension:         Response
```

Figure 2. A Data Approximation.

already saw, such as Role and InModel. Some of the most common attributes are those under DescriptorForGenericAttribute. These generic attributes serve as facets that can belong to any type of attribute. For example, as shown in figure 3, any attribute can have a Modality facet. Possible values are required, required-unchanging-value, optional, derivable, or annotation when associated with a particular class of data item. Similarly, any attribute of a data item, when associated with a specific data item, can have the values computed or stored. The CandidateValues facet for an attribute can also be specified; a default is that any specialization of this attribute is a candidate value if an attribute appears in the taxonomy by name. Data type is another generic attribute. Large taxonomies of specific data types—in mathematics, in an application domain such as signal processing or payroll, or within the domain

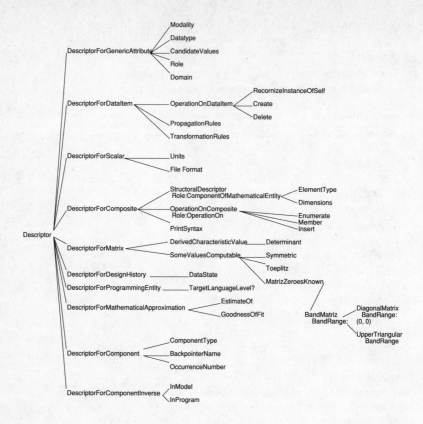

Figure 3. Attributes of Data Items.

of programming itself—are often useful and are recorded as the Domain. Within the application domain, some of the data types directly reflect the structural Role of the data item (for example, responses and sensitivities in the tool sensor modeling domain are both Data types and Roles in a model description).

Figure 3 also shows a sampling of attributes that apply to specific types of data items, most from the domain of abstract mathematical objects. If any attribute has a value that is frequently used, then a new, named object with this value filled in is used as a subcategory in the Descriptor hierarchy. For example, under DescriptorForComposite, the StructuralDescriptor attribute has its Role facet set to ComponentOfMathematicalEntity, and the OperationsOnComponent has its Role set to OperationOn. All subclasses inherit these roles so that matching and knowledge-acquisition functions that need to find all the operations on, or components of, a data item can be written in the most general terms.

Some examples of attributes representing the structural relationship of a subpart to its composite object are shown in figure 4. In programming (Com-

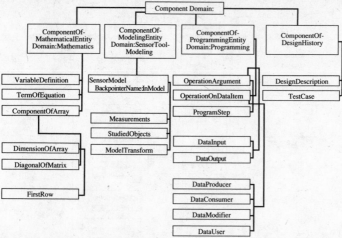

Figure 4. Structural Relationships within Data Items.

ponentOfProgrammingEntity), some classes of relationships that are frequently used are the data input and output of an OperationArgument and the
producers and consumers of data of an OperationOn component associated
with procedures or programs. Many relationships have facets from figure 3
that indicate the component type (usually in the Role facet, but in the case
where all attributes are unique, the name of the attribute also serves as the
component type or role), the occurrence number for ordered sets of similar
values, and the back-pointer object. An example of a back pointer can be
seen in figure 1 when the Measurements attribute (a specialization of the
SensorModel component) is added to a specific sensor model Model-M1. At
this point, the object Z, which is the value filling the Measurement attribute,
is given an InModel attribute with value Model-M1.

Transformational relationships resemble structural relationships. If a derivational history is viewed as a data item, then the transformational relationship
between data items is a structural relationship within the derivation history.
The attributes of a transformation relationship indicate the previous data item
and the transformation applied. The system can infer interesting mathematical
properties, such as whether a mapping is isomorphic, from the transformation
type. A selection from a hierarchy of transformation relationships is shown in
figure 5. A useful representation for complex transformations is an operation
invocation record with data input and output values for the particular operation application instance; transformation attributes mirror the program description attributes. The RoleMappings attribute associated with a representation decision is useful in determining how to bring constraints from the
mathematical and modeling domains into the programming domain.

Comparative relationships between data items (figure 6) help the system

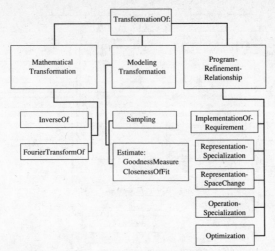

Figure 5. Transformation Relationships among Data Items.

express constraints between items and help determine the similarity of items for knowledge acquisition. The relationships are also used in the matching process. Some relationships are assertions that cause propagation; others simply record facts of a relationship. Relationships can be computed when needed rather than stored (for example, sibling, alternative, transform sequence), and results can be cached for efficiency.

Checking, Propagating, and Acquiring Data Descriptions

We have seen a number of data attributes that are useful for storing back pointers and derived values at data-creation time, determining the quality of a match, and simplifying the organization and acquisition of new objects. I turn now to summarizing the processes by which data descriptions are checked, propagated, and acquired.

Checking Data Descriptions

The notion of checking a data item has several meanings. At run time, DAROS checks whether an actual data value, given by the user or passed by another part of the program, satisfies the abstract description of the data item and constraints on the data item. DAROS needs different types of checking at design time and knowledge-acquisition time (not implemented) to determine which of two data descriptors is more specific. At design time, checking is used in the matching process to make sure that a data item that is attached as the input or output to an operation is at least as specific as the data type representing the constraint on this argument; at knowledge-acquisition time, it is used to check the legality of user insertions of objects into a hierarchy (objects must be

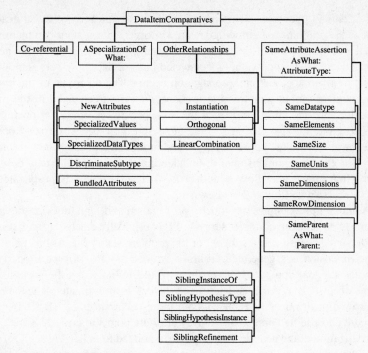

Figure 6. Comparative Relationships between Data Items.

more specific than the objects given as their immediate generalization).

The definition of more specific is fairly straightforward for data objects that appear in scientific programming, which tend to be arrays rather than complex, irregularly composed structures. For primitive object descriptions, more specific simply means that the first object is a descendant of the other object in the taxonomic hierarchy. For complex descriptors, more specific means, at a minimum, that the object classes of the descriptors are in a specialization relationship in a taxonomy. There can also be domain-specific attributes (for example, dimensions and units) whose values must be in a specialization relationship. In addition, the descriptors' subparts have to obey the specialization relationship; so, DAROS has to do a recursive, structured tree walk. All subparts or dimensions that are in the less specialized object must also be present (or specialized) in the more specialized object. Data objects that are sibling types, say, two user-defined matrix objects, are sometimes in a specialization relationship. The same sort of tree-structure walk and attribute comparison will determine the relationship of sibling types.

Propagating Data Descriptions

As noted in Refinement by Means-End Analysis, at design time, it helps to propagate information about data types, data attributes, data creation, and the use of data in operations. This propagation is essentially a symbolic evaluation of the program to help with design. However, information can be propagated both forward and backward through a program description. When a more specific data-type value is connected (with a data flow between operations) to a less specific one, propagation occurs. The data type of the operation input or output that was the less specific type is changed to the more specific type, and all other uses of the less specific type by other operations in a program are also changed to the more specific type. Also, many operations have constraints between output and input that can cause new information (for example, dimensions) to be added to the less specific data description when a new data flow is added or when a data type is propagated in response to a data flow added elsewhere.

A number of examples of property propagation at design time are shown in figure 1. As another example, suppose EP is originally created as an EstimatedProperty because it is a subgoal of the problem statement. At this point, its RowDimension is a generated arbitrary symbol, say P1, of type Property. If another subgoal computed the error, it would initially also be specified in terms of this P1. When it is determined that EP is an estimate of X, then P2, the row dimension of X, replaces both these occurrences of P1. P2 is more specific because its DimensionOfArray attribute points to array X, which is a specialization of the generic PropertyMatrix pointed to in P1.

If the run-time system is sophisticated enough, information about specific data types and creation and transformation history should also be propagated to the descriptions of concrete data items. Here, information can only be propagated in the forward direction. For example, recall the discussion on displaying plots of responses in Data Input and Output. If one of the run-time input to DAROS is a true response called Re87, then the labels used on the induction response plot can automatically be set to Re87-shallow, and so on, without explicitly specifying any naming and parameter passing to the user interface.

Many alternative techniques for propagating data descriptions exist: special-purpose code, production rules, if-added rules, attribute grammars, and so on. Most of them can be made to propagate descriptions, but it is preferable if the same declarative form can be used for type checking and multidirection propagation at design time and for propagation of attributes to concrete data output at run time. Because the refinement process is incremental, specialized global flow algorithms that are rerun whenever there is a demand are probably inappropriate.

The prototype system DAROS uses constraints to handle the propagation as well as the type checking of data attributes. The constraint system, CONMAN (Wald 1989) was a previously existing component of the HYPERCLASS system in which DAROS was implemented. In CONMAN, constraints are defined by both Boolean conditions, which should be satisfied by an attribute value or a set of attribute values, and actions to be taken after modifying values. Before a value is modified, the condition is tested against the new value. If the test succeeds, any associated action routines are applied, the attribute value is modified, and any values that depend on the changed value are notified of the change so that they can also be updated. CONMAN has a test mode so that a set of changes can be explored to determine if any violations would be caused without actually setting any values from the original modification or any chained actions. The constraint actions can include error-correction routines or back-pointer maintenance. The list of other attributes to be notified of changes is automatically computed from the constraint expression. Simple constraints can be represented as expressions in facets on attributes, but complex constraints that equally apply to several attributes, especially those that frequently appear, can be represented as constraint objects. In DAROS, most constraints are represented as specially defined constraint objects associated with data-type objects such as DataMatrix. These constraints are checked whenever values with these data types are set (all attributes have a data-type facet). If a new value is specified that is more specific than the old value, then the associated constraint object actions propagate the new data type to other attributes using the previous value. Thus, the list of uses of a specific data item is constantly updated by the constraints. In addition, if data-value monitoring has been enabled for the data object, then the display is updated after any change to the value. The actions are conditional, depending on whether the update takes place at design time or run time.

If it were desired at design time that the alternative design histories could simultaneously be maintained so that multiple refinements could be explored in parallel, a context or reason maintenance mechanism would be needed. This mechanism is not directly supported by CONMAN and is not implemented in DAROS. Because the system needs to check the compatibility of operations by propagating constraints in both directions, the system would have to either check compatibility in a special context (to avoid the premature propagation of results into the entire program description) or maintain dependency links on all assertions about data values. Although a context mechanism was available and was used in the interpretation chain system (Kant 1988), this capability was not considered critical enough to implement in the prototype.

Acquiring Data Descriptions

Errors at run time, for example, the absence of a required attribute such as a dimension, signal an opportunity for knowledge acquisition. In the case of a missing attribute, a constraint is probably missing. Similarly, a conflict in propagated values indicates that one of the constraints might be wrong. Tools for locating the sources of conflicting constraints and maintaining a stack of editing tasks are, of course, desirable, as are static knowledge base consistency checkers.

Sophisticated descriptions of data structure and attributes should facilitate the acquisition of domain knowledge. In addition to simplifying the addition of data that resembles existing forms, a rich data representation will indicate additional questions to ask the user about operations using the data. For example, it will be easier to automate asking the user about whether a mathematical modeling operation has an inverse or whether its output is an estimate of some other quantity. Similarly, constraints on data associated with operations that produce or consume a newly defined data type provide clues about the structure of the data representation, as in defining SensitivityMatrix in figure 2.

As indicated in Data and Operation Acquisition, separating domain-specific attributes from mathematical and programming attributes helps organize knowledge bases. The system should use the abstract, domain-oriented specification of operations rather than the program-specific representation to propagate the abstract data properties to the abstract data items that result from the operations. An indication of which ancestors to search for inheritance of specific attribute types would improve the efficiency of knowledge representations that do not cache all attributes.

After the construction of a program or a complex operation is complete, the user can choose to remember the structure for future use. This process includes making sure that all (sub)structure input and output that are appropriate to the top level are moved up and generalized, inferring the constraints on the top-level input and output from all the intermediate constraints, generalizing the data types used during inference to those contained in the permanent knowledge base, and recording the configuration itself in the permanent knowledge base.

For example, after solving the example problem of how to compute an EstimatedProperty, DAROS creates a new operation with an input that is a ForwardMatrixModel (not Model-M1) and an output that is an EstimatedProperty (not X'). It also infers constraints, for example, that the row dimensions of the output and the response matrix and sensitivity matrix of the model are the same. It does not propagate problem-specific facts such as the number of data points in the actual value of X'.

Conclusions

Detailed descriptions of data, especially constraints on the input and output data of operations, help an automated software design system control the search for refinement steps. The means-ends approach to selecting design steps compares descriptions of the desired output (available input) to descriptions of operation output (input) to reduce the number of possibilities considered and determine the closest matches. In addition, the system identifies potential optimizations and next steps in processing chains by inspecting stored attributes of available data and desired attributes on operation input. Representation conversion is assisted by structural descriptions of data items.

Knowledge bases for software design should include both domain and design knowledge; general mathematical knowledge is also often useful. Separating attributes of data items by domain, mathematics, and programming roles makes it possible to have some permanent objects purely in one category for clarity of representation. Role mapping helps to create concrete programming constructs that cross category boundaries. This mapping can be done as part of knowledge acquisition or as a temporary move needed during a specific design process.

Generic attributes of knowledge representation systems (for example, data types, roles, candidate values, modality, and back pointers) help in matching and knowledge acquisition. Comparative relationships between attributes also facilitate acquisition and matching. Useful attributes for programming in the mathematical domain also include units and dimensions and derivable components. Programming attributes cover a wide range, from data type and operation structure for small programming steps to refinement and transformation links. Many domain-specific specializations of all these classes of attributes and relationships are needed to complete a software design knowledge base. A rich structure of interconnections makes it easier to explain, compose, and reuse knowledge base concepts.

The DAROS prototype was developed for, and evaluated on, a family of problems that compared the differences in accuracy between linearizing forward and inverse models for nuclear logging data deconvolution problems. More was done on paper (a series of eight experiments) than was implemented (just a few of the examples). The features of the system that the domain expert liked best were the brevity of the specifications and the automatic monitoring of data through labeled graphs, especially when the parameters could be changed in near real time. Less visible features such as the constraint mechanism enabled this capability. Although not enough alternative operations were implemented to quantify how much useful filtering could be achieved based on best match, at least the most obvious choices were eliminated. One knowledge-acquisition capability integrated into DAROS was the ability to generalize the results of a problem-solving session and define a new compound operation with an abstracted set of input and output. Additional knowledge-acquisition scenarios were detailed on paper, and limited implementation experiments on adding new concepts were separately done. One disadvantage of DAROS was that it was implemented on top of a system that was rather large and not widely available. The successor system (chapter 8) addresses this problem and also explores the use of forward chaining rather than means-ends analysis for a problem. This system, called SINAPSE, adopted the use of explicit representations of array dimensions and the checking and propagation of array properties prototyped in DAROS. However, because it is implemented in another language, the details of the mechanics differ. SINAPSE has been successful in the domain of finite-difference algorithm synthesis.

Acknowledgments

Joseph Wald designed the array-manipulation language used here in the format-conversion examples. Charles Watson patiently explained the application-domain examples (but is not responsible for any remaining misrepresentations). Patricia Carando gave helpful feedback on an earlier version of this chapter. Ursula Wolz helped clarify many knowledge representation and knowledge-acquisition issues by working through the examples in detail and analyzing and improving the prose in earlier versions of this chapter. Dorothy Setliff and Michael Lowry gave careful readings to a draft of this chapter.

References

Balzer, R. 1985. A 15-Year Perspective on Automatic Programming. *IEEE Transactions on Software Engineering* SE-11(11): 1257–1267.

Barstow, D. R. 1986. A Perspective on Automatic Programming. *Readings in Artificial Intelligence and Software Engineering* 10:537–559.

Brachman, R. J., and Schmolze, J. G. 1985. An Overview of the KL-One Knowledge Representation System. *Cognitive Science* 9(2): 171–216.

Green, C. C, and Barstow, D. R. 1978. On Program Synthesis Knowledge. *Artificial Intelligence* 10.

Greenspan, S. J.; Borgida, A.; and Mylopoulos, J. 1986. A Requirements Modeling Language and Its Logic. *Information Systems* 11(1): 9–23.

Kant, E. 1988. Interactive Problem Solving Using Task Configuration and Control. *IEEE Expert* 3(4): 36–49.

Kant, E. 1986. On the Efficient Synthesis of Efficient Programs. In *Readings in Artificial Intelligence and Software Engineering*, eds C. Rich and R. Waters, 157–184. San Mateo, Calif: Morgan Kaufmann.

Kant, E. 1983. On the Efficient Synthesis of Efficient Programs. *Artificial Intelligence* 20(3).

Kant, E.; Daube, F.; MacGregor, W.; and Wald, J. 1990. Knowledge-Based Program Generation for Mathematical Modeling. Presented at the Second International Conference on Expert Systems for Numerical Computing, Purdue University, March.

Kotik, G. 1984. Knowledge-Based Compilation of High-Level Data Types, Technical Report KES.U.83.5, Kestrel Institute.

Neighbors, J. M. 1984. The Draco Approach to Constructing Software from Reusable Components. *IEEE Transactions on Software Engineering* SE-10(11): 1257–1267.

Nestor, J. R.; Newcomer, J. M.; Giannini, P.; and Stone, D. L. 1990. *IDL: The Language and Its Implementation*. New York: Prentice-Hall.

Rich, C. 1981. A Formal Representation for Plans in the Programmer's apprentice. In Proceedings of the Seventh International Joint Conference on Artificial Intelligence, 1044–1052. Menlo Park, Calif.: International Joint Conferences on Artificial Intelligence.

Smith, D. R.; Kotik, G. B.; and Westfold, S. J. 1985. Research on Knowledge-Based Software Environments at Kestrel Institute. IEEE Transactions on Software Engineering SE-11(11): 1278–1295.

Smith, R. G., and Carando, P. J. 1986. Structured Object Programming in STROBE, Technical Report, Schlumberger-Doll Laboratory for Computer Science, Austin, Texas.

Smith, R. G.; Barth, P. S.; and Young, R. L. 1987. *A Substrate for Object-Oriented Interface Design*. Cambridge, Mass.: MIT Press.

Wald, J. 1989. Implementing Constraints in a Knowledge Base. In *Expert Database Systems: Proceedings from the Second International Conference,* ed. L. Kerschberg, 163–183. Benjamin Cummings.

8

Scientific Programming by Automated Synthesis

Elaine Kant, Francois Daube, William MacGregor, and Joe Wald

The goal of the program synthesis performed by the SINAPSE system is to minimize the time required for scientists and engineers to design and implement mathematical models. SINAPSE helps users formulate problems if they use standard classes of governing equations and can also guide the user through the design decisions for the algorithms that it can generate. The bulk of the system concerns the automatic generation of the implementation so that the scientist or engineer is not forced to learn details of the target hardware and language to transform the equations into efficient code on a range of target architectures. Finally, the system supports revision at the specification, rather than the implementation, level. We are initially focusing on the synthesis of finite-difference programs from models based on partial differential equations.

Scientific problem solving seems to be a promising application domain for automatic program synthesis. Let's first consider how the benefits typically advertised can be achieved for the synthesis of scientific programs and then look at the costs.

In the ideal program synthesis system, programs are easy to specify in terms natural to the end user. The automated implementation prevents careless errors. Programs can be optimized for different target machines and programming languages by simply changing the specification. Modification and reuse are facilitated by the clarity of the specifications and the codification of programming and application knowledge. Overall, because the user can quickly experiment with different specifications and implementations, productivity is dramatically increased.

In scientific applications, problems can naturally and concisely be specified in terms of the mathematics of the application, and much implementation knowledge is readily available in books and journal articles. Three-dimensional (3D) models are especially suited to automation. The 3D models contain long, complex arithmetic expressions and boundary conditions compared to most existing one-dimensional (1D) and two-dimensional (2D) codes. Until the advent of new parallel supercomputers, it was simply not feasible to compute 3D models for large input. Because models at Schlumberger must be run on gigabyte-sized data sets, the speed of the target code is important. This requirement presents us with an opportunity to free the modelers from learning the intricacies of optimizing for new architectures and from hand coding error-prone details. The integration of symbolic mathematics into code generation enables the error-free case analysis of boundary conditions for complex geometries and the inclusion of high-order finite-difference operators into time-varying 3D problems. Modifications to either the models or algorithms are also usually specified easily. Not only are individual mathematical models reused fairly often, but also the existence of several common formulations makes it profitable to be able to access similar models and see what implementations worked for them. Preliminary experiments with SINAPSE has demonstrated that within its domain of expertise, generation time for a program is under 10 minutes (most examples take just 1 or 2 minutes).

To be fair, we must consider the potential costs of program synthesis. One of the major issues is the large investment to analyze, abstract, and codify a new application domain. There are gaps in our knowledge of useful abstractions to map even the lowest application level onto computational models. However, the investment in domain modeling can pay off if algorithms (for example, finite-difference) or algorithm components (for example, approximation of derivatives by difference expressions) are frequently used, and the same model is frequently modified. It is not necessary for the system to make all the algorithm choices; simply providing a system to combine various choices in a consistent manner is extremely useful. The codification of enough programming knowledge to generate efficient code has similar costs and trade-offs but has been done enough times now that the benefit-cost ratio is more predictable. Although the target code that SINAPSE generates is readable and includes many comments, we do not directly address the issue of debugging, which can be a real problem because imperfect systems mean that end users will be looking at the target code despite our best intentions to shield them from having to do so. Finally, we must consider the costs of maintaining the synthesis system and making it available on different platforms; the specifications and design history are much less useful for program evolution without the automated system to implement them. This issue is still open because we currently have no detailed plans for technology transfer. However, we are deriving enough benefit in both research and application that we expect our work to be worthwhile for the next few years.

In summary, we believe that the domain of mathematical modeling, although complex, is tractable. It is rich enough that there is a payoff to speeding the implementation process. We believe an application-specific synthesis system (with user specification of many algorithm decisions rather than total automation) can be developed faster than generic tools for parallel programming and can incorporate more specialized algorithm elaborations and optimizations.

The beginning of this article outlines the problem-solving framework used in the SINAPSE system and then gives an example of the synthesis process. After a discussion of search control and design histories, each of the stages in program development is discussed in turn, considering its concepts, representations, and reasoning strategies. Open issues and a summary discussion conclude the article.

Problem-Solving Framework

The problem-solving framework discussed here was developed over the first year of the project and came from a variety of sources, including previous experience by the developers and others in program synthesis. To specialize this knowledge to the scientific programming domain, we reverse engineered a few existing programs and then generalized them. We are now working with domain experts on new codes that they want to develop. After summarizing the framework, we discuss how our choice of implementation platform follows from our analysis of the problem-solving styles.

The Scientific Programming Process

The synthesis of programs for mathematical modeling begins at the level of domain modeling (Barstow 1986; Arango 1988) and then moves to the mathematics of the underlying physical phenomena. Synthesis then proceeds to high-level algorithms and to detailed algorithms in a pseudocode. Eventually, the end result must be numeric codes in a specific language such as Fortran or C that execute on high-performance floating-point processors and the visualization of results. Only through the direct expression of the mathematics of physical processes and the automatic generation of programs consistent

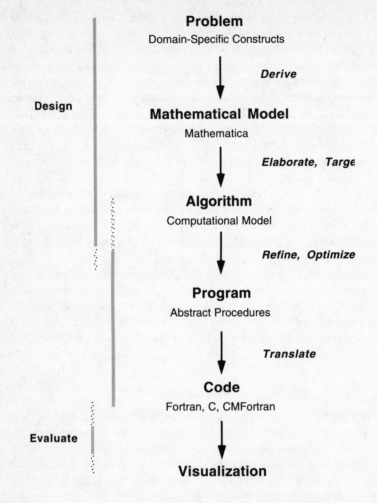

Figure 1. A Problem Solving Framework for Mathematical Modeling.

with the mathematics will the scientist be able to easily optimize, retarget, and modify mathematical modeling codes.

The SINAPSE system is based on this problem-solving framework for mathematical modeling, which is illustrated in figure 1. This section gives an overview of the activities and representations at and between each level; the next sections provide detailed examples. Although the figure shows a linear progression, it is assumed that feedback and revision cycles can occur at any stage (the extent to which these cycles are implemented is discussed in Search Control).

Each stage in the framework corresponds to a different level of program description detail and can involve different concepts, representations, and reasoning techniques. We can think of each level as an abstract machine with several components we call *domains of knowledge* (Neighbors 1989). Although SINAPSE addresses each of these levels to some degree, it concentrates on supporting the transitions from mathematics to code.

The system starts with a problem description. It is expressed in terms of application-domain key words, with operations at the level of "compute the forward model" for a problem in the domain of "wave propagation." Models are described in terms such as "StressStrain" formulation and "Elastic."

From the problem formulation, the system derives a more complete specification of the mathematical model through domain knowledge and symbolic manipulation. A model is expressed in terms of constructs such as partial differential equations (PDEs) and data input descriptors and graphic output requirements. SINAPSE uses the equation representation from MATHE-MATICA (see Implementation Platform) to represent these mathematical models as lists of PDEs. Alternatively, the user can directly build directly the set of equations in MATHEMATICA.

The next program synthesis step is to elaborate the model into an abstract algorithm schema. The schemas serve as algorithm outlines; many comments about program structure, which will also appear in the target code, are inserted at this step. The algorithm schemas are targeted toward specified architectural classes (such as serial, shared-memory parallel, or massively parallel). Algorithms are expressed in terms of mathematical concepts such as difference expressions and regions of a grid. Some computational models are particularly appropriate for specific architectures. For example, *stencils* (neighborhood operators such as adding together all array values that are one away from a central point on any dimension), can efficiently be implemented in microcode in massively parallel architectures. Elaboration into an algorithm schema requires design decisions such as what order approximation to use and which difference method to use.

Next, the algorithm is refined and optimized to construct a generic program. Refinement rules use algorithm schema representations as skeletons on which to attach detailed descriptions of individual algorithm steps. Additional constructs are needed to specify data handling and various kinds of parallel executions. The intermediate details of transforming from algorithm to program should be transparent. The system is responsible for having sufficient refinement rules to generate efficient programs for a reasonable variety of architectures and software environments, preferably without asking the user any questions.

Finally, detailed target language knowledge helps translate the program into code in a specific executable language such as Fortran for the CONNECTION MACHINE or C. Representation decisions such as using arrays (versus functions or lists) and details of calling external numeric analysis routines are made at this stage. The final translation to code is easily accomplished with simple parsing rules using syntax tables and action rules.

Visualization of the results, although important to understanding the solution and evaluating the program, is not a focus of the SINAPSE system. Thus, although we provide several graphic output routines for our examples, we do not attempt to automatically generate these display programs.

Implementation Platform

Scientific problem solving requires both symbolic and numeric reasoning. Program synthesis requires a powerful symbolic language with rules, pattern matching, and the ability to represent objects. In addition, one of our goals is to design a practical, portable program synthesis system so that if we continue to be successful, we can make our work widely available without excessive recoding. Although not the only possible solution for our requirements, MATHEMATICA has proved to be a satisfactory environment for both the rapid prototyping and the continued development of SINAPSE.

With a scientific programming application domain, it makes sense to incorporate a symbolic manipulation system in the problem-solving environment. Symbolic manipulation can facilitate a wide range of the scientific modeler's preliminary activities, from the derivation of mathematical models to the creation and analysis of numeric experiments; such techniques can capture the mathematics of physical phenomena, apply simplifications or substitutions to adapt standard formulas to the particular situation, and attempt analytic solutions. During synthesis, we can apply analytic techniques to determine, for example, whether a particular set of parameters matches convergence criteria. Many transformational steps are conveniently represented as algebraic or mathematical transforms, and the power of symbolic manipulation is readily applied. Typical examples of transformations are series approximations of derivatives and the substitution of variables to effect a change of coordinates.

If we can use the same system for symbolic manipulation and program synthesis, then we can combine the mathematics of the problem formulation, the procedural knowledge of abstract algorithms, and the concrete description of numeric programs in a tightly knit representational scheme with no manual copying or cumbersome representation conversions. Representative symbolic manipulation systems are MACSYMA (Symbolics 1987), REDUCE (Rayna 1987), MAPLE (Char et al. 1985), SCRATCHPAD (Jenks 1984), and MATHEMATICA (Wolfram 1988). The first two are powerful, fast, and well-debugged computer algebra systems. They are written on top of Lisp, and source code is available for some versions; in addition, these two systems are reasonably convenient for program synthesis programming. However, these systems are not always well received by the mathematical modeling community, which is used to programming in Fortran and appreciates the nice user interface that MATHEMATICA provides for expressing computations and graphing results. Adding the Lisp layer and/or other layers for rule-based or object-oriented programming can make startup time and portability even more of a problem. MAPLE, which is written in C, is widely used but is not as convenient for combining with program synthesis. SCRATCHPAD is not yet commercially available and might not be as convenient for coding transformations.

Because of its availability and suitability for both symbolic manipulation and programming, we are using MATHEMATICA as the implementation platform for SINAPSE. MATHEMATICA is a rich environment, with capabilities for symbolic algebra and calculus, numeric computation, 2D and 3D POSTSCRIPT graphics, programming, expression translation into Fortran and C, and an interface to the host operating system. MATHEMATICA's existing mix of symbolic and numeric computation eases the transition from the rough ideas in a problem description into mathematics and from mathematics into algorithms (and even makes it easy to document the results in reports). MATHEMATICA's evaluation paradigm, which causes repeated simplification of all expressions until there are no changes, is a mixed blessing. Although repeated evaluation is often desirable for simplification and rule-based programming, it is sometimes hard to control when the goal is to examine and manipulate expressions to build them into programs. As a practical matter, MATHEMATICA is approachable by, and potentially of value to, mathematical modelers even without the SINAPSE extensions. It is also available on virtually all platforms used by engineers.

Because some of the basic primitives we use (such as differentiation) are in MATHEMATICA and because the algorithms (such as finite difference) could directly be coded and interpreted in MATHEMATICA, people sometimes wonder why the SINAPSE system is needed at all. In fact, SINAPSE supplies a number of capabilities not available in MATHEMATICA. It adds application-specific refinement knowledge, knowledge of how to generate code that is efficient for very large data structures or parallel architectures, and a record of design history. Interpretation of MATHEMATICA programs is useful for prototyping, but even on moderate-sized arrays, the code is slow. Also, the accuracy and stability of built-in algorithms is not always appropriate to the problem. In addition, although MATHEMATICA can generate Fortran expressions, it cannot generate complete programs, and the code that it produces is not particularly efficient.

Related Work

Our goal of supporting scientific modeling is common to many other projects. With problems that involve the solution of partial differential equations, the ALPAL system is the closest in spirit to what we are trying to accomplish and has made impressive progress (Cook 1988). It calls on MACSYMA for some of its symbolic manipulation needs. Some similar research is under way for finite-volume problems (Steinberg and Roache 1990).

An extensive system in the same application domain but one that is not as relevant to the program synthesis approach is ELLPACK (Dyksen and Gritter 1989). Also, a project at Rutgers University (Russo, Kowalski, and Peskin 1989) uses an object-oriented Prolog for the classification of numeric concepts and the solution of ordinary differential equations. Gibbs (Wilson 1983) proposes a scientific programming environment on top of Fortran. Several other examples of automated numeric modeling are given in Abelson et al. (1989) along with an inspiring vision of an intelligent computer assistant.

This chapter is not the place for a complete survey of program synthesis. We should say that under more convenient circumstances, we might have tried to extend an existing system. However, even KIDS (chapter 19), a well-developed, knowledge-based software development system for transforming formal algorithm specifications into correct and efficient programs, does not specifically address numeric programming. Using KIDS or REFINE alone (Smith, Kotik, and Westfold 1985) would have required adding a symbolic manipulation system, as was done for the generation of FFT algorithms (King et al. 1989) (which used MACSYMA). (Other related approaches involve the use of domain knowledge in requirements and specification acquisition—for example chapter 3.) The ELF system (chapter 9) is one of the closest in spirit to application-driven systems. Although in a totally different application area (VLSI), it shares an interest in the explicit representation of algorithms and domain knowledge to produce efficient code for a family of related specifications.

An Example of the Synthesis Process

This example of the synthesis process shows ow a problem is set up, how the mathematical model is derived, how the target program is produced, and how changes are made.

Setting Up a Problem

The SINAPSE system assumes that the user wants to synthesize a mathematical modeling program. The first question it asks the user is the area of application:

> You have a choice for Domain.
> 1: WavePropagation
> 2: ElectroMagnetics
> 3: Nuclear
> ...
> 6: OtherDomain
>
> H: Help
> S: SelectionInformation
> F: ForceChoice
> O: OtherInteractions

Our example comes from the wave-propagation area. In this domain, geo-

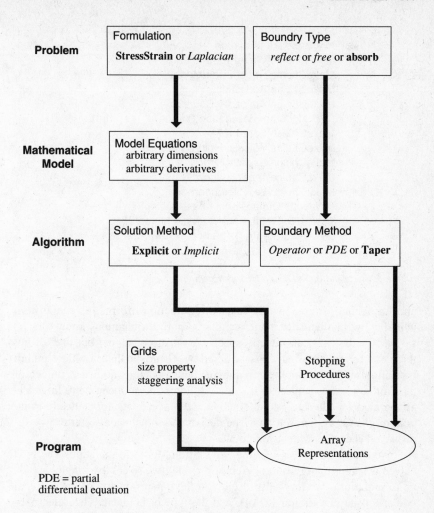

Figure 2. Pictorial Representation of Design Decisions.

physicists use seismic and sonic surveys to understand the structure of the earth's subsurface. Pressure waves are sent through a geologic formation, and the reflected echoes are recorded at a set of receivers. Forward modeling can be used to simulate the propagation of the pressure waves to optimize the placement of source and receivers for a survey or to help geophysicists verify conclusions by creating synthetic seismic traces that can be compared to field data. Such models are also useful to developers of sonic tools.

Once the application-domain choice is made, a standard set of model formulations is available. The choices offered this time are StressStrainModel

```
(* model formulation *)
MakeChoice[WavePropagation];
MakeChoice[StressStrainModel];
MakeChoice[Acoustic];
MakeChoice[AbsorbingBoundary];
    (* algorithm description *)
MakeChoice[Fortran77];
MakeChoice[SolveByFiniteDifference];
MakeChoice[ExplicitMethod];
MakeChoice[TaperBoundary];
MakeChoice[LazyNeighborhood];
sfWave2d[Dimensions] ~has~ Memo[{x,y}];
sfWave2d[DefaultOrder] ~has~ Memo[2];
sfWave2d[Stagger] ~has~ Memo[True];
```

Figure 3. Specification in Design History Form.

and Laplacian Model. In this case, the SelectionInformation menu item would show that actually, there are many more formulations known to the system (or the user can directly specify a set of equations) but that all but these two formulations have been filtered by a heuristic that says they are not typically used in this application domain. The modeler who insists on one of these other choices can select it using the ForceChoice menu item. In general, the modeler can select an alternative and proceed, ask for status information, or change system settings. The design decisions made so far can be re-displayed at each new decision point.

For our example, we select the StressStrainModel formulation. The next choice is between an Elastic or Acoustic model (we select the simpler acoustic formulation). We must also decide on the dimensionality of the problem (we specify a 2D version $\{x, y\}$), and the type of boundary (we select Absorbing over Reflecting and other choices). The dimensionality is asked as a question, allowing user type-in rather than a choice of numbered alternatives, so that the modeler can specify arbitrary names for the dimensions. When SINAPSE requests numeric values or expressions for properties in this free-form style, a default is always offered.

Most of the design decisions made by the modeler occur during model formulation and later during algorithm selection. Figure 2 outlines the choices available and the specific choices that lead to one example. The representation of such decisions is discussed in Representations. These choices can be made interactively, with SINAPSE prompting the user through increasingly specific choices, as described here, or simply reading from a file where the choices can be listed in any order, as shown in figure 3.

Deriving the Mathematical Model

From the previous set of choices, the system has enough information to set up the equations for the model. The example model consists of three first-order, coupled partial differential equations relating the time and space derivatives of the stresses S and particle velocities U. Spatially dependent parameters are ρ, the density of the medium, and λ, a stiffness index.

$$\frac{\partial Sxx[x,y,t]}{\partial t} = \lambda[x,y](\frac{\partial Uy[x,y,t]}{\partial y} + \frac{\partial Ux[x,y,t]}{\partial x}) \tag{1}$$

$$\frac{\partial Ux[x,y,t]}{\partial t}\rho[x,y] = \frac{\partial Sxx[x,y,t]}{\partial x} \tag{2}$$

$$\frac{\partial Uy[x,y,t]}{\partial t}\rho[x,y] = \frac{\partial Sxx[x,y,t]}{\partial y} \tag{3}$$

The system can normalize these equations, determining whether there are any dependencies in the computation order and putting the unknowns onto the left-hand sides of the equations.

Outlining the Algorithm

Another set of decisions is now made to determine which kind of numeric approximation algorithm to use. First, the modeler specifies the target architecture and language in case they affect the algorithm choice. Here, we simply specify Fortran77 for a conventional architecture such as a Sun-4. If CONNECTION MACHINE Fortran were chosen instead, additional algorithm implementations and constructs, such as operations on subranges and microcode stencils (highly efficient neighborhood operators) would be available for later choices.

For a basic equation solution technique, we choose to approximate the equations with the discretization technique of finite differencing (alternatives are solving analytically or solving in a transform space). *Finite-difference methods* estimate the derivative of a function at a point as a linear combination of function values at a small number of neighboring (discretized) grid points. The new system of equations relates variable values at current time t to values at earlier time steps. When the values of variables at time t can directly be expressed in terms of previous values, the method is said to be explicit. When the solution of a system of equations is required at each time step, the method is said to be implicit. The selection of a particular method can depend on the accuracy needed, the length of the simulation, and stability requirements. For our example, we select the explicit method.

The number of neighboring points chosen for the approximation depends on the accuracy desired and the order of the function derivative. The modeler can specify any integer. We choose the simple but low-accuracy value of two for our first-order derivative.

Boundary conditions, which specify the behavior of variables at the boundaries of the grid through particular equations or operators, are an important part of the design of a finite-difference program. In the example, we select a tapered region around the grid to absorb incoming waves by multiplying all values in the region by exponentially decaying coefficients.

The dependency analysis previously mentioned is used to determine the allowable staggering. *Staggering* evaluates the derivatives of different quantities at grids that are offset from each other. This technique can significantly improve the accuracy of a reduced computation (with increasing grid spacing). The user specifies whether to use staggering where it is allowed.

Additional properties (grid size, time-step size, region of tapering, quantities changed by source, quantities read at receivers) are needed to elaborate a complete program, but in most cases, these properties can be inferred from the problem class using inheritance (see Representations). Because of the inference capability, SINAPSE specifications tend to be fairly concise.

The choices of algorithm method and method details determine the overall structure of the program, again using the inheritance structure to assemble algorithm fragments. To implement finite-difference techniques, SINAPSE builds a program structure with declarations, time-stepping loop, boundary conditions, and input and output statements (for example, to save entire wave-field snapshots or signal traces at the receivers). The result is an algorithm skeleton that looks something like the following. (MATHEMATICA uses square brackets for function calls, curly braces for lists, and a right arrow for a replacement operator):

```
Initialization
    InitSources
    InitTapers
TimeStepLoop
    ForEachQuantity Q in {Sxx, Ux, Uy}
        ForEachPoint Pt in Grid[{x, y}]
            Approximate[Equation[Q], Pt, order->2]
        PostStep
        UpdateTapers
        UpdateSource
        ReadReceivers
```

Refining the Program

The detailed refinements of solution methods are encoded as MATHEMATICA rules. For example, to implement the time-stepping loop, SINAPSE has rules that use MATHEMATICA's pattern-matching capabilities to scan the differential equations and replace continuous functions by their discretized approximations. Additional rules produce finite-difference assignment statements and convert representations in functional notation into array operations with the necessary declarations.

One of these rules, called Approximate, takes as arguments the equation for computing a quantity, the quantity, a point at which to compute it (here, assume a normal point $\{x, y\}$ not on a boundary), and the order of approximation (number of points in the weighted sum). The rule defines the new value (at time $t + 1$) to be the previous value of the quantity expression (here, $Ux[x, y, t]$) plus the discretized form of all the derivatives on the right-hand side of the normalized equation. In the following Approximate rule, Normalize, UnknownExpr, Assign, and ApproximateRhs are all SINAPSE-defined functions. The := notation indicates a rule definition. Single baseline bars after variable names indicate the first appearance of a single-element variable. This example is a simple illustration of MATHEMATICA's pattern language, which allows typed arguments, predicate testing in argument matching, a matching of the formal parameters to lists of arguments or other structures, and many other pattern expressions. All subsequent uses of the same variable must match the same value.

```
Approximate[equation_, quantity_, Pt_, order_] :=
    eqn = Normalize[equation];
    quant = UnknownExpr[quantity, Pt, t];
    assign[quant, quant + ApproximateRhs[rhs[eqn], order]]
```

In approximating the expression on the right-hand side, we replace all derivatives (assume there are no cross-terms in the partials) with their discretizations. There are actually several sorts of discretization rules, but the system chooses one that uses the center of the averaged points (slightly offset because of staggering) to determine the weight for each point. The arithmetic operators, $Sum[expr, \{i, L, U\}]$ summation notation (*expr* is typically a function of *i*, which ranges from L to U), and *expr* /. *x* -> *y* replacement notation (all instances of *x* at any level in expr are replaced by *y*) are all part of MATHEMATICA; weight is a SINAPSE-defined function.

```
CentralDiscretize[deriv_, var_, order_, offset_] :=
    evalPt = (order + 1)/2 + offset;
    Sum[weight[order,evalPt,i] * (deriv /. {var -> var + i-evalPt}),
            {i,1,order}]
```

The application of CentralDiscretize to the partial derivative of Ux with respect to t (see equation 2), for example, results in

$(Sxx[x, y] - Sxx[1 + x, y]) / rho[x, y]$.

The enumeration of the grid can be complex if all the boundaries are treated differently. However, in the simple case on a sequential machine, it is simply a nested loop. The result of program refinement is a pseudocode program. The notation *all*[{*var, init, final*}, *parallel/sequential, expression*] is part of the SINAPSE intermediate programming language.

```
sequential[
        comment["Initialize sources"], <code>,
        comment["Set up absorbing taper"], <code>,
        comment["Time loop"],
        all[{t, 1, Size[t]}, sequential,
                <code for other quantities>,
                comment["Discretization for updating Ux"],
                    all[{x, 1, -1 + Nx}, parallel,
                                all[{y, 1, Ny}, parallel,
                                            assign[Ux[x, y],
                                                        Ux[x, y] -
        (Sxx[x, y] – Sxx[1 + x, y]) / rho[x, y]]]],
                <code for other quantities>
                ]
        comment["Update Taper Boundary conditions"], <code>,
        comment["Add source contribution"], <code>,
        comment["Interpolate receivers signals"], <code>
        ]
```

Producing the Target Code

From the pseudocode plus the declaration information, SINAPSE generates target language code using simple syntactic rules. The entire process, from problem formulation to target code, takes less than one minute of central processing unit time on a Sun-4/110. Table 1 outlines the composition of the complete target program for our small example and for a similar 3D code with more complex equations. Some sample Fortran and C fragments for the code are shown in figure 4.

Visualization

One of the best ways to understand the output of a mathematical modeling program is to generate graphic representations of the data. We provide several kinds of displays. One program output is a set of values representing seismic echoes at a set of vertically aligned receivers. Figure 5 presents a MATHEMATICA display of this output. The synthesized programs can also output snapshots of wave fields at a sequence of points in time. We have a manually written program for a Silicon Graphics machine that displays such output as animation sequences. A few frames from this sequence are shown in figure 6.

Making Changes

A program specification can be developed interactively, as we saw, or can be read from a file developed by a knowledgeable user that essentially predefines answers to some or all system questions. The alternatives and parameter values resulting from the interaction sequence (combined with any prespecified statements) form the design history of a program, which is use-

Fortran77: (about 250 lines total)
```
    REAL Sxx(512, 512)

    ...
    DO 10400 it=1,tMax
    DO 10270 ix = 1, -1 + Nx
    DO 10260 iy = 1, Ny
    Ux(ix,iy) = Ux(ix,iy) – (Sxx(ix,iy) – Sxx(1 + ix, iy))
   &/rho(ix,iy)
10260 CONTINUE
```

Fortran9X: (about 200 lines total)
```
    REAL Sxx(512, 512)
    ...
    DO 10240 it=1,tMax
            Ux(1:-1 + Nx,1:Ny) = Ux(1:-1 + Nx,1:Ny) –
   &(Sxx(1:-1 + Nx,1:Ny) – Sxx(2:Nx,1:Ny))/rho(1:-1 + Nx,1:Ny)
10240 CONTINUE
```

C: (about 215 lines total)
```
    float Sxx[512][512]

    ...
    for(it=1;it<=tMax;it++)
            for(ix=1; ix<=-1+Nx; ix++)
                    for(iy=1; iy<=Ny; iy++)
                            Ux[ix][iy] = Ux[ix][iy] –
                                    (Sxx[ix][iy] – Szx[ix][1 + ix])/rho[ix][iy] + ...
```

Figure 4. Generation of Code from Math Code.

ful for documentation, design revision, or alternative comparisons. The interaction history can be saved in a specification file that can later be edited or
loaded into the system. Any type of change can be made in the file version of
the specification by text editing, and most changes can be made interactively
by selecting from a list of alternatives presented to the user. In either case,
the synthesis process is restarted, using the new choice set. Irrelevant decisions are ignored, and any new questions that have not had answers already
specified are asked interactively.

SINAPSE has generated several dozen finite-difference programs. A simple
example of a modification is changing the dimension specification from
fdmme[*Dimensions*] = {*x,y*} to *fdmme*[*Dimensions*] = {*x,y,z*}, which results
in a 3D version of a wave-propagation program (manual implementation of
3D programs are quite tedious, especially when there are complex cases
around the boundaries). Other variations are using implicit, rather than explicit,
methods, changing the finite-difference operator's order, changing the boundary conditions, and averaging material values around critical transition regions.

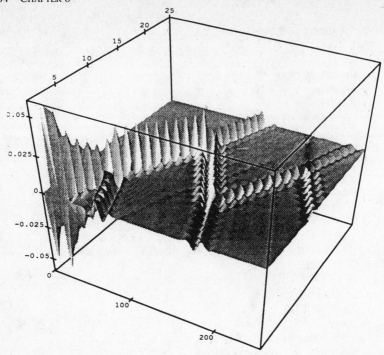

Figure 5. Seismic Echoes.
An initial impulse is generated at time t = 0 (on the left) and propagates through a two-dimensional solid. As time advances (to t = 300 going right and downward), the wave partially reflects from first one interface between materials with different compressional velocities (at depth d = 5) and then from a second interface (at d = 15).

Most of the programs generated have been in Fortran77 because of user preferences for portable codes. However, SINAPSE has also produced a few C programs and is beginning to produce Fortran9X code for our Connection Machine. The Fortran9X code that SINAPSE generates is currently not highly optimized, but by hand tuning less than 10 percent of the generated code, we were able to achieve code that takes only 4 seconds each time step to simulate the propagation of a wave through a 64 x 64 x 128 grid.

The specifications for the programs SINAPSE has generated are all on the order of 50 lines. From these specifications, between 200 and 5000 lines of target language code are generated in one to 10 Sun-4/110 minutes (the average time is under 3 minutes).

Search Control

In pursuit of efficiency and compatibility with our implementation platform, we are experimenting with a fairly simple form of search control that builds

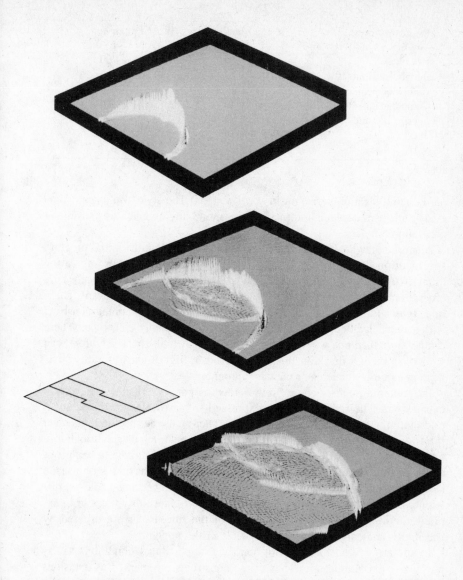

Figure 6. A Sequence of Snapshots Showing a Wave Field Propagating in a Simulated Seismic Experiment.

An impulsive source is discharged at time zero in an idealized two-dimensional elastic (solid) medium. A spheric wave propagates away from the source and is partially reflected at the two interfaces of the faulted dipping bed shown in the schematic. These 200 x 200 resolution images are taken from an animation sequence displayed on a Silicon Graphics workstation.

Program Action	Code Lines	In 3D Example
Commons and declarations	75	100
Read Data	50	200
Initialized variables	30	100
Computed main equations	25	600
Computed boundary values	30	150
Interpolated and output result	<u>45</u>	<u>50</u>
Total	255	1200

Table 1.

on the simplification paradigm in MATHEMATICA. The style also shares some goals with partial evaluation methods in optimizing as much as possible at generation time.

A simple view of SINAPSE search control would be that the initial program specification is simply evaluated (repeatedly simplified according to the usual MATHEMATICA style) to produce a program in the target language. Many program transformation rules will be applied as they become relevant. These rules typically replace the simple use of an abstract programming construct with a more detailed expression in terms of less abstract constructs. There can be more than one way to refine a construct. A refinement, therefore, can embody a design decision that moves from a high-level program speci-fication to a more concrete, executable program.

Programming constructs are represented as parameterized MATHEMATICA expressions. The refinements are expressed by MATHEMATICA replacement rules with the same name as the construct. There must be specific refinement rules for all constructs; the system does not use planning or conditioning to find applicable transformations. The refinement rules can have a pattern of arguments on the left-hand side and arbitrary computations on the right-hand side. In MATHEMATICA, there can be several rules with the same name but dif-ferent applicability constraints encoded in the left-hand side pattern or in ex-plicit conditions on the right-hand side of the rule. Rules are ordered by specificity, and only the first of the matching rules applies.

In SINAPSE, we code rules with nontrivial applicability conditions as ex-plicit decision alternatives. Thus, some constructs are marked as decisions and have alternative rules that do not share the name of the construct. Selec-tion from the rules is not done in the usual MATHEMATICA manner. Instead, the alternatives are explicitly listed with the construct name. When trying to evaluate the construct, a set of heuristics is first applied to the alternatives, and then the user is consulted if the system cannot resolve the matter.

The arguments to a heuristic rule are (a subset of) the alternatives for refining the decision plus the arguments to the decision construct itself. The heuristic returns a subset of its input alternatives. Thus, heuristics that are basically applicability conditions simply return their input if the alternative is relevant or remove it from the input list if it is not. More sophisticated preference rules are possible, but we have not yet determined any that are appropriate for our applications.

SINAPSE also allows the design decision questions to be answered in advance. Whether from a specification file or the early interactive dialog, the answers are stored as a pointed heuristic about how to make a choice.

The initial specification that SINAPSE evaluates is actually a combination of the mathematical model (or application-specific description) and a standard series of tasks that make sure all questions about the specification are answered; analyze the specification, construct a program skeleton, insert declarations, insert the code body based on the specification; generate a complete program; and then allow the user the options of compiling, executing, and displaying the results. The design decision questions are asked in advance so that the user can respond to them in an order that seems natural from a specification point of view and then walk away from the terminal rather than asked at irregular intervals in an implementation-determined order.

Design Histories

Because programming is an iterative process with much feedback, it is critical to be able to explore a variety of alternatives at the level of algorithm choice as well as the implementation level. This exploration requires the ability to both look at program output and trace results to the relevant specifications to easily record and revise design decisions. SINAPSE has no automated mechanisms for tracing target code to specification, but many of the refinement rules do insert a comment in the code they generate that can be used to help the tracing process. SINAPSE does record design histories, which although basic, are useful for documenting, revising a design, and trying out multiple alternatives.

SINAPSE can be used to construct a simple tree of alternative implementations (no graphs or truth maintenance). To revise a program, the user asks the system for a list of the decisions that were recorded. The system then replays the synthesis and again presents the alternatives for the decisions selected for change and lets the user select a new one.

SINAPSE only records the decisions that are part of the specification, not those that are indirectly made by MATHEMATICA's rule ordering. A typical program would have a few dozen recorded decisions and hundreds of unrecorded rule applications. Because the system's use of MATHEMATICA's evaluation paradigm results in so many unrecorded decisions and because the synthesis only takes a few minutes (no more than 10 on any of our existing examples), SINAPSE does not attempt any sophisticated replay mechanisms. It simply removes the heuristics that make the decision the user wants to change and restarts the synthesis process. Instead of trying to precompute what part of the design history is still relevant, it simply recomputes it as needed. Decisions from the previous run that are made irrelevant by the change are simply ignored and will not be written out when a new design history is saved. Currently SINAPSE assumes that heuristics check preconditions and override saved choices that might not be legal any longer. More sophisticated and safer techniques could be used here, but to date, they have not been necessary, so we have not spent any energy implementing them.

Problem Formulation

The problem description can be expressed to SINAPSE with application-domain key words that the system can use to derive a mathematical model. Alternatively, the user can directly formulate the mathematical model (as in Mathematical Model Description).

Concepts

The application concepts involve general physical objects such as time, spatial geometries (with dimensions, regions, boundaries), and materials. Other concepts are intrinsic physical properties of materials (such as density, stiffness), measurements of variable physical quantities (such as stress, particle velocity), and an abstract notion of mathematical modeling (model types such as elastic or acoustic). Currently, the only operation on models known to the system is solving them by forward simulation. The names of the application domains themselves (such as seismic wave propagation or heat diffusion) are also concepts.

Representations

SINAPSE has fairly primitive representations for the application constructs. For those that have a discrete set of alternative values (such as elasticity or isotropy), SINAPSE has a decision representation that includes only the decision name; a set of alternatives; and, possibly, heuristic rules for selecting between alternatives (the user typically must make the choice however). Related sequences of these choices are stored together in a decision sequence, so SINAPSE can ask questions in an order that makes sense for the end user rather than when they come up during program refinement.

Some concepts do not have fixed sets of values (such as the names of spatial dimensions). These concepts are represented as properties, which are a special type of decision (and, therefore, can be included in decision sequences). Properties can have default values that the user can confirm or override.

In all SINAPSE, there are about two dozen decisions with several alternatives for each and about four dozen properties. Text strings are associated with each decision, decision alternative, and property name to explain the terms to the user.

Corresponding to each named application domain is a class object that can have specialized decisions, properties, or values that override those of the superclass. For example, here are some fragments from SINAPSE showing how definitions in WavePropagation sometimes override the definitions in its superclass BasicDomain. The a ~fn~ b notation is a MATHEMATICA infix syntax for binary functions of the form $fn[a, b]$.

```
BeginClass[BasicDomain]
BasicDomain[EquationSetUp] ~hasPropertySeq~
    {Equations, Variables, Boundaries};
BasicDomain[Equations] ~has~ AskUserInput["Equations List:"];
NewChoice[Boundaries];
AddAlternatives[Boundaries,AbsorbingBoundary,ReflectingBoundary, . . .];
. . .

EndClass[];

BeginClass[WavePropagation, BasicDomain];
WavePropagation[EquationSetUp] ~hasPropertySeq~ {Elasticity, Isotropy,
    Dimensions, Coefficients, Equations, Variables, Boundaries}
WavePropagation[Equations] ~hasMemo~ WaveEquationGenerator[];
```

Reasoning Techniques

To help users formulate problems, SINAPSE walks them through a decision tree of choices of problem domain and model characteristics. The tree is the consequence of the collection of decisions sequences, any item of which can be another decision sequence (more general control structures might eventually be necessary, but to date, we have gotten by without them). Although the details can vary depending on the choice of problem domain, typically, decisions concern model properties (elasticity, isotropy) and equation formulations (stress-strain, Laplacian, Maxwell). Heuristics can apply, for example, to filter the set of choices presented to the user to those that are likely to be relevant to the selected application domain. One of the choices of equation formulation is "user-specified," so that the modeler can directly provide the equations to the system if none of the built-in types is appropriate.

Mathematical Model Description

If the user has not directly specified the mathematical modeling equations, SINAPSE derives them from the problem formulation. Application-domain knowledge and symbolic manipulation are used to put the equations into a fully specified form.

Concepts

At the mathematical modeling level, specification concepts include many general mathematical constructs such as equations, partial derivatives, independent and dependent variables, and coefficients. Operations include normalizing and solving equations and determining properties such as the highest-order derivative or determining whether an equation is elliptical, hyperbolic, or parabolic.

Fully specified models must also have boundary conditions (possibly different models for the boundary regions), must have any source signal described, and must know what is being solved for and what measurements of the solution are to be made (what variables are to be output at what spatial locations and time periods). Error estimates or other derived quantities, although not part of the model, are also frequently included in a specification.

Representations

Representations at the mathematical modeling level continue to use the decision and property representations from the problem formulation level and also use MATHEMATICA notation for equations, derivatives, arithmetic expressions, and so on. The property representation is used to record the different types of variable roles. An extended form of the property representation permits equations (or other boundary operators) to be associated with spatial regions. The domain-specific knowledge for converting key-word and property concepts (such as stress-strain model formulation in dimensions $\{x,y\}$) into mathematical notation is expressed as MATHEMATICA rules.

Here are two examples of equations illustrating the extended property representation. Equation 4 is the default case. Equation 5 is true only at the right-hand x boundary. $MM\$$ is a pointer to the current context. It is normally set to something like $sfWave2d$ (for specification file Wave, two dimensions). MATHEMATICA not only evaluates all arguments to a function, it also evaluates the function name itself. The definitions with the more specific arguments are placed earlier in MATHEMATICA's rule list, so the second definition would only match a request for $MM\$[Equation, Sxx, \{1, x\}]$, whereas the first definition would match for $MM\$[Equation, Sxx, \{1,y\}]$ and would have matched the first request if the second definition were not present. The MATHEMATICA notation $D[f,x]$ gives the partial derivative of f with respect to x.

$$MM\$[Equation, Sxx, Case\_] =$$
$$D[Sxx[x,y,t], t] == lam[x,y](D[Ux[x,y,t], x] + D[Uz[x,y,t], x]) \tag{4}$$

$$MM\$[Equation, Sxx, \{1, x\}] =$$
$$D[Sxx[x,y,t], t] == 0; \tag{5}$$

A specification can also include information about data objects such as types (real, complex), dimensions (scalar, array of responses by properties), and properties (diagonal or Toeplitz array). This information need only be provided for objects explicitly mentioned by the user and when the system cannot infer the information from application-specific knowledge.

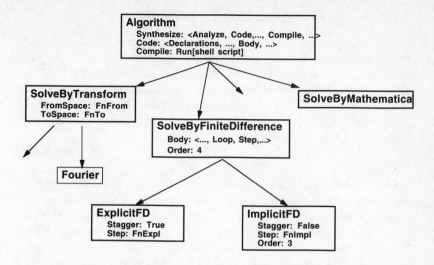

Figure 7. An Algorithm Class Hierarchy.

Reasoning Techniques

In deriving the mathematical model from the problem formulation, SINAPSE uses mostly explicit, domain-specific rules. More general problem-solving methods are not appropriate because this phase is basically a matter of expanding definitions rather than searching for solutions. Getting the appropriate set of equations is relatively straightforward. The rules typically expand a concept, such as turning "stress-strain formulation" into a set of partial differential equations. The rules are parameterized by formulation type, model properties, dimensions, and so on. These rules are written in MATHEMATICA and use symbolic simplifications. For example, if a coefficient in a standard equation formulation is specified as zero, the whole term is automatically simplified to zero ($MM\$[mu] = 0$ for the acoustic case in the following rule). The set of statements is taken from some rules setting up equations such as equation 1. Scan applies the function in its first argument to the list in its second. The function SetEquation, when called with dimen = x, creates equation 4.

```
Scan[SetEquations, NormalDimensions];
SetEquation[dimen_] :=
      MM$[Equation, SVar[dimen, dimen], Case_] = NormalEqn[dimen];

NormalEqn[dimen_] :=
      Simplify[(MM$[lambda]+2MM$[mu]) DuNormal[dimen] + . . . ];
DuNormal[dim_] := D[UFn[dim], dim];
```

Algorithm Elaboration

Another important part of a specification of a mathematical modeling program is the type of numeric approximation algorithm to be used. Although the system can have heuristics for automatically making such choices, typically the trade-offs between numeric accuracy and stability and computation time are quite complex and not completely understood or formalizable. Thus, our philosophy is to concentrate more on providing reusable algorithm components and less on techniques for automated decisions.

Concepts

At the algorithm level, control constructs, algorithm types, and some more detailed mathematical notations are added to the mathematical modeling constructs. A rough notion of target architectures (serial, massively parallel, shared memory, vector, and so on) is needed so that an appropriate algorithm type can be selected. The algorithms themselves are expressed in terms of partial orderings of sequential and parallel blocks and enumerations over regions.

Algorithm types are another class of concepts that become important at this level. Examples include analytically solving a set of equations, or solving them by a finite-difference method, or solving in a transform space. Algorithms can have *subtypes* (explicit and implicit finite-difference methods) and can share common subparts (discretization of equations, time-step loops). More detailed mathematical concepts at this level include difference equations, grids, and specialized boundary operators.

Representations

At this level, SINAPSE continues to use decisions to represent named concepts with enumerated values, such as target architecture and algorithm type, and continues to use properties for more arbitrary value sets, such as what order series approximation to use for the discretization method. In addition, the algorithm contents are represented as algorithm schemas (as in chapter 9) using a small set of control constructs and named subparts, and they are stored in a hierarchy and can inherit some of their subparts from more general algorithm classes. Object-oriented representations have been found useful by others working in the area of numeric computing (Kowalski 1987; Barras et al. 1990). Figure 7 presents a simplified graphic view of the current hierarchy of problem classes.

Because MATHEMATICA does not provide built-in inheritance, we have implemented a simple form of inheritance using default rules. Each class has one default rule that says to look for the value in the superclass of the current class. The default rule is always the last rule in the list of rules for a class. Multiple inheritance is implemented by explicitly listing what other class to inherit from for the properties that are to be inherited off the main branch. An arbitrary expression can be evaluated to compute the class from which property values are to be inherited.

The algorithm schemas serve as skeletons on which to attach more detailed descriptions of individual algorithm steps. The individual steps are again expressed in MATHEMATICA notation augmented with SINAPSE control and data abstractions and other key-word concepts such as the approximate operation. These key words are refined by transformation rules.

The basic form of the algorithm goes through several steps as decisions are made. We give simplified versions here for concise presentation. Substeps are indicated by indenting. For a SolveByFiniteDifference, the basic steps are a set of initializations followed by a time-stepping loop. Each time step in the loop computes the next approximation and then updates boundaries and sources if needed and computes the values seen at the receivers:

```
Initialization
        InitSources
        InitBoundary
TimeStepLoop
        MainFiniteDifferenceMethod
        PostStep
                UpdateBoundary
                UpdateSource
                ReadReceivers
```

Choosing ExplicitMethod refines the main method using the default order of approximation (ImplicitMethod would have a different main method and would change the default order):

```
Initialization
    . . .
TimeStepLoop
    ExplicitMethod (order->4)
    PostStep . . .
```

Choosing the taper boundary method refines the Initialization and PostStep processing:

```
Initialization
    InitSources
    InitTapers
TimeStepLoop
    ExplicitMethod (order->4)
    PostStep
        UpdateTapers
        UpdateSource
        ReadReceivers
```

The dimensions chosen $\{x, z\}$ and the defaults for the source signal and receiver reading complete the decision-making process. The discretization methods fill out the main part of the time-stepping loop.

```
Initialization
    . . .
TimeStepLoop
    ForEachQuantity Q in {Uz, Szz. . .}

        ForEachPoint Pt in Grid[{x, z}]
                Approximate[Equation[Q], Pt, order->4]
    PostStep
        . . .
```

Reasoning Techniques

Algorithm elaboration requires design decisions of the sort already discussed, such as which difference method to use or what order approximation to use. Although, in general, we leave the choices to the modeler, heuristics are sometimes helpful. For example, an analytic heuristic can determine what orders are likely to be stable under the known convergence criteria given the previously made decisions.

Where there are analytic techniques for making choices, MATHEMATICA is a convenient representation and computing engine for them, with built-in calculus and simplification functions. We do not attempt decisions that would require theorem proving or complex backward chaining.

Most data structures in the scientific programming we have done to date are arrays or simple files of records. Thus, to date, all our data representation decisions have not had a major impact on the algorithm chosen and, in fact, can automatically be made by the system. (An exception is the solve-in-transform-space example, where the choice of the algorithm was driven by the modeler's knowledge that there would be a particularly efficient representation.) Thus, even though a data representation choice might eventually make sense at the algorithm level, they are all currently considered program refinement at the next level down.

Writing transformation rules is easy because evaluation within MATHEMATICA is essentially rule based, although iterative, recursive, and functional programming styles are accommodated as well. Multiple definitions of rules can be made, some giving specializations to be used when more specific argument values are known. In MATHEMATICA, evaluation is a repeated process of applying rules (which look like function definitions) and reevaluating after every step. For example, the program

(op = Print; y = a + b; op[y]; a = 3; b = 5; op[y])

first prints $a + b$ then prints 8. The implementation of our system makes use of this MATHEMATICA property to effect continual refinement of a program specification as well as to simplify symbolic expressions. Rule specialization and repeated evaluation facilitate implementing the concept of *partial evaluation* (producing specialized, optimized programs from general definitions and specific arguments).

Program Refinement

Program refinement continues the introduction and elaboration of lower-level constructs.

Concepts

Most of the domain-specific detailed refinement of the algorithm steps occurs at this level. For example, the program description is filled with the details of how to enumerate all the regions of the grid (central, boundaries, corners) and which discretization operators to use for each region. An understanding of the arithmetic and control operations available in the target architecture and language is required to describe the types of enumeration. Properties of data structures (dimensions of arrays, nonzero array locations such as diagonal and data type of elements) are propagated through expressions, and domain-specific simplifications of terms take place.

Representations

The end result of program refinement should be a fully specified program in an intermediate language that abstracts away from the details of data representations and enumerations. This language is not yet fully developed. The internal forms of data declarations, including any newly inferred properties, are part of the language as well as abstract enumeration statements. Program descriptions at this level can also include statements in a slightly more detailed language called MATHCODE that is described in the next section.

In intermediate stages, SINAPSE also mixes in some MATHEMATICA statements that include calls to other rules, which, in turn, expand to call other rules and eventually expand into constructs in the intermediate language.

Reasoning Techniques

The elaboration of algorithm steps is accomplished with rules written in MATHEMATICA that expand into MATHEMATICA arithmetic expressions or statements in SINAPSE's internal language that do not expand any farther. Because repeated evaluation is built into MATHEMATICA, we need no special rule interpreter to ensure that the most specific rules apply when there are several similar rules.

Some of the reasoning at this level propagates properties and types and dimensions through expressions and applies domain-specific expansions, simplifications, and optimizations. All the properties we have worked with to date can be updated with the type of forward chaining in the simplification rules that are automatically applied, or we have written simple backward-chaining rules for computing whether specific properties are true. Backward-chaining rules are applied on demand (typically as conditions on other rules).

As an example, consider the set of finite-difference operators. This set of rules implements knowledge of function interpolation by polynomials of arbitrary order. The symbolic differentiation operators already in MATHEMATICA can then be used to compute the weights of arbitrary finite-difference operators. For example, the rule

```
LagrangePoly[k,x] :=
     Sum[y[i] Product[If[j !=i,
                          (x − x[j])/(x[i] − x[j]),
                          1],
                 {j,1,k}],
          {i,1,k}]
```

produces the polynomial

$$\sum_{i=1}^{k} y_i \prod_{j,j \neq i}^{k} (x - x_j) / x_i - x_j)$$

This polynomial is used by the rule FD$Operator to produce the weights of an operator. For example, FD$Operator[1,5/2,4,1] $\Rightarrow$ 1/24, which is the weight of the first point for a central, fourth-order operator computing first derivatives.

Implementation rules select particular constructs for the entities described in the algorithmic formulation of the problem. Some rules use the staggering information to generate loop statements or knowledge of operator symmetry to factor terms in the main loop of the program.

Target Generation Code

Most of the details of data representation and control flow and local optimization take place at the code- generation level. Our goal is to generate programs that run efficiently on multiple architectures. To minimize complexity, we factored this goal in two subgoals.

The first target code-generation subgoal is to generate high-quality generic code. The MATHCODE language is the representation for the generic code. This code captures the essence of the implementation but not the details and includes data representation choices, related declarations, expanded operations for accessing the representations, and insertion of parallel constructs where possible and serialization of parallel constructs if necessary. Currently, SINAPSE has only a modest amount of knowledge about optimization for parallel architectures. For example, a different data-compression strategy is used for averaging materials values when generating code for the Connection Machine than for a sequential machine. The Connection Machine version avoids a double indexing scheme that saves space but cannot be executed in parallel.

The second subgoal is to translate the generic code into a compilable program in a specific language. Target language rules translate the program into the syntax of a specific executable language such as Connection Machine Fortran or C. The translation to code is easily accomplished with simple parsing rules using syntax tables and action rules. Although the algorithms and operations have already been picked with some knowledge of the target architecture, it is at this level that the details of the available language options are taken into account.

Concepts

Choices made at the first stage of the program-refinement level include those for data representation (such as diagonal, tridiagonal, or normal layout for arrays) and input and output techniques (read from file, interactively ask user, store in file, display on terminal). Data representation details such as storage location and layout, whether through direct construction or compiler directives, are handled at this level. Array operations are checked to make sure that the argument and result arrays conform and that some coercions are performed. Another decision that must be made is whether to call external numerical analysis routines or generate internal subroutines.

In the second stage of code generation, the translation of MATHCODE to Fortran or C source text is primarily a syntax transformation that is performed mechanically with no specification or implementation decisions in the sense of the earlier discussion. Because the MATHCODE language is restricted to basic numeric operators and simple control statements, the translation is easily accomplished. The language is principally a subset of MATHEMATICA, although it has been extended with statically typed variables, procedures, and constructs to express parallelism.

The translation of MATHCODE to Fortran or C attempts to preserve uniform semantics to the extent practical. For example, integer, real, string, and Boolean data types are available in each target language, and the semantics of the MATHCODE compound statement If, Do, and While are essentially similar across target languages. A parallel function is defined that lists a set of expressions that can be evaluated in parallel. A parallel function is translated to either a parallel or sequential construct in the target language, depending on the availability of real parallelism in the target language execution environment.

Representations

The internal representation of data objects is extended from conceptual dimensions, type, and properties to include a physical representation, reference expression, and input-output method. The physical representation is used to check array conforming and later is the source for declaration statements. MATHEMATICA functions are used to implement the elaboration of physical representations and to check conformance.

The lower level of code generation marks the abrupt and final transition from program representation in the symbolic manipulation system to the program representation as Fortran or C source text. No further program transformations are performed by SINAPSE after this transition; the program units are compiled, linked, and executed in the traditional manner.

Reasoning Techniques

The decision mechanism already described is used by the system to make representation decisions such as whether to store only the nonzero elements of special arrays (such as those having the property diagonal). At this level, we attempt to have SINAPSE make all the decisions without help from the user because the distance from the specification can mean that the user has less contact with the decision (for example, an array for which a decision is needed can be a temporary variable introduced by the system).

Optimization rules are transformations made to improve time or space performance. These rules are similar to refinement rules but, typically, transform a complex pattern of constructs into another complex expression of constructs at the same level of refinement. Therefore, no decisions are associated with optimization rules. SINAPSE has some global points at which optimizations of a certain type are considered; other rules are associated with the symbol in the pattern that seems most relevant to applicability and are automatically applied. Although we do not yet have enough examples to determine which technique is most useful, explicitly applied rules seem easier to understand and debug.

Translation from MATHCODE to the target language is accomplished by a conventional recursive-descent parser coupled to action rules. Parser rules match MATHCODE constructs and bind to parameter instantiations; the bindings are passed to action rules that emit target language syntax. The translation is actually accomplished in two passes to ease restrictions on statement ordering for the levels above. The translator is extremely compact (about 2000 lines) because of the regularity of the language and the use of MATHEMATICA patterns to define the parsing rules and target language–dependent action rules.

Open Issues

As we continue to work toward the goal of practical application, three major areas motivate research and experimentation: the adaptation of SINAPSE to new applications, code generation for multiple architectures, and data management. Other important areas such as visualization (Boubez, Froncioni, and Peskin 1990) and input geometries are being addressed by other research groups and are not considered here.

Code Generation for Multiple Architectures

Questions about code generation for multiple architectures include What knowledge is needed by the program synthesis process to target and optimize algorithms? At what level in our refinement framework should this knowledge reside? When is it sufficient to assume one, standard virtual machine, for example, Fortran 9X? What performance predictors must be known to perform optimization? What performance predictors can be supplied at an early stage to help guide the transformation process?

SINAPSE currently has constructs representing whether actions can be performed in parallel or must be performed in sequence. We will continue to augment SINAPSE with such constructs. For example, neighborhood operators are useful constructs for all architectures; on a massively parallel architecture, they can even be written as calls to microcode instructions for maximal efficiency.

A major open issue in code generation is the modeling of a parallel architecture. Our plan is to incrementally develop such models to accommodate the transformation rules. That is, our transformation rules will be parameterized by properties of the architecture (for example, number of processors, communications costs, startup and incremental costs for operations). This approach allows us to use crude rules to get results early and provides an evolutionary path to develop general-purpose reusable rules.

Parallel architectures usually have some kind of distributed memory. Another open issue in code generation is deciding where to locate data and how to move it. Although we expect to initially rely on compiler defaults, we recognize that these decisions have paramount effect on performance and are working on automatically generating compiler directives.

Data Management

A sizable portion of a modeling program is devoted to data management—reading and writing data sets. Data sets, stored in one or more files, contain such elements as model parameters and geometry descriptions. Subroutines to read and write data sets are complicated by requirements to parse input files, validate input, convert formats, and traverse data structures. If data sets are large, input-output performance can be important. If data sets are very large (for example, must be stored on tape), sequential processing might be necessary, severely constraining algorithm design.

Thus, input-output complicates programs for these two principal reasons: the persistence of data sets stored in files, which gives rise to problems with file naming, access control, variable bindings, and format conversion, and the performance of file access relative to primary memory access, which interferes with algorithm design and optimization.

What approaches might be adopted in SINAPSE to attack the data management problem? When performance is not the dominant concern, a variety of approaches increase the convenience of data access. For example, data sets can be made self-describing through standardized formats and read and written through standardized function libraries. Formal grammars can be used to describe data sets and automatically synthesize access functions. Data dictionaries can be created to expand the name space of a program beyond its local variables.

When performance is the dominant concern, the problems become entwined with the algorithm design and require a quantitative approach. Again, different approaches are possible. Data sets can be implemented as abstract data types with explicit cost models for movement from element to element. Data sets can be designed to remember the performance statistics of their past history and feed the information to predictive models. If contention for resources exists, an accurate cost model can require queueing analysis or simulation of the target computing system.

Adapting to New Applications

The generality of SINAPSE knowledge is an important concern for potential users. Currently, we have powerful techniques for a narrow problem (explicit finite-difference programs for initial boundary-value problems). What balance do we strike between power and generality in the long term? We expect to emphasize power in narrow domains but extend generality in a bottom-up, example-driven manner. Thus in the near term, we will continue to add algorithm and application knowledge to enable us to handle new problems such as acoustic wave propagation in a steady fluid flow. For example, to achieve this goal, we will probably need to mix explicit and implicit methods. Although we will develop sufficient breadth to demonstrate feasibility and uncover the necessary representation space, the range of desired synthesis knowledge is ever increasing. Therefore, we will also provide tools with which end users can easily extend the system. We hope to show that there is a critical mass of domain knowledge and that the end user can add new knowledge to a reasonable extent.

Tools to automate knowledge incorporation require formal definitions of domain knowledge, which can vary in form for specification constructs, mathematical approximation rules, optimization rules, and decision-making heuristics. We attempt to simplify knowledge addition by using a single syntax and programming style (MATHEMATICA rules with additional structure imposed). Also, we minimize the number of different constructs and ensure that users do not need detailed understanding of SINAPSE internals; constructs are limited to those helpful either in describing the domain, specifying the functional behavior desired, or selecting among alternative algorithms (for example, terms such as numeric stability). The high-level constructs of the MATHEMATICA language itself should simplify the specification of the actual content of the new mathematical techniques.

Most new knowledge will be added for a particular problem-solving session, but at the same time, the user should generalize and abstract. When a user notices a problem (missing or incorrect behavior), the system must help determine the category of knowledge involved, find repair rules, fix the specific problem (including propagating changes to dependent functions, related performance properties, and so on), and generalize the solution (considering new places for using components and modifying similar components). Previewing dependent changes before action is desirable.

We expect classification schemes and the principles of abstraction and object-oriented design to continue to help in organizing related information for reuse or specialization. Hierarchies of techniques for modifying knowledge also appear useful. For example, modification techniques include adding heuristics, alternatives, or new decisions; reordering heuristics or decisions; and modifying implementation rules. Initial tools will include interactive support for such organization; possible techniques for longer-term automation are case-based classification and access and reasoning by analogy.

Current Distribution of Knowledge. At the time of this writing, SINAPSE contains approximately 13,000 lines of MATHEMATICA source code. A top-level breakdown is system interaction and control, 20 percent of the code; model formulation and algorithm selection, 15 percent; program refinement, 30 percent; and code generation, 30 percent. The remaining 5 percent consists of example program specifications. We estimate that somewhat more than half of the existing system could be reused for the synthesis of other types of scientific programs.

The system interaction code is relatively stable and is not expected to grow as much as the application-related parts of the system. This code should be completely reusable in applications in other branches of scientific programming. Of this code, about 35 percent is user interface related, 55 percent defines primitives used for defining properties and decisions and setting up algorithm hierarchies, and the remaining 20 percent is related to making and recording design decisions.

Most of the model formulation and algorithm selection knowledge (about 80 percent) consists of algorithm class descriptions in terms of relevant properties and skeletons of algorithm bodies. Application-specific model formulation only accounts for about 20 percent. We expect this part of the system to grow significantly as we take on additional applications. Although the overall knowledge structures would change with different application domains, about a third of the current properties and algorithm schemas are in the top parts of the algorithm hierarchy and would likely carry over, as would additional fragments at lower levels.

Program-refinement knowledge is almost all about finite-difference algorithms; less than 10 percent concerns solving problems in a transform space. This section of the system will probably grow most rapidly as we extend our application domains.

The code-generation component includes a higher-level section, with conditional and Boolean simplification, array-dimensional analysis and conforming, and representation selection and optimization (40 percent). The lower-level code generation (60 percent) includes a parser; a declarations processor; and detailed syntax rules for Fortran, Connection Machine Fortran, and C. We expect the higher-level code- generation component to grow moderately as we add more optimizations for different types of architectures. This code should be reusable in applications for other branches of scientific programming.

Although we don't count visualization as part of the system proper, we also have 500 lines of MATHEMATICA for developing simple material files and 2000 lines of C for Silicon Graphics display programs.

End User Knowledge Addition. Here, we make a few preliminary comments about how easy it is for developers to add new knowledge. These observations are based on some recently made, carefully recorded small changes and on an analysis of the existing code organization.

One set of small changes we made recently was to add a new kind of finite-difference operator called *upwind differencing*. Previously, all our code assumed the use of central differencing without explicitly representing the choice. Actually, there were several variants, differing according to method (explicit, implicit) and whether or not the derivative was taken with respect to time. The main change was to explicitly name the operator type and unify the calling procedures. This change took 5 new lines of property and property default definitions in the class files. It took 24 lines of slightly revised existing code to explicitly define the 4 existing operator types and 2 lines to define the new operator. However, 29 lines of code that implicitly invoke the operators were removed. The net change to the system was only 2 lines added, but about 45 lines of code were manipulated over a period of about 4 hours by one of the experienced system developers.

A related set of changes was made so that different operators could be used depending on the specific equation and quantity being differentiated (previously, only time derivatives were treated independently). The operator function definitions and calls to the generic operator required changes to 4 lines. One new operator was also added (4 lines changed, 6 added), and another generalization concerning the interaction between operators and boundaries was made (9 lines). Overall, about 25 lines were touched over a period of about 3 hours; again, a rate of about 10 lines each hour.

One of the more difficult problems for the end user, assuming that s/he knows some of the basics of the system organization and the MATHEMATICA language, is how to find the code that needs to be modified. Especially in the kind of modifications done here—generalizing a hard-wired assumption—this task might not be easy. SINAPSE currently provides only a few simple tools to help inspect its internal structure. For example, the user can get displays of the class hierarchies and algorithm skeletons but not automatic entry into the correct files for a particular construct (unfortunately, the MATHEMATICA programming environment is not state of the art for an interpreted language in terms of built-in object-oriented function, tracing and debugging, function updating, or performance monitoring).

Adding a new alternative for an existing choice is slightly easier. We have not yet collected any data on this type of choice, but we can make some backward estimates by inspecting the current system structure. For example, two kinds of boundary-handling methods we can isolate are the taper method and the LIAO operator. These methods each involve 3 lines to assert their existence and about 5 lines to insert initialization and update calls into the algorithm skeletons. Another change made was to add the option to average the values of materials at boundaries. This change required only 4 lines to insert a call for averaging and make the default to not average. The code to actually implement these methods is much more complex (150 to 300 lines each, which takes weeks to develop), but the interfaces to the rest of the system appear fairly straightforward (at least with hindsight).

Summary

The SINAPSE system currently synthesizes finite-difference programs from the symbolic description of mathematical models based on partial differential equations. Several kinds of boundary conditions, including the use of additional equations, are supported. We implemented techniques such as grid staggering and material averaging to match the quality of existing commercial programs. The intermediate MATHCODE code generated by the system is translated to Fortran, Fortran9X, or C, depending on the target specified by the user.

The program synthesis framework assumed in SINAPSE includes levels for domain-specific problem formulation, mathematical modeling equations, abstract algorithms, pseudocode programs, and executable code. The entire system is implemented in MATHEMATICA, which provides support for rules, functions, and symbolic manipulation. Somewhat different representations and reasoning strategies are used in different levels. The first few levels involve mostly key-word design decisions directly made by the user. The transition to abstract algorithms involves composing algorithm schema fragments (in a generic language). The algorithm schemas are arranged in an object hierarchy with the design decisions and schema components represented as object properties that are inherited, specialized, or added at the appropriate level. Refinement to pseudocode is made with mathematically detailed algorithm refinement rules that exploit MATHEMATICA's algebraic manipulation capabilities. These middle stages use forward rule applications based on the earlier design decisions. No target code is produced until the last step, which involves more forward rule applications, some system-determined representation decisions, and some language-independent optimizations. Thus, although the system is domain specific and does not include as many choices of data structure and algorithm refinement as a more general program synthesis system, it is still definitely a program synthesis system rather than a code generator. There are no "big switch" decisions that select large fragments of code. None of the algorithm fragments are more than 25-lines long (the largest chunks involve input-output), and most fragments will be expanded differently depending on the equations involved, the other algorithm choices, and the data representation choices made at later levels.

Although much work remains in extending the system to more of the application domain and generating better code for parallel architectures, the current SINAPSE system demonstrates that the approach is suitable for scientific programming in general. Specifications are usually less than 20 percent of the size of the generated code, which takes only minutes to synthesize. New chunks of code, such as for different boundary or difference operators, can be added in time on the order of days and then reused in other applications. We estimate that at least half the system would be reusable in different scientific programming applications. The system has already generated more working application code than the 13,000 lines that it contains.

Acknowledgments

We could not have built a knowledge-based program synthesis system without the advice of some domain experts, and we are grateful to Michael Oristaglio, Curt Randall, and Charles Watson for their time and patience. We also thank Barbara Gates, Stephane Launay, Juan Leon, and Newman Shee for programming support. David Barstow, Barbara Gates, Juan Leon, Ted Linden, Reid Smith, and Jeremy Wertheimer made helpful comments on previous versions of this chapter.

References

Abelson, H.; Eisenberg, M.; Halfant, M.; Katzenelson, J.; Sacks, E.; Sussman, G. J.; Wisdom, J.; and Yip, K. 1989. Intelligence in Scientific Computing. *Communications of the ACM* 32(5): 546–562.

Arango, G. 1988. Domain Engineering for Software Reuse. Ph.D. thesis, Dept. of Information and Computer Science, Univ. of California at Irvine.

Barras, P.; Blum, J.; Paumier, J. C.; Witomski, P.; and Rechenmann, F. 1990. Eve: An Object-Centered Knowledge-Based PDE Solver, Technical Report, CSD-TR-963, Purdue Univ.

Barstow, D. 1986. A Perspective on Automatic Programming. In *Readings in Artificial Intelligence and Software Engineering,* eds. C. Rich and R. C. Waters, 537–559. San Mateo, Calif.: Morgan Kaufmann.

Boubez, T. I.; Froncioni, A. M.; and Peskin, R. L. 1990. A Prototyping Environment for Ordinary Differential Equations, Technical Report, CSD-TR-963, Purdue Univ.

Char, B. W.; Geddes, K. O.; Gonnet, G. H.; and Watt, S. M. 1985. *Maple User's Guide*. Waterloo, Ontario, Canada: Watcom.

Cook, G. O. 1988. A Tool for the Development of Large-Scale Simulation Codes, Technical Report UCID-21482, Lawrence Livermore National Laboratory.

Dyksen, W. R., and Gritter, C. R. 1989. Elliptic Expert: An Expert System for Elliptic Partial Differential Equations. *Mathematics and Computers in Simulation* 31:333–342.

Jenks, R. D. 1984. A Primer: Eleven Keys to New Scratchpad. *Lecture Notes on Computer Science* 174:123–147.

Kowalski, A. D. 1987. An Object-Oriented Prolog Representation of Quasilinear Partial Differential Equations. Presented at the International Symposium on AI Expert Systems and Languages in Modeling and Simulation, Barcelona, Spain, June.

King, D.; Mullen, T.; Rice, B.; Topping, P.; and Weyland, N. 1987. Knowledge-Based FFT and Convolution Synthesis for Any Number of Points. *Mathematics and Computers in Simulation* 31:441–451.

Neighbors, J. M. 1989. Draco: A Method for Engineering Reusable Software Systems. In *Software Reusability*, eds. T. J. Biggerstaff and A. J. Perlis, 295–320. New York: Association of Computing Machinery.

Rayna, G. 1987. *Reduce—Software for Algebraic Computation*. New York: Springer-Verlag.

Russo, M. F.; Kowalski, A. D.; and Peskin, R. L. 1989. An Object-Oriented Knowledge-Based Approach to the Automatic Synthesis of Numerical Programs for Differential Equations. Draft.

Smith, D. R.; Kotik, E. G.; and Westfold, S. J. 1985. Research on Knowledge-Based Software Environments at Kestrel Institute. *IEEE Transactions on Software Engineering* SE-11.

Steinberg, S., and Roache, P. 1990. Using MACSYMA to Write Finite-Volume Solvers, Technical Report, CSD-TR-963, Purdue Univ.

Symbolics. 1987. MACSYMA User's Guide. Symbolics, Inc., Cambridge, Mass.

Wilson, K. G.1983. GIBBS: A Proposed Scientific Program Development System, Laboratory of Nuclear Studies, Cornell Univ.

Wolfram, S. 1988. *A System for Doing Mathematics by Computer*. Redwood City, Calif.: Addison-Wesley.

On the Automatic Selection of Data Structures and Algorithms

Dorothy Setliff

Real-world very large scale integration (VLSI) design tools often exhibit two salient features: They must address a variety of technologies, and as they grow to accommodate new technologies, they increase in size and complexity. As a result, many such tools evolve into large, baroque systems. The rapid pace of technology evolution has placed a burden on the design and implementation of these tools. As a result, the development of adequate tools generally lags behind the introduction of new technologies. This chapter presents ELF, a system for transforming flexible, high-level specifications for integrated circuit (IC) and printed circuit board (PCB) routers into working software. The ELF system provides an automatic programming environment that integrates domain knowledge with automatic program synthesis techniques. To demonstrate this idea, I describe the selection process for a variety of router applications. The successful synthesis of varied algorithms supports my central argument that the integration of specific knowledge of the target domain within a program synthesis environment is useful for synthesizing real-world design tools.

This article is organized as follows: The next section reviews the target domain: VLSI wire routers. Introduction to ELF and the Selection Stage provides a high-level introduction to the three stages of the ELF synthesis architecture (input, selection, and code generator stages), its internal knowledge representations, and some implementation details. ELF Architecture: The Selection Stage provides a detailed analysis of the operation of the selection stage. Selection Stage Examples presents experimental results on a variety of ELF-synthesized routers and includes discussions on how domain knowledge influenced the selection of algorithm and data-structure implementations. The closing section presents conclusions.

Target Domain: Wire Routers

In VLSI design, *physical design* refers to the process of reducing a structural description of a piece of hardware to the geometric layout of IC. Physical design is typically a two-step process: placement and routing. *Placement* arranges the relevant electronic components, for example, transistors, gates, and logic blocks, to minimize some consumable hardware, for example, the total area, or the amount of interconnection. The goal of placement is to make it feasible for the subsequent routing phase to interconnect all components.

Maze Routing

Routing electrically interconnects all components. At the least, routing must be able to embed all the wiring connections, but routing also seeks to minimize the amount of wiring. My work on tool synthesis focuses on a particular class of mature, successful routing algorithms: maze routers. Maze routers form a broad and adaptable class of routers known also as Lee routers or Lee-Moore routers (Hightower 1983; Lee 1961; Ohtsuki 1986; Soukup 1981). The basic ideas behind a simple maze router are similar to those of classical search problems.

Consider the following routing problem: A set of components to be interconnected has already been placed on a surface, for example, a chip or PCB. Each component has one or more interconnection terminals. Each set of two or more terminals that must be wired together is called a *net*. A typical maze-routing problem is to route a set of nets, one at a time, in some arbitrary order. A maze router is used when the shortest connection path or, more generally, the least cost connection path is desired. Because only one wire is routed at a time, and previously routed wires become obstacles for future wires, the order of routing these nets is crucial. The simplest possible routing problem here is to connect nets that are constrained to having only two terminals in a single conducting layer and attempt to find the shortest possible routing path.

There are four phases in a maze routing algorithm: setup, expansion, backtrack, and cleanup. In the setup phase, the routing area is forced onto a simple two-dimensional grid of cells. The grid represents the routing search space. Each cell in this grid has an associated *traversal cost*, or the cost of using this cell as part of the interconnection. The simplest implementation gives the unit cost of all cells except those that cannot be traversed at all because they are occupied by previous wires; these cells are simply regarded as unreachable during the search. An unrouted net, consisting of a source and a target terminal, is then selected to enter into the next phase, expansion.

The basic idea of expansion is to start from one terminal of the net to be routed, the source terminal, and then search outward until the target terminal is reached. For example, this search could be implemented by first examining all paths that are a distance of one cell from the source, then a distance of two cells from the source, then three cells, and so forth. At any time in this search, the cells being examined constitute a *wavefront* of cells that expand outward from the source cell. There are several options for performing the expansion process. Conventional search terminology suffices to define these options. If expansion searches all cells at a distance i from the source cell before looking at those cells at a distance $i + 1$, as in the previous example, the expansion is performing a *breadth-first* search. If, instead, the expansion preferentially searches those cells that are known to be closer to the target, the expansion is performing a *depth-first* search. Most commonly, the expansion searches the least costly cell on the wavefront (using a *best-first* search), assuming that individual cells in the grid have their own individual cost to traverse them. The expansion algorithm is similar to Dijkstra's algorithm for finding the least costly path between two nodes in a weighted graph (Aho, Hopcroft, and Ullman 1974). The physical characteristics of the components, terminals, and nets affect which expansion style works best.

Once the target is reached, we can proceed with the backtrack phase to find the actual wiring path. In the simplest case, as each cell is expanded, information is embedded in the cell, indicating the direction of expansion used to enter the cell. In particular, this directional information can be traced backward from the target cell, adding each cell to the actual connection path until the initial source net cell is reached; in this way, we trace the final path backward, from target to source.

Finally, the cleanup phase reinitializes the grid to show the existence of this backtracked connection path as an obstacle to future wirings. These four phases are then repeated for each remaining net to be routed. The four phases are discussed in more detail in Setliff (1989).

Maze Router Variations

Maze router implementations come in many variants. In general, a given maze router implementation must address the following domain-related characteristics:

Fabrication characteristics pertain to the physical environment of the carrier on which the router operates. Some fabrication characteristics that affect maze router implementations are the existence of multiple routing layers; preferred routing directions on different routing layers; constraints on the placement or adjacency of *vias* (vias form connections between different routing layers) in the grid; and wiring angle constraints, such as whether diagonal (45°) wires are permitted in addition to rectilinear wires.

Application characteristics pertain to router operation within the target application. One critical application characteristic that affects maze router implementations is whether a detailed router or a global router is desired. *Detailed routers* decide on the precise physical location of individual wire segments. For *global routers,* the carrier is divided into regions, and the global router chooses only through which regions each wire will be placed, not exactly where within a region. A subsequent detailed router will then perform all the intraregion wiring. Global routers are used when wiring congestion is a serious problem or when the size of the routing problem is great enough to require this type of hierarchical breakdown.

Algorithm characteristics affect router efficiency. Common algorithm characteristics include net ordering, expansion phase selection (breadth first, depth first, or best first), wavefront data-structure constraints, routing detour limits (how far a wire is allowed to meander past its minimum possible length), and backtrack optimization.

Maze routers are a particularly good domain for research on tool generation for three basic reasons. First, maze routers are technology and application dependent. This reason ensures an interesting range of algorithms. Second, maze-routing algorithms are mature and fairly straightforward, keeping the focus entirely on the synthesis task and not on debugging the routing techniques themselves. Finally, these algorithms require complex elaborations to adapt them to specific uses, and these elaborations require both routing expertise and general knowledge of programming mechanics. This reason makes maze routing an interesting application for investigating the use of general and domain-specific knowledge in program synthesis.

Introduction to ELF and the Selection Stage

This section describes the features and implementation details of ELF's automatic program synthesis architecture. ELF automatically builds implementations for data structures and algorithms to best fulfill the requirements of the routing application. The final data-structure and algorithm implementation is the culmination of a sequence of design decisions. Each design decision uses general or domain-specific knowledge. I first introduce the representations for data structures, algorithms, domain-specific knowledge, and design decisions. I then review the three broad stages of ELF: input, selection, and code generator.

```
LOOP path_not_found IS TRUE END
   LOOP   site IN same_cost OF wavefront END
   TEST   site NOT expanded AND
          site IN limits AND
          path_not_found IS TRUE END
      ASSIGN path_not_found TO check_target WITH site END
      ASSIGN cost TO cost + cost_function END
      PUT site IN wavefront OF cells WITH cost END
      REMOVE site FROM wavefront OF cells WITH same_cost END
   ENDTEST
   ENDLOOP
ENDLOOP
```

Figure 1. Example ADL Algorithm Specification

Knowledge Representation in ELF

ELF operates on abstract representations of algorithms and data structures. Algorithms are represented in a custom-designed language called the algorithm development language (ADL), which is essentially a much simplified variant of SETL (Schonberg, Schwartz, and Sharir 1981; Liu 1979).

Figure 1 illustrates an ADL template for the expansion phase. This ADL template examines each cell in the set "wavefront" and references it through "site." The "test" statement checks each cell for expansion validity, for example, that it has not already been expanded or is even full. If the cell passes the validity test, then the code checks to see if the target has been reached, and if not, it expands into the cell. The ADL descriptions are not themselves executable. The intent is not to have a large library of ADL styles, each differing only slightly. Instead, ADL relies on relatively few abstract algorithm styles.

The important characteristic of the ADL language is that it specifies only simple computations and uses sets and set operations to reference all complex data objects. Like SETL, ADL does not coerce these sets into specific implementations. For example, in figure 1, the set "wavefront" is only known to be accessed by "same_cost." In the actual implementation, "wavefront" can be implemented as some complex structure, such as an array of linked lists or as a doubly linked list.

Data structures are represented as a composition of basic templates similar to those in Kant (1983). Templates for primitive structures such as one-dimensional arrays and linked lists are directly supported; these templates have attribute slots for obvious characteristics such as size and access time, which are part of the information necessary to judge the merits of a particular structure. The composition of structures is permitted using a simple parent-child attribute, so that, for example, I can construct an array of lists of trees of arrays, and so forth. Figure 2 shows a typical template for a hierarchically

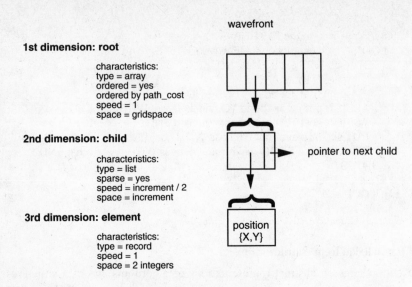

1st dimension: root

characteristics:
type = array
ordered = yes
ordered by path_cost
speed = 1
space = gridspace

2nd dimension: child

characteristics:
type = list
sparse = yes
speed = increment / 2
space = increment

3rd dimension: element

characteristics:
type = record
speed = 1
space = 2 integers

Figure 2. Wavefront Data-Structure Representation.

composed array-of-lists structure, in this case, the wavefront data structure. For simplicity, I refer to each layer of such a hierarchically composed structure as a dimension of this structure. The structure in the first dimension is called the *root structure*. Each dimension is annotated with information about the expected domain-specific requirements, for example, that the structure is sparse, that it is ordered, and that the indexes to access its ordered components have a particular form. In figure 2, the illustrated data structure has three dimensions. The *root dimension* is an array, and it is ordered using the range of values determined by another data structure called path-cost. The second, or *child*, dimension is a list and consists of the third dimension's grid position information as well as the necessary pointer to the next child in the list.

ELF uses domain-specific design knowledge to make design decisions. Both design knowledge and design decisions are represented within rules. ELF is a rule-based system written in OPS5 (Brownston et al. 1985), running under Unix 4.3. The following classes of knowledge are identified: (1) design generation knowledge, (2) program synthesis knowledge, and (3) design interaction knowledge.

Design generation knowledge is expertise about the implementation of the domain. This knowledge is represented as the ramifications of critical sets of combinations of data-structure and algorithm implementations. This knowledge representation is in a many-to-many style. Examples of this class of knowledge are *router structure knowledge* (knowledge of what constitutes a solution for the application problem) and *routing phase requirement knowl-*

ALGORITHM_SELECTION_refine_expansion_phase:
 Given minimizing execution time AND
 Given Dependency Analysis statistics for expansion modification
  algorithm candidates for expansion decision AND
 Given one algorithm candidate timing estimates is less than
  others THEN

Select that algorithm candidate option .

Figure 3. Design Decision Rule Using Design Interaction Knowledge.

edge (knowledge of what can fulfill the solution requirements). An example of router structure knowledge is information about routing phase behaviors along with algorithm and data-structure suitabilities, that is, rules about the ability of a particular data-structure choice to cope with a particular application. An example of routing phase requirement knowledge is information about which algorithms are useful in a particular routing phase. *Program synthesis knowledge* is information about the syntactic and semantic requirements of the target application language (in this case, C). Examples of this class of knowledge are data-structure implementation characteristics and coding expertise. *Design interaction knowledge* is information about how the two previous knowledge classes interact. Interactions are mostly the result of the inherent interdependencies among data-structure implementations within an algorithmic structure.

ELF utilizes these sources of knowledge to make design decisions. A *design decision* either proposes, selects, or refines various implementations. Design decisions are represented as a set of ordered goals and subgoals within rules. An example rule (in an English language representation of an OPS5 rule) is given in figure 3. This rule shows that the resolution of a required decision to select an algorithm to implement the router expansion phase using design interaction knowledge of the projected timing estimates of the algorithm modifications.

The following subsection overviews the ELF synthesis architecture and its use of these knowledge sources.

Overview of the ELF Synthesis Architecture

The ELF synthesis architecture comprises three stages, as illustrated in figure 4. First, the input stage reads all application specifications from the user. This stage uses these specifications, along with design generation knowledge, to propose the set of design decisions required to complete the routing application. Solution candidates for each design decision are placed in candidate sets. There is one candidate set (composed of one or more entries) for each design decision.

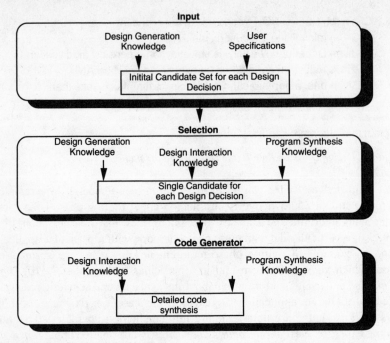

Figure 4. ELF Synthesis Architecture.

The second stage, selection, uses all three knowledge classes to make design decisions involving the design of data structures and algorithms. The method of making design decisions is an important issue. The separation of data-structure and algorithm design decisions is a key point in this stage. I discuss this stage in detail in the next section.

The third stage, code generator, uses program synthesis knowledge and design interaction knowledge to transform the design decisions into executable code. Like the PSI/SYN system (Kant 1983; Barstow 1979), the code generator stage generates final code through a sequence of small transformations. The process starts from the ADL abstract algorithm representation, progresses to an intermediate representation for the code to be synthesized, then finishes with the executable code.

ELF Architecture: The Selection Stage

This section focuses on the details of design decision making in the selection stage of the ELF synthesis architecture. The selection stage integrates the data-structure selection ideas explored by Low (1978) and Rowe and Tonge (1986) as well as the algorithm selection ideas studied by McCartney (chapter 13) and Smith (chapter 19). The design decision process uses all three knowledge sources as a guide to the selection of data-structure and algorithm

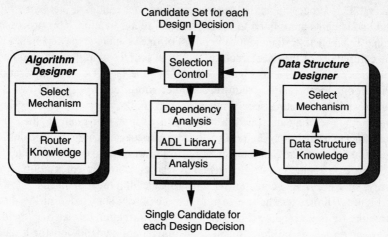

Figure 5. Modules of the Selection Stage.

implementations. Each design decision is typically the design of either an algorithm or data structure. Figure 5 illustrates the selection process. The input to this stage are candidate sets for each design decision required by the particular application. Selection is implemented by four modules: selection control, dependency analysis, data-structure designer, and algorithm designer. The selection control module regulates the interaction between the data-structure and algorithm selection modules by only allowing a designer module to progress on a design decision one step at a time before allowing the other module to evaluate the effects of this step. In this way, the interdependency of algorithm and data-structure implementation design decisions dominates the selection process.

The dependency analysis module is a slave to the two designer modules. This module analyzes the ADL algorithm representations and computes the expected costs of this algorithm over the current data-structure design decision candidate sets. Recall that in the ADL language, there is no explicit data-structure implementation. The dependency analysis module analyzes the ADL representation of each algorithm alternative along with the current data-structure representation state. Its output is the cost and interdependency information for each design decision required in this application. Previous design decisions affect this information and can act as constraints on other design decisions within the two designer modules.

The Data-Structure Designer Module

The data-structure designer module is concerned with design decisions that involve the building of relevant data structures. Building data structures is a two-tier process. First, a data-structure candidate must be preferred over the others. This process is called *selection*. Then, the candidate data structure and its elements are refined to create the final representation. This process is called *refinement*. Refinement can consist of one or more steps depending on the complexity of the data structure. All three sources of knowledge aid both selection and refinement. Figure 6 illustrates the use of design generation knowledge in the data-structure designer module. This rule shows the ramifications of routing specifications (for example, number of routing layers) on the use of a data structure within an algorithm (for example, the number of accesses is low). The result is the refinement of a data-structure design decision from an array implementation to an array-of-lists implementation. The previous selection design decision (the current implementation is an array) acts as a design constraint and is propagated in the refinement.

Figure 7 illustrates the use of program synthesis knowledge in the data-structure designer module. This rule looks at information provided by the dependency analysis module to select an integer implementation for a data-structure design decision. In this case, variable V was found to range over data-structure S; therefore, if S is an array, then V should be an integer.

Finally, Figure 8 illustrates the use of design interaction knowledge in the data-structure designer module. This rule combines a user directive to minimize the space required by the application with the previous selections made the algorithm designer module in the expansion phase design decision to select a list implementation for the data-structure design decision.

The Algorithm Designer Module

The algorithm designer module is the companion to the data-structure designer module and is used to select and refine algorithm design decisions. Similar to the data-structure designer, this module uses a two-tier process that first selects the initial candidate algorithms and then refines the selected algorithm to complete the router design. The algorithm designer module uses design interaction knowledge in conjunction with the algorithm cost computations provided by the dependency analysis module to both select and refine algorithm schemas to reflect the routing application characteristics. Figure 3 illustrates the use of design interaction knowledge in the algorithm designer module.

The refinement of algorithm design decisions often involves the generation of other design decisions. For example, in Figure 9, the refinement of the expansion phase design decision to a depth-first search places restrictions on the net composition; that is, they cannot be multiterminal nets. This refinement results from the inability of the depth-first expansion to accurately measure the notion of moving closer to multiple targets. In this case, the algorithm designer module produces a new design decision, net composition, with a relevant candidate set incorporating multiterminal to two-terminal net transformation algorithms.

I explicitly acknowledge the interdependence of algorithm and data-struc-

DATA_STRUCTURE_SELECTION_layers_influence:
  Given the number of routing layers <= 2 AND
  Given a gridded router type AND
  Given this data structure is:
    number of accesses in algorithm is low
    sparse
    current implementation is an array THEN

Refine the selection to an array of lists.

Figure 6. Use of Design Generation Knowledge in the Data-Structure Designer Module.

DATA_STRUCTURE_SELECTION_first_dimension_array:
  Given an array is in candidate set for data structure S AND
  Given S is ordered by data structure V THEN

Select integer for V.

Figure 7. Use of Program Synthesis Knowledge in the Data-Structure Designer Module.

DATA_STRUCTURE_SELECTION_wavefront_as_list:
  Given expansion phase selection is best-first AND
  Given want to minimize space consumption AND
  Given data structure S is sparse THEN

Select a list as the root type for data structure S.

Figure 8. Use of Design Interaction Knowledge in the Data-Structure Designer Module.

ture selection. For example, a specific implementation for each essential data structure (such as the routing grid) must be selected based on the needs of particular algorithm selections and vice versa. Constraint propagation in and between the data-structure designer module and the algorithm designer module enforces interdependence. Constraint propagation is provided through the dependency analysis module data-structure and algorithm cost metrics.

Selection Stage Examples

To illustrate the use of the domain-specific knowledge in the selection stage, I review several examples of automatic data-structure and algorithm selec-

ALGORITHM_SELECTION_add_decomposition:
    Given expansion phase selection is depth-first AND
    Given have multi-terminal nets THEN

Make a design decision to decompose net
Candidate set includes: minimum spanning tree, steiner tree.

Figure 9. Introducing a New Design Decision in the Algorithm Designer Module.

tion for router software. I present two sets of experiments. The first experiment set illustrates the breadth of knowledge available in the selection stage, and the second set illustrates the depth of knowledge available in the selection stage. In each experiment set, I first review the input specifications for the routing application. I then detail the selection traces for the router expansion phase, the data structure representing the routing search area (called the wavefront) and the data structure representing the routing area (called the grid). Finally, I compare the synthesized results against synthetic or industrial benchmarks.

Gate-Array Routers

This subsection looks at a suite of four global routers for gate arrays. In this set, individual cells in the routing grid represent large areas, called *routing channels*, on the chip; accordingly, these cells each have a capacity for wires to traverse them. The cost of traversing a cell is a function of the previous demand for wires to traverse this cell. Traversal costs act as a load-balancing heuristic in that congested cells are more expensive to traverse.

In the first routing application, GA1, the user specified a global router, for a congested, grid-based carrier (that is, the gate-array chip) having two routing layers; each net is a multiterminal net rather than the simpler two-terminal net. The user also directed ELF to emphasize the speed of routing over the routing space requirements. The second routing application, GA2, differs from GA1 in that ELF was directed to minimize routing space requirements. The third gate-array routing application, GA3, differs from GA1 in that ELF is required to build a router requiring the decomposition of the input net into two terminal nets using a minimum spanning-tree algorithm (Aho, Hopcroft, and Ullman 1974). The fourth gate-array routing experiment, GA4, is similar to GA2 but allows diagonal (45°), as well as the normal rectilinear, wiring between routing cells. This set of experiments demonstrates the flexibility available in ELF for accommodating modifications to the underlying router technology without having to modify executable router code. These experiments stress the expansion phase and wavefront data-structure design decisions.

Design Decision	Router GA1	Router GA2	Router GA3	Router GA4
Expansion search phase Wavefront data structure Routing Grid data structure	best-first array of array array of array	depth-first list array of list	depth-first array of array array of array	depth-first list array of list

Figure 10. Gate-Array Router Synthesis Selections.

Figure 10 summarizes the design decisions for the expansion phase, wavefront data structure, and routing grid data structure for each of the four routers.

The selection process begins with the selection control module. This module begins the iterative design decision process with the data-structure designer module. The first key design decision is the building of the routing grid data structure. The grid implementation design decision is a direct result of technology restriction and is most closely tied to technology. For all these routers, the size of the target application is small enough to allow full representation of the gate-array routing area through an array implementation, even though the routing areas are relatively sparse over the actual physical area. For each of the routers GA1 to GA4, the root data structure is selected to be an array. This selection is not the total implementation for the grid data structure and is more fully refined later.

The second key design decision is the expansion phase algorithm. It is at this point that the selection process varies. Algorithm selection is dependent on the cost metrics provided by the dependency analysis module. The user preferences to minimize either routing speed or routing space requirements focus attention on the relevant cost metrics (speed or space estimates). Because both GA1 and GA3 seek to minimize routing speed, the relevant cost computation is the time-cost computations. Figure 11 details the sequence of cost computations derived for GA1 to GA4 as selection proceeds. Each row shows the effect of either a proposed algorithm refinement or the application of domain knowledge.

The GA1 router initially ranks the depth-first search style over the best-first search style. Domain knowledge of the effects of a gate-array application on the depth-first search operation, namely, that gates themselves are routing blockages, causes a reevaluation of the cost computations. In addition, domain knowledge of the effects of limiting the physical search area (called a *bounding box*) lowers the time cost of the best-first search by decreasing the effective search space. There is no change to the depth-first time cost because the depth-first algorithm being compared already has an implied bounding box as part of its implementation. The user requirement to handle multiterminal nets also benefits the best-first search style because this style is not easily amenable to multitarget search paths. The algorithm designer se-

Time Cost	GA1		GA2		GA3		GA4	
	Best first	Depth first	Best first	Depth first	Best first	Depth first	Best first	Depth first
Initial cost:	224	184	224	184	224	184	224	184
Gate Array :	224	196			224	196		
Add bounding box:	210	196	210	196	210	196		
Add multi-node:	204	224	204	224				
Add diagonal:							316	204
Add bounding box:							280	180
cost % difference:	10%		10%			7%		55%

Figure 11. Gate-Array Expansion Phase Time-Cost Computations.

lects the best-first search style, with the necessary refinements used to revise the cost estimates. The GA3 router also initially ranks the depth-first search style as faster than the best-first search style. In this case, ELF knows that it only needs to route two terminal nets (recall that multiterminal nets must be decomposed into two terminal nets in GA3). Depth-first schemes can search fast, but ELF's particular strategy is most effective when restricted to two-terminal problems. The algorithm designer selects the depth-first search style for GA3.

The GA2 and GA4 routers seek to minimize routing space requirements. The relevant cost computations are the space-cost computations. Figure 12 details the space-cost computations for GA2 and GA4. The blank entries indicate that a particular experiment did not use the domain knowledge on the same horizontal line to revise the space-cost computations.

For GA2, the space-cost computation enabled the design decision to select the depth-first expansion, but for GA4, the relevant cost computations were too close to definitively make a selection. The secondary cost computations, namely, the time-cost computations in figure 11, were used to verify the expansion selection preferred using the space-cost computations. For example, the cost estimates for GA4 reflected the impact of diagonal (45°) wiring. All cells in the routing grid have eight neighbor cells to be examined during expansion. GA1 to GA3 only need to examine the four compass neighbors and can ignore the four diagonal neighbors. Because ELF knows that the number of cells to be examined strongly determines the running time of the router and because this router appears as though it will examine many more cells than if only rectilinear wires were permitted, ELF selects the depth-first expansion with the explicit aim of reducing the total number of cells visited during the expansion process.

The selection stage now focuses back on the grid data-structure design de-

Space Cost	GA2		GA4	
	Best first	Depth first	Best first	Depth first
Initial cost:	52,412	26,412	13,102	7,988
Gate Array :	52,412	29,712		
Add bounding box:	32,940	28,756		
Add multi-node:	32,748	28,728		
Add diagonal:			14,112	7,988
Add bounding box:			7,236	7,189
cost % difference:		12%		1%

Figure 12. Gate-Array Expansion Phase Space-Cost Computations.

cision. For routers GA1 and GA3, the user directive to minimize routing time combines with domain knowledge of the application size to produce a two-dimensional array implementation for the grid. For routers GA2 and GA4, design generation knowledge (figure 6) produces an array-of-lists implementation for the grid. Specifically, ELF observed that the numerous blockages in the grid because of nonporous gates are not available for wiring channels. Accordingly, it simply decided to omit them from the grid and generate the extra code to dynamically compute their location when it needs them. This type of decision making is a nice example of how ELF can produce working applications that surprise even its designers. Because ELF was never instructed not to use a sparse array for the routing grid (that is, there was no routing rule prohibiting sparse array structures for the routing surface), ELF created the structure and the code to manage it.

The fourth key design decision is the wavefront data structure. Routers GA1 and GA3 were optimized for speed, not space. For these routers, ELF chose a traditional path-cost–indexed array of lists for the wavefront, which minimizes execution time. However, for routers GA2 and GA4, this indexed wavefront structure was predicted to be somewhat large; so, to optimize space, a simple one-dimensional ordered list was chosen. This data-structure implementation is clearly slower to search but is likely to require less dynamic memory use.

To test the function and correctness of each of the ELF-synthesized routers, the design team ran a 900-gate, 1100-net benchmark. Performance statistics for these routers are given in figure 13. The original user directives on favor-

Router	Memory Use (bytes)	CPU Time (VAX 8800 sec.)	% Wires Routed
GA 1	14606	87.7	100%
GA 2	6456	132.5	100%
GA 3	8208	115.5	100%
GA 4	9376	59.5	100%

Figure 13. Synthesized Gate-Array Router Performance Comparison.

ing speed or space were accommodated. Note that GA1, which was synthesized for speed, did indeed complete the task in less time, about 50 percent faster than GA2. However, GA2, which was synthesized to conserve memory space, required 6 kilobytes (KB) of space compared to 14 KB for GA1. Router GA3 executed more slowly than GA1, even though both were tuned for speed. The difference is the change in the backtrack phase to handle the decomposed two-terminal nets. As expected for this small problem, all four routers succeeded in routing all the nets.

Practical Gate-Array Router

In this example, ELF was directed to produce a PCB router for an industrial application. A PCB router must deal not only with wire capacities but also with via capacities (which allow the wire to change layers on PCB). The cost of using a via is much greater than a wire, which increases the complexity of the design problem.

Again, the selection process begins with the data-structure module and grid data-structure design decision. The grid data-structure implementation must be consistent with the fabrication constraints. Specifically, the grid data structure must account for vias. The grid data structure was first selected to be an array to meet the user direction to minimize routing time. The increased space costs were considered, but a two-dimensional of array implementation was the result of refinement because the requirements of the PCB physical domain resulted in a reasonably sized array. The grid data structure is shown in figure 14. Note that the grid implementation represents all the physical commodities (for example, wires and vias) available within the grid unit.

The second key design decision is the expansion algorithm. This design

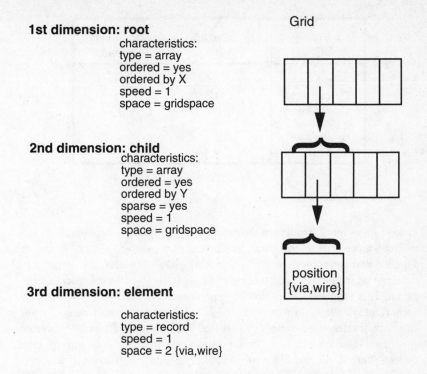

1st dimension: root
characteristics:
type = array
ordered = yes
ordered by X
speed = 1
space = gridspace

2nd dimension: child
characteristics:
type = array
ordered = yes
ordered by Y
sparse = yes
speed = 1
space = gridspace

3rd dimension: element

characteristics:
type = record
speed = 1
space = 2 {via,wire}

Figure 14. Grid Data-Structure Representation for Printed Circuit Board Router.

decision is domain knowledge intensive. Each expansion must check if the reached cell might cause the use of a via if the reached cell is not on the same physical layer as the expanding cell. The expansion phase options are best-first or depth-first search-type algorithms. The cost computations for the two algorithms are shown in figure 15. Domain knowledge of the granularity of the circuit board application increases the cost computation for the best-first expansion. The best-first expansion time cost is penalized by the wave-front size and its corresponding time cost. The depth-first expansion is penalized by the expected congestion difficulties. The algorithm designer chooses the depth-first search on the basis of a lower routing time cost.

This application requires that the instantiation of the expansion take into account the effects and use of vias. Design interaction knowledge creates the necessary new design decisions and their respective candidate sets required to handle vias in the expansion phase design decision. For example, the expansion design decision must include checks on via consumption. Further, the complication is only performed after satisfying two expansion constraints: wire availability and the necessity of via use. These new design de-

Time Costs	Best-first search	Depth-first search
Initial cost	92	N1
Granularity	l12	61
Congestion	l12	90
% difference:		24%

Figure 15. Expansion Phase Time-Cost Computations.

cisions act as modifications to the expansion phase design decision.

From these broad constraints, ELF produced a working router. To test the function and correctness of this ELF-synthesized PCB router, the design team obtained an industrial board routing example from Digital Equipment Corporation. This example is regarded by experts as being unroutable by automatic tools (Doreau 1989). In particular, the board is extraordinarily dense, requiring manual interaction to finish its wiring. The board has about 2900 connections in 111 square inches. This example is particularly appealing, even though there is no real hope of completely routing it, because it has been used inside Digital as a test of the quality of externally supplied vendor routers. A direct comparison is surveyed in figure 16.

Specifically, note that neither router finishes all connections: ELF completes 91 percent of the nets, and this particular production run finishes 94 percent. The production solution is only somewhat better but requires significantly more memory space because the production system represents all six PCB layers, even though only two layers are routable. Both ELF and the production solution used a similar number of vias. This result is considered successful given ELF's current knowledge of routers.

Conclusions

In this chapter, I suggested that for real-world applications such as VLSI design software, automatic program synthesis is workable. However, I strongly believe that it is essential to integrate both generic program synthesis knowledge and domain-specific knowledge to create practical program synthesis environments. Toward this end, a program synthesis architecture was developed that relies on using these two critical knowledge sources to select appropriate algorithms and data structures and then transform these selections into executable code. A prototype system, ELF, working in the domain of IC

Experiments	Space Required (bytes)	Routing Time (VAX 8800 sec.)	Wires Routed	Wirelength (inches)
PCB router	41K	489	2552/2792	3696
Digital Production- Quality Router	2.2MB	512	2594/2792	4090

Figure 16. Comparison with a Production Router.

and PCB wire-routing tasks, demonstrates the feasibility of these ideas. Specifically, ELF demonstrates the necessity of the careful integration of domain knowledge with program synthesis knowledge to guide the selection of the necessary algorithms and data structures. I illustrated the selection of data structures and algorithms for both gate-array and PCB routers and demonstrated the successful performance of the synthesized routers.

References

Aho, A.; Hopcroft, J.; and Ullman, J. 1974. *The Design and Analysis of Computer Algorithms.* Reading, Mass.: Addison Wesley.

Barstow, D. 1979. An Experiment in Knowledge-Based Automatic Programming. *Artificial Intelligence* 12:73–119.

Brownston, L; Farrel, R.; Kant, E.; and Martin, N. 1985. *Programming Expert Systems in OPS5.* Reading, Mass.: Addison Wesley.

Doreau, M. 1989. Private correspondence, Carnegie-Mellon University, February 1989.

Hightower, D. 1983. The Lee Router Revisited. In Proceedings of ICCAD, 1983: IEEE ICCAD Conference. Washington, D.C.: IEEE Computer Society.

Kant, E. 1983. On the Efficient Synthesis of Efficient Programs. *Artificial Intelligence* 20(3): 253–306.

Lee, C. 1961. An Algorithm for Path Connections and Its Applications. *IRE Transactions on Electronic Computers,* September, 246–265.

Liu, S. 1979. Automatic Data Structure Choices in SETL. Ph.D. diss., Courant Institute of Mathematical Sciences, New York Univ.

Low, J. R. 1978. Automatic Data Structure Selection: An Example and Overview. *Communications of the ACM* 21(5): 376–385.

McCartney, R. 1987. Synthesizing Algorithms with Performance Constraints, Technical Report, Dept. of Computer Science, Brown Univ.

Ohtsuki, T. 1986. Maze Running and Line Search Algorithms. In *Layout Design and Verification*, ed. T. Ohtsuki, 99–132. Amsterdam: North Holland.

Rowe, L., and Tonge, F. 1978. Automating the Selection of Implementation Structures. *IEEE*

Transactions on Software Engineering 4(6): 494–506.

Schonberg, E.; Schwartz, J.; and Sharir, M. 1981. An Automatic Technique for the Selection of Data Representations in SETL Programs. *ACM Transactions on Programming Language and Systems* 3:126–143.

Setliff, D. 1989. Knowledge-Based Synthesis of Custom VLSI Router Software. Ph.D. diss., Electrical and Computer Engineering Dept., Carnegie-Mellon Univ.

Soukup, J. 1981. Circuit Layout. In Proceedings of the IEEE 69, 1281–1304. Washington, D.C.: IEEE Computer Society.

❧ SECTION FOUR ❧

Knowledge Compilation

The goal of knowledge compilation research is to combine the domain-independent advantages of knowledge interpreters with the efficiency advantages of specialized hand-derived algorithms. Knowledge interpreters such as expert system shells solve problems by interpreting domain-specific knowledge bases using general-purpose inference algorithms, such as backward chaining and constraint propagation. To obtain generality, they cannot exploit the special properties of any particular problem or domain and, hence, are inefficient compared to specialized algorithms. In contrast to knowledge interpreters, knowledge compilers derive efficient specialized algorithms by compiling, not interpreting, domain-specific knowledge and design knowledge. The research goal is knowledge compilers that effectively exploit large and diverse bodies of explicitly represented task-specific knowledge to derive efficient task-specific algorithms.

Search control is a dominant theme of the chapters in this section. Knowledge compilers are themselves domain independent, in contrast to the domain-specific program synthesizers described in the previous section. The number of possible inputs and outputs for a domain-independent synthesizer is much larger than for a special-purpose synthesizer, so the search space is much larger. Without search guidance, knowledge compilers are as inefficient during program synthesis as knowledge interpreters are during problem solving.

Tom Dietterich, Jack Mostow, and James Bennett organized an influential workshop on knowledge compilation in 1986 with the sponsorship of ACM and Oregon State University. Many authors in this book attended this workshop, which attracted researchers from the fields of automatic programming, logic programming, and machine learning. The goal of knowledge compilation research is to combine the domain independent advantages of knowledge interpreters with the efficiency advantages of specialized hand-derived algorithms.

The first three authors, Jack Mostow, Christopher Tong, and Wesley Braudaway, are all members of the Artificial Intelligence and Design Project at Rutgers Universi-

ty. One of the project's goals is to automate the synthesis of efficient computer-aided design software. In contrast to the domain-specific approach of Setliff's research described in the previous section, they are seeking general principles applicable across many domains. Robert McCartney, currently on the faculty at the University of Connecticut, describes work begun with his Ph.D. dissertation research at Brown University on the efficient derivation of efficient programs in computational geometry. Robert Hall, currently a member of AT&T Bell Laboratories, summarizes his recent Ph.D. dissertation research at the Massachusetts Institute of Technology on a knowledge-based approach to program optimization.

Mostow's chapter first reviews the emerging field of knowledge compilation. The chapter then describes the DIOGENES system that synthesizes heuristic search algorithms, a line of research extending back to Mostow's Ph.D. dissertation research at Carnegie Mellon University. DIOGENES synthesizes programs by interactively transforming high-level specifications formulated as generate-and-test algorithms into efficient code. Some transformations move constraints from tests in the original algorithm into generators in the final algorithm, so that the final algorithm never generates many unacceptable solutions. This movement of constraints into generators is called constraint incorporation and is more fully described in Braudaway's chapter. At each step of a transformational derivation, DIOGENES computes the applicable transformations, and the user selects one of them. Thus, initially the user provides the search guidance. However, when the user modifies a specification, the XANA subsystem of DIOGENES replays the original transformation sequence with appropriate modifications to derive a new algorithm. Thus, DIOGENES can reuse the search knowledge encapsulated in the original transformation sequence.

Tong's chapter describes a divide-and-conquer approach to search control in knowledge compilation. Feasibility and effectiveness rules classify the problem constraints into separate groups that are then transformed into algorithm components by specialized knowledge compilers. Tong's graduate students have been building these specialized knowledge compilers; one of them is the RICK compiler described in Braudaway's chapter. The separate algorithm components are then composed into a final algorithm. To date, Tong's research has focused on spatial configuration problems and is illustrated with the example of synthesizing a program that lays out the floor plan of a house.

Braudaway's chapter summarizes part of his recent Ph.D. research and illustrates the importance of coordinating algorithm design and representation (data structure) design. Braudaway's RICK compiler is a specialist for incorporating local constraints into generators. To incorporate local constraints into a hierarchically defined generator, the representation of the constraints must be compatible with the hierarchical decomposition of the generator. RICK solves this compatibility problem through a least commitment approach to deriving the hierarchical decomposition of the generator. The initial specification abstractly represents a generator, with no a priori commitment to its hierarchical decomposition. RICK coordinates constraint incorporation with the derivation of the hierarchical decomposition of a generator, thus avoiding the need to backtrack during program synthesis.

McCartney's chapter first describes the MEDUSA system developed during his Ph.D. dissertation research. MEDUSA has automatically synthesized dozens of planar intersec-

tion algorithms in computational geometry. Part of the specification given to MEDUSA *is a performance constraint on the final algorithm.* MEDUSA *spends more time when given a tighter performance constraint, thus trading program synthesis efficiency for the efficiency of the resulting algorithm. McCartney's chapter then describes a framework for search control during program synthesis that was implemented in* MEDUSA. *The key is to decompose the search space into independent or quasi-independent search spaces.* MEDUSA'S *search space is defined by a hierarchy of tasks and subtasks. McCartney defines two types of subtask independence—functional independence and cost independence—and shows how* MEDUSA *uses them to control search during program synthesis. Cost constraints provide early pruning during program synthesis. The use of asymptotic cost complexity considerably simplifies the propagation of cost constraints and leads to greater cost independence because lower-order terms are ignored.*

Robert Hall summarizes his Ph.D. dissertation research on automatically optimizing computer programs by removing redundant computations. The mechanism he studied is the redistribution of intermediate results by adding extra data flow links from the output of intermediate computations to the input of other computations. This approach introduces a limited form of function sharing that is also characteristic of other engineering disciplines, such as mechanical design. Opportunities for redistribution arise in many contexts, including the adaptation of preexisting software components to particular problems. Hall's optimizer takes as input a partial specification of a program, a structural representation of a program based on data and control flow, a partial proof of correctness, and a set of test cases. Plausible redistribution candidates are found through test-case filtering; their safety is then certified using either limited automated reasoning or further empirical testing and incremental automatic debugging. Explanation-based generalization is used to derive correctness conditions that can be used in both the candidate search phase and the certification stage.

The chapters in this section illustrate a variety of knowledge-based approaches to search control during program synthesis. Mostow's DIOGENES *system reuses previous transformational derivations by adapting them to modified specifications. Tong's system classifies problem constraints into categories that are handled by specialized knowledge compilers, such as Braudaway's* RICK *compiler.* RICK *avoids search by taking a least commitment approach to refining the generator representation in test incorporation. McCartney's* MEDUSA *system decomposes a search space into independent or quasi–independent search spaces by making use of functional independence and cost independence of subtasks. Hall's optimizer combines analytic and empirical techniques to provide search guidance in deriving redistributions.*

Search control is also a dominant theme of the chapters in the next section on formal derivation systems. The approaches overlap; for example, like DIOGENES, *some of these formal systems can reuse previous transformational derivations. In the next section, the metalevel programs that provide search guidance are called tactics and strategies. The chapters are more formal and mathematical than the chapters in this section.*

A Transformational Approach to Knowledge Compilation:

Replayable Derivations of Task-Specific Heuristic Search Algorithms

Jack Mostow

This chapter describes an emerging area of research called knowledge compilation and how it can improve computer-aided design (CAD). Productivity in certain areas of design has grown increasingly dependent on CAD tools, computer programs that automate the analysis, synthesis, or evaluation of designs. Many such tools have been developed to perform specialized design tasks or help human designers perform them more efficiently by taking over some of the computational details. Although good tools make it possible to create designs faster than by hand, they are time consuming and expensive to construct. The most efficient tools are typically limited to narrow applications—hard to modify when the task changes and infeasible to reuse for other design tasks.

The development of new CAD tools is sometimes a limiting factor in design for rapidly evolving technologies. Consider what happens when a new fabrication technology (such as gallium arsenide in VLSI) or a new style of design (such as systolic circuits) is invented. Such an advance cannot be exploited until it is possible to design artifacts that make use of it. If the design process requires CAD tools, they must first be developed. For example, at the Spring 1989 Defense Advanced Research Projects Agency VLSI Contractors' Meeting, many researchers reported that brittle and buggy CAD tools were a principal bottleneck in developing novel circuit designs. Thus, methods for developing better CAD tools faster could substantially accelerate progress in design areas that rely on them. They could also make it feasible to automate specialized design tasks that are currently performed by hand because it is too expensive to develop CAD tools for them.

The traditional approach to developing new CAD tools is to manually develop specialized algorithms. The disadvantage of this approach is the cost of algorithm development and maintenance. A specialized algorithm or tool is rarely reusable for other applications, thanks to the specialization that provides its efficiency. Modifying a specialized algorithm to keep pace with changing technology is difficult and error prone—a phenomenon all too familiar to developers of CAD tools.

To reduce the cost of software development and maintenance, expert system shells provide a *knowledge interpretation approach* in which a generic shell operates on a domain-specific knowledge base. In this approach, the user specifies easily understandable domain-specific rules, which are then interpreted by the general-purpose shell to solve instances of the problem. Ideally, the rules are easy to modify and maintain. No explicit algorithm development is necessary, but the rules must be written for the particular type of interpretation engine used by the expert system shell, for example, backward chaining, constraint propagation, or problem decomposition. The overwhelming disadvantage of knowledge interpretation is that it is inefficient compared to the speed of specialized algorithms: Because the algorithms and data structures used by the interpreter must be generic, they cannot exploit idiosyncrasies of any particular domain.

The Knowledge Compiler Approach

The knowledge interpreter, or generic shell, approach and the specialized algorithm approach represent contrasting trade-offs between generality and power. The former provides tools that are easy to build and modify but is inefficient, and the latter achieves efficiency but at the cost of flexibility. How can we combine the advantages of both approaches to eliminate their disadvantages?

The *knowledge compilation approach* seeks to combine the efficiency of specialized algorithms with the simplicity, understandability, modifiability, and reusability of explicit knowledge representations by automating the translation of such representations into efficient algorithms. Thus, knowledge

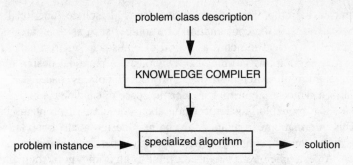

problem class description

KNOWLEDGE COMPILER

problem instance ──────▶ specialized algorithm ──────▶ solution

Figure 1. The Knowledge Compiler Approach.

compilation can be described as the automated transformation of explicitly represented knowledge about some class of problems into an efficient algorithm for solving instances of this class. This approach is illustrated in figure 1.

Because the structure of a specialized algorithm exploits knowledge about a particular design task, it can be much faster than a general algorithm or an expert system shell that directly interprets an explicit representation. However, because the knowledge is represented in an explicit, declarative, application-neutral form, it should be easy to modify and reuse for other tasks. Similarly, the compilation methods are represented in a general form that can be reused to create algorithms for other design tasks. Therefore, the knowledge compilation approach, if successful, should make it much easier to develop new CAD tools without sacrificing their efficiency.

Knowledge compilation aims at a long-term payoff. We expect that the effort invested in developing knowledge compilers will make new algorithms and tools much easier to build. When the application requirements change, they will be recompiled with significantly less effort—and fewer bugs—than modifying the code by hand, as is done today. Once knowledge compilation reaches this stage, it should more than repay the research effort invested in it.

The problem addressed in this chapter consists of finding a design (in some medium) that satisfies certain criteria, where the space of possible designs and the criteria to be satisfied are givens. Such problems include many design synthesis problems solved by CAD tools for parametric design (which consists of choosing values for a known set of parameters) and configuration design (which consists of combining components from a known set). However, this type of synthesis problem is by no means specific to design; for example, it includes many scheduling and routing problems. Conversely, it does not include the difficult process of defining the space of possible solutions and the appropriate criteria to satisfy—a crucial aspect of design.

The space of possible configurations is generally huge or even infinite. For VLSI design, we might think of the space of possible configurations as all the combinations of choices for what to put (metal, semiconductor, insulator) at each point on the chip. The solution criteria would include functional requirements as well as the consumption of resources such as time, area, and power. Even if we treat the chip as a grid of one-square-micron cells, the number of configurations is immense. Obviously, a practical design algorithm cannot afford to search more than a tiny fraction of this space.

Specialized synthesis algorithms reduce the space of candidate solutions to a tractable size by exploiting information about the class of problems they solve. This information can include the common design goals, book knowledge about the domain, simplifying assumptions, experience, empirical data, and so on. An example of a specialized synthesis algorithm in the domain of VLSI is a programmed logic array (PLA) (Savage 1983) generator, which is specialized to synthesizing circuits laid out in a regular array of a certain form. In extreme cases, there is sufficient information to eliminate search altogether; that is, the algorithm constructs the solution without considering alternative candidates. In other cases, the search is reduced to a much smaller space of choices but is not completely eliminated.

Research in knowledge compilation seeks to automate the process whereby information about a class of problems is used to reduce the amount of search needed to find solutions. For design problems, this research addresses such questions as How can knowledge about a domain be converted into the forms needed for design? and How can heuristics for searching the design space automatically be discovered? These questions are hard.

To answer them, research in knowledge compilation is more or less following this historical sequence: First is the manual construction of specialized algorithms. Many such algorithms have been constructed to solve practical problems. From the viewpoint of research on knowledge compilation, they constitute data on the phenomena of interest—examples of how various kinds of information can be exploited to reduce search. Second is the rational reconstruction of such algorithms, case studies analyzing how they could have been generated by computer (Mostow and Swartout 1986; Mostow and Voigt 1987). The purpose of these studies is to make explicit the underlying methods used in developing the algorithms. Third is the development of knowledge compilation methods capable of generating new algorithms. These methods codify the heuristic algorithm design ideas identified in the case studies. To derive new algorithms, they must be formulated in more general terms than their specific applications that appear in the case studies. Much of the research on knowledge compilation is at this stage, including the DIOGENES project reported here. Fourth is the development of practical knowledge compilers for growing classes of problems. To be practical, a knowledge compiler must have enough methods to generate a useful range of algorithms.

Knowledge compilation overlaps algorithm synthesis and automatic programming in its goal of synthesizing efficient programs and its methods for doing so. In fact, the distinction between them is somewhat tenuous at best and is more a question of research emphasis than a clear-cut difference in content. Research in knowledge compilation has focused on how to bring as much domain knowledge as possible to bear on the synthesis process and has mainly concentrated on deriving algorithms for specialized single-domain applications similar in scope to expert systems. In contrast, research in algorithm synthesis has focused on how to derive algorithms that are as efficient as possible and has mainly concentrated on deriving rather general algorithms that can be applied to many domains.

Overview of DIOGENES

DIOGENES is an experimental knowledge compiler. It takes a problem statement as input and produces an algorithm as output. The problem statement describes a space of possible solutions and lists the criteria that an acceptable solution should meet. Thus, DIOGENES is well suited to the sort of design synthesis problems naturally specified in this form, provided it can derive good heuristic algorithms for solving such problems.

DIOGENES is based on an iterative model of the process of designing heuristic algorithms, a model in which the work can be shared between human and computer. This model takes the form of a *nested loop*, where the outer loop formulates the specification of the problem class, and the inner loop implements an efficient algorithm to meet the specification. The need for iteration arises because the resulting algorithm might not be acceptable. Acceptability depends on how much of the class the algorithm handles, the quality of the solutions it produces, and the efficiency with which it runs. If the algorithm is unacceptable, the specification is reformulated, or the implementation strategy is changed, and the algorithm is reimplemented accordingly. This process repeats until an acceptable algorithm is obtained.

The algorithm synthesis process performed by DIOGENES should not be confused with the processing performed by the synthesized algorithm. The algorithm itself inputs a specification of a particular problem instance and finds a solution. The problem instance specification includes a value for each input parameter that appears in the specification of the problem class. How much search (if any) is used by the algorithm to find a solution depends on how much knowledge about the problem class is incorporated in the algorithm.

DIOGENES operates interactively. It transforms a specification into an algorithm by applying a sequence of transformations chosen by the user from its catalog. The user is responsible for evaluating the acceptability of the resulting algorithm and deciding whether and how to modify the specification. DIOGENES partially implements a modified specification by replaying the applicable portion of the original transformation sequence, and the user completes the implementation by selecting additional transformations to apply. DIOGENES was used to derive algorithms for several versions of a simple mechanical gear train design problem as well as a small fragment of a VLSI circuit router.

I now introduce the gear train problem and use it to illustrate two iterations of the DIOGENES algorithm design process, interrupting to describe how DIOGENES represents and executes algorithms, transformations, and derivations. In the first iteration, a naive formulation of the problem is specified and transformed into an algorithm that turns out to be unacceptable. In the second iteration, a revised specification is partly implemented by replaying the derivation of the first algorithm, and the implementation is then completed by applying some additional transformations. The example is concluded by discussing how this algorithm could further be improved. DIOGENES is evaluated and compared with other knowledge compilers, and the future prospects for this approach.are assessed

Example Design Task: Choosing Gear Train Ratios

The example task arises in the course of designing a gear train such as the one depicted in figure 2. A gear train consists of a series of gear pairs attached to rotating shafts. A gear pair consists of one gear driving another. The ratio of the number of teeth on each one determines the ratio of the rotational speeds of the shafts to which they are attached. For example, the first gear pair in figure 1 consists of the 30-tooth gear on the first shaft driving the 20-tooth gear on the second shaft, so that the second shaft rotates 1½ times faster than the first shaft. Because the gear train has three gear pairs with ratios 30:20, 30:20, and 40:30, it produces an overall rotational speedup of 3 from the first (input) shaft to the last (output) shaft. This gear train has the mechanically desirable properties of being fairly short—only three gear pairs—and evenly spreading the speedup over them.

The task consists of choosing what sequence of gear ratios to use. (We ignore such issues as how to lay out the gears and shafts or choose the materials that they are made of.) A problem in this class is characterized by a desired speedup ratio and a set of standard gear pairs available for achieving it; more precisely,

Given a desired ratio R and a set of standard gear ratios, find a sequence, s, of them that
- Is standard: (for all x in s) x is in StandardRatios
- Is short (that is, has few gear pairs): Small(Length(s))
- Is fairly uniform: (for all x in s) x ≈ Average(s)
- Achieves the desired ratio: Product(s) = R

How a Specification Is Formulated for DIOGENES

This model of heuristic algorithm design begins with an incompletely specified problem statement in which the space of possibilities is well defined, but the solution criteria are somewhat ambiguous. To make them

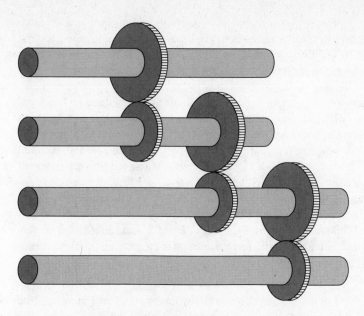

Figure 2. A Gear Train with Gear Ratios 3/2, 3/2, 4/3 and Speedup of 3.

more precise, these criteria must be formulated as constraints or preferences. Each constraint must be satisfied, and the preferences should be optimized subject to the constraints.

Suppose we decide to treat all four criteria in the gear train problem as constraints. This formulation can be paraphrased as "find a short uniform gear train that achieves the desired ratio." As we see later, alternative choices lead to other formulations with different behavior.

How a Specification Is Represented in DIOGENES

To reason about the formulated design problem, DIOGENES must somehow represent it. An extensional representation of the space of possible designs is impractical because there are too many; for example, there are infinitely many sequences of standard gear pairs. Instead, DIOGENES represents the space as an algorithm for searching it. This intensional representation provides a concise encoding of the space. The so-called algorithm might be terribly (even infinitely) inefficient, but this inefficiency doesn't matter because the purpose of the algorithm is representation, not execution. By representing the design problem in the language of algorithms, we can use algorithm transformation techniques to transform the initial algorithm into an efficient one.

In principle, an algorithm could be represented in almost any programming language. However, some representations are much easier to reason about than others. DIOGENES represents search algorithms in terms of three kinds of algorithm components (Mostow 1988, 1989b): generators, testers, and sorters. In addition, DIOGENES has schemas for higher-level constructs such as the generate-and-test method and depth-first search defined in terms of these components.

A *generator* emits successive elements of some set or sequence. The notation [S] –x→ indicates a generator for the set S, where the name x refers to any element of S. DIOGENES has various types of generator constructs, of which the following are relevant to our example: (1) an *enumerator,* denoted m..n, counts from m to n; (2) a *Cartesian product,* denoted S^n , generates all n-tuples of elements in the set S; and (3) a *Kleene product,* denoted S*, generates all sequences of elements in the set *S*, that is, all strings over the alphabet S. A *tester*, denoted <C>, filters generated elements that violate the test C. A *sorter*, denoted –S→ Sort(P), orders the set S according to the preference P. For example, our initial formulation of the gear train problem is represented as follows:

[Reals*] –s→ <Standard> → <Short> → <Uniform> → <AchievesRatio>.

Here [Reals*] denotes a Kleene product over the set of real numbers (the alert reader can realize that every gear ratio must be a rational number because each gear has an integral number of teeth; however, the initial formulation of a problem is rarely perfect, as this example illustrates), and the notation –s→ binds the name s to each sequence of reals; so, the problem formulation can be paraphrased as

Generate all sequences of real numbers.
    For each sequence *s,*
        Test if it's <u>standard, short, uniform,</u>and achieves the desired ratio.

(The underlined constraints are explained later.)

Internal Schematic Representation of Algorithms in DIOGENES

The notation previously used is (in somewhat cleaned-up form) the external form that DIOGENES presents to the user, and is designed for human readability. However, for internal purposes, DIOGENES uses an object-oriented representation designed to support execution, inference, and transformation.

The DIOGENES internal representation has a schema for each type of generator (and other algorithm component) with appropriate slots. For example, the schema for Enumerator has LowerBound and UpperBound slots to represent the range m..n and a Counter slot to encode its current state. Schemas for higher-level constructs have slots for algorithm components. For example, the schema for GenerateAndTest has a Generator slot and a Test slot. Similarly, the schema for KleeneProduct has a BaseGenerator slot.

An algorithm is encoded in DIOGENES by instantiating some schema, that is, filling in its slots with objects of suitable types. These objects can be algorithm components represented as schema instances themselves, in which case the overall representation of the algorithm is a hierarchical structure of schemas. The external notation shown earlier is automatically produced from this internal structure by a prettyprinter. The actual output of the prettyprinter for this example is

```
[[[[[[*REALNUMBERSET*]]^* –s->
<ALL(ITEM,S)<ITEM MEMBERSHIP *STANDARDGEARSET*>>]->
<(NONOPERATIONAL-TEST SHORTSEQUENCE)(S)>]->
<(NONOPERATIONAL-TEST UNIFORMITY)(S)>]->
<LISTPRODUCT(S) = *RATIO*>]
```

For clarity, a more readable version will be used throughout the rest of the chapter. DIOGENES does not have a parser in the opposite direction (from the external notation into schematic structures), in part because the external notation does not specify schema types and is not required to have a unique parse.

How Algorithms Are Executed in DIOGENES

The operational semantics of the internal representation is defined by a recursive object-oriented interpreter for each schema. The interpreter for each type of generator defines how it responds to the same uniform protocol inspired by (Wile 1982). An Initialize message causes a generator to initialize its internal state. A Pulse message causes the generator to emit a value for its current state and to move to its next state. An Exhausted? message causes the generator to check whether it has anything left to emit. Such an interpreter was implemented for every schema used in DIOGENES. The purpose of this exercise was to work out the precise semantics. A compiler would provide more efficient execution but would take more effort to implement.

The interpreter for each generator specifies how to respond to each kind of message based on its current slot values, invoking other generators as needed. To illustrate, consider a GenerateAndTest whose Generator slot is filled by the generator G and whose Test is the predicate P. (In the DIOGENES external notation, it is written simply as [G] → <P>.) It responds to an Initialize message simply by relaying it to G. It responds to Pulse by pulsing G until G emits an element that satisfies P. It responds to Exhausted? by looking ahead to see if any such elements remain. As this example illustrates, each interpreter is simple because it does only a small amount of work, recursively passing the rest down to its slots. Moreover, the uniform protocol provides a useful kind of modularity in that the code for the interpreter does not depend on how the slots are instantiated. For example, the interpreter described for GenerateAndTest works no matter how its Generator slot is instantiated; it does not need to know what type of generator G is to properly invoke it. Thus, composition constructs such as GenerateAndTest provide the procedural glue that defines the composition. Other composition constructs reorder the output of a generator, apply a mapping to each element, nest two or more generators, or perform some kind of iteration. For example, if the generator G generates the elements of set S, then an instance of the KleeneProduct schema that has G in its BaseGenerator slot ([G*] in the DIOGENES external notation) will generate all sequences over the alphabet S.

Thus, the DIOGENES internal representation for the initial formulation of the gear train problem is a cascade of four nested GenerateAndTest components, one for each of the four tests. The innermost one, summarized in the external notation as [Reals*] –s→ <Standard>, is internally represented as shown in figure 3.

The Generator of the GenerateAndTest is a KleeneProduct that generates all (too many to count) sequences of real numbers. The Test is a UniversallyQuantifiedTest that is satisfied by a sequence only if every element of the sequence satisfies its Predicate. The Predicate checks if a given individual gear ratio is in the StandardRatios set ("item" refers to the element to be tested). Thus, the overall output of the GenerateAndTest is the set of all sequences of standard ratios. Of course, this set can be computed more efficiently, is now described.

How an Algorithm Is Derived in DIOGENES

The DIOGENES approach to converting a problem specification into an efficient algorithm consists of applying a series of speedup transformations chosen from a catalog. The series of transformations depends on the design problem and the implementation strategy. At each step, DIOGENES computes the set of applicable transformations, the user chooses one, and diogenes applies it.

Some of these transformations move constraints into generators. For example, one of the DIOGENES transformations applies to any GenerateAndTest whose Generator is a KleeneProduct and whose Test is a UniversallyQuantifiedTest that tests each sequence to see if every element satisfies some predicate P. The transformation moves the test earlier to generate only those sequences whose elements satisfy P. That is, it rewrites [G*] –s→ <forall x in s P(x)> as [([G] → <P>) *] –s→ . Before the transformation, the KleeneProduct forms all sequences over the alphabet generated by G; each such sequence is then tested. After the transformation, the KleeneProduct forms sequences over the restricted alphabet of elements that satisfy P; each such sequence is guaranteed to satisfy the original test.

In terms of schemas, this transformation operates as shown in figure 4. (The DIOGENES transformations are procedurally implemented in Common Lisp rather than in any specialized language designed for the concise expression of transformations on schemas. Before any effort was invested in designing such a language, it seemed advisable to develop a catalog of transformations to ascertain what kinds of constructs such a language might require.) In particular, it rewrites the innermost GenerateAndTest of the example as

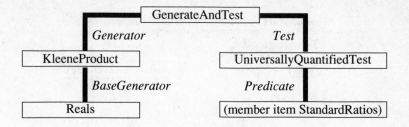

Figure 3. Internal Schematic Representation of an Algorithm Fragment.

the KleeneProduct shown in figure 5. This KleeneProduct first forms the subset of Reals that are standard ratios and then generates all sequences of them. Because the set StandardRatios is a subset of Reals, the GenerateAndTest can be eliminated. This speedup is accomplished by a transformation that simplifies [G] –x→ <x in S> to [S] when S is a subset of the elements generated by G.

As this example illustrates, determining whether a rule is applicable can involve some deduction. DIOGENES uses generic deduction rules attached to schemas, such as the fact that every element output by a GenerateAndTest satisfies the Test predicate. It has a rudimentary mechanism for propagating such information, which can be useful in ascertaining the applicability of a transformation. For example, one such transformation simplifies a Generate-AndTest to its Generator if the Test is redundant; that is, it is already satisfied by every generated element. Proving this condition requires information about the context in which the Test occurs. Constraint propagation is used to provide this information.

At this point the standard ratio constraint has fully been incorporated; that is, it requires no run-time testing because the transformed algorithm only generates sequences of standard ratios. Similarly, the short gear train constraint, which is formulated as *gear train length = 1 gear pair,* is incorporated by transforming the KleeneProduct into a generator of singleton sequences. By applying such transformations to the initial problem formulation, DIOGENES is able to incorporate the constraints previously underlined and obtains the following simple algorithm:

[StandardRatios[1]] –s→ <AchievesRatio> .

This algorithm can be paraphrased as follows:

Enumerate all standard ratios.
    For each one,
        Test if it achieves the desired ratio.

This algorithm is fast but rarely succeeds because it works only when the desired ratio happens to be one of the standard ratios. Thus, the efficiency of

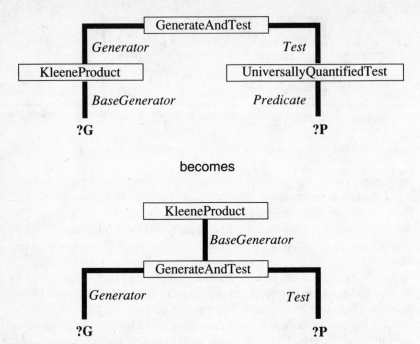

Figure 4. A Transformation in DIOGENES.

the algorithm is acceptable, but its coverage is not. In our example, the user recognized this deficiency simply by inspecting the algorithm. However, it appears straightforward to automatically detect by running the algorithm on a set of typical problem instances and noticing that it often fails to find a solution. Either way, deficient coverage indicates that the problem specification was inappropriately formulated.

How a Specification Is Revised for DIOGENES

Failure to solve an acceptable percentage of the problem class suggests that the problem specification is overconstrained. In this example, the cause of the deficient coverage is a decision to treat the short gear train criterion as a constraint that the gear train must be of length 1. To remedy the deficiency, the user relaxes this constraint into a preference for shorter gear trains. The revised formulation is represented as follows:

[Reals* → Sort(Length)] –s→ <Standard> → <Uniform> → <AchievesRatio> .

It can be paraphrased as

Generate all sequences of real numbers.
Sort them in order of increasing length.

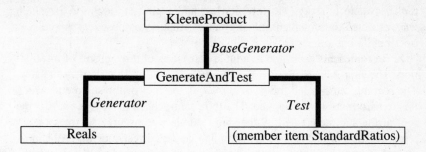

Figure 5. Effect of Applying a Transformation.

For each sequence *s*,
Test if it's standard, uniform, and achieves the desired ratio.

In this example, there is only one preference, but in more complex problems, there can be multiple, conflicting preferences. In such cases it is necessary to decide how to integrate them. Mostow and Swartout (1986) describe some general methods for integrating preferences. Mostow and Voigt (1987) show how some of these methods were used to integrate several (often conflicting) medical preferences in the course of deriving different versions of the therapy selection algorithm used in the expert system MYCIN.

How a Derivation Is Replayed by XANA

A change in the specification makes it necessary to reimplement the algorithm because the previous algorithm is no longer appropriate. However, many of the same implementation decisions incorporated in the original algorithm are still appropriate, even though the algorithm as a whole is not. Therefore, it makes sense to replay whichever decisions still apply rather than to force the user to repeat them. DIOGENES has a mechanism developed by Greg Fisher called XANA (Greek for "again") (Mostow and Fisher 1989; Mostow, Barley, and Weinrich 1989) that replays the subset of transformation steps from the implementation of the original algorithm that still apply to the revised specification.

Replaying a derivation involves a number of technical issues (Mostow 1989a), including the capture and representation of decisions in a form that can be replayed, the correspondence between old and new objects, and the appropriateness of replaying a given step. XANA captures decisions by simply recording each transformation step. As illustrated in figure 6, the DIOGENES transformations operate on hierarchical schema structures represented as trees whose nodes are schema names and whose arcs are slot names. Because the DIOGENES transformations can rearrange existing tree structure, XANA required significant extensions to the replay method used in the circuit design replay system BOGART (Mostow, Barley, and Weinrich 1989, 1990), which was restricted to refinement transformations that decompose leaves into sub-trees but do not modify existing tree structure.

XANA represents each step as a tuple consisting of three pieces of informa-tion. The first item is the name of the transformation rule used in the step. The second item, called the *source node*, is the root of the subtree to which this transformation was applied. The third item, called the *target node*, is the root of the subtree created by the step to replace the source subtree. XANA'S representation of nodes is designed to handle the correspondence problem. A node that appears in the initial specification is designated by the unique se-quence of arcs (slot names) leading to it from the root. For example, if the initial fragment shown in figure 6 represented the entire specification, then the node for Reals would be designated by the sequence (Generator BaseGenerator) because the root is a GenerateAndTest whose Generator is a KleeneProduct whose BaseGenerator is Reals.

A node created by a transformation step is designated by two pieces of in-formation: the transformation step and the unique sequence of arcs leading to the node from the root of the substructure created by the step. For example, the GenerateAndTest created by the transformation step shown in figure 6 is designated by the step and the singleton sequence (BaseGenerator) because the root of the subtree created by the step is a KleeneProduct whose BaseGenerator is the new GenerateAndTest.

This naming scheme is recursive because nodes are designated in terms of steps, and vice versa. Ultimately, every node is designated by the chain of steps that led from the initial specification to the creation of the node.

Given this scheme, XANA finds the new node corresponding to an old one simply by reinterpreting the same designation in the new context. That is, be-cause the old node is designated by instructions for finding it, XANA finds the corresponding new node by simply following those instructions starting from the root of the revised specification. (Actually, XANA achieves the same effect more efficiently by caching correspondences as it replays the derivation.) This process fails in contexts where the instructions cannot be followed. For example, the sequence (Generator BaseGenerator) cannot be applied to the root of the second tree in figure 6 because the KleeneProduct schema it rep-resents has no slot named Generator.

To replay a series of steps, XANA finds the new node corresponding to the source node for each step and applies the transformation rule for the step. If the corresponding node does not exist or if it violates the preconditions of the rule, the step is assumed to be inappropriate in the new context and is skipped. Skipping a step does not preclude replaying a later step, as long as the source node of the later step still has a corresponding new node that satisfies the preconditions of the rule.

In the example, XANA replays about half of the steps in the original deriva-

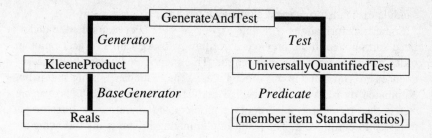

becomes

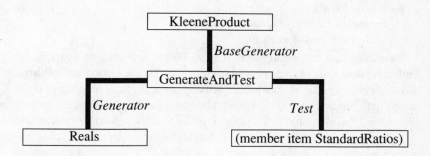

Figure 6. XANA Represents Steps as Transformations on Trees.

tion, producing the following algorithm:

$[0 \ldots \infty]$ -n$\rightarrow$ [StandardRatios^n] -s$\rightarrow$
Sort(Length) $\rightarrow$ <Uniform> $\rightarrow$ <AchievesRatio> .

This algorithm can be paraphrased as follows:

For n from 0 to infinity,
Generate all sequences of n standard ratios.
<u>Sort them by length.</u>
For each sequence *s,*
Test if it's uniform and achieves the desired ratio.

This algorithm eliminates some of the inefficiencies in the problem specification but requires further speedup to make it reasonably efficient. Fortunately, additional improvements that were not applicable to the original formulation are now possible.

How an Algorithm Is Improved in DIOGENES

DIOGENES speeds search algorithms primarily by reducing the number of candidates they consider (as opposed to, say, speeding the consideration of each candidate). Transformations can reduce search in various ways.

Some transformations eliminate expensive steps. For example, the underlined sorting step in the previous algorithm sorts sequences of gear ratios in order of increasing sequence length. This step is redundant because sequences are generated in this order already. The redundant sorting step is not eliminated by replaying the original derivation because there is no sorting step in the original formulation of the problem and, therefore, no transformation step to eliminate it. The result of eliminating it here is the following algorithm:

$$[0 \ldots \infty] \text{ -n} \rightarrow [\text{StandardRatios}^n] \text{ -s} \rightarrow \text{<Uniform>} \rightarrow \text{<AchievesRatio>} .$$

This algorithm can be paraphrased as

> For n from 0 to infinity,
>> For each sequence s of n standard ratios,
>>> Test its ratio and <u>uniformity.</u>

By eliminating the sorting step, it is no longer necessary to generate the (infinite!) set of all sequences of standard ratios before testing any of them. Consequently, the set of candidates actually considered is reduced to those tested until the first solution is found. The execution time of this transformed algorithm is proportional to b^n, where b is the number of standard ratios, and n is the sequence length of the first solution found. Here, b is called the *branching factor* of the search, that is, the number of choices at each point, and n is the *depth*, that is, the number of choice points on the successful path to a solution. Although this exponential-time algorithm terminates in finite time (assuming a solution exists), it will be slow unless the set of standard ratios is small, and the solution is a short gear train.

Another general transformation speeds a search algorithm by reducing the branching factor of the search. For example, the choice of gear pairs can be restricted by moving the underlined uniformity test earlier in the search process. Instead of generating a sequence of *n* gear pairs and then testing it for uniformity, the test is applied before generating the sequence. Here, a sequence is defined to be uniform if every element is close to the average of the sequence:

$$\text{Uniform(s)} = (\text{for all x in s}) \; x \approx \text{Average(s)} .$$

Thus, the improved algorithm looks as follows:

$$[0 \ldots \infty] \text{ -n} \rightarrow [\text{StandardRatios} \text{ -x} \rightarrow \text{<x} \approx \text{Average(s)>}]^n \text{ -s} \rightarrow \text{<AchievesRatio>}$$

This algorithm can be paraphrased as follows:

> For n from 0 to infinity,
>> For each standard gear ratio,
>>> Test if it's close to average.
>> For each sequence of n such ratios,
>>> Test if it achieves the desired ratio.

This algorithm is faster than the previous algorithm by the exponential factor r^n, where r is the fraction of standard ratios that are close to the average ratio of the gear pairs in the gear train. This speedup is obtained by eliminating the consideration of nonuniform sequences.

However, the expression "close to average" is nonoperational because the average cannot be computed until the complete gear train is generated. This expression must be operationalized to make the algorithm executable. As this example illustrates, to apply a useful transformation, other transformations might also be needed.

The term average is actually somewhat imprecise. There are various types of averages, including arithmetic, geometric, and harmonic. Imprecision in the problem specification can be exploited by choosing the most computationally expedient interpretation. For reasons that will soon become clear, it is here the geometric average, defined as

GeometricAverage(s) = Product(s) $^{1/\text{Length}(s)}$ if s is non-empty .

DIOGENES must rewrite the geometric average of a sequence of gear pairs as an expression that can be computed before the sequence is generated. To do so, it exploits the fact that problem constraints can be used to deduce values. In particular, the expression Product(s) , denoting the product of the ratios in the generated sequence s , can be rewritten as the desired ratio R based on the AchievesRatio constraint. Similarly, Length(s) is known to be n at the point in the algorithm where the average is needed. Thus, the expression GeometricAverage(s) , which is nonoperational at the point in the algorithm where it occurs, can be rewritten as the operational expression $R^{1/n}$. We can now see the computational motivation for interpreting Average as GeometricAverage. If we interpreted Average instead as, say, ArithmeticAverage(s) , defined as Sum(s)/Length(s) , there would be no way to predict its value before the sequence s is completely generated.

Of course, interpreting an underspecified problem based solely on computational expedience runs the risk of violating important considerations omitted from the problem specification. It is important to make sure that decisions about the specification make sense in the domain. However, it is worthwhile to point out that human developers of practical heuristic systems make many choices motivated primarily by computational considerations— choices that either have little known impact on domain-level considerations, or else embody trade-offs necessary for efficiency (Mostow and Swartout 1986; Swartout and Balzer 1982). Judging the appropriateness of a decision with respect to criteria omitted from the specification is outside the scope of DIOGENES and, therefore, is the responsibility of the user.

The restriction that s be non-empty can be enforced by starting n at 1 instead of 0. The resulting operational algorithm is

$[1 .. \infty] -n \rightarrow [\text{StandardRatios} -x \rightarrow \langle x \approx R^{1/n} \rangle]^n -s \rightarrow \langle \text{AchievesRatio} \rangle$.

It can be paraphrased as

> For n from 1 to infinity,
>> For each standard gear ratio,
>>> Test if it's close to $R^{1/n}$.
>> For each sequence of n such ratios,
>>> Test if it achieves the desired ratio.

This algorithm still takes time exponential in the length of the solution (number of gear pairs in the gear train) but with a much lower branching factor. (The exact value depends on how the relation "close" [≈] is defined.) The algorithm is efficient enough to be respectable and to illustrate the DIOGENES transformational approach.

How an Algorithm Could Further Be Improved

A fully optimized algorithm is too complex to derive here, but it is worthwhile to list some of the methods that could be used. Transformations were defined on paper for these methods, but not all of them were implemented in DIOGENES, and some are implemented in less than full generality for want of a sufficiently powerful deduction mechanism for tasks such as theorem proving, expression simplification, and symbolic algebraic manipulation. Rather than implement such a mechanism, it could make sense to use an already-existing one, such as the RAINBOW engine in the KIDS program-transformation system (chapter 19).

Treat a Constraint as a Budget and Interpolate: If the desired ratio is treated as a budget to be distributed over the elements of the generated sequence, the portion of it that remains unspent after generating some of the elements can evenly be redistributed over the rest. In the gear train example, if the first ratio in a sequence happens to be somewhat larger than $R^{1/n}$, the target value for the next ratio is readjusted to be somewhat smaller. The idea of budgeting was developed in DONTE (Tong 1988), where it was used for circuit design, and generalized into a knowledge compilation method in MENDER (Voigt and Tong 1989; chapter 11), where it was applied to a floorplan design task.

Trade Coverage for Speed: The search can be reduced by abandoning a partial sequence as soon as its product exceeds R. This transformation assumes that every standard ratio is greater than 1, which is not necessarily the case; thus, it restricts the algorithm to problems (or at least solutions) in which every ratio is greater than 1. This example illustrates the important point that speedup transformations can introduce simplifying assumptions that restrict the class of problems covered or the space of solutions generated.

Impose a Canonical Order: The initial problem statement is expressed as finding a sequence of gear ratios, but the order of elements within the sequence is unimportant. Rather than generate the same gear train in all possible orders, the search can be reduced by imposing some canonical order, say, from small to large. Thus the choice for the ith element in the sequence restricts the $i + 1$th element to be equal or greater. This restriction reduces the branching factor of the search by eliminating alternative orderings of the same gear train.

Identify Exploitable Properties: Related to the idea of introducing a simplifying assumption is the idea of identifying and exploiting a property left implicit in the initial problem formulation. An example of such a property is the fact that every gear ratio is a rational number. This property might be exploited by explicitly representing each ratio as a pair of integers of the form <numerator, denominator>, where both integers can be represented as bags of prime factors. The product of ratios is a pair of the same form and can be simplified by canceling factors common to the numerator and denominator. Suppose the desired ratio R is a rational number and must be achieved exactly. In the example in figure 2, a gear pair consisting of a 30-tooth gear and a 20-tooth gear might be represented as $<2^1 * 3^1 * 5^1 , 2^2 * 3^0 * 5^1 >$, and the goal ratio of 3 might be represented as $<2^0 * 3^1 * 5^0 , 2^0 * 3^0 * 5^0 >$. It might then be possible to speed the generation of an acceptable sequence of gear ratios by favoring the addition of elements that insert factors required in the goal (such as the 3 in the numerator) and penalizing the addition of elements that insert extraneous ones. However, such reasoning about mathematical representations is sophisticated and would be challenging to automate in any general fashion.

Trade Optimality for Speed: Another way to reduce search is to keep only the best k partial sequences, say, those closest to the interpolated ratio. This method, called *beam search* (Barr and Feigenbaum 1981, Volume 1, pp. 350-351), reduces run time from an exponential function of the solution length n to a linear function of k^n. The cost of this reduction is that beam search can occasionally miss the optimal solution, namely, when the partial sequence it begins with is not one of the k most promising ones.

Propagate Constraints: Because the desired value of Product(s) is known, the last gear pair must have the desired ratio R divided by the product of the first $n-1$ ratios. Instead of generating possible values for the last element, it can be computed directly and then checked to see if it qualifies as a standard ratio.

Use Finite Differencing: This method eliminates a repeated computation of some expression by updating its value whenever necessary (Paige and Koenig 1982). For example, when a new ratio is added to the end of the sequence being generated, it is not necessary to recompute the expression "the product of the ratios chosen so far" from scratch. Instead, the value of this expression can simply be updated by multiplying the previous product by the new element.

Evaluation of DIOGENES

DIOGENES was sufficiently implemented to derive several algorithms but is far from covering any meaningful class of problems. Despite its incomplete status—in fact, because of it—one should ask what it would take for DIOGENES (or knowledge compilation in general) to work.

The answer has three parts: First, a correct problem specification must somehow be developed. Second, a set of methods adequate to implement the specification is required. Third, there must be some means of choosing the appropriate combination of methods to apply. Each issue is now illustrated by analyzing what DIOGENES does about it.

Getting the Specification Right

Specification is an iterative process. The initial specification given to a knowledge compiler is liable to be an inaccurate and incomplete description of the problem that really needs to be solved. Errors must be exposed and corrected. Ambiguities must be resolved. Coverage and quality must sometimes be compromised for efficiency.

If we look at the specification process itself as a kind of search, we can see that it involves both the capability to propose specification changes and the capability to decide which changes to actually make.

Some of the DIOGENES transformations propose specification changes in the form of transformations that choose interpretations for ambiguous terms (for example, average) or introduce simplifying assumptions (for example, all ratios exceed 1).

Assumptions made during knowledge compilation should be checked against data or theory. Knowledge compilation methods that alter the problem specification can be viewed as introducing assumptions about the domain. Such assumptions might be verified analytically against a domain theory, tested empirically against a set of benchmark problems, or put to the user as questions.

In DIOGENES, the user must decide which transformations to apply and, thus, which assumptions and specification changes to approve. Such decisions generally appear to require domain-specific expertise and, thus, must be made by the user. However, the DIOGENES mechanism for replaying derivations does provide indirect support for iterative algorithm design by accelerating the reimplementation of a modified specification.

Getting an Adequate Set of Methods

The adequacy of a knowledge compiler's methods depends on their correctness and generality. Knowledge compilation methods must be debugged. Unless these methods can be proven correct, they can introduce bugs that must be found and fixed as part of knowledge compilation.

DIOGENES leaves the user responsible for writing correct transformation rules. The RAINBOW inference engine (Smith 1982) used in the KIDS program-transformation system (chapter 19) appears powerful enough to verify individual applications of some transformation rules, but verifying a rule in the abstract can be much harder, for example, when the rule is expressed procedurally or when its correctness depends on deep domain properties.

The methods used in a knowledge compiler should be general enough to amortize the cost of developing and implementing them. Although developing a specialized design algorithm by hand is difficult, it is generally easier than developing a knowledge compiler that can synthesize such an algorithm. To be worthwhile, a knowledge compiler must help construct enough algorithms to pay for the cost of its development. That is, it must satisfy the following inequality:

(cost of building the knowledge compiler) + (cost of using it to derive N algorithms)
  < (cost of developing the same algorithms by hand) .

The more algorithms the knowledge compiler can derive, the easier it is to pay off. However, some tasks are so complex that it is worthwhile to develop tools to help solve them, even if the tools only apply to this task. In such cases, a one-shot knowledge compiler might pay off even though it is only applied to a single task.

The DIOGENES methods are its transformations, and they apply to multiple domains, not just gear train design. Some of them have been used to help derive algorithms for selecting therapies in MYCIN (Mostow and Voigt 1987), playing the card game of Hearts (Mostow 1981, 1983a), or routing wires in VLSI (Kelly 1988). A few of the DIOGENES transformations that simulate general deduction mechanisms were implemented in a nongeneral fashion in lieu of constructing such mechanisms. As of June 1989, DIOGENES had 56 rules, of which 41 were general transformations on search algorithms, 2 embodied knowledge specific to the gear train problem, and 13 deduced constraints on the data flowing through the algorithm or propagated such constraints from one point to another.

The repertoire of methods used in a knowledge compiler should cover enough problems to be useful. Just because each method is general doesn't mean that the set of them is enough to solve many problems. The DIOGENES repertoire is its catalog of a few dozen transformations, which is not enough to cover any interesting class. It remains to be seen how large a catalog must be to be useful—dozens of transformations? Thousands? Is any finite catalog sufficient? The answer to this question will largely determine the amount of work needed to bring the transformational approach to the point of practical application.

The user should be able to compensate for gaps in the system's methods. If the knowledge compiler is only complete enough to cover 90 percent of the steps needed to derive a good algorithm, it should let the user supply the other

10 percent. This flexibility would greatly extend its scope because the class of algorithms derivable with a given set of methods is much smaller than the class of almost derivable algorithms. If the application frequency of the methods follows a Zip distribution, or an 80-20 rule in which 20 percent of the methods covers 80 percent of the steps, not only would a catalog of the most frequently used methods be useful, but a complete catalog would likely be impractical.

However, it remains to be seen what class of users can understand an interactive knowledge compilation system well enough to supply the missing steps or how the system can explain the state of a derivation clearly enough that the user can see what is needed.

In DIOGENES, users can intervene only by creating or editing a transformation rule. From the user's viewpoint, it could be easier to directly edit the algorithm, and let the system infer a new rule, as in the LEAP learning apprentice system for Boolean circuit design (Mitchell, Mahadevan, and Steinberg 1985).

Controlling the Knowledge Compilation Process

An automatic knowledge compiler must be able to choose an appropriate series of methods to apply. If the methods are represented as transformation rules, this search-control problem means choosing a sequence of rule applications.

In DIOGENES, the user chooses the sequence of transformation rules to apply and the expressions to apply them to. DIOGENES computes which rules are applicable at each point (typically half a dozen) and applies the rules chosen by the user, although it automatically fires certain rules that perform deductions. Even a trivial algorithm takes over 10 transformation steps to derive; nontrivial algorithms can require dozens or more. Transformations are chosen to speed the algorithm or pave the way for others that do. It remains to be seen how to automate these choices, although some analysis (Fawcett 1988) indicates that the search-control techniques used in one of the DIOGENES precursors (Mostow 1983b, 1983c) might help. If the catalog is both large and incomplete, the search control problem becomes especially difficult, somewhat like navigating across a large expanse of rough terrain without knowing in advance which ravines can be bridged.

Capturing the knowledge compilation process in the machine offers a way to replay previous decisions. A record of these decisions captures the tradeoffs and assumptions incorporated in the final algorithm. It can be edited and replayed to accommodate specification changes (design iteration) or derive algorithms for similar design problems (design by analogy) (Mostow 1989a; Mostow, Barley, and Weinrich 1989). Thus, a transformation sequence is much more reusable than the resulting algorithm or the solutions it outputs.

DIOGENES can replay transformation sequences using XANA (Mostow and Fisher 1989). XANA works for the design iteration case; that is, it helps automate the inner loop of reimplementing a modified specification.

Related Work

To put DIOGENES in context, it is now compared with a number of other systems. The prototypical knowledge compiler automatically maps a well-defined specification of a problem into a complete, correct implementation entirely at compile time. Therefore, one can characterize different systems in terms of the classes of problems they address and the ways in which they vary from this prototype.

The class of problems solved by a knowledge compiler is characterized by the range of specifications they can input and the range of implementations they can output. The class of specifications DIOGENES can, in principle, take as input lies toward one end of a spectrum of generality because it allows any specification expressed in terms of generators, testers, and sorters. The KIDS program-transformation system (chapter 19) lies even further toward the general end of the spectrum, because its specification language is broad. Generic program-transformation systems developed by Partsch (1986, 1989), Darlington and Burstall (Darlington 1976; Burstall and Darlington 1977), Cheatham (1981), Paige (Paige 1986; Paige and Henglein 1987), and others can be viewed as lying at this end as well (for a survey of this work, see Partsch and Steinbruggen [1983] as well as some of the more recent work reported in Mostow [1985] and Rich and Waters [1986]). At the opposite end lies ELF (chapter 9), which is specialized to the domain of maze routing, as well as other domain-specific approaches to automatic programming (Barstow 1985). Somewhere in between lies KBSDE (chapter 11), which applies to a class of constraint-satisfaction problems involving spatial configuration. KIDS and KBSDE input well-defined specifications and produce correct implementations, and DIOGENES and ELF sometimes fill in details of the specification or make heuristic trade-offs as they proceed.

Some knowledge compilation systems, including DIOGENES, KBSDE, KIDS, and ELF, produce complete implementations, but others only produce individual components of an implementation. KBSDE comprises subsystems that produce such components: RICK (chapter 12) synthesizes constrained generators that generate all candidates satisfying certain problem constraints, MENDER (Voigt and Tong 1989) synthesizes patchers that repair candidates that violate constraints; and HiT (Mohan and Tong 89) synthesizes hierarchical problem-solving architectures in which abstract solutions are generated to satisfy some of the problem constraints and then refined into concrete solutions that satisfy the other constraints. LEAP (Mitchell, Mahadevan, and Steinberg 1985) and SCALE (Tong and Franklin 1989) produce decomposers that split problems into subproblems that can be solved more or less independently. FAILSAFE (Mostow and Bhatnagar 1987), its successor FAILSAFE-2 (Bhatnagar and Mostow 1990), and ABSOLVER (Mostow and Prieditis 1989) synthesize heuristics for state-space problem solvers: The FAILSAFE systems synthesize pruners, and ABSOLVER synthesizes sorters in the form of admissible evaluation functions.

Knowledge compilers vary in terms of the amount and type of guidance they require. Like DIOGENES, KIDS is an interactive system in which the user selects a sequence of transformations to apply, and the system applies them, recording the transformation sequence so that it can later be replayed. In contrast, KBSDE, ELF, and ABSOLVER automatically operate at compile time.

Some machine learning systems can be viewed as performing knowledge compilation at run time by using other information in addition to the problem specification. In LEAP, this information consists of example problem decompositions performed by the user. In SCALE and the FAILSAFE systems, the information consists of experience extracted from traces generated in the course of problem solving. LEAP, SCALE, and FAILSAFE all use explanation-based learning (Mitchell, Keller, and Kedar-Cabelli 1986) to convert such information into a useful form. The DESIGNER-SOAR algorithm design system (chapter 22) uses SOAR'S built-in chunking mechanism (Laird, Rosenbloom, and Newell 1986; Laird, Newell, and Rosenbloom 1987) to learn from its experience. The chunks learned in the course of designing an algorithm can be used later in the same design or in the design of subsequent algorithms.

Finally, knowledge compilers can be characterized by the level at which their output is expressed, which reflects which kinds of implementation decisions have been made and which ones are still open. DIOGENES and KBSDE produce algorithms composed of function-level components such as generators and testers. At this level, which roughly corresponds to the point where current high-level compilers can take over, the search space explored by the algorithm has been fixed, but lower-level details such as data-structure selection are left open. KIDS synthesizes algorithms in a high-level programming language that the REFINE compiler (Reasoning Systems 1987) can then compile. ELF goes all the way down to C code.

Power versus Generality for Knowledge Compilers

One principle suggested by the knowledge compilers surveyed is a trade-off between a knowledge compiler's generality (defined by what input problems it can solve) and its power (defined by the quality of its output and how much help it needs from the user to produce it). The knowledge compiler approach mentioned the power-versus-generality trade-off as it applies to algorithms: The narrower the problem class an algorithm covers, the more powerful it can be. The same trade-off applies one level higher, to knowledge compilers. That is, by restricting which classes of problems are addressed, it is possible to devise more powerful knowledge compilers that exploit the restrictions. For example, DIOGENES and KBSDE are restricted to problems expressed in terms of search. They exploit this restriction in the representations they use, which are tailored to express search algorithms rather than other kinds of algorithms. Thus in a representation with a built-in schema for depth-first search, it is not necessary to rederive a depth-first search algorithm from first principles; it is sufficient to map a given problem onto the schema and determine how the components of the schema should be instantiated. However, the domain of all search problems is broad. How can additional leverage be obtained by further restricting this domain?

The ELF system (chapter 9) embodies an interesting answer to this question. ELF synthesizes VLSI maze-routing programs from high-level specifications. Because each maze router solves a different class of routing problems, ELF can be viewed as a knowledge compiler specific to the domain of maze routing. Maze routers find wiring paths to connect two or more points on a circuit layout. They use variations of the same basic algorithm, depending on the type of routing problem they solve.

ELF exploits its restriction to the maze-routing domain in several ways. First, ELF's representation includes routing-specific features, such as the expected degree of congestion in the routing area and the size of the bounding box within which the router will search for a wiring path. This representation facilitates the concise specification of problems. Thus, the user can specify the problem simply by providing values for a number of familiar domain-specific features rather than having to figure out how to map it into more general computational terms and formulate a complex specification.

Second, ELF uses a built-in generic algorithm for maze routing. Instead of having to derive this algorithm from first principles, it only needs to figure out how to instantiate its components. KIDS and DIOGENES gain similar leverage from built-in schemas for some general types of search, but ELF takes the same idea further along the generality-versus-power trade-off curve.

Third, ELF's representation facilitates the concise specification of maze routers in domain-specific terms. For example, ELF has a built-in rule that says to use a larger bounding box if the routing area is congested. This rule concisely captures an important relationship in a form ready to apply during the construction of a maze router because the specification provides information about the expected degree of congestion. By building in domain-specific concepts such as congestion, the developer of the domain-specific knowledge compiler made it possible for subsequent users of the knowledge compiler to refer to these concepts without having to define them.

Conclusion

What are the future prospects for knowledge compilation? To assess this approach in the proper context, it is appropriate to ask how far it will have to get to pay off.

Ideally, one might want a completely general knowledge compiler that automatically produces efficient design algorithms for real domains. However, this utopian goal far exceeds the payoff point. A useful knowledge compiler need not be fully automatic, as long as it's easier for the user to assist the compiler than to develop an algorithm by hand. Similarly, a useful knowledge compiler does not need to be perfectly general—just enough to amortize the cost of its development. In fact, the first practical knowledge compilers might well be restricted, such as the ELF maze router generator (chapter 9), to narrow problem domains in which there are many different problem subclasses requiring their own efficient algorithms.

Thus, the goal of knowledge compilation is ambitious, but fail-soft in the sense that it could pay off handsomely without achieving full automation or complete generality. In particular, even interactive or specialized knowledge compilers might greatly accelerate the development of new CAD tools, thereby dramatically enhancing the productivity of designers, especially in the new and rapidly changing domains characteristic of modern technology.

Thus, knowledge compilation remains a promising area. Its potential payoff is considerable because it offers to combine the efficiency of specialized algorithms with the reusability of expert system shells and knowledge bases. Knowledge compilation can be viewed as "automating design automation," that is, the development of CAD tools. Just as CAD tools can make the design process faster, more reliable, and better documented by moving it into the computer, knowledge compilation should achieve the same advantages for the process by which CAD tools are developed. Moreover, progress is tangible. Current systems can already derive useful programs sufficiently complex that they would be difficult and error prone to develop by hand, let alone modify.

However, scaling up to more complex applications will require progress in several directions. To scale up to larger knowledge bases, larger search spaces, and larger designs, knowledge compilers will need to integrate many of the approaches now separately being investigated. To handle harder problems, the algorithms they synthesize will need to combine different kinds of components, including generators, testers, sorters, patchers, and decomposers. The architectures of these algorithms will need to fit the problems they solve, so that each piece of knowledge will be applied at the right point. Although some knowledge compilers based on fixed architectures might produce enough algorithms to be useful, escaping this restriction will require the flexibility to tailor the architecture to the problem. To further reduce the amount of search required to solve problems, some knowledge compilers will learn from their problem-solving experience to speed from one problem to the next or even while solving a single problem. As the example of ELF suggests, the first practical knowledge compilers will probably sacrifice generality to automate the synthesis of good algorithms for restricted domains by exploiting domain-specific representations and algorithm design knowledge. It might become possible to combine domain specific knowledge compilation methods with more general ones, but it will require the ability to translate among the multiple representations involved.

Finally, knowledge compilation requires a considerable amount of knowledge, both domain-specific and algorithmic. It's clear that the DIOGENES catalog of a few dozen transformations is far from complete even for the limited domain of gear train design, let alone for the general class of heuristic search algorithms. ELF, which is restricted to the narrow domain of maze routing, covers this domain well but represents a dissertation's worth of development effort. KIDS, which synthesizes a broader range of algorithms, represents years of effort by a number of researchers, and applying it to a given problem still requires the user to encode a specification of the task, definitions of concepts in the domain, and lemmas for reasoning about them. In short, developing the body of machine-representable knowledge needed to build and use practical knowledge compilers will take a massive knowledge-acquisition effort. The feasibility of the knowledge compilation approach might turn out to depend on the extent to which the burden of acquiring this knowledge can be transferred from human to machine by replacing manual knowledge engineering with machine-aided knowledge acquisition (for example, of transformations) and machine learning (for example, of heuristics).

Acknowledgments

I would like to thank Richard Cooperman and Greg Fisher for implementing DIOGENES; Tom Fawcett and Kevin Kelly for contributing to earlier work; Chris Tong, Phil Franklin, Armand Prieditis, and William Cohen for commenting on earlier drafts; Jeremy Wertheimer and Allen Goldberg for their useful reviews; Susan Finger, Robert McCartney, and Michael Lowry for giving such helpful editorial guidance; and the members of the Rutgers University AI/Design Project for providing good ideas and a stimulating environment.

References

Barr, A., and Feigenbaum, E. A., eds. 1981. *The Handbook of Artificial Intelligence,* volume 1, 350–351. Los Altos, Calif.: William Kaufmann.

Barstow, D. 1985. Domain-Specific Automatic Programming. *IEEE Transactions on Software Engineering* SE-11(11):1 321–1336.

Bhatnagar, N., and Mostow, J. 1990. Adaptive Search by Explanation-Based Learning of Heuristic Censors. In Proceedings of the Eighth National Conference on Artificial Intelligence, 895–901. Menlo Park, Calif: American Association for Artificial Intelligence.

Burstall, R. M., and Darlington, J. 1977. A Transformational System for Developing Recursive Programs. *Journal of the ACM* 24(1): 44–67.

Cheatham, T. E. 1981. An Overview of the Harvard Program Development System. In *Software Engineering Environments*, ed. H. Hunke. New York: North Holland.

Darlington, J., and Burstall, R. M. 1976. A System which Automatically Improves Programs. *Acta Informatica* 6:41–60.

Fawcett, T. 1988. A Control Strategy for Heuristic Search Algorithm Design, Working Paper, 104, AI/Design Project, Rutgers Univ.

Kelly, K. 1988. Router Derivation #1, Working Paper, 103, AI/Design Project, Rutgers Univ.

Laird, J. E.; Rosenbloom, P. S.; and Newell, A. 1986. Chunking in Soar: The Anatomy of a General Learning Mechanism. *Machine Learning* 1(1): 11–46.

Laird, J. E.; Newell, A.; and Rosenbloom, P. S. 1987. Soar: An architecture for General Intelligence. *Artificial Intelligence* 33(1): 1-64.

Mitchell, T. M.; Mahadevan, S.; and Steinberg, L. 1985. Leap: A Learning Apprentice for VLSI Design. In Proceedings of the Ninth International Joint Conference on Artificial Intelligence, 573–580. Menlo Park, Calif.: International Joint Conferences on Artificial Intelligence.

Mitchell, T. M.; Keller, R. M.; and Kedar-Cabelli, S. T. 1986. Explanation-Based Generalization: A Unifying View. *Machine Learning* 1(1):47—80.

Mohan, S., and Tong, C. 1989. Automatic Construction of Hierarchical Generate-and-Test Algorithms. In Proceedings of the Sixth International Workshop on Machine Learning, 483-484. San Mateo, Calif.: Morgan Kaufmann.

Mostow, J. 1990. Towards Automated Development of Specialized Algorithms for Design Synthesis: Knowledge Compilation as an Approach to Computer-Aided Design. *Research in Engineering Design* 1(3): 167–186.

Mostow, J. 1989a. Design by Derivational Analogy: Issues in the Automated Replay of Design Plans. *Artificial Intelligence* 40(1–3): 119–184.

Mostow, J. 1989b. An Object-Oriented Representation for Search Algorithms. In Proceedings of the Sixth International Workshop on Machine Learning, 489–491. San Mateo, Calif.: Morgan Kaufmann.

Mostow, J. 1989c. Towards Knowledge Compilation as an Approach to Computer-Aided Design. In Proceedings of the National Science Foundation Engineering Design Research Conference, 475–490. Washington, D.C.: National Science Foundation.

Mostow, J. 1988. An Object-Oriented Representation for Search Algorithms, Working Paper, 107, AI/Design Project, Rutgers Univ.

Mostow, J., ed. 1985. Special Issue on Artificial Intelligence and Software Engineering. *IEEE Transactions on Software Engineering* SE-11(11): 1253–1408.

Mostow, D. J. 1983a. Machine Transformation of Advice into a Heuristic Search Procedure. In *Machine Learning*, eds. J. G. Carbonell, R. S. Michalski, and T. M. Mitchell, 367–403. San Mateo, Calif.: Morgan Kaufmann.

Mostow, J. 1983b. Operationalizing Advice: A Problem-Solving Model. In Proceedings of the Second International Machine Learning Workshop, 110–116. Urbana-Champaign, Ill.: Univ. of Ill.

Mostow, J. 1983c. A Problem-Solver for Making Advice Operational. In Proceedings of the Third National Conference on Artificial Intelligence, 279—83. Menlo Park, Calif.: American Association for Artificial Intelligence.

Mostow, J. 1981. Mechanical Transformation of Task Heuristics into Operational Procedures. Ph.D. thesis, Computer Science Dept., Carnegie-Mellon Univ.

Mostow, J., and Bhatnagar, N. 1987. Failsafe—A Floor Planner That Uses EBG to Learn from Its Failures. In Proceedings of the Tenth International Joint Conference on Artificial Intelligence, 249–255. Menlo Park, Calif.: International Joint Conferences on Artificial Intelligence.

Mostow, J., and Fisher, G. 1989. Replaying Transformational Derivations of Heuristic Search Algorithms in DIOGENES. In Proceedings of the DARPA Workshop on Case-Based Reasoning, 94–99. Washington, D.C.: Defense Advanced Research Projects Agency.

Mostow, J., and Prieditis, A. E. 1989. Discovering Admissible Heuristics by Abstracting and Optimizing: A Transformational Approach. In Proceedings of the Eleventh International Joint

Conference on Artificial Intelligence, 701–707. Menlo Park, Calif.: International Joint Conferences on Artificial Intelligence.

Mostow, J., and Swartout, W. 1986. Towards Explicit Integration of Knowledge in Expert Systems: An Analysis of MYCIN's Therapy Selection Algorithm. In Proceedings of the Fifth National Conference on Artificial Intelligence, 928–935. Menlo Park, Calif.: American Association for Artificial Intelligence.

Mostow, J., and Voigt, K. 1987. Explicit Integration of Multiple Goals in Heuristic Algorithm Design. In Proceedings of the Tenth International Joint Conference on Artificial Intelligence, 1090–1096. Menlo Park, Calif.: International Joint Conferences on Artificial Intelligence.

Mostow, J.; Barley, M.; and Weinrich, T. 1990. Automated Reuse of Design Plans in Bogart. In *Artificial Intelligence in Engineering Design*, eds. C. Tong and D. Sriram. Forthcoming.

Mostow, J.; Barley, M.; and Weinrich, T. 1989. Automated Reuse of Design Plans. *International Journal for Artificial Intelligence in Engineering* 4(4): 181–196.

Paige, R. 1986. Programming with Invariants. *IEEE Software*, 56-69.

Paige, R., and Henglein, F. 1987. Mechanical Translation of Set-Theoretic Problem Specifications into Efficient Ram Code—A Case Study. *Journal of Symbolic Computation* 4(2).

Paige, R., and Koenig, S. 1982. Finite Differencing of Computable Expressions. *ACM Transactions on Programming Languages and Systems* 4(3): 402–454.

Partsch, H. 1989. From Informal Requirements to a Running Program: A Case Study in Algebraic Specification and Transformational Programming. *Science of Computer Programming* 11(3): 263–297.

Partsch, H. 1986. Transformational Program Development in a Particular Program Domain. *Science of Computer Programming* 7(2): 99–242.

Partsch, H., and Steinbruggen, R. 1983. Program Transformation Systems. *ACM Computing Surveys* 15(3): 199–236.

Reasoning Systems. 1987. REFINE User's Guide. Reasoning Systems, Inc., Palo Alto, Calif.

Rich, C., and Waters, R. C., eds. 1986. *Readings in Artificial Intelligence and Software Engineering*. San Mateo, Calif.: Morgan Kaufmann.

Savage, J. E. 1983. Three VLSI Compilation Techniques: PLA's, Weinberger Arrays, and Slap, A New Silicon Layout Program. In *Algorithmically Specialized Computers*, eds. L. Snyder, L. J. Seigel, H. J. Seigel, and D. Gannon. New York: Academic.

Smith, D. R. 1982. Derived Preconditions and Their Use in Program Synthesis. In *Proceedings of the Sixth Conference on Automated Deduction*, ed. D. W. Loveland, 172–193. Lectures Notes in Computer Science 138. New York: Springer-Verlag.

Swartout, W., and Balzer, R. On the Inevitable Intertwining of Specification and Implementation. *Communications of the ACM* 25(7): 438–440.

Tong, C. 1988. Knowledge-Based Circuit Design. Ph.D. thesis, Computer Science Dept., Stanford Univ.

Tong, C., and Franklin, P. 1989. Tuning a Knowledge Base of Refinement Rules to Create Good Circuit Designs. In Proceedings of the Eleventh International Joint Conference on Artificial Intelligence, 1439–1445. Menlo Park, Calif.: International Joint Conferences on Artificial Intelligence.

Voigt, K., and Tong, C. 1989. Automating the Construction of Patchers That Satisfy Global Constraints. In Proceedings of the Eleventh International Joint Conference on Artificial Intelligence, 1446-1452. Menlo Park, Calif.: International Joint Conferences on Artificial Intelligence.

Wile, D. S. 1982. Generator Expressions, Technical Report, USC/Information Sciences Institute.

11

A Divide-and-Conquer Approach to Knowledge Compilation

Christopher Tong

In this chapter, I describe research in an emerging area of AI called knowledge compilation (Dietterich 1986). *Knowledge compilation* converts explicitly represented domain knowledge into an efficient algorithm for performing some task in this domain. Knowledge compilation techniques for computer-aided design (CAD) applications are being developed. Design synthesis problems can often be formulated in terms of searching for a solution in a well-defined but potentially enormous space of possibilities, for example, a space of possible cell configurations and wire routings in very large system integration (VLSI) design. Although general-purpose, operations research algorithms are sometimes adequate for coping with such problems, these methods often fail to fully exploit idiosyncratic properties of a particular task or to make sufficient use of available domain knowledge. By taking advantage of such domain-specific information, knowledge compilation techniques can potentially generate specialized algorithms that outperform general-purpose algorithms. Knowledge compilation also has the potential to generate algorithms for specialized tasks not easily handled by general-purpose approaches.

Knowledge Compilation

The view of knowledge compilation presented here can best be characterized in terms of a three-level hierarchy. Each level in the hierarchy corresponds to a different way of describing knowledge-based systems. At the *knowledge level* (Newell 1982), a system is described in terms of the class of problems it will be required to solve, the criteria that determine acceptable solutions, and the domain knowledge needed in the problem-solving process. Knowledge-level descriptions specify the task to be performed without prescribing the method of performing it. At the *function level*, a system is described in terms of functional components, such as generators, testers, and patchers. These components are high-level abstractions of actual code. They are configured into a variety of architectures in order to represent a variety of search algorithms. At the *program level*, a system is described in terms of a conventional programming language such as Lisp, Prolog, or C. The actual procedures and data structures used to implement search algorithms are described at this level. The relationships among these three levels are described more fully in Tong (1987).

These levels can be related to the standard software-engineering terms of requirements, specifications, the design, and the implementation. Requirements are fuzzy knowledge-level descriptions. Specifications are complete and correct knowledge-level descriptions. A function-level description is a restricted kind of design. A program-level description (or, simply, program) is an implementation.

Knowledge compilation converts a knowledge-level specification of a task into a function-level search algorithm. The search algorithm is required to correctly implement the knowledge-level specification. For this reason, the algorithm must somehow incorporate the knowledge found in the knowledge-level description. Once such a function-level description is constructed, existing automatic programming tools can be used to generate a program-level description. For example, my notion of the function level roughly corresponds to the input level of several existing automatic programming tools such as REFINE (Smith, Kotik, and Westfold 1985).

The function level serves as a planning island that decomposes the task of designing a search algorithm into two parts. In principle, our knowledge compilation research need only be concerned with the first part (compiling the knowledge level into the function level), leaving the second part (compiling the function level into the program level) to be handled by conventional automatic programming systems. For this reason, I expect the function-level concept to provide considerable leverage for research in compiling search algorithms.

Compilation of Specifications for Spatial Configuration Tasks

The Knowledge-Based Software Development Environment (KBSDE) project (Tong 1986) has been studying issues in knowledge compilation. KBSDE has initially been focusing on developing knowledge compilation techniques that are applicable to spatial configuration design synthesis problems. I define a spatial configuration as an object composed of standard parameterized parts arranged in positions and orientations to meet a specified set of spatial constraints. Spatial configurations arise in a variety of design applications, including VLSI design, mechanical design, architectural design, and urban planning. Many such design tasks can be given a knowledge-level specification having the following general form:

Generate($s \mid T(s) \wedge P(s)$) ,

or "Generate an object s of type T that satisfies predicate P." The type definitions $T(s)$ specify the (usually hierarchical) structure of object s in terms of its parts, subparts, and so on.[1]

The solution constraints $P(s)$ specify any additional criteria that the object s must meet to be a valid solution, for example, spatial constraints on the positions and orientations of components and constraints relating the parts to each other. The goal is to synthesize efficient algorithms from such specifications.

The domain of house floor planning is one example of a spatial configuration design task. The knowledge-level specification for a class of simple floor-planning tasks is shown in figure 1. The specification requires finding an object s of data type Floorplan. A floor plan comprises a number of individual rooms; thus, type Floorplan has components $R_1, \ldots, R_n$. Each room can be represented by a corner point, a length, and a width; hence, type Room has components $<x,y,l,w>$. The specification also requires that the floor plan satisfy the Acceptable predicate. This predicate is a conjunction of five different spatial constraints that an object must meet to be an acceptable solution to the problem. Individual floor-planning problem instances can differ in the house length, the house width, and the number of rooms in the house.

This research has initially focused on generating a family of algorithms that are particularly appropriate to spatial configuration tasks. We are developing knowledge compilation methods that generate search algorithms composed of the following types of function-level components and architectures, among others. (These components and architectures are described more fully in Incorporating Knowledge into Search Algorithms.) *Generators* produce a stream of objects of a particular data type. *Testers* filter objects that violate given constraints. *Constrained generators* produce a stream of objects of a particular data type that also satisfy a given constraint, without resorting to explicit testing (for example, integers that are greater than five are produced by simply initializing the generator at five). *Hill-climbing patchers* modify objects that fail to satisfy a given constraint, to make them satisfy the constraint. *Generate-and-test architectures* use a generator to produce a stream of objects of a given data type and a tester to filter the objects failing to satisfy given constraints. *Generate-test-and-patch architectures* combine a gener-

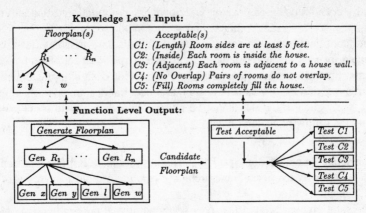

Figure 1.
The Floor-Planning Design Problem and an Inefficient Generate-and-Test Algorithm.

ate-and-test architecture with a hill-climbing patcher. Multiple abstraction-level architectures initially generate an abstract solution satisfying some of the constraints and then generate a fully specified solution that is a refinement of the abstract solution and also satisfies the remaining constraints.

Researchers expect KBSDE to achieve considerable leverage as a result of focusing on the specialized type of knowledge compilation problem previously defined. This specialization was chosen in light of a principal lesson learned during previous research in the area of automatic software generation. Previous efforts to develop general automatic programming tools met with only limited success. Somewhat more success was achieved by specializing either the input or the output of the compilation process. The input can be specialized by focusing on a class of problems that share a common structure, for example, set-theoretic fixed-point problems (Paige and Henglein 1987), or problems that share common knowledge, for example, problems arising in the domain of oil well logging (Barstow 1985). The output can also be specialized by developing methods specifically designed to generate a specialized class of algorithms, for example, divide-and-conquer algorithms (Smith 1985), global search algorithms (Smith 1988), or local search algorithms (chapter 20). KBSDE involves specialization of both the knowledge-level input (to spatial configuration problems) and the function-level output (to search algorithms composed of a particular family of function-level components). Therefore, we expect KBSDE to avoid the pitfalls of excessively general approaches and build on the success previously achieved through specialization.

A Divide-and-Conquer Model of Knowledge Compilation

A more precise characterization of knowledge compilation is possible as a result of restricting the types of problems to be compiled and the types of algorithms to be synthesized. In particular, I can now define what it means for a function-level search algorithm to correctly incorporate a knowledge-level description. A knowledge-level description is said to be incorporated if two conditions are met: (1) each constraint appearing in $T(s)$ or $P(s)$ must be assigned to at least one function-level component responsible for enforcing the constraint and (2) each function-level component must actually be capable of enforcing the constraints assigned to it. Knowledge compilation can, thus, be viewed as a process of mapping knowledge-level constraints onto function-level components.

Compilation Choices. Constraints can be assigned to function-level components in a variety of ways. The efficiency of the resulting algorithm depends on how individual constraints are assigned to function-level components. Consider the following two alternative ways of implementing the knowledge-level specification of the floor-planning task shown in figure 1: One rather naive approach would synthesize the generate-and-test algorithm shown in figure 1. This algorithm could be synthesized by converting the type description $T(s)$ (that is, Floorplan(s)) into a generator and converting the solution constraints $P(s)$ (that is, Acceptable(s)) into a tester [Liew and Tong 1987]). The generator of this algorithm successively outputs all objects of type Floorplan. It does so using a hierarchy of generators corresponding to the hierarchical decomposition of floor plans given in figure 1. Thus, an object of type Floorplan is created by invoking a room generator to create each room. An object of type Room is created by invoking a positive integer generator for each parameter of a room description. After a candidate solution has completely been generated, the candidate is passed to the testing component of the algorithm. The tester determines whether the candidate floor plan satisfies the constraints specified by the Acceptable predicate. For this purpose, the tester simply applies a sequence of tests corresponding to the conjuncts appearing in the definition of $P(s)$.

A more sophisticated knowledge compiler might synthesize the algorithm shown in Figure 2. This algorithm is organized in terms of a two-level problem-solving architecture. At the abstract level, the algorithm uses a constrained generator that incorporates the constraint C4 (no overlap) to generate abstract solutions to the floor-planning problem. Each abstract solution constitutes an incomplete description of an actual solution. It describes only the topological and directional relationships between rooms R1, R2, and R3 without precisely describing their sizes, shapes, or positions. At the base level, abstract solutions are refined into complete solutions that also satisfy constraints C1, C2, C3, and C5. A constrained generator produces floor plans that satisfy constraints C1 (length), C2 (inside), and C3 (adjacent) and that are consistent with the directional constraints in the abstract solution. Finally, a hill-climbing patcher modifies these floor plans to satisfy the constraint C5

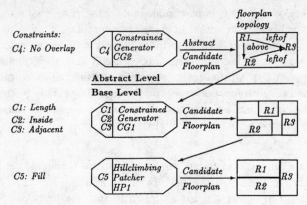

Figure 2. A More Sophisticated Floor-Planning Algorithm.

(fill). The hill-climbing patcher repeatedly modifies the candidate floor plan in a manner that increases the total area covered. The patcher terminates when the entire house area is filled.

A Divide-and-Conquer Strategy. The KBSDE project has adopted a divide-and-conquer approach to knowledge compilation. This approach involves (1) decomposing the problem by classifying constraints into groups and assigning each group to a single function-level component responsible for satisfying the constraints in the group, (2) implementing each function-level component by invoking a compiler that specializes in constructing components of this type (each specialized compiler takes a set of constraints as input and synthesizes a function-level component that enforces the constraints), and (3) composing the function-level components into the problem-solving architecture under construction.

The classification of constraints plays a central role in the process previously outlined. Classification serves to map each knowledge-level constraint onto a function-level component responsible for enforcing this constraint. The mappings must all be feasible; that is, each constraint must be mapped to a function-level component capable of enforcing this constraint. The mappings must also be effective; that is, constraints must be mapped to function-level components in a manner that results in an efficient search algorithm.

The issue of feasibility can be illustrated by the constraints C1 ("Room sides are at least 5 feet") and C5 ("Rooms completely fill the house") from the floor-planning example shown in figure 1. Constraint C1 can feasibly be mapped to a constrained generator, as was done in generating the sophisticated algorithm shown in figure 2. This mapping is feasible because C1 is a local constraint; that is, it depends on a single variable appearing at a leaf in the floor-plan part hierarchy. In contrast to this mapping, constraint C5 cannot feasibly be mapped to a constrained generator of individual rooms because C5 is a global constraint on all the rooms; that is, it depends on the entire candidate solution. Constraint C5 can nevertheless be assigned to a tester (as in the naive algorithm) or a hill-climbing patcher (as in the sophisticated algorithm). In general, KBSDE will use feasibility rules to determine which function-level components could potentially implement a given constraint. Feasibility rules are discussed in Incorporating Knowledge into Search Algorithms.

In many situations, a given constraint can feasibly be mapped to more than one function-level component. Not all feasible mappings lead to equally efficient algorithms. For instance, the sophisticated algorithm of figure 2 is much more efficient than the naive generate-and-test algorithm of figure 1. In general, KBSDE will use effectiveness rules to heuristically determine which constraint assignments to function-level components lead to the most efficient algorithms. Examples of effectiveness rules are provided in Controlling the Compilation Process.

The divide-and-conquer approach of KBSDE offers an important advantage over unrestricted transformational models of knowledge compilation (Tappel 1980). Such systems typically involve a combinatorially explosive search process in the absence of a control structure that places tight restrictions on the application of transformations. In contrast, a divide-and-conquer approach splits the compilation problem into parts that are handled by specialized compilers. Because the compilers operate with relative independence, the divide-and-conquer approach avoids the combinatorial explosion inherent in unrestricted transformational systems. Therefore, the control problem is considerably simplified.[2]

Basic Research Questions and Answers

Researchers are addressing a number of research issues to develop KBSDE into a system that can synthesize important classes of heuristic algorithms in a cost-effective manner. The most important of these issues are outlined here. Each issue is stated in the form of a question. Associated with each question is a general description of the type of answer that is emerging from our research:

Q: How can a large family of search algorithms be described in terms of a small set of basic function-level components?

A: These algorithms can be described as specification of various types of function-level components and architectures for organizing these components into complete algorithms.

Q: In what ways can a given type of constraint be correctly incorporated into a search algorithm that finds an object satisfying the constraint?

A: A set of feasibility rules indicates whether a given type of constraint can correctly be incorporated into a given type of component. For each type of function-level component, a specialized compiler incorporates constraints into this type of component.

Q: What is the most effective way to incorporate a given type of constraint into a search algorithm that finds an object satisfying the constraint?

A: The most effective approach is to use a set of effectiveness rules that indicate which assignments of component constraints will result in efficient search algorithms. Asymptotic complexity analyses and empirical efficiency measurements support the effectiveness rules.

Q: How can researchers quickly incorporate a given set of constraints into a search algorithm?

A: Researchers can use a divide-and-conquer control structure that uses feasibility and effectiveness rules to assign constraints to function-level components and invokes a specialized compiler to construct each component type.

Research in these areas is presented in the following sections. Research aimed at developing specialized compilers for mapping constraints from the knowledge level to the function level is discussed in Incorporating Knowledge into Search Algorithms. Research on methods of determining the effectiveness of mappings and methods of quickly controlling the compilation process is discussed in Controlling the Compilation Process.

Incorporating Knowledge into Search Algorithms

In this section, I address the question of characterizing a large family of algorithms in terms of a small set of function-level components. I also discuss how particular types of constraints can correctly be incorporated into a search algorithm (that finds an object satisfying the constraint).

This research has focused on methods of mapping knowledge-level constraints into the following types of function-level components: generators, testers, constrained generators, hill-climbing patchers, and multiple abstraction-level architectures. KBSDE project researchers began developing a specialized compiler for each component type. Prototype versions of each system currently exist (at varying levels of development). Preliminary sets of feasibility rules were developed in parallel with the building of these compilers. The following subsections review the status of these specialized compilers. They also present preliminary feasibility rules for each compiler.

Synthesizing Generators and Testers of Composite Objects

Generate and test can be viewed as a default algorithm for solving problems of the form

Generate($s \mid T(s) \wedge P(s)$)

because the procedural embedding is so direct:

Generate(s | T(s));
Test(s,P(s));
Return(s).

This pseudocode should be interpreted as Generate an s that is an instance of $T(s)$. Test the predicate $P(s)$ on s. If the Test fails, backtrack to the Generate; if the Test succeeds, Return the value of s. (If the Generate runs out of values that can be generated, return failure.)

Although generate-and-test algorithms tend to be slow, they can be necessary when more sophisticated algorithms cannot be constructed. KBSDE contains relatively straightforward methods for constructing generate-and-test algorithms (Liew and Tong 1987). Related methods are described in Bennett and Dieterich (1986); Holte (1990); and Smith, Kotik, and Westfold (1985). As illustrated in figure 1, generators are constructed from the type constraints $T(s)$, and testers are constructed from the solution constraints $P(s)$. Generators of composite objects are constructed by recursively building a generator for each component and combining the component generators into a control structure that generates the full Cartesian product. Generators of primitive objects can extensionally be represented as lists (for example, Left, Right, Up, Down) or as intervals of integers (for example, [1,10]). KBSDE constructs testers by unfolding predicate definitions. Universally and existentially quantified expressions are converted into iterative procedures. Each quantified variable is associated with a data type. The data type definition is used to construct a generator of values of the quantified variable. KBSDE's methods for compiling generators and testers are implemented as part of the RICK (refinement-based constraint incorporator for compiling knowledge) compiler (chapter 12).

Mapping Constraints into Constrained Generators

A simple generate-and-test architecture is extremely inefficient for all but trivial problems. For example, for a 9- x 9-foot house with 4 rooms, the problem solver in figure 1 generates a space containing 10^{16} candidate solutions (4 rooms, each having 4 parameters that each range over 10 values). Only a small number, 288, of these solutions are acceptable, satisfying constraints C1 through C5. The size of this space is clearly exponential in the number of rooms. With a uniform distribution of acceptable solutions in the space of candidate solutions, the generate-and-test problem solver will generate roughly $10^{16} \div 288 \approx 3 \cdot 10^{13}$ candidates before finding a solution. This problem solver is exponentially slow.

The RICK compiler (chapter 12) specializes in mapping constraints at the knowledge level into constrained generators at the function level. RICK takes as input a hierarchical data type description $T(s)$ and a collection of constraints $C_1(s),...,C_n(s)$. The output of RICK is a constrained generator that generates all composite objects of type T that satisfy constraints $C_1,..., C_n$. Constrained generators produced by RICK are required to operate in polynomial time in the size of their input plus their output (for example, for the floor-planning example, size is a function of the number of rooms, the house length, and the house width). In the absence of this condition, a constrained generator could simply be constructed by hiding a generator and a tester inside a black box. The polynomial bound guarantees that constrained generators will operate without the explicit testing of candidates. The polynomial time is typically used to evaluate functional expressions (for example, for lower and upper bounds on the range of legal values or for the entire set of legal values) in the current context. Constraints incorporated in a constrained generator do not also need to be tested; hence, the backtracking that accompanies testing is eliminated.

A constraint P on a composite object that can be localized to part of the solution is called a *localizable constraint* . If a localizable constraint can additionally be incorporated into the primitive part generators, it is called a *local constraint*. Intuitively, local constraints are those that constrain relatively small portions of the entire solution. RICK specializes in localizing constraints to part generators and incorporating the localized constraints by constructing constrained generators. The localization activity (sometimes called *test movement*) is worthwhile in its own right, even if constraints cannot fully be incorporated; the smaller the parts being tested, the smaller the amount of superfluous backtracking.

RICK uses a combination of two strategies for incorporating a set of constraints $C_1,..., C_n$ into a generator of parts with type T_p. Neither strategy is sufficient by itself. One strategy enumerates all objects of type T_p and tests them against constraints $C_1,..., C_n$ at compile time. By remembering which objects satisfy the constraints, this effort would be amortized over future problem-solving episodes. Unfortunately, this strategy fails if the type predicate T_p describes a large or infinite set of objects. A second strategy attempts to directly incorporate constraints $C_1,..., C_n$ by adjusting upper or lower bounds used in defining a generated range of values. For example, the constraint $x \geq 5$ can be incorporated into a generator of positive integers by adjusting the integer generator's bounds from $[1,\infty]$ to $[5,\infty]$. Unfortunately, not all constraints can directly be incorporated in such a simple manner.

RICK modifies and combines these two strategies in a manner illustrated in figure 3. Suppose that RICK were given the constraints C2 (inside) and C3 (adjacent) as input. The modified *enumeration strategy* systematically generates abstract cases, rather than individual objects, at compile time. Each abstract case represents an entire set of individual objects. RICK enumerates abstract cases in two steps:

In the first step, RICK divides each constraint C_i into a number of abstract cases representing different ways of satisfying constraint C_i. The abstract cases are derived from the different values that can be assumed by the existentially quantified variables in the predicate calculus representation of the constraint. For example, the constraint Adjacent (C3) has the following form: "For each room, there exists some house side and some room side such that

1. *Enumerate Abstract Cases*
   of each Constraint

2. *Select Consistent Combinations*
   of Abstract Cases

3. *Incorporate each Consistent*
   Combination into a Separate
   Generator

$P = Rooms\ INSIDE\ house\ \wedge\ Rooms\ ADJACENT\ to\ house\ wall$

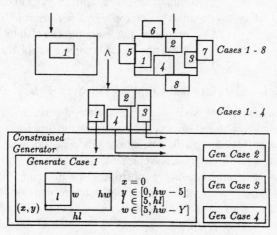

Figure 3. RICK'S Synthesis of Constrained Generators.

the room side is contained in the house side." The room side can take on 4 possible (abstract) values (Left, Top, Right, Bottom), as can the house side. Of the 16 possible combinations, only 8 are actually consistent. Hence, the Adjacent constraint has 8 abstract cases associated with it. In contrast, the Inside constraint (C2) has only a single associated case because its predicate calculus expression has no existentially quantified variables.

In the second step, RICK examines each combination of abstract cases of constraints $C_1,..., C_n$ and determines which combinations are mutually consistent. For example, four of the eight combinations of constraints C3 (Adjacent) and C2 (Inside) are found to be consistent. The modified *direct incorporation strategy* is then applied to each consistent combination of abstract cases. RICK builds a separate generator for each consistent combination rather than a single generator for the entire problem. Each case is implicitly defined by a set of constraints. RICK then applies techniques for mapping constraint sets (of certain restricted types, for example, local and linear constraints) into bounded intervals. For example, in processing the constraints Inside (C2) and Adjacent (C3), RICK synthesizes the constrained generator shown at the bottom of figure 3. The complete constrained generator operates by successively calling each of four separate generators. Each of the four output a stream of rooms adjacent to a single house side.

A prototype version of RICK was implemented and successfully tested in the floor-planning domain. In particular, RICK was shown to incorporate the constraints C1 (length), C2 (inside), and C3 (adjacent) into a constrained generator, using the procedure previously outlined. Experience in building the RICK prototype has provided insights into the feasibility of building constrained generators. Local constraints (on small parts of the solution) that are also linear (that is, linear combinations of parameter values) can always be incorporated into a constrained generator. The floor-planning domain indicates that some types of linear, nonlocal constraints can also be incorporated into constrained generators. Nevertheless, a complete set of feasibility rules remains to be developed.

Mapping Constraints into Hill-Climbing Patchers

In the best of cases, RICK would build a constrained generator that only generates (in polynomial time) objects that satisfy all the problem constraints. In this case, the compiled algorithm is simply this generator with no tester. In general, though, no single solution representation will allow all constraints to become local (or even localizable) constraints; the likelihood of there being no perfect solution representation increases with the number of constraints. With respect to a given problem representation, the remaining global constraints appear to require the generation of much or all of the solution before they can be evaluated or reasoned about. For example, with respect to a solution representation in which the top-level parts of a floor plan are rectangular rooms, the constraint "The rooms must completely fill the rectangular house" appears to require many if not all the rooms to be placed and sized before this constraint can be evaluated. Constructing a constrained room generator that is guaranteed to generate (in a clairvoyant manner) individual rooms (in polynomial time) in such a way that together they will fill the house (and also satisfy a host of other constraints) seems difficult if not impossible. Currently, RICK makes uses of a heuristic that examines constraints and labels them local, localizable, or global on the basis of their syntactic form. The solution object must satisfy all P, where

$$P(s) = P_{local}(s) \text{ and } P_{localizable}(s) \text{ and } P_{global}(s) .$$

RICK creates a constrained generator of objects of the required type T that satisfy $P_{local}(s)$ and $P_{localizable}(s)$. For example, in the following example house floor-planning task, RICK is capable of incorporating four out of five problem constraints:

P_{local}(floorplan) $\wedge$ $P_{localizable}$(floorplan) $\equiv$ C1 $\wedge$ C2 $\wedge$ C3 $\wedge$ C4

P_{global}(floorplan) $\equiv$ $C5$:$\forall$ P [interiorPoint(P,house) $\rightarrow$ $\exists$R,P1 [room(R) $\wedge$
interiorPoint(P1,R) $\wedge$ coincides(P,P1)]]
("The rooms must completely fill the rectangular house.")

Thus, RICK constructs a constrained generator that generates floor plans with rooms that are of minimal dimensions, are inside the house, and do not overlap. However, the rooms cannot fill the house interior. Testing a global constraint is not the only way to use it in problem solving. The (partially implemented) MENDER compiler (Voigt and Tong 1989) specializes in mapping constraints at the knowledge level into hill-climbing patchers at the function level. Hill-climbing patchers attempt to modify an object to satisfy given constraints. They modify an object by applying a series of patching operations that operate in a hill-climbing control structure (that is, guided by an evaluation function). Hill-climbing patchers are constructed by synthesizing a set of patching operations and implementing a control mechanism to select from among competing patching operations. The first task is simplified by restricting patching operations to be changes in parameter values of a generated object (for example, changes in the length, width, or position of a room rectangle).

Not all changes in parameter values are appropriate in a hill-climbing patcher. Selected patches are restricted to those that improve the degree to which an object satisfies the given constraint. To measure the degree of constraint satisfaction, MENDER converts the Boolean constraint into a numeric evaluation function. For example, constraint C5 (fill), "The rooms must fill the house," can be converted into an evaluation function that counts the number of points on the house floor that are covered by rooms:

$f(S) = \sum_{Room \in input\ set\ of\ rooms} length(Room) \cdot width(Room)$.

Iterative patching that always increases the value of this function will eventually lead to a filled house, that is, when the value of $f(S)$ is $length(house) \cdot width(house)$.

MENDER is initially focusing on compiling constraints that define resource-assignment problems. Such problems involve assigning parts of a resource (for example, the floor space of a house) to consumers of this resource (for example, room rectangles). One particular type of resource-assignment problem is called a "consume all" problem. A *consume all problem* requires that each unit of a resource be assigned to some consumer. Constraint C5 (fill), "The rooms must fill the house," is an example of a consume all problem. Another type of resource-assignment problem is called "obey partial ordering." Such problems involve an ordering relation defined over units of the resource, for example, the total ordering of the time slots of a scheduling problem. Constraints on resource assignments to consumers can then be phrased in terms of the ordering on resources. For example, precedence constraints among jobs can be expressed in terms of the ordering of time slots.

MENDER is being implemented using a set of generic constraint schemata. Each schema will correspond to a different type of resource-assignment problem. Whenever a constraint successfully matches a schema, information associated with this schema will be used to synthesize an evaluation function. For example, the schema defining consume all problems is associated with a method for constructing evaluation functions that measure the amount of the resource that has yet to be consumed. A schema defining obey partial ordering problems would likewise contain a method for constructing evaluation functions suitable for this type of problem. Feasibility rules for MENDER correspond to the generic constraint schemata. Each generic schema specifies a class of constraints for which it is feasible to construct a hill-climbing patcher. A particular constraint can be handled by MENDER only if it matches a schema from the library.

MENDER is partially implemented. The current version of MENDER is capable of automatically deriving an evaluation function for constraints of the consume all type. The system successfully generated an evaluation function and a set of legal patching operations for the floor-planning constraint C5 (fill), as previously described. MENDER is also capable of incorporating the evaluation function and patching operations into a greedy control structure, which selects the patching operation that makes the greatest improvement.

Empirical studies have shown how the generate-test-and-patch algorithm can further be improved by equipping the patcher with a look-ahead mechanism for heuristically selecting modifications that circumnavigate local minima (the central danger of greedy hill climbing).

Mapping Constraints into Multiple Abstraction-Level Architectures

Often, a constraint on a composite object can be expressed as a constraint on functions of composite object parts. I now show that in this case, a multilevel generate-and-test algorithm can be constructed. Suppose our design problem requires constructing an object s of type T with parts $p1$ and $p2$ of types $T1$ and $T2$, respectively. Suppose also that there is a constraint P on the parts, expressed in terms of functions f and g:

$Generate(s \mid T(s) \wedge s = <p1,p2> \wedge T1(p1) \wedge T2(p2) \wedge P(f(p1),g(p2)))$.

This problem can be solved with the following generate-and-test algorithm:

Generate(p1 | p1 ∈ domain(T1));
Generate(p2 | p2 ∈ domain(T2));
Test(<p1,p2>, P(f(p1),g(p2)));
Return(<p1,p2>) ,

where *domain(Ti)* is the set of all objects of type *Ti* (which we presume can be enumerated). This algorithm returns a solution $s = <p1,p2>$, satisfying P (if one exists). However, given additional knowledge about the range of the functions f and g, we can construct the following more complex but some-times more efficient generate-and-test algorithm:[3]

Abstract Level

Generate(a1 | a1 ∈ range(f(domain(T1))));
Generate(a2 | a2 ∈ range(g(domain(T2))));
Test(<a1,a2>, P(a1,a2));

Base Level

Generate(p1 | p1 ∈ domain(T1));
Test(p1, f(p1) = a1);
Generate(p2 | p2 ∈ domain(T2));
Test(p2, g(p2) = a2);
Return(<p1,p2>).

I call such a problem solver a multilevel generate-and-test algorithm. As an example, the design problem might be to synthesize a two-room house floor plan whose total area is AREA:

$Generate(s \mid Floorplan(s) \land s = <p1,p2> \land Room(p1) \land Room(p2)$
$\land AREA = Area(p1) + Area(p2))$.

The simple, single-level generate-and-test floor planner would generate lengths, widths, and positions for each room and then sum the areas of the rooms to check the constraint. The multilevel floor planner is based on what is, in effect, an abstraction of each room (having position, length, and width) into a single number, its area. The multilevel generate-and-test algorithm can be viewed as taking place on two levels: an abstract level and a base level. The abstract generate-and-test algorithm generates two area numbers that sum to the right total AREA. These numbers are passed down to the base level, where they serve as constraints (through tests);[4] the base-level gener-ate-and-test algorithm generates rooms until it creates those with the appro-priate areas:

Generate(a1 | a1 ∈ range(Area(domain(Room))));
Generate(a2 | a2 ∈ range(Area(domain(Room))));
Test(<a1,a2>, AREA = a1 + a2);

Generate(p1 | p1 ∈ domain(Room));
Test(p1, Area(p1) = a1);
Generate(p2 | p2 ∈ domain(Room));
Test(p2, Area(p2) = a2); Return(<p1,p2>).

Note that in some cases, it is also possible to synthesize a refinement oper-ator that directly computes refinements from abstractions using an inversion (or partial inversion) of the functions that would otherwise explicitly be test-ed at the base level. For example, one such refinement operator might take area $a1$, pick a real value for the length l of room $p1$ such that $0 < l \le a1$, and then compute width w of room $p1$ to be $a1/l$. Synthesis of such refinement operators is, however, beyond the scope of the current research. Techniques have been developed for evaluating and constructing efficient hierarchical generate-and-test algorithms from design problem specifications (Mohan and Tong 1989; Mohan 1989). These techniques are being implemented in a program called HiT. Like some other techniques for preprocessing constraint networks (Dechter 1989), HiT partitions the constraint set into parts. However, unlike these other techniques, HiT reformulates the network in a special manner based on constraints that have function symbols (for example, "area" in $area(r1) + area(r2) = AREA$).

Multilevel problem solvers have also been constructed by hand and experiments have been carried out to measure the improvement in efficiency over a single-level problem solver. Based on these experiments and on standard cost models for database query processing (Ullman 1982), a cost model that can be used to estimate the efficiency of a particular multilevel problem solver has been developed and is being tested (Mohan 1990). Roughly speaking, the cost model predicts that a multilevel generate-and-test algorithm will be more efficient than the single-level algorithm (that is, its benefit will outweigh the overhead of its additional level) in problem domains where P is a tight constraint; the ranges of f and g are smaller than the domains of $p1$ and $p2$; and it is relatively easy to find abstract objects $a1$ and $a2$ for which corresponding base-level objects $p1$ and $p2$ exist, where $f(p1) = a1$ and $g(p2) = a2$ (perhaps through appropriately restrictive definitions of the ranges of f and g). The base-level objects that correspond to the abstract objects are called the refinements of the abstract objects.

Controlling the Compilation Process

Q: What is the most effective way to incorporate a given type of constraint into a search algorithm that finds an object satisfying the constraint?

A: The most effective way is to use a set of effectiveness rules that indicate which assignments of component constraints will result in efficient search algorithms. Asymptotic complexity analyses and empirical efficiency measurements support the effectiveness rules.

Q: How can we quickly incorporate a given set of constraints into a search algorithm?

A: A divide-and-conquer control structure can be used that involves feasibility and effectiveness rules to assign constraints to function-level components and that invokes a specialized compiler to construct each component type.

The Divide-and-Conquer Control Strategy

When fully implemented, KBSDE will use a divide-and-conquer approach to control the knowledge compilation process. Three subtasks arise in the di-

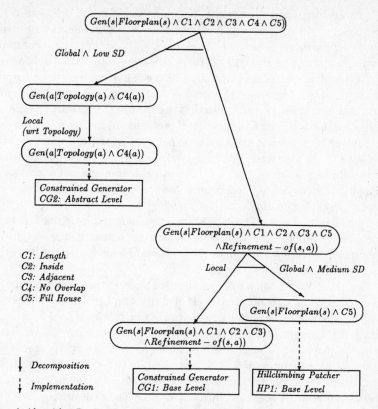

Figure 4. Algorithm Design Subproblems Created by Divide-and-Conquer.

vide-and-conquer approach: decomposing the knowledge-level specification into implementation subproblems, implementing the algorithm components, and composing each algorithm component into the problem-solving architecture under construction. The decomposition step divides a single knowledge compilation problem of the form

$Generate(s \mid T(s) \land P(s))$

into multiple knowledge compilation subproblems. Each subproblem has the form "Construct an algorithm component that enforces constraints $C_1,...,C_n$." An example problem decomposition hierarchy is shown in figure 4. This diagram illustrates how the sophisticated house floor-planning algorithm in figure 2 might have been synthesized by the proposed divide-and-conquer strategy. The specialized compilers proposed earlier in Incorporating Knowledge into Search Algorithms are responsible for implementation. Each compiler will also be responsible for composing the algorithm component it creates into the problem solver under construction.

Two distinct types of decompositions that figure in the proposed divide-and-conquer strategy are interlevel partitioning and intralevel partitioning: *Interlevel partitioning* divides the responsibility for enforcing constraints across two levels of abstraction. Two knowledge compilation subproblems result from this type of decomposition. One subproblem specifies an abstract problem solver. The abstract problem solver is required to produce an abstract solution satisfying all constraints assigned to the abstract level. A second subproblem specifies the base-level problem solver. The base-level problem solver is required to produce an actual solution satisfying all constraints assigned to the base level. The base-level solution must also be a refinement of the abstract solution. Each of these two subproblems can further be decomposed before being implemented. *Intralevel partitioning* divides the responsibility for enforcing constraints among algorithm components within a single abstraction level. This type of decomposition results in one knowledge compilation subproblem for each algorithm component that is assigned responsibility for any constraints. These subproblems are solved by implementing the specific algorithm components.

Constraint classification rules will be used to decide on the appropriate partitioning of constraints between levels of abstraction and between components within a single level of abstraction. *Feasibility rules* will be used to determine which partitionings lead to subproblems that can be compiled. *Effectiveness rules* will be used to decide which partitionings lead to efficient search algorithms. Both types of rules will be formulated in terms of constraint features. Preliminary constraint features include locality, linearity, solution density, and abstraction value. A constraint might be local or global, depending on the size of the part of the solution to which it refers. A constraint can have a solution density with respect to some space (the proportion of the space that satisfies the constraint). A constraint can have an abstraction value that measures the benefit of using this constraint to build a new abstraction level relative to a single-level algorithm. The abstraction value depends, among other things, on the time to generate an acceptable abstract solution, the time to generate a base-level refinement of an abstract solution, and the likelihood that each abstract solution can be refined into an actual solution. These constraint features should be useful in predicting feasibility and effectiveness; however, a complete set of constraint features remains to be developed.

Preliminary Effectiveness Rules

I now present an initial set of effectiveness rules. Although I do not yet have any formal justification for the utility of these rules, I try to provide suggestive intuitions based on the system-building experiences of the researchers in this project and others.

First is to map all local and localizable constraints into a constrained generator whenever possible. Map the remaining local constraints into testers on the individual parts to which they are localized. This rule attempts to synthesize an algorithm that performs no search at all. When the ideal of no search is not attainable, the rule prefers algorithms that prune partial solutions and backtrack early over algorithms that test entire solutions and search exhaustively.

Second, if the search space is small or the solution density SD of a global constraint is high, then map the global constraint into a tester. This rule recommends a simple generate-and-test algorithm when the number of solutions is large relative to the size of the solution space. The generate-and-test is cost effective because backtracking will likely only occur a small number of times. This rule also recommends a simple generate-and-test approach for small search spaces because generators and testers usually incur less overhead than other function-level components.

Third, if the solution density SD of a global constraint is medium, then map the global constraint into a hill-climbing patcher. In medium-density solution spaces (with uniformly distributed solutions), a candidate solution that fails to satisfy a global constraint is likely to be close enough to an acceptable solution that a hill-climbing patcher can correct the failure using a short sequence of modifications.

Fourth, if the solution density SD of a global constraint is low, then map the constraint into the abstract level of a multilevel problem solver. When solutions are sparse, the overhead of finding and refining an abstract solution will likely be a worthwhile price to pay to guarantee satisfaction of the global constraint.

The operation of these preliminary effectiveness rules is illustrated in figure 4. The decomposition process begins when rule 4 is used to assign constraint C4 (no overlap) to be handled by an abstract problem solver. (We assume that C4 is the only global constraint with a low solution density.) HiT might then decide that floor-plan topologies result in a more efficient multilevel problem solver than all other abstractions under consideration. Thus, the abstract problem solver would be required to generate a topological floorplan description a that is consistent with constraint C4. Since constraint C4 is local with respect to the abstract solution representation, rule 1 would then recommend assigning C4 to a constrained generator of floorplan topologies. The base-level problem solver would be required to generate a refinement of the abstract solution a that satisfies the remaining constraints C1,C2,C3, and C5. Because constraints C1 (length), C2 (inside), and C3 (adjacent) are all local, rule 1 would recommend that they be handled by a constrained generator. Assuming that constraint C5 (fill) has medium solution density, rule 3 would assign C5 to a hill-climbing patcher. The resulting sophisticated algorithm would have the form illustrated in figure 2.

Experiments are currently being conducted to see whether the divide-and-conquer approach actually works in practice. Several research issues must be addressed. The preliminary set of constraint features previously proposed must be elaborated. In particular, researchers are developing criteria for precisely defining such constraint features as low, medium, or high solution density; local or localizable constraint; and abstraction value. Cost-effective means are being developed for evaluating such constraint features as the solution density of a constraint. Preliminary effectiveness rules will be evaluated by carrying out asymptotic complexity analyses and empirical efficiency measurements of the algorithms they generate.

Three further areas of research that require investigation if the divide-and-conquer approach is to become practical are (1) managing interactions among knowledge compilation subproblems; (2) composing algorithm components into a globally coherent algorithm; and (3) engineering the specifications into a compilable form. These topics are examined in the next two subsections.

Subproblem Interactions and Composing Algorithm Components

The knowledge compilation subproblems created by the divide-and-conquer strategy interact. Several particular types of interactions among subproblems have been observed:

Using Consistent Representations: To ensure that algorithm components can be composed, a divide-and-conquer strategy must arrange that consistent solution representations are used by all algorithm components at a given level of abstraction. For example, if a tester refers to particular parts of the solution, they must correlate with the solution parts generated upstream in the control flow.

Sharing Subproblems: Similar or identical subproblems can appear at multiple points in the problem-decomposition hierarchy resulting from our divide-and-conquer strategy. For example, to implement the hill-climbing patcher HP1 shown in figure 4, MENDER must construct a generator of patching operations that do not violate the previously achieved constraints C1, C2, or C3. The RICK compiler faces the same task in building the constrained generator CG1. The divide-and-conquer control strategy must detect such situations to avoid a duplication of efforts.

Ordering Subproblems: Subproblems must be processed in an order consistent with dependencies among the subproblems. For example, when HiT is used to process an abstract-level subproblem, it output a refinement constraint that must be incorporated into the base-level problem solver. This constraint must be available to compilers such as RICK or MENDER that process the base-level subproblems. Therefore, HiT must be invoked prior to these other compilers. As a second example, suppose that the solution density of a constraint is to be estimated by actually running a component of the problem solver (for example, a constrained generator) and collecting statistics. So that the required component is available, the knowledge compilation subproblems must be processed in an appropriate order. (Chapter 13 has some further ideas regarding subproblem interactions in algorithm design.)

Purpose-Directed Knowledge Engineering

The knowledge-level specification of a design task, *Generate*(*s* | *T*(*s*) ∧ *P*(*s*)), has two components, *T*(*s*) and *P*(*s*). The engineering phase in this model of knowledge compilation is a preprocessing step that attempts to find a way of expressing both *T*(*s*) and *P*(*s*) to make subsequent knowledge compilation as effective as possible. Hence, we are developing techniques for engineering the solution representation *T*(*s*) and reformulating the solution constraints *P*(*s*) to enhance opportunities for effective compilation.

Engineering **T(s)**: For the kinds of design tasks being considered, type *T*(*s*) is invariant in the sense that the types of all the parts in the part hierarchy are fixed at compile time. For example, one such type decomposition is illustrated in figure 1: Floor plans can be viewed as having parts of type Room. Rooms are rectangles. Rectangles can be viewed as having parts: <*x,y,l,w*> (a corner point, a directed length, and a directed width).

T(*s*) can be engineered in the sense that alternative type decompositions are possible. For example, rectangles can be decomposed into parts in other ways such as <*leftSide, topSide, rightSide, bottomSide*> and <*x1,y1,x2,y2*> (two opposite corner points).

That *T*(*s*) can be engineered means that constraint features can be engineered, too, insofar as certain constraint features are functions of the solution representation. For example, constraint C3, "Each room adjacent to house wall," is global with respect to the <*x,y,l,w*> representation of a room but local with respect to the <*leftSide, topSide, rightSide, bottomSide*> representation.

Given that *T*(*s*) (and, consequently, such constraint features as locality) can be engineered, how should we engineer it? Our proposed ideal is

> Engineer the solution representation to maximize the number of constraints that are local (or localizable) with respect to it.

All constraints that are local can be incorporated into a relatively efficient constrained generator (that is, one that takes polynomial time in the sum of the size of the generator input and output). In the best case, researchers would engineer the representation of *T*(*s*) so that all the constraints look local and create a polynomial-time design algorithm. Failing this capability, they engineer the representation of *T*(*s*) to make as many constraints as possible look local.

Engineering **P(s)**: *P*(*s*) can be engineered in that the same constraint can often be expressed in many different ways. During compilation, the problems of choosing a representation for *P*(*s*) and *T*(*s*) interact in that *P*(*s*) contains constraints on solution parts, and *T*(*s*) defines the solution parts that will be generated. Engineering $P(s)$ (and $T(s)$) should ensure that all the solution parts mentioned in $P(s)$ appear in the representation of $T(s)$. As a negative example, consider "Each room is inside the house" expressed as "Each point p in the room rectangle must be contained in the house rectangle." Suppose $Room(r)$ is represented by $<x(r),y(r),l(r),w(r)>$. There is no direct way to evaluate the constraint against a candidate solution generated by picking values of $x, y, l,$ and w because the constraint refers to objects (point p) not explicitly mentioned in the room representation.

The process of engineering $T(s)$ has been facilitated by using a knowledge base containing a semantic network representation of generic solution part types. For example, they have a knowledge base containing such common geometric part types as rectangles, lines, points, and so on. The specification for a new design task is related to the generic data types through such statements as "All rooms are rectangles" and "All houses are rectangles." The generation of alternative representations for $T(s)$ is facilitated because each object type definition (for example, the one for Rectangle) in the generic knowledge base can have alternative type decompositions stored in it (for example, $<x,y,l,w>$).

The process of engineering $P(s)$ has been facilitated by caching rules for translating between alternative type decompositions with an object type definition (for example, $<x,y,l,w> \rightarrow <x1,y1,x2,y2>$: $x1 \leftarrow x$; $y1 \leftarrow y$; $x2 \leftarrow x+l$; $y2 \leftarrow y+w$). A constraint referring to objects in one representation can be reformulated into one using objects in another representation by applying such rules.

Each of the specialized compilers (RICK, MENDER, and HiT) relies on the constraints in $P(s)$ matching a limited number of normal forms (schemas). If they do not match, they can sometimes be reengineered so that they do match. For automating the process of reengineering $P(s)$, researchers are considering such goal-directed techniques as antecedent derivation (Smith 1982) and explanation-based learning (Mitchell, Keller, and Kedar-Cabelli 1986) for generalizing over a number of acceptable designs (constructed using a strawman generate-and-test version of the algorithm).

Discussion and Related Work

In this chapter, I described the KBSDE project, which is conducting research in knowledge compilation. In particular, research has studied how to compile knowledge-based systems that solve simple spatial configuration problems.

Knowledge compilation and algorithm design are phrases reflecting different views on (and different methodologies and benchmarks for) the same automated software design process. I now consider the implications of these different viewpoints.

Knowledge Compilation

The phrase knowledge compilation places an emphasis on the input to the automated software design process (knowledge) and suggests the effective exploitation of large and diverse bodies of available task-specific knowledge as a research goal. The synthesized algorithms are, typically, knowledge-based systems. Progress occurs when new types of knowledge can be (semi) automatically exploited. For example, I discussed how to exploit two new types of knowledge for creating design algorithms: an object class (or type) hierarchy and a set of schemas for classifying solution constraints. Being able to exploit object-oriented knowledge and create object-oriented algorithms opens the door to handling a new set of knowledge-intensive tasks. Work in knowledge compilation takes its cue from at least two sources: coherent problem types whose specifications have some structure that can be schematized and existing knowledge-based systems. With the first source, the KBSDE project focused on design problems with the form "Generate a composite object of known type T and satisfying P." It further studied regularities in the substructure of both T (for example, known part typing) and P (for example, partitioning P into P_{local}, $P_{localizable}$, and P_{global}). The project continues such studies, exploring, for example, how regularities in the part interconnections (for example, doors between rooms in a floor plan) can be effectively exploited. It is possible that the analytic reasoning problems described in Van Baalen (1988) might also form a coherent problem type. Characterizing such regularities in problem descriptions is necessary to successfully view knowledge compilation as a classification process.

With the second source, several existing knowledge-based systems have been rederived, for example, the MYCIN THERAPY ADVISOR (Mostow and Voigt 1987) or a system for designing mechanical gear trains (chapter 10).

This chapter focused on compiling complete and correct specifications. However, because of the specification's complexity (presumed by the knowledge compilation viewpoint), a problem specification can be incomplete or incorrect. Thus, we should probably think of knowledge compilation as an activity embedded in a larger system redesign process. The larger process can also involve:specification acquisition (Fickas 1987), specification modification (chapter 4), incremental recompilation (Swartout and Balzer 1982; chapters 5 and 10), and the rational reconstruction of the system on the basis of new insights (Tong and Franklin 1989).

Algorithm Design

The phrase algorithm design emphasizes the output of the high-level phase of software design (an algorithm). Typically, the problem specifications themselves are relatively simple (although the domain theory need not be) and presumed to be correct (but possibly incomplete—see chapter 19). Work in this area takes its cue from at least two sources:

First are coherent algorithm types described in textbooks on data structures and algorithms (for example, Aho, Hopcroft, and Ullman [1974] or Nilsson [1984]). Here, progress occurs when a new type of algorithm can be synthesized (divide-and-conquer [Smith 1985], heuristic search [Mostow 1983], and so on). Characterizing such regularities in algorithm components and configurations is necessary to successfully view algorithm design as a classification process.

Second are well-studied algorithms described in textbooks from computer science (chapter 19), operations research (chapter 20), geometry (Tappel 1980; Steier and Kant 1985; chapter 13), and graph theory (chapter 19; Cai and Page 1987). Progress occurs when a new well-known algorithm (for example, the simplex method) can be synthesized.

Algorithm Optimization and Implementation

Both knowledge compilation and algorithm design researchers tend to focus on the high end of the software design process. The synthesized algorithm is often suboptimal (for example, because it is expressed as an instance of a generic schema). Thus, algorithm design is often followed by (or interleaved with) such optimization techniques as finite differencing (Paige and Koenig 1982; chapter 19), partial evaluation (chapters 15 and 19), the redistribution of results (chapter 14), and simplification.[5]

The synthesized algorithm is often expressed in a high-level language; thus, synthesis is often followed by (or interleaved with) an implementation process that efficiently translates the algorithm into a programming language such as Lisp; implementation involves activities such as data-structure selection (Schwartz 1975; Kant and Barstow 1978; Smith, Kotik, and Westfold 1985; Paige and Henglein 1987; Van Baalen 1988) and complexity analysis (Kant and Barstow 1978; chapter 13).

Extensions of the Knowledge Compilation Model as Classification

One of the long-term goals is to develop ideas to handle increasingly harder design problems, for example, design algorithms that do run-time information gathering, conduct more complex forms of redesign than hill climbing in a parameter space, or reason about the behavior of components when the artifact under design is a system. To apply the classification approach, feasibility and effectiveness rules need to be identified for incorporating solution constraints into each of these new design algorithm components.

Alternatives to the Model of Knowledge Compilation as Classification

Existing knowledge compiler technology can usefully be compared along the narrow focus–to–broad focus spectrum. Some compilers are specialized; for example, the ELF system (chapter 9) specializes in compiling global routers for varying VLSI technologies. The KBSDE compiler described here addresses a different and somewhat broader class of algorithms for spatial configuration tasks. Finally, the DIOGENES compiler (chapter 10) addresses the still broader class of heuristic search algorithms. These compilers appear to obey the standard power-generality trade-off. The models of knowledge compilation also grow progressively weaker as the breadth widens, culminating in such weak models as a transformational model of knowledge compilation (chapter 10) or a model of knowledge compilation as formal derivation. A clear, short-term goal for the field of knowledge compilation is to identify a set of coherent task types of intermediate generality (for example, such as spatial configuration) and build a knowledge compiler for each one. A worthy long-term goal is to enable the more specialized compilers to augment their capability with the weaker methods of the more general compilers when some novel task description does not fit the schema associated with specialized compilers.

Alternatives to Knowledge Compilation

Knowledge compilation depends on the possibility of acquiring or factoring out knowledge and heuristics that apply over an entire class of problems (the possible input to the synthesized algorithm). This observation makes apparent an inherent limitation of such a compile-time approach. Some information can be specific to a particular problem instance. In such a case, run-time information gathering (through deduction, constraint propagation, and so on) can be a more cost-effective way to produce this information than knowledge compilation. Some knowledge might not apply over an entire problem class but only over a subset of the problems that can be characterized. Depending on the nature of the characterization, either performing compile-time case analysis or learning conditionally applicable knowledge by generalizing from run-time examples might be the appropriate approach.

Acknowledgments

Special thanks to the KBSDE project members—Wes Braudaway, Sunil Mohan, and Kerstin Voigt—for their major contributions to the ideas reported here. Thanks to Chun Liew for building the original KBSDE knowledge compiler. Thanks to Lou Steinberg, Jack Mostow, and the other members of the Rutgers University AI/Design Project for providing a creative research environment. Thanks to Tom Ellman, Wes Braudaway, and Kerstin Voigt for their tremendous help with the figures and text of an earlier version of this chapter. Thanks to Mike Lowry and Rob McCartney for their helpful comments on an earlier draft. Finally, thanks to Sri Da Kalki for the rest.

Notes

1. Note that unlike abstract data types, these type definitions do not specify the behavior of operations on the data type; the definitions are purely structural.

2. A related advantage results from the fact that the specialized compilers can be developed in parallel and with relative independence by separate investigators. Thus, no graduate student lies on the critical path of another.

3. Recall that the interpreted algorithm backtracks to the last Generate whenever a test fails, or a generator runs out of values.

4. It is also sometimes possible to incorporate such constraints in the base-level generator.

5. Simplification is in everyone's algorithm design method!

References

Aho, A.; Hopcroft, J.; and Ullman, J. 1974. *The Design and Analysis of Computer Algorithms.* Reading, Mass.: Addison Wesley.

Barstow, D. 1985. Domain-Specific Automatic Programming. *IEEE Transactions on Software Engineering* SE-11(11): 1321–1336.

Bennett, J., and Dietterich, T. 1986. The Test Incorporation Hypothesis and the Weak Methods, Technical Report, TR 86-30-4, Dept. of Computer Science, Oregon State Univ.

Cai, J., and Paige, R. 1987. Binding Performance at Language Design Time. In Proceedings of the Fourteenth ACM Symposium on Principles of Programming Languages, 85–97. New York: Association of Computing Machinery.

Dechter, R. 1989. Tree Clustering for Constraint Networks. *Artificial Intelligence* 38:353–366.

Dietterich, T., ed. 1986. Proceedings of the Workshop on Knowledge Compilation. Menlo Park, Calif.: American Association for Artificial Intelligence.

Fickas, S. 1987. Automating Analysis: An Example. In Proceedings of the Fourth International Workshop on Software Specification and Design. Washington, D.C.: IEEE Computer Society.

Holte, R. 1990. Efficient Candidate Elimination through Test Incorporation. In Change of Representation and Inductive Bias, ed. D. Benjamin, 223–230. Boston: Kluwer.

Kant, E., and Barstow, D. 1978. The Refinement Paradigm: The Interaction of Coding and Efficiency Knowledge. *IEEE Transactions on Software Engineering* 9:287–306.

Liew, C. and Tong, C. 1987. Knowledge Compilation: A Prototype System and a Conceptual Framework, Working Paper 47, AI/Design Project, Rutgers Univ.

Mitchell, T. M.; Keller, R. M.;and Kedar-Cabelli, S. T. 1986. Explanation-Based Generalization: A Unifying View. *Machine Learning* 1(1): 47–80.

Mohan, S. 1990. Constructing Hierarchical Solvers for Functional Constraint-Satisfaction Problems. Submitted to the 1991 IEEE Conference on Applications of Artificial Intelligence. Also Working Paper 172, AI/Design Project, Rutgers Univ.

Mohan, S. 1989. Automatic Construction of Hierarchical Problem Solvers. Ph.D. proposal, Computer Science Dept., Rutgers Univ.

Mohan, S., and Tong, C. 1989. Automatic Construction of a Hierarchical Generate-and-Test Algorithm. Presented at the Sixth International Machine Learning Workshop, Ithaca, N.Y., June 26–27.

Mostow, J. 1983. Learning by Being Told: Machine Transformation of Advice into a Heuristic Search Procedure. In Machine Learning, eds. R. Michalski, J. Carbonell, and T. Mitchell, 367–403. San Mateo, Calif.: Morgan Kaufmann.

Mostow, J., and Voigt, K. 1987. Explicit Integration of Multiple Goals in Heuristic Algorithm Design. In Proceedings of the Tenth International Joint Conference on Artificial Intelligence, 1090–1096. Menlo Park, Calif.: International Joint Conferences on Artificial Intelligence.

Newell, A. 1982. The Knowledge Level. *Artificial Intelligence* 18:87–127.

Nilsson, N. 1984. *Principles of Artificial Intelligence*, 2d ed. San Mateo, Calif.: Morgan Kaufmann.

Paige, R., and Henglein, F. 1987. Mechanical Translation of Set-Theoretic Problem Specifications into Efficient Ram Code—A Case Study. *Journal of Symbolic Computation* 4(2): 207–232.

Paige, R., and Koenig, S. 1982. Finite Differencing of Computable Expressions. *ACM Transactions on Programming Languages and Systems* 4(3): 402–454.

Schwartz, J. 1975. Automatic Data Structure Choice in a Language of Very High Level. *Communications of the ACM* 18(12): 722–728.

Smith, D. R. 1988. Structure and Design of Global Search Algorithms, Technical Report KES.U.87.12, Kestrel Institute, Palo Alto, California.

Smith, D. 1986. Top-Down Synthesis of Divide-and-Conquer Algorithms. *Artificial Intelligence* 27(1): 43–96. Also in *Readings in Artificial Intelligence and Software Engineering*, eds. C. Rich and R. Waters, 35–61. San Mateo, Calif.: Morgan Kaufmann.

Smith, D. 1982. Derived Preconditions and Their Use in Program Synthesis. In Proceedings of the Sixth Conference on Automated Deduction, ed. D. Loveland, 172–193. Lecture Notes in Computer Science 138. New York: Springer-Verlag.

Smith, D.; Kotik, G.; and Westfold, S. 1985. Research on Knowledge-Based Software Environments at Kestrel Institute. *IEEE Transactions on Software Engineering* SE-11(11): 1278–1295.

Steier, D., and Kant, E. 1985. The Roles of Execution and Analysis in Algorithm Design. *IEEE Transactions on Software Engineering* SE-11(11): 1375–1386.

Swartout, W., and Balzer, R. 1982. On the Inevitable Intertwining of Specification and Implementation. *Communications of the ACM* 25(7):438–440.

Tappel, S. 1980. Some Algorithm Design Methods. In Proceedings of the First National Conference on Artificial Intelligence, 64–67. Menlo Park, Calif.: American Association for Artificial Intelligence.

Tong, C. 1987. Toward an Engineering Science of Knowledge-Based Design. *Artificial Intelligence in Engineering* (Special Issue on AI in Engineering Design) 2(3): 133–166.

Tong, C. 1986. KBSDE: An Environment for Developing Knowledge-Based Design Tools. Presented at the Knowledge Compilation Workshop, September 24–26, 1986.

Tong, C., and Franklin, P. 1989. Toward Automated Rational Reconstruction: A Case Study. In Proceedings of the Sixth International Machine Learning Workshop, 302–307. San Mateo, Calif.: Morgan Kaufmann.

Ullman, J. 1982. *Principles of Database Systems*. Rockville, Maryland: Computer Science Press.

Van Baalen, J. 1988. Overview of an Approach to Representation Design. In Proceedings of the Seventh National Conference, 392–397. Menlo Park, Calif.: American Association for Artificial Intelligence.

Voigt, K., and Tong, C. 1989. Automating the Construction of Patchers That Satisfy Global Constraints. In Proceedings of the Eleventh International Joint Conference on Artificial Intelligence, 1446–1452. Menlo Park, Calif.: International Joint Conferences on Artificial Intelligence, Inc.

12

Automated Synthesis of Constrained Generators

Wesley Braudaway

In this chapter, I present a method from the Knowledge-Based Software Development Environment (KBSDE) project discussed in chapter 11. This method compiles a search algorithm component called a constrained generator from a declarative specification of a design synthesis task. This work falls within the research area of knowledge compilation (Dietterich 1986) that focuses on compiling explicitly represented domain knowledge into an efficient algorithm that performs some task in this domain.

The Knowledge Compilation Solution to Design Problems

The KBSDE project is initially focusing on the development of knowledge compilation techniques applicable to spatial configuration design synthesis problems. A *spatial configuration* is an object that is hierarchically composed of parts arranged in positions and orientations to satisfy a specified set of spatial constraints. These problems require the synthesis of an object s of type T. T defines the hierarchical structure of s in terms of its parts, subparts, and so on (for example, a house with room parts and side subparts). The solutions to these problems must satisfy a set of constraints P defining valid solutions (for example, spatial constraints on the positions and orientations of the components of s).

An earlier study (chapter 11) showed that a hierarchical generate-and-test problem solver can be compiled from a declarative language representing these spatial configuration problems. It is generally accepted that generate-and-test problem solvers are only effective for use on simple problems. One optimization technique for improving the efficiency of a generate-and-test problem solver is test incorporation (Dietterich and Bennett 1986). *Test incorporation* involves test movement, constraint incorporation, or both. *Test movement* regresses tests back into the generator process to achieve early pruning without affecting the correctness of the problem solver. *Constraint incorporation* (Tappel 1980) modifies the generator so that it enumerates only those values that satisfy a particular problem constraint; the resulting generator is a *constrained generator*. Without the use of explicit testing, these constrained generators only produce solution candidates that satisfy the constraint. Because of this incorporation of constraints into the generators, the testers for the constraint can be removed from the generate-and-test architecture. Problem-solving efficiency is significantly increased with the use of these constrained generators.

Incorporating a constraint from $P(s)$ into a hierarchical generator structure created for $T(s)$ requires that it be factorable into one or more of the primitive generators. This incorporation can only be done if the constraint, represented using the same terms defined in $T(s)$, is local; that is, it only constrains a small set of primitive generators. This definition depends on the representation used for $T(s)$ and $P(s)$. Some constraints are inherently global where no representation exists that allows them to be local. The compilation method described in this chapter only applies to constraints that can be defined as local.

Constraint incorporation modifies the primitive generators so that they only produce solutions that satisfy the constraint. The domain knowledge from which this generator structure is created can contain predefined representations called *alternative type descriptions* T. For example, a room rectangle can be expressed in terms of the coordinates of two diagonally opposed corner points or in terms of its four sides. Because not all these alternatives allow the constraint to be local, they do not equally facilitate constraint incorporation. A *structure mismatch problem* occurs when a solution representation $T(s)$ and the corresponding hierarchical generator structure are chosen, causing constraint incorporation to fail. I examine two forms of this problem. The *constraint factoring problem* occurs when a representation used to express a constraint does not allow it to be factorable into constraints on the individual primitive generators. This problem is complicated by the need to find a single representation so that $P(s)$ contains constraints on solution parts that are all defined within $T(s)$. This second problem is called the *compatible factoring problem*.

One approach to the two structure mismatch problems is a least commitment, top-down refinement compiler called RICK (refinement-based constraint incorporator for compiling knowledge). RICK incorporates constraints by refining constraints into constrained generators, rather than regressing and incorporating testers for the constraints into an existing generator structure. RICK takes a set of alternative hierarchical data type descriptions T and a collection of local constraints $C_1(s), \ldots, C_n(s)$. The output of RICK is a constrained generator that generates all objects of type T that satisfy constraints $C_1, \ldots, C_n$. RICK transforms any global constraints into testers; however, this chapter does not discuss this process. By engineering the hierarchical type description T from the defined alternatives, RICK avoids the compatible factoring problem. Through this engineering, RICK defines a solution representation $T(s)$ that is compatible with the representation of each constraint. By using the abstract portion of $T(s)$ (the nonprimitive part levels of the hierarchical type description) during the refinement of the constrained generators, RICK also avoids a premature commitment to a primitive generator structure that can lead to the constraint factoring problem for local constraints.

This chapter describes the approach applied by RICK and its solution to the two structure mismatch problems. The second section defines the class of domains for which this method applies and illustrates the example domain of house floor-planning problems. The third section illustrates the structure mismatch problems using examples from the house floor-planning domain. The fourth section discusses the concepts behind this approach and illustrates their implementation in RICK. The fifth section evaluates this approach by stating some limitations and identifying extensions to the RICK compiler. I compare this work with related research in the sixth section and then summarize the chapter.

The Example Problem Domain

For many spatial configuration design problems, the hierarchical structure of the artifact s (for a class of problems) is predefined; for example, house floor plans can consist of rectangular rooms, which, in turn, consist of sides and corners. The design task remaining for the problem solver is to fill in and interconnect the structure by assigning values to the unspecified artifact parameters in a way that is consistent with the spatial constraints. This type of problem, *parameter instantiation* (Steinberg and Ling 1990), can be solved by constraint-satisfaction problem solvers (Dechter and Pearl 1988) but is less efficient than a problem solver that has incorporated the problem's constraints. Spatial configuration design tasks can also require the dynamic synthesis of interconnecting parts. For example, doors can be synthesized on de-

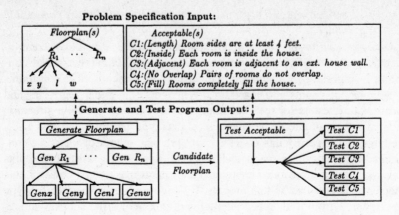

Problem Specification Input:

Floorplan(s)	*Acceptable(s)*
R_1 $\cdots$ R_n	*C1:(Length) Room sides are at least 4 feet.*
	C2:(Inside) Each room is inside the house.
	C3:(Adjacent) Each room is adjacent to an ext. house wall.
x y l w	*C4:(No Overlap) Pairs of rooms do not overlap.*
	C5:(Fill) Rooms completely fill the house.

Figure 1.
The Floor-Planning Design Problem and an Inefficient Generate-and-Test Algorithm.

mand to satisfy a spatial constraint that two rooms be connected. I postpone
the discussion of RICK's solution to this synthesis subproblem, presenting it
in The Evaluation of This Approach. RICK constructs a problem solver for
these spatial configuration problems where the constraints are hard constraints that define feasible solutions (and not soft constraints that define the
relative optimality of feasible solutions). Currently, RICK only compiles problem solvers for design problems that are not overconstrained, a solution that
satisfies all the constraints can be found.

To illustrate these ideas, I use the problem of constructing house floor
plans. The problem-class specification given to RICK defines a solution as an
object *s* of data type Floorplan that satisfies the Acceptable predicate. A floor
plan comprises a number of individual rooms $R_1, \ldots, R_n$. The size of the
floor plan and the number of rooms define individual problem instances for
this floor-planning problem class. The problem solver produced by RICK for a
problem class is able to solve any of its problem instances. The Acceptable
predicate is a conjunction of five different spatial configuration constraints
(top of figure 1) that a floor plan must meet to be an acceptable solution.
Constraints C1, C2, and C3 are local constraints using the proper representation, and their incorporation is demonstrated. Constraints C4 and C5 are
global constraints, although I discuss an extension to RICK that partially incorporates C4.

Each object that is part of the hierarchical solution representation $T(s)$ is a
specialization of some generic object contained in a knowledge base of common knowledge. For example, the room parts of the floor plan are instances
of the generic rectangle object. As mentioned previously, this knowledge
base contains alternative object type descriptions for these generic objects. In

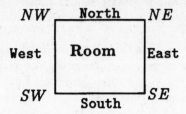

Figure 2. A Room Representation.

the case of the Floorplan object, rectangular rooms can be composed of any combination of the following parts: its four sides (west, north, east, and south); its four corners (SW, NW, NE, and SE); its two diagonals (Positive-Diagonal, Negative-Diagonal); its parameters $<x, y, l, w>$, where (x,y) is the coordinate of the SW corner, and l, w are the magnitudes of the south and west rectangle sides, respectively; and other parts. The hierarchical floor plan in figure 1 only illustrates one alternative representation of a room. A room representation composed of room sides and room corners is depicted in figure 2. These alternatives will be selected by RICK to engineer an adequate solution representation $T(s)$ for use during compilation. Along with the part-composition alternatives, these hierarchies contain the relevant structural constraints common to rectangular objects (for example, the west room side is perpendicular to the north room side.)

Constraint Incorporation and the Structure Mismatch Problem

A simple, hierarchical, generate-and-test problem solver for the floor-planning domain and its correspondence to the problem specification is shown in figure 1. The generator creates a candidate solution containing descriptions for each of the n rooms specified by a particular problem. Each room is generated by assigning values (0 through 9 in the 9- x 9-foot house problems) to its parameters using the representation $<x,y,l,w>$. The generators are invoked in the sequence (x, y, l, w) for each room. After all the generators have been invoked, the testers evaluate the candidate solution for satisfaction of the problem constraints. A failure of any test results in chronological backtracking through the generator sequence to find a new candidate solution.

For a 9- x 9-foot house with 4 rooms, this problem solver (figure 1) has a generation space containing 10^{16} candidate solutions (4 rooms, each having 4 parameters that each range over 10 values). Only a small number, 288, of these solutions are acceptable, satisfying constraints C1 through C5. This generation space is clearly exponential in the number of rooms. Assuming a uniform distribution of acceptable solutions in the space of candidate solutions, the generate-and-test problem solver will generate roughly $10^{16} \div 288 \approx 3 \cdot 10^{13}$ candidates before finding a solution. This problem solver is inefficient.

Constraint incorporation can be used to improve the efficiency of the problem solver. For example, constraint C1 is easily incorporated by changing the lower bounds of the length and width generators from 0 to 4. The roughly $9.8 \cdot 10^{15}$ candidate solutions that violate C1 will not be generated, leaving a search space of roughly $1.7 \cdot 10^{14}$ candidate solutions (4 rooms, each having 4 parameters, 2 ranging over 10 values, and 2 ranging over 6 values).

The Constraint Factoring Problem

Unfortunately, incorporating a constraint can be difficult when a problem constraint on the entire solution cannot be partitioned into constraints on individual parameter generators. This case can occur when a hierarchical object type T is chosen that does not allow the local constraint to be factored into the solution representation $T(s)$. For example, with the generator structure in figure 1, it is difficult to incorporate constraint C3, expressed as[1]

$$\forall R \exists RS,HS[room(R) \rightarrow sideof(RS,R) \wedge sideof(HS,house) \wedge segmentof(RS,HS)] .$$

That is, all rooms must share a side with a house side. The *segmentof(RS,HS)* predicate unfolds into the conjunction stating that segment RS must lie on the same line containing segment HS, and the end points of segment RS must lie between the end points of segment HS on this line. Assume that constraint C2 has already been incorporated so that only rooms inside the house are generated. If we represent a room by its $<x, y, l, w>$ parameters (figure 3a) (where $<x, y>$ corresponds to corner SW, and $<l,w>$ are the room's length and width in the x, y direction from corner SW, respectively), constraint C3 simplifies to[2]

$$x(R) = 0 \vee y(R) + w(R) = hw \vee x(R) + l(R) = hl \vee y(R) = 0 .$$

This constraint implies that a room must either have its west side on the west side of the house, its north side on the north side of the house, and so on. Because this constraint refers to all room parameters and has disjuncts that refer to different parameters, there is no easy way to factor it into constraints on the primitive generators. Therefore, this constraint factoring problem inhibits constraint incorporation.

Note, however, that the constraint refers to the containment (segmentof) of a room side within a house side. A more adequate object type would represent a room rectangle by any two perpendicular side objects (each side object, in turn, having a location and a length)(figure 3b). Given this representation, we could incorporate constraint C3 (adjacent) by simply modifying the generator of one room side to place it along one of the four house sides. This example suggests an obvious method for incorporating a constraint: Shift the representation of either the constraint, the generator, or both until incorporation succeeds. Automatic problem reformulation is a difficult re-

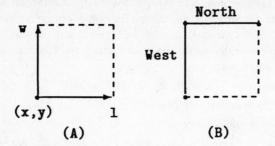

Figure 3. Alternative Room Representations.
A: The < x,y,l,w > room representation.
B: The perpendicular room side representation.

search problem with many unresolved issues (Korf 1980; Benjamin 1990). In the next section (Knowledge Compilation as Top-Down Refinement), I present an alternative approach to knowledge compilation that reduces the combinatorial explosion that is involved in searching a space of representations.

This constraint factoring problem is liable to occur in test (constraint) incorporation approaches that incorporate after the generation structure has been designed. Consider the data flow, transformational approach to constraint incorporation taken by Tappel (1980) and Mostow (chapter 10). Their approach refines the generate-and-test (or heuristic search) algorithm by manipulating a data flow graph representation of the problem solver. The data flow graph represents the problem solver by using a node in the graph to represent a generator or tester step. The nodes are ordered according to their occurrence during execution. Tappel and Mostow use test incorporation to refine the data flow graph by moving the tester nodes closer to the generator nodes they affect and maintain the correctness of the represented process. This approach, without using representation reformulation, has committed to a problem solver architecture using a particular solution representation $T(s)$ of the problem to be solved. By prematurely committing to a solution representation and generator structure, this approach cannot avoid the constraint factoring problem, and constraint incorporation can be inhibited. The data flow network only represents the sequence of generators and testers. With this information, test incorporation can only manipulate the order of these processes in the problem-solving sequence. To avoid the constraint factoring problem, more knowledge is needed about the problem's alternative type descriptions so that the solution representation can be reformulated with respect to the problem constraints.

The Compatible Factoring Problem

The second structure mismatch problem is the compatible factoring problem.

This problem occurs when an adequate object type description T and corresponding generator structure are chosen for one constraint (that is, a representation that allows the constraint to be local) that is not compatible with the adequate representations for the other constraints. For example, suppose constraint C1 is expressed as

$$\forall R, \exists L, W[room\ (R) \rightarrow [length(L, R) \wedge L \geq 4] \wedge width(W, R) \wedge W \geq 4]]\ ,$$

where the predicate definitions for length and width are provided as

$$length(L,R) \equiv L = l(R);\ width(W,R) \equiv W = w(R)\ .$$

This constraint can easily be incorporated into the l and w generators when $T(s)$ defines a room by its four parts $<x,y,l,w>$, as in figure 3a. Although this representation allows the incorporation of constraint C1, it was previously shown to be an inadequate representation for constraint C3. Therefore, the $<x, y, l, w>$ solution representation cannot be used to simultaneously incorporate both constraints C1 (length) and C3 (adjacent). This compatible factoring problem occurs because the constraints are not expressed in terms of common or compatible terminology.

To avoid the compatible factoring problem, a hierarchical solution representation $T(s)$ is engineered during compilation to allow all constraints in the given problem class to be expressed using the same terminology. Using $T(s)$, RICK can incorporate all local constraints and avoid the structure mismatch problem.

This engineered representation $T(s)$ must be complete. That is, all attributes of the object represented by $T(s)$ must be computable from the information contained in $T(s)$. For example, a room cannot completely be described by a single corner but can be described by two adjacent sides. Therefore, a representation of a room by its west and north side would be complete.

More formally, for any object a from the set of problem objects O, let $g(a)$ be some property of a (for example, the area of a room). Let r be some component of the representation $T(s)$, and let I be the mapping from the representation components to the objects (the *interpretation map*). A representation is complete if

$$Complete(T(s),O,I) \equiv \forall g\ \exists f\ \forall a\ \forall r[a \in O \wedge r \in T(s) \wedge I(r) = a \rightarrow g(a) = f(r)]\ .$$

Intuitively, this equation states that computable properties of a represented object should mirror the same properties of this actual object.

Knowledge Compilation as Top-Down Refinement

The approach applied in RICK is least commitment, top-down refinement that achieves constraint incorporation by refining the local spatial constraints of P into constrained generators of objects that satisfy P, thus constructing the generator structure using iterative refinement. In contrast, previous approaches regress and incorporate testers into an existing generator structure. RICK takes a set of alternative hierarchical data type descriptions T from which to engineer the solution representation and a collection of local constraints $C_1(s), \ldots, C_n(s)$ from P. The output of RICK is a constrained generator that generates all objects of type T that satisfy constraints $C_1, \ldots, C_n$. Each constrained generator must produce a single value in polynomial time with respect to the size of the problem (for the floor-planning example, size is a function of the number of rooms, the floor-plan length, and floor-plan width.) In the absence of this condition, a constrained generator could be constructed by simply hiding a generator and a tester inside a black box. The polynomial bound guarantees that constrained generators will operate without explicitly testing the candidates and will improve the problem solver's performance.

To construct a constrained generator, in principle, a compiler could simply enumerate all candidates that can be generated and save, in the constrained generator, only those candidates that satisfy the constraints to be incorporated. During execution of the compiled problem solver, the constrained generator would enumerate the saved candidates. Because it is known that the candidates satisfy the incorporated constraints, the testers for the constraints and the backtracking they initiate will not be needed. This approach is clearly ineffective for constructing constrained generators because the initial candidate space can be large and possibly infinite, in which case the compiler could not produce a complete generator. Also, the storage requirements of such a constrained generator could not be satisfied.

Another approach to constraint incorporation is as follows: Suppose the problem specification defines an object, x, of type integer and the constraints $x \geq 5$ and $x \leq maxInt$. Contained in the catalog of basic generator types is a sequence generator, $Generate(p, [start, stop, incr])$, that generates a parameter, p, starting from the initial value, $start$, and generating successive values by increments of $incr$ until stopping with the last value, $stop$. These constraints specify extremes for the range of the generated object x and can easily be incorporated to create the constrained generator $Generate(x, [5, maxInt, 1])$. However, by itself, this direct incorporation strategy will not succeed for hierarchically structured objects and more complex constraints.

RICK modifies and combines these two strategies of enumeration and direct incorporation in a manner illustrated in figure 4. Suppose that RICK were given the constraints C1 (length), C2 (inside), and C3 (adjacent) as input. For each constraint, a set of abstract cases that satisfy the constraint can be derived. Each abstract case represents an entire set of individual objects of type T (that is, a set of solutions). For example, constraint C2 (inside) defines the single abstract case of a room completely contained within or adjacent to the external house walls. This abstract case can be represented by the following set of inequalities:

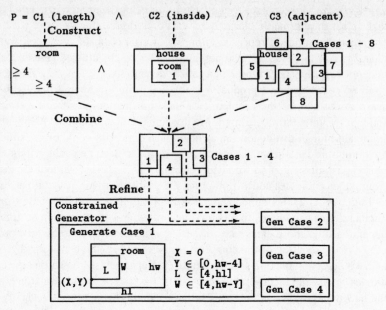

Figure 4. RICK's Synthesis of Constrained Generators.

X coord (SW (house)) ≤ X coord (SW(room)) ≤ X coord(NE(house))

Y coord (SW (house)) ≤ Y coord (SW(room)) ≤ Y coord(NE(house))

X coord (SW (house)) ≤ X coord (NE(room)) ≤ X coord(NE(house))

Y coord (SW (house)) ≤ Y coord (NE(room)) ≤ Y coord(NE(house))

RICK constructs a constrained generator by enumerating these abstract cases in two stages. In the first stage, RICK refines each constraint Ci into a generator of abstract cases representing the different ways of satisfying constraint Ci. For example, constraint C3 (adjacent) is refined into a generator of eight cases. Constraints C1 (length) and C2 (inside) are each refined into single case generators. In the second stage, RICK uses these generators to enumerate each combination of the abstract cases satisfying constraints $C_1, \ldots, C_n$ and determines which combinations are mutually consistent. For example, four of the eight combinations of constraints C1 (length), C2 (inside), and C3 (adjacent) are found to be consistent. The modified direct incorporation strategy is then applied to each consistent combination of abstract cases. RICK builds a separate generator for each consistent combination rather than a single generator for the entire problem. For example, in processing the constraints C1(length), C2 (inside), and C3 (adjacent), RICK synthesizes the constrained generator shown at the bottom of figure 4. The constrained generator operates by successively calling each of four separate generators. Each case generator produces a stream of rooms that are adjacent to a single house side, are inside the house, and satisfy the minimum dimension requirements. The complete RICK algorithm is

RICK-Compiler $(T(s)$ alternative representations, $C_1(s), \ldots, C_n(s))$:
    Construct a representation for $T(s)$ from the alternatives;
    For each local constraint C_i
        Construct a Case Generator;
    Collect consistent abstract case combinations;
    Refine the abstract constrained generator using a primitive representation.

The following subsections discuss each algorithm step in detail.

Construct the Solution Representation $T(s)$

This subsection demonstrates the construction of the solution representation $T(s)$ from the constraints C1 to C5. This task is also described in Braudaway (1990). The goal of this construction is to ensure that all the solution parts mentioned in $P(s)$ appear in the representation of $T(s)$.

Consider constraint C1 (length) expressed as

$$\forall R, \exists L, W[room(R) \rightarrow length(L,R) \wedge width(W,R) \wedge L \geq 4 \wedge W \geq 4],$$

where the predicate definitions for length and width are also provided as

$$length(L,R) \equiv L = l(R); width(W,R) \equiv W = w(R).$$

The l and w parameters are the known length and width primitive components of a rectangle. To obtain the object parts referenced by this constraint, the constraint's predicates are unfolded until all quantified variable sorts (type definitions) are known. For this constraint, the component being constrained is room, which is defined in the problem description to be an instance of the rectangle generic object. This definition serves as an index into the knowledge base of generic objects to access the type description alternatives. The constraint's references include the l and w parts of a room rectangle, which are known in the generic knowledge base to represent the magnitude of a rectangle's north and west sides, respectively. The constructed object type will contain the link from these primitive components, l and w, to the nonprimitive components they represent. Therefore, any constraint reference to l or w will explicitly reference the north or west side, respectively. Figure 5 illustrates the constructed solution representation for this constraint.

Now suppose that constraint C3, stating that each room must share a side with a house side, is expressed as

$$\forall R \exists RS, HS[room(R) \rightarrow sideof(RS,R) \wedge sideof(HS,house) \\ \wedge segmentof(RS,HS1)],$$

where the sideof predicate is defined as

$$sideof(RS,R) \equiv [RS = west(R)] \vee [RS = north(R)] \vee [RS = east(R)] \\ \vee [RS = south(R)].$$

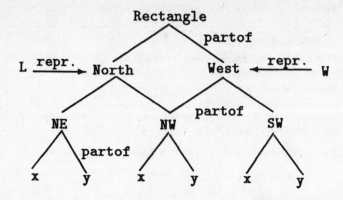

Figure 5. Solution Representation Constructed for the Side Magnitude Constraint.

The *segmentof(RS,HS)* predicate was intuitively defined previously. As before, the component being constrained is room, which is defined in the problem description as an instance of rectangle. The constraint's references include the north, south, west, and east rectangle sides. The east and south components are not defined in the previous type description (figure 5); therefore, the type description is modified by adding the absent links or components that are referenced by the current constraint. The east and south components are added to the representation, giving a solution representation $T(s)$ for the two constraints (figure 6).

A solution representation is complete (formally defined earlier) if a complete set of lower-level components, defined in the knowledge base of generic objects, is either present or derivable for each domain object. In the case of rectangles, these lower-level components are the four rectangular corners SW, NW, NE, and SE. The room representation in figure 6 contains all primitive corners, so it is a complete object type. The representation in figure 5 does not contain the rectangle corner SE; however, the SE corner can be derived from the represented corners SW, NW, and NE using the rectangle constraints about the equality of opposite-side magnitudes and the constraints on parallel sides and perpendicular sides. Therefore, the solution representation in figure 5 is also a complete representation of the room rectangle object.

Construct a Case Generator

To facilitate a least commitment approach, RICK refines a constraint into a generator of abstract cases. This generator is partial because it only generates those parts of the (hierarchical) solution $T(s)$ specified in the constraint. The generator is also abstract because the generated parts are expressed in terms of abstract objects (the nonprimitive part levels of the hierarchical type description).

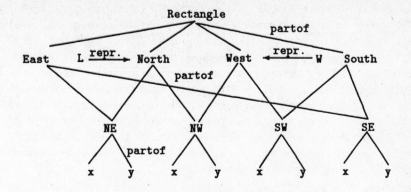

Figure 6. Unified Solution Representation for Both Constraints.

Suppose RICK is given constraint C3 (adjacent):

$\forall R \exists RS, HS[room(R) \rightarrow sideof(RS,R) \wedge sideof(HS,house)$
$\wedge\ segmentof(RS,HS)]$.

RICK first determines which object from $T(s)$ that can be generated is constrained by C3. This context is identified by the universally quantified variable, R in this case, whose defining sort predicate (type definition), $room(R)$ in this case, specifies an object in $T(s)$. This context indicates that the resulting case generator will contribute to room generation.

RICK then transforms each quantified variable into a subgenerator whose values are defined by the sort predicate for this variable. This quantifier range is obtained by unfolding the predicate's definition, which is contained as part of the problem specification. For example, variable RS is defined by the predicate $sideof(RS,R)$, where R is a room previously defined. This predicate unfolds into the disjunctive list (west, north, east, south) and becomes the range of the RS subgenerator for this constraint.

All other predicates, if any, on the left of the implication will define the conditions under which this case generator can be applied. All other predicates on the right of the implication will define the output of the created case generator (that is, the abstract case). For constraint C3, one possible unfolding of the $segmentof(RS,HS)$ predicate is the following specification: $corner1(RS) \in Points(HS) \wedge corner2(RS) \in Points(HS)$. This specification states that each corner of the room side RS can be assigned from the set of points contained on the generated house side HS.

Because there are multiple subgenerators in this case generator (one for HS and one for RS), RICK checks each subgenerator combination (that is, each case) to determine if the case is consistent with the structural constraints of the context (for example, the rectangular room in this example). Each consistent case is recorded in the case generator. For this example, it is known that the end points of a rectangle's (the type description for room and house) sides are distinct points. The west and east sides of a rectangle are vertical (that is, the x values of each point contained on the side are equal); the south and north sides of a rectangle are horizontal. From this information, the abstract case $RS = west$ and $HS = north$ is inconsistent because the corners of the west room side cannot be distinct points and also be assigned from *Points(HS)*. Only the 8 consistent cases from the 16 combinations will be recorded in an association list $G001$ accessed by HS. This value extensionally represents the function that $RS = $ *the set of room sides parallel to the given HS*. The resulting abstract case generator is

Select a House Side, HS, from $\{W, N, E, S\}$
  Generate a Room Side, RS, from $\{W, N, E, S\} \cap G001(HS)$
    with $Corner1(RS) \in Points(HS) \wedge$
      $Corner2(RS) \in Points(HS)$.

Notice, that this case generator includes the case where an east room side can be contained within a west house side. This case is consistent with constraint C3, although I show that this case is not consistent with constraint C2 (inside). The abstract case generator, therefore, represents all different ways of satisfying the incorporated constraint. Also, this abstract case generator is partial in that it only generates a room side. In contrast, a complete generator would construct complete room rectangles.

Which constraints can be reexpressed in this way? Almost by definition, for a constraint to be reexpressible as a generator of partial solutions, it must be a local constraint; that is, it must constrain only a generated part of the solution. For this reason, I have focused on the incorporation of the three constraints C1 to C3 (figure 1) that are local to individual rooms.

The previous abstract case generator is expressed in terms of abstract objects, such as room sides and house sides, instead of primitive parameters such as $x, y, l,$ or w. This formulation of the generator is motivated by the constraint itself, which only specifies these abstract objects and makes no commitment to their primitive parameter representation. Several representation alternatives are usually possible; to unnecessarily commit to a particular one might make the incorporation of other constraints difficult or impossible (because of the constraint factoring problem). I replaced the constraint factoring problem with the new problem of combining several abstract case generators into a single consistent constrained generator.

Collect Consistent Abstract Case Combinations

In our floor-planning example, RICK creates three abstract case generators, one for each of the local constraints C1 to C3 (figure 1). From constraints C1 (length) and C3 (adjacent), RICK produces two room-side generators, and from constraint C2 (inside) it produces a generator for each diagonally opposed room corner SW and NE. Combining these abstract case generators is complicated by the interactions that occur between them. To say that generators interact means that at least one combination of values that can be generated is inconsistent. For example, each room must both be inside the house (C2) and have at least one side on the house boundary (C3).

Each combination defined by the cross-product of each generator's abstract cases must be evaluated for consistency. This consistency checking is conducted in the same manner as that used during the construction of abstract case generators. RICK stores the consistent cases in an abstract constrained generator. Figure 7 illustrates RICK's application of this method to the floor-planning domain. Each abstract case combination is depicted as a different path in a search tree. For example, the left most path in the tree is constructed when the abstract case generator for constraint C3 (adjacency) produces the values [*HS = House West Side, RS = Room West Side*], the next leftmost path corresponds to [*HS = House West Side, RS = Room East Side*], and so on.

After generating a particular path in the search tree (a particular case combination), the set of constraints defining the case (output of the abstract case generator) is checked for consistency. For example, the case combination [*HS = House West Side, RS = Room East Side*] implies that the east room side must be placed on the west house side:

$$Xcoord(SE(RS)) = Xcoord(SW(HS)) . \tag{1}$$

Because all the constraints in this domain are linear, algebraic constraints (see The Evaluation of This Approach for a discussion of this limitation), RICK uses the simplex method to determine their consistency (that is, the existence of a feasible solution to these constraints).[3]

Consistency checking determines that the previous constraint (equation 1) is inconsistent with constraint C2 (inside):

$$Xcoord(SW(HS)) \leq Xcoord(SW(RS))$$

and a constraint associated with rectangles in general

$$Xcoord(SW(RS)) < Xcoord(SE(RS)) .$$

The inconsistency of these constraints follows by transitivity, which intuitively indicates that the abstract case has forced the SW room corner outside the house.

As illustrated in figure 7, four of eight abstract cases are found to be consistent (those not crossed out in the figure), and are collected into an abstract constrained generator for room generation:

Select a House Side, *HS*, from {*W, N, E, S*}
  Generate a Room Side, *RS*, from {*W, N, E, S*} ∩ *G*002(*HS*)
    with *Corner*1 ∈ *Points*(*HS*) ∧
    *Corner*2 ∈ *Points*(*HS*) .

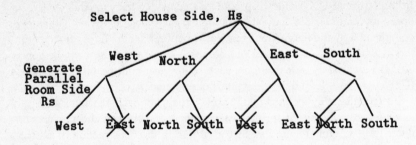

Figure 7. Paths Formed during Simulation.

The term $G002(HS)$ records the four consistent cases as an association list accessed by *HS* and extensionally represents the function that $RS = the set of$ *room sides that correspond to the given HS*.[4] Therefore, this step has resolved the interaction between constraint C3 (adjacency) and constraint C2 (inside).

By using an abstract portion (nonprimitive parts) of the solution representation $T(s)$ in these steps, this modified enumeration strategy is feasible because the number of abstract cases is relatively small. The pruning of inconsistent abstract cases removes entire equivalence classes of inconsistent solution candidates produced by a complete generator.

Refine the Abstract Constrained Generator
Using a Primitive Representation

After combining the abstract case generators, the resulting abstract constrained generator must be refined into a complete generator consisting of a set of primitive parameter generators. This task is accomplished by directly incorporating the constraints for each consistent abstract case into a primitive generator for this case. Constraint incorporation was completed in the previous step. Thus, all complete generators refined from the abstract constrained generator will have the same generation space (even though it will be represented differently). Because RICK only distinguishes between alternative algorithms based on the size of their constrained generation spaces, it views all the refinements as equally good and can construct any one of them. In the floor-planning example, these alternative refinements correspond to the various alternatives for representing a rectangle in terms of primitive parameters (for example, $<x,y,l,w>$).

In actuality, the alternative problem solvers are not equally good: Lower-level differences in data and program structures cause differences in space and time complexity. Ideally, selection should be based on criteria for data- and program-structure optimization. In the current prototype system, the user selects the desired alternative, which is then translated into Lisp.

```
(GENERATE-OBJECT ROOM
    (ENUMERATE BRANCH '(WEST NORTH EAST SOUTH))
    (CASE BRANCH
        ((WEST) ;place room on house west side.
            (GENERATE X 0)
            (GENERATE Y (0 (- hw 4)))
            (GENERATE L (4 hl))
            (GENERATE W (4 (- hw Y))))
        ((NORTH) ;place room on house north side.
            (GENERATE X (0 (- hl 4)))
            (GENERATE Y hw)
            (GENERATE L (4 (- hl X)))
            (GENERATE W (4 hw)))
        ((EAST) ;place room on house east side.
            (GENERATE X hl)
            (GENERATE Y (4 hw))
            (GENERATE L ((- hl) -4))
            (GENERATE W ((- Y) -4)))
        ((SOUTH) ;place room on house south side
            (GENERATE X (0 (- hl 4)))
            (GENERATE Y 0)
            (GENERATE L (4 (- hl X)))
            (GENERATE W (4 hw))))) >
```

Figure 8. Generator Created by Constraint Incorporation.
The CASE statement defines a conditional generator range that depends on the value of BRANCH. [A B] is the generation sequence from A to B, with an increment of 1.

When applied to the floor-planning example, this method incorporates the three local floor-planning constraints C1 to C3. The resulting problem solver (figure 8) generates each room by picking a room location (X,Y) from a point on a house side. The room specification is completed by generating length and width values (starting from the required minimums) that place the room inside the house with respect to the room's location (X,Y).

This problem solver generates roughly $6 \cdot 10^{10}$ candidate solutions for a 9- x 9-foot house with 4 rooms (figure 8). For each of the 4 rooms, there are 4 ways to pick a house side; for each of these cases, there are 21 ways to pick a room side that is a subsegment of this house side. Also, there are 6 ways to pick the perpendicular magnitude. Thus, the total number of candidate solutions is $(21 \cdot 6 \cdot 4)^4$.

This number is a reduction in complexity of five orders of magnitude from the inefficient, generate-and-test problem solver previously shown. RICK was extended to also incorporate constraint C4 (no overlap). The problem solver resulting from incorporating this constraint has a generation space of 12,216 candidates (288 of which are solutions) for this 9 x 9 example.

The Evaluation of This Approach

In this section, I describe some of the limitations of RICK's prototype approach. From these limitations, I identified and implemented several extensions that enhance RICK's scope and potential for scale-up. Although these extensions were implemented, a complete discussion of the results and their implications are beyond the scope of this chapter. Earlier, this chapter presented the underlying issues and framework of the initial RICK prototype. Here, I refer to this initial prototype as RICK-1 and describe the enhanced implementation as RICK-2.

Incorporating Only Local Constraints

Expressed in terms of a particular hierarchical type description T, some constraints are local, factorable into simple constraints on primitive part generators, and others are global, constraining the entire solution or interrelating several parts of the solution. As indicated earlier, RICK-1 is only able to incorporate local constraints. For example, constraint C1 (length) can feasibly be mapped into a constrained generator because C1 depends on a single variable appearing at a leaf in the floor-plan part hierarchy. In contrast, constraint C5 (fill) cannot feasibly be mapped into a constrained generator because C5 is a global constraint in all predefined, alternative representations; that is, it depends on the entire candidate solution. Nevertheless, constraint C5 can be mapped into a tester (as in the naive algorithm) or a hill-climbing patcher. This later mapping is being considered in other research (Voigt and Tong 1989; see chapter 11).

The extension in RICK-2 for this limitation is a restricted constraint-propagation capability, defined within the constrained generators, for semiglobal constraints. A semiglobal constraint depends on a portion of the candidate solution that is larger than a leaf in the part hierarchy but is smaller than the entire solution. The propagation is restricted in the sense that when extending a partial solution by adding a new object, the constrained generator can reference previously generated components to dynamically synthesize new constraints on the currently generated object. If the constrained generator satisfies these new constraints, then, by implication, the semiglobal constraint relating the current component to other component(s) will also be satisfied.

For example, consider the constraint that all rooms must be adjacent to at least one other room. In the constrained generator for room Ri, RICK-2 constructs a routine that chooses a room PR from the set of previous rooms. The routine creates a set of constraints that room Ri's generator must satisfy for room Ri to be adjacent to the selected room PR (for example, $Xcoord(SW(Ri)) = Xcoord(SE(PR))$ and $Ycoord(SE(PR)) \leq Ycoord(SW(Ri)) \leq Ycoord(NE(PR))$). Alternatively, the routine can postpone the satisfaction of the adjacency constraint by placing room Ri on a list of preferred previous rooms. With this action, the routine gives some future room generator the responsibility of satisfying this constraint on room Ri. This option is only allowed as long as there are future rooms to be generated. The last room generator must also try to position its room adjacent to all previous rooms that have not satisfied this constraint (that is, preferred rooms) if possible. If the current generator is unable to satisfy the constraints created by the routine, then chronological backtracking on the routine's choice points (and possible earlier choice points) occurs.

Constraint C4 (no overlap) is a special case of a semiglobal constraint. Because C4 defines a relationship between pairs of rooms, RICK-2 can produce a more efficient constraint-propagation strategy that does not rely as heavily on backtracking. The details of this result will be reported at a later date.

Incorporating Only Linear Algebra Constraints

RICK-1 constructs constrained generators from constraints that define structural relationships between components of $T(s)$. For some domains, these constraints are linear, algebraic constraints on the composite objects (that is, linear combinations of parameter values). This limitation allows the use of the simplex method during RICK-1's combine step to check the consistency of the composed abstract cases. It also allows RICK-1's refine step to use the *direct incorporation strategy* (that is, adjusting lower and upper bounds on the range of generated values) to incorporate the constraints into primitive parameters.

RICK-2 can handle other types of constraints by extending its combine step to include other processes that evaluate the consistency of a set of constraints (for example, integer programming or symbolic evaluation). RICK-2 was extended to allow constraints whose predicates define functional algorithm components and constraints that define relationships between sets. RICK-2's refine step can further be extended with other automatic software design strategies (for example, Paige and Henglein [1987]) that will allow it to transform a set of consistent constraints into a primitive algorithm component.

Creating Only Extendable Incremental Refinement Problem Solvers

The generate-and-test problem-solving architecture produced by the RICK-1 compiler can be characterized as an incremental refinement architecture. However, RICK-1's resulting problem solver is only capable of *monotonic refinement*; that is, a solution is constructed by a generation structure that only extends a partial solution into a more complete solution. During generation, an object in a partial solution is not modified when it adds a new object to the partial solution. In the floor-planning domain example, the generator extends a partial solution by adding a new room without modifying any existing rooms.

Some problems necessitate the use of refinement that modifies objects within the partial solution. For example, Flemming et al. (1986) define a type of spatial configuration domain, called *topological configuration*, which generates a rectangular topology (rectangles with left-of, right-of, above, and below parameters whose values are other rectangles) called an *orthogonal structure*. When a partial solution is extended by adding a new rectangle to the orthogonal structure, the existing rectangles are refined by modifying their parameters to include their new relationship to the newly added rectangle. The prototype version, RICK-1, is incapable of producing this type of refinement problem solver.

To obtain the more general incremental refinement problem solver needed in some domains, the compiler requires more declarative information about the structure of $T(s)$. Included in the information about the parts contained in $T(s)$ is information describing how the parts are composed to form object s. In the topology domain, this information describes how an orthogonal structure is inductively composed with the addition of a new rectangle. In the extended RICK-2 compiler, the hierarchical object description $T(s)$ is augmented with a declarative composition rule. This rule defines the context under which the objects that can be generated are combined as well as a description of the addition and deletion tasks that must to be made to existing objects to extend a partial solution of type $T(s)$. With this extension, RICK-2 can produce an iterative refinement problem solver that is capable of not only extending partial solutions but also modifying existing objects in a partial solution to produce a correctly composed $T(s)$. This extension is restricted to only those operations needed to compose object parts into a valid object of type $T(s)$.

Compiling Only Parameter Instantiation Problems

In general, for structure synthesis problems, the hierarchical structure of the object to be synthesized cannot be known at compile time. The problem specification defines a set of refinement rules from which objects are synthesized to dynamically solve the problem (at run time). Although RICK-1's top-down refinement compilation process chooses the structure of the synthesized object $T(s)$ from a set of alternatives, it does so at compile time, and the structure of all alternatives is explicitly represented. Therefore, RICK-1 is not capable of handling general structure synthesis problems.

I have extended RICK-2 to handle a broader class of structure synthesis problems than the class of parameter instantiation problems. In particular, RICK-2 is capable of synthesizing connector objects as well as constructing component objects. When a relationship between multiple objects is defined by the propagation of new constraints (as previously defined for semiglobal constraints), it might be necessary to connect these objects with a connector (for example, a door in the floor-planning domain or a wire in a circuit layout problem). When this interaction is satisfied by the constrained generator, it can instantiate a new generator for the connecting object and post new constraints on this generator that must be satisfied. This approach extends RICK-2's scope by dynamically adding connector objects, such as doors, to the structure of object *s*; however, the structure of the connector objects must be known a priori for RICK-2 to create a generator that can be dynamically instantiated.

Scaling This Approach for More Complex Problems

A spatial configuration problem is given to RICK-2 through a problem specification and a knowledge base of generic objects. The knowledge base contains the declarative composition rules discussed previously and alternative type descriptions *T* for generic objects such as rectangles. Represented with each part in the alternative type descriptions are the relevant structural constraints (for example, "East and West rectangle sides are parallel"). The problem specification contains the list of objects in the problem, the type of each object from the knowledge base, the type of problem defined by a reference to a composition rule in the knowledge base, and the problem class constraints given in first-order predicate calculus. The remainder of the RICK-2 compiler is domain independent for the class of spatial configuration problems.

RICK-2 was demonstrated for two classes of spatial configuration problems, as defined by the two composition rules developed to date. These problems are geometric configuration problems for objects generated on a grid system within a bounded area and topological configuration problems (defined previously) for objects generated within an orthogonal structure. Tests are being conducted on variations of the floor-planning domain and single-layer circuit layout problems for both the geometric and topological domain classes. New classes of spatial configuration problems can be added by adding more composition rules and generic objects to the knowledge base.

RICK-2 is being combined with other compilation methods within the KBSDE project to compile problem solvers that perform at an acceptable level for more complex problems. Because the KBSDE compiler maps problems into the function level (chapter 11), defining a problem solver in terms of functional components, other automatic programming tools (for example, REFINE [Reasoning Systems 1987]) can be used to further refine the problem solver into an existing programming language such as Lisp or C. By applying RICK-2 as part of a larger compiler, I expect to be able to compile a problem solver that performs in a manner analogous to Flemming's ROOS1 system (Flemming et al. 1986). This includes ROOS's application to building floorplan design, analog board layout, service core design, and other problems (Coyne and Flemming 1990).

Related Work

To facilitate the comparison of this work with related work in automated software design, it is useful to view knowledge compilation as a design process that designs a problem solver from the specification for a class of problems. I contrast three approaches according to their model of the design process and the manner in which domain knowledge is used to produce reasonably efficient algorithms.

Knowledge Compilation as Iterative Redesign

Tappel (1980) defines test and constraint incorporation as modifications to a data flow graph representing the components of the algorithm to be synthesized. A test refers to certain solution components; hence, these solution components must be generated before the test can be run. Tappel's approach moves a test backward in the algorithm's data flow graph until it is placed just after the generators of these referenced solution components. An attempt is also made to modify the generator so that only values that satisfy the test are enumerated. Tappel's approach takes a generate-and-test algorithm as input and iteratively redesigns it by incorporating constraints.

The strategy used by DIOGENES (chapter 10) is similar to Tappel's but applies a transformational approach to modify an initial generate-and-test algorithm (for possibly overconstrained problems) into a more efficient heuristic search algorithm. This approach uses domain knowledge that has been embedded in some or all of the transformations. However, the design knowledge for controlling the compilation process is supplied by the user of the DIOGENES system (who selects among applicable transformations). The design model used by both of these strategies is hill-climbing that iteratively redesigns a problem solver to improve its efficiency (although some steps do not directly improve efficiency but enable other optimization steps).

RICK constructs constrained generators of solutions whose feasibility is defined by problem constraints. In contrast with the iterative redesign approaches, which incorporate constraints after a complete problem solver is created, RICK refines the problem constraints into partial solution generators (which are then merged), thus simultaneously designing the problem solver and incorporating constraints. By using a least commitment approach for representation selection, RICK decouples the issues of incorporating constraints and representing generated solutions that the iterative redesign approach must handle together.

Knowledge Compilation as Top-Down Refinement

CYPRESS (Smith 1988), using KIDS (chapter 19), focuses on mapping declarative knowledge into a global search algorithm. A global search algorithm splits a set representation for all candidate solutions of a problem into subsets and extracts solutions from the subsets when possible. This approach uses declarative domain knowledge in the form of procedural schemas. For example, one global search schema enumerates all bounded sequences over a finite set. The method refines the problem specification into an algorithm by choosing the domain-specific schema that best matches the problem domain. This algorithm schema is refined through theorem proving (and program transformations) to fill in the details of the algorithm. Constraints are formulated and incorporated during this instantiation of the procedural schema.

The RICK compiler refines the constraints into abstract case generators, which are combined into a single abstract case generator; this single abstract case generator is refined into a problem solver that generates complete solutions. RICK's refinement steps have a smaller grain size then those used by CYPRESS. CYPRESS constructs (by instantiation) a single algorithm. In contrast, RICK composes an algorithm structure out of a set of constrained generators tailored to the given problem class.

CYPRESS, and STRATA (Lowry 1990; chapter 20) can reason about problem specifications that constrain the behavior of data manipulation. RICK, however, handles structural (object-oriented type) constraints on objects. KIDS and STRATA were applied to problems defined on recursive data types such as lists, sequences, and sets. In contrast, the structural constraint type of problem (which includes spatial configuration) defines a finite set of objects where constructing an acceptable solution means assigning values to all the attributes to satisfy the structural constraints.

Knowledge Compilation as Representation Design

DRAT (Van Baalen 1988) designs a representation for analytic reasoning tasks given in predicate calculus. A problem solver uses the representation to translate a problem statement (a set of facts) into a structure that can be inspected to answer questions about the facts. DRAT searches a library of specialized representations to find a representation that maximizes the number of constraints incorporated into the behavior of the representation (that is, data structure).

This goal is similar to RICK's task of selecting a representation that allows constraint incorporation from a library of alternatives. The representations in DRAT's library include standard methods that operate on the representation. RICK's alternative type descriptions are more declarative in that they only contain structural constraints on the objects within the library. DRAT also enforces constraints in a data structure by designing active value functions into the representation. RICK enforces constraints by compiling them into the solution generation process. The domains for which DRAT and RICK apply are also different. DRAT handles the class of problems that identify and reason about extensional sets, and RICK handles domains that construct artifacts in spatial configuration problems.

Summary

Complete incorporation of a constraint into a generator is a difficult task, especially when the constraint (expressed in terms of the generated parameters) has a structure that is not factorable into constraints on the individual parameter generators. In this chapter, I described and illustrated the results of the RICK program, which avoids structure mismatch problems by viewing constraint incorporation as top-down refinement from constraints into constrained generators. RICK incorporates a problem constraint by refining it into an abstract case generator that is guaranteed to satisfy the constraint (abstractly). These generators are then combined into a single abstract generator. During combination, interactions between cases are resolved by simulating the generators and collecting only those generated combinations that are proven to be consistent. Because the constraints are fully incorporated into the combined generator, further refinement into a complete generator of primitive parameters will not create a structure mismatch problem.

RICK produces problem solvers that solve spatial configuration design problems. It was demonstrated using the house floor-planning domain. RICK is being applied to variations of the floor-planning task as well as circuit design and topology configuration tasks. I also discussed the scale-up potential of RICK to more complex domains such as building layout design. RICK currently consists of 21,000 lines of Lisp code and compiles the example floor-planning problem solver in roughly 25 minutes of central processing unit time on a Sun Sparcstation.

Acknowledgments

Special thanks to Chris Tong for his support, leadership, and contributions to the ideas reported in this chapter. I am grateful to the members of the Rutgers University AI/Design Project for the ideas and stimulating environment they provide. I would like to thank Elaine Kant, Mike Lowry, and Chris Tong for their helpful comments on earlier drafts.

Notes

1. We are using the convention of uppercase for variables and lowercase for predicates and constants.

2. The elements *hl* (house length value in the *x* direction) and *hw* (house width value in the *y* direction) are parameters whose values are problem specific.

3. I realize in retrospect that I should have used an integer programming method to guarantee the soundness of the answer because the coordinates are integer valued. The approach can be extended by using routines that check the consistency of other classes of (nonlinear) constraints. Note that this floor planner cannot be implemented as a linear program, primarily because some of the constraints C1 to C5 are expressed as disjunctions.

4. This mapping associates west room side with west house side, north room side with north house side, and so on.

References

Benjamin, P., ed. 1990. *Change of Representation and Inductive Bias*. Boston: Kluwer.

Braudaway, W. 1990. Constraint Incorporation and the Structure Mismatch Problem. In *Change of Representation and Inductive Bias*, ed. P. Benjamin, 193–207. Boston: Kluwer.

Coyne, R. F., and Flemming, U. 1990. Planning in Design Synthesis: Abstraction-Based Loos. In *Applications of Artificial Intelligence in Engineering*, ed. J. S. Gero, 91–111. Berlin: Springer-Verlag.

Dechter, R., and Pearl, J. 1988. Network-Based Heuristics for Constraint-Satisfaction Problems. *Artificial Intelligence* 34:1–38.

Dietterich, T., and Bennett, J. 1986. The Test Incorporation Theory of Problem Solving (Preliminary Report). In Proceedings of the Workshop on Knowledge Compilation, 145–161. Menlo Park, Calif.: American Association for Artificial Intelligence.

Dietterich, T., ed. 1986. Proceedings of the Workshop on Knowledge Compilation. Menlo Park, Calif.: American Association for Artificial Intelligence.

Flemming, U.; Coyne, R.; Glavin, T.; and Rychener, M. 1986. Roos1—Version 1 of a Generative Expert System for the Design of Building Layouts. In Proceedings of the International Joint Conference on CAD and Robotics in Architecture and Construction, 157–166. New York: Nichols.

Korf, R. 1980. Toward a Model of Representation Changes. *Artificial Intelligence* 14(1): 41–78.

Lowry, M. R. 1990. Strata: Problem Reformulation and Abstract Data Types. In *Change of Representation and Inductive Bias*, ed. D. P. Benjamin, 41–66. Boston: Kluwer.

Paige, R., and Henglein, F. 1987. Mechanical Translation of Set-Theoretic Problem Specifications into Efficient Ram Code—A Case Study. *Journal of Symbolic Computation* 4(2): 207-232.

Reasoning Systems. 1987. REFINE User's Guide. Reasoning Systems, Inc., Palo Alto, California.

Smith, D. 1988. Structure and Design of Global Search Algorithms, Technical Report KES.U.87.12, Kestrel Institute, Palo Alto, California.

Steinberg, L., and Ling, R. 1990. A Priori Knowledge of Structure versus Constraint Propagation: One Fragment of a Science of Design, Working Paper, 164, AI/Design Project, Rutgers Univ.

Tappel, S. 1980. Some Algorithm Design Methods. In Proceedings of the First National Conference on Artificial Intelligence, 64–67. Menlo Park, Calif.: American Association for Artificial Intelligence.

Van Baalen, J. 1988. Overview of an Approach to Representation Design. In Proceedings of the Seventh National Conference on Artificial Intelligence, 392–397. Menlo Park, Calif.: American Association for Artificial Intelligence.

Voigt, K., and Tong, C. 1989. Automating the Construction of Patchers That Satisfy Global Constraints. In Proceedings of the Eleventh International Joint Conference on Artificial Intelligence, 1446-1452. Menlo Park, Calif.: International Joint Conferences on Artificial Intelligence.

13

Subtask Independence
and Algorithm Synthesis

Robert McCartney

Algorithm synthesis can be defined as the translation from a functional specification of a task to an operational one; that is, given what to do, determine how to do it. A central problem in automating algorithm synthesis is search control; unless a system does better than exhaustively searching through the space of possible designs, it will never be able to scale up to reasonably general domains and techniques.

The focus of this chapter is on the search-limiting effects of sibling independence on the design process. Tasks are siblings if they are subtasks of the same task; sibling tasks are independent if the successful synthesis of one has no effect on the synthesis of the others, and the failed synthesis of any subtask leads to the failure of the decomposition containing it (hence, the success or failure of other siblings becomes irrelevant). If by some method, we could quickly find out whether a decomposition will succeed or fail, we could reduce the effort expended in synthesis. Requiring subtasks in a decomposition to be independent is such a method; we can individually consider their syntheses, making it easier to detect failure and reducing the effects of any ordering decisions that we make.

The underlying model of algorithm synthesis (and the experimental test bed for many of these ideas) is the algorithm synthesis system MEDUSA, which I describe in the first part of the chapter. Given this model, I discuss sibling independence in terms of functional interactions (functional independence) and constraint propagation (cost independence).

MEDUSA: A Model of Algorithm Synthesis

MEDUSA (McCartney 1988) was developed to explore algorithm synthesis techniques and was designed with the following goals in mind: (1) synthesis should be done without user intervention; (2) algorithms will be produced to meet some given performance constraints; and (3) the synthesizer should be reasonably efficient, that is, be considerably better than exhaustive search. These three goals are all closely related to search control. The first goal means that no external guidance will be available to help avoid search, forcing the search strategies (and, more generally, all the knowledge needed to perform the tasks) to be internal to the synthesizer. The second goal limits the possible range of solutions for a task and, furthermore, provides a metric for judging the value of a solution. The third goal emphasizes the development of search-limiting strategies that will allow synthesizers to scale up to larger problems and amounts of knowledge.

In general, algorithm synthesis is difficult; it requires large amounts of domain and design knowledge, and much of design appears to be complex manipulations and intuitive leaps. We have attempted to circumvent these problems by working with a restricted set of synthesis methods in a restricted domain. The underlying hypothesis is that a fairly restricted set of methods can be used to produce algorithms with clean design and adequate (if not optimal) performance. The domain used to develop and test MEDUSA is the planar intersection problem from computational geometry. This domain has a number of characteristics that make it a good test area: (1) nearly all objects of interest are sets, so most algorithmic tasks can be defined in terms of set primitives; (2) a number of tasks exist that are not hard (that is, linear to quadratic complexity; algorithms in this range are practical for reasonably large problems); (3) although all the objects are ultimately point sets, most can be described by other composite structures, for example, lines and planar regions, so object representation is naturally hierarchical; (4) problems in this domain are solvable by a variety of techniques, some general and some domain specific. Choosing the proper technique from a number of possibilities is often necessary to obtain the desired performance. The test problems (with associated performance constraints) used in developing this system are given in table 1.

These problems have many similarities (minimizing the amount of domain knowledge needed) but differ enough to demand reasonable extensibility of

Task	Cost Constraint
Detect whether two convex polygons (*N* sides total) intersect.	*N*
Report the intersection of two convex polygons (*N* sides total).	*N*
Detect whether two simple polygons (*N* sides total) intersect.	*N log N*
Report the intersection of two simple polygons (*N* sides total).	*(N + S) log N*
Report the connected components in a set of *N* line segments.	(N + S) log N
Report the connected components in a set of *N* isothetic line segments.	*N log N + S*
Report the intersection of *N k*-sided convex polygons.	*N k log N*
Report the intersection of *N* half planes.	*N log N*
Report the intersection of *N* half planes.	N^2
Report the intersection of *N* isothetic rectangles.	*N*
Report the intersection of *N* arbitrary rectangles.	*N log N*
Report the area of the union of *N* isothetic rectangles.	*N log N*
Report the perimeter of the union of *N* isothetic rectangles.	*N log N*
Report the connected components of a set of *N* isothetic rectangles.	*N log N + S*
Detect if any three points in a set of *N* points are colinear.	N^2
Detect if any three points in a set of *N* points are colinear.	N^3
Detect if any three lines in a set of *N* lines share an intersection.	N^2
Report all lines intersecting a set of *N* vertical-line segments.	*N log N*
Report all lines intersecting a set of *N* x-sorted vertical-line segments.	*N*

Table 1. Test Problems for Algorithm Synthesizer.
S refers to the number of pairwise intersections between segments or polygon sides.

techniques. MEDUSA is implemented in Lisp. It uses and modifies a first-order predicate calculus database using the deductive database system DUCK (Mc-Dermott 1985). The database contains knowledge about specific algorithms, general design techniques, and domain knowledge and is used as a scratch-pad during synthesis. Useful DUCK features include data dependencies for truth maintenance, data pools for maintaining different contexts, and a convenient bidirectional Lisp interface that supports procedural attachment and user extensions to the underlying control mechanisms.

The Synthesis Process

The synthesis process in MEDUSA is characterized by three features: It proceeds from the top down, it is cost constrained, and subtasks can only be generated in a small number of ways.

MEDUSA synthesizes algorithms from the top down; it starts with a functional description of a task and either finds a known algorithm that performs the desired function within the cost constraint or generates a sequence of subtasks that is functionally equivalent to the task. This process continues recursively on the subtasks until all are associated with a sequence of known algorithms (primitives). This process naturally leads to a hierarchical structure in which the algorithm can be viewed at a number of abstraction levels . Furthermore, it allows the synthesis process to be viewed as generation with a grammar (with the known algorithms as terminals).

Synthesis is cost constrained; a performance constraint (maximum cost) that the synthesized algorithm must satisfy is included in the task specification. Researchers' position is that an algorithm is not sufficiently described until its complexity is known with some (situation-dependent) precision. Asymptotic time complexity on a Ram was chosen as the cost function because it is the standard metric used for algorithms on a sequential machine; this choice has effects on synthesis control (see Using Asymptotic Costs), but other metrics would work as well. Two reasonable alternatives to using a cost constraint that are precluded by practical considerations are (1) having the synthesizer produce optimal (or near-optimal) algorithms or (2) having the synthesizer produce the cheapest algorithm possible given its knowledge base (both of these are in terms of run-time performance). To produce an optimal algorithm, the system must be able to determine what the optimal performance is; this task is difficult, requiring a different set of techniques from design. Producing the cheapest possible algorithm is comparable in complexity to producing every possible algorithm for a task, unless we can provide an infallible mechanism to choose among decompositions. This process is likely to be exponential in the total number of subtasks, making it impractical for all but the shortest derivations.

A key function in MEDUSA (as in any hierarchical problem solver) is *subtask generation*; given a task description, decompose it into a sequence of subtasks whose execution is functionally equivalent to the task. One of the ways researchers simplify synthesis in this system is to use only four methods to generate subtasks.

The first method uses schemas to generate equivalent skeletal algorithms. A *skeletal algorithm* is an algorithm with known function but with some parts (its subtasks) incompletely specified. For example, an algorithm to report all intersecting pairs from a set of objects ($A(s) = \{(x,y) \mid x \in s \land y \in s \land x \neq y \land x \cap y \neq \varnothing\}$) can have a two-object intersection test as its subtask. The schemas range from those generating specific algorithms (for example, a sort algorithm with a generic comparison function) to general algorithmic paradigms (for example, binary divide and conquer). These schemas are a convenient way to express general paradigms and allow generalizations of known algorithms whose subtasks can be designed to exploit specific task characteristics. The execution cost of a skeletal algorithm is specified as a function of its subtasks' costs.

The second subtask generation method is to transform the task into an equivalent one using explicit domain information. This process allows the use of logical equivalence in decomposing tasks. For example, the fact "for any polygons A and B, A contains B if and only if B is a subset of A, and their boundaries do not intersect" allows the decomposition of a containment test of two polygons into a conjunction of the tests for subset and boundary intersection.

The third subtask generation method uses case decomposition. Suppose that there is some set of cases, at least one of which is true (a disjunction). A way to perform a task under these circumstances is to determine a case that is true, then solve the task given this case. An algorithm that handles this situation requires two subtasks for each case: one that tests whether the case holds, another to do the original task given the case holds. We restrict this algorithm by considering only disjunctions where exactly one disjunct is true (termed oneofdisjunction by de Kleer [1986]). Care is taken to ensure that the case decomposition chosen is relevant to the task at hand.

The fourth way to generate a subtask is to use some dual transform; specifically, transform a task and its parameters into some dual space, and solve the equivalent task there. This technique can be effective, allowing the use of algorithms and techniques from related problems and domains, but is difficult to control unless it is possible to predict that a problem is easier in some other domain. For example, suppose we want to detect whether any three points in a finite point set are colinear. Given that we have a transform that maps a line to a point and vice versa, and if two objects intersect in the primal if and only if they intersect in the dual, then we can recast this problem as, first, map the points in the input set to a set of lines and, second, detect whether any three lines in this line set share an intersection.

Of the four decomposition methods, skeletal algorithms are the most general; with minor modifications, they could be used to implement the other three. Because these modifications affect control during synthesis (in particular, the current implementation requires that skeletal algorithms have functionally independent subtasks), the methods were separately implemented to allow greater flexibility in control strategies. For details, see McCartney (1988).

Example: Detect Intersection of Two Convex Polygons

The synthesis process can be illustrated with an example (figure 1): Synthesize an algorithm that can determine whether two convex polygons intersect and that runs, in the worst case, in time proportional to the total number of vertices. For notational convenience, I label the polygons A and B.

First, the task is decomposed into four disjoint cases using domain information: The polygon boundaries intersect, A contains B, B contains A, or the polygons do not intersect. Because the cost of the task (using this decomposition) is the sum of its subtasks, each subtask has the linear time constraint. This simple propagation of the parent's constraint will also apply to the rest of the subtasks in this example.

Working first on the boundaries intersect case, we synthesize an algorithm to see if the boundaries intersect. We use a skeletal algorithm, a *sweep-line algorithm* to detect line-segment intersection (Preparata and Shamos 1985), which applies because a polygon boundary is a set of line segments (actually it is slightly more complicated because adjacent segments in each boundary

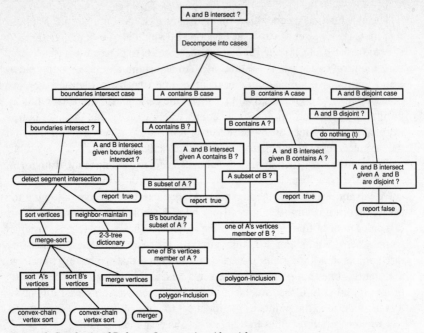

Figure 1. Synthesis of Polygon Intersection Algorithm.
Tasks are represented by rectangles, known and skeletal algorithms by ovals.

intersect at an end point, but these intersections can be filtered without in-creasing the time complexity). This sweep-line algorithm has two compo-nents (subtasks): one to sort the vertices of the segments in X-order, one to perform a dynamic neighbor-maintain algorithm on the segments in Y-order. To sort the vertices in X-order, we use a skeletal merge-sort algorithm: Its subtasks are (1) sort A's vertices, (2) sort B's vertices, and (3) merge the two sorted vertex sets. The two sorts can each be accomplished using a known al-gorithm that sorts the vertices of a convex chain in linear time. The third sub-task can be accomplished by using the standard linear-time merge algorithm (with constant-time comparisons).

The dynamic neighbor-maintain is a dictionary algorithm (Aho, Hopcroft, and Ullman 1974). Set items are line segments; they are to be put into some structure on the basis of their relative Y positions. The input to this algorithm is a linear number of queries; the queries used are insert, delete, and report-neighbors (that is, for a given segment, return the segments directly above and below it). This subtask is done by using the known algorithm 2-3-dy-namic sort, a dictionary implemented with a 2-3 tree that supports a superset of the necessary queries. The cost of this algorithm is the sum of the costs of its queries, each of which is equal to the log of the cardinality of the working set (the excess of inserts over deletes) at the time of the query. The working set cardinality here is bounded by the number of line segments in the two sets that intersect some vertical line; because the polygons are convex, the number of boundary segments intersecting any line is bounded by a constant. Because the number of queries in the neighbor-maintain task is linear, and the working set cardinality is bounded by a constant, this algorithm satisfies the linear constraint.

Detecting whether the polygons intersect, given that the boundaries intersect, is done using the known algorithm "report true," because boundary intersection implies intersection.

Next, we work on the *A contains B* case, first trying to get an algorithm to see if the case holds. We have the additional information that the boundaries do not intersect because we already tested this case and would only reach this point if the test were false. By definition, *A* contains *B* if and only if *B* is a subset of *A*, and their boundaries do not intersect. Because the boundary intersection is null, an equivalent task is to determine whether *B* is a subset of *A*. *A* and *B* are bounded regions, so *B* is a subset of *A* if and only if *B*'s boundary is a subset of *A*. Because *A* is a bounded region, and its boundary does not intersect *B*'s boundary, either *B*'s boundary is a subset of *A*, or *B*'s boundary and *A* are disjoint. Therefore, it suffices to check whether any non-null subset of *B* is a subset of *A*, so for simplicity, we use a singleton subset of *B* (any member) and test for inclusion in *A*. We can perform this test using a known polygon-point-inclusion algorithm on polygon *B* and any vertex of *A*, with performance that is linear in the number of *B*'s vertices. This test determines whether *A* contains *B*. The second part of this case, determining whether the polygons intersect given that *A* contains *B*, is equivalent to "report true."

Next, we work on the *B contains A* case, with the added preconditions that the boundaries do not intersect, and *A* does not contain *B*. It differs slightly from the previous case because the task *A subset of B?* is equivalent to one point of *A* being in *B* because of the added precondition that *A* does not contain *B*. Otherwise, it is just the previous case with the parameters reversed.

Finally, we work on the *A and B disjoint* case, with the added preconditions that the boundaries do not intersect and that neither polygon contains the other. These added preconditions imply that *A* and *B* are disjoint; so, determining whether the case holds is equivalent to "do nothing (always true)," and determining whether the polygons intersect given that they are disjoint is equivalent to "report false." Therefore, this question can be resolved using the following sequence of operations (with cost proportional to the sum of the number of sides of the two polygons):

Run detect-segment-intersections algorithm using the following components:
- Sort the polygon vertices using merge sort with components
  - sort each polygon's vertices using convex-chain-vertex sort
  - merge the two polygon's vertices.

> • Use 2-3-dynamic-sort for dictionary during scan.
> If detect-segment-intersections returns true, report true
> else Do a polygon-point-inclusion test for polygon A, any vertex of B.
>   if it shows inclusion, report true
>   else Do a polygon-point-inclusion for polygon B, any vertex of A.
>   if it shows intersection, report true
>   else report false.

This example illustrates the process of decomposing tasks, propagating constraints, and composing the results into an algorithm. I did not discuss chosing among alternative decompositions or ordering the subtasks for synthesis; I discuss these issues later. The example corresponds to behavior observed in MEDUSA before schemas for sweep-line algorithms were added to the knowledge base, schemas that led to an alternative synthesized algorithm.

Synthesis Mechanics

Synthesis can be represented by a single routine that takes a task and (1) generates an equivalent decomposition (subtask sequence), (2) calls itself for each subtask in its decomposition that is not completely specified, and (3) computes the cost of the task as a function of the costs in the decomposition. The cost constraints propagate forward from task to subtask; the costs percolate back from subtask to task. The important control mechanisms are those that pick from a group of possible decompositions, choose which active task to work on, propagate constraints and combine costs, and instantiate tasks.

Choosing among Alternative Decompositions. A problem inherent in synthesis is the possibility of combinatorial explosion as a result of multiple decomposition choices. Unless it is always possible a priori to choose a decomposition that will lead to a solution whose performance is within the constraint, sometimes synthesis will reach a dead end (no decomposition possible or time constraint violated). In these cases, some form of backtracking must be done. Unless severely limited, this backtracking will lead to exponential time for synthesis. To reduce backtracking, MEDUSA uses a sequence of heuristics to choose the candidate most likely to succeed. The heuristics used in MEDUSA are partly dependent on implementation decisions made regarding independence (see Choice Heuristics and Results).

Independence and Synthesis Order. If the subtasks in a decomposition are independent, the order in which the subtasks are synthesized is unimportant. This situation is not always the case; consider the case- determination tasks in the example. The fact that the boundaries did not intersect was important to the solution of the containment determinations, and the facts that the boundaries did not intersect and that neither polygon contained the other made the task of testing whether A and B were disjoint into a trivial one. In general, the testing of any conjunction, disjunction, or oneofdisjunction of predicates is highly order dependent because each predicate test is dependent on which predicates were already tested. It might be that not all orderings lead to a solution within the time constraint; so, part of the synthesis task is to determine this order of execution.

Propagating Constraints and Combining Costs. Because much of the control of the system is based on costs, it is necessary to manipulate and compare cost expressions. In this model, *costs* are symbolic expressions that evaluate to integers; they are arithmetic functions of algorithm costs, set cardinalities, and constants. There is an expression manipulator that can simplify such expressions, symbolically compare them, and propagate constraints to subtasks given the task constraint and the task cost as a function of the subtask costs. The use of asymptotic costs simplifies propagation and combining as well as the promotion of subtask independence, as discussed in Using Asymptotic Costs.

Task Instantiation. Sibling independence is based on the relationships among the sibling subtasks at instantiation time, that is, when a particular decomposition is chosen for a task, and the components of this decomposition are made into tasks. Assuming that the functional description of a subtask is equivalent to preconditions and postconditions, the instantiation of a subtask involves replacing parameters with the appropriate arguments from the parent task; making instances of any uninstantiated variables; and asserting the preconditions and postconditions into the task's context, which is typically the context of its parent (a case where subtasks are instantiated into different contexts is discussed in Order Independence). This process assumes applicative algorithms; the postconditions cannot reflect changes to the input because both are asserted into the database and assumed to lead to no contradiction. Instantiation of sibling subtasks must ensure that variable bindings (instantiated parameters) are consistent across subtasks.

Comparing MEDUSA to Other Synthesis Systems

MEDUSA is an intellectual descendent of the PSI project (Barstow 1979; Kant 1979) because it depends on large amounts of domain knowledge and uses efficiency information to guide search. More specifically, it has a number of features in common with other algorithm design systems, particularly KIDS (chapter 19), STRATA (chapter 20), and DESIGNER-SOAR (chapter 22). All these systems design algorithms from functional specifications, primarily work from the top down, and attempt to synthesize efficient algorithms. The differences are primarily those of emphasis; the different systems are attacking overlapping parts of the same problem. A few examples follow:

First, search control is a central feature in MEDUSA, as it is in DESIGNER-SOAR. In the latter, search is directed by means-ends analysis and becomes more effective with experience. In MEDUSA, search control is based on local characteristics, including efficiency information, and does not improve with experience.

Second, encoding algorithmic paradigms as templates is important in MEDUSA, KIDS, and STRATA. The tactics encoded in KIDS and STRATA tend to be generally applicable and, as a result, are individually more complex. MEDUSA tends to have a larger number of more specific schemas to encode a particular tactic; for example, divide and conquer is handled by two schemas in MEDUSA, one for equal-sized decompositions and one for one-rest decompositions. Both would fit under the general divide-and-conquer tactic in KIDS.

Third, problem reformulation is central in STRATA, where a problem specification is abstracted before design. This reformulation is a generalization of the use of duality in MEDUSA and is emphasized much more in the STRATA research. Both problem reformulation and duality relate to DESIGNER-SOAR'S use of multiple problem spaces; in all these cases, the system attempts to find a design space that facilitates a solution. Given the overall similarities, it is expected that the search-control techniques used in MEDUSA could be transferred to other algorithm design systems.

Functional Independence

Two siblings are functionally independent if their functional descriptions can completely be specified at instantiation time. As an example, consider a task to sort the union of a number of disjoint sets of numbers; we can use a merge-sort task with the following subtasks: map a sort function over the input set (producing a set of sorted sets) and merge the sorted sets into one set.

Suppose the input and output sets of this task are A, a set of disjoint number sets, and B, a set of numbers that is a permutation of the reduction by the union of A (that is, B is the sorted set whose members are those found in the union of all the members of A). We instantiate the subtasks by making A the input of the map subtask and B the output of the merge subtask and make a new instance C, a set of sorted number sets that is the output of the map subtask and the input to the merge subtask. As part of instantiation, the preconditions and postconditions are asserted, notably that C is a set of sorted sets and that each of its members is a permutation of a member of A.

The input to the second subtask here is the output of the first, which forces an order onto the execution of the subtasks. Because the preconditions of the merge subtask (that is, its input is a set of sorted disjoint number sets) are known at instantiation time, we can synthesize these siblings in any order. Having an algorithm to do the map subtask doesn't change the synthesis of the merge, and vice versa: The success or failure in synthesis of either subtask is independent of the synthesis of the other. For the task to succeed (be synthesized), however, both subtasks must succeed; if no solution can be found for either one of the subtasks at any point in the synthesis, then the task can fail without regard to the other subtask.

The basic characteristic of functionally independent siblings is that their successes and failures are isolated because the solution of one leaves the others' task descriptions unchanged. Suppose we synthesize an algorithm for a subtask with either more general preconditions or more specific postconditions, that is, one that is more widely applicable or does more than the specification. With functional independence as presented here, this situation has no effect on previous or subsequent siblings in the sequence, even when the one's output is the other's input. If taken into account, however, one sibling's extra function could lead to the success of a another sibling that would otherwise fail.

Suppose we were to allow such dependence. If a sibling were to fail with its given specification, it could still succeed if another sibling (or siblings) could be synthesized with more general preconditions or more specific postconditions. To determine whether this case exists, however, it might be necessary to synthesize all possible solutions for subtasks that can succeed as specified (and subsequently attempt to synthesize those that would have failed for each solution). The amount of effort (in terms of number of retrys) could be lessened by always attempting to find solutions that are generally applicable with the most specific result. However, typically, no unique solution has both more general preconditions and more specific postconditions than all of the others, and solutions with more general preconditions or more specific postconditions are often more difficult to synthesize. The potential for exhaustive search leads to general dependence being too expensive in terms of synthesis time.

Order Independence

Even though the problems inherent in allowing siblings to be functionally dependent might be too difficult to overcome in general, we can consider a subclass of these, called *order-dependent siblings*. These are siblings where more than one possible execution order exists, and the preconditions of a subtask are dependent on its position in the execution order; that is, each sibling can add facts to the contexts of subsequently executed siblings, and these facts are known at instantiation time. This situation is more restricted than general functional dependence because the changed preconditions are a function of the order alone and not the implementation of the other subtasks; once the order is specified, the siblings are functionally independent. Significantly, the changes to the preconditions of a task are exactly specified by its position in the order of execution, a fact that can be used to limit the number of synthesis attempts for any subtask to the number of its siblings.

Consider the task (from the example) of determining the truth value of the conjunction (*and* (*subset A B*)(*null?* (*intersection* (*boundary A*)(*boundary B*)))); it has two subtasks, one to evaluate (*subset A B*), another to evaluate (*null?* (*intersection* (*boundary A*)(*boundary B*))). The subtasks can be evalu-

Evaluate (*subset A B*)
if (*subset A B*)
   then Evaluate (*null? (intersection (boundary A)(boundary B))*)
            given (*subset A B*)
     if (*null? (intersection (boundary A)(boundary B))*)
        then report true
        else report false
   else report false

Evaluate (*null? (intersection (boundary A)(boundary B))*)
if (*null? (intersection (boundary A)(boundary B))*)
   then Evaluate (*subset A B*) given (*null? (intersection (boundary A)(boundary B))*)
     if (*subset A B*)
        then report true
        else report false
   else report false

Figure 2. Alternative Orderings for Subtasks
of (and (subset A B)(null? (intersection (boundary A)(boundary B)))).

ated in either order because they are in a conjunction, the second is evaluated only if the first is true. We combine these subtasks in one of two ways depending on the order of execution (figure 2), and the context of the second subtask includes the fact that the conjunct tested in the other task is true.

The possible orderings of a set of order-dependent subtasks (and the resulting context changes on subsequent tasks) are known once the decomposition is chosen. One way of dealing with this situation is to make each possible ordering an alternative decomposition. The problem is that for *n* subtasks we have *n!* possible orderings of the subtasks, which is a lot of potential decompositions. Furthermore, a naive search through them to find an ordering that works can waste a lot of information, particularly regarding the subtask interactions in success and failure. We consider two alternatives to the naive approach: dynamically using multiple contexts and using subtask failures to filter the remaining choices.

The Multicontext Method. One solution for order-dependent siblings (the one used in MEDUSA) is to leave the execution order unspecified at instantiation time and construct the execution order during synthesis of the subtasks. In the multicontext method, the order in which the tasks are synthesized provides the order of execution. This task is accomplished by associating a separate context with each sibling and modifying the other siblings' contexts whenever a subtask is completed. The precise modification depends on how the subtask results will be combined; if evaluating a conjunction, when a subtask completes, its conjunct is added to the context of each of its unfinished siblings (which are also reset to active status). To synthesize an algorithm to evaluate the conjunction $c_1 \wedge c_2 \wedge \ldots \wedge c_k$, we can use the following algorithm (where t_j is the task to evaluate c_j):

Given a set of active tasks $t_1, t_2, \ldots, t_k$:
    1. Work on active tasks until one (t_i) succeeds
        If unsuccessful
        then fail $t_1, t_2, \ldots, t_k$

        else   put t_i into finished state
                reset unfinished tasks in $t_1, t_2, \ldots, t_k$

                add c_i to unfinished tasks' contexts
                go to 2.

    2. If all are finished,
        then report them in order synthesized
        else go to 1.

Once a task finishes in step 1, we reset unfinished tasks and add c_i to their contexts. If $t_1, t_2, < \ldots, t_k$ are the unfinished tasks on entry to step 1, and t_i is the task that finishes, the addition of c_i to each of the other contexts converts these tasks into ones to evaluate $c_1 \mid c_i, \ldots, c_{i-1} \mid c_i, c_{i+1} \mid c_i, \ldots, c_k \mid c_i$ because we synthesize tasks with respect to their contexts. The use of contexts allows us a good bit of freedom to choose which active task to work on. We can perform work on the tasks within the conjunction in any order, spreading the work among the subtasks as we choose until one succeeds. This method is guaranteed to find a synthesis order of the subtasks if one exists without interleaving (that is, if there is a sequence such that the synthesizer could find an algorithm for each conjunct given the previous conjuncts in the sequence were true); adding a precondition to a task can only increase the number of possible decompositions. Adding a precondition requires that we distinguish between independent and dependent tasks that fail; if a dependent sibling fails, it might still succeed if a sibling's synthesis succeeds and modifies its context. In MEDUSA, the state, waiting-for-siblings, is used for dependent siblings that cannot be synthesized in their current context but have siblings that might still finish. Because the context of an independent sibling cannot be modified by its siblings, once an independent sibling cannot be synthesized, it fails. This difference is illustrated in figure 3, which shows the possible state and transitions for a task in MEDUSA, with dependent and independent referring to order independence.

Consider the synthesis of the conjunctive example *(and (subset A B)(null? (intersection (boundary A)(boundary B))))*. With symmetry, there are three possibilities: both tasks can succeed independent of order, both can fail independent of order, and one can only be done in the context of the other being true (for example, *(subset A B) | (null? (intersection (boundary A)(boundary B)))* can suc-

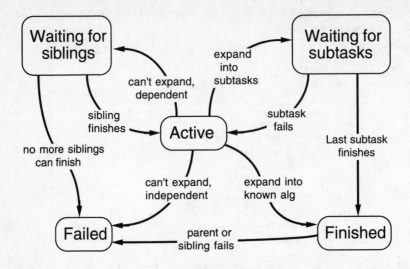

Figure 3. States and Transitions for Tasks.

ceed, but (*subset A B*) alone cannot. In the first case, the synthesis order is unimportant, but the second subtask will be reset when the first succeeds. In the second (both fail) case, both subtasks will be attempted because failure of the first is not assured until the second fails. In the last case, the order is important; if we choose the sibling that cannot be done independently, we can exhaust its possibilities, then reset it to active (with the added information in its context) on the success of the other and succeed on the second attempt.

The Filtering Approach. A lot of the inefficiency in the naive approach of considering every ordering is the result of wasting information gained through success and failure. We could use this information, however, in a scheme that works as follows: choose an ordering and instantiate the subtasks and synthesize the subtasks as independent siblings. If the chosen sequence works, all is fine. If, however, a subtask fails, we use this information to eliminate some of the untried orders and not unnecessarily throw away successful subtask syntheses. If we fail on a given ordering, we filter (remove from consideration) all sequences that have a subset of the failed subtask's predecessors before it in the sequence. Furthermore, if we have been successful on some number of the subtasks starting from the beginning, we only need to consider sequences that have the same sequence prefix for these successes. In this case, we can keep these subtasks' solutions. For example, suppose we have order-dependent siblings *a, b, c,* and *d*; choose the order abcd to try; and fail on *c* after successfully synthesizing *a*. Because *c* was unsuccessful, we can eliminate all sequences with *c* preceded only by a subset of $\{a,b\}$, and because a was successful without predecessors, we only need to consider sequences headed by a. This situation leaves those sequences beginning with a and having d precede c – *abdc, adbc,* and *adcb*. If we were extremely unlucky in choosing the orders, we could still fail an exponential number of subtasks before succeeding or failing. To avoid this possibility, we further restrict ourselves to working on the subtasks in the order that they will be executed. With this restriction, the range of the possible number of subtasks succeeding and failing is the same as for the multicontext method. In MEDUSA, the multicontext method is used; because the only order-dependent subtasks allowed are conjunctions, disjunctions, and oneofdisjunctions, the intercontext modifications are straightforward. This approach was chosen over the filtering approach in part because the underlying mechanisms to handle dynamic contexts had already been implemented and were being used for other purposes.

Success and Failure

Order-dependent and order-independent siblings behave differently in regard to success and failure; in particular, a dependent sibling can fail (exhaust all possible solutions) as many times as it has siblings, but an independent sibling can only fail once. In comparing this behavior, we can compare the extra work caused by choosing a nonoptimal synthesis order. The following comparison is based on using the multicontext implementation for order-dependent siblings; a comparison of this approach with the filtering approach is presented later in this section.

Extra work because of nonoptimal synthesis order is any work done on a subtask before it fails as a result of the failure of an independent sibling, or it is reset because of the success of a dependent sibling (as implemented, all work done on a subtree is discarded on reset because the changed context can lead to different possibilities. Minimizing this extra effort calls for different strategies. In the independent sibling case, this work is caused by the failure of a subtask; to minimize the work, find failures before doing work on other tasks, and find them on the shortest path in the derivation. In the dependent sibling case, extra work is caused by the success of one task resetting the others and causing any work already done on the reset tasks to be discarded; to minimize this effort, find successes by choosing a sequence of synthesis and execution, then work on each task to completion in this order. The strategy depends on choosing a sequence well a priori, which can be difficult.

The amount of extra work can be much greater for the dependent sibling case. Consider two decompositions, each with n subtasks, one dependent, one independent. The worst situation in the independent case is to succeed on $n - 1$ subtasks, then fail on the final one, leading to $n - 1$ subtrees worth of waste—the work done to successfully synthesize $n - 1$ subtasks. In the dependent case, the worst situation is to fail all but one subtask and then succeed on the last one; at this point, all the sibling-wait siblings are reset with changed context. The same situation can happen for the remaining $n - 1$ siblings, and so on, until the last step when we succeed on the final sibling with the $n - 1$ context modifications. The amount of wasted work here corresponds to the $n(n - 1)/2$ subtask failures. Unless the amount of work necessary to fail on a task is significantly less than the amount needed to succeed (which is counter to both intuition and practice with MEDUSA), the additional effort involved in synthesizing dependent siblings can be substantial.

The previous comparison would essentially be the same for the filtering approach. Extra work corresponds to the effort spent on failing subtasks when followed by a successful subtask (when some other order is being attempted). No extra work is done on tasks that do not reach either success or failure before a sibling success because work is strictly done sequentially, which makes the filtering approach superior if choosing promising sequences can effectively be done. In the worst case, the behavior is the same as the multicontext approach: fail on $n-1$ orders because of the first subtask, then $n - 2$ because of the second, and so on.

The total amount of work in terms of subtask successes and failures for independent and dependent sibling decompositions (each with n subtasks) is shown in table 2. It should be realized, however, that the number of sibling subtasks of a given conjunction or disjunction can typically be small. In MEDUSA's domain of geometric algorithms, the maximum number of dependent siblings in a decomposition seen in practice is five.

Cost Independence

Siblings are said to be cost independent if their performance constraints (established at instantiation time) do not include the costs of their siblings. The effect of such independence is to isolate their syntheses compared with their costs. As was the case with functional dependence, the lack of independence can lead to a good deal more effort in synthesis as failure becomes more difficult; that is, the inability to synthesize a subtask during synthesis does not mean that the decomposition containing it must fail.

In this section, I first examine how cost dependence is related to constraint propagation. I discuss how such dependence affects the synthesis process and identify some strategies that attempt to make it better. I look at how using asymptotic costs as a cost metric can eliminate cost dependence in certain cases and characterize those cases where it is effective. Finally, I discuss a number of other cost metrics in regard to cost independence.

Constraint Propagation

Constraints are propagated from task to subtask at subtask instantiation. If there is a single subtask that is equivalent to the task, the constraint is propa-

	Failure		Success	
	S	F	S	F
Independent	$0, n-1$	1	n	0
Dependent	$0, n-1$	$n, n(n-1)/2 + 1$	n	$0, n(n-1)/2$

*Table 2. Range of Number of Subtask Successes
(S) and Failures (F) for n Subtask Decompositions.*

gated as is. In the general case, the cost of the task is an expression in the costs of its subtasks. To propagate under these circumstances, we set the cost expression equal to the constraint and solve for the subtask costs, resulting in the constraints for the subtasks.

Suppose we have a task gen-intersect to report the intersection of two finite sets in time $f(x)$, where x, is the sum of the set cardinalities. Further, each set is represented as either a list or a bit vector (both are represented in the same way, but representation is not known until execution time). This task can be performed by testing for the representation, then doing either an intersection using lists (list-intersect) or an intersection using bit vectors (bv-intersect). Suppose the representation check takes unit time; relating the costs, we get

$Constraint(gen\text{-}intersect) \quad = f(x)$
$\quad\quad Cost(gen\text{-}intersect) = 1 + max(Cost(list\text{-}intersect), Cost(bv\text{-}intersect))$

Setting the cost equal to the constraint, we calculate the following:

$Constraint(list\text{-}intersect) \quad = f(x) - 1$
$Constraint(bv\text{-}intersect) \quad = f(x) - 1$

That the constraints are independent is not surprising because only one of the subtasks is executed. This situation is generally not true, however; more commonly, all the subtasks are executed in some order. Suppose we have a task to evaluate some function applied to some mapping over a set; specifically, let max-dist be the task to determine the maximum distance from the origin of a point set. This function can be described as the maximum of the set produced by mapping the distance-from-origin function over the point set. The cost here can be expressed as the cost of the mapping (the set size times the cost of each individual mapping) plus the cost of applying the function to the mapped set. Suppose our constraint here is $K |x|$, where $|x|$ is the size of the set, leading to the following cost and constraint equations:

$Constraint(max\text{-}dist) \quad\quad = K|x|$
$Cost(max\text{-}dist) \quad\quad\quad = Cost(max\text{-}apply) + |x| \cdot Cost(dist\text{-}calc)$

where *max-dist* is the task to apply the maximum function to the set, and *dist-calc* is the function to calculate the distance for an individual point. Using the equality as before, we find the following constraints:

$$Constraint(max\text{-}apply) = K\,|x| - |x| \cdot Cost(dist\text{-}calc)$$
$$Constraint(dist\text{-}calc) = K - Cost(max\text{-}apply)\,/\,|x|$$

In this form, because the constraints include the costs of the siblings, these subtasks are not cost independent. Because this statement is true, we cannot tell if the solution to a subtask performs within its constraint until the synthesis of the other is completed.

Synthesis and Cost Dependence

In the cost-independent case, the synthesis mechanisms are straightforward: Each subtask has its own constraint independent of its siblings, so it can succeed or fail (in cost terms) without regard to its siblings results. In the dependent case, however, it is necessary to consider the interactions. One method is to synthesize one sibling (subject to the constraint of its sibling's cost being nonnegative), then substitute its cost into the other's constraint and synthesize it. With the example of the previous section, choosing to synthesize max-apply first, we would synthesize an algorithm for max-apply with a constraint of $K|x|$ and substitute the max-apply cost into the dist-calc constraint, then synthesize dist-calc.

The difficulty with this technique regards failure. If we fail on the synthesis of the first subtask, we are done. If, however, we fail on the second subtask after synthesizing the first, we can try to synthesize a less expensive algorithm for the first, then (if successful) try the second again with a looser constraint. This sequence of operations can be repeated several times, particularly if a large number of possible solutions to the first subtask exist, or there are more than two cost-dependent siblings.

There are two less naive alternatives to this strategy that can lead to some performance improvement: (1) synthesize the cheapest possible algorithm for the first subtask, which leads to the loosest possible constraint for the second and (2) choose a constraint for the first that apportions the cost among the subtasks, then synthesize it and substitute the cost into the second. Both of these alternatives have drawbacks. If the amount of work needed to synthesize an algorithm is inversely related to its cost, then finding the cheapest algorithms can waste a good deal of work when unnecessary. It is not obvious how constraints can be chosen in the second case; the benefits over the naive approach depend on making reasonably good guesses. The need to distinguish one subtask as first could be eliminated by allowing work on more than one, but at a cost of greater complexity (similar to the order-dependent subtask schemes in Order Independence).

Using Asymptotic Costs

When discussing algorithms, it is common practice to use asymptotic costs ("Big-Oh") on a Ram as a metric for execution time. $O(f(x))$, the asymptotic value of a function $f(x)$, denotes the set of all functions $g(x)$ such that

$$\exists\ K,N\ \forall x\ (x > N) \to K\ g(x) \geq f(x)\ .$$

The practical effect of making this replacement is to simplify $f(x)$ by ignoring leading lower-order terms and leading constants when making comparisons. (For more details, see Knuth [1973]). Asymptotically comparing algorithms is equivalent to comparing them as their input size gets arbitrarily large and considerably simplifies arithmetic.

Suppose we use asymptotic costs in the previous example. Because we ignore constant terms, the original costs and constraints become

$$Constraint(max\text{-}dist) = O(|x|)$$
$$Cost(max\text{-}dist) = O(Cost(max\text{-}apply)) + O(|x| \cdot Cost(dist\text{-}calc))$$

Setting the costs and constraint equal, we can solve for the constraints (asymptotically):

$$Constraint(max\text{-}apply) = O(|x|)$$
$$Constraint(dist\text{-}calc) = O(1)$$

In this form, the subtasks are cost independent, with the independence resulting from the cost measure.

More generally, if we can express the task cost as the sum of a constant number of terms, and each term contains at most one subtask cost expression (that is, an expression $Cost(x)$, where x is a subtask), then we can express the constraint of each subtask without using any of the other subtask costs. Grouping the additive terms on the basis of the subtask costs, we find (for k subtasks):

$$\text{given: } Cost(task) = \sum_{1 \leq i \leq k} C_i$$
$$\text{use: } Constraint(task) = C_i \text{ to calculate } Constraint(S_i)$$

where C_i is the sum of all terms containing the cost expression for subtask S_i. If these conditions hold (using asymptotic costs), the siblings are cost independent.

Even using asymptotic costs, we can still get cost-dependent siblings. Consider the following example: The task is to sort a set based on some pairwise comparison function; the constraint is quadratic in $|x|$, the size of the input set. This task, sort-set, can be broken into two subtasks, p-compare, which does the pairwise comparison, and gen-sort, which is a generic sorter that uses p-compare for as many comparisons as it makes. Because the cost of a sort is proportional to the number of comparisons it makes, we have the following:

$$Constraint(sort\text{-}set) = |x|^2$$
$$Cost(sort\text{-}set) = Cost(p\text{-}compare) \cdot Cost(gen\text{-}sort)$$

Setting the cost equal to the constraint and solving for subtask costs, we obtain

$$Constraint(p\text{-}compare) = |x|^2 / Cost(gen\text{-}sort)$$
$$Constraint(gen\text{-}sort) = |x|^2 / Cost(p\text{-}compare)$$

Each of these task's constraint is dependent on the cost of the other. Rather than synthesizing each subtask to its own constraint, we need to synthesize both such that the product of their costs is within the parent's constraint. This approach can largely nullify any benefits gained (in terms of search control) from synthesizing to a constraint. In MEDUSA, we did not allow cost dependence; to do a generic sort such as the one in the example would require a mechanism to apportion the constraints at instantiation time.

Alternative Cost Models and Independence

When designing MEDUSA, the asymptotic worst-case time cost on a Ram was chosen for two reasons: simplicity of computation and naturalness as a measure for algorithm complexity. Other options included a more exact worst-case cost measure, some combined measure of space and time, and average (expected) time performance. The primary advantage of using asymptotic costs is that in many cases (those specified in the previous section), constraints can be propagated to subtasks that do not involve their siblings' costs. This position would not be true if we used a more exact measure (one that considered constant factors). Whether this propagation would be possible for a combined space-time measure depends on how we do the measurement and how we combine subtask costs. The obvious combination of space and time is as a product (more exactly, the integral of space used with respect to time). Suppose we have a task T with two subtasks A and B that are sequentially executed, so the space used by the first is available for reuse by the second. In this case, we can propagate constraints as with independent subtasks:

$$Cost(T) = (Space(A) \cdot Time(A)) + (Space(B) \cdot Time(B)) .$$

That is, as long as we are only interested in asymptotic space-time behavior, we can just propagate to each subtask. If, however, sequential execution is not possible, so the subtasks cannot share space, the costs become

$$Cost(T) = (Space(A) + Space(B)) \cdot (Time(A) + Time(B)) .$$

In this case, the cross-product terms keep us from independently propagating the constraints—the same problems seen with the multiplicative costs in the sort example—with the added complexity of considering space as well as time.

Using expected costs could be beneficial because the performance characteristics of average cases can be more useful to an algorithm designer than the worst case. For some algorithms, the worst case corresponds to a situation that rarely appears (as an example, consider the simplex algorithm that virtually always performs well in practice but has exponential worst-case performance). However, using expected costs demands that assumptions be made regarding the distributions of the costs for known algorithms, which can be highly situation dependent. Constraint propagation and cost combination would be more complicated because computations would be made with random variables. These difficulties aside, the loss of independence is not a problem inherent in using expected time as a cost measure.

Choice Heuristics and Results

Given an implementation that includes multicontext order-dependent siblings, there are two primary choices: which decomposition to use for a particular task and which active task to work on. We developed heuristics for both.

Heuristics were used to choose among alternative decompositions. These heuristics provided a preference for certainty over uncertainty and independence over dependence. For the purposes of this chapter, these preferences mean that known algorithms were favored over all others, and decompositions into independent subtasks were favored over decompositions into dependent subtasks (dual transformations were favored least and handled by a different mechanism). As a result, the use of dependent siblings was avoided whenever possible. For example, the problem in Example: Detect Intersection of Two Convex Polygons was solved differently (using a sweep-line algorithm) once the schemas for sweep-line algorithms were added to the knowledge base.

Various heuristics were tested for choosing among decompositions into independent subtasks. A number of these used additional information; a typical performance was associated with the various decompositions, to be used only for the purpose of choosing among alternatives. We compared the following strategies: (1) ignoring the typical performance, (2) choosing the alternative with least typical cost, and (3) choosing the alternative with the greatest typical cost that fit within the constraint. The most effective of these strategies (empirically) was the third one because it tended to find simple (to synthesize) solutions when they existed (for more details, see McCartney [1988]).

Choosing the active task on which to work was largely based on preferences established at decomposition time. It is most efficient to work depth first on the tasks in the proper order. If the order is incorrect, a fair amount of effort can be expended on tasks that fail; in the worst case, the number of failed dependent subtasks is quadratic in the number of dependent subtasks (table 2). When a task is decomposed, an order for the subtasks is hypothesized; the system then works on them in this order (depth first) with two modifications. First, if one path of the derivation tree gets too far ahead of the others, they are allowed to catch up. This approach avoids a task succeeding or failing on a long path when a sibling could succeed on a short one. Second, if an order-dependent subtask fails (goes into a wait state until a sibling succeeds), when it is reset, it is given less preference—the more a task fails, the more it is avoided.

For this process to perform well, the preferences established at decomposition time need to be reasonably good. Establishing these preferences here was a domain-dependent process: Top preference was given to simple set predicates (such as null tests), least preference was given to a predicate that involves (directly) the desired result of the decomposition, and the rest were equally rated. The rationale for the top preference is that simple set predicates tend to have simple solutions; the rationale for the least preference is that it is only in those cases where the desired result of the computation is difficult to get that we would partition the problem instead of directly solving it. The ordering of the four cases in the polygon-intersection example illustrates how these preferences can work: The test for the boundary intersection was done first because it is a simple set predicate; the test for the sets being disjoint was done last because the question led to the decomposition; and the two containment tests were arbitrarily done second and third.

A certain amount of deductive effort is involved in getting all the equivalent decompositions, much of it on decompositions that will be filtered out the heuristics. MEDUSA reduced this wasted effort using a *lazy fetching approach:* Rather than fetching all the equivalent decompositions, it fetches all equivalent known algorithms and sets up closures to fetch the others (one for independent decompositions, one for dependent). This approach fits well with our known-independent-dependent filter heuristic explained in the previous section: If a known algorithm exists, the actual fetching of the others is never done, similarly with independent versus dependent algorithms. Because we get closures for all the equivalent decompositions, we can always fetch them if they are needed during backtracking.

Conclusions

Search-limiting strategies often involve a trade-off between exhaustive search and completeness: In avoiding exhaustive search, we sacrifice the ability to find some solutions that could otherwise be found. Using only independent subtasks (in both functional and cost terms) is such a strategy; search is limited, and its control is greatly simplified, particularly in terms of ordering decisions. If subtasks are independent, the criteria for each one's success are fixed when the task is decomposed. Because these criteria are independent of solutions obtained for the sibling subtasks, the subtasks can independently be synthesized and evaluated. Consequently, a subtask will be taken to completion (success or failure) one time at most, and at this completion, it is known whether the subtask succeeded or failed. By contrast, in the dependent case at decomposition time, the criteria for overall success are known, but the individual subtask criteria can be changed by, or depend on, results from other subtasks. In this situation, a subtask can be taken to completion many times, depending on the number of possible solutions for its siblings.

Rather than completely eliminating dependent subtasks, we examined how the independence requirement could be loosened without causing the exhaustive search problems that independence avoids. We separately examined functional dependence and cost dependence.

Order-dependent siblings are functionally dependent in that the preconditions of subtasks are affected by the order of their execution. Importantly, these effects are known and exclusively result from this order. The search problems can still be severe because N subtasks can be executed in $N!$ orders. If we merely generate an ordering, attempt to synthesize the subtasks, and choose another ordering when we fail, we could fail an exponential number of subtasks before a solution is found (and would always fail an exponential number of subtasks if no solution were possible). I presented two approaches that could be considered intelligent backtracking. Both methods (multicontext and filtering) use failure information to eliminate possibilities that must fail and keep the subtask solutions that can be used in an overall solution if one exists. When a subtask fails in context in the multicontext approach, any successful subtasks are kept, and the failed subtask is not attempted again unless its context is changed. When an ordering fails in the filtering approach, the prefix of successful subtasks is kept, and all orders with the failed subtask in the same position are eliminated. In this way, for both methods, the maximum number of subtask failures is quadratic in the number of subtasks. Both of these methods improve the naive approach of trying all the orders until one succeeds without making synthesis less complete; any solutions found using the naive approach can be found using either of the other two approaches.

Cost-dependent siblings can cause similar search problems because in this case, a sibling does not have an exact constraint until its dependent siblings are finished. If it fails at this point on the basis of insufficient resources (no solution possible within its constraint), it is necessary to try to synthesize its siblings at a lower cost, then try it again (with a looser cost constraint). This "fail-redo sibling-retry" cycle can recur an arbitrary number of times.

Using asymptotic time as a cost measure reduces the cost-dependency problem in a simple way: If a task cost is an additive function of its subtask costs, the costs are not dependent (see Using Asymptotic Costs). This approach does not completely eliminate the problem; the example of the generic sorter illustrated a case leading to a multiplicative cost function. In MEDUSA, the problem was eliminated for the generic sorter by constraining it to having constant-time comparisons; we could have retained more flexibility by having more schemas corresponding to different comparison times. Generalizing this approach leads to a possible solution for such cases: Provide a mechanism to generate a discrete set of cost-allocation combinations, akin to the use of all possible orders in the filtering approach for order dependence. If the number of dependent subtasks were small, and the number of possible cost combinations could be restricted, an intelligent backtracking scheme could be effective for this problem as well.

References

Aho, A.; Hopcroft, J.; and Ullman, J. 1974. *The Design and Analysis of Computer Algorithms.* Reading, Mass.: Addison-Wesley.

Barstow, D. R. 1979. An Experiment in Knowledge-Based Automatic Programming. *Artificial Intelligence* 12:73–119.

de Kleer, J. 1986. An Assumption-Based TMS. *Artificial Intelligence* 28:127–162.

Kant, E. 1979. A Knowledge-Based Approach to Using Efficiency Estimation in Program Synthesis. In Proceedings of the Sixth International Joint Conference on Artificial Intelligence, 457–462. Menlo Park, Calif.: International Joint Conferences on Artificial Intelligence.

Knuth, D. E. 1973. *The Art of Computer Programming*, volume 1, 2d ed. Reading, Mass.: Addison-Wesley.

McCartney, R. 1988. Synthesizing Algorithms with Performance Constraints. Ph.D. thesis, Dept. of Computer Science, Brown Univ.

McDermott, D. 1985. The Duck Manual, Technical Report, 399, Dept. of Computer Science, Yale Univ.

Preparata, F. P., and Shamos, M. I. 1985. *Computational Geometry: An Introduction*. Berlin: Springer-Verlag, 1985.

Program Improvement by Automatic Redistribution of Intermediate Results: An Overview

Robert J. Hall

General tools make it easy to solve many different problems. Unfortunately, using a general tool to solve a specific problem often yields an inefficient solution. The reason is simple: The general tool was designed to handle harder problems, so it might do more work than necessary in a given context.

In some engineering domains, general tools are widely used. Mechanical engineers, for example, exploit catalogs of standard parts as much as possible to reduce production costs. Because the precise part for the specific job is unlikely to be available in a catalog, the designer must find a standard, more general part that handles the job. Accordingly, mechanical designs often sacrifice performance to be able to use low-cost standard parts.

By comparison, software engineers seldom reuse standard parts (except low-level ones, such as programming language primitives, library routines, and operating system tools), even though such practice appears to have major benefits. It would yield more correct code because the reused code has already been tested and debugged. Code would be produced faster because no time is spent on producing reused subroutines. Also, the code would be more readable because reused components would be modular and well documented. Readability is a crucial cost consideration because debugging and maintenance usually dominate the cost of a large software project.

A major reason for this lack of widespread reuse in software engineering is the inefficiency phenomenon previously discussed. Software by nature has extremely complex, layered subgoal hierarchies; hence, using standard parts at many levels of a software design would lead to piling the inefficiencies of many such general-tool uses. This approach can result in unacceptable performance in the final, composed solution. Thus, programmers currently tailor their code to the specific task, exploiting constraints in the problem context to regain efficiency. Unfortunately, the tailored solution has many significant drawbacks: It takes longer to write the code, the resulting programs tend to have a tangled and unclear structure, the necessity of producing more new code increases the potential for error, and unreadable programs are hard for others to understand and modify.

A primary goal of this research is to invent a way to automatically tailor general data and procedural abstractions to their contexts of use, thereby avoiding the general tool inefficiency problem in software reuse. I implemented a system capable of automatically performing powerful but routine tailoring operations based on the fundamental engineering design principle of function sharing. The system is fully automatic in that it quickly runs to completion without human intervention. Full automation has a price, however, because the problem of verifying that a program optimization preserves correctness is, in general, uncomputable.[1] The optimizations found by the system are guaranteed to preserve correctness only on the set of test cases given as input; as a result, programs optimized by the system must be used with some external form of certification (either at compile time or run time). See Correctness for further discussion of this issue.

Computational solutions to problems that are both formally uncomputable and practically difficult always involve trade-offs. Typically, one must give up some degree of a desired property in return for a practical algorithm. This research is no exception; the main technical contributions of this work are in the trade-offs made for practicality. Key Ideas in the Implementation highlights these trade-offs.

Function Sharing

Function sharing is when one structural component serves more than one purpose in a design. This research attempts to automate the introduction of function sharing into program designs. Many of the insights gained also carry over to other design domains.

Examples in Design. Function sharing is ubiquitous in engineering problem solving. Ulrich (1988) says that

> if automobiles were designed without function sharing they would be relatively large, heavy, expensive and unreliable. But because elements like the sheet-metal body perform many functions (electrical ground, structural support, aerodynamic faring, weather protection, and aesthetics among others) automobiles can be manufactured relatively inexpensively and can perform relatively well (p. 76).

Ulrich's work explores the introduction of function sharing into the designs of mechanical devices. Here are some examples from other domains: In electronic design, fanout is a simple example of function sharing. A bus structure is a more complicated example that saves quadratic wiring costs by using a single set of wires to mediate communication among functional units. Architects design the walls of buildings to perform several functions at once: structural support of the building, separation of interior spaces, decoration, and sound insulation. In software engineering, well-known optimization techniques such as common subexpression elimination, loop fusion, and memoization introduce function sharing in limited ways.

The Adaptation Problem. To introduce function sharing into a design, one must solve two problems: finding a candidate for sharing and adapting the design to make it work. Consider the process of improving a container for popcorn to work not only as the shipping package but also the cooking vessel in a microwave oven. The original idea is simply the observation that the same container can, in principle, serve both purposes. Significant problem-solving remains to be done, however: In addition to its original requirements of strength, food preservation, and low cost, it must also be capable of expanding because the cooked popcorn fills a larger volume; there should be no metal in it; and it should withstand a larger range of temperatures. Satisfying these additional constraints requires general design problem-solving expertise; I call this problem the *adaptation problem*.

By contrast, consider going from the initial design of a car in which a ground wire runs from the tail light to the battery to another design in which the metal car body acts as the ground wire. Almost no additional design is necessary beyond the initial observation that the car body can serve the purpose of the ground wire. In this case, the adaptation problem is trivial.

In this research, I have restricted my attention to those optimizations requiring only trivial adaptation; that is, the only adaptation considered is the introduction of (extended) data flow from a new source (value producer) to a target (value user) together with the elimination of any arc from the old source to the target. This type of adaptation can be implemented using only additional local variables, input arguments, and return values as the means of communicating a value from its point of computation to its (shared) points of use (what I mean by extended data flow). No additional subroutine calls are added, and the only changes to types of subroutine calls are those required to implement extended data flow. I term this restricted kind of function-sharing optimization the redistribution of intermediate results, or just redistribution.

The decision to study only redistribution (rather than general function sharing) has both advantages and disadvantages. The key advantage is that it allows me to study the problem of automating the introduction of function sharing into programs without developing a general theory of automated program design. It also drastically limits the search for optimizations by allowing the system to ignore any optimization that adds new computations. Even with this simplification, however, search control is still a problem (see Candidate Generation).

The obvious disadvantage of studying only redistribution is that the system will be able to perform fewer optimizations. Consider, for example, a program whose original design operates on two different representations (say, array and pointer based) of the same list, and suppose the program requires both representations of the list to be sorted. (Such a design is plausible if one reusable component constructs and operates on the array representation, and some other reusable component constructs and operates on the pointer-based representation.) It is unlikely that the sorted array representation can directly be used by the routines requiring a sorted linked list. However, solving the adaptation problem would result in a design that converted the sorted array into a sorted linked list and saved it for later use, thus eliminating a costly sort in favor of a linear-time conversion.

Significance of the Work

The problem of automatic program improvement is of interest to both the AI and software-engineering communities. From an AI perspective, optimization is a key step in the design process; design, in turn, is an important kind of human problem solving. Furthermore, design optimization is hard enough that it shares a fundamental property with many other problems of AI: Its inherent difficulty requires computational solutions that trade power for tractability. AI researchers should view this research as a case study in the computational trade-offs and techniques required to implement an intuitively motivated principle of design optimization—the introduction of function sharing—in the software domain. Further, I believe that many of the insights gained directly carry over to other design domains as well. Note, however, that although this approach is motivated by intuitions about how humans optimize designs, I have not attempted to rigorously study or duplicate human cognitive behavior.

From a software-engineering perspective, automated program improvement is important in that better optimizers allow programmers to write programs more quickly and clearly and worry about less detail. In particular, better optimizers can perform more of the tailoring required to reuse software modules among different applications, thereby saving separate development costs. Software engineers should view this research as an attempt to demonstrate an approach to automatic program optimization that is qualitatively more powerful than conventional approaches and well suited to facilitating the reuse of software components. Note, however, that the research is still in the exploratory stage; so, it is too early to make hard claims about the ultimate usefulness of the techniques. In particular, the implemented system has not yet been engineered for optimal performance.

An Example

This section illustrates how the system can perform the powerful but routine optimizations currently done by (human) hand. The system was successfully applied to several (currently, 26) programs from three different domains, including the following example. This example is kept simple so that it can briefly be treated here. (More complex examples are mentioned in Optimization Phenomena Captured and explored in detail in Hall [1990]). It requires more input than just the traditional source-language structural representation; the system uses teleological structure (possibly obtained during the design process) to assist in optimization. This additional input is discussed here and in Additional Input Information.

Suppose we want to write a Common Lisp program to reverse a list (presumably forgetting that the language provides a primitive to do so). We don't want it to destructively modify the input list, so we decide to use only side-effect–free Lisp primitives in writing the program. Here is our first pass:

```
(DEFUN MY-REVERSE (L)
  "Reverses the input list nondestructively"
  (IF (NULL L)
      NIL
      (APPEND (MY-REVERSE (REST L))
              (LIST (FIRST L))))))
```

This program is clearly correct as long as the input is a finite Lisp list (that is, a CDR chain of cons cells ending in NIL). In addition, it was quickly constructed from preexisting software components, in this case, the standard Common Lisp language primitives. We didn't have to implement any of the subroutines, and we didn't have to worry about side effects. Unfortunately, this implementation uses too much time and space to be practical—both are proportional to the square of the length of the input list because APPEND copies its first input on every recursive invocation of MY-REVERSE. The system discovers optimizations that turn this inefficient implementation into one using only linear time and space. The optimized program (the following Lisp code) creates only one new cons cell for each cell of the input list and maintains a tail pointer for the new list as it is constructed.

```
;; returns two values:
;; reversed list and last-cons of reversed list
(DEFUN MY-REVERSE-2 (L)
  "Reverses the input list nondestructively"
  (IF (NULL L)
      (VALUES NIL NIL)
      (MULTIPLE-VALUE-BIND (REVD-TAIL LAST-CONS)
          (MY-REVERSE-2 (REST L))
        (LET ((NEW-LAST (LIST (FIRST L))))
          (VALUES (APPEND-2 REVD-TAIL NEW-LAST LAST-CONS)
                  NEW-LAST)))))

(DEFUN APPEND-2 (L1 L2 LAST-L1)
  "Performs APPEND within MY-REVERSE-2"
  (NCONC-2 L1 L2 LAST-L1))

(DEFUN NCONC-2 (C1 C2 LAST-C1)
  "NCONC within APPEND-2.
  If C1 is not NIL, then LAST-C1 must be the last-cons of it"
  (IF (NULL C1)
      C2
      (PROGN
        (RPLACD LAST-C1 C2)
        C1)))
```

Applying the System. A fundamental limitation of current compiler-based approaches to optimization is the fact that they accept only a program's structure (expressed in a standard programming language). They cannot exploit any freedoms that might exist in the program's specification, simply because there is no way for the programmer to express them. By and large, the optimized program must compute values identical to those computed by the original. (Some approaches exploit limited, implicit specification information such as the knowledge that newly allocated memory cells are all equivalent.)

I explored two generate-and-test algorithms for discovering redistributions, each incorporating several stages of filtering. IBR (invariant-based redistribution) operates by simply trying out each candidate and directly evaluating the program's overall correctness using test input and given effective optimization invariants (defined later). In contrast, IEBR (invariant- and explanation-based redistribution) incorporates an additional filtering step based on computing an approximate weakest precondition for each target (its target condition) that is sufficient to guarantee overall correctness. That is, any object satisfying the target condition can be used as input to the target and still maintain program correctness. A source whose value fails to satisfy the target condition of a target in some test case is eliminated from consideration. The two approaches differ in their required input and their performance characteristics. I later discuss (see Experiments) experiments that compare them, but for brevity, I only demonstrate IEBR.

IEBR requires the following input:

First is a structural representation of the program and those of any called subroutines. Specifically, the program must be represented as a data flow program, consisting of boxes (subroutine calls) with ports (acting as input parameters and return values), flow arcs (representing equality between ports), conditionals (allowing conditional execution of boxes), and program ports (acting as overall program input and output). This program representation has the intuitive, parallel-execution operational semantics usually attached to data flow programs (Rich and Waters 1990). I adopted this structural representation because it makes key features, such as ports and data flow, explicit and hides irrelevant details, such as program syntax and variable names. Figure 1 illustrates the data flow representation corresponding to the MY-REVERSE program, and figure 2 shows those of APPEND and its subroutine NCONC. Note that side effects are modeled as in standard denotational semantics using explicit stores. Note also that the representation does handle recursive programs.

Second is a set of representative test-case input for the program. The system incorporates an evaluator capable of executing programs on given input and recording trace data. The system uses these data in the search phase to screen candidate optimizations by evaluating target conditions. It turns out that a single, well-chosen test-case input is sufficiently representative of MY-REVERSE's behavior to allow all and only correct optimizations; one such test case is the cons cell and store representation of the abstract list (0 1 2 3 4 5).

Third is a collection of effective optimization invariants that together specify all properties of the program's input-output relation that must be preserved by the optimizer. These are ground-evaluative statements of input-output function, expressed in quantifier-free conjunctive normal form with free variables (implicitly universally quantified) and special systematically named logical constants denoting ports within the program. Some or all of these invariants can be relative in that they can express a relation between the optimized program's output and those of the unoptimized program. (This concept generalizes the traditional notion of input-output specification.) The system can, of course, use any sufficient approximation to the actual specification, but a more restrictive specification allows less optimization freedom; hence, the resulting program might be less efficient. The optimization invariants used for MY-REVERSE can be paraphrased in English as follows:

> For a given input, the output of the optimized program must be equal to that of the original program viewing both output as abstract lists; that is, corresponding CARs must be identical, but the cells making up the list itself might be different.
> The program can only modify newly allocated memory cells.

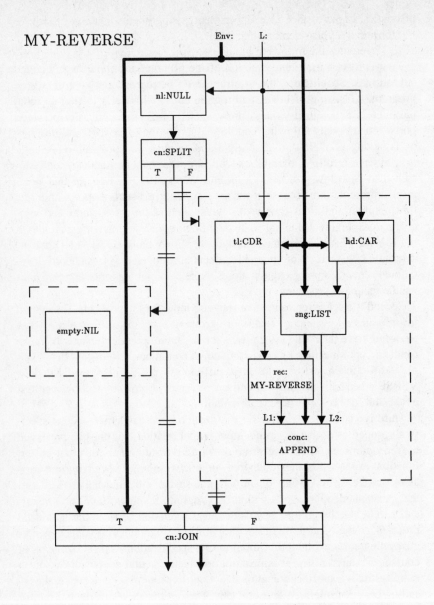

Figure 1. Structural Representation of the Recursive MY-REVERSE Program. Thin arcs represent standard data flow; thick arcs represent environments; arcs with two short cross-segments denote control flow (used here only to indicate conditional execution). This representation is similar to the plan calculus described in Rich and Waters (1990). A box is labeled with an instance identifier, a colon, and a type identifier.

The first statement is relative, in that it refers to the output of the unoptimized program. Note that instead of using the well-known and easily formalized top-level specification of list reversal, here I use a relative optimization invariant to demonstrate the technique. In this case, the two are logically equivalent, but in general, the relative invariant is more conservative but easier to formalize.

Fourth is a proof that the program's structure correctly implements its top-level specification based on domain axioms and program structural axioms. Because it is difficult to formalize and prove program specifications, the system can accept proofs of *quasi-specification*—formal constructs capturing some specification freedoms but not others. The proof and specification input for MY-REVERSE were automatically constructed by a quasi-specification proof generator for side-effect free list programs (see Incomplete Design Information). Proofs are basically trees with typed nodes. The type of the node indicates the inference step used to conclude the clause at the node from the clauses of the children. The key inference steps allowed are binary (propositional) resolution and free-variable instantiation. Leaf (axiom) types include domain axiom, structural axiom, and propositional-with-equality tautology.

Remark on Notation: It is useful to be able to systematically refer to elements within a program. To this end, I defined a path-name notation for program structure. Each path name begins with a $ and the top-level program name followed by a sequence of identifiers separated by periods. Referring to figure 3, the program port labeled L would be designated by the path name $MY-REVERSE.L; the conc:APPEND box is denoted $MY-REVERSE.CONC (of type APPEND); the L1: input port to this box is denoted $MY-REVERSE.CONC.L1; the cpy:COPY-LIST box within the implementation of $MY-REVERSE.CONC (see also figure 2) is denoted $MY-REVERSE.CONC.CPY; and so on.

Intuitively, it is clear where all the space inefficiency (and much of the time inefficiency) in MY-REVERSE comes from: Every recursive invocation of MY-REVERSE makes a new copy of the reversed tail within APPEND. Of course, APPEND must copy its first input list to avoid destroying it. Used in MY-REVERSE, however, this copy operation is unnecessary because the reversed tail is always made of fresh cons cells, and it is not used after the call to APPEND. Thus, we can greatly improve the performance of MY-REVERSE by eliminating the unnecessary copy operation. Note that this operation is exactly what compilers incorporating copy elimination might do. Remember, however, that this operation is only one phenomenon captured by redistribution.

The system discovers this optimization as follows: Rather than trying to examine each of the exponentially many sets of source-target pairs, the system takes an indirect approach. It only considers groups of pairs that together allow the elimination of a box; moreover, it considers boxes in descending order of estimated cost within the program. It crudely estimates the computa-

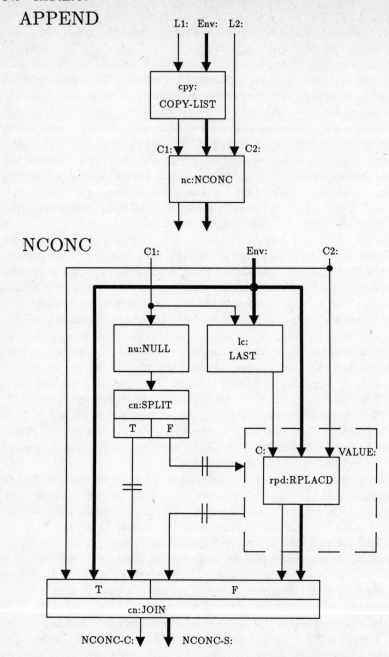

Figure 2. Structural Representation of the APPEND and NCONC Subroutines. These are the structural models used by the system.

tional (time and space) costs of each box in the design, taking into account its nesting position within any recursions. For example, the box $MY-RE-VERSE.CONC.CPY is estimated to have cost (3, 3), meaning it contributes a quadratic amount to both the time (first component) and the space (second component). (In general, a box's cost is (i, j), where $i - 1$ is the exponent of the run-time cost, and $j - 1$ is the exponent of the space cost, $i, j > 0$. $i = 0$ *or* $j = 0$ means that the box has zero cost in time or space. Cost pairs are totally ordered lexicographically.) This cost estimate is straightforward to compute given the cost values for the computational primitives.

Considering each box, in turn, in descending order of cost, the system tries to eliminate each of the box's output by finding redistributions that eliminate arcs emanating from them until the box's output are entirely disconnected from the rest of the program. To decide whether a given source-target pair candidate should be accepted, the system first derives an approximation to the weakest logical condition on the target that an object connected to the target must satisfy to maintain overall program correctness. I term this condition the *target condition, tc_t (.)*, for the target t. Assuming this condition is operational—that is, the system can evaluate its truth on concrete data values without reexecuting the altered program on the test cases—the system evaluates $tc_t(s)$ for each candidate source s on each given test case. If s passes this test for each test case, then the redistribution pair (s, t) is accepted.

In the example, to get rid of the memory cell output of the copy box, the system derives the target condition for the target $MY-REVERSE. CONC.NC.C1, which can be paraphrased as follows: (1) viewed as an abstract list in the store. $MY-REVERSE.CONC.NC.ENV, the value must represent the reversed tail of the input list to MY-REVERSE; (2) the memory cell structure making up this list must be fresh with respect to the store of the top-level call to MY-REVERSE; and (3) the memory cell structure making up this list must be disjoint from that of $MY-REVERSE.CONC.NC.C2.

This condition is automatically derived from the input proof by a technique related to explanation-based generalization (DeJong and Mooney 1986). It is easier to test for and prove correct than simply "it might be anything as long as the revised MY-REVERSE still satisfies the original top-level specification." The target condition is easier to test because it can be done without altering the program or reexecuting the test cases (unlike the top-level specification). It is easier to prove because it refers to a local area of the program rather than the entire program.

Using this search and testing procedure twice (once as previously shown and once for the store target $MY-REVERSE.CONC.NC.ENV), the system discovers two redistributions that eliminate the copy box: The source $MY-REVERSE.REC.L-OUT takes over as input to the target $MY-REVERSE.CONC.NC.C1, then $MY-REVERSE.REC.ENV-OUT takes over as input to the store target $MY-REVERSE.CONC.NC.ENV (figure 3). Note

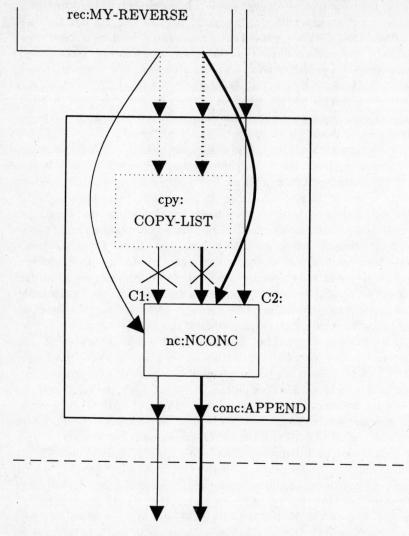

Figure 3. First Optimization Step for MY-REVERSE.
This diagram shows a closeup of a portion of the MY-REVERSE program (figure 1),
with the implementation of the APPEND box shown within its boundary. $MY-RE-
VERSE.CONC.CPY was eliminated by rerouting two data flow arcs and removing
dead code. (The crossed-out arcs and the dotted boxes and arcs are unused structure
eliminated in creating the optimized version.)

that the redistributions are implemented using extra flow arcs and input arguments to the revised (local) implementation of APPEND.

This modification improved the space use to exactly one new cons cell to each cons cell in the input list. In general, this allotment is the best space use possible for a nondestructive reverse.

The run time is still quadratic, however. Almost every time NCONC calls LAST, it must iterate down the cells making up the list to find the last cons cell in the list. It turns out, however, that every time NCONC actually needs to know the last cons of the list, MY-REVERSE-1 has already computed it in the previous recursive invocation! After being appended to the reversed tail of the tail, the output of the sng:LIST box one level down in the recursion is now the last cons. Hence, if we could pass this pointer upward a level to the input of the $MY-REVERSE.CONC.NC.RPD box, we could avoid the costly last cons iteration. Continuing the optimization process (still examining boxes in cost order), the system eventually discovers this optimization and implements it as in figure 4. Note that this redistribution involves adding new auxiliary output values to the MY-REVERSE program.

In summary, note the following facts: First, MY-REVERSE-2 is linear in both time and space, whereas the original implementation was quadratic. Linear is the best possible condition. Second, the optimizations introduced by the system consisted only of creating specialized versions of the original subroutines, with some unnecessary calls eliminated. The system did not rely on a large library of highly specific program transformations. Third, even though the output of the optimized program is not identical at the cons cell level to that of the original, the modified program still satisfies the given optimization invariants. Fourth, the code is not readable or clear, but because it will not be maintained (it can automatically be regenerated), it doesn't need to be. (In practice, using an interactive theorem prover to certify optimizations might require that the system justify optimizations to the user, but in any case, this approach won't require readable source code.)

Optimization Phenomena Captured

A wide range of optimizations can be expressed in terms of redistributions. The examples briefly presented here are discussed in detail in Hall (1990).

Recall that a redistribution requires finding a new source to connect to a given target, allowing one to eliminate the old source's computation (if the old source is not used elsewhere). One large class of redistributions arises when the new source's value is identical to the old source's value. Often, however, a value that is not identical to that of the old source can be substituted for the purposes of the target. One large class of this type is based on eliminating unnecessary copy operations; the new source is simply whatever

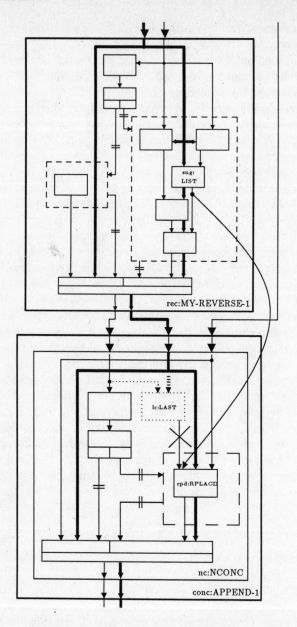

Figure 4. The Second Optimization Step for MY-REVERSE.
This diagram shows a closeup of a portion of MY-REVERSE-1, including the changes
made by the second round of optimization. Implementations of subroutines are shown
within solid-box boundaries. The redistribution indicated by the curved arrow allows
the elimination of the LAST box. It is implicitly applied at all levels of recursion.

was to be copied by the copy box, and the old source is the output of the copy box. Another such class enables the removal of code whose sole purpose is to maintain unnecessary and costly data invariants. Still another class of optimizations, loop fusions, has examples of both identical-value and non-identical-value redistributions. Given these observations, the single mechanism of redistribution conceptually unifies many optimization phenomena that are separately treated in the conventional compiler literature. Moreover, by virtue of using more input information, the approach can be applied at all levels of abstraction rather than only at the language level.

Identical-Value Redistributions

The most obviously correct redistributions are those in which the new source's value is identical to the old source's value.[2] A particularly simple special case of such a redistribution, where the old and the new sources are computed by syntactically identical expressions—is known in the compiler literature as *common subexpression elimination* (Aho, Sethi, and Ullman 1986).

There are many occasions when considerations of readability and clarity lead one to code multiple computations of the same value within a program. Consider the following correct implementation of the polynomial evaluation formula

$$poly(C, X) = \sum_{i=0}^{|C|-1} C_i X_i,$$

where C is a finite list of coefficients (in increasing order of subscript), and x is a number:

```
(DEFUN POLY (C X)
  (LET ((SUM 0))
    (DOTIMES (I (LENGTH C))
      (SETQ SUM (+ SUM (* (NTH I C) (EXPT X I)))))
    SUM))
```

This formula uses quadratic time for two reasons: First, iteration, $i + 1$ of the loop in POLY calculates x^{i+1} (in time proportional to $i + 1$) by recursively calculating x^i and then multiplying by x. However, iteration i of POLY just computed x^i, so this value could correspondingly be shared at each level of the recursion. Second, iteration $i + 1$ of the loop in POLY traverses the list C from the beginning (within *NTH*, which calls *NTHCDR*) to find (*NTH* $(i + 1)$ C), taking time proportional to $i + 1$. This computation finds (*NTHCDR* $(i + 1)$ C) by recursively finding (*NTHCDR* i C) and then taking CDR. (*NTHCDR* i C), however, was computed in iteration i of POLY, so it could be shared for each i.

The system discovers and carries out these two optimizations, resulting in a linear-time program.

Identical values can be shared in a program on many occasions. For example, earlier redistributions can create opportunities for later identical-value redistributions. In MY-REVERSE, the first optimization, consisting of two nonidentical-value redistributions, enabled the single identical-value redistribution of the second optimization.

Copy Elimination

Nondestructive operations on structured data types often take the conceptual form of copy and modify: The program makes structurally disjoint copies of (some of) the input objects and then performs a destructive operation on the copies to produce the result. The APPEND program used in MY-REVERSE is an example because it copies its first argument and then destructively modifies part of it to attach the second input list. Frequent use of operations such as APPEND often leads to programs that are inefficient in both time and space because of unnecessary copying. (Such a problem with the original MY-REVERSE led to the first optimization.) Note that this inefficiency is inherent in the specification of APPEND, not in its implementation. Only by realizing that the specification of a given call to APPEND is overly general can the optimizer remove the extraneous copy.

Copy-and-modify operations do not need to be coded in a style as explicitly structured as the system's APPEND; frequently, the copying happens along with other operations as the result list is built. For example, the standard recursive implementation of APPEND has this property. The system is capable of removing these unnecessary copies as well. Moreover, it can eliminate user-defined copy operations on user-defined data structures at all abstraction levels in exactly the same way as it does for copies of lists—by using the extra information in the input teleological structure.

Data Invariant Suspension

Another general class of redistributions centers on the idea of *data invariant suspension.* Concrete representations of data abstractions are often constructed by defining an abstraction function from a concrete type—a subset of a (possibly mutable, possibly recursive) record type—to the abstract type. The appropriate subset of the record type is defined by a set of constraints on the allowed values of the record fields. Each constraint is termed an invariant because it is a property that must be maintained by any module that operates on the representation. Examples of invariants include (1) a linked list used to represent a set contains no duplicate entries, (2) a binary search tree representing a set is balanced, and (3) each node in a pointer-based representation of a directed graph contains lists of both forward and backward pointers to neighbors.

Invariants must be maintained by modules that operate on the data structures if and only if their truth is required to prove the correctness of the specification of the program in which they are used. In a given context, the optimizer can suspend a data invariant (that is, not maintain it locally) as long as the top-level program remains correct. The optimizer can then eliminate any subcomputations whose only purpose is to locally maintain the suspended invariant. Note that I allow specifications to constrain the overall efficiency of a program as well as its function; thus, invariants whose purpose is only to maintain the efficiency of other operations (such as keeping a binary search tree balanced) can be suspended in certain contexts, such as when the efficiency to be gained exists only in modules and is not subsequently used by the program.

As an example of invariant suspension, consider the linked-list representation of a set. The operation of adding a new member to a set (set-add) must check to see if the added element is already an element of the list to avoid duplicating an entry. The only purpose of such a check is to maintain the no-duplicates invariant. The no-duplicates invariant is then assumed true in implementing operations such as set cardinality. However, the usual implementation of the set membership operation will be correct even if the list contains duplicates. Thus, if a program were, say, to do several set-adds followed only by some membership tests (and not return any of the set objects as return values) then the no-duplicates invariant could be suspended over this portion of the program. The set-adds would not need to do the extra checking; they could simply push the new element onto the front of the list. Each set-add would cost only a constant amount of time instead of time proportional to the length of the list.

Note that I am not claiming that all invariants are associated with code that is for one purpose only. It is frequently the case that subroutines perform more than one function in a program. Thus, suspending just one of the invariants maintained by such a module would not allow its elimination. The system is most effective at introducing function sharing into designs where the individual boxes have single (or few) purposes. My observation is that it is usually possible to find such structural models of programs, although these models do not always correspond with the most natural implementations. Often, it is better to let the optimizer introduce function sharing in a context-sensitive way rather than just use a partially shared implementation everywhere.

Generalized Loop Fusion

In the conventional compiler literature, a *loop fusion* (or jamming) is the action of merging two iterations over the same range when no data flow conflicts can be proven between the two loops. For example, a loop that sums the odd numbers in an array can be fused with one that sums the even numbers, saving one round of incrementation and bound checking. Typically, such iterations must explicitly be bounded, and the ranges must be identical. Redistribution optimizations can capture more general loop fusions by a judicious choice of program representation.

In this research, loop fusions are distinguished by the fact that the shared value is a temporal sequence of values generated by iteration. These general loop fusions do not necessarily involve same-length sequences of identical values because loops with different termination criteria can have their overlapping ranges fused, and corresponding elements can differ.

The system uses a representation of loops based on Waters's Series Expressions (Steele 1990) that requires significant back-end compiler support (in the form of a macro package). Note that even though the macro package does nontrivial postprocessing, the adaptation problem is still solved by my system using only (series) data flow rerouting. This advantage comes from using a powerful representation.

A *series data object* is a mathematical sequence of Lisp data values (that is, a function from $\{0 \ldots k\}$, for some k, to standard Lisp data values). At the implementation level, each series object is used to represent the sequence of values taken on by some variable on successive iterations of the compiled loop. See the appendix of Steele [1990] for explanations of the series functions used here.

As an example of generalized loop fusion, consider the following Common Lisp program, EQUAL-AFTER-SUBSTITUTION? In this original form, it has two loops. The first loop consumes linear space in constructing an intermediate list representing the substituted list; this list is then scanned by the EQUAL program. Subsequently, the intermediate list is discarded. Note that both loops are implicit in the series representation.

```
(DEFUN EQUAL-AFTER-SUBSTITUTION? (NEW OLD L1 L2)
  "True iff L2 is EQUAL to the result of substituting
   NEW for OLD in L1"
  (EQUAL (SUBSTITUTE NEW OLD L1) L2))
```

The Lisp primitives are structurally modeled as follows:

```
(DEFUN EQUAL (L1 L2)
  "Lisp EQUAL"
  (LET ((MARKER (MAKE-SERIES (GENSYM))))
    (COLLECT-AND
      (#MEQ (CATENATE (SCAN L1) MARKER)
            (CATENATE (SCAN L2) MARKER)))))

(DEFUN SUBSTITUTE (NEW OLD LIST)
  "Simplified Lisp SUBSTITUTE"
  (COLLECT
    (#MSUBIFEQ (SERIES NEW) (SERIES OLD) (SCAN LIST))))

;;; Helper for SUBSTITUTE
(DEFUN SUBIFEQ (NEW OLD X)
  (IF (EQ OLD X) NEW X))
```

This Lisp code corresponds to the data flow representation used. The models are presented in Lisp for expository purposes; the system accepts only the data flow representation.

Series expressions have the advantage of making iterations explicit structural elements of programs; thus, they become elements that can be shared among different users. The iteration implicit in SUBSTITUTE is over the elements of the first list argument, L1, to EQUAL-AFTER-SUBSTITUTION? The iteration in EQUAL is over both the result list of SUBSTITUTE and the second input to EQUAL-AFTER-SUBSTITUTION? The system introduces function sharing here by replacing the (SCAN L1) in EQUAL with a series data flow from the output of (#MSUBIFEQ . . .) from SUBSTITUTE. This data flow obviates the COLLECT in SUBSTITUTE; so, the intermediate list output of SUBSTITUTE is not created. Furthermore, the iteration is now controlled by COLLECT-AND, which can terminate before the end of the input list is reached. The resulting program has a single loop over the input list *L1*. The improved version saves substantial time and space.

Key Ideas in the Implementation

Space constraints do not allow a full exposition of the implementation; details can be found in Hall (1990). The remainder of this chapter summarizes the key ideas and trade-offs made to obtain a practical system.

Given unlimited time and space resources, a (nonexistent) perfect theorem prover for the domain, and a (nonexistent) practical theory of program efficiency, it would be easy to find the optimal set of redistributions to improve any program. One could separately test each subset of the quadratically many source-target pairs in the program and evaluate each one for correctness and degree of program improvement, picking the best one. Unfortunately, this approach is impossible. The correctness problem and the problem of evaluating program efficiency are uncomputable, and there are exponentially many sets of source-target pairs to try.

Instead, I broke down the problem of finding the best set of source-target pairs to reroute into two subproblems. First is *candidate generation:* Which of the exponentially many sets of source-target pairs should we consider? Second is *candidate screening:* Given a source-target pair, how can we quickly evaluate its likelihood of correctness?

The two optimization algorithms, IEBR and IBR, use the same approach to candidate generation, based on box-cost estimation. They differ in their methods of candidate screening and in the additional input information (beyond the program's structure) they require.

Additional Input Information

Requiring more input information is an extra burden for the user; thus, it represents a trade-off between ease of use and increased performance. I argue that the extra input are not too difficult to provide, particularly if the system is to be used in an integrated program design environment.

This research can potentially be applied in two principal ways: either as a stand-alone optimizer used directly by programmers or as a subprocess of a larger automated design system, such as the Programmer's Apprentice (Rich and Waters 1990) or KIDS (chapter 19). When used in the larger context, it is reasonable to expect that the extra information is produced as a natural part of the machine-mediated design process; hence, it represents little or no extra effort. In the stand-alone case, various techniques can be applied to make the programmer's job easy enough to be worthwhile.

Optimization Invariants. Current optimizing compilers are fundamentally limited in power because they do not have access to the extra information possessed by the human programmer. In the absence of some statement of optimization invariants, such as a top-level specification, the optimizer can only make program changes that can be proved to preserve correctness based on the specifications of the language primitives. For example, can COPY-LIST in the following program be removed (that is, replaced by IDENTITY)?

```
(DEFUN F (X L)
  "Prepends X to L"
  (CONS X (COPY-LIST L)))
```

The answer depends on what specification the routine *F* is required to satisfy. The replacement is allowed unless the specification includes the requirement that the output cells be fresh. For example, the replacement would be disallowed if *F* were used in

```
(DEFUN DANGER (X L)
  "Appends X.L to L"
  (NCONC (F X L) L)),
```

but it would be allowed if *F* were only used here:

```
(DEFUN SAFE (X L)
  "Appends X.L to L"
  (APPEND (F X L) L))
```

A standard compiler is forced to assume the worst and not make the replacement; there is no way to provide it with a weaker specification than the most conservative. My system, however, accepts and exploits a statement of optimization invariants for each program. For *F*, if freshness is required, the programmer must explicitly give an optimization invariant enforcing it; otherwise, the system need not preserve it. Feather and London (1982) investigate the issue of exploiting specification freedoms in the context of automatically implementing high-level program specifications.

Explanations. The intuition behind the IEBR algorithm is that it is easier to find a substitute for a value (and know that the substitute is adequate) if we know the purpose(s) the value serves. The target condition given earlier for $MY-REVERSE.CONC.NC.C1 was an English paraphrase of such a purpose description.

A key idea of this research is that the earlier purpose description can automatically be derived from a proof of the top-level specification of MY-REVERSE. Typically, a programmer will know why (s/he believes that) the program is correct. From this knowledge, s/he can derive descriptions of the purposes of intermediate results and use such descriptions to justify optimizations. IEBR captures this notion using a new form of explanation-based generalization, called *parent-child clause unioning* (PCCU). See Hall (1990) for further discussion of this technique. Rather than attempting to automatically derive the correctness explanation for the entire program (an impractical task), the system relies on user input, proofs from the software library, and the automatic generation of proofs of quasi-specifications.

Incomplete Design Information

Both algorithms require extra input information that can be difficult to supply. Fortunately, in each case, optimizer performance can be traded for ease of use.

To use IBR, the programmer must provide effective top-level optimization invariants (such as a top-level specification) for the program. (*Effective* here means that the system must be able to computationally evaluate them on given concrete data values.) It is well known that top-level specifications are difficult to formalize for complex programs. IBR, however, can use relative invariants because it has access to the unoptimized program that is assumed correct. For many programs, this ability makes the job of providing invariants trivial because the effective specification can simply test for equality with the original output. In other cases, such as in MY-REVERSE, the original output values can be used to check some abstract properties of the new output, but other portions of the specification must still be formalized by the programmer. In still other cases, the original output values provide no help at all in checking the output values of the optimized program. In most instances, however, a relative specification is more conservative than a nonrelative specification could be but easier to formalize.

To use IEBR, the programmer must provide a proof that the program's structure satisfies the given top-level specification. IEBR would likely be impractical if the user were forced to provide a complete proof of a complete specification for each program to be optimized. Two observations address this difficulty: First, much of the proving and specifying can take place when the library of reusable modules is built rather than when the modules are used to develop a new program. Thus, the costs for library modules are effectively amortized to zero over all uses of the library. Second, a trade-off can be made: The user can sacrifice some optimization performance in return for usability. To support this trade-off, the system can accept a proof of a *quasi-specification* in place of a proof of a true specification. A quasi-specification is a statement of program behavior that can refer to internal program values, unlike true specifications that can refer only to input and output values. The key property of quasi-specifications is that we can prove classes of them automatically, allowing IEBR some useful optimization freedom. Hall (1990) discusses quasi-specifications in detail.

I have implemented algorithms to support the fully automatic production of proofs of quasi-specifications for programs that operate on abstract lists. These proofs accurately capture such properties as side-effect behavior and abstract list equality but are overly restrictive regarding other behavior such as the actual abstract list function. Generally, automatic production must be implemented differently for different domains of programs because different domains have different invariants and properties that must systematically be captured.

In summary, the user does not need to do any difficult manual proofs or even define a complete formal specification to use IEBR; the system can automatically perform these actions. Of course, the system will then miss some optimizations because it cannot get as much information as it can from a proof of a true specification.

Candidate Generation

The system's solution to the candidate generation problem represents a trade-off between search completeness and tractability. Both IBR and IEBR use the same heuristic search-control strategy based on a crude cost-estimation technique that considers only those sets of pairs that would allow the system to immediately eliminate a box. Once a box is eliminated, the system then tries to eliminate more boxes, with the iteration terminating when all boxes with a cost estimate greater than a threshold (the box-cost threshold) have been considered.[3] More costly boxes are considered before less costly ones, and boxes within a box are considered after the box itself. The system can occasionally miss the best set of source-target pairs because the best set requires eliminating a low-cost box before a high-cost box or because the best set of pairs cannot be partitioned so that each group is associated with eliminating a box. This problem is a version of the well-known local maximum problem that plagues all hill-climbing algorithms. The heuristic seems to perform well in practice, however.

Candidate Screening

The second aspect of the search problem is *candidate screening*. A (human or machine) procedure for deciding whether a given source-target pair maintains overall program correctness is likely to be computationally costly.

Thus, the search phase should discard as many faulty candidates as possible. (If the system is used without a compile-time certifier [see next subsection], the issue of candidate screening is even more important.) Of course, some candidates can be eliminated simply on syntactic grounds: based on either a static-type clash or a *causality conflict* (that is, when the proposed source's value is partially determined by the target's value). Such simple tests are not enough, however. In even moderate-sized programs, hundreds or thousands of candidates can remain, of which only a few, possibly tens, are actually valid redistributions.

The key idea for solving this problem centers on the idea of using concrete test-case input: If the program resulting from a source-target redistribution is incorrect on a given test case, then the redistribution candidate can certainly be discarded. This situation represents a trade-off: The negative aspect is that test cases for complex programs can be difficult to compute and store. Positive aspects include that it provides excellent filtering; test cases are usually available in the design environment, and unlike automated theorem proving, it is easy to compute test case output given the program.

I have designed and experimented with two different approaches that exploit this idea. The approach taken in IBR is the simpler of the two: First, structurally carry out the source-target redistribution, and then reexecute each test case, evaluating the correctness of the overall program output using the effective optimization invariants given as input. If the results are not correct, the structural change is retracted.

IEBR, however, avoids reexecuting the test cases for most pairs. As discussed in An Example, it first derives the target condition, $tc_t(.)$, for each target t considered. It performs this derivation using PCCU (DeJong and Mooney 1986). It then evaluates whether the source candidate satisfies the target condition in every concrete test case. Once a pair passes this target condition test, the redistribution is structurally carried out, and the test cases are reexecuted. Top-level optimization invariants are then checked (as in IBR) to make sure the redistribution hasn't rendered some prior pair invalid.

At the cost of some optimization power, variants of IEBR can be made to operate even in the absence of optimization invariants and even without ever reexecuting a test case (Hall 1990).

Correctness

The system produces a set of source-target pairs that preserve correctness on the test cases when it is used to optimize the program. This statement does not, of course, imply that the program remains correct on every input. The system trades correctness for the ability to consider powerful optimizations. It is obviously undesirable for an optimizer to introduce errors into the user's program (the user typically introduces enough on his/her own). One can deal with this problem in two different ways: Attempt to certify all kept redistributions at compile time, or use automatic tools to support run-time debugging of erroneous optimizations.

Compile-Time Certification. One idea is to use an automated theorem prover to try to prove each conjecture. If the theorem prover fails after a certain amount of effort, reject the candidate. A given scheme for limited, incomplete reasoning defines the notion of *routine optimizations,* those provable by the system, and *deep optimizations,* those not provable. The hope would be to properly engineer the trade-off between proving cost and optimizer performance.

Using a theorem prover has the advantage of guaranteeing that the optimizations preserve correctness. The disadvantage, however, is that current theorem provers bog down with problems of significant size. Thus, significant advances in the state of the art are required to make this approach practical for complex programs.

Probably the most practical near-term approach to compile-time certification is to have a human guide the theorem prover to the proofs. This approach would both preserve correctness and be computationally practical. The undesirable feature is that it is not fully automated and would require the user to think hard about low-level implementation details.

Note that IEBR supports these methodologies much better than IBR: IEBR only conjectures changes to the program whose justification (if it exists) can be viewed as a perturbation of the original input correctness proof. (That is, all that needs to be proved is simultaneous satisfaction of the target conditions of the redistribution pairs rather than the entire altered program.) Thus, IEBR tends to restrict attention to the more routine, easier-to-prove redistributions. This point is a significant one in IEBR's favor. IBR gives no help at all along these lines.

Run-Time Debugging. The notion of efficient program checking introduced by Blum and Kannan (1989) provides another means of coping that does not rely on automated theorem proving. Intuitively, an efficient program checker is a separate program (assumed correct) that can check the output of the original program in a relatively insignificant amount of time. My proposal is to check the optimized program's output every time it is run (using an efficient program checker); if it is found to be incorrect, then signal the user and offer to reoptimize the program using the input for the faulty run as an additional test case. (Of course, the reoptimization can ignore all source-target pairs that were shown incorrect in the previous run. This approach saves most of the time of reoptimization.) The result of the reoptimization will be a program that is more often correct than the original optimized version.

This approach is practical as long as the checking is efficient: The run times of the optimized program and the checker together must be significantly less than that of the original program alone. Blum and Kannan (1989) develop a theory of efficient program checking related to this idea but do not apply it to program optimization; hence, their definition of an efficient program checker is different than mine.

Note that an efficient checker cannot be relative because it would be forced to run the unoptimized program (to get those output) every time it checked a run of the optimized program. Such a strategy obviously violates the efficiency condition. Note, however, that the optimizer can still use a relative optimization invariant during optimization; it is only forbidden at program use time.

Experiments

Both algorithms have been run on 26 examples. Most of the examples are in the domain of a simple pointer-based representation of abstract lists, similar to but simpler than the list representation in Lisp. (MY-REVERSE is one such program.) Some examples are simple numeric programs, such as POLY, and some operate on a list representation of sets, the set representation built as the next abstraction layer on the abstract list representation. The most complex example (that is, the one that takes the longest to completely optimize) is an implementation of the merge-sort algorithm for sorting lists of numbers. The box-cost threshold was set as low as possible; the only boxes not considered for elimination were zero-cost boxes (constants). Simply to give an idea of the speed of the algorithms, the complete search and optimization of MY-REVERSE took 158 seconds for IEBR and 346 seconds for IBR. (The system is implemented in Common Lisp on a Symbolics 3670.) For IEBR, 24 boxes were considered, 31 target conditions were derived, and 223 source-target pairs were tested using target conditions. IBR examined the same 24 boxes and executed the test case 223 times during optimization. For comparison, IEBR required 14,980 seconds (4:09:40) to optimize the merge-sort program, and IBR required 59,081 seconds (16:24:41). IEBR considered 370 boxes, derived 475 target conditions, and considered 22,858 source-target pairs. IBR executed 4,893 test-case recomputations in considering 318 boxes (16,425 source-target pairs). The optimizations carried out included loop fusions and copy eliminations; they were somewhat different from IEBR to IBR, although the two result programs essentially were equally efficient.

IBR is always at least as powerful as IEBR (and usually more); when both are usable, IBR improves the program at least as much as IEBR and sometimes more. (This statement must be qualified to reflect the quality of the input to the algorithms; if IBR gets a more conservative specification than IEBR, then IEBR will perform better. The statement applies to cases in which the same top-level specification is used for both.) Furthermore, its input requirements are much easier to meet for many programs, although seemingly not for complex programs with complex high-level specifications.

However, there are cases on which IBR cannot be run because it is too difficult to formalize the optimization invariants. (There are variants of IEBR that can operate on programs without optimization invariant input.) Furthermore, even if IBR can be run, it is much more expensive than IEBR because it requires running the test cases hundreds or thousands of times. This fact is particularly true for complex programs. (Evaluating a target condition is generally much simpler computationally than reexecuting the entire program.) IBR is also more prone to generate false conjectures because of test-case coincidences than IEBR. Another drawback is that the program surgery required to carry out the candidate redistributions costs IBR much more than IEBR because there are so many more. (IEBR carries out only redistributions passing the target condition test; IBR carries out every pair considered.)

Pairs of examples were run that were carefully controlled for relative input size relationships to demonstrate a significant difference in the growth of the cost functions of the two algorithms. With this technique, IEBR performs significantly better than IBR, particularly as the size of the input program increases. For most of the examples, IBR usually took between three and six times as long as IEBR to complete the search. The largest advantage achieved by IEBR was a factor of nine.

On one example, IBR was slightly faster than IEBR. This result is explained by the fact that the more powerful IBR is able to eliminate a box early on that IEBR does not eliminate; hence, IEBR had to search the box's substructure, but IBR didn't. This interaction of power and speed effectively reduces the run-time advantage of IEBR over IBR in cases where the input explanatory structure is too weak to allow full generalization.

Examples were also chosen to explore various types of optimizations, including all the examples given in this chapter. Thus, examples were run demonstrating identical-value redistributions, copy elimination, data invariant suspension, and generalized loop fusions.

Literature Review

This section relates this research to previous approaches to improving program performance. It also discusses relations with other branches of AI research.

Program Improvement and Redesign

Several areas of research in this area are relevant.

Traditional Compiler Techniques. One way to view the redistribution of intermediate results is as an attempt to generalize many traditional compiler techniques to apply to arbitrarily high-level abstractions. Techniques such as common subexpression elimination, copy elimination, and loop fusion (Aho,

Sethi, and Ullman 1986) are fundamentally limited by the level of their source languages. That is, they can only exploit the semantics of the data types that are primitive to the language because they cannot capture and fully exploit the semantics of user-defined types. This problem stems from having no access to the true specifications of the programs or the domain theory that connects the structure to the specification. For example, a Fortran optimizer can only exploit the algebraic laws of integers, arrays, and other low-level types, knowing nothing of the laws of higher-level types such as sets, mappings, and graphs.

I include in the category of traditional compiler techniques the operations of type inference and automatic data-structure choice and aggregation performed by the SETL compiler (Freudenberger, Schwartz, and Sharir 1983). SETL is a much higher-level language than most; hence, the optimizations that its compiler performs have greater impact on program performance. Nevertheless, these optimizations are still limited to the semantics of language primitives. The optimizer demonstrates a great deal of ingenuity in determining when certain optimizations regarding sets and mappings can be performed, but the language cannot capture any extra semantic information about higher-level, user-defined abstractions. Although it might infer that a particular copy operation on a set is unnecessary, it will not be able to infer the analogous fact about a copy operation on a user-defined type. Because no language will ever predefine anywhere near all the useful programming abstractions, it is doubtful whether the traditional approach toward optimization will ever achieve the flexibility and power of a human expert.

Low-Level Program-Transformation Systems. The program-transformation school (Partsch and Steinbruggen 1983; Cheatham 1984; Darlington 1981; chapter 18) takes the view that optimization should take place as a process of program transformations, usually at the source code level. Each transformation must provably preserve program correctness. Consequently, each transformation has a set of applicability conditions that must be verified. An as-yet unattained goal of the research is that these conditions be automatically checked so that program correctness is guaranteed no matter how the human influences the process.

Fully automatic approaches to choosing the sequence of transformations are not generally capable of producing efficient code because the search space is too large and because it is too difficult to determine the relative efficiency of the results. Consequently, most transformational approaches are semi-automatic in that a human must guide the selection process (also, the human must sometimes assist in verifying applicability conditions). This line of research cannot be termed a success because the process of (a human) guiding the transformations is difficult and tedious. Each transformation is relatively low level, so many are required to carry out any particular optimization. Optimizing a large program from its clear but inefficient specification requires too many small-grain steps to be feasible. (There is, however, ongoing research into structuring the transformation process; see Fickas [1985] for one approach and Meertens [1986] for many views on this subject.)

A particular branch of this field (Wile 1981; Scherlis 1981) investigates specializing data type implementations to their contexts. Although these approaches discuss some of the transformations possible, they again do not discuss the issue of automating the search. In particular, there is no discussion of explanatory structure or the use of correctness information in guiding the search.

It is possible that the search-control ideas developed in this research (focus on eliminating a box at a time in order of estimated cost) might be applicable to program-transformation technologies; I have not looked into this connection as yet.

High-Level Program-Transformation Systems. KIDS (chapter 19) is an interactive program-transformation system incorporating many powerful transformation tools, such as algorithm designers, an inference system, a finite-differencing subsystem, and a partial evaluator. This program is qualitatively different from the other program-transformation approaches in that the human guidance is in terms of much higher-level operations. This approach ameliorates the search problems faced by the lower-level transformation systems.

In fact, a redistribution module would, I believe, fit in well in the KIDS environment as another available automatic transformation step because it can perform tasks the other steps can't. For example, Smith mentions several shortcomings in the final program output by KIDS for the *k* queens problem: It performs unnecessary list-member checks and unnecessary copy operations. I gave examples here of how my system can get rid of these things. However, the KIDS environment could probably be easily adapted to maintain the teleological information needed by the redistribution system because all the steps are automated.

Similar in philosophy to KIDS is the Programmer's Apprentice (Rich and Waters 1990). It, too, contains various types of experts (a designer, a program recognizer, and a requirement assistant) and a general inference system (Cake). In principle, it is capable of taking much higher-level and less precise initial problem statements than KIDS but is less automated. I believe that a redistribution subsystem would fit into the Programmer's Apprentice for much the same reasons as it would with KIDS: It provides necessary capabilities not already available, and the environment naturally provides most of the extra teleological information as a by-product of the design and analysis processes.

Finite Differencing. Finite differencing (Paige and Koenig 1982) is a method for improving programs by replacing repeated all-at-once computations with more efficient incremental versions. The implementation in RAPTS (Paige 1983) is semiautomatic in that a user must decide which instances of differencing to apply and whether an instance is desirable. The system is given a sizable base of specific differentiation rules, each of which applies to some pattern of operations expressed in SETL. For example, one such rule says that the expression, # S (size of the set S), can incrementally be maintained by initially calculating the size of S, for every addition to S adding 1 to it, and for every deletion subtracting 1 from it.

Although finite differencing is an elegant idea, expressing this idea in terms of a large rule base of highly specific instances has significant problems. The biggest problem is that to exploit the idea of differencing to its fullest, the system would require new differencing rules for any new abstraction. This problem is not simply the standard expert system complaint, however. Typical expert systems solve relatively fixed problems, where the expertise only changes slowly. By contrast, the designer creates new abstractions to meet the specific needs of each new problem. Therefore, in order for the rule-based implementation of finite differencing to be considered a complete theory, it must also account for how the rules are (automatically) derived from the definitions of the abstractions. Other finite-differencing problems include difficulties in deciding which rules to apply and whether a given rule will improve program efficiency.

With regard to redistribution, I believe that much of the finite-differencing behavior can be seen as an application of the redistribution principle. A principled approach to redistribution would, therefore, supply a partial answer to the problem previously mentioned. Finite differencing could then be seen as an emergent behavior rooted in deeper principles. Of course, rules are not bad as such. Transformation rules automatically compiled from experience (those that could otherwise be automatically derived in a principled but slow way) can be useful for speeding the process.

Memoizing. Mostow and Cohen (1985) investigate automating the well-known technique of *memoizing,* that is the idea of a subroutine maintaining a cache of its output values for those input for which it has already computed an answer. If the subroutine is ever called more than once on the same input, the answer is looked up in the cache the second and succeeding times rather than recomputed. Mostow and Cohen explore the addition of caches to Interlisp functions with an eye to building a fully automatic tool. Unfortunately, it appears that this problem is too difficult because side effects and large data structures make the technique difficult to justify in many cases. I believe the chief problem in this approach is, again, that the memoizer has neither knowledge of, nor control over, the design process because like a compiler, it takes in only the Interlisp source code. It must always assume the worst possible cases of use for any given subroutine, cases that could possibly be ruled out if extra information relating to purpose and correctness were known. Memoizing can potentially be used to implement equal-value redistributions, but I have not explored this technique.

Tupling. Pettorossi (1984) defines *tupling* as the combination of two initially separate functions into a single, vector-valued function so that their implementations can share partial results. He proposes it as a program transformation but does not discuss automating the search. The essence of the technique is interesting in comparison with my approach to redistribution. My system avoids the need for tupling, viewing the program as virtually flattened, so that all intermediate results are available to be shared (limited only by execution ordering of the boxes and recursion constraints). The system tracks the module boundaries, but is free to add new input and output ports to boxes to achieve sharing. I believe tupling can be viewed as a transformation that could help implement redistribution in a general program- transformation system.

Automatic Programming Approaches to Efficiency. Automatic programming systems usually implement a top-down refinement approach to program design, always staying within abstraction boundaries. This approach contrasts with my system, which is primarily concerned with breaking these boundaries to gain efficiency. Thus, my system is complementary to these systems. The most interesting point of comparison with my system is the method of deriving and using cost information to guide the search.

Kant's (1983) LIBRA system is designed to be a search-control expert that guides the stepwise refinement process of the PSI (Green 1976) synthesis system. LIBRA guides the search by performing an incremental symbolic analysis of the efficiency of the evolving design, obtaining optimistic and achievable performance estimates. The refinement is then controlled using a branch-and-bound method. LIBRA spends most of its time performing algebraic manipulation to simplify quantitative cost estimates of the overall program. McCartney's (1987) MEDUSA system designs efficient algorithms in the domain of computational geometry problems. McCartney's approach augments the stepwise refinement paradigm of Kant's approach with domain knowledge of general problem-decomposition techniques. MEDUSA uses analytic knowledge in a similar way to LIBRA, that is, to provide a cost function for use with a branch-and-bound search.

I avoided the complexity of maintaining a quantitative cost estimate of the entire program at each step by only deriving qualitative cost estimates of portions (boxes) of the program.

Both LIBRA and MEDUSA would have trouble producing the optimized implementations achievable with redistribution, simply because they operate within abstraction boundaries. It would be very interesting to integrate my system with these systems. Moreover, because they perform stepwise refinement, much of the teleological information (including the specifications and module correctness proofs) would be a natural by-product of the software library and the initial design process and could then be used by my system.

Replanning and Designing Extensible Software. Linden (chapter 23) proposes using much the same additional information—specifications and teleological information—to support the evolution and redesign (for a changing specification) of software systems. Although not directly relevant to program optimization, this work nevertheless points out other valuable uses of this extra information. This work is still another reason to move toward integrated software development environments that can support the type of automated documentation required for both approaches.

Explanation-Based Generalization

Target conditions are derived from proofs using a novel technique related to explanation-based generalization (DeJong and Mooney 1986). Although there are many approaches to explanation-based generalization, they all take in an explanation of why a given concrete example belongs to a concept and extract a generalized, operational definition of concept membership from it. The technique used is basically the operation of turning constants to variables and back propagating constraints through operators.

My system contrasts with this system in that the input is an explained program, but the concepts to be learned are conditions on portions of the program. Thus, the explanation is not of why a single concrete example satisfies a single concept but, rather, why many different structural elements work together to satisfy a goal. The system then learns an approximation to the role of each structural element in the correctness of the design. Each of these roles is a target condition. Thus, each single explanation encodes many concepts.

Another difference is in the technique of generalizing: My system uses PCCU in resolution proof trees (Hall 1990), which is different from standard approaches to explanation-based generalization. Standard approaches generalize both the concept at the root of the tree and the conditions at the leaves of the tree through a form of variabilization. PCCU does not attempt to generalize the clause at the root of the proof tree (which explanation-based generalization does to get a proof of concept membership in terms of a free variable) because the proofs it operates on are not direct proofs of concept membership. Rather, the proofs establish global program properties, and the PCCU technique infers implicit concept membership conditions (target conditions) from these proofs. As such, variabilization is neither appropriate nor desirable. However, given a particular proof tree, the PCCU technique extracts more general leaf conditions than do standard explanation-based generalization techniques and is able to generalize selected proof leaves rather than simply all the leaves. (For further technical discussion of PCCU, see Hall [1990].)

Although there is work on using explanation-based generalization to acquire programming methods from experts, I have not seen any that uses explanation-based generalization to derive facts about elements of a given program to perform optimization.

Conclusions

The redistribution of intermediate results captures a wide range of powerful optimizations. This ability is to be expected because it is a limited form of one of the most basic principles in all design optimization, function sharing. This research investigated the automation of this idea. The success of the implemented prototype serves as an initial demonstration of the feasibility of the approach; however, much remains to be done to produce useful tools for programmers. Overall, I believe the techniques here hold significant promise for eventual application.

Experiments have demonstrated the usefulness of the additional input to the optimization process beyond the program's structure. In particular, having an effective representation of the program's function enables optimizations that are qualitatively more powerful than those achievable from the source code alone. Moreover, also having the proofs connecting program structure to program function both allows more programs to be optimized and qualitatively speeds the optimization process, as can be seen in the typical speed advantage enjoyed by IEBR over IBR.

Experiments and analysis seem to show that the algorithm based on computing target conditions from explanations, IEBR, enjoys significant advantages over the brute-force approach of IBR. In addition to the speed benefits, IEBR's exploitation of program teleology has these advantages: First, it restricts attention to optimizations that are more easily proved correct; and, hence might be more practical to safely use. Second, IEBR is less susceptible to test-case inadequacies (unfortunate coincidences) that lead to the introduction of program bugs. If these advantages bear out under testing in a practical setting, they would represent strong arguments for integrated software development environments where teleological information is formalized along with the design and is subsequently used by automated tools.

Limitations

Here, I summarize the limitations of the approach, which exist at many levels of description:

First, as an approach to facilitating the reuse of software modules, function sharing is limited in that it is not a universal technique. Other techniques, such as partial evaluation and finite differencing, easily capture optimizations that function sharing does not get at all. The reverse is also true, however.

Second, the redistribution of intermediate results is more limited than function sharing in general in that it introduces no new code into the design; hence, useful optimizations are missed even if only simple additions are required. I expect that this research will serve as a starting point for exploring function sharing with nontrivial adaptation problem solving.

Third, each of the trade-offs made for practicality makes the system less powerful. For example, the system can give answers (conjectures) that introduce bugs into the program if the test cases have unfortunate coincidences in them, it can miss the best optimizations if eliminating an inexpensive box is required to enable eliminating a costly box, and IEBR can miss optimizations if a quasi-specification proof (not incorporating enough information) is used.

Fourth, the redistribution of intermediate results is sensitive to the idiosyncrasies of the input program's structure. That is, small changes to a program's structure can have significant effects on optimization results.

Future Work

This research raised many issues for future research and engineering: First, redistribution optimizations within recursive programs are often thwarted by the need of the base case for a different redistribution than is needed by the recursive case. It should be relatively simple to extend the theory to handle this problem. Second, cases have arisen requiring simple but nontrivial adaptation problem solving, such as moving boxes into or out of the scope of a conditional. Future research should investigate at least these limited cases. Third, the system needs to be re-engineered for maximum efficiency and integrated into a larger program design environment, preferably one with powerful automatic theorem-proving capabilities. This ability would allow investigation of whether the technology will ultimately be useful.

Acknowledgments

Special thanks are owed to Chuck Rich for many valuable discussions. Thanks also to Dick Waters, Tomas Lozano-Perez, John Guttag, Doug Smith, and Peter Szolovits for discussing the issues presented here and to David Steier, Ted Linden, and Michael Lowry for reading and commenting on drafts.

Notes

1. This fact follows easily from Rice's theorem (Hopcroft and Ullman 1979).

2. Unless otherwise noted, I always use "identical" and "equal" as synonyms denoting the mathematical sense of equality; this use is not the same, for example, as the Lisp relation EQUAL.

3. Recursion complicates the definition of "all boxes" in a program. See Hall (1990) for details.

References

Aho, A.V.; Sethi, R.; and Ullman, J. D. 1986. *Compilers: Principles, Techniques, and Tools.* Reading, Mass.: Addison-Wesley.

Blum, M., and Kannan, S. 1989. Designing Programs That Check Their Work. In Proceedings of the Twenty-First Symposium on the Theory of Computation, 86–97. New York: Association for Computing Machinery.

Cheatham, T. E. 1984. Reusability through Program Transformation. *IEEE Transactions on Software Engineering* SE-19(5): 589–595.

Darlington, J. 1981. An Experimental Program Transformation and Synthesis System. *Artificial Intelligence* 16:1–46.

DeJong, G., and Mooney, R. 1986. Explanation-Based Learning: An Alternative View. *Machine Learning* 1:145–176.

Feather, M. S., and London, P. E. 1982. Implementing Specification Freedoms. *Science of Computer Programming* 2:91–131.

Fickas, S. F. 1985. Automating the Transformational Development of Software. *IEEE Transactions on Software Engineering* SE-11(11): 1268–1277.

Freudenberger, S. M.; Schwartz, J. T.; and Sharir, M. 1983. Experience with the SETL Optimizer. *ACM Transactions on Programming Languages and Systems* 5(1): 26–45.

Green, C. C. 1976. The Design of the PSI Program Synthesis System. In Proceedings of the Second International Conference on Software Engineering, 4–18. Washington, D.C.: IEEE Computer Society.

Hall, R. J. 1990. Program Improvement by Automatic Redistribution of Intermediate Results, Technical Report, AI-TR-1251, Artificial Intelligence Laboratory, Massachusetts Institute of Technology.

Hopcroft, J. E., and Ullman, J. D. 1979. *Introduction to Automata Theory, Languages, and Computation*. Reading, Mass.: Addison-Wesley.

Kant, E. 1983. On the Efficient Synthesis of Efficient Programs. *Artificial Intelligence* 20:253–306.

McCartney, R. D. 1987. Synthesizing Algorithms with Performance Constraints. In Proceedings of the Sixth National Conference on Artificial Intelligence, 149–154. Menlo Park, Calif.: American Association for Artificial Intelligence.

Meertens, L. G. L. T., ed. 1986. Program Specification and Transformation: Proceedings of the IFIP TC2/WG 2.1 Working Conference on Program Specification and Transformation. Amsterdam: North-Holland.

Mostow, J., and Cohen, D. 1985. Automating Program Speedup by Deciding What to Cache. In Proceedings of the Ninth International Joint Conference on Artificial Intelligence, 165–172. Menlo Park, Calif.: International Joint Conferences on Artificial Intelligence.

Paige, R. 1983. Transformational Programming—Applications to Algorithms and Systems. In Proceedings of the Tenth Annual ACM Symposium on Principles of Programming Languages, 73–87. New York: Association of Computing Machinery.

Paige, R., and Koenig, S. 1982. Finite Differencing of Computable Expressions. *ACM Transactions on Programming Languages and Systems* 4(3): 402–454.

Partsch, H., and Steinbruggen, T. 1983. Program Transformation Systems. *ACM Computing Surveys* 15(3): 199–236.

Pettorossi, A. 1984. A Powerful Strategy for Deriving Efficient Programs by Transformation. In Proceedings of the 1984 ACM Symposium on Lisp and Functional Programming, 273–281. New York: Association of Computing Machinery.

Rich, C., and Waters, R. 1990. The Programmer's Apprentice. New York: Association of Computing Machinery.

Scherlis, W. L. 1981. Program Improvement by Internal Specialization. In Proceedings of the Eighth ACM Symposium on Principles of Programming Languages, 41–49. New York: Association of Computing Machinery.

Steele, G. 1990. *Common Lisp: The Language*, 2d ed. Pensauchen, N.J.: Digital.

Ulrich, K. 1988. Computation and Preparametric Design, Technical Report, AI-TR-1043, Artificial Intelligence Laboratory, Massachusetts Institute of Technology.

Wile, D. 1981. Type Transformations. *IEEE Transactions on Software Engineering* SE-7(1): 32–39.

Formal Derivation Systems

Formal derivation systems are based on a combination of two approaches, both overviewed in the introduction. The first approach is to apply rules of inference to a specification and a domain theory to prove that for every legal input, there exists a legal output. If the proof is constructive, then a program can be extracted from the proof. This technique is a generalization of logic programming, in which an answer is extracted from a proof for a particular input. This approach was pioneered by Cordell Green and Richard Waldinger in the late sixties. The second approach is to apply correctness-preserving transformations to a specification to incrementally refine it into a program. This approach was developed by many people both in America and Europe. As shown by the chapters in this section, these two approaches are complementary.

The transformation rules in the previous sections on domain-specific program synthesis and knowledge compilation are mainly developed through a knowledge engineering approach. These transformation rules are acquired through introspection, consultation with a domain expert, or some other knowledge elicitation technique. In contrast, the transformations and inference rules used in formal derivation systems are rigorously based on logic. Consequently, the chapters in this section are more mathematical than those in previous sections. The advantage of a rigorous foundation is that a program synthesized with a formal derivation system is verifiably correct.

As in the knowledge compilation section, search control is a dominant theme. Guiding a formal derivation system through a large search space requires substantial design knowledge. The systems described in this section are interactive; the user makes high-level design decisions, and the systems carry out these decisions. However, even with high-level human guidance, the search space is still combinatorially explosive. Therefore, design knowledge is encapsulated into metalevel programs called tactics or strategies. Tactics control the application of basic transformation or inference steps. The replay of derivation histories is another method for search guidance.

Considerable progress has been made since the pioneering research of Green and

Waldinger. The early work showed that the formal approach was mathematically feasible through examples such as simple straight-line programs and sorting algorithms. The chapters in this section show that the formal approach can scale up to much harder problems, such as synthesizing rule-based algorithms, signal-processing algorithms, and linear programming algorithms. This task was accomplished by addressing the search-control issues and formalizing design and domain knowledge. Within the next decade, the break-even point should be reached, where it is easier to develop a program with a formal derivation system than by hand. In addition, research is being pursued for scaling up program synthesis from programming in the small (programs consisting of less than a thousand lines of code) to programming in the large (systems currently requiring many person-months or person-years of effort).

This section includes a variety of American and European authors. Jan Komorowski, a faculty member at the Norwegian Institute of Technology, is a founder of the partial deduction method for logic programming. Wolfgang Bibel, a professor at the Technical University of Darmstadt, is one of the founders of the knowledge-based approach to program synthesis and recently served as conference chair for IJCAI-89. Jeremy Wertheimer's chapter summarizes his Master's thesis research at the Massachusetts Institute of Technology and the Kestrel Institute, a research institute founded and directed by Cordell Green. Uday Reddy, a faculty member at the University of Illinois, applies his past research on term-rewriting systems to program transformation. Douglas Smith and Michael Lowry are research scientists at the Kestrel Institute. Smith's chapter describes KIDS, an advanced program synthesis environment that incorporates a wide spectrum of techniques. Lowry's chapter describes part of his Stanford Ph.D. dissertation research that was carried out within the KIDS environment. Maritta Heisel, Wolfgang Reif, and Werner Stephan are members of the research staff at the University of Karlsruhe in Germany. Their chapter describes research encompassing program verification, program modification, and program synthesis.

Komorowski's chapter describes a transformational method for refining logic programs called partial deduction. Partial deduction uses partial information to do partial proofs and then encapsulates the leaves of the incomplete proof in a new, more efficient residual program. Komorowski compares partial deduction for logic programs to the fold-unfold transformations for functional programs introduced by Burstall and Darlington. As in other transformational methods, search control is a dominant issue. Two tactics are described for controlling search: Opening is a tactic for expanding definitions, and abbreviating is a tactic for collapsing a sequence of function calls into a single call. Komorowski has implemented the PAL environment for transformational refinement of logic programs. PAL supports programming methodologies based on refining data abstractions, procedural abstractions, and metalinguistic abstractions. Future work includes developing tools to help navigate the tree structure of a derivation.

Bibel's chapter describes a vision of software engineering called predicative programming in which all aspects of software development are formalized and automated. Predicative programming is based on logic; the objective is to allow humans to communicate with a software development environment in declarative, rather than algorithmic, terms. Bibel describes past work on LOPS and current work on XPRTS, both transformational implementation systems that refine declarative specifications into efficient Prolog code. Tactics and strategies can be added as control modules to XPRTS.

Wertheimer's chapter describes the application of formal derivation methods to AI algorithms, in particular, rule-based algorithms. He presents a formal derivation of a version of the RETE *pattern matcher, a many-pattern–many-datum algorithm used in* AI *production systems such as* OPS5 *and* SOAR. *An initial derivation was done in the* KIDS *system described later in this section. Ultimately, his research could be part of an attempt to map and formalize the design space of rule-based systems.*

Wertheimer's chapter illustrates the algebraic approach to transformational development that is also used in other chapters in this section. The initial specification for pattern matching is concisely formulated in terms of algebraic structures such as lattices. The derivation relies on distributive laws in the form of equations that define how pattern-matching operations distribute over abstract data types. Distributive laws simplify derivation steps that would otherwise require inductive proofs. The algebraic approach can also clarify the mathematical properties underlying a problem and, thereby, guide the generalization of the derived algorithm. For example, Wertheimer defines the semantics of his simplified RETE *algorithm in terms of the valuation structures for the semantics of first-order logic. This technique enables him to succinctly define an extension to the algorithm that handles negation on the left-hand side of rules.*

Reddy's chapter describes the FOCUS *system, an interactive program-transformation system based on term rewriting. Term rewriting is a limited form of inference with equations that has much smaller search spaces than more general inference techniques. Reddy describes the trade-off of power versus generality with this special inference technique and compares it with other approaches. Reddy's chapter also describes the* FOCUS *utilities for recording, editing, and replaying derivations. Derivations are organized as tree structures that allow exploring alternate derivation paths. This method also facilitates modifying software by making incremental changes to the specification and then replaying the derivation. Future work includes improving the replay system and extending* FOCUS *with tactics.*

Smith's chapter describes KIDS, *an interactive program-transformation system that supports the full spectrum of program development activities.* KIDS *provides tools for domain theory development, high-level algorithm design, program optimization, and data type refinement.* KIDS *provides a graphic interface in which a user selects part of a specification or partially refined program and then chooses a program development operation. All the operations in* KIDS *are high level, thereby shielding the user from low-level control decisions. A unique aspect of* KIDS *is the algorithm design tactics, including tactics for divide and conquer and global search. Most of the operations use* RAINBOW, *a directed inference system that subsumes theorem proving, formula simplification, and the derivation of necessary and sufficient conditions.* RAINBOW *provides particularly good support for reasoning with distributive laws, thereby facilitating the algebraic approach previously described. The chapter illustrates the* KIDS *capabilities with an example from the domain of radar and sonar signal processing.* KIDS *has been used to design and optimize algorithms for over 50 problems.*

Lowry's chapter describes an algorithm design tactic for local search algorithms, also known as hill-climbing algorithms. This design tactic was implemented as an extension to the KIDS *system. The design tactic was developed using a methodology called design analysis. The key to the design tactic is a formalization of the intuitive notion of a natural perturbation that was informally described in previous work on local search algorithms. An abstract theory for the class of local search algorithms was developed using this formalization. The design tactic derives a local search algorithm from a problem specification by developing an interpretation from this abstract local search theory to the problem domain and then instantiating a program schema. As an example, the automatic derivation of the simplex algorithm is described.*

Heisel, Reif, and Stephan describe KIV, an interactive formal development shell for imperative programs. KIV is based on dynamic logic, in which other programming logics such as that of Hoare and Dijkstra can be derived. KIV has a multilevel control architecture. At the bottom are the basic inference rules of dynamic logic. Derived rules are fixed schematic proofs in dynamic logic. Tactics and strategies are implemented as programs in PPL, a functional metalanguage. Tactics are goal-subgoal generators that are more complex than derived rules. Strategies select derivation steps according to a method. Most strategies are interactive and require the user to supply additional information during program generation. Two strategies from the literature implemented in KIV are described in their chapter. The first strategy is Gries's method for developing individual programming constructs such as LOOPS and conditionals. The second strategy is Dershowitz's method for developing programs by modifying previous programs. This strategy includes substrategies for analogy, transformation, synthesis, and classical verification. An advantage of PPL'S representation is that different strategies can freely be combined and interleaved. Future work includes support for programming in the large.

Synthesis of Programs in the Partial Deduction Framework

Jan Komorowski

The goal of this research is to develop a framework for a complete software design methodology. A complete methodology includes a calculus for designing specifications, a calculus for the incremental refinement of specifications, and a programming environment that implements the calculi and that allows the user to experiment with the specifications. More specifically, this programming methodology is based on partial deduction (Komorowski 1981, 1989). The aim of this work is a rapprochement between formal software engineering and knowledge-based methods.

Another motivation for this work is an observation that several methods proposed for automating the design of software, some of which are discussed in this volume, share a refinement and specialization paradigm. It seems that this paradigm takes the form of partial evaluation, as in functional programming, or partial deduction, as in logic programming.[1] In general, *partial deduction* is concerned with generating a correct (residual) program given a program and context conditions for its use.

Partial Deduction: A Brief History

The original motivation for partial deduction was the optimization of Prolog programs, but it appears today that partial deduction is a rather omnipresent and unifying principle in computer science. For example, Bry (1989) shows that partial deduction yields Alexander and magic set methods for deductive databases, van Harmelen and Bundy (1988) point to the similarity of explanation-based learning and partial deduction, and Hoppe (1990) investigates the relationship of partial deduction to nonmonotonic and default reasoning. Furthermore, the partial deduction theorem is applicable to Prolog and to system languages in the Prolog family (that is, Parlog, Concurrent Prolog, GHC, Andora Prolog, and so on).

Partial deduction is a transformational method. Because it is difficult to build sophisticated autonomous transformation systems that understand the transformations and programs being transformed and that can make a number of intricate decisions, such as trading space for time, researchers took a typical AI approach in which the human programmer and the machine cooperate toward solving a problem. The currently mechanizable part of transformational knowledge is expressed in a sophisticated theorem prover in the form of tactics and with the use of partial deduction parameters. The tactics and parameters contribute to taming the unruly combinatorial explosion if a blind and unrestricted approach is taken. It is then the programmer's role to communicate the points of interest and suggest paths to explore. PAL, an advanced partial deduction environment that was implemented, facilitates this communication. It is anticipated that with time, part of the accumulated knowledge of transformations can gradually be transferred to the environment.

The specific aims of this presentation are to introduce the principle of partial deduction and demonstrate its applicability to automating software design. In particular, a refinement calculus called replacement-in-context that uses the tactics and partial deduction parameters and a programming environment that supports program synthesis based on partial deduction are presented.

Structure of the Presentation

Knowledge-Based Transformational Programming presents some of the concepts and motivation behind this work. The next section is an introduction to partial deduction. It starts with an informal presentation and a few examples and is followed by formal definitions and a theorem that states the soundness and completeness of partial deduction. Tactics and parameters of partial deduction are presented both formally and with examples in Partial Deduction Tactics and Parameters. Replacement-in-Context uses the results of the previous section to introduce a calculus for the incremental transformation of programs that is called replacement-in-context. A description of the PAL environment is provided in the next section and is followed by Sample Developments, which contains excerpts from sample developments. Finally, Partial Deduction and Software Design discusses the role of partial deduction in software design, and the last section presents my conclusions and suggests some topics for future research.

It is assumed that the reader has a rudimentary knowledge of logic programming or has some background in Prolog. For an excellent introduction to logic programming and Prolog, see Nilsson and Maluszynski's (1990) book. For simplicity, I restrict attention to logic programs without negation. Such programs are called *definite-clause programs* or, for short, definite programs. The technical results are, however, for *normal programs*, that is, programs that include negation. Example Prolog programs used here follow the standard Edinburgh notation with variables starting with capital letters or underscores and constant names with lowercase letters.

Related Work

Partial deduction was first introduced to logic programming in 1981 in my thesis (Komorowski 1981, 1982) but has only recently received a lot of attention. Most of the work has concentrated on the theory of partial deduction (for example, Lloyd and Shepherdson [1990]) and the problems of implementing a partial deduction engine. A comparison of the performance of the five most often cited engines can be found in Lam (1989). With the possible exception of Lakhotia's (1989) ProMix, work on environments for partial deduction is scarce.

Clearly, there is a relationship with the partial evaluation of Lisp (Haraldsson 1977; Beckman, et al. 1976) and functional programs. For a collection of articles on these and related topics, see Bjørner, Ershov, and Jones (1987). This research is also related to, for example, Back's (1988) work on the theory of refinement calculus.

In the broad context of automating software design, partial deduction seems to play a central role as a general mechanism that expresses the refinement or specialization of specifications and programs. Several of the contributions in this volume, such as the KIDS system (chapter 19), knowledge compilation (chapters 10 and 12), knowledge-based refinement in software development (chapter 23), logics for software specification (chapter 16), and refinement calculi and systems (chapters 15, 18, and 21), seem to share one underlying principle of specialization to a varying degree. For example, a generic search algorithm can be specialized to a depth-first search procedure, a general plan for design decisions can be refined with domain-specific knowledge to realize a particular engineering application, or a high-level specification can be refined into a parallel algorithm using the knowledge of a particular hardware architecture.

Knowledge-Based Transformational Programming

Computer programs are concerned with how-to or procedural knowledge, and most of today's programming languages are algorithmic and built to support the expression of this procedural, process-oriented knowledge. Mathematics, logic, and much of the high-level communication among people and between software designers and computers is declarative; that is, it is in the form of what-is knowledge. *Logic programming* is a declarative approach to programming in which the programmer specifies the what-is part as a collection of clauses (roughly, a Prolog program), and the computer provides the how-to part expressed in a general theorem prover (for example, a Prolog interpreter). This approach can be powerful when it works. One of the main problems is that a general prover cannot make intelligent choices in search for a solution, so it usually performs an exhaustive search. Good programmers will try to improve on the performance of their programs by using deep knowledge of the prover and several programming tricks. This approach defeats the purpose of logic programming and is expensive to realize because it usually takes time, money, and insight to refine this declarative knowledge into the procedural how to. One additional advantage is lost in this process: A lucid and conceptually simple specification is clobbered by the optimizations, and the often informal character of the improvements can invalidate the correctness of the result.

I believe that knowledge-based transformational programming founded on partial deduction offers a plausible alternative to informal and ad hoc program development and refinement. Before I give a general outline of this kind of programming, let us look into the often-used parallel between programming and cooking. This time let both programming and cooking be knowledge based.

I am not a good cook, but my wife and I like eating some of our national meals, that is, Polish and Swedish. In the past when I told my wife that I would cook a Polish stuffed duck or Lithuanian *kolduny,* she would not know how I was going to prepare them, and vice versa. I had little idea of how to marinate *gravlax*—the delicious sweet and salty(!) Swedish salmon. After some years, we both gained an insight into each other's national cuisines and now manage to prepare a good meal. The same is true with programming. If an inexperienced programmer is requested to design a program for inverting a matrix, he/she will probably have an idea of what he/she wants the program to do, but it will take time before he/she comes with a concrete program that satisfies the specification $A \times A^{-1} = I$.

It is unlikely that he/she will be able to prove its correctness either. Ideally, such a specification could automatically be transformed into a program.

Like the inexperienced cook (I cannot prepare many of my wife's superb sauces or desserts because I lack much of her background knowledge), the novice programmer lacks knowledge of data structures, programming constructs, efficiency of the underlying hardware, and so on. However, if I were an experienced cook, I could probably relate the Swedish desserts to the general knowledge of desserts and specialize or refine the general case to a Swedish instance. Knowledge-based cooking and knowledge-based compilation seem to be similar in many aspects. Assume that there is a repository or a knowledge base of data structures and their properties, programming constructs and their efficiency, and typical solutions to some programming problems. Given a programming task, we would then specialize a general case to the problem at hand. This situation is a bit of a utopian dream, but when the domain was restricted, a number of projects reported success because the knowledge base was limited in size, and the search was manageable.

Thus, it seems that we witness a gradual formalization of the art or craft of programming. Rules of programming are formally expressed in a mechanizable form that can be used by computers to synthesize software. In this scenario, the general but usually inefficient knowledge is correctly specialized with respect to a specific use. Such a specialization process is probably best handled by knowledge-based transformational programming. It is knowledge based because in contrast to the strictly mathematical approach to transformations, the use of heuristics and user's guidance is both allowed and encouraged. Many of the contributions to this volume strengthen the conjecture that indeed, it might be the right approach to the problem of improving the software quality. One such class of applications that has been successfully realized in the partial deduction framework is the specialization of metalinguistic abstractions in which metainterpreters are compiled to their implementational language. The compilation can be automatic, and most importantly, it does not require writing a compiler.

Transformations capture much of the essence of knowledge transfer. The what-is declarative knowledge is completed by providing the how-to knowledge, and a specification that was initially either non-executable or possibly inefficient becomes usable from the computational point of view. Because it is possible to define correct refinement calculi, transformations can incrementally be done and without the need to manage entire programs. The logic-based transformations are particularly appealing because they add the additional property of the specification implying the result of a transformation. The most important contribution of transformational programming is that it can reconcile the declarative nature of specifications with the procedural character of most computer programs.

An important remaining question is whether there are several essentially different mechanisms or, possibly, one single principle common to several of the approaches presented in this book. My hypothesis is that this single principle is partial deduction and partial evaluation. Time and improved knowledge of the applications and a better understanding of the principle will show to what degree I am correct in this statement.

Several important details are still missing in this scenario, and many of the partial deduction transformations must be user initiated, but to date, the experience is encouraging. Using a simple principle and a limited set of tools, researchers can obtain complex and sophisticated programs. Some of these programs, such as the last example described in this chapter, would be nontrivial to obtain with nontransformational methods.

In the remainder of this chapter, I look into partial deduction and the possibility of compiling by specialization and synthesis from the user-provided knowledge. This area is related to what traditional software engineering calls the refinement of specifications. I should add that the research on how to automate the generation of the user's knowledge, that is, how to obtain the first specification, is ongoing. This research combines knowledge compilation with machine learning methods and is based on partial deduction.

Partial Deduction

This section introduces the concept of partial deduction informally by using examples and formally by providing a minimum of necessary definitions and the partial deduction theorem.

Partial Deduction by Example

As the name suggests, partial deduction is a kind of an unfinished proof or derivation. Partial deduction was patterned on a partial evaluation of Lisp programs developed by Beckman et al. (1976), which was conceived as a specialization technique and used as a programming tool. For example, if an argument of a *plus* function is known at compile time to be 1, then it can be replaced by its specialized version *add1*. Generally, if a condition B is known to be true at compile time, then a specialization of a programming language statement *if B then S_1 else S_2 with respect to B is S_1*. The resulting S_1 is called a *residue*. In Prolog, partial deduction could be illustrated as follows. Let the program be

    p(f(X), h(a, Z)) :- q(X).
    p(g(X), h(b, Z)) :- r(X).
    r(k(U)) :- s(U).

and the goal be :- p(g(Y), h(S, S)). Partial deduction of the clauses with respect to the goal can give a residual program

    p(g(k(U)), h(b, b)) :- s(U).

Partial evaluation concerns transformations of imperative or functional programs. However, partial deduction transforms logic programs, that is, logical theories. If appropriately defined, it adds a logical interpretation of the relationship between the original program and the residue. Namely, the residue is implied by the original program (thus, partial deduction is sound), and under

certain conditions, the residue implies the original program, thus giving rise
to the completeness of partial deduction. Another important difference is the
result of unification. In partial evaluation, a value of an argument is only carried down or forward through the computation, but in partial deduction, partially instantiated arguments can be propagated both forward and backward.
(This propagation is explained in the next chapter.) Partial deduction and
evaluation share a similar implementational technique. They are implemented as modifications to an interpreter or metainterpreter of the programming
language, that is, on an operational semantics. Partial deduction is easier to
implement because the evaluation order of arguments is based on unification.

All the examples presented here could be recreated by tediously simulating a modified Prolog interpreter. The idea of partially deducing programs
can be shown on a sequence of refinements to a family relationship program.
The programs are intentionally incomplete. The first one specifies the relations grandparent, grandfather, grandmother, and father, but no definition is
given for parent or mother.

```
grandparent( X, Z) :-
      grandfather( X, Z).
grandparent( X, Z) :-
      grandmother( X, Z).

grandfather( X, Z) :-
      father( X, Y), parent( Y, Z).

grandmother( X, Z) :-
      mother( X, Y), parent( Y, Z).

father( george, henryk).
father( henryk, jan).
father( henryk, stan).
father( victor, helena).
```

A partial deduction of the program with respect to grandfather(A, C) is

```
grandfather(george, Z0):-
      parent(henryk, Z0).
grandfather(henryk, Z0):-
      parent(jan, Z0).
grandfather(henryk, Z0):-
      parent(stan, Z0).
grandfather(victor, Z0):-
      parent(helena, Z0).
```

The partially deduced program, also called the *residual program*, was obtained by performing all possible derivations with the goal grandfather(A, C)
and interrupting them whenever atoms parent or mother were selected.[2] The
goal with the instantiations and the dangling unresolved literals are then used

to construct a new clause called a *resultant*. For example, one such derivation is

   :- grandfather(X0, Z0)
   :- father(X0, Y0), parent(Y0, Z0)
   :- parent(henryk, Z0)

where variable X0 is instantiated to george and variable Y0 to henryk; hence, the first resultant is grandparent(george, Z0):- parent(henryk, Z0).

There is good intuitive justification for the construction of a resultant. For example, in the previous example, the atom grandfather(george, Z0) is provable when parent(henryk, Z0) is. Furthermore, note that although partial deduction mimics a Prolog-style execution there is at least one important difference; for the previous family program and goal, Prolog would fail because neither parent nor mother predicate is defined.

These notions are precisely defined later. At this moment, let us notice that goals express context information about how the program is to be used. This information is propagated to the program, but the program can also propagate information to the goal and subgoals and through itself. This propagation, which is a form of data flow analysis, is essential in obtaining a specialized program. In the first residue, the goal was uninstantiated, and the program propagated the information from a subgoal such as father(X0, Y0) instantiated to father(george, henryk) backward to grandfather and forward to parent.

The residue can be subject to further refinements. Let us add a definition of parent

   parent(A, B) :- father(A, B).
   parent(A, B) :- mother(A, B).

and perform another partial deduction, this time with respect to (hence abbreviation *wrt)* grandfather(A, stan). The derivation will now be interrupted only when the predicate mother is selected.

   grandfather(george, stan).
   grandfather(george, stan):-
      mother(henryk, stan).
   grandfather(henryk, stan):-
      mother(stan, stan).
   grandfather(henryk, stan):-
      mother(jan, stan).
   grandfather(victor, stan):-
      mother(helena, stan).

Notice that in addition to propagation, partial deduction prunes some branches. First, the grandparent and grandmother definitions were pruned. In the second partial deduction, any possibilities of finding the grandfathers of Jan, who is Stan's brother, were discarded.

The reader can verify two interesting facts: If the first program is completed with the definitions of parent and father and partially deduced with respect to grandfather(A, stan), then the residual program will be the same as the one that we incrementally obtained. Similarly, if a definition of predicate mother is added to the completed program or to the residual program then the results of standard derivations (for example, using Prolog execution) of the program and the residue with the goal grandfather(A, stan) or its instances give precisely the same success and fail answers. An example from the author's family is

```
mother( henriette, henryk).
mother( anna, helena).
mother( helena, stan).
mother( helena, jan).
```

The answers are grandfather(george, stan) and grandfather(victor, stan). The interested reader can, of course, experiment with his(her) own family names as well as other relationships. A good place to start is with the definitions of aunt and uncle. The results can be residual definitions for the maternal and paternal aunts and uncles.[3]

In general, partial deduction is concerned with generating a correct residual program given a program and context conditions for its use. In other words, it concerns the soundness property of partial deduction: What is derivable from the residue must be derivable from the original program. As the precious example indicates, partial deduction can also be complete, possibly under some restrictions. Completeness of partial deduction means that the residue that was obtained with respect to some atom derives the atom's instances if the original program does.

I conclude this example with a partial deduction of a recursive program such as the well-known appending of lists:

```
append( [], L, L).
append( [X|Xs], Ys, [X|Zs]) :-
      append ( Xs, Ys, Zs).
```

where atom append([A1, A2, A3], Bs, Cs) expresses a context condition for the use of the program. Partial deduction will generate a specialized, one-line program append([X0, X1, X2], Ys0, [X0, X1, X2| Ys0]). for appending to lists of three elements. The reader should be able to easily simulate the construction of the resultant.

Definitions and the Partial Deduction Theorem

This subsection reviews the theoretical foundations for partial deduction and establishes a basis for an implementation of a partial deduction engine. Definitions 1 to 5 specify partial deduction. Definitions 6 to 12 state sufficient conditions for the completeness of partial deduction. The partial deduction theorem is the main technical result. With minor changes the presentation follows Lloyd and Shepherdsson (1991).

As I said earlier, partial deduction is a form of program transformation. Given a program P and a goal G, partial deduction produces a residual program P' that is specialized with respect to the goal G. The residual P' should have the same semantics as P with respect to G; that is, ideally, the computed and the correct answers for G in P' should be equal to answers for G in P. It is also expected that G should be more efficiently executed in P' than in P.

Partial deduction is sound for definite-clause programs. Soundness of a partially deduced program means that if P' is a partial deduction of a program P *wrt a goal* G, then the correct computed answers for G in P' are correct computed answers for G in P, and if G fails in P', then it fails in P. A residual program is computationally weaker but complete in the sense that if there is a refutation of $P \cup \{G\}$, then there is a refutation of $P' \cup \{G\}$, and if a goal fails in P, it fails in P'. However, this fact is true only for G and instances of G. Intuitively, a residual program P' contains only the relevant information that is indicated by G; for goals that are not instances of G, computations will, in general, fail, although the original program P might succeed.

A standard technique for defining partial deduction is based on the proof-theoretic semantics using SLD resolution. (SLD is a permuted acronym for linear resolution with a selection function for definite clauses. SLDNF adds negation by failure.) Recall that partial deduction engines are obtained as modifications to interpreters or metainterpreters. The construction is as follows: Partial (or "unfinished") derivations for G in P (and partial derivation trees) are constructed first. Then, P' is obtained as an appropriate selection of instantiated clauses that label the derivation trees. To this end, the notions of goal, SLD derivation, and SLD tree are suitably generalized.[4,5] The generalizations allow us to extend the notion of derivation to an "unifinsihed" derivation, that is, a finite derivation that can be neither a success nor a failure.

Definition 1 (Resultant): A resultant is a formula $A_1, \ldots, A_m \leftarrow B_1, \ldots, B_n$, where $m > 0$, $n \geq 0$, and $A_1, \ldots, A_m$ and $B_1, \ldots, B_n$ are atoms.

Definition 2 (SLD Derivation of a Resultant): Given a fixed computation rule $\mathfrak{R}$, an SLD derivation of a resultant R_0 is a finite or infinite sequence of resultants: $R_0 \to_{\mathfrak{R}} R_1 \to_{\mathfrak{R}} R_2 \to_{\mathfrak{R}} \ldots$, where for each k

R_k is of the form
$$A_1, \ldots, A_m \leftarrow B_1, \ldots, B_{i-1}, B_i, B_{i+1}, \ldots, B_n$$

R_{k+1} (if any) is of the form:
$$(A_1, \ldots, A_m \leftarrow B_1, \ldots, B_{i-1}, C_1, \ldots, C_j B_{i+1}, \ldots, B_n) \theta$$
if (1) the $\mathfrak{R}$-selected atom in R_k is B_i, (2) there is a standardized apart program clause $H \leftarrow C_1, \ldots, C_j$;[6] and (3) B_i and H have a most general unifier θ.

Definition 3 (Partial SLD Trees): The (partial) SLD tree of a resultant R_0

under $\mathfrak{R}$ is a rooted tree whose root is R_0 and where a node R_i is either a leaf or has the children $\{R_{i+1} \mid R_i \rightarrow_{\mathfrak{R}} R_{i+1}\}$.

Definition 4 (Partial Deduction of an Atom): A partial deduction of an atom A in a program P is the set of all nonfailing leaves of an SLD tree of $A \leftarrow A$. A *failing leaf* contains a selected atom that does not unify with any clause of the program.

The assumption that A is an atom can be relaxed to allow a finite set of atoms, $\mathbf{A} = \{A_1, \ldots, A_k\}$, and a partial deduction of $\mathbf{A}$ in P is the union of partial deductions of $A_1, \ldots, A_k$ in P. These partial deductions are called *residual predicates*.

Definition 5 (Partial Deduction of a Program): A partial deduction of P with respect to $\mathbf{A}$ is a program P' (also called a *residual program*), obtained from P by replacing the set of clauses in P whose heads contain one of the predicate symbols appearing in $\mathbf{A}$ with a partial deduction of $\mathbf{A}$ in P.

A condition restricting arbitrary partial deductions to those that intuitively are specializations has to be imposed to guarantee completeness and, for the case of normal programs, even the soundness of partial deduction.

Definition 6: Let S be a set of first-order formulas and $\mathbf{A}$ a finite set of atoms. S is called $\mathbf{A}$-closed if each atom in S containing a predicate symbol occurring in an atom in $\mathbf{A}$ is an instance of an atom in $\mathbf{A}$.

Next, follow the definitions of the coveredness and independence conditions.

Definition 7: If A and B are atoms, and a substitution θ exists such that $A\theta = B$, then we say that B is an instance of A, and that A is more general than B.

Definition 8: Let A and B be atoms. We say that A and B have a common instance if an atom C exists such that C is an instance of both A and B.

Definition 9: Let $\mathbf{A}$ be a finite set of atoms. We say that $\mathbf{A}$ is independent if no pair of atoms in $\mathbf{A}$ have a common instance.

Definition 10: Let P be a definite program. The dependency graph of P is the directed graph in which nodes are the predicate symbols in P, and there is a directed arc from p to q if a clause C exists in P in which p is the predicate symbol in the head of C, and q is the predicate symbol in a literal in the body of C.

Definition 11: Let P be a definite program and G a definite goal. We say that G depends on a predicate symbol p in P if there is a path from a predicate symbol in G to p in the dependency graph for P.

Definition 12: Let P be a definite program, G a definite goal, A a finite set of atoms, P' a partial deduction of P *wrt* A, and $P*$ the subprogram of P' consisting of the definitions of predicate symbols in P' on which G depends. We then say that $P' \cup \{G\}$ is **A**-covered if $P^* \cup \{G\}$ is **A**-closed.

The following theorem (Lloyd and Shepherdson 1990) shows that the coveredness and independence conditions are sufficient to ensure the computational equivalence of the original and residual programs.

Theorem 1; Let P be a definite program; G a definite goal; **A** a finite, independent set of atoms; and P' a partial deduction of P *wrt* **A** such that $P' \cup \{G\}$ is **A**-covered. We then have the following:

1. $P' \cup \{G\}$ has an SLD refutation with computed answer θ if and only if $P \cup \{G\}$ *does*.

2. $P' \cup \{G\}$ has a finitely failed SLD tree if and only if $P \cup \{G\}$ *does*.

Recall that the results were presented here for definite programs but that the original theorem is formulated for normal programs.

Partial Deduction of Prolog and Related Languages

Partial deduction is applicable to Prolog and other logic programming–related languages. I restrict myself to pure Prolog, that is, Prolog without side effects and nonlogical constructs. Because of Prolog's depth-first search, the order of clauses in the residual program must follow the lexicographic order of the clause sequences used in their derivations. In addition, the partial deduction theorem is applicable to systems languages in the Prolog family (that is, Parlog, Concurrent Prolog, GHC, Andora Prolog, and so on), but a full treatment of partial deduction in these languages requires a deeper analysis of the commit operators.

Partial Deduction Tactics and Parameters

Partial deduction is a generalization of an unfold transformation method and instantiation. It can produce more efficient programs. Its main strength comes from the ability of unification to propagate data structures using the derivation trees to the resultants. This approach is a form of data flow analysis that I originally recognized and called forward and backward data-structure propagation (Komorowski 1982).

The unfold and fold transformations for functional languages were originally introduced by Burstall and Darlington (1977). Their goal was to create a system for computer-aided programming. Unfold and fold transformations can informally be explained as follows. Consider the following set of grammatical rules:

1. $S \rightarrow A\,C\,B$
2. $A \rightarrow K\,L$
3. $D \rightarrow L\,C\,B$

Unfolding rule 2 in the right-hand side of rule 1 results in $S \rightarrow K\,L\,C\,B$.

Folding this result with rule 3 produces S → K D. In the context of functions, we can say that *unfolding* replaces a function call with the body of the function, and *folding* is a reverse operation in which a sequence of calls is usually replaced by one function call. Folding can dramatically improve efficiency. Burstall and Darlington showed how a function computing the nth element of the Fibonnacci series is improved by folding with its exponential complexity reduced to linear.

Clark (1978) and Hogger (1982) show that such transformations provide an additional advantage when applied to logic programs because the transformed program is logically implied by the original program, although such transformations (both in the functional and logic framework) are only partially correct. A remaining problem is total correctness. Theorem 1 shows that partial deduction is indeed totally correct. Informally, under the assumptions of the theorem, the residual program terminates if and only if the original program does. Hence, partial deduction is potentially an appropriate mechanism for program transformation.

Before partial deduction can effectively be used, however, a few problems have to be solved. First, partial deduction as previously defined does not include foldinglike transformations, and some important results known in the case of the transformation of functional programs cannot be obtained in its framework, (for example, a transformation from an exponential to a linear Fibonacci function). Second, the knowledge required to answer the question when to fold or unfold is complex and hard to establish. Hence, it is difficult to build a sophisticated autonomous system that would understand partial deduction and the program being transformed, could trade space for time, and would know when to prune the derivation tree. The problem of deriving new recursive definitions for folding is, in fact, generally unsolvable, although algorithms for some folding cases have been designed (Pettorossi and Proietti 1989).

Rather than attempting to design an autonomous partial deduction system, I informally defined two tactics (Komorowski 1989) that let the user indicate where and how partial deductions can be performed. I proved their correctness in Komorowski (1990a) and slightly extended to account for nonrecursive abbreviations in Komorowski (1990b). In addition, I defined a parameter for partial deduction that allows controlling the depth of unfolding and a parameter that enables the handling of undefined predicates. In what follows, I review the tactics and parameters and illustrate their application with examples. Then, I present a method for the incremental development of programs using extended partial deduction.

Opening

Controlling unfolding is generally undecidable because it amounts to the termination problem. Several heuristic solutions are possible, but it seems that a conservative approach to unfolding that allows only one step is often useful in the context of program development. I found that the atoms that are to be unfolded are usually those that define an implementation of the abstract data types used by the specification. This result leads to a logic programming methodology in which programs are designed with as little concern for the actual implementation of a data type as possible. In such a scenario, a selection of an implementation is made from a repository of implementations. Hence, the first tactic is designed so that the programmer can indicate what choices should be made and which information is to be propagated through the rest of the specification. It supports the data-abstraction methodology.

Definition 13 (Opening of Predicates): Let A be a finite, independent set of atoms; G a definite goal; and P a definite program where $P = P_1 \cup S$ for some disjoint P_1 and S, where S is a set of definitions of some predicate symbols. I call P_1 a source and S an axiomatization. Let P' be a partial deduction of P wrt A such that $P' \cup \{G\}$ is A-covered, where the predicates of the atoms selected by the computation rule are the predicates of the heads of the clauses in S. Such partial deduction is called the opening of predicates S in P wrt A.

Remark: Opening is trivially correct by the partial deduction theorem.

Example of Opening. Let us obtain a residual program for the enqueue and dequeue operations for queues. Let enq and deq define the two operations but with no commitment about which kind of list is actually used for representing queues. The enq and deq operations become the source.

```
enq(E, Q, NewQ) :-
        make_list(E, Elist), conc(Q, Elist, NewQ).
deq(Q, E, NewQ) :-
        make_list(E, Elist), conc(Elist, Q, NewQ).
```

From a repertoire of implementations of lists, the difference lists are chosen.[7] Clauses defining these lists become the axioms:

```
make_list(Elt, [Elt| Es]-Es).
conc(X-Y, Y-Z, X-Z).
```

Finally, partial deduction is called with the wrt set $A = \{enq(E, Q, NQ), deq(Q, E, NQ)\}$:

```
enq(E0, X0-[E0| Es0], X0-Es0).
deq(X0-X1, E0, [E0| X0]-X1).
```

The residue defines constant-time queue-manipulation operations. One might argue that such programs can manually be written. I believe that it is much easier to obtain them by using partial deduction. In fact, most beginners and even some intermediate programmers do have problems in writing such programs without a hitch. Furthermore, in most cases, it is easier to develop a program first with the standard lists and then have it automatically transformed to use the difference lists.

Continuation Points

Opening is conservative, and it can happen that the programmer has enough knowledge to relax the conditions for opening. To this end, there is a parameter for partial deduction in the form of continue declarations. They are used as conditions for sundry openings.

Definition 14 (Conditional Opening): Let $B \in S$, where S is an axiomatization. If B is the atom selected by the computation rule, then B is opened either if it is the first selection of the predicate or if a user-defined continue declaration is satisfied.

Definition 15 (Continue Declarations): A *continue declaration* for a predicate B of an axiom is a clause of the form

'$continue'(B, Numb) : $- C_1, \ldots, C_n$,

where Numb ≥ 1 is the number of previous openings, $n \geq 0$, and C_is are literals.

Continue declarations are necessary to obtain meaningful residual programs with recursive predicates. The correctness of the resulting residual program is not compromised by continue declarations, although their use can cause nontermination of the partial deduction engine. Usually, the continue declaration will specify conditions for opening recursive predicates for which the argument on which recursion is performed is, for example, a ground term or a finite list. The opening conditions are actively being researched, but the underlying undecidability of the termination problem means that only heuristic solutions will be found.

A continue declaration was actually used in the example of the residual program for appending to three-element lists, but for simplicity it was omitted. This declaration is '$continue'(append(Ls, _, _), _) :- nonvar(Ls). It allows opening provided that the first argument of append is a nonvariable. Clearly, a list of three or fewer elements is a nonvariable, and opening can proceed until it terminates with the empty list.

Abbreviating

The second tactic is called *abbreviating* and is a generalization of folding that was introduced by Burstall and Darlington (1977). Abbreviating is similar to folding, but it adds unification-based instantiation. Thus, substitutions can be propagated both forward and backward, whereas in folding, instantiations are, practically, only in the forward direction. As in folding, abbreviating can change the logic of a specification because a sequence of literals can be assigned a new name. If the name is recursively defined, the result often has a new but equivalent logic.

Definition 16 (Abbreviating): Let P be a program; A a finite, independent set of atoms: $H \leftarrow L_1, \ldots, L_k$ a standardized apart clause of P; and

$A\sigma \leftarrow L'_1, \ldots, L'_k, B_1, \ldots, B_n$ a resultant in an **A**-covered SLD derivation of $P \cup \{\leftarrow A\}$. Finally, let θ be a substitution such that $L'_1, \ldots, L'_k = (L_1, \ldots, L_k)\theta$ with $H\theta$ not unifiable with any other head of a clause of P. Then the clause $A\sigma \leftarrow H\theta, B_1, \ldots, B_n$ is the result of abbreviating the sequence $L'_1, \ldots, L'_k$ with H and is called an abbreviated resultant.

We can correctly extend partial deduction by allowing abbreviating steps in derivations that result from the following corollary.

Corollary : An abbreviated resultant follows from P if and only if the corresponding nonabbreviated resultant does, that is, resultant $A\sigma \leftarrow L'_1, \ldots, L'_k, B_1, \ldots, B_n$ follows from P if and only if resultant $A\sigma \leftarrow H\theta, B_1, \ldots, B_n$ does.

A proof is straightforward and can be found in Komorowski (1990b). Examples that illustrate abbreviating follow.

Futures

From the definition of partial deduction, it follows that if an undefined predicate is selected by the computation rule then the derivation fails, and no resultant is created for this derivation. This behavior is undesirable in incremental program development because it is unlikely that all definitions are provided from the beginning. It is also possible that a definition is externally defined and included in another file (or module). In fact, in my second example of partially deducing a family program, the derivations were interrupted whenever the (undefined) mother and parent predicates were selected. To avoid failing with such derivations, a parameter allows suspending undefined predicates. The check for undefined predicates is automatically performed for a requested pair of a source and an axiomatization. Thus, the required behavior in the first residue of the family example is, in fact, obtained with '$external'(parent (Y0, Z0)) and '$external'(mother(X1, Y0)). where the clauses defining grandparent, grandfather, and grandmother constitute the source, and the remaining clauses are axioms. Without these parameters, the residual program would be empty. Similarly, in obtaining the second family residue, the future declaration was only mother since predicate parent was already defined.

Replacement-in-Context

By now, it is generally accepted that programming is an interactive and incremental activity. Rarely, if ever, are specifications or programs written in one breath. I believe that a similar observation applies to transformational programming. A refining condition is established, and an intermediate residual program synthesized for which another condition is found, and so on, leading to a sequence of residual programs. The heuristics and the parameters for declaring futures and continuations provide important elements of an incremental refinement methodology. For example, the opening tactic is a method for introducing context conditions that are (globally) true (compare axioms). However, conditions might only hold locally. For example, one of the arguments of a predicate can be established as a list of pairs rather than any list, with the condition not holding for all uses of the predicate. Abbreviating is likely to be used in such cases. Eventually, there will be a number of conditions and invariants, and it is unlikely that all of them can be established a priori. Hence, rather than finding all of them at once, it is much more plausible to work in an incremental fashion. The question is whether such methodology is correct. The answer is positive, but first, a more precise formulation is needed.

Let us write $P \sim_A P'$ if P' is an (extended) partial deduction of P wrt $\mathbf{A}$. From the partial deduction theorems and from the soundness of abbreviating it immediately follows that if $P \sim_A P'$, then $P \vdash P'$. Hence, if $P_0, P_1, \ldots, P_n$ is a sequence of programs such that $P_0 \sim_A P_1 \sim_A \cdots \sim_A P_n$, then $P_0 \vdash P_1 \vdash \ldots \vdash P_n$. From the properties of syntactic consequence, it follows that $P_0 \vdash P_n$. In addition, because it is obviously the case that $P \sim_A P$, it follows that $\sim_A$ is a preorder. The idea is now to apply partial deduction to subprograms rather than to the entire program. To this end, we need definition 17.

Definition 17 (Subprogram): T is a subprogram of P (denoted $P[T]$) if $T \subseteq P$, and all definitions for goals appearing in T are contained in T.

For simplicity, it is assumed that there is only one definition, called entry point to T, from which clauses are selected as input clauses for derivations from T. Assume that $P[T] \sim_A P[T']$ holds for some A, but $T \sim_A T'$ does not. In principle, we can partially deduce the entire program $P[T']$, but it might be expensive. It is much more convenient to be able to transform parts of a program in an incremental fashion. To this end, we need a context condition under which $T \sim_A T'$ holds, that is, some condition B such that

(1) $P[T] \sim_A P[B \cup T]$

   and

(2) $(B \cup T) \sim_A T$

By monotonicity and the transitivity of $\sim_A$, we obtain $P[T] \sim_A P[T']$. Intuitively, point 1 says that B is a context condition that holds at the entry point to T. (Methods for obtaining B can be, for example, the inductive assertion method for logic programs of Drabent and Małuszyński [1988] or the abstract interpretation of Nilsson [1989]). Following Back (1988), I call this method of transformational programming replacement-in-context. An example illustrating it is presented later.

The Pal Environment

Few practical systems support a general transformational methodology. A notable exception is, for example, the KIDS system for program development

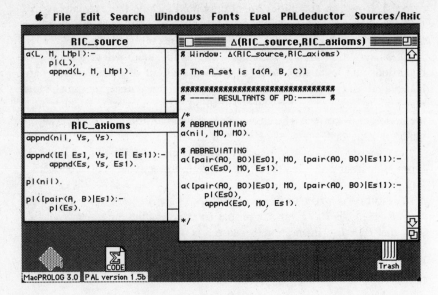

Figure 1. The PAL *Environment.*

(chapter 19). However, most of the work in transformational programming has been theoretical, and many claims have been made in its favor based on manual refinements. The goal behind implementing PAL was to provide a practical tool for the study of transformational programming in logic programming. The system can be used for transforming Prolog programs because it knows about several evaluable predicates (built-in procedures), but no attempt was made to handle their partial evaluation[8] or maintain the original order of subgoals in the bodies of procedures. This problem is usually not serious, but it will be alleviate in the next version of the system. The cut-and-assert built-in procedures are not partially evaluated.

The PAL environment that supports the replacement-in-context methodology was implemented in the LPA MacProlog system on the Macintosh computer family. It is an *embedded system*, which means that all the facilities of the Prolog language and environment are available to the programmer at any time with the partial deduction function added to, rather than put on top of, the Prolog environment. PAL is illustrated in figure 1.

In addition, there are tools for creating and selecting sources, axiomatizations, wrt sets, continuations, and futures. Special-purpose debugging facilities allow graphic and code tracing of the partial deduction process. The interface uses menus, dialog windows, and buttons for parameter setting. A minor but important convenience of PAL is its smart algorithm for preservation of the user's names of variables, which avoids the confusion over internal variable names such as _103 that haunt Prolog users. The implemented partial deduction engine is an extended metainterpreter type.

The usual mode of work is as follows: The programmer creates a source and an axiomatization by selecting entire windows or clauses in the windows. The partial deduction engine is then invoked, and a dialog window is displayed where a number of parameters such as tracing, external predicates, and so on, can be selected. The residual program is written to a new window that is named Δ(Source, Axiomatization). The code in the window contains its name, the wrt set, and the residue. This approach allows restoring the history of a development. On completion of the residue, the window can be chosen as a new source or axiomatization. An example screen is shown in figure 1.

It was found that the implementation of the partial deduction engine is satisfactory and that the environment is convenient to use for small and medium-long refinements. Not surprisingly, long refinement sessions quickly become messy. A specific graphic tool that helps navigate in the tree structure of the refinements is needed. Theoretical foundations for such a tool for any refinement calculus have been laid down, and a prototype was implemented by Waxlax (1990), but it has not been integrated into the environment.

In addition to the partial deduction of logic programs, PAL supports the partial deduction and evaluation of other languages. For example, by partially deducing a pure-Prolog interpreter for Scheme wrt to a Scheme function definition, these functions can be compiled into Prolog code. More importantly, Scheme interpreter's code can be itself compiled by providing appropriate continue declarations. Although the efficiency of this process is low because of the number of levels of metainterpretation, the possibility itself is attractive. In principle, it means that instead of writing a partial evaluator for each language, one only needs to provide a pure-Prolog interpreter for the language and a set of continuation declarations. This task is substantially less complicated than writing a partial evaluator.

Sample Developments

I start with a simple example illustrating replacement-in-context. The development also demonstrates the use of abbreviating. Let T be the familiar appnd[9] program (the first two clauses in the RIC_axioms window) for which a condition pl(X) (defined by the third and fourth clause in this window) holds for the first argument of the definition in T, as expressed by the definition of a(X, Y, Z) (the clause in the RIC_source window). The residue is written in % ABBREVIATING groups. Opening the third and fourth axioms gives the first resultant, and opening the second and fourth axioms and abbreviating with the source produces the second resultant. A snapshot of the screen after the residue is obtained is shown in figure 1.

In the abbreviating mode, every derivation contains abbreviated resultants, if such were possible to create, and the resultant that was used as the basis for abbreviating as the last clause in each % ABBREVIATING group. This arrangement means that if no abbreviating was successful, there will be just one clause in every % ABBREVIATING group. A residual program is then obtained by selecting exactly one clause from each group. For example, in figure 1, the first % ABBREVIATING group contains just one clause because there was no abbreviating possible in this derivation, and the second group contains two clauses, meaning that one abbreviating was made. The first clause is the result of abbreviating, and the second one is the clause that was abbreviated.

After this introductory example, I develop a nontrivial program. Consider the issue of computing the length of the longest increasing sublist of the elements of a given list. A naive solution is to find all increasing sublists and then to find the longest sublist. Clauses C_1 and A_1 to A_6, with obvious definitions for Boolean operators length and max, specify a solution that follows. (Excerpts from a session with PAL were annotated for this example.) The task is to find a better program that finds the longest sublist more efficiently, that is, in one pass of the input list. This example is an automated version of a manual development presented by Pettorossi and Proietti (1989). The curious reader can try to develop such a program and prove it correct without the help of this transformational methodology. It is likely to be a much more tedious task.

```
% Window: MAX-UPS. source1
C₁. max_ups(L, Max):- ups( L, LL), maxlength( LL, Max).
```

```
% Window: MAX-UPS. axioms
A1. ups( [], []).
A₂. ups( [H], [[H]]).
A₃. ups( [H,H1|T1], [[H]|Y]) :- H > H1, ups( [H1|T1], Y).
A₄. ups( [H,H1|T1], [[H|Y1]|Y]) :- H =< H1, ups( [H1|T1], [Y1|Y]).

A₅. maxlength( [], 0).
A₆. maxlength( [H|T], M) :-
          maxlength( T, M1), length( H, N), max( N, M1, M).
```

The first partial deduction with abbreviating with max_ups is done wrt max_ups(L, Max) and with the futures 'external'(max(N0, M10, M0)). 'external'(length(H0, N0)).

```
% Window: Δ(MAX-UPS. source1,MAX-UPS. axioms)
% The A_set is [max_ups(L, Max)]
% ────── RESULTANTS OF PD:────── %

% ABBREVIATING
max_ups([], 0).
```

% ABBREVIATING
max_ups([H0], Max0):-
        maxlength([], M0), length([H0], N0), max(N0, M0, Max0).

% ABBREVIATING
max_ups([H0, H1| T10], Max0):- max_ups([H1| T10], Max1), H0>H1,
        length([H0], N0), max(N0, Max1, Max0).

max_ups([H0, H1| T10], Max0):- H0>H1, ups([H1| T10], X0),
        maxlength(X0, M0), length([H0], N0), max(N0, M0, Max0).

% ABBREVIATING
 max_ups([H0, H1| T10], Max0):- H0=<H1,
        ups([H1| T10], [H2|T11]), maxlength(T11, M0),
        length([H0| H2], N0), max(N0, M0,Max0).

All but one call to ups was eliminated. ups([H1|T10], [H2|T11]),
maxlength(T11, M0) is not an instance of the body of C_1; hence, abbreviating could not be done in the last clause. A good strategy is to introduce a
new definition that contains as its body the literals that could not be abbreviated and in the head all the variables occurring in the body. I add clause C_2
for the predicate new to MAX-UPS. source1 and name the new source
MAX-UPS. source2.

% Window: MAX-UPS. source2
C_1. max_ups(L, Max):- ups(L, LL), maxlength(LL, Max).

C_2. new(H1, T1, Y1, M1):- ups([H1|T1], [Y1| Y]), maxlength(Y, M1).

Replacing MAX-UPS. source1 with MAX-UPS. source2 and leaving all other
parameters unchanged leads to a successful abbreviation in the last derivation.

    . . .

% Window: Δ(MAX-UPS. source2,MAX-UPS. axioms)
    . . .

% ABBREVIATING
max_ups([H0, H1| T10], Max0):- new(H1, T10, Y10, M10),
       H0=<H1,length([H0| Y10], N0), max(N0, M10, Max0).
max_ups([H0, H1| T10],Max0):- H0=<H1, ups([H1| T10], [H2| T11]),
       maxlength(T11, M0), length([H0| H2], N0), max(N0, M0, Max0).

The remaining problem is a development of an explicit recursive definition
for new. Let the source remain MAX-UPS. source2, but the axioms A_1 to A_4
are chosen as MAX-UPS. newaxioms, and let the wrt set consist of new(H,
T, Y, M). Opening the axioms and abbreviating with the source produce a
new definition of new:

% Window: Δ(MAX-UPS. source2,MAX-UPS. newaxioms)
% The A_set is [new(H, T, Y, M)]
% ——— RESULTANTS OF PD:——— %

% ABBREVIATING
new(H10, [], [H10], M10):- maxlength([], M10).

% ABBREVIATING
new(H10, [H0| T10], [H10], M10):-
    max_ups([H0| T10], M10), H10>H0.

new(H10, [H0| T10], [H10], M10):-
    H10>H0, ups([H0| T10], X0), maxlength(X0, M10).

% ABBREVIATING
new(H10, [H0| T10], [H10| T11], M10):- new(H0, T10, T11, M10),H10=<H0.
new(H10, [H0| T10], [H10| T11], M10):-
    H10=<H0, ups([H0| T10], [T11| T12]), maxlength(T12, M10).

Finally, opening maxlength in max_ups and new produces

max_ups([], 0).
max_ups([H0], M100):- length([H0], N0), max(N0,0, M100).
max_ups([H0, H1| T0], M100):- max_ups([H1| T0], M101),
    H0>H1, length([H0], N0), max(N0, M101, M100).
max_ups([H0,H1| T0], M100):- new(H1, T0, T110, M101), H0=<H1,
    length([H0|T110], N0), max(N0, M101, M100).

new(H100, [], [H100], 0).
new(H100, [H0| T0], [H100], M100):- max_ups([H0| T0], M100), H100>H0.
new(H100, [H0| T0], [H100| T1],M100):- new(H0, T0, T1, M100), H100=<H0.

The current implementation of the algorithm for abbreviating changes the order of some subgoals. If the resultants are to be executed by Prolog, a re-ordering of the goals is necessary. This problem will be alleviated in the next version of the system. Notice the preservation of symbolic names for Prolog variables.

Partial Deduction and Software Design

Partial deduction makes several contributions to software design. In the following subsections, I look at some of them.

The Back-End and the Front-End Tools

Traditionally, partial deduction has been used as a *back-end tool* to obtain more efficient programs. Efficiency gains for a residual program can be discussed in the terms of the size of the derivation trees. One efficiency factor is the length of a derivation. From the definition of resultant, it immediately follows that because input clauses in a residual program are resultants, then the length of a derivation is usually shortened. However, pruning, or eliminating the failing branches, reduces the number of alternatives or the width of the derivation tree. Note also that resultants are more specific, in the sense that variables in the original clauses can become instantiated to nonvariable terms. One advantage is that when using more specific clauses, unification can be performed at earlier stages of derivations. This fact implies that failed derivations can be shorter. Another advantage is that compilers and tools that analyze Prolog programs often work better with instantiated arguments rather than with variables in procedure heads and with procedure calls in the bodies that instantiate the variables. For example, if heads are more specific, then compilers generate better control information. In conclusion, partial deduction allows the propagation of local information throughout a program.

Partial deduction can create problems. If an uncontrolled approach to partial deduction is taken, in particular, by allowing too many unfolding steps, the resulting residual program can become exponential in the number of the clauses constituting the program. If a source clause $A \leftarrow B_1, \ldots, B_n$ is opened with axioms $B_1, \ldots, B_n$, and each B_i is defined by $k > 0$ clauses, then the residue can have k^n resultants. Countermeasuring this exponential growth is a motivation behind the tactics and parameters of partial deduction. The tactics trade automatic but blind generation of programs for an informed but partly human-supported synthesis.

Partial deduction serves as a *front-end tool* because it not only optimizes programs by some improvements to their internal structure, it also synthesizes new programs from specifications and how-to knowledge. For example, using the abbreviating tactic, the $O(n^2)$ *max_ups* program is correctly transformed to a linear one. Other examples that were developed include the transformation of a naive sort with $O(n!)$ complexity to an $O(n^3)$ sorting program. The construction of residual programs from resultants is an interesting case of the so-called extraction of programs from proofs, an advocated method of program synthesis. Among other things, it provides an intuitive explanation for why partial deduction is sound and, to some degree, complete. A resultant is a summary of successful proof steps, and the residual predicate is the sum of the corresponding resultants. A proof with the resultants resumes where partial deduction interrupted, which is the only way that the proof can be obtained.

An interesting example of applying a refinement calculus based on partial deduction to software design is the work by Nilsson (1990) on a design of abstract machines for logic programming languages. The starting point is an abstract and simple interpreter for the source language. With a sequence of refinements (opening and abbreviating) wrt to some typical input programs, the interpreter is transformed until it reaches a suitable level of abstraction. The input programs compile by partial deduction into machine code, and the refined interpreter compiles into an abstract machine for the machine code. He demonstrates the power of the methodology by reconstructing control instructions for Warren's ABSTRACT MACHINE (1983) for a propositional subset of Prolog.

Another interesting application of partial deduction to software design is its use to generate programs for modular logic programming by Bugliesi, Lamma, and Mello. The authors use partial deduction to perform hypothetical reasoning in an inheritance network and to retrieve and synthesize residual programs.

The Support for Programming Methodologies

Partial deduction supports a variety of important programming methodologies by alleviating several of the problems usually associated with them. These methodologies are data abstraction, procedural abstraction, and metalinguistic abstraction.

Data abstraction is the technique of isolating the parts of a program that deal with how data objects are represented from those parts of a program that deal with how data objects are used. This technique makes programs easier to design, maintain, and modify. Its drawback is that it sometimes causes a decrease in efficiency. The propagation of data structures by opening can usually restore the efficiency.

Another important methodology is *procedural abstraction*. Recall that procedural abstraction is a method of decomposing a program into independent parts that accomplish identifiable tasks that can be used as modules in defining other procedures. Procedural abstraction fits the declarative programming paradigm. At the abstraction level, there is no concern with how the procedure computes its values, only the fact that it computes. As with data abstraction, a possible disadvantage results from information hiding: The internal information is not available to other procedures. Partial deduction appears to promote interprocedural optimization by removing layers of procedural calls and propagating local data structures.

The third example is metalinguistic abstraction. Abelsson and Sussmans (1985) state that "metalinguistic abstraction is the establishment of new descriptive languages. . . . [G]iven a language, if we can implement in that language an evaluator for a second language then our computer will also be able to evaluate [programs] of that latter language. This method of implementing a language is known as constructing an embedded language." The compilation of metainterpreters by partial deduction is a prime example of support for an important methodology. Finally, the refinement calculus supports both the top-down and bottom-up stepwise refinement of programs.

Conclusions

Partial deduction appears to be a simple but powerful principle in computer science. Here, I showed that it also can be a basis for a systematic development of programs. Because the issue of unfolding is generally undecidable, I designed two correct tactics and parameters that heuristically help the user direct partial deduction. The otherwise unruly search problem plaguing many transformational systems becomes manageable.

Partial deduction is implemented in the PAL system, an environment for developing nontrivial programs. It is the first practical environment for studying sequences of transformations of logic programs. It is well documented and can be made available to interested researchers from the author at the University of Trondheim.[10] Examples of larger programs developed with PAL include the compilation of Scheme functions to Prolog code, the redevelopment of an editor for structures by Komorowski and Małuszyński (1987), and a few search algorithms.

It appears that partial deduction and the proposed programming methodology contribute to a reconciliation between the declarative what-is and procedural how-to programming. A specification or an inefficient high-level program that is concerned with the declarative aspects of a problem can systematically be refined into a more efficient how-to program.

Several issues remain: Visual paradigms for navigation in long refinement sequences, heuristics for automatically introducing Eureka definitions as well as additional tactics are important practical issues. Applications of the methodology to the development of parallel logic programs, programs in other languages, and knowledge-based systems will be explored in the future. One particularly interesting question emerging after the study of several contributions to this collection is a verification of the hypothesis that partial deduction and partial evaluation are the mechanisms for most of the knowledge compilation approaches to software design. Other remaining topics are the controversy over the equation Explanation-Based-Generalization = Partial Deduction and the relationship of partial deduction to nonmonotonic and default reasoning.

Acknowledgments

I would like to thank R. J. Back for helpful comments on the topics treated here and Johan Lahtivuori for his excellent work on the PAL system as well as many interesting discussions. The comments of reviewers were helpful in improving the quality of this presentation. Last but not least, special thanks to Anna, who contributes beautifully to my well being in many more ways than just by preparing *gravlax*.

Notes

1. Beneficially influenced by Lisp partial evaluation, I used the phrase "partial evaluation in logic programming" when I introduced the principle to logic programming. Obviously, "partial deduction" is a better phrase in the context of logic.

2. All examples quoted here were generated in the PAL environment.

3. The Swedes are precise about grandparents, aunts, and uncles. For example, mother's mother is called mormor, and father's mother is farmor.

4. An SLD derivation corresponds to a Prolog computation and consists of resolution steps. It can be finite or infinite. If it is finite, it can be a success or a failure.

5. An SLD tree is a tree of SLD derivations. A Prolog interpreter constructs and searches an SLD tree using backtracking when a failure is reached.

6. Each time a clause is to be used in a resolution step, the variables of the clause must be given new and unique names. This technique is similar to providing new and unique locations for actual parameters in recursive procedures of other programming languages.

7. A *difference list* is a representation that maintains a pointer to the end of the list and, thus, allows constant-time insertion at the end of the list. It has certain drawbacks in most Prolog implementations because it is prone to errors due to the lack of the so-called occur check. However, carefully used, it offers substantial efficiency gains.

8. The term partial evaluation is used in this context because the evaluable predicates of Prolog do not have a declarative semantics, and they are evaluated by the underlying implementation language.

9. LPA Prolog complains when the user tries to redefine system predicates, hence the intentional misspelling of the word append.

10. Norwegian Institute of Technology, Department of Computer Science and Electrical Engineering, The University of Trondheim, N-7034, Trondheim, Norway.

References

Abelson, H.; Sussman, G.; and Sussman, J. 1985. *Structure and Interpretation of Computer Programs.* Cambridge, Mass.: MIT Press.

Back, R. J. R. 1988. A Calculus of Refinements for Program Derivations. *Acta Informatica* 25:593–624.

Beckman, L.; Haraldsson, A.; Oskarsson, O.; and Sandewall, E. 1976. A Partial Evaluator and Its Use as a Programming Tool. *The Journal of Artificial Intelligence* 7(4): 319–357.

Bjorner, D.; Ershov, A. P.; and Jones, N. D., eds. 1987. *Workshop on Partial Evaluation and Mixed Computation.* Lecture Notes in Computer Science. Springer-Verlag.

Bry, F. 1989. Query Evaluation in Recursive Databases: Bottom-Up and Top-Down Reconciled. Presented at the First International Conference on Deductive and Object-Oriented Databases, December, Kyoto, Japan.

Bugliesi, M.; Lamma, E.; and Mello, P. Partial Deduction for Structured Programming. Submitted for Publication.

Burstall, R. M., and Darlington, J. 1977. Some Transformations for Developing Recursive Programs. *Journal of ACM* 24(1): 44–67.

Clark, K. 1978. Negation as Failure. In *Logic and Data Bases,* eds. H. Gallaire and J. Minker, 293–322. New York: Plenum.

Drabent, W., and Maluszyński, J. 1988. Inductive Assertion Method for Logic Programs. *Theoretical Computer Science* 59(1): 133–155.

Haraldsson, A. 1977. A Program Manipulation System Based on Partial Evaluation. Ph.D. diss., Dept. of Computer and Information Science, Linköping Univ.

Hogger, C. J. 1982. Derivation of Logic Programs. *Journal of ACM* 28(2): 372–392.

Hoppe, T. 1990. Explanation-Based Generalization, Partial Deduction and Non-Monotonic Reasoning, Technical Report, University of Berlin. Draft.

Komorowski, J. 1990a. Elements of a Programming Methodology Founded on Partial Deduction—Part 1. In Proceedings of the International Symposium on Methodologies for Intelligent Systems, ed. Z. Ras. North Holland.

Komorowski, J. 1990b. Towards a Programming Methodology Founded on Partial Deduction. In

Proceedings of the European Conference on Artificial Intelligence. London: Pitman.

Komorowski, J. 1989. Towards Synthesis of Programs in the Framework of Partial Deduction. Presented at the Workshop on Automating Software Design, Eleventh International Joint Conference on Artificial Intelligence, August, Detroit, Mich.

Komorowski, J. 1982. Partial evaluation as a Means for Inferencing Data Structures in an Applicative Language: A Theory and Implementation in the Case of Prolog. In Proceedings of the ACM Symposium on Principles of Programming Languages, 255–267. New York: Association of Computing Machinery.

Komorowski, J. 1981. A Specification of an Abstract Prolog Machine and Its Application to Partial Evaluation. Ph.D. diss., Dept. of Computer and Information Science, Linköping Univ.

Komorowski, J., and Małuszyński, J. 1987. Logic Programming and Rapid Prototyping. *Science of Computer Programming* 9:179–205.

Lakhotia, A. Promix User's Manual, Technical Report, CES-89-05, Computer Engineering and Science Dept., Case Western Reserve Univ.

Lam, J. K. K. 1989. Control Structures in Partial Evaluation of Pure Prolog. Master's thesis, Univ. of Saskatchewan.

Lloyd, J. W., and Shepherdson, J. C. 1991. Partial Evaluation in Logic Programming. *Journal of Logic Programming*. Forthcoming.

Nilsson, U. 1990. Towards a Methodology for the Design of Abstract Machines of Logic Programming Languages. Submitted for Publication.

Nilsson, U. 1989. A Systematic Approach to Abstract Interpretation of Logic Programs. Master's thesis, Dept. of Computer and Information Science, Linköping Univ.

Nilsson, U., and Maluszynski, J. 1990. *Logic, Programming, and Prolog*. New York: Wiley.

Pettorossi, A., and Proietti, M. Decidability Results and Characterization of Strategies for the Development of Logic Programs. In Proceedings of the International Conference on Logic Programming. Cambridge, Mass.: MIT Press.

van Harmelen, F., and Bundy, A. 1988. Explanation-Based Generalisation = Partial Evaluation. *Journal of Artificial Intelligence* 36:401–412.

Warren, D. H. D. 1983. An Abstract Prolog Instruction Set, TN 309, SRI International, Menlo Park, California.

Waxlax, P. 1990. An Environment for Supporting Derivations in a Refinement Calculus (in Swedish). Master's thesis, Åbo Akademi Univ.

16

Toward Predicative Programming

W. Bibel

Software production is a rapidly expanding multibillion dollar business. The products coming from this business, however, are far from satisfactory. Thus, around 1970, the term software crisis emerged. Because a crisis is something that is overcome after a limited period, the term is not used any more; however, the problems are worse today, at least from the user's point of view. For business, the situation is not bad at all because unsatisfactory software raises the appetite for a new product, and thus, it raises the selling figures.

There is little hope that this situation will change in the near future. The reason is that the production of fundamentally better software would mean making radical changes that involve universities, industry, and governments. The situation must be critical in terms of the costs involved before a chance for improvement exists.

This pessimistic perspective should not prevent at least a few of us from taking little steps toward a different and better approach, far away from the mainstream activities in software engineering. I have devoted a substantial part of my work to such an approach, which since 1974 I have called *predicative programming.*[1]

To a large extent, programming is a *reasoning* process carried out on the basis of a body of various kinds of knowledge. Typically, the skills of people available for this activity are not among the best developed. Hence, machine support would be extremely desirable for assuring the abstraction and precision required for a satisfactory result. To provide suitable support, it is best to aim in principle (but not necessarily in practice) at a full automation of the whole process to get a better understanding of the mechanisms involved. This approach potentially requires a full formalization of all parts involved (including high-level requirements, end user needs, and environment to the extent that models for these parts have been rationalized). Although many formalisms exist for the context of programming, only logic formalisms are rich enough to meet these requirements. Logic is especially capable of modeling the reasoning processes involved in programming.

The problem here is that a research program of huge dimensions is required, one that can never be realized if it is carried out by a few individuals in an unconcerted way. Because of the enormity of this effort, only a few tiny pieces are surveyed that might eventually fit into the whole puzzle. These pieces come from the work pursued over more than a decade by a number of people under the perspective just outlined.

In the next section, I present a short review of the predicative programming paradigm. The following section then reviews the LOPS system. I briefly explain the strategies used and illustrate their application with the familiar problem of determining the maximum of a set. The architecture of the system is explained, which, in its newest version, is realized on top of the experimental program-transformation system XPRTS. An evaluation of the results of LOPS, including a list of problems still to be solved, completes this review.

To address whether it is worthwhile to invest the enormous efforts necessary to make a system such as LOPS available for real-life applications, The Amenities of Programming describes the unpleasant situation in current software practice. This situation begs for radical improvement. In Concurrent Software Production, I speculate about what direction we would have to move to achieve such improvement. I argue for the need for a method of concurrent software production and make a case for predicative programming.

Predicative Programming

The basic paradigm of predicative programming comes from the following observation: If people communicate about complex mechanisms, then the information explicitly exchanged is of a mainly declarative, as opposed to algorithmic, nature. In cases where persons do explicitly communicate algorithms, these are exclusively simple ones, such as a short sequences of actions. Predicative programming is meant to enable people to communicate with computers in the same fashion. Note that this statement means that computers are to share implicit algorithmic information with people that is usually not made explicit in communication.

Declarations are generally concerned with objects, their properties and relations, and general statements involving these concepts. Predicate logic is the common language for dealing with exactly these concepts. Thus, it provides the most natural formal language for representing declarations of this kind, hence the term predicative. The use of logic as a language for formalizing declarative statements as programs on the declarative level is one of the major aspects of predicative programming.

Formalizing declarations might be necessary, but it is obviously not sufficient for programming purposes. A method that transforms declarations into algorithms and efficiently executable programs is also needed. Today, such an idea does not appear strange anymore because Prolog takes as its input what can be regarded as a purely declarative statement and interprets it in an algorithmic way. This technique is made possible by the deductive machinery available in logic, especially by proof procedures.

In 1975, I first explored the possibility of using proof techniques to achieve a more comfortable and reliable approach to programming (Bibel 1975a, 1976b). Although this work made its first appearance at roughly the same time as Prolog, from the beginning, it was aimed at a more general goal. It was not restricted to horn-clause logic, as was Prolog. Also, it did not compromise in terms of a purely predicative style of programming, while Prolog was, strictly speaking, functional in nature.

Because the efforts of this project are greater, more than just an effective prover for horn logic is needed. Even if the approach could be achieved as in Prolog, the prover would still have to cope with more than horn logic. There seems no way that a general prover can yield computed output from given input on the basis of purely declarative programs (as in Prolog) simply because of the enormous complexity of the prover's underlying search space; thus, a different paradigm is needed here. Proof mechanisms need to become involved in the process of transforming the declarative program into an equivalent one that can efficiently be executed. Research experience shows that the transformation can be achieved if guided by a few general strategic schemes and supported by various kinds of knowledge.

Again, research experience shows that the nature of the target program resulting from the transformation is such that little automatic manipulation is needed to transform it into a Prolog program. Therefore, I refer to programs resulting from this transformation as problem specifications on the deductive level.[2] In certain applications, one could content with such a deductive specification and simply use a (deductive) Prolog interpreter (or compiler) for execution.

However, the execution techniques currently used in Prolog are excellent for prototyping and for applications less demanding in performance, but they are not satisfactory for many computationally costly applications in which performance is a crucial issue. In these cases, the compilation of a deductive program into a functional or imperative one is needed that makes heavy use of destructive assignment, for example. Recent results (Bibel 1986, 1988) suggest that the current Prolog compilers have not at all exhausted the potential in this respect. For example, I mention the detection of recursive cycles in the deductive structure of the problem as one of the issues involved here (Bibel 1988). The transformation from the declarative to the deductive level and the subsequent compilation into efficient code are two other important aspects of predicative programming.

The LOPS System

The major obstacle for predicative programming was the task of transforming programs given at the declarative level into those at the deductive level. To overcome this obstacle, a strategic method was developed (Bibel 1980) as part of the LOPS (logical program synthesis) project (Bibel and Hörnig 1984).

In communicating a programming task to the computer on the declarative level, the user is repeatedly prompted for input variables and their requirements as well as for output variables and their requirements on these in relation to the input variables. From this information, the system configures a declarative problem specification in first-order logic. From the specification, a program on the deductive level is eventually obtained by rewriting logical formulas in a stepwise fashion, starting with the specification. Each of these transformations, achieved through rewriting, aims at making the formula capable of being evaluated in an increasingly efficient way until a program is reached that can be executed in a high-level programming language (such as Prolog) with sufficient performance. The sequence and the details of the transformational steps are guided by a few basic strategies of a general nature and supported by a knowledge base. Thereby, an essential role is played by a theorem prover. In this process, user interaction is not excluded in practice.

Further details of this process are given in the following subsection. The system architecture and the experimental results are then discussed. In the remainder of the section, an evaluation of this approach is attempted.

The Strategies

From the information gathered in the initial dialogue with the user, LOPS composes a declarative specification of the following form:

$$\forall \textit{<input-variables>} \; \exists \textit{<output-variables>} \; (\textit{input-condition} \rightarrow \textit{output-condition}) \, .$$

In shorter but less mnemonic form the same formula reads

$$\forall \, i \, \exists \, o \, (IC(i) \rightarrow OC(i,o)) \, .$$

For illustration, I use the well-known problem of determining the maximal element m in a set S with some ordering:

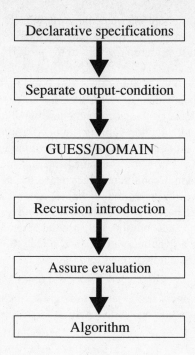

Figure 1. The LOPS Strategies.

$\forall S \exists m (SET(S) \rightarrow m \in S \wedge S \leq m)$.

The literal $S \leq m$ is an abbreviation for $\forall x (x \in S \rightarrow x \leq m)$.

The formula captures the problem in the most natural way. It provides a purely declarative specification with no computational content of any use.[3] Because the output condition will be subject to a number of transformations to reach the deductive level, I introduce a name for it with the following formula.

$\forall S \forall m (SET(S) \rightarrow (MAX(S,m) \leftrightarrow m \in S \wedge S \leq m))$.

In effect, the transformations apply to this formula. For simplicity, quantifiers are deleted from here on. The transformations are activated by the strategies shown in figure 1 (Bibel 1980).

The separation of the output condition (performed by a component called GET-SOC in LOPS) applies to the case of multiple output variables, so it cannot be illustrated with my current example that features only a single output variable. The first strategy that applies is GUESS, in close cooperation with DOMAIN. To understand the idea behind these two strategies, imagine the situation as it stands. By way of the specification formula, we claim the existence of an object m satisfying a certain condition. In the absence of any computational means for getting hold of it, making a reasonable guess is all we can do. "Reasonable" in this context means that we should restrict our guess to the objects that are in some sense relevant to the problem or, in this case, the objects in the given set.

Such is the intuitive idea behind GUESS and DOMAIN. Because intuition is not what we can expect from LOPS, this idea has to be realized in a purely syntactic way. LOPS does so by introducing a new variable g in relation to the output variable m and selecting a proper subcondition for restricting the range of g from the output condition. The subcondition in this case turns out to be $g \in S$ on the basis of syntactic considerations (such as the number of subformulas in the output condition, which leave the system with a choice among two alternatives in the current example) as well as knowledge available in the knowledge base that provides information about the difficulty in evaluating the selected subcondition. Because the other alternative in our example would involve a quantifier, a clear preference results with the chosen alternative, leading to the transformed formula

$$SET(S) \to (MAX(S,m) \leftrightarrow g \in S \wedge m \in S \wedge S \leq m \wedge (g = m \vee g \neq m)) \,.$$

The last conjunct simply expresses that the guess might be right or wrong. The system prefers a certain disjunctive normal form, so the formula is transformed to

$$SET(S) \to (MAX(S,m) \leftrightarrow g \in S \wedge (m \in S \wedge S \leq m \wedge g = m \vee m \in S \wedge S \leq m \wedge g \neq m)).$$

We are a step closer to a computational form because we now distinctly have two different cases, one for $g = m$, the other for $g \neq m$. We achieved these two cases using a strategy that works for any specification whatsoever, applying to all strategies used in LOPS. The strategies' generality provides the unique strength of LOPS.

Note that the popular divide-and-conquer strategy is subsumed by GUESS and DOMAIN along with the subsequent LOPS operations described shortly, which together result in a more general behavior. This generality results because the guess element can be interpreted in the subsequent process in various ways. I describe one process (the deletion of g from S). Another method of interpretation is as the midelement of a list that is split into two smaller lists. These interpretations are determined in a goal-oriented manner by subsequent strategic considerations on the basis of the specification and the knowledge base.

Because the strategies applied to a specification result in transformations, one is reminded of transformational approaches often used in software construction. In contrast to these approaches, there are no fixed transformation rules available here; rather, the rules are generated in a flexible way by general strategic guidelines from the formula under consideration.

What I illustrate with GUESS and DOMAIN could be continued with the remaining strategies in an analogous way. Because LOPS is well documented in the literature, I only give a brief summary of the remaining steps.

The system recognizes that the first case can be evaluated in a computationally satisfactory way after minor manipulations. Thus, the next strategy of recursion introduction (performed by a component called GET-REC in LOPS) turns its attention to the second case. To select a recursion scheme in the knowledge base, lemmas are generated that the theorem prover is asked to prove. For example, the formula

$$SET(S) \wedge g \in S \rightarrow (m \in S \leftrightarrow m \in S \backslash g \wedge g \neq m)$$

is generated on the basis of strategic considerations similar to those in GUESS and DOMAIN. The lemma is easily verified by the prover, and thus, the recursion is discovered. However, in the literal remaining, besides the recursive term, an occurrence of the unknown m still resides that obviously cannot be evaluated. This fact is discovered by the strategy EVAL, which substitutes this occurrence by the recursive term after asking the prover for the verification of the generated lemma.

At this point, the system is basically done with synthesis because the resulting formula is more or less a Prolog program. To come to terms with the "more or less," Neugebauer (1991) has a method of assigning modes to the variables that allows the completely mechanical extraction of a Prolog program (or any other program for that matter) from the resulting formula. Variables can be in input (+), output (-), or logical (? or just a blank) mode. This mode information is carried through the entire synthesis. For example, the initial formula actually reads as follows.

$$\forall S \, \forall m \, (SET(S) \rightarrow (MAX(S^+, m^-) \leftrightarrow m \in S \wedge S \leq m)) \,.$$

Here, S is explicitly labeled as an input variable and m an output variable. The target language imposes restrictions on how modes are propagated through the formula. Also, the modes restrict the sequences of literals in the resulting formula to those that allow a feasible execution in the target language. The complete synthesis, along with the modes in this example, finally leads to the following formula.

$$SET(S) \rightarrow (MAX(S^+, m^-) \leftrightarrow g^- \in S^+ \wedge (g^+ = m^- \wedge S^+ \leq m^+ \vee$$
$$MAX(S^+ \backslash g^+, m^-) \wedge g^+ \leq m^+ \wedge g^+ \neq m^+)).$$

Read this formula from left to right (as the interpreter for Prolog does, assuming this language is the chosen target language) to understand the computational information carried by the modes. For example, the literal $g^- \in S^+$ tells the system that this literal is to be executed with S as an input resulting in some g such that the literal holds. Therefore, membership in a set must be among the knowledge available to the system in its knowledge base for which it can provide routines from its library, an obviously fair requirement. After the successful execution of this literal g, its mode is changed to input mode. Therefore, in the subsequent equality literal, m can be determined for the first of the two cases and the inequality thus tested, and so on. Because this approach is a purely mechanical way to computationally interpret the formula, it should be obvious why the formula can now easily be translated by LOPS into the following Prolog program:

```
max(S,M)     :-  isset(S), max1(S,M).
max1(S,M)    :-  member(G,S), max2(S,M,G).
max2(S,M,G)  :-  setminus(S,G,SmG), max1(SmG,M), less(G,M),!.
max2(S,M,M)  :-  setless(S,M).
```

The predicates in the bodies of these clauses not defined here are of a general nature and, thus, are assumed to be available in the knowledge base as library routines.

Note that the literals in the last formula were already written in a sequence to be executable when traversed from left to right. Although for general logical formulas, this case is obviously not true (just reverse the sequence in this case, for example), the modes provide a mechanism to determine the sequences that can be executed among all possible ones. The method thus reduces the search space of possible derivations of deductive programs as well as the need for backtracking during the execution of the resulting program.

Determining the sequence of disjunctions is not as obvious as determining that of conjunctions and, therefore, was not illustrated in my example. Thus, the resulting maximum program is not the best possible one in terms of efficiency. A similar technique, which is not yet implemented, that uses modes for predicate symbols would make the system recognize that the subgoal setless(S,M) in the last clause of the program is, in fact, not needed (Neugebauer 1991). After this modification, the program realizes the best possible Prolog algorithm for the maximum problem.

To summarize, LOPS is based on a few general strategies. These strategies are used as guidelines for the generation of transformations in a particular problem specification. In the process of generating transformations, the syntactic properties of the specification formula are exploited, and general knowledge is assumed to be available to the system. The kind of syntactic information exploited and knowledge used is illustrated by the current example.

As I noted, generality is one of the important features characterizing the LOPS approach. Space does not permit the detailed demonstration of this generality. Strong evidence for this generality is provided by the fact that a wide variety of problems were synthesized along precisely the same strategic lines. Among these problems are computing the subset (or sublist) relation; merging lists; sorting lists; finding a spanning tree in a graph; and computing the square root, the quotient, and remainder (Fronhöfer 1984, 1985; Neugebauer 1986; Neugebauer, Fronhöfer, and Kreitz 1988). The synthesized algorithms are as efficient as the best known in the literature.

Although the strategies seem general enough to avoid excluding interesting algorithms, they restrict the search for algorithms to a point where program synthesis seems feasible for practical applications. As the study of the sorting problem demonstrates (Neugebauer 1986), the alternatives left open by the strategies are indeed essential alternatives. At least in the case of sorting, they cover the different sorting algorithms known from the literature (such as selection-sort, merge-sort, insertion-sort, quick-sort).

System Architecture

The LOPS project was initially carried out under difficult conditions, leading to a heterogeneous software package. Therefore, within the ESPRIT project ALPES (advanced logical programming environments), a complete reimplementation was undertaken (Neugebauer, Fronhöfer, and Kreitz 1989; Neugebauer 1987; Kreitz 1987). The software is now more flexible for change or extension as well as more professional from a software-engineering point of view. In a nutshell, it can be described as follows:

Rather than committing the implementation to the strategies used in LOPS, the new implementation strives to provide a general formula transformation tool that can be specialized in various ways, one of which is the LOPS system. This general tool, called XPRTS (experimental program-transformation system) (Neugebauer, Fronhöfer, and Kreitz 1989), is designed in a strictly modular way. It allows the manipulation of formulas on various abstraction levels. Its architecture is shown in figure 2.

XPRTS has a *transformation unit* (TU) that provides basic manipulations of formulas, represented as trees, such as copying, truncation, expansion, and comparison. These manipulations are activated through any of several hierarchical control unit layers (CU_i, $i \geq 0$). On the lowest level CU_0, only a few basic control constructs are provided that allow, for example, for the conditional processing of manipulations or the definition of (recursive) procedures. The higher levels allow the expression of more abstract strategies, so that, for example, a LOPS strategy such as GUESS would be a command explicitly known to CU_2 (four levels were realized). The remaining modules of the whole system shown in figure 2 fulfill the functions suggested by their names.

XPRTS is operative, and the LOPS strategies are realized within it. A number of the syntheses mentioned in the previous subsection can be demonstrated in an interactive way with this version of LOPS based on XPRTS. That is, remaining gaps, such as the lack of an operative interaction with the theorem prover (TP), cause lemma verification to be done manually. A system kernel is written in C, but the remaining system is written in XPRTS interpreted (super-) user language. The entire system is integrated within the ALPES prototype system, where it acts as a program development support system. The Alpes prototype system itself is a C-Prolog programming environment, offering many other programming support functions besides the LOPS functions,

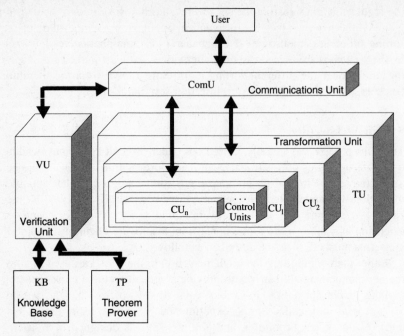

Figure 2. The Architecture of XPRTS.

such as browsing, debugging, data typing, and program analysis and transformation (Fronhöfer and Neugebauer 1987; Fronhöfer and Furbach 1989).

Project Evaluation

LOPS has certainly fulfilled researchers' initial expectations. It demonstrated that an important part of software design, that is, the generation of algorithms from a given declarative specification, can be automated for a wide variety of algorithms on the basis of a uniform and general strategic approach. The problems remaining after this experiment are the following:

The first problem is one of complexity in breadth (as opposed to depth). How can one get the numerous bits of knowledge necessary for a truly powerful LOPS into the knowledge base? Even for the simple problems considered in the current LOPS version, obtaining this knowledge required a major undertaking of a tedious nature. It is hard to conceive of people trying to obtain all the necessary details for a realistic system. Thus, an automated form of knowledge acquisition seems indispensable.

A second major problem relates to the fact that software production is more than the generation of algorithms. In fact, some even argue that the generation of algorithms is a negligible part of it. Although such an extreme position seems wrong—whatever the problem, some algorithmic behavior is always involved in its solution—developing the remaining part of a software design system was not part of the LOPS project. Some of the preceding chapters of this book are devoted to this topic.

A third major problem with the LOPS approach (or any other known approach for that matter) is that it suffers from the same problems as other software on the market. Although it was carefully designed, modularized, and what have you, it is still unreliable software, difficult for someone not involved in its design and implementation to understand, and, thus, difficult to change. For this reason, C. Kreitz, one of the persons involved in the project, strongly argues for a more formalized approach to the development of a system such as LOPS. He proposes an intuitionistic-type theory as a formalism in which both the reasoning necessary for system development as well as the system itself can be represented (Kreitz 1991). NuPRL (Constable et al. 1986) is used to realize the necessary formal proofs. In Kreitz (1990), the GUESS strategy of LOPS is formalized to illustrate the idea. Here, GUESS becomes a theorem in the metatheory and is easily verified with the help of NuPRL, which guarantees the correctness of the transformations generated. The perspective of this approach is that all strategic information is formalized in the same way. Thus, given a particular problem specification, the respective theorems are instantiated for this particular case and a program is extracted from the proof of these specialized theorems.

A major gap not closed in the LOPS project for a number of circumstantial reasons is the lack of a link to a theorem prover. In a companion project, a prover called SETHEO (Letz et al. 1991) was built on the basis of the connection method (Bibel 1983, 1987). As opposed to LOPS, which uses a top-down approach to programming, SETHEO supports a programming language called Lop that operates on an even higher level than Prolog because it allows full use of first-order logic. Despite this generality, SETHEO offers remarkable performance with several tens of kilo logical inferences per second (KLIPS). However, even with the theorem prover, much work still needs to be done (Bibel 1991). In regard to the relation with LOPS, one can view it in two ways: LOPS needs a prover such as SETHEO for the proof of the lemmas generated, but Lop, based on SETHEO, needs a system such as LOPS as its natural extension to a high-level programming language.

Other authors are working along similar lines. Probably the most closely related project is the KIDS system developed by D. Smith (chapter 19). Just as LOPS is built on top of XPRTS, KIDS is built on top of REFINE. Also like LOPS, KIDS starts from a logical problem specification, uses various tactics for creating algorithms, makes significant use of a deductive inference system, does all sorts of rewriting, and so on.

There are a number of differences between the two basic systems. The most significant difference is that KIDS' mature and impressive performance has yet to be matched by some version of LOPS. Some of the performance differences might be the result of Lops' unbalanced state of development. Further, what is achieved in KIDS by selecting a global search tactic on the basis of an abstract global search theory, LOPS handles with its strategies, especially GUESS and DOMAIN. For example, consider the problem of determining Costas arrays (chapter 19). As a logical formula, this problem can be stated as follows:

$$\forall n \, \exists \, c_1, \ldots, c_n$$
$$(\forall i, j = 1, \ldots, n \, (c_i \in \{1, \ldots, n\} \land (i \neq j \rightarrow c_i \neq c_j)) \land$$
$$\forall i = 1, \ldots, n-1, \, j, k = 1, \ldots, n-i \, (j \neq k \rightarrow c_{j+i} - c_j \neq c_{k+i} - c_k)).$$

In this case, it is straightforward for the system to guess at some $c_i \in \{1, \ldots, n\}$. As a consequence of this action, LOPS is forced to consider the structure, shown in figure 2 in chapter 19, that, in the case of KIDS, resulted from involved deliberations that were partially performed by the user.

Another similar system is Focus, developed by U. Reddy (chapter 18). However, because LOPS emphasizes the strategic part of synthesis, a comparison with Focus seems unreasonable without considering its strategic part AutoFocus, which is not yet completed.

The KIV system (chapter 21) is based on the verification methodology and is hard to compare with the strictly constructive approaches of KIDS and LOPS.

The Amenities of Programming

A general lesson learned from the LOPS project is the tremendous size of the task of building a software construction system. Is it worthwhile to undertake such an enormous task? To answer this question, let us look at the current reality with existing software. Although it might seem farfetched, I consider user interfaces, explaining in the next section what synthesis might offer them. The example is interesting because anyone using computers is subject to the shortcomings of user interfaces.

Today, the more advanced computer systems offer an option between a menu-driven and a command-oriented human interface. Let us consider the menu-driven option first. At any given level, the user can choose among a small set of options presented as icons or key words in a menu. Any of these options either leads to a different level with another menu or activates a particular command.

The user is expected to understand the meaning of the icons and the key words, which also means understanding the classification underlying the decision tree represented by the menus and the commands offered for execution. A help option usually supports this understanding.

Menu-driven systems of this kind are considered user friendly, and for limited and restricted applications such as text processing, they are useful. If we think of complex systems, however, the weaknesses of such systems become obvious. First, to expect the user to have such extensive knowledge means a substantial burden on his(her) part. The help option only alleviates this burden to a limited degree because the help information grows exponentially with the system's complexity. In addition, for the experienced user, running through a number of menus before being able to execute a certain command is a nuisance. Thus, the menu-technique is not preferred in complex systems.

In the extreme, command-oriented systems consist of a single menu containing a list of all available commands along with a description of their use and meaning. This listing is provided to the user in the form of a user's guide or user's manual. Would-be programmers have to be prepared to read a couple of hundreds of pages and remember them before doing useful work. I am not talking here of memorizing poems, mind you, but of attaching some meaning to a letter such as j or a sequence like $^\wedge x^\wedge c$, in fact to hundreds of cryptic sequences of key strokes. Often, the meaning depends on the system's actual status, thus complicating things even further.

This approach is fine for the specialist who spends much of the time with one or two systems; however, we can forget it for the average individual who uses the computer as a tool at irregular intervals to support his(her) work on projects of varying kinds. What would such people need?

Generally speaking, the system shouldn't distract the user's attention from his(her) work. That is, it should take little effort to communicate a command to the system, for example, striking one key or, at most, a few of them. However, the user's awareness of the fixed associations of meanings to keys must not be anticipated by the system. Can we reconcile these seemingly contradictory needs?

Some progress toward such ends might still be possible with the current technology. In particular, the help function could be made even more state sensitive, thus more focused. In addition, it could consider the statistical likelihood of a certain command being sought by the user at any given state. Thus, calling help at any given moment would present, say, at most five options with brief descriptions; in 95 percent of the cases, the required command would be included. The remaining 5 percent of these cases would require further paging through the context-sensitively ordered list of commands. In particular, the customization of the system to the skills and needs of a particular user should be foreseen, and the help function should be adapted accordingly. Such a system would more actively respond to the user's needs.

Unfortunately, the solution just outlined is not easy to achieve. It asks for the design of complex systems, resulting in serious problems with respect to installation, adaptation, and maintenance. Even if these problems could be managed, the result would still be an inflexible system from the user's point of view.

Humans like to create their individual interfaces in interaction with the rest of the world. For technological hardware like cars, for example, this desire can be fulfilled only in part with different varieties to choose from. Computers are different in that they provide intellectual, not physical interfaces that require more differentiation. They allow any interface you might want. Why then impose fixed interfaces on users? As a consumer, I want to buy an interface that I am able to mould according to my own taste and to my capabilities. However, I want to do so without becoming a system programmer. Just by telling the interface system what I dislike about the current option, I want it to reconfigure itself to meet this preference (after possibly offering advice about my idea). Am I dreaming? Not if we take serious approaches such as the one taken in LOPS. Before discussing these approaches, let us just touch on a number of other problems with the current state of affairs.

Because current systems are already complex, never expect them to properly function or even to suit modest demands in all cases. Subsequent system versions, which users certainly want to install in order to keep their environment up to date, are released in a due amount of time. Experience tells us that the tasks of fixing problems, incorporating new versions, adapting existing hardware and software, and so on keep a technician busy full time for even a small installation. More importantly, because the problems arising in daily use are becoming increasingly complex, you had better look for a technician who is really smart. Some of us might have already sensed a mood of despair in our labs.

To this point, our discussion has more or less been concerned with the problems involved in doing the right thing at a given time to achieve an immediate behavior, as desired. To a great extent, programming concerns foreseeing the future needs of behavior without being able to anticipate the circumstances under which these needs arise. Typically, during programming, we only have a rough idea of the task requirements on a global level. Therefore, it is no surprise that the software that is eventually produced is often more a disappointment than a success. The wish for a change in the result comes the day the package is delivered.

Perhaps the most frustrating of all these problems is the fact that not all software production is additive. Relatively minor changes often require fully rewriting major parts of a system. Often, such rewriting has to be carried out by a new team of programmers. Because becoming familiar with code is a demanding task, there is even more readiness to redo the whole program. Paradoxically, in intellectics,[4] it has even become a virtue to throw away written software in the hope that the next version is an improvement. This attitude reminds me of the time when secretaries had to retype manuscripts again and again and again without ever achieving a correct version. Think about how much more difficult programming is in comparison to typing!

What is offered as a remedy for these problems in the software-engineering literature? You find countless pages filled with such topics as computer-aided software engineering (Case); the application of development techniques; life-cycle support; verification, validation, and testing approaches; high-level language programming; data structures, abstract data types, hierarchical types, and operations; and integrated programming environments. I might be shortsighted, but I simply cannot see a solution to the fundamental problems discussed here in any of these concepts. Indeed, I did not come across any article that outlined a scenario in which any of these concepts would lead us to a more desirable future.

Because the software engineers should know, it seems that no brighter future is possible. However, a few (compared to the masses of software engineers) researchers have heralded a fundamentally different approach. Their background is often in intellectics or logic. Sometimes, the key words are automatic programming or program synthesis or computational logic. Some of this work deserves a closer inspection, and this book has made a valuable step in this direction. In the next section, I describe a scenario that is more desirable, doing so at the risk of wishful thinking.

Concurrent Software Production

Although software engineers correctly speak of the life-cycle of software, thereby referring to various phases (requirements, specification, and so forth), they actually treat these phases in a sequential way, a fact that is evident in the terminological use of the word phase. A more appropriate approach would be to think of the specialists for each of these phases sitting around a table together, doing their work in a concurrent way. Like concurrent manufacturing, we could speak of *concurrent software production*.

I describe producing software in this way in detail in Bibel (1985). The basic point is simply that it would be desirable to have the various phases of the life-cycle intimately interact with each other. For example, it would help to have an immediate feedback from the team that implements the software for those who set up the requirements to check whether the requirements are indeed met by the actual implementation. Similar arguments apply to other pairs of phases. No one would seriously disagree with such an idea but the issue is whether this idea could ever be realized.

Imagine that systems such as LOPS or KIDS (chapter 19) are sufficiently maturing for realistic software production. Thus, a rising degree of automation would result that could make concurrent programming feasible. First, note that a close inspection of these systems shows that they could even handle partial problem descriptions. In this way, immediate feedback could be provided during the phase of problem shaping. Once the design phase is completed, the compiled version of the declarative specification program would henceforth be used for execution. In other words, synthesis and compilation, being time consuming, would be done only once.

However, the heuristic information that is used during the synthesis and compilation would be kept *along* with the program. If the user wants changes, s/he would specify them. On the basis of this additional declarative specification (together with the specification of the available program), the synthesis and compilation would have to be redone, but the heuristic information that was kept would considerably speed the synthesis process. In fact, in the case of minor changes, it could make the process possible in a fully automated way.

Thus, programs would become *additive,* a feature that is of the utmost desirability in overcoming the problems previously discussed. Simply, if you have two systems, one consisting of the necessary changes and the other being the available program, and just add them together; through the synthesis and compilation mechanism, binding them functionally together, they still remain a program.

Note that software of this kind would overcome the problems previously described. For example, anyone could customize a system's interface the way s/he likes without having to become acquainted with the system language simply by specifying his(her) desires in a declarative way. In addition, processes such as fixing problems, incorporating new versions, and adapting existing hardware and software would be a lot easier if they could be carried out on the declarative level.

For example, a user interface such as the one discussed in the previous section is such a program. Imagine that it was designed in just the way it was outlined. Now assume I want to impose a change on it; for example, I want to delete strings of text with three mouse clicks, a process I cannot perform with my editor here. This process would work as follows.

The system is put into configuration mode. In interaction with the system, the requirement is specified in a semiformal form of communication. The system checks for any inconsistencies with its own specification. If inconsistencies exist, the consequences of removing them in favor of the desired change are explained to the user. Otherwise, the new piece of specification is added to the specification of the entire system (that is stored with it). By following the heuristic information (that is also stored, replacing the system programmer in a concurrent programming session), synthesis and compilation is performed, with new changes required only at the points where the new piece of specification becomes relevant. Note that no search is needed for the unchanged parts because all heuristic information is kept. My conjecture is that in this example of deleting text with mouse clicks, no search would be caused for the synthesis by the specification change because it is so marginal. Although changes of this sort are indeed marginal, imagine how useful such an additive system would nevertheless be.

True, realizing the dream of additive systems in general and responsive user interfaces in particular begs the solution to a number of hard problems well known in intellectics (Bibel 1975b, 1985). The (semi)automatic synthesis of an algorithm from a logical description such as in LOPS is only one of these problems. Dealing with incomplete, perhaps incorrect, descriptions and acquiring the details of a huge knowledge base are two others.

None of these problems is close to being solved. In fact, notwithstanding this book, nearly no one seems interested in their solution, at least no one from the software-engineering community.[5] This situation probably exists because there is little reward in attacking such hard problems for which real progress is visible only on close inspection; that is, individual referees or appointment committees would not often recognize the relative achievement. Thus, the prospects for a realization look rather grim. Perhaps the only hope might be the prospect that the situation will predictably become so bad, as traditional systems become even more complex, that all involved will get mad and start looking for radical change.

Conclusion

In this chapter, I pursued two different but closely related goals. I tried to present the principles of predicative programming in the perspective of the current situation with software production. Further, I briefly surveyed the work done during the LOPS project.

The second of these goals was treated in The LOPS System. There is the hope that the reader gained a feeling for the nature of this work; this discussion played an important role in our pursuing the first goal. That is, the experience gained in this project makes us believe that predicative programming is a feasible idea and that LOPS is the way to take to realize it.

In contrasting current software practices with the predicative programming approach, I tried to justify the need for radical change in these practices. Given the complexity of the task of realizing predicative programming to some extent, I do not expect such a change happen in the near future. However, the attractiveness of the prospects of this research, such as the possibility of concurrent programming, makes me believe that a change will occur at some point in the future.

Acknowledgments

I appreciate the valuable comments from Christoph Kreitz, Michael Lowry, Gerd Neugebauer, and Uday Reddy, with his student Steve Hasker, on earlier versions of this chapter. Sunny Ludvik polished the English. These contributions considerably improved the presentation.

Notes

1. The term *predicative programming* was coined first in Bibel (1975a,1975b) but was recently used in a slightly different sense by Hehner (1984).

2. In Bibel (1976a), I used the term *strategic definitions* to express the same idea.

3. One might think of a generate-and-test algorithm for its interpretation, but which objects should be generated in the first place? Note that the interpreter would not see, as humans do, that only those in *S* make useful candidates.

4. I refer here to the fields of AI and cognitive science.

5. Note that the researchers among the software engineers are only a tiny fraction; in turn, those represented in this book are only a small fraction of this tiny number.

References

Bibel, W. 1991. Perspectives on Automated Deduction. In *Festschrift for W. W. Bledsoe*, ed. R.S. Boyer. Utrecht: Kluwer Academic.

Bibel, W. 1988. Advanced Topics in Automated Deduction. In *Fundamentals of Artificial Intelligence II*, ed. R. Nossum, 41–59. Lecture Notes in Computer Science 345. Berlin: Springer.

Bibel, W. 1987. *Automated Theorem Proving*, 2d ed. Braunschweig: Vieweg Verlag.

Bibel, W. 1986. Predicative Programming Revisited. In *MMSSSS'85—Mathematical Methods for the Specification and Synthesis of Software Systems,* eds. W. Bibel and K. Jantke, 24–40. Berlin: Springer.

Bibel, W. 1985. Wissensbasierte Softwareentwicklung. In Wissensbasierte Systeme–1. Intern. GI Kongress, eds. W. Brauer and B. Radig, 17–41. Fachberichte Informatik 112. Berlin: Springer.

Bibel, W. 1983. Matings in Matrices. *Communications of the ACM* 26:844–852.

Bibel, W. 1980. Syntax-Directed, Semantics-Supported Program Synthesis. *Artificial Intelligence* 14:243–261.

Bibel, W. 1976a. Synthesis of Strategic Definitions and Their Control, Technical Report, 7610, Fakultät für Mathematik, Technische Universität München.

Bibel, W. 1976b. A Uniform Approach to Programming, Technical Report, 7633, Fakultät für Mathematik, Technische Universität München.

Bibel, W. 1975a. Prädikatives Programmieren. In *GI–2. Fachtagung Über Automatentheorie und Formale Sprachen, ed . H. Brakhage*, 274–283. Berlin: Springer.

Bibel, W. 1975b. Programmieren in der Sprache der Prädikatenlogik. Habilitation Thesis, Mathematics Dept., Technische Universität München. Draft.

Bibel, W., and Hörnig, K. M. 1984. LOPS—A System Based on a Strategical Approach to Program Synthesis. In Automatic Program Construction Techniques, eds. A. Biermann, G. Guiho, and Y. Kodratoff, 69-89. New York: MacMillan.

Constable, R. L.; Allen, S. F.; Bromley, H. M.; Cleaveland, W. R.; Cremer, J. F.; Harper, R. W.; Howe, D. J.; Knoblock, T. B.; Mendler, N. P.; Panangaden, P.; Sasaki, J. T.; and Smith, S. F. 1986. *Implementing Mathematics with the NuPRL Proof Development System*. Englewood Cliffs, N.J.: Prentice-Hall.

Fronhöfer, B. 1985. The LOPS Approach: Towards New Syntheses of Algorithms. In *Öesterreichische Artificial Intelligence Tagung,* eds. H. Trost and J. Retti, 164–172. Berlin: Springer.

Fronhöfer, B. 1984. Heuristics for Recursion Improvement. In *ECAI-84—Proceedings of the 6th European Conference on Artificial Intelligence*, ed. T. O'Shea, 577–580. Amsterdam: North-Holland.

Fronhöfer, B., and Furbach, U. 1989. Alpes—A Programming Environment for Logic Programming. In *Wissensbasierte Systeme–3. Intern. GI Kongress,* eds. W. Brauer and C. Freksa,

496–506. FB Informatik 227. Berlin: Springer.

Fronhöfer, B., and Neugebauer, G. 1987. ESPRIT Project 973 Alpes—Advanced Logical Programming Environments. In Wissensbasierte Systeme–2. Intern. GI Kongress, eds. W. Brauer and W. Wahlster, 388–39. FB Informatik 155. Berlin: Springer.

Hehner, E. 1984. Predicative Programming. *Communications of the ACM* 27:134–151.

Kreitz, C. 1991. Towards a Formal Theory of Program Construction. *Review d'Intelligence Artificielle* 4(3): 53-79.

Kreitz, C. 1990. The Representation of Program Synthesis in Higher-Order Logic. In GWAI'90, ed. H. Marburger, 171–180. Berlin: Springer.

Kreitz, C. 1987. Towards a Flexible LOPS Implementation: An Example of XPRTS Programming, ATP-79-X-87, Technische Universität München.

Kreitz, C.; Neugebauer, G.; and Fronhöfer, B. 1988. Logic-Oriented Program Synthesis, FKI-90-88, Technische Universität München.

Letz, R.; Schumann, J.; Bayerl, S.; and Bibel, W. 1991. SETHEO—A High-Performance Theorem Prover for First-Order Logic. *Journal of Automated Reasoning*. Forthcoming.

Neugebauer, G. 1991. Pragmatische Programmsynthese. Ph.D. thesis, Technische Hochschule Darmstadt.

Neugebauer, G. 1987. User's Manual for XPRTS, ATP-78-X-87, Technische Universität München.

Neugebauer, G. 1986. Synthesis of Sorting Algorithms with the LOPS Approach, ATP-56-III-86, Technische Universität München.

Neugebauer, G.; Fronhöfer, B.; and Kreitz, C. 1989. XPRTS—An Implementation Tool for Program Synthesis. In *GWAI'89*, ed. D. Metzing, 348–357. Berlin: Springer.

17

A Derivation of an Efficient
Rule System Pattern Matcher

Jeremy Wertheimer

Formalizing algorithm derivations is a necessary prerequisite for automating algorithm design. This chapter describes a derivation of an algorithm for incrementally matching conjunctive patterns against a growing database. This algorithm, which is modeled on the Rete algorithm used in the OPS5 production system (Forgy 1982), forms a basis for efficiently implementing rule-based systems. The highlights of this derivation are a formal specification for the rule system matching problem, the derivation of an algorithm for this task using an algebraic model of conjunctive and disjunctive variable substitutions, and the optimization of this algorithm to handle incremental processing of new data.

The result of this work is a derivation, starting from a formal specification, of an algorithm similar to the Rete network. This description is at a higher level of abstraction than the description presented in Forgy (1982).

This derivation was implemented using program transformations, some of which are described in Algorithm Derivation and in Optimization. A detailed presentation of this derivation and an earlier implementation can be found in Wertheimer (1989).

The sections in this chapter present (1) a brief introduction to the goals of this work and the application domain studied; (2) an overview of the derivation and related work; (3) a discussion of the context of this work, including the exploration of program design spaces, transformational programming, and an algebraic approach to programming; (4) a specification of the rule system matching task; (5) a description of the Rete algorithm and the simplifications made to this algorithm for the purposes of this chapter; (6) a formalization of the specification; (7) a derivation of an algorithm and representation; (8) an optimization of this derived algorithm to handle the incremental processing of additions to the database; (9) the correspondence of this optimized algorithm to the Rete matcher; (10) the correspondence between the structures introduced in the derivation and the model-theoretic semantics of first-order logic; and (11) some conclusions.

Background

Programs are still written and rewritten in a manual ad hoc manner. A goal of automatic programming research is to foster an alternative approach to programming. This approach involves gathering, organizing, formalizing, and implementing programming knowledge. Researchers have begun to use this approach to automate the development of small programs. Currently, this approach is mostly used with small programs, and it does not directly address the management of complexity issues that arise with and dominate programming in the large. However, even automating programming in the small could be of enormous value to all programmers.

One goal of this approach is to build a library of programming knowledge that embodies the common collection of algorithms, data structures, and techniques that are the basis of programming. One objective is to use this library to build automatic programming systems. A second benefit that comes from this approach is the development of sharper understandings of current algorithms and techniques. This chapter is intended as a contribution toward both of these goals. As such, it should be of interest both to readers interested in automatic programming and to those interested in this particular application domain.

This chapter focuses on the application domain of AI programming. Specifically, the focus is on rule-based systems, an important class of AI programs. The term rule-based system is used here to encompass those systems derived from the paradigm of logical inference, including production systems, theorem-proving systems, and deductive databases.

Rete Derivation Overview

The basic task considered here is the efficient implementation of a rule system pattern matcher. The core of this task involves efficiently finding all matches between a set of rules and a database. The algorithm derived here is modeled on the Rete matcher (Forgy 1982) used in the OPS5 production system (Brownston et al. 1985). This matcher efficiently finds all matches for a rule base and a database and then incrementally updates this set of matches as the database is modified.

The heart of the derivation is a mathematical model of the information computed and manipulated in performing this task. The representations used in the final program are directly derived from this model. The structures in this model are similar to the structures used in the model-theoretic semantics of first-order logic. This connection is discussed in Correspondence to Model Theory.

Earlier work (Manna and Waldinger 1981; Eder 1985; Rydeheard and Burstall 1986) dealt with deriving the unification algorithm, a generalization of the single-pattern–single-datum pattern matcher. Also, several articles were published that describe formal models of rule-based systems (Robinson 1987). The work described here deals with deriving an algorithm for the many-pattern–many-datum pattern match problem. The attempt to formalize the structures in the Rete matcher led to the introduction of an extension to the formalizations previously cited. In general, the result of matching a pattern and an expression is a substitution, which specifies the appropriate bindings for the variables in the pattern so that the pattern matches the expression. This derivation introduces disjunctive substitutions to represent the results obtained from matching a pattern against several possible data in a database. The formal derivation of the matcher is based on a correspondence between the structure of the specification and a structure constructed from these disjunctive substitutions. Specifically, the derivation uses a homomorphism from a set algebra used in the specification to a lattice of disjunctive substitutions. (Briefly, a *homomorphism* is a mapping between structures that preserves operations. For example, a logarithm is a homomorphism from positive real numbers under multiplication to real numbers under addition.)

This mathematical model leads to an initial algorithm that satisfies the functional specification for the matcher but does not satisfy the performance requirements. However, by application of the general-purpose techniques of finite differencing (Paige and Koenig 1982) and partial evaluation (chapter 15), this initial implementation can be transformed into an algorithm similar to the Rete matcher. Therefore, the result of this work can schematically be expressed as

Rete = Formal Specification
+ Lattice Construction Based on Homomorphism to Specification
+ Finite Differencing Based on Distributive Laws
+ Partial Evaluation

(This chapter does not discuss the use of partial evaluation. See Wertheimer [1989] for a discussion of this technique.)

The substitutions used in this derivation are equivalent to the valuation structures used in the model-theoretic semantics of first-order logic. This connection suggests an extension of the derived algorithm to handle negation. It also raises the possibility that the Rete algorithm could be derived starting directly from the semantics of first-order logic.

This chapter presents a formal program derivation. This derivation was implemented using program transformations. A first implementation was done using the REFINE wide-spectrum specification language and KIDS (the Kestrel interactive development system) (chapter 19). The derivation was subsequently reimplemented in Common Lisp and greatly expanded. Although the complete details of these implementations are not presented in this chapter, selected transformations are presented. For the purposes of presentation, the programs presented in this chapter are written in a pidgin-Algol form that closely resembles REFINE code.

The next three sections discuss some context for this work, including the organization of programming knowledge in program design spaces, the use of program transformations to implement derivations, and the use of algebraic techniques to formalize program derivations.

Program Design Spaces

This work began as an effort to formalize some of the programming knowledge used in implementing rule-based systems. This chapter presents a detailed formalization of a small part of this design space.

The approach used here involves examining several programs from the literature that belong to a particular application domain, for example, rule-based systems; constructing a taxonomy of these programs based on the different design decisions that they embody; and rederiving these programs (or simplified versions) using formal specifications, domain models, formally defined representations, and transformation rules.

The goal of this work is to build libraries containing formal domain models, mathematical structures for use in implementing domain models, and common programming techniques for efficiently implementing these structures.

This work involves an attempt to map the design space of rule systems as described by the various design decisions that differentiate the programs in this domain. Figure 1 shows a portion of the rule-based system design space.

Although programs in this design space share a common domain model—the paradigm of rule-based inference—they differ in various design decisions. One basic difference concerns how the rules are selected and applied. A system can be forward chaining, where rules are applied to data to

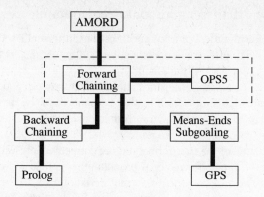

Figure 1. Rule System Design Space.

yield new data; backward chaining, where rules are applied to goals to yield subgoals; or means-ends, where a distance metric is used to apply the rule most relevant to reducing the current gap between data and goals.

Within a control paradigm, such as forward chaining, programs can differ in other design decisions. For example, the AMORD system (de Kleer et al. 1978), a forward-chaining system similar to OPS5, differs from OPS5 in that it does not have a Rete network. In AMORD, the matching of conjunctive patterns is handled by using a facility that allows the right-hand side of a rule to contain arbitrary Lisp code, including code to add a new rule. An AMORD rule can match a single pattern and then create a new rule to handle the matching of any remaining patterns.

Another example of differing design decisions involves indexing the patterns in the rule base. Instead of matching a new datum against all the rule patterns, the system can first use a quick approximate matcher—such as a test for equal predicate symbols—to filter rule patterns that cannot possibly match a given datum.

A third example of design decisions involves mechanisms for handling assumptions and retraction. Mechanisms that have been used for this function include context systems and truth maintenance systems.

Achieving the ultimate goal of codifying and formalizing programming knowledge requires both the high-level mapping of the design space previously described, and the detailed formalization and implementation of the pieces of this design space. This chapter presents a portion of this detailed formalization, a beginning for the piece dealing with the formal derivation of OPS5.

Although the task of filling in these design spaces with formal derivations, as done in this chapter, can be time consuming, it seems to be a reasonable direction toward building the library of programming knowledge that allows the development of knowledge-based automatic programming tools.

Transformational Programming

To automate algorithm design from specifications, a formalism is needed for describing the manipulations of specifications and programs. This work uses the program-transformation formalism.

One advantage of program transformations is that they can encode common programming knowledge in a form that is independent of the particular target program. Another advantage of the transformational approach is that it guarantees the correctness of the final program, provided that the initial specification is correct and that all of the transformations are correctness preserving.

One problem with transformational programming is that it is often considerably more difficult to construct a formal derivation of a program than to simply write the program. Also, even given a sufficient library of transformations, it is a complex task to decide the order in which to apply the transformations. Higher-level tools for organizing the strategy and tactics of transformational development will probably be required before this technology becomes widely used. The KIDS system (chapter 19) is a start in this direction.

Another problem is that there are various ways of encoding a given piece of programming knowledge. Although it seems appealing to encode knowledge in the most flexible manner possible, there are often trade-offs between flexibility and efficiency. For example, several of the transformations used in this derivation arise from general algebraic laws. It seems preferable to encode them as axioms rather than transformations. However, this approach requires the use of theorem-proving technology, which can often be difficult to efficiently exploit. Smith's (1982) work on RAINBOW is an interesting step in the direction toward directing a theorem prover for use in an automatic programming system.

This chapter describes a manually directed algorithm derivation. An ultimate goal of this type of work is to eventually have automated systems perform these derivations. Because part of the purpose of doing this derivation was to identify useful transformations, the derivation was done first, and then transformations were created to implement this derivation. For the purposes of this chapter, the implementation of the derivation using program transformations served mostly as a verification that the steps had properly been carried out and that all necessary steps had been enumerated.

Toward an Algebra of Programs

Perhaps the most fundamental approach to advancing software design is to change the programmer's conception of the nature of programs. One appealing direction for this change is to consider programs as formal mathematical objects and subject them to formal reasoning and manipulation.

One approach to developing a formal theory of programs is to concentrate on functional programs. Backus (1978) discusses constructing an algebra of programs using the functional language FP. Functional programs have the advantage of being much easier to reason about than programs with state because like mathematical objects, functional expressions have the same value in any context. However, efficiency considerations have dictated that most real-world programming be done using imperative languages.

In the development described in this chapter, the simple structure provided by the use of functional programs facilitated focusing on the semantics of the data being manipulated. The finite-differencing technique provided a useful framework for optimization. This separation of concerns can probably be fruitfully applied in many other program design situations.

The development of programming knowledge in various domains can be considered to proceed through the stages of experimentation, codification, formalization, and automation. An example of experimentation is the development by Forgy of the Rete algorithm. An example of codification is a textbook such as that by Aho, Hopcroft, and Ullman (1974). An example of formalization is the work of Meertens (1987) and Bird (1987), which aims to produce algebraic theories of common data structures, such as lists, and their operations. An example of automation is the KIDS interactive transformation system (chapter 19).

Much of the formalization work previously mentioned deals with common data structures such as lists and sequences. The derivation in this chapter is an example of applying these algebraic techniques to new representations derived for particular application domains. This work involves pieces of codification, formalization, and automation.

Most formal derivations, including the one presented in this chapter, have been done after the fact. The preliminary state of current knowledge and the exigencies of programming in the real world do not usually allow the luxury of using formal methods for writing new and innovative programs. Perhaps this situation will change as more experience is gained with formal methods. It might then be possible to bring the clarity and precision of the best presentations of programs to the development of new programs.

Rule System Specification

This section briefly describes the operation of a rule system. This description is formalized below in Formal Specification.

Consider the rule system shown in figure 2. The system contains two main data structures: a database (*db*) and a rule base (*rb*). The rules in the rule base contain two fields: a left-hand side (LHS), and a right-hand side (RHS). The rules are modeled on the inference rules in a logical system. The LHS of a rule consists of a set of patterns, which are symbolic expressions containing variables. A pattern from an LHS can be matched against a datum in the database by finding a substitution that replaces the variables in the pattern with terms, so that the resulting pattern is equal to the datum. The LHS of a rule can be matched against the database by finding a single substitution

```
 1   function rule-system(rb, db) =
 2       repeat
 3           cs ← {⟨r, σ⟩ | r ∈ rb ∧ σ ∈ match-conj(lhs(r), db)}
 4           if cs = ∅ then return db end if
 5           cs-elt ← conflict-resolution(cs)
 6           if cs-elt = ∅ then return db end if
 7           r ← cs-elt.1, σ ← cs-elt.2
 8           db ← db ∪ {instantiate(rhs(r), σ)}
 9       end repeat

10   function match-conj(patterns, db) =
11       Rep({σ | ∀ₚ∈ₚₐₜₜₑᵣₙₛ ∃_d∈db instantiate(p, σ) = d})
```

Figure 2. Rule System Specification.

under which each of the patterns in LHS matches some datum in the database. If such a substitution exists, the rule is applicable to the database. For a given database and rule base, several rules might be applicable, and the same rule might be applicable with several different substitutions. The conflict set is the set of pairs of applicable rules and corresponding substitutions. The terms conflict set and conflict resolution are taken from the domain of production systems. (The Rete algorithm was first implemented in the OPS5 production system.) In these systems, the order in which rules are run is critical to the proper operation of the system. If several rules are applicable in a given state, the rules are said to be in conflict, and a special procedure is called to resolve this conflict and select which rule to run. For the purposes of this chapter, the details of conflict-resolution strategies can be ignored. The conflict-resolution procedure is simply defined to return either some element of the conflict set or the empty set.

A rule can be applied in the forward direction by matching LHS of the rule against the database and then instantiating RHS of the rule with the substitution that resulted from the matching and adding the result to the database. On each cycle of a rule system, the system computes the conflict set, invokes the conflict-resolution procedure to select a single rule-substitution pair from the conflict set, and applies this rule to the database. The interpreter repeats this cycle of operations until the conflict set is empty (or some other termination condition is satisfied).

The major inefficiency in this specification is the recomputation of the conflict set, which involves matching all the rules and all the data and occurs after every modification of the database. A more efficient approach would be to compute the conflict set for the initial database and rule base and, thereafter, incrementally update the conflict set as changes are made to the database. The next section describes how the Rete matcher implements this efficient approach.

Rete Description

This section describes the Rete network (Forgy 1982) (Brownston et al. 1985). The key feature of the Rete network is the compilation of the rule base into a token-passing data flow network that incrementally accepts changes to the database and produces corresponding changes to the conflict set. This section describes the simplified Rete network that is considered in this chapter. The simplifications are described in the next section.

Because the parts of the Rete network generated by different rules are basically independent, this explanation concentrates on the Rete network for a single rule.

Figure 3 shows a Rete network for the rule

$(f\ ?x)\ \&\ (g\ ?y)\ \&\ (h\ ?x\ ?y) \Rightarrow (p\ ?x\ ?y)$.

A Rete network is composed of three types of nodes: match nodes (called 1-input nodes in Rete), combine nodes (called 2-input nodes in Rete), and rule nodes (called Terminal nodes in Rete). Three types of tokens are passed between the nodes: database-change tokens, substitution tokens, and rule-substitution match tokens.

The rest of this section describes the operation of the Rete network. This description is organized by tracing the progression of a token in the network (figure 3).

The task of the matcher is to accept database-change tokens and output the corresponding changes to the conflict set. The changes to the database are input to the network on the bus shown at the top of the figure.

Match Nodes

The nodes at the top of the figure, labeled $(f\ ?x)$, $(g\ ?y)$, and $(h\ ?x\ ?y)$, represent matching nodes for the various patterns in the rule. There is one matching node for each pattern in the rule. (In the full Rete network, there would be one matching node for each pattern in the rule base.) A match node has a single input port and a single output port.

Copies of all new data tokens enter on the bus at the top of the figure and are distributed to all match nodes in the network. A match node processes a new data token by matching it against the node's pattern. If the datum and the pattern match, a token containing the resulting substitution is passed out the output port of the match node. If the datum and pattern do not match, no token is passed out the match node.

Combine Nodes

Tokens passed from the output ports of match nodes are sent to the input ports of combine nodes. A combine node has two input ports, referred to as the left input and the right input. (The ports are functionally symmetrical.) Each of the input ports of a combine node has a memory associated with it.

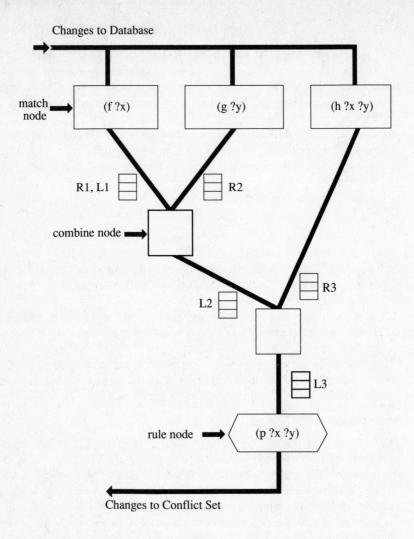

Figure 3. A Rete Network.

This memory holds all the tokens that have been received at this port since the network was initialized. A combine node has a single output port.

The role of a combine node is to combine the substitution tokens from its left and right parent nodes and generate a stream of substitution tokens that are consistent with the substitutions received at its left and right input ports. Each output substitution must be consistent with some substitution received at the left input and some substitution received at the right input.

The combine node functions as follows: When a new token is received at the left input port of a combine node, it is inserted into the left input memory and combined with all the elements in the right input memory of the node. If the results of any of these combinations are valid substitutions, these results are passed out the output port of the combine node.

The corresponding process is performed when a token is received at the right input port of a combine node. The token is inserted into the right input memory and combined with all the tokens in the left input memory. Any valid combinations are passed out the output port.

Rule Nodes

A fan-in tree of combine nodes is built for all the patterns in LHS of a rule, as shown in figure 3. The output port of the final combine node is connected to the input port of a rule node. When a substitution is received at the input port of a rule node, the node passes a token containing the rule and the substitution out its output port. These tokens, which describe the additions to be made to the conflict set, are gathered on the output bus and pass out the Rete network.

Simplifications

The focus of this chapter is on the central feature of the Rete algorithm: the computation of the conflict set and the incremental recomputation of this set as the database is modified. The matcher derived in this chapter has the same basic structure as the Rete algorithm and performs the same incremental update of the conflict set as does the Rete algorithm. However, it is a simplified version of the Rete algorithm. This section discusses the features of the Rete algorithm that are not covered in this derivation.

First, the Rete algorithm allows rules to have patterns marked with negative signs, which are used to implement a version of logical negation. A rule containing such a negated pattern is run only if none of the data in the database matches against this pattern. The algorithm derivation presented here only deals with positive patterns. An extension to this derivation to handle negation is discussed in Correspondence to Model Theory.

Second, in logical deduction, the only result of applying an inference rule is to deduce a new statement. In the formalization of commonsense reasoning and the engineering of rule systems, it is found useful to also allow rules to retract deductions and remove terms from the database. The OPS5 system provides this facility. When a term is removed from the database, the Rete network removes all entries from the conflict set that involved matching against this term. This facility is not present in the matcher derived in this chapter. It could be added to the matcher within the framework developed in this chapter.

Third, in most rule systems, a number of patterns are likely to appear in several rules. It is inefficient to repeat the computations of the matches to these patterns for each rule. A better scheme is to share the results of matching a pattern among all the rules that include this pattern. The Rete network performs this sharing.

This chapter focuses on deriving the central architecture and features of the Rete matcher: the division of the matching work among a network of nodes and the incremental update of the conflict set as changes are made to the database.

Formal Specification

The first step in performing a derivation involves formalizing the specification. To formalize the specification previously presented, let V, the set of variables, and C, the set of constants, be two disjoint sets. Let T, the set of terms, be the free semigroup generated by $V \cup C$, that is, the set formed by closing $V \cup C$ under the application of a binary operation. For example, if Lisp's cons function is used as the semigroup operation, the T becomes the set of all s-expressions that can be constructed from the atoms in $V \cup C$. Let G, the set of ground terms, be the set of all elements in T that do not contain any variables. With these definitions, the database in a rule system, db, is represented as a subset of G.

The LHS of a rule contains a set of terms that can be matched against data in the database. In many rule-based systems, the order of the patterns in the left-hand sides of the rules have carefully been hand tuned by the programmers in an attempt to improve the performance of the systems (Smith and Genesereth 1985). To accurately model these systems, LHS of a rule would have to be represented as a sequence. This chapter retains the semantics of logic, where the elements in a conjunct are unordered. The RHS of a rule contains a single term that can be instantiated and added to the database. If a rule is modeled as a tuple of LHS and RHS, then the set of rules, R, is equal to the set $2^T \times T$, and the rule base in a rule system, rb, is a subset of R.

A substitution is a partial function from V to G. Let E denote the set of all substitutions. The Greek letters σ, τ, and υ are used to denote substitutions, and S, S_1, and S_2 are used to denote sets of substitutions.

A term p can be instantiated with a substitution σ by replacing all the variables in p with their images in σ. If any of the variables in p are not in the domain of σ, the result is undefined. The notation p^σ is used to denote this instantiation, and the term p is referred to as a pattern. The inverse of instantiation is matching. The result of matching a pattern p and a datum d is a substitution σ such that $p^\sigma = d$ (if such a substitution exists; otherwise, the match fails).

For the rule system specification shown in figure 2, the matching is handled by the code in line 3 in the rule-system function and line 11 in the match-conj (match-conjunction) function. This code assigns the set of all rule-and-substitution tuples to cs such that the rule is in the rule base and that for all patterns in LHS of the rule, some datum in the database exists such that the pattern is equal to the datum when instantiated with the substitution.

That is, the conflict set contains all rules that match against the database paired with their corresponding substitutions. Line 4 checks that the conflict set is non-empty. Line 5 calls the conflict-resolution procedure to select one rule-and-substitution tuple from the conflict set. Line 6 checks that a valid rule-and-substitution tuple was returned by the conflict-resolution procedure, and line 7 extracts the rule and the substitution from this tuple. Line 8 instantiates RHS of the selected rule with the selected substitution and adds the result to the database. Because the set of substitutions in line 11 is an unbounded set, a representation function (Rep) is used to denote a concrete representation of this set. (The formalism of representation functions is used to map from abstract domain objects to their corresponding concrete implementations. These representation functions are the inverse of the abstraction functions used in Liskov and Guttag [1986].) The representation is discussed in detail in the next section.

The next section presents a direct implementation of this specification. This implementation is correct but inefficient. The Optimization section presents an optimized implementation that follows the technique, used in the Rete network, of incrementally updating the conflict set as changes are made to the database.

Algorithm Derivation

This section presents the derivation of an initial implementation of the specification shown in figure 2. The core of the algorithm involves computing the conflict set as a function of the database and rule base as specified by

$$cs \leftarrow \{<r, \sigma> \mid r \in rb \wedge \sigma \in \text{match-conj}(\text{lhs}(r), db)\}$$

where

$$\text{match-conj}(\textit{patterns}, db) = \text{Rep}(\{\sigma \mid \forall_{p \in \text{patterns}} \exists_{d \in db} \text{instantiate}(p, \sigma) = d\}).$$

The first part of this specification can easily be implemented as

$$cs = \bigcup_{r \in rb} \{<r, \sigma> \mid \sigma \in \text{match-conj}(\textit{lhs}(r), db)\}.$$

Therefore, this section focuses on implementing match-conj. The specification for match-conj requires finding the substitutions that simultaneously provide matches in the database for all the patterns in LHS of a rule. This conjunctive substitution task can be divided into computing matches of individual patterns and combining sets of substitutions. An expression for match-conj can progressively be constructed from the following subexpressions:

$$\text{match}(p, d) = \text{Rep}(\{\sigma \mid p^\sigma = d\}) \tag{1}$$

$$\text{match-pattern-db}(p, db) = \text{Rep}(\bigcup_{d \in db} \{\sigma \mid p^\sigma = d\}) \tag{2}$$

and

$$\text{match-conj}(\textit{patterns}, db) = \text{Rep}(\bigcap_{p \in \text{patterns}} \bigcup_{d \in db} \{\sigma \mid p^\sigma = d\}). \tag{3}$$

A key idea behind this derivation is the explicit representations of sets of substitutions for the conjunctive match problem that arises from matching all the patterns in a rule and for the disjunctive match problem that arises from matching a pattern against all the terms in a database.

It is important to note that the sets of substitutions in equations 1 through 3 are unbounded sets, which can be seen from the fact that if a substitution σ is in one of these sets, then any substitution τ that is an extension of σ—that is, any τ that agrees with σ on all the variables on which σ is defined and is also defined on some additional variables—is also in the set. For example, if $\sigma = \{x \mapsto 1\}$ is in one of these sets of substitutions, then $\tau = \{x \mapsto 1, y \mapsto 2\}$ is also in the set. The unbounded nature of these sets is necessary for the set representing a conjunctive match of two patterns p and q to be equal to the intersection of the sets representing the matches to p and to q .

These infinite sets of substitutions cannot directly be stored in an implementation. What is needed to implement this scheme is a finite representation that captures the information in these sets. Furthermore, the combining operations in the representation should be homomorphic to the set-combining operations in equation 3. This situation allows moving the representation function in equation 3 past the union and intersection, thereby allowing the use of the match function as specified in equation 1. The remainder of this section presents the derivation of such a representation.

One natural representation arises from representing a set of mappings by the substitution that represents the intersection of the mappings. For example, the set of all mappings that map x to 1 would be represented by the mapping $\{x \mapsto 1\}$; that is, $\mathrm{Rep}(\{\sigma \mid x^\sigma = 1\}) = \{x \mapsto 1\}$.

To formalize this representation, the set E can be ordered so that a substitution τ is $\prec$ a substitution σ if and only if τ is an extension of σ,

$$\tau \preceq \sigma \leftrightarrow \forall_{x \in V} (x^\tau = x^\sigma \text{ or } x^\sigma = \omega) \tag{4}$$

(where ω denotes undefined), and a set of substitutions can be represented by its greatest element under this ordering. This ordering is based on considering the substitutions as mappings. Alternatively, this ordering could be expressed in terms of the operation of the substitutions in instantiating patterns. This alternative definition for the ordering is given by

$$\sigma \preceq \tau \leftrightarrow \forall_p \forall_d (p^\tau = d \rightarrow p^\sigma = d).$$

The structure consisting of the set of substitutions E with the ordering given in equation 4 forms a *semilattice,* which will be referred to as the substitution semilattice (SSL) (figure 4). Details on lattice theory can be found in Bell and Machover (1977) and Curry (1977). Briefly, a *poset* (partially ordered set) is a set with a reflexive, antisymmetric, and transitive binary relation $\leq$ defined on the elements of the set; a semilattice is a poset with a greatest lower bound binary operation $\wedge$ defined on the elements of the set; and a *lattice* is a poset with both the greatest lower bound $\wedge$ and a least upper bound $\vee$ defined on the elements of the set. Note that this derivation involves two structures: a semilattice and a lattice. The ordering in the semilattice, SSL, is denoted by $\sigma \preceq \tau$, and the greatest lower bound in this semilattice is denoted by $\wedge_1$. The ordering in the lattice, DSL (introduced later), is denoted by $\Upsilon < \Phi$, and the greatest lower bound and least upper bound in the lattice are denoted by $\wedge$ and $\vee$.

The greatest lower bound of two elements in SSL represents the consistent combination of the two substitutions; that is, it is an extension of both of the substitutions and, therefore, contains all the variable bindings of both substitutions, as long as the two substitutions do not disagree on any variable on which they are both defined. If there is a disagreement, the result of the greatest lower bound is the bottom element ($\perp$). This greatest lower bound can be expressed as

$$\sigma \wedge_1 \tau = \begin{cases} \lambda x \ (\text{if } x^\sigma = \omega \text{ then } x^\tau \text{ else } x^\sigma) & \text{if } \sigma \cong \tau \\ \perp & \text{otherwise} \end{cases}$$

where the symbol $\cong$ denotes weak equality: $\sigma \cong \tau \leftrightarrow \forall_x (x^\sigma = x^\tau \text{ or } x^\sigma = \omega \text{ or } x^\tau = \omega)$. A bottom element $\perp$, defined such that $\forall_{\sigma \in E} \ \sigma \wedge_1 \perp = \perp$ and $\forall_{\sigma \in E} \perp \preceq \sigma$, can be added to SSL to represent the result of combining two inconsistent substitutions (that is, two substitutions that disagree on the binding of a variable).

Unfortunately, this representation does not accommodate all the sets of substitutions that are of interest. For example, the set of substitutions that represents all the matches between the pattern (p x) and the database {(p 1), (p 2)}, is given by $\{\sigma \mid x^\sigma = 1 \text{ or } x^\sigma = 2\}$. This set does not have a greatest element, and therefore it does not have a representation in this semilattice.

The representation can be modified to accommodate disjunctive substitutions such as these. Instead of representing a set of substitutions S by a single greatest element, it can be represented by a set of maximal elements:

$$\text{Rep}_2(S) = \{\sigma \in S \mid \neg \exists_{\tau \in S} \ \sigma \prec \tau\}.$$

Note that for every element σ in S , there is some element τ in $\text{Rep}_2(S)$, such that $\sigma \preceq \tau$. The capital Greek letters Υ, Φ , Ψ, and Γ are used to denote sets of maximal elements in E .

These sets of maximal elements can be ordered by the following extension to the ordering previously used. Let a set of substitutions Υ be less than ($\leq$) a set of substitutions Φ if and only if every substitution in Υ is less than ($\preceq$) some substitution in Φ :

$$\Upsilon \leq \Phi \leftrightarrow \forall_{\sigma \in \Upsilon} \ \exists_{\tau \in \Phi} \ \sigma \preceq \tau. \tag{5}$$

The result of this set and ordering is a new lattice, which will be referred to as the disjunctive substitution lattice (DSL) (figure 5). The ordering given in equation 5 can also be expressed, as done for $\preceq$, in terms of the operation of the substitutions in instantiating patterns. This alternative definition is given by

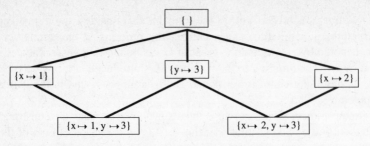

Figure 4. Illustration of the Ordering on Substitutions.

$\Upsilon \leq \Phi \leftrightarrow \forall_p \, \forall_d \, [(\exists_{\sigma \in \Upsilon} \, p^\sigma = d) \rightarrow (\exists_{\tau \in \Phi} \, p^\tau = d)].$

Whereas the SSL structure is a semilattice, this DSL structure is a lattice, with both a greatest lower bound and a least upper bound. These operations are given by

$$\Upsilon \vee \Phi = \Upsilon \cup \Phi \qquad\qquad (6)$$

and

$$\Upsilon \wedge \Phi = \{\sigma \mid \exists_{\tau \in \Upsilon} \, \exists_{\upsilon \in \Phi} \, \sigma = \tau \wedge_1 \upsilon\}.$$

Actually, equation 6 is a slight oversimplification. In cases where

$$\exists_{\sigma \in \Upsilon} \, \exists_{\tau \in \Phi} \, [(\sigma \prec \tau) \text{ or } (\tau \prec \sigma)] \,,$$

the value of $\Upsilon \vee \Phi$ can be simplified using identities. For example,

$$\{\{x \mapsto 1\}\} \vee \{\{x \mapsto 1, y \mapsto 2\}\} = \{\{x \mapsto 1\}\} \,.$$

These cases do not arise in this derivation, because $\vee$ is always applied to sets of substitutions that represent alternative matches for the same pattern. Consequently, these substitutions have the same domains, and their least upper bounds cannot be reduced using identities. In these cases, equation 6 holds. Let DS be the subset of 2^E that contains all disjunctive substitutions where all the substitutions in the disjunct have the same domain:

$$DS = \{S \mid S \in 2^E \, \& \, \forall_{\sigma \in S} \, \forall_{\tau \in S} \, \text{domain}(\sigma) = \text{domain}(\tau)\} \,.$$

All the disjunctive substitutions that arise in the programs in this chapter are contained in DS.

This new representation fits the desiderata mentioned at the beginning of this section because Rep_2 is a lattice homomorphism from the lattice $<2^E, \subseteq, \, \cup, \cap>$ to the lattice $<DS, \leq, \vee, \wedge>$, and therefore,

$$\text{Rep}_2(S_1 \cup S_2) = \text{Rep}_2(S_1) \vee \text{Rep}_2(S_2) \qquad\qquad (7)$$

$$\text{Rep}_2(S_1 \cap S_2) = \text{Rep}_2(S_1) \wedge \text{Rep}_2(S_2) \qquad\qquad (8)$$

(Any powerset, such as 2^E, forms a lattice under the subset relation.)

Finally, with this homomorphism, an algorithm for the specification in equation 2 can be derived:

$$\text{match-conj}(\textit{patterns}, \textit{db}) \quad = \text{Rep}_2(\bigcap_{p \in \text{patterns}} \bigcup_{d \in db} \{\sigma \,|\, p^\sigma = d\})$$

$$= \bigwedge_{p \in \text{patterns}} \bigvee_{d \in db} \text{Rep}_2(\{\sigma \,|\, p^\sigma = d\})$$

$$= \bigwedge_{p \in \text{patterns}} \bigvee_{d \in db} \text{match}(p, d) \,.$$

To implement this derivation, transformations can be constructed using equations 1, 7, and 8. Also, some transformations are needed to convert between quantified set formers and set operations. Some of these transformations are shown in figure 6. The format used for presenting transformations is a slightly simplified version of the REFINE format. In this format, symbols prefaced with @ signs are variables, and double arrows (– –>) denote transformations. Of these transformations, T1 to T3 are applicable to any code, but T4 and T5 are specific for this representation. (The reduce function combines all the elements in a sequence using a binary operation. In this chapter, as in REFINE , the map and reduce functions can be applied to sets as well as sequences. Also, the map, reduce, and scan functions are extended to operate on any number of sequences.) The resulting code, including the code derived from the lattice definitions, is shown in figure 7. For typographical purposes, ssl-meet, dsl-meet, and dsl-join are used as synonyms for $\wedge_1$, $\wedge$, and $\vee$. The code for the rule-system procedure can be directly taken from the specification in figure 1. Code for match and instantiate is shown in figure 8. For this derivation, the code for match and instantiate was coded by hand. Details for automatically deriving simple single-pattern–single-datum matching functions can be found in the references cited in Rete Derivation Overview.

Optimization

The major source of efficiency in the Rete matcher is its incremental update of the conflict set as the database is modified. This incremental updating can be obtained by finding the finite difference of the computation of the conflict set with respect to additions to the database. This finite differencing can be achieved by using distributive laws to distribute the computation of the conflict set over the update of the database, which consists of the union of the old database and the new data. The general plan for implementing this optimization is to reorganize the computation of the conflict set to save all the intermediate results and then use these intermediate results in computing the new value of the conflict set that arises from modifying the database. This section presents the details of this optimization.

The main step in this optimization is the finite differencing of the computation of the conflict set. Surrounding this main step are several preparatory and cleanup steps. The initial preparatory steps are performed to make the intermediate results of the match computations available for finite differencing.

First, the rule-system function is converted into a recursive form for ease

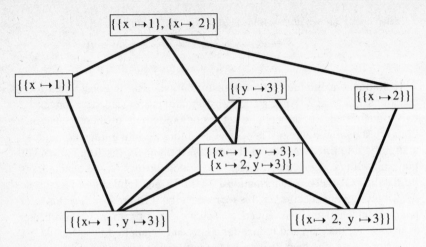

Figure 5. Illustration of the Ordering on Disjunctive Substitution.

```
T1: { @expr | ∀ (y) (y ∈ @S => @formula) } -->
    unary-intersection({ {@expr | (@formula)} | (y) y ∈ @S })

T2: { @expr | (y) y ∈ @S } --> map(λ (y) @expr, @S)

T3: unary-intersection(@S) --> reduce('∩,@S)

T4: Rep(@S1 ∩ @S2) --> DSL-Join(Rep(@S1),Rep(@S2))

T5: Rep({@e | (@e) instantiate(@p,@e)=@d}) --> Match(@p,@d)
```

Figure 6. Some Transformations Used in the Initial Implementation.

of manipulation. In general, functional programs, because of their simpler structure, are easier to manipulate than imperative programs. Next, the match-conj function is folded (Burstall and Darlington 1977) into the rule-system function to make the intermediate computations within match-conj available for manipulation (figure 9).

At this point, to simplify the presentation, the rule system is simplified to deal with a single rule, as shown in figure 10. (This simplified rule-system function is named rule-system-s.) Code for the full many-rule system appears at the end of this section.

Next, the outer reduce computation is replaced by a scan computation to save the intermediate results from each pattern. (See transformation T6 in figure 13.) The scan function, also know as the prefix function, is similar to reduce except that it builds a list of intermediate values. For example, for the sequences w, x, y, and z and the function f, $z = \text{scan}(f,w,x,y)$ implies that $z_0 = w_0$ and that $z_i = f(z_{i-1},w_i,x_i,y_i)$ for $i > 0$. The function last-elt selects the

```
function match-conj(patterns, db) =
  reduce('dsl-meet,
         map(λ (p) reduce('dsl-join
                           map(λ (d) match(p,d),
                               db)),
             patterns)

function dsl-meet(ds1,ds2) =
  { s | s1 ∈ ds1 & s2 ∈ ds2 &
        s = ssl-meet(s1, s2) & defined?(s) }

function dsl-join(ds1,ds2) =
  ds1 ∪ ds2

function ssl-meet(s1,s2) =
  let dom = domain(s1) ∪ domain(s2)
    if ∃ (x) (x ∈ dom & d1 = s1(x) & d2 = s2(x)
                & defined?(d1) & defined?(d2)
                & d1 ≠ d2)
    then undefined
    else { x ↦ if defined?(s1(x)) then s1(x) else s2(x)
             | x ∈ dom }
```

Figure 7. Initial Implementation of Match-Conj and Related Functions.

```
function match(p,d) =
  if constant?(p)
     then if p=d
          then { ∅ }
          else ∅
     else if variable?(p)
          then {{p ↦ d}}
          else if constant?(d)
               then ∅
               else dsl-meet(match(first(p), first(d)),
                             match(rest(p), rest(d)))

function instantiate (p,s) =
  if constant?(p)
     then p
     else if variable?(p)
          then if defined?(s(p))
               then s(p) else p
          else cons(instantiate(first(p),s),
                    instantiate(rest(p),s))
```

Figure 8. The Match and Instantiate Functions.

```
function rule-system (rb, db) =
  let cs = { <r,s> | r ∈ rb &
              s ∈ reduce('DSL-Meet,
                          map(λ (p) reduce('DSL-Join,
                                            map(λ (d) match(p,d),
                                                db)),
                              lhs(r))) }
    if cs = ∅ then db
    else let cs-elt = conflict-resolution(cs,db)
          if cs-elt = ∅ then db
          else let r = cs-elt.1, s = cs-elt.2
                let delta = { instantiate(rhs(r),s) }
                  rule-system(rb,db ∪ delta)
```

Figure 9. Result of Folding Match-Conj into the Recursive Version of Rule-System.

```
function rule-system-s (rule, db) =
  let cs = { <rule,s> |
              s ∈ reduce('DSL-Meet,
                          map(λ (p) reduce('DSL-Join,
                                            map(λ (d) match(p,d),
                                                db)),
                              lhs(rule))) }
    if cs = ∅ then db
    else let cs-elt = conflict-resolution(cs,db)
          if cs-elt = ∅ then db
          else let r = cs-elt.1, s = cs-elt.2
                let delta = { instantiate(rhs(r),s) }
                  rule-system-s(rule,db ∪ delta)
```

Figure 10. Simplified Version of Rule-System for a Single Rule.

```
function rule-system-s (rule, db) =
  let R = map(λ (p) reduce('DSL-Join,map(λ (d) match(p,d),
                                          db)),
              lhs(rule))
    let L = scan('DSL-Meet, R)
      let cs = map(λ (s) <rule,s>, last-elt(L))
        if cs = ∅ then db
        else let cs-elt = conflict-resolution(cs,db)
              if cs-elt = ∅ then db
              else let r = cs-elt.1, s = cs-elt.2
                    let delta = { instantiate(rhs(r),s) }
                      rule-system-s(rule,db ∪ delta)
```

Figure 11. Result of Transforming Reduce into Scan and Folding R and L.

last element of a sequence. Two variables, R and L (corresponding to the right and left memory values in the Rete network), are introduced to hold the intermediate results both before and after the scan with DSL-Meet (figure 11).

As a final preparation for finite differencing, the recursive call inside rule-system is unfolded once, as shown in figure 12. This step makes the values of R, L, CS, and delta computed during one matching cycle (in the upper set of computations in figure 12) available for use in computing the corresponding values during the next matching cycle (in the lower set of computations in figure 12).

At this point, the distributive laws for DSL-Meet and DSL-Join are applied in order to finite difference the computation of R, L, and CS in the unfolded recursive call. Because the sequences L and R and the set CS grow monotonically (the only changes made to them involve adding elements), the new values for these variables can be computed by computing the additions to be made—which are called the deltas—and adding these additions to the old values. The bases for the finite differencing are the associative law for $\vee$ and the distributive law for $\wedge$ over $\vee$:

$$V_{d \in db1 \cup db2}\ \{\sigma \mid p^\sigma = d\} = V_{d \in db1}\ \{\sigma \mid p^\sigma = d\} \vee V_{d \in db2}\ \{\sigma \mid p^\sigma = d\}$$
$$(\Upsilon \vee \Phi) \wedge (\Psi \vee \Gamma) = (\Upsilon \wedge \Psi) \vee (\Upsilon \wedge \Gamma) \vee (\Phi \wedge \Psi) \vee (\Phi \wedge \Gamma) .$$

These laws can be used to compute the following finite-difference equations:

$$R1_i = V_{d \in db \cup delta}\ \{\sigma \mid p^\sigma = d\} \tag{9}$$

$$= V_{d \in db}\{\sigma \mid p^\sigma = d\} \vee V_{d \in delta}\ \{\sigma \mid p^\sigma = d\}$$

$$= R_i \vee V_{d \in delta}\ \{\sigma \mid p^\sigma = d\}$$

$$L1_i = L1_{i-1} \wedge R1_i\ (\text{for } i \geq 2)$$

$$= (L_{i-1} \cup Ldelta_{i-1}) \wedge (R_i \cup Rdelta_i) \tag{10}$$

$$= (L_{i-1} \wedge R_i) \cup (Ldelta_{i-1} \wedge R_i) \cup (L_{i-1} \wedge Rdelta_i) \cup (Ldelta_{i-1} \wedge Rdelta_i)$$

$$= L_i \cup (Ldelta_{i-1} \wedge R_i) \cup (L_{i-1} \wedge Rdelta_i) \cup (Ldelta_{i-1} \wedge Rdelta_i) .$$

From these equations, the values for R1 and L1 can be written in terms of the values of R and L and the updates to these values:

$$R_i\quad = V_{d \in db}\ \{\sigma \mid p^\sigma = d\}$$

$$Rdelta_i = V_{d \in delta}\ \{\sigma \mid p^\sigma = d\} \tag{11}$$

$$R1_i\quad = R_i \cup Rdelta_i \tag{12}$$

$$L_i\quad = L_{i-1} \wedge R_i$$

$$Ldelta_i = (Ldelta_{i-1} \wedge R_i) \cup (L_{i-1} \wedge Rdelta_i) \cup (Ldelta_{i-1} \wedge Rdelta_i) \tag{13}$$

$$L1_i\quad = L_i \cup Ldelta_i \tag{14}$$

Because only one element is added to the database at a time, delta is usually much smaller than db. Therefore, the computations in equations 11, 12, 13, and 14 are less expensive than the computations in equations 9 and 10

```
function rule-system-s (rule, db) =
  let R = map(λ (p) reduce('DSL-Join,map(λ (d) match(p,d),
                                                 db)),
            lhs(rule))
    let L = scan('DSL-Meet, R)
      let cs = map(λ (s) <rule,s>, last-elt(L))
        if cs = ∅ then db
        else let cs-elt = conflict-resolution(cs,db)
                if cs-elt = ∅ then db
                else let r = cs-elt.1, s = cs-elt.2
                        let delta = { instantiate(rhs(r),s) }
                          block rule-system-s1
                          let R1 = map(λ (p)
                                          reduce('DSL-Join,
                                                 map(λ (d) match(p,d),
                                                         db ∪ delta)),
                                      lhs(rule))
                            let L1 = scan('DSL-Meet, R1)
                              let cs1 = map(λ (s) <rule,s>, last-elt(L1))
                                if cs1 = ∅ then db ∪ delta
                                else
                                  let cs-elt1 = conflict-resolution(cs1,
                                                            db∪delta)
                                  if cs-elt1 = ∅ then db ∪ delta
                                  else let r1 = cs-elt.1, s1 = cs-elt.2
                                          let delta1 = { instantiate(rhs(r1),s1) }
                                            rule-system-s(rule,(db ∪ delta)
                                                            ∪ delta1)
```

Figure 12. Result of Unfolding the Recursive Call in the Simplified Rule-System.

because fewer pattern matches and combining operations are required.

Some of the transformations used to perform this optimization are shown in figure 13, and the relevant fragment of the resulting code is shown in figure 14. Of these transformations, T6 to T9 are valid for any code, whereas T10 is only valid if the function being scanned distributes over union; that is, if $f(w \cup x, y \cup z) = f(w, y) \cup f(w, z) \cup f(x, y) \cup f(x, z)$.

Finally, the nested computation is unfolded into a procedure, and the recursive call is modified to use this procedure and pass the appropriate values. This procedure completes the optimization steps for the simplified single-rule rule system. For the many-rule case, the values of R and L have to be converted into sequences that hold the appropriate values for all the rules. Actual Lisp code for this final program is shown in figure 15.

Correspondence to Rete

The correspondence between the implementation previously derived and the Rete network is illustrated in figure 3. The correspondence can be seen by identifying the L_i and R_i values in the programs with the contents of the left and right input memories of the combine nodes in the Rete network.

A goal of this derivation is to capture the operations that comprise the Rete algorithm using mathematical operations. The match function models the operation of the match nodes in the Rete algorithm. It takes a pattern and a datum as arguments and returns substitutions (elements of SSL) that are analogous to the substitution tokens generated by the match nodes in Rete. The operation of the combine nodes in Rete is modeled by the meet operation in SSL, which computes the consistent combination of two substitutions in SSL. DSL captures operations on whole sets of substitutions. An object in DSL can represent the contents of a left or right memory in a Rete node, and the meet operation in DSL can model the operation of a combine node over a period of time by computing all consistent combinations of all the substitutions in the input memories.

Correspondence to Model Theory

The original model for rule-based systems is the paradigm of deductive inference. This section discusses the correspondence between the algorithm derived in Algorithm Derivation and the model-theoretic semantics of first-order logic. This direct relationship between the domain structures and the implementation structures yields many advantages. It provides for the explanation and verification of the features implemented so far and provides directions for implementing extensions. This section briefly reviews the model-theoretic semantics of first-order logic and discusses the correspondence of the semantic model to the representation and algorithm previously derived. A discussion of semantics can be found in texts on logic and model theory, for example, Bell and Machover (1977).

Consider a first-order language L consisting of variable symbols, function symbols (consider constants to be 0-ary functions), and predicate symbols. Consider a model for this language, called a *structure*, consisting of a universe U, and a mapping from each n-ary function symbol in L to an n-ary operation on U and from each n-ary predicate symbol in L to an n-ary relation on U.

A *valuation* σ is a structure together with an assignment of a value $x^\sigma \in U$ to each variable x. Given a valuation σ, a value can be assigned to any term in L using the following rules:

1. $(f(t_1, \ldots, t_n))^\sigma = f^\sigma(t_1^\sigma, \ldots, t_n^\sigma)$.
2. $(P(t_1, \ldots, t_n))^\sigma = \top$ if $< t_1^\sigma, \ldots, t_n^\sigma > \in P^\sigma$, $\perp$ otherwise
3. $(\alpha \wedge \beta)^\sigma = \top$ if $\alpha^\sigma = \top$ and $\beta^\sigma = \top$, $\perp$ otherwise.
4. $(\alpha \vee \beta)^\sigma = \top$ if $\alpha^\sigma = \top$ or $\beta^\sigma = \top$, $\perp$ otherwise.
5. $(\neg\alpha)^\sigma = \top$ if $\alpha^\sigma = \perp$, $\perp$ otherwise.
6. $(\alpha \to \beta)^\sigma = \top$ if $\alpha^\sigma = \perp$ or $\beta^\sigma = \top$, $\perp$ otherwise.

This definition is known as Tarski's truth definition and forms the basis of the model-theoretic semantics of first-order logic.

To apply this model to a rule system, consider LHS of a rule as a term in a language and the database as a structure. A rule can be run if its LHS is true in the database, that is, if a valuation σ exists such that $LHS^\sigma = \top$ (where $\top$ denotes truth). From the Tarski definition, a conjunct in LHS of a rule is true under a valuation σ if all of its clauses are true under σ. That is, the problem

```
T6: reduce(f,S) --> last-elt(scan(f,S))

T7: map(f,a ∪ b) --> map(f,a) ∪ map(f,b)

T8: reduce(f,a ∪ b) --> f(reduce(f,a),reduce(f,b))

T9: map(λ (x) f(g(x),h(x)), S) --> map(f,map(g,S),map(h,S))

T10: scan(f,map('∪,S,T)) -->
     map('∪,scan(f,S),
         scan(λ (fts-fs,t,fs,s) f(t,fs) ∪ f(s,fts-fs) ∪ f(t,fts-fs),
              T, cons(NIL,(scan(f,S))), S))
```

Figure 13. Transformations to Finite-Difference R1, L1, *and* CS1.

```
function rule-system-s (rule, db) =
  ...
  block rule-system-s1
   let Rdelta = map(λ (p)
                      reduce('DSL-Join,
                             map(λ (d) match(p,d), delta)),
                    lhs(rule))
    let R1 = map('∪,R,Rdelta)
    let Ldelta = scan(λ (Ldelta,Rdelta,L,R)
                        DSL-Meet(Rdelta,L) ∪
                        DSL-Meet(R,Ldelta) ∪
                        DSL-Meet(Rdelta,Ldelta),
                      Rdelta, cons(NIL,L), R)
     let L1 = map('∪,L,Ldelta)
      let csdelta = map(λ (s) <rule,s>, last-elt(Ldelta))
      let cs1 = cs ∪ csdelta
   ...
```

Figure 14. Result of Finite-Difference R1, L1, *and* CS1.

of finding all matches for a rule in a database can be seen as the problem of finding all possible assignments to the variables in a conjunctive term under which the term is true in a given universe.

With the rule system interpreted this way, the following interpretations can be given to the structures used in the derivation: The semilattice SSL consists of valuations, $\preceq$ is an ordering on valuations, and $\wedge_1$ is a binary operation on valuations; the lattice DSL consists of sets of valuations, $\leq$ is an ordering on sets of valuations, and $\wedge$ and $\vee$ are binary operations on sets of valuations; and the procedure match-rule takes a LHS, and a universe *db* and returns the maximal valuation under $\preceq$ from the set $\{\sigma \mid LHS^\sigma = \top\}$.

This correspondence provides a clear semantics for the Rete algorithm in terms of the usual model-theoretic semantics of first-order logic. This correspondence also provides directions for implementing one of the extensions outlined in Simplifications. For example, the facility for handling negated patterns in LHS of a rule can be obtained by directly implementing the interpretation for negation in the semantic definition previously shown. The direct implementation of this specification consists in matching a negated pattern $\neg P(t_1, \ldots, t_n)$ (which represents a negated predication) if and only if a valuation does not exist

```
(DEFUN RULE-SYSTEM (RB DB)
  (LET ((R (MAPCAR #'(LAMBDA (RULE)
                       (MAPCAR #'(LAMBDA (P)
                                   (REDUCE #'DSL-JOIN
                                           (MAPCAR #'(LAMBDA (D)
                                                       (MATCH P D))
                                                   DB)))
                                 (LHS RULE)))
                     RB)))
    (LET ((L (MAPCAR #'(LAMBDA (R) (SCAN #'DSL-MEET R))
                     R)))
      (LET ((CS (MAPCAN #'(LAMBDA (RULE L-ELT)
                            (MAPCAR #'(LAMBDA (S) (CONS RULE S))
                                    (LAST-ELT L-ELT)))
                        RB L)))
        (LET ((CS-ELT (CONFLICT-RESOLUTION CS DB)))
          (IF (NULL CS-ELT)
              DB
              (LET ((DELTA (LIST (INSTANTIATE (RHS (CAR CS-ELT))
                                              (CDR CS-ELT)))))
                (RULE-SYSTEM1 RB (UNION DB DELTA) R L CS DELTA))))))))

(DEFUN RULE-SYSTEM1 (RB DB R L CS DELTA)
  (LET ((RDELTA (MAPCAR #'(LAMBDA (RULE)
                            (MAPCAR #'(LAMBDA (P)
                                        (REDUCE #'DSL-JOIN
                                                (MAPCAR #'(LAMBDA (D)
                                                            (MATCH P D))
                                                        DELTA)))
                                      (LHS RULE)))
                        RB)))
    (LET ((R1 (MAPCAR #'(LAMBDA (R RDELTA)
                          (MAPCAR #'UNION R RDELTA))
                      R RDELTA)))
      (LET ((LDELTA (MAPCAR #'(LAMBDA (L R RDELTA)
                                (SCAN #'(LAMBDA (YD XD Y X)
                                          (UNION (DSL-MEET Y XD)
                                                 (UNION (DSL-MEET YD X)
                                                        (DSL-MEET YD XD))))
                                      RDELTA (CONS NIL L) R))
                            L R RDELTA)))
        (LET ((L1 (MAPCAR #'(LAMBDA (LDELTA L)
                              (MAPCAR #'UNION LDELTA L))
                          LDELTA L)))
          (LET ((CSDELTA (MAPCAN #'(LAMBDA (RULE LDELTA-ELT)
                                     (MAPCAR #'(LAMBDA (SUBST)
                                                 (CONS RULE SUBST))
                                             (LAST-ELT LDELTA-ELT)))
                                 RB LDELTA)))
            (LET ((CS1 (UNION CS CSDELTA)))
              (LET ((CS-ELT1 (CONFLICT-RESOLUTION CS1 DB)))
                (IF (NULL CS-ELT1)
                    DB
                    (LET ((DELTA1 (LIST (INSTANTIATE (RHS (CAR CS-ELT1))
                                                     (CDR CS-ELT1)))))
                      (RULE-SYSTEM1 RB (UNION DB DELTA1) R1 L1 CS1 DELTA1)))))))))))
```

Figure 15. Final Rule-System Code.

under which the pattern $P(t_1, \ldots, t_n)$ is true, that is, if a binding does not exist to the variables in $P(t_1, \ldots, t_n)$ under which $P(t_1, \ldots, t_n)$ matches an element in the database. This implementation corresponds to the closed-world assumption described in Reiter (1978).

Conclusions

The goal of this chapter was to analyze the rule system matching problem and derive an efficient algorithm for it. Mathematical structures were used to provide semantics for the data manipulated in the computation, and the data representations were designed by considering these mathematical structures. A finite-differencing program optimization was implemented by distributing the match computation over the updates to the database.

The substitutions manipulated in this algorithm are similar to the valuation structures used in the model-theoretic semantics of first-order logic. This connection to model theory provides direction for extending the algorithm to handle negation. It also suggests that a Rete-like algorithm could directly be derived from the semantics of first-order logic and optimized using general-purpose techniques such as finite differencing and partial evaluation.

The techniques used in this derivation—(1) formalizing a problem in terms of (possibly unbounded) sets and mappings, (2) implementing the specification by constructing an implementation of objects and operations homomorphic to the sets and mapping in the specification, and (3) optimizing this initial algorithm using techniques such as finite differencing—might be applicable to other algorithm design problems.

The development of algebraic techniques for software design might allow programmers to once again move to a higher level of abstraction (analogous to the move from assembler language to higher-level languages), with the concomitant benefits of greater programmer efficiency and improved program correctness.

Acknowledgments

I would like to thank Charles Rich, my master's thesis adviser, for his support and patience; Reid Smith for support during my visits to Schlumberger Palo Alto Research; Doug Smith and Cordell Green for support during my visit to Kestrel Institute; Lee Blaine, Peter Ladkin, Tom Pressburger, Jeff Siskind, and Doug Smith for many fruitful discussions about this work; and Joyce Nachimson for her encouragement. This chapter was improved by comments from Wes Braudaway, Maritta Heisel, Michael Lowry, Robert Mc-Cartney, Wolfgang Reif, Werner Stephan, and Andreas Wolpers.

References

Aho, A. V.; Hopcroft, J. E.; and Ullman, J. D. 1974. *The Design and Analysis of Computer Algorithms*. Reading, Mass: Addison-Wesley.

Backus, J. 1978. Can Programming Be Liberated from the von Neumann Style? A Functional Style and Its Algebra of Programs. *Communications of the ACM* 21:613–641.

Bell, D., and Machover, M. 1977. *A Course in Mathematical Logic*. Amsterdam: North Holland.

Bird, R. S. 1987. An Introduction to the Theory of Lists. In *Logic of Programming and Calculi of Discrete Design*, ed. Manfred Broy, 5–42. NATO Advanced Science Institutes Series, series F, number 36. Berlin: Springer-Verlag.

Brownston, L.; Farrell, R.; Kant, E.; and Martin, N. 1985. *Programming Expert Systems in OPS5.* Reading, Mass.: Addison-Wesley.

Burstall, R. M., and Darlington, J. 1977. A Transformation System for Developing Recursive Programs. *Journal of the ACM* 24:44–67.

Curry, H. 1977. *Foundations of Mathematical Logic.* New York: Dover.

de Kleer, J.; Doyle, J.; Rich, C.; Steele, G. L., Jr.; and Sussman, G. J. 1978. AMORD: A Deductive Procedure System, Memo, 435, Artificial Intelligence Laboratory, Massachusetts Institute of Technology.

Eder, E. 1985. Properties of Substitutions and Unifications. *Journal of Symbolic Computation* 1:31–46.

Forgy, C. 1982. Rete: A Fast Algorithm for the Many Pattern–Many Object Pattern Match Problem. *Artificial Intelligence* 19:17–37.

Liskov, B., and Guttag, J. 1986. *Abstraction and Specification in Program Development.* Cambridge, Mass.: MIT Press.

Manna, Z., and Waldinger, R. 1981. Deductive Synthesis of the Unification Algorithm. *Science of Computer Programming* 1:5–48.

Meertens, L. G. L. T. 1987. An Abstracto Reader Prepared for IFIP WG 2.1, CS-N8702, Center for Mathematics and Computer Science, Amsterdam.

Paige, R., and Koenig, S. 1982. Finite Differencing of Computable Expression. *ACM Transactions on Programming Languages and Systems* 4:402–454.

Reiter, R. 1978. On Closed-World Data Bases. In *Logic and Data Bases,* eds. H. Gallaire and J. Minker, 55–76. New York: Plenum.

Robinson, J. A. 1987. Notes on Logic Programming. In *Logic of Programming and Calculi of Discrete Design,* ed. Manfred Broy, 109–144. NATO Advanced Science Institutes Series, series F, number 36. Berlin: Springer-Verlag.

Rydeheard, D. E., and Burstall, R. M. 1986. A Categorical Unification Algorithm. In *Category Theory and Computer Programming,* eds. D. Pitt, S. Abramsky, A. Poigné, and D. Rydeheard, 493–505. Lecture Notes in Computer Science, volume 240. Berlin: Springer-Verlag.

Smith, D. R. 1982. Derived Preconditions and Their Use in Program Synthesis. In *Sixth Conference on Automated Deduction,* ed. D. W. Loveland, 172–193. Lecture Notes in Computer Science, volume 138. Berlin: Springer-Verlag.

Smith, D. E., and Genesereth, M. R. 1985. Ordering Conjunctive Queries. *Artificial Intelligence* 26:171–215.

Wertheimer, J. M. 1989. Derivation of an Efficient Rule System Pattern Matcher, Technical Report, 1109, Artificial Intelligence Laboratory, Massachusetts Institute of Technology

18

Design Principles for an Interactive Program-Derivation System

Uday S. Reddy

Approaches to program derivation or design are usually classified as program synthesis techniques (Bibel 1980; Manna and Waldinger 1979; Smith 1985) or program-transformation techniques (Balzer, Goldman, and Wile 1976; Barstow 1979; Broy and Pepper 1981; Burstall and Darlington 1977; Scherlis 1981). Some researchers argue that program synthesis techniques are currently suitable for only small problems, whereas transformation techniques have the potential to scale up (Rich and Waters 1986; Introduction). The reason for this argument seems to be in the deduction methods used with the two techniques: Synthesis is usually based on inference, whereas transformation is usually based on replacement.[1] *Inference* means the axioms and rules supplied to the program-derivation system are expressed as implications, and the logical operations of the system derive either necessary conclusions of premises (forward reasoning) or sufficient antecedents of goals (backward reasoning). In contrast, *replacement* means that the axioms supplied to the system are expressed as equations or rewrite rules, and the logical operations replace expressions by other equivalent expressions. Equational reasoning is not always adequate (for example, to derive the kind of algorithms derived in Smith [1985]), but inferential reasoning suffers from large search spaces. For example, consider an axiom such as $(x = y) \Rightarrow (x \geq y)$. A forward-reasoning system that replaces $x = y$ with $x \geq y$ is losing a lot of information. Similarly, a backward-reasoning system that tries to achieve x ≥ y by trying to achieve $x = y$ is giving itself a hard problem. Simply too many antecedents imply a given goal and too many conclusions might be drawn from a given premise. In contrast, a deduction system that works by replacement can only replace $x \geq y$ by another formula with the same amount of information, for example, $(x = y) \vee (x > y)$. Usually, there are not very many such formulas. Some of the recent research in theorem proving recognizes the usefulness of replacement with respect to the search space problems (Bibel 1987; Brown 1986; Hsiang 1982; Murray and Rosenthal 1988; Potter and Plaisted 1988; Zhang and Kapur 1988).

Search space is one of the main criteria determining the effectiveness of automated program-derivation systems. Imagine that we present a specification to an automated system, and it returns 20 different programs, most of which are unreasonable. Perhaps, it is not worth the trouble examining all the output programs and choosing one as opposed to writing one by hand. There are a variety of solutions to the search space problem. One solution is to tell the system about the expected form of the output program. This information can be used by the system to guide itself through the search space and eliminate the unreasonable output programs that the search leads to. However, specifying output program schemes can be a large problem in itself. Feather (1982, p. 18) notes that the effort required for this specification seems to grow "faster than the scale of the programs." Another solution is to make the system interactive, so that the user can guide the system along the right path and choose among alternatives whenever choices arise. It should be simpler to make choices at the choice points rather than in the final programs because choices multiply when they are combined. The interactive paradigm also makes it possible to incorporate genuine program design; by *design*, I mean not only decision making but also invention or synthesis.

The design of an interactive system raises its own issues. First, the program-derivation procedures should be human oriented (unlike clausal resolution [Robinson 1965] or Knuth-Bendix completion [Knuth and Bendix 1970], for example). The user should be able to understand all the activities performed by the system to the extent that he/she can perform them on his(her) own. The system's behavior should be reasonably predictable without complex interactions. The system should also be able to explain itself when required. Most of all, the search spaces should be reasonably small so that the user is not swamped with numerous possibilities as a result of any operation.

Because the user and the system have to cooperate in performing derivations, many of the system's internals have to be opaque to the user. For example, what is the state of the program at a particular point in a derivation? What part of the specification is made defunct by prior derivation, and what part of it is still active? A system that interacts with the user only through a dialogue (like a conventional interactive programming system) is unsatisfactory in this respect. The state of the derivation is kept internally in such a system, and the user can only view parts of it by querying. It is also necessary to provide the user with a static, rather than a dynamic, picture of the program-derivation state. Thus, it is necessary to maintain a program derivation as a data object that is extended (rather than modified) as the derivation progresses. The derivation object should be visible to both the user and the system so that they can operate on it together by sharing responsibilities.

I outline here the design principles of an experimental program-derivation system called *Focus* that was built with these concerns in mind. Focus blurs the distinction between program synthesis and program transformation by using a uniform set of operations for both deriving programs from logical specifications and transforming programs into more efficient ones. However, the emphasis of automation is on logical, rather than heuristic, aspects of program design. In this sense, it is closer to program synthesis systems than transformation systems. Program derivations are represented in Focus as trees, and a tree editor called TREEMACS (Hammerslag, Kamin, and Campbell 1985; Hammerslag 1988) is used to manipulate them.[2] Focus appears to the user as an extension of TREEMACS by providing program-derivation operations in addition to its tree-editing operations. The nodes in a derivation tree contain either derivations of program components designed by the user or program properties proposed by the user. Some nodes also contain subgoal information, such as case analysis, generated by the system. Visibility rules govern the information accessible to a node. Each node looks at a different program-derivation state, even though the derivation tree is itself static. Each node draws information (in the form of rules) from the rest of the tree and contributes some information to it. The system keeps a record of these dependencies. The system also keeps a record of all the derivation activity performed within each node, which is meant to be used during modification of specifications and derivations. The details of derivation tree structure are discussed in Structure of Program Derivations.

The deduction techniques of Focus are primarily based on *term rewriting*, that is, equational logic with oriented equations. The orientation of equations is along the direction of improved performance. Thus, a rewrite rule $A \rightarrow B$ means that A is equal to B and also that A can be replaced by B to improve performance. Although the application of a rewrite rule always improves performance, it might do so at the cost of increased program size (perhaps infinitely). The form of rules also distinguishes this situation. Thus, each rule contains logical information, performance information, and program size information. The form of the rules and the logical operations that they are used with are described in Interactive Control of Program Transformation.

Although I am convinced of the need for inferential reasoning, I am not yet sure what form it should take. Some ideas on controlling search in such reasoning are already known (Smith 1985). I am also investigating deduction mechanisms for inferential reasoning that mimic some aspects of term rewriting, such as the use of pattern matching and finite termination (Bronsard and Reddy 1990b).

It is through the equations, rewrite rules, and oriented deduction techniques that the problems of search space are addressed. Equations, in general, involve fewer alternatives than implicative rules. Second, the oriented use of rules allows information to be propagated in a preferred direction. Because the orientation is based on well-founded orders, the system can blindly rewrite terms to normal forms with the guarantee of termination. Note that rewriting can still lead to multiple normal forms, which means that the search space is not completely eliminated. However, the overall approach based on rewriting generally leads to smaller search spaces than would be possible using implicative rules.

The rewrite rules previously mentioned do not contain any design information. The Focus system does not attempt to perform any design (creation of focuses). It merely helps in realizing the design decisions made by the user. In this sense, it is similar to the KIV system (chapter 21), but the logical operations implemented by Focus are of a much larger grain size.

For performing large derivations, it is also useful to compile and use libraries of tactical design rules that achieve desired program-derivation goals. For this purpose, my group is designing a tactical design system called Auto-Focus that acts as an automatic driver for Focus in carrying out standardized program design tasks. This two-tiered architecture allows the separation of logical and heuristic aspects of program design. I only discuss the Focus system in this chapter because AutoFocus is still in a preliminary design stage.

Overview of Focus

A specification supplied to Focus is written in the language of Focus. It usually consists of two sets of rules: definitions and properties. *Definition rules* define the function and predicate symbols used in the specification. *Property rules* state theorems (and occasionally axioms) that can be taken for granted during the program-derivation process. The types of function and predicate symbols are also declared using notations similar to those found in functional languages such as Standard ML (Milner 1984). In addition to types, functions and predicates can have additional preconditions under which they are well defined. The system checks that the specifications are well-formed under the stated preconditions. Libraries of such specifications can be built and loaded into other derivation structures.

The functional language subset of the Focus language includes Boolean connectives, if-then-else expressions, and a *let* construct. The latter is of the form *let* $t = e_1$ *in* e_2, where t is a constructor term , and e_1 and e_2 are expressions. (*Constructors* are uninterpreted function symbols introduced in type definitions). A *let* term of the above form is well defined if e_1 evaluates to a term that matches t. Its value is then the value of e_2 under the bindings obtained from the pattern match. Definitions expressed in the functional language subset can be translated into conventional functional languages.

Another important subset of the Focus language deals with definite descriptions. This subset was originally described in Reddy (1987), where it was called a *functional logic language*. It is also related to other notations for definite descriptions in mathematical logic (Pottinger 1988). The main construct in this subset is of the form *The* $e[x^*]$ *: p,* where e is an expression, x^* is a set of variables bound in the construct, and p is a Boolean formula. Its meaning is the unique value of e for all x^* satisfying p. If there is no such unique value of e, then the expression is not well defined. Definitions expressed using definite descriptions can be translated into logic programming languages such as Prolog but not into conventional functional languages. Other major subsets of the Focus language include a language of indefinite descriptions (which is useful if there are multiple solutions satisfying a formula) and a language of set comprehensions. Finally, the propositional subset supports quantifications *Exist* x^* *: p* and *All* $(x^* : p)$ q.

To illustrate the use of Focus, I consider two examples. The first one is well-suited for program transformation, that is, for replacement-based reasoning, whereas the second one requires inferential reasoning.

Figure 1 shows the specification of a simple lexical scanner that extracts a list of words from a list of characters. The specification is taken from Darlington (1976) and Feather (1979) with some modifications. The input to the scanner is a string (list) of characters, each character being an alphanumeric character or a space. The output of the scanner should be the list of words in the input, where a *word* is a consecutive sequence of alphanumeric characters bounded by spaces.

Note that the scan function is defined in terms of two auxiliary functions, *fword* and *rword*, that extract the first word and the remainder of the string after the first word respectively. Each of these functions traverses the initial part of the input string, which is clearly a duplication of work. The specification is presumably written in this form in the interest of modularity and ease of understanding. The program- transformation objective is to eliminate the repeated traversal of the string involved in *fword* and *rword*.

Proceeding somewhat naively, the user can consider unfolding the definitions of *fword* and *rword* in *scan,* realize that *scan* cannot be defined recursively, and postulate a new function scanword that generalizes the second clause (definition rule) of *scan*. The specification of this function looks like the following:

```
external
  type char
  function alpha : char → bool
        /* check if alphanumeric character */
definitions
  type list(t) = Nil + t.list(t)
  type word = list(char)
  function scan : list(char) → list(word)
  scan(Nil) → Nil
  scan(char.s) → fword(char.s).scan(rword(char.s))
  function fword : list(char) →word
        /* the first word */
  fword(Nil) → Nil
  fword(c.s) {alpha(c)} → c.fword(s)
  fword(' '.s) → Nil
  function rword : list(char) → list(char)
        /* the remainder of the word */
  rword(Nil) → Nil
  rword(c.s) {alpha(c)} → rword(s)
  rword(' '.s) → skip(s)
  function skip : list(char) → list(char)
        /* skip spaces */
  skip(Nil) → Nil
  skip(c.s) {alpha(c)} → c.s
  skip(' '.s) → skip(s)
```

Figure 1. Specification of Scan Function.

scanword(s) = fword(s).scan(rword(s)) .

This specification of *scanword* can be transformed to a recursive program and then utilized in redefining *scan*. This derivation yields the final program:

```
scan(Nil) → Nil
scan(char.s) → scanword(char.s)
scanword(Nil) → Nil. Nil
scanword(c.s) {alpha(c)} → let x1. x2 = scanword(s) in (c.x1).x2
scanword (' ' . s) → Nil.scan(skip(s))
```

Alternatively, the user might notice that this program ties up too much implicit stack space during the recursive processing of *scan* and postulate a different auxiliary function, such as

getword(s) = (fword(s), rword(s)) .

This function can also be transformed to a recursive program and utilized in redefining *scan* as follows:

scan(Nil) → Nil
scan(char.s) → let (x1,x2) = getword(char.s) in x1. scan(x2)
getword(Nil) → (Nil, Nil)
getword(c.s) {alpha(c)} → let (x1,x2) = getword(s) in (c.x1, x2)
getword(' '. s) → (Nil, skip(s))

Any number of other design options are possible. For example, it is possible to obtain a completely iterative (tail recursive) program by producing a reversed list of words. One can postulate the functions

scanloop1(s, word, words) = apnd(rev(scan(rword(s)),
                                   rev(apnd(rev(fword(s)), word).words)
scanloop2(s, words) = apnd(rev(scan(skip(s))), words)

and similarly transform them into iterative definitions and use them in redefining *scan*. To give a flavor of how such transformations are achieved using Focus, I show the derivation of the first alternative in figure 2.

The lines labeled by *focus* are the specifications entered by the user. The first focus indicates a desire to redefine the case *scan(char.s)*. The second focus gives the specification of the new function *scanword*. The user then invokes an operation called *expand* that splits the specification into cases. Each case is then automatically simplified and rewritten using the rules available to the system, and the desired program is obtained for *scanword*. The user then invokes a rewrite operation on the first focus. The right-hand side of the definition is rewritten to an application of *scanword,* thereby using the newly derived program of *scanword*. I return to this example after discussing the various program-manipulation operations of Focus and show how these results are obtained.

As a second example, the maximum of a list of integers can be specified as follows:

function max : *list(int)* → *int*
precondition max(l) : *l* ≠ *Nil*
max(l) = The z: z ∈ *l & All (e: e* ∈ *l) e* ≤ *z* .

The specification states that the maximum of l is the element z of l such that every element e of l is less than or equal to z. Note that the function is well defined only under the precondition $l \neq Nil$. This specification cannot be executed in a functional programming language. However, it can be translated to a logic programming language, such as Prolog (Clocksin and Mellish,1981), where it requires time quadratic in the length of the list. With Focus, the specification can be transformed to the following functional program that is linear in the length of the list:

max(h. Nil) → h
max(h,t) {t ≠ Nil} → let z = max(t) in if z ≤ h then h else z

The derivation of this program is discussed in Examples.

focus scan(char.s) = fword(char.s).scan(rword(char.s))
rewrites to: scan(char.s) = scanword(char.s)

focus scanword(s) = fword(s).scan(rword(s))
introduction rule: fword(s).scan(rword(s)) scanword(s)
derived rules: fword(s) $\to$ let x1.x2 = scanword(s) in x1
          scan(rword(s)) $\to$ let x1.x2 = scanword(s) in x2

cases from fword(s)
   1. scanword(Nil) = Nil.scan(rword(Nil))
   simplifies to: scanword(Nil) = Nil.Nil
   2. scanword(c.s) {alpha(c)} = (c.fword(s)).scan(rword(c.s))
   simplifies to: scanword(c.s) {alpha(c)} = (c.fword(s)).scan(rword(s))
   rewrites to: scanword(c.s) {alpha(c)} = let x1.x2 = scanword(s) in (c.x1).x2
   3. scanword(' '.s) = Nil.scan(rword(' '.s))
   simplifies to: scanword(' '.s) = Nil.scan(skip(s))

Figure 2. Derivation of a Program for scan(char.s)

Interactive Control of Program Transformation

Performance savings during program transformation come from three sources:
(1) performing computation steps (that are otherwise done at run time) at transformation time, (2) applying properties of program components to achieve substantial reductions in computation costs, and (3) creating or identifying contexts in which program components can be optimized or specialized.

The first of these savings is similar to the savings obtained by constant
folding in compilers and partial evaluation (Ershov 1982; Jones, Sestoft, and
Sondergaard 1985; chapter 15). By itself, it does not achieve much reduction
in computation costs. However, when it is used together with specialization
and design, it can lead to significant savings. In any case, partial evaluation is
essentially required during program transformation, and it is necessary to
make it as painless and automatic as possible.

Applying properties is also essentially required during program transformation, but it is not as straightforward as partial evaluation. Given an expression, several properties can apply to different subexpressions, and a judg-
ment needs to be made about which choice leads to the optimal savings. It
might also be necessary to massage or condition an expression to a particular
form so that a property becomes applicable.

Creating contexts for optimization is perhaps the most important activity during transformation. This activity can range from simple unfoldings of procedure
calls to the intelligent design of new program components (which can combine
several components into one or split a single component into multiple ones).

Whenever a new component is to be designed, one starts with a specification of the component and derives an implementation of it. Once this procedure is done, the previous specification becomes a property of the component. Thus, component design and property application closely interact with each other.

Partial Evaluation

Partial evaluation means performing all computations that are possible using the information available in an expression. It essentially involves unfolding function applications using the function definitions. Unless it is done carefully, partial evaluation can easily produce infinite unfoldings of expressions with little savings in computation costs. For example, consider the following function to test for membership in a list:

$$e \in l = \text{if } l = nil \text{ then False else } e = hd(l) \text{ or } e \in tl(l) . \tag{1}$$

Given a trivial application of $\in$, such as $a \in x$, repeated rewriting using this definition rule (equation 1) produces an infinite unfolding. This problem is well known in the work on partial evaluation, and successful partial evaluators require the user to annotate function applications to control such unfoldings (Sestoft 1985). However, such annotations only provide a partial solution to the problem. An application that appears as $a \in x$ in the program text can be instantiated in some context to $a \in a.y$. Although there is no benefit to unfolding $a \in x$, unfolding the instance $a \in a.y$ allows it to be simplified to True. Static annotations in program text cannot distinguish between such situations.

The solution to the problem is to use better notation for expressing definitions so that the beneficial contexts for rewritings are made explicit. One notation, used by Burstall and Darlington (1977) in NPL and subsequently adopted in other functional languages (Burstall, MacQueen, and Sanella 1980; Milner 1984; Turner 1985) is to use pattern-directed rules. The $\in$ function can be defined in this notation as

$$e \in Nil \to \text{False}$$
$$e \in h.t \to e = h \text{ or } e \in t . \tag{2}$$

With these rules, $a \in x$ cannot be rewritten, but $a \in a.y$ can be rewritten as

$a \in a.y$
$\quad \to a = a \text{ or } a \in y$
$\quad \to \text{True or } a \in y$
$\quad \to \text{True} .$

Another notation is that of conditional rewrite rules. With this notation, the second rule in equation 2 can be modified to

$$e \in h. t \{e = h\} \to \text{True}$$
$$e \in h. t \{e \neq h\} \to e \in t . \tag{3}$$

Now, $a \in a.y$ can be rewritten to True, but $a \in b.y$ cannot be rewritten unless it is known whether $a = b$ or $a \neq b$.

In Focus, definition rules such as equations 2 and 3 are called *simplification rules*. They imply that their use during rewriting does not incur an unacceptable overhead in program size. They also have to satisfy the strong termination property: Every rewrite sequence obtained by repeated application of simplification rules must be finite. Note that equation 1 does not satisfy this property. The strong termination property, together with the requirement that definition rules be nonoverlapping, ensures that all expressions have unique normal forms with respect to the simplification rules. This arrangement allows the transformation system to blindly simplify all expressions and rules to their normal forms without user intervention. Definitions such as equation 1 can still be expressed, but they are not used in the automatic rewriting process (see Setting Contexts by Expansion).

Application of Properties

Properties of program components (functions, procedures, abstract data types, and so on) come from three sources: (1) they can be supplied as part of the initial problem specification (as domain knowledge), (2) they can be proved on the fly as logical consequences of definitions, or (3) they can arise from the specifications of newly designed program components.

In general, such properties can be expressed in two forms: as oriented rewrite rules that can blindly be applied to improve performance and as equations that are not oriented in any direction. Examples of equations that cannot be oriented are properties such as associativity and commutativity, which do not, by themselves, achieve any improvement in performance. Examples of oriented property rules are

$$e \in apnd(l, m) \rightarrow e \in l \text{ or } e \in m \, ,$$

which avoids the cost of constructing an appended list, and

$$last(rev(a. x)) \rightarrow a \, ,$$

which replaces an $O(n)$ computation by a constant time computation. Such properties can be proved using techniques similar to program transformation (Reddy 1989, 1990b). The oriented property rules must also satisfy the strong termination property in conjunction with simplification rules used for function definitions.

For ensuring termination, Focus implements a flavor of well-founded orders for rewrite systems called *recursive path orderings* (Dershowitz, 1982). These orderings are based on user-specified precedence orders over the function symbols. The recursive path orderings are not always adequate for all rewrite rules one wants to express. However, they reduce much of the tedium involved in ensuring termination.

Rewriting by property rules can produce multiple results. Given an expression, there can be many subexpressions that can be rewritten, and multiple rewrite rules can apply to them. For example, consider the rewrite rules

$$apnd(apnd(x,y), z) \rightarrow apnd(x, apnd(y,z)) \tag{4}$$

and

$$apnd(rev(x), y) \rightarrow revap(x, y) \, . \tag{5}$$

The functions *apnd* and *rev* are the list append and reversal functions, and *revap* is a specialized function that reverses its first argument and appends it to the front of the second argument. Given these functions, the expression $apnd(apnd(rev(x), y), z)$ can be rewritten in two different ways:

$apnd(apnd(rev(x), y), z)$
　　　$\rightarrow apnd(rev(x), apnd(y, z))$ using 4
　　　$\rightarrow revap(x, apnd(y, z))$ using 5,

and

$apnd(apnd(rev(x), y), z)$
　　　$\rightarrow apnd(revap(x, y), z)$ using 5.

Neither an innermost nor an outermost rewriting strategy can enumerate all possible rewritings, and exhaustive enumeration of all rewritings can be expensive.

There are a variety of solutions to this problem. The simplest solution is to manually control one or more rewrite steps and then use default innermost or outermost rewriting strategies (both of which are provided in Focus) for the remainder of the rewriting. To manually control a rewriting step, a subexpression of the given expression is specified. Focus applies all possible rewrites to the chosen subexpression, and the desired rewrite result can be chosen.

A second solution is to add additional rewrite rules to the rule base so that the multiple rewrite results can further be rewritten to a single normal form. Because rewrite rules denote equality, the multiple rewrite results are logically equal. In the previous example, $revap(x, apnd(y,z))$ and $apnd(revap(x,y), z)$ are equal because they are both equal to $apnd(apnd(rev(x), y), z)$. Thus, it is valid to add a new rewrite rule

$apnd(revap(x, y), z) \rightarrow revap(x, apnd(y, z))$

provided it does not violate the strong termination property and the rewrite is judged to improve performance. To add such rewrite rules in Focus, the user creates a focus node (see focusing) with the initial expression, generates all possible normal forms using a Focus operation, chooses the preferred normal form, and invokes another Focus operation to add rewrite rules mapping all other normal forms to the preferred one. The recursive path orderings (mentioned previously in connection with termination) can also be used to automatically decide the orientation of rewrite rules derived in this fashion.

When creating libraries with large rule bases, it is desirable to ensure that all expressions have unique normal forms so that the user of the library does not have to deal with the multiple normal form problem. A rewrite system that satisfies the unique normal form property is said to be *confluent*. The Knuth-Bendix completion procedure can be used to add additional rewrite

rules to a rewrite system until it becomes confluent (Dershowitz and Jouannaud 1989; Huet and Oppen 1980; Knuth and Bendix 1970). Unfortunately,
it is not always practical to complete rewrite systems in this way. One often
finds that the completion procedure generates a large (even infinite) number
of new rewrite rules. However, even in such cases, it is desirable to make the
rewrite system as confluent as practically possible. The Focus system provides operations to incrementally complete a rewrite system so that a desired
number of new rewrite rules can be added. This process is done under user
control, much like the expansion operation that is discussed later.

In some contexts, it might not be desirable to insist on unique normal
forms. It might indeed be necessary to consider multiple normal forms and
decide among them based on external factors such as sizes of data objects.
For example, a set can be represented by a search tree or a bit-vector representation based on such factors, and each representation would involve different normal forms. Although Focus allows multiple normal forms at a local
level, the associated overhead in user interaction makes it awkward to deal
with them. Other approaches, such as maintaining separate libraries that incorporate different orientations of preference, would work better. Another
possibility is to use types to decide the applicability of rules so that the terms
of a particular type still have unique normal forms. The choice between
search tree and bit-vector representation can then be made globally in terms
of types rather than locally with multiple normal forms.

Setting Contexts by Expansion

Transforming most specifications involves, in an essential way, unfolding
one or more function applications appearing in it. Such unfolding is called
expansion and is almost always interactively issued by the user.

Nonterminating definitions such as equation 1 are expressed as expansion
rules (written using $\longrightarrow$ as opposed to $\rightarrow$). To optimize $a \in a.y$ using equation 1 expressed as an expansion rule, the user needs to issue an expand com-
mand, whereupon it is expanded to

   if $a.y = Nil$ then False else $a = hd(a.y)$ or $a \in tl(a.y)$.

This form subsequently simplifies to True (assuming hd is defined by simplification rules).

Expanding the application $a \in x$ using equation 1 merely involves rewriting.
However, if the definition (equation 2) were used, expanding $a \in x$ still achieves
a similar effect. Suppose the expression occurs in a specification of the form:

   $f(a, x) = \ldots a \in x \ldots$.

Its expansion then yields the following two cases:

   $f(a, Nil) = \ldots$ False $\ldots$
and
   $f(a, h.t) = \ldots a = h$ or $a \in t \ldots$.

Such cases are obtained using an operation called *narrowing* (Fay 1979; Reddy 1987). This operation essentially involves *unifying* the expression against the left-hand sides of definition rules to obtain the most general rewritable instances of the expression.

Expanding $a \in x$ using the conditional rules (equation 3) involves a generalization of narrowing for dealing with conditions, called *conditional narrowing*. It yields the cases

$f(a, Nil) = \ldots$ False $\ldots$

$f(a, h.t)\ \{a = h\} = \ldots$ True $\ldots$

and

$f(a, h.t)\ \{a \neq h\} = \ldots a \in y \ldots.$

Thus, although the use of pattern-directed or conditional simplification rules avoids infinite unfoldings of expressions during rewriting, it does not preclude the expansion of expressions that do not have sufficient information for simplification. Generally, such expansions do not achieve any savings by themselves but allow the expanded definitions to be simplified in their particular contexts.

Setting Contexts by Folding

Another consideration arising from nonconfluent property rules is that rewriting is not complete for equational reasoning. To replace an expression A by an expression B, it might be necessary to first replace A by C using a rewrite rule backward and then rewrite C to B. Such equational proofs are called *peak proofs* because they can be written in the form

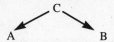

Following Burstall and Darlington (1977), the backward rewriting of A to C is called *folding*. However, unlike Burstall and Darlington, Focus uses folding only for setting the context for a forward rewriting step, not for the introduction of function applications. We can temporarily fold A to the less efficient expression C provided that it facilitates rewriting it to a more efficient expression B. As might be expected, folding is done only at the user's request, and the user might have to specify varying degrees of information to control it. Usually, the principal function symbol to be introduced as a result of folding is specified.

Folding is an expensive operation both in terms of time and search space. For example, if a rule such as

hd(h.t) $\rightarrow$ h

is used for folding, absolutely any expression e can be folded to *The hd(e.t)* [*t*]: *True*. Therefore, controlling the use of folding has been a major design problem in program-transformation systems. The most common use of folding in the framework of Burstall and Darlington is to introduce the application of a function. In the Focus framework, this process becomes an instance of forward rewriting rather than folding (see Focusing). The use of folding to achieve replacement peak proofs should be distinguished from this use. Compared to the introduction of a function application, it rarely occurs. Note also that the Knuth-Bendix completion process (see Setting Contexts by Expansion) can reduce or eliminate the need for folding.

Focusing

All the user actions mentioned in the earlier sections are for controlling the operation of Focus. However, the main design activity in performing program derivations is *focusing*. This activity mainly involves postulating new functions that are expected to have efficient implementations and are useful for optimizing the existing functions. Such new functions combine existing functions, specialize them to specific contexts, or generalize them to allow efficient processing. Various techniques for designing such functions have been proposed in the literature (Burstall and Darlington 1977; Feather 1979; Paige and Koenig 1982; Reddy 1990a; Scherlis 1981). Other than postulating functions, focusing also involves postulating properties that can be proved and then integrated into the rule base. One can also design new data representations by defining abstraction and representation functions and then postulating focus functions for the representation types using the original functions on the abstract types.

To design a function f, one starts with a specification of the form

$$f(x) = D , \tag{6}$$

where D is an expression stated in terms of existing functions. A program for f is then derived using expansion, simplification and rewriting. Once the derivation of a program for f is complete, the specification equation (equation 6) becomes a property of the derived program, and it can be used as a property rule. In fact, it can naturally be oriented backward as a rewrite rule $D \to f(x)$. The rationale is that the derived program for $f(x)$ would be more efficient than the expression D; thus, any instance of D should be rewritten to the corresponding instance of $f(x)$ so that the efficiency of the program can be exploited. Such back-oriented specifications are called *introduction rules* because they introduce a newly developed program component in a larger context.

More interestingly, such an introduction rule can be used within the derivation of $f(x)$ itself. Once an expansion operation is performed on D, any instance of D occurring in the generated cases can recursively use the savings obtained by the new program being developed. Thus, within the derivation of a function, the function's introduction rule has the effect of recursion introduction. It is well recognized that recursion introduction must be performed using some form of induction, lest one derive silly (and incorrect) programs of the form $f(x) = f(x)$ (Manna and Waldinger 1979). The induction method used in Focus is based on the well-founded term-rewriting order. Because the definition rules are strongly terminating, all rewrite sequences are finite, and any term obtained by rewriting a given term is smaller in this sense. Because the expand operation implicitly involves a rewrite step, the expanded specification can freely be as an induction hypothesis in the generated cases. Thus, the induction principle remains in the background and is automatically satisfied by the program-manipulation operations of Focus. See Reddy (1989, 1990b) for a technical justification of this method.

Internal Rules

The semantics of all the primitive constructs of the Focus language is captured by a large set of built-in property rules and a set of inference rules that derive new property rules from given user rules. For example, notice that the if-then-else construct satisfies the distributivity law

$f(\dots \text{ if } p \text{ then } a \text{ else } b, \dots) \; = \; \text{if } p \text{ then } f(\dots, a, \dots) \text{ else } f(\dots, b, \dots)$,

and the let construct satisfies the selection rule

$\text{let } c(t_1, \dots, t_n) = c(d_1, \dots, d_n) \text{ in } e \; = \; \text{let } t_1 = d_1, \dots, t_n = d_n \text{ in } e$.

Complete axiomatizations for some of these constructs can be found in Bloom and Tindell (1983), Bronsard and Reddy (1990a), and Guessarian and Meseguer (1987).

The semantics of the language also interacts with user-supplied property rules; so, it is necessary to derive new rules from the given ones. For example, if one side of an equation has an if-then-else expression, it is necessary to consider its effect in contexts where the condition might be true or false:

$$\frac{\text{if } p \text{ then } e_1 \text{ else } e_2 = d}{\begin{array}{c} e_1 \{p\} = d \\ e_2 \{not(p)\} = d \end{array}} .$$

The semantics of the let construct interacts with constructor applications, necessitating the following inference rule:

$$\frac{c\,(e^*) = d}{e_i = \text{let } c(x^*) = d \text{ in } x_i} , \qquad\qquad (7)$$

where c is a constructor. If one side of an equation has a definite description, then an equivalence is derived for its condition

$$\frac{(\text{The } e\,[x^*] : p) = d}{p = (e = d)} \qquad\qquad (8)$$

if all x^* occurs in e. A major part of the Focus development effort was devoted to finding and efficiently implementing the properties and inference rules to axiomatize the language.

Examples

To illustrate the various program-derivation operations previously discussed, I reconsider the two examples mentioned in Overview of Focus. First, let us look at the derivation of the program for *scan(char.s)* using *scanword,* shown in figure 2. The user creates focuses for the two functions and invokes an expand operation on the second focus. When this focus is expanded, its specification is oriented backward as an introduction rule. This rule eventually causes the parent focus to be rewritten using a call to *scanword.* Note that the inference rule (equation 7) yields two derived rules from the introduction rule, which are able to rewrite the component terms *fword(s)* and *scan(rword(s))*.

To expand the *scanword* focus, the leftmost-outermost subexpression *fword(s)* is chosen for expansion by default. The user can override the default by specifying a subexpression to be expanded. (For example, expanding *rword(s)* would lead to another derivation but, in this case, to the same final program). Expansion of *fword(s)* yields three cases that are directly obtained by considering the three definition rules of *fword.* For each case, the system automatically simplifies the expressions obtained and then attempts to rewrite them using known property rules. The only rewriting in this example is in the second case, where *fword(s)* and *scan(rword(s))* are rewritten using (the derived rules of) the introduction rule of *scanword.*

The total effort required of the user involves creating the two focuses, issuing an expand command, and, finally, closing the focus nodes for accepting the programs derived in them. This process can be contrasted with the effort required in the ZAP system (Feather 1979), where it is necessary to specify what the expected form of the output program is, which functions can be unfolded during the derivation, and which functions can be used in the final program. The extra detail in the use of the ZAP system is necessary to control the search. Focus is able to proceed more autonomously and still produce desired results because the rules in Focus encode performance information through the orientation of property rules. In this example, the only property rules are introduction rules obtained from the expanded specification, which are back oriented along the direction of improved performance. Because these rules can freely be used, there is no need to specify the expected form of the program.

The second example previously mentioned is the derivation of a linear time program for the maximum of a list. Figure 3 shows this derivation.

Note that the specification here involves a precondition $l \neq Nil$ that is written to the left separated by a ::. The precondition can be assumed while rewriting the specification, but it does not appear in the derived program.

The derivation proceeds by first performing an expansion (on the subexpression $z \in l$). The definition rules (equation 2) are used for this purpose.

focus l ≠ Nil :: max(l) = The z : z ∈ l & All (e : e ∈ l) e ≤ z

introduction rule: The z : z ∈ l & All (e : e ∈ l) e ≤ z {l ≠ Nil} → max(l)

derived rules: (1) z ∈ l & All (e : e ∈ l) e ≤ z {l ≠ Nil} → z = max(l)

(2) All (e : e ∈ l) e ≤ z {l ≠ Nil & z ∈ l} → z = max(l)

(3) max(l) ∈ l {l ≠ Nil} → True

(4) All (e : e ∈ l) e ≤ max(l) {l ≠ Nil} → True

(5) e ≤ max(l) {l ≠ Nil & e ∈ l} → True

cases from z ∈ l

l.   Nil ≠ Nil :: max(Nil) = The z : False & All (e : e ∈ l) e ≤ z
     eliminated

2.   h.t ≠ Nil :: max(h.t) = The z : (z = h or z ∈ t) & All (e : e ∈ h.t) e ≤ z

simplifies to: max(h.t) =   (if All (e : e ∈ t) e ≤ h then h);

The z : z ∈ t & h ≤ z & All (e : e ∈ t) e ≤ z

cases on condition t = Nil

2.l. max(h.Nil) = (if All (e : e ∈ Nil) e ≤ h then h);

The z : z ∈ Nil & h ≤ z & All (e : e ∈ Nil) e ≤ z

simplifies to: max(h.Nil) = h

2.2. t ≠ Nil :: max(h.t) = (if All (e : e ∈ t) e ≤ h then h);

The z : z ∈ t & h ≤ z & All (e : e ∈ t) e ≤ z

rewrites to: t ≠ Nil :: max(h.t) = (if All (e : e ∈ t) e ≤ h then h);

(if h ≤ max(t) then max(t))

rewrites to: t ≠ Nil :: max(h.t) = (if max(t) ≤ h then h);

(if h ≤ max(t) then max(t))

Prove All (e : e ∈ l) e ≤ m {l ≠ Nil} → (max(l) ≤ m)

Figure 3. Derivation of max.

This step yields two cases: when $l = Nil$, $z ∈ l$ is False and when $l = h.t$, $z ∈ l$ is $z = h$ or $z ∈ t$. The first case is eliminated because it does not satisfy the precondition $l ≠ Nil$. The second case simplifies to a nondeterministic choice by distributing the conjunction and *The* constructs over disjunction. The first choice branch turns out to be of the form *The z: z = h* . . . . Because z is uniquely determined at this point, the expression is convertible to *if . . . then* h. Such an if expression, with the else-part missing, is defined only if the condition is true. Note that the introduction rule for *max* gives rise to a number of derived rules. The first of these is derived by the inference rule (equation 8), and the others are obtained from this rule by considering the semantics of logical connectives and equality.

The user then introduces further case analysis on case 2 using the condition $t = Nil$. The motivation for this step is to enable recursive calls to *max* (which is only possible when $t \neq Nil$). The first case here simplifies to the desired form. Case 2.2, still has two choice branches, only the second of which is rewritable using the introduction rule of *max*. In fact, this rewriting is done using the first derived rule of the introduction rule, which replaces two of the conjuncts $z \in t$ and *All* ($e: e \in Nil$) $e \leq z$ by $z = max(l)$. Again, because z is uniquely determined, the expression is put in the *if* form. To introduce a recursive call in the first branch, the user needs to perform more work. She/he needs to state and prove the property

$$All\ (e : e \in l)\ e \leq m\ \{l \neq Nil\} \rightarrow (max(l) \leq m)\ .$$

Note that $\rightarrow$ in this rule denotes oriented equality, not implication. It is interesting that this property cannot be proved using equational reasoning alone. It needs to be transformed into two implications, each of which can then be proved using resolution- or natural deduction–style techniques. The introduction rule of *max* and its various derived rules can be used in this proof. Rewriting by this property rule then introduces a recursive call in the first choice branch and the desired program is obtained. The final definition in case 2.2, is further optimized by eliminating repeated subexpressions and converting the choice to an if-then-else expression, but I omit these details here. An important fact to be established in this process is that the choice branches are consistent. When both the branches are defined (that is, $h = max(t)$), they evaluate to the same value, h. Thus, the derivation we exhibited here not only derives an efficient program for *max* but also establishes that the specification is well defined (that is, a value satisfying the maximum property exists and is unique).

It is interesting to contrast this derivation with derivations that can be performed in the KIDS system (Smith 1985; chapter 19) and the LOPS system (Bibel 1980; chapter 16). Whereas the specification of *max* here uses a definite description (stating that there is a unique value with the maximum property), the specifications in these systems use indefinite descriptions (stating that there is some value with the maximum property). The derivation in LOPS makes the additional assumption that the specification is well defined. In contrast, the focus derivation establishes the specification to be well defined by showing the existence and uniqueness of a value with the maximum property. This fact explains some of the extra effort involved in the focus derivation. For example, in case 2.2, the LOPS derivation can assume that the maximum exists; so, it must be h whenever $h \leq max(t)$ is False. This assumption obviates the auxiliary property that was proved here. Similarly, if any value satisfying the maximum property is considered acceptable, then $max(t)$ can be accepted whenever $h \leq max(t)$, and the first choice branch need only be considered when $max(t) < h$. The derived rule (5) and the transitivity of $<$

are enough to show the condition required for the first choice branch. Again, the property proved would be obviated.

Why, then, do I insist on using definite descriptions (as opposed to indefinite descriptions) and verifying such descriptions to be well defined? The second question is answered by considering correctness concerns. Focus is not only meant to automate part of the programming process but also to assist the programmer in developing correct programs. It does not assume that specifications are always well defined because it is easy to write ill-defined specifications. Note, for example, that omitting the precondition $l \neq Nil$ makes the specification ill defined. Such omissions can have disastrous consequences in an automated system because the system can then introduce an application of *max* in a context where the precondition does not hold. Coming to the first question, I do not necessarily insist on the use of definite descriptions. The user could replace *The* with *Any* and redo the derivation of the program. However, using an indefinite description would provide less information to the system and achieve less automation than using a definite description. For our example, the derived rules 1 and 2 of the introduction rule would not be available, which means that rewriting the second choice branch in case 2.2, would not be possible. The effect of the rules would have to be obtained by inferential reasoning using the other derived rules (3, 4, and 5). The derivation in Smith (1985) shows how this process can be done, but this alternative is less attractive when the search space of inferential reasoning is considered.

The KIDS and LOPS derivations also make a prior choice about the structure of the final program; that is, that it should be defined by induction on the list argument. This choice permits certain decisions to automatically be made; for example, $max(h.t)$ should be defined in terms of $max(t)$, and hence, a case analysis on the condition $t = Nil$ is required. In the Focus derivation, this case analysis is invoked by the user. At a higher level of detail, it can be noted that Focus possesses no knowledge of the list data structure involved in this derivation. The instantiations for the variable l are directly obtained from the definition of the $\in$ function. In contrast, both KIDS and LOPS depend on knowledge of how to construct recursive programs on specific data structures. The generality of the Focus approach would become apparent when data structures of a user's own construction are used or when algorithms with unconventional structure need to be derived (Reddy 1990a). However, researchers envision that the AutoFocus driver for Focus will have to incorporate tactical knowledge similar to KIDS and LOPS regarding data structures and algorithm structures. The separation of logical and heuristic information in this fashion achieves both automation (when routine problems of standardized structures are involved) and generality (when new structures need to be handled).

Structure of Program Derivations

So far, I have dealt with the techniques of program derivation. In this section, I discuss the system-level and life-cycle issues addressed in the Focus effort.

Documenting Derivations

A program development system must organize the derivations of programs into a suitable structure so that the programmer can easily comprehend them. To this end, one finds that there are two kinds of documentation required of program derivations. The first kind serves the same purpose as a program listing in the conventional software life cycle. It should be usable by program designers and maintainers to understand the program implementation and its structure. However, in contrast to conventional listings, this kind of documentation also provides the history and the rationale of the implementation. Note, first, that the specification is the best readable account of the system. As the program derivation proceeds the components of the system are increasingly specialized in the context of their use (Scherlis 1981). Thus, the components of the final implementation cannot be understood in isolation. They have to be understood in relation to the more abstract components found in the specification. In practice, the system undergoes several changes in structure and abstraction in going from the most abstract specification to the most efficient implementation. The components to be found at each stage should then be understood in relation to the components of the earlier stages. A documentation of these relationships and the products of various stages of derivation is called a *derivation history.*

In addition to the products of the stages of the derivation and their relationships, the second kind of documentation includes all the necessary details of the derivation activity itself. This additional level of detail is not necessary to understand the program structure and rationale, but it is necessary to make changes. Radical changes that necessitate discarding the whole derivation and implementation are rare. Instead, most changes require minor modifications to the specifications and can be propagated to the implementations by following the prior derivation activity. A *derivation script* serves this purpose.

The early efforts toward documentation of derivations (Feather 1979; Wile 1983) did not make this distinction between derivation histories and derivation scripts. The methods given in Darlington (1981) seem to contain some elements at the derivation history level, but they contain low-level operations as well (such as unfold and fold). Another feature of these approaches is that they document derivations at a metalevel in terms of operations on programs. I believe that the high-level documentation of derivations should mainly contain program-level information. In this context, we can draw an analogy with mathematical proofs. In writing proofs, we manage to communicate the reasoning and rationale for proof steps without mentioning the basic logical inference rules involved in them. One would like derivation histories to be descriptions at the level of such proofs. (Derivation scripts are akin to descriptions at the level of mechanically verifiable proofs). The notion of derivation trees is central to the high-level descriptions that Focus constructs.

Derivation Trees

Let us show how the tree structure arises through a sample scenario. Suppose we are trying to derive an efficient program for an expression e. We postulate a focus for it as

$$p(x_1, \ldots, x_n) = e \, .$$

Sometimes, the expression e can directly be transformed into a more efficient form by a case analysis on its variables (such as for *scanword*). However, more often, we have to choose another expression s for which an efficient program can be derived. This new expression s can be a subexpression of e, a collection of subexpressions that have common subcomputations, or even a generalization of e. The choice of the expression s is a crucial design decision based on the programmer's insight into the nature of the computation. In general, a focus cannot be as simple as the example used here. It can be a focus on an abstract data type involving several procedures and focus expressions, or it can specify several procedures in terms of a single focus expression , and so on. However, independent of the structure of the focuses, the tree structure is involved in all of them.

Having chosen to form a focus on the expression s, we have a hierarchy such as

> *Focus* $p(x_1, \ldots, x_n) = e$
>   *Focus* $q(y_1, \ldots, y_n) = s \, .$

The focus on s is subsidiary to that of e because the development of s is an integral part of the development of e. When the development of s is complete, we have an efficient procedure for it in terms of q. We then need to realize these gains in the parent focus, which involves rewriting e to some e' using the back-oriented introduction rule $s \to q(y_1, \ldots, y_n)$.

The new expression e' might still need further development. We might have to choose another internal focus expression s' and continue this process:

> *Focus* $p(x_1, \ldots, x_n) = e$
>   *Focus* $q(y_1, \ldots, y_m) = s$
>   *program:* $q(y_1, \ldots, y_m) = \ldots$
>   *Focus* $q'(z_1, \ldots, z_k) = s'$
>   *program:* $q'(z_1, \ldots, z_k) = \ldots$
> $\vdots$
>
>   *program:* $p(x_1, \ldots, x_n) = \ldots$

Now, we only need to note that each subsidiary focus can, in turn, have other subsidiary focuses, and it is clear that we have a tree structure. In fact, the tree structure of focuses closely resembles the block structure of programs. (However, unlike block structure, the focus tree structure does not impose any scope discipline). There is, of course, no unique way to organize a derivation into a tree. The program designer is free to structure it as he/she sees fit. For example, instead of making the focus of q' subsidiary to the original focus node of p, the designer can open a new focus node for p with the specification e' and derive the procedure q' as a part of this focus.

I find that this flexibility in how the derivation is organized into trees and how the trees themselves are developed to be important. It allows the designer to layer the tree by the levels of abstraction desired. Flexibility in the order of development allows one to leave parts of a subtree incomplete and work on other subtrees. It also allows one to come back and modify a previously developed subtree even if its exported information has already been used in the other subtrees. Equally important is a user interface that allows the designer to directly work with the tree rather than a textual representation of it. This approach allows the designer to examine the high-level structure of the tree and ignore the internal details of the various subtrees. To facilitate this approach, the Focus system uses a programmable tree editor called Treemacs (Hammerslag, Kamin, and Campbell 1985; Hammerslag 1988) for its user interface. The tree editor provides functions to selectively view parts of the tree, walk around the tree, and create and delete nodes. The functions of the Focus system, such as opening and closing focus nodes and other transformation operations discussed in the last section are also provided through this interface.

The derivation history, characterized earlier as the high-level documentation describing the history and the rationale of the implementation, is now merely the focus tree, with each focus node displaying two pieces of information: its specification and the derived program. Figure 4 shows a sample derivation history for the implementation of *scan*. (This history includes a focus for *scanskip* in addition to the two focuses developed in figure 2).

Program-Derivation State

Even though the organization of a program derivation is represented as a tree, the process of program derivation is a sequential process. Each derivation step takes an input program and produces an output program. For example, if we view the derivation tree of figure 4 as a derivation step, its input program has the rule

scan(char.s) → fword(char.s).scan(rword(char.s)) ,

whereas the output program has the rule

scan(char.s) → scanword(char.s)

in its place. The input program does not have the procedures *scanword* and *scanskip*, but the output program does. If we perform another program-

```
focus scan(char.s) =
                    fword(char.s).scan(rword(char.s))
```
program:
```
scan(char.s) → scanword(char.s)
```

```
    focus scanword(s) = fword(s).scan(rword(s))
    program:
    scanword(Nil) → Nil.Nil
    scanword(c.s) {alpha(c)} → let x1.x2 = scanword(s) in (c.x1).x2
    scanword(' '.s) → Nil.scanskip(s)
    introduction rules:
    rword(s).scan(rword(s)) → scanword(s)
    rword(s) → let x1.x2 = scanword(s) in x1
    scan(rword(s)) → let x1.x2 = scanword(s) in x2
```

```
        focus scanskip(s) = scan(skip(s))
        program:
        scanskip(Nil) → Nil
        scanskip(c.s) {alpha(c)} → let x1.x2 = scanword(s) (c.x1).x2
        scanskip(' '.s) → scanskip(s)
        introduction rules:
        scan(skip(s)) → scanskip(s)
```

Figure 4. A Derivation History of scan

derivation step after that of figure 4, for example, to make *scan* tail recursive, then the input to this step would be the output program of figure 4. Not only are programs transmitted between such derivation steps but also all other kinds of rules, such as property rules, introduction rules, and specifications (old programs). We call the sum total of all the rules so transmitted a *program-derivation state.*

In systems that only present a dynamic view of this program-derivation process (for example, Popart [Wile 1983] and KBEMACS [Waters 1985]), there is only one program-derivation state active at any time. It is not possible to go back to an earlier state and examine the differences between it and the current state except by retracting derivation steps. This approach makes it hard for the user to track what was accomplished and what is left to be done. In contrast, the derivation trees of Focus present a static view of the entire program-derivation process. Different parts of the tree refer to different derivation states. For this purpose, the nodes of a derivation tree can be viewed as organized in a sequential fashion, from top to bottom. If a node is opened above the tree of figure 4, its input state would be the state that existed prior to the derivation of figure 4. It is possible, for example, to prove a property in such a node and then rederive the tree of figure 4 to take the new property into account. There is no need to retract or delete the tree in order to make such a modification.

This static picture of the program-derivation process is achieved by distributing the program-derivation state throughout the tree instead of keeping a single global state. Each node contributes some rules to the state. The rules visible to a node are the rules contributed by the nodes that precede it in the textual top-to-bottom reading of the tree. These nodes include a node's predecessor nodes (at the same level) and their descendants, its ancestor nodes, and their respective predecessors and descendants. The rules contributed by the node's descendants are also visible. However, as I discuss shortly, there is some dynamic character to this contribution. A node can contribute global rules that are visible to all other nodes according to the visibility rules. It can also contribute local rules that are only visible to its descendants. Examples of local rules are the focus specifications and back-oriented introduction rules of a focus node that is not yet closed.

The derivation process represented by a derivation tree is, thus, statically represented. However, the derivation process within a single node is dynamic. Notice (for example, in figure 2) that each node has a state, namely, the focus equation. This state is called a *focus state* as opposed to the program-derivation state. The focus state dynamically changes as various derivation operations, such as simplification and rewriting, are performed. It is not possible to go back to an earlier state except by retracting such operations. More significantly, the creation of a subsidiary focus node is also considered a derivation operation in this context. For example, in figure 2, the top node for *scan(char.s)* is first created, then a subsidiary focus for *scanword(s)* is created. Finally, a rewriting step is performed in the top node after the subsidiary focus is closed. This sequencing is important because the rewriting step involves the introduction rule of *scanword*, which is contributed by the subsidiary focus only after it is closed. Any operations performed on the top node before the closing of the subsidiary focus do not have access to this introduction rule.

Derivation Scripts and Replay

With the formal derivation methodology, program modification involved in conventional software maintenance translates to specification modification and derivation replay. Modifying a specification invalidates one or more focus nodes in a derivation because the definitions and properties used in these nodes are no longer present. To reconstruct a valid derivation, we would have to redo the derivations of these nodes. In the process, we might also have to modify the specifications of subsidiary focuses and redo their derivations. In the worst case, we might have to abandon the entire prior derivation and start all over. However, I believe starting over is rarely necessary. Often, the modifications needed are small and incremental. The system support needed for such rederivations is, first, tracking dependencies between nodes and rules so that the invalidated nodes can be identified and, second, replaying derivations of focuses in the context of altered rule bases or specifications.

In using Focus, one finds that replay is useful not only for modifications but also for initial derivations. One such use is the correction of errors and dead ends during a derivation. While performing a derivation, it is possible to make mistakes or typos that need to be corrected before the derivation can be completed. More significantly, one often finds it necessary to add preconditions or strengthen inductive hypotheses after some derivation effort. Replay can be used to redo the prior (partial) derivation after making corrections. Wile (1983) also notes this application of replay. Another application of replay is to reuse solutions of problems for other different but analogous problems.

To facilitate replay, the system stores a record of the operations performed on each derivation node. Such records are called derivation scripts. Note that the program designer never needs to directly construct the derivation scripts (unlike in Darlington [1981], Feather, [1979], and Wile [1983]). He/she only manipulates the specifications and programs; the records of the activity are automatically constructed by the system. An entry in a script describes the operation performed, any parameters to the operation (such as a particular subexpression to be rewritten), and a description of the results. The result descriptions are meant to be used for matching the intermediate results obtained during replay, allowing failures to be detected immediately. (However, researchers found the space requirements for storing intermediate results excessive in practice. Through a system option, the result descriptions are almost always purged when derivations are stored on disk, and this feature has not been useful. Summary descriptions of results, such as the number of normal forms obtained in a rewrite operation, are retained in spite of the purge, and they are used during replay). A rudimentary replay mechanism, which blindly and automatically replays the derivation of a focus tree using these scripts, was implemented and has extensively been used.

This rudimentary replay mechanism is, of course, highly inadequate. Replay is essentially used to propagate changes; so, the results obtained during replay are bound to be different to varying degrees. Replay must be both tolerant and sensitive to such differences. The tolerance is exhibited in adapting derivation operations to slightly modified expressions in specifications. For example, if some subexpression fails to get rewritten during replay, the replay must proceed unless an operation is required to be performed on the failed subexpression. Sensitivity is required to detect differences that will necessarily cause the replay to fail at some later stage. It is necessary to alert the user about such failures, but at the same time, the system should not burden the user with every small difference encountered during replay. (In this context, a useful analogy is the behavior of a compiler when errors are found in source programs. A single error in the program often causes a flurry of related error messages because of the lack of tolerance and sensitivity on the part of the compiler). These requirements motivated the design of a new intelligent replay mechanism. This mechanism is still under implementation; so, I cannot report on experience with it.

To distinguish between essential and inessential differences in replay results, the replay mechanism must possess some knowledge of what is achieved by each step of the derivation, called its *tactical achievements*. These achievements are essentially discovered by watching the user "over the shoulder." Any number of criteria can be used to formulate tactical achievements. Researchers are currently experimenting with marking certain subexpressions of specifications as critical for the derivation and tracking their status through the derivation operations. The criticality is determined by constructs and function symbols that must not appear in the final programs. If a critical subexpression is affected differently by an operation during the original derivation than during the replay, the situation is flagged as a potential failure.

To promote tolerance, the replay mechanism assumes that the specification on which replay is to be performed is at best analogous to the original specification. A variety of analogical mapping techniques are used to ignore harmless differences.

To maintain the integrity of derivation trees, the replay mechanism is used to make fresh copies of focus trees rather than overwrite existing trees. When the replay is complete and successful, the copy created by replay can be accepted at the user's insistence. The exported rule bases of the original tree and the copy are then compared to detect differences. If any rules of the original tree are deleted or replaced by new ones, then the nodes dependent on such rules are flagged as invalid, and they need to be replayed to reestablish the consistency of the derivation.

Conclusion

I outlined the main design principles of the interactive program-derivation system Focus. The important characteristics of the system are its human-oriented deduction procedures, its emphasis on small search spaces, and the novel organization of program derivations as tree structures. The derivation tree structure presents to the user a static, rather than dynamic, picture of the derivation process and permits the flexible development of derivations.

At the time of this writing, a first-order functional language subset was completely implemented, and a variety of program transformations were performed using it. Logic programming features such as quantifiers were also implemented, but the completeness of the implemented deduction techniques is not yet resolved. Algorithm synthesis problems (such as the example of *max*) were tried, but this kind of activity is currently not well supported by the system because of the lack of inferential (first-order) reasoning facilities. In recent work (Bronsard and Reddy 1991), researchers formulated rewritinglike mechanisms for inferential reasoning that will go a long way in supporting algorithm synthesis.

The most interesting derivations performed to date lie somewhere between program optimization and algorithm synthesis. These problems arose in considering the self-application of Focus and are documented in Reddy (1990a). The overall objective in these problems is program improvement, but achieving the desired improvement involves identifying specialized properties maintained by the programs, building theories of such properties, and then specializing the programs in the context of such properties. The work involved in these problems is significantly larger than conventional program transformations, but at the same time, the programs do not fall under well-defined algorithmic structures. For solving such problems, Focus fills the important gap between program-transformation systems such as those described by Barstow (1979) and Burstall and Darlington (1977) and algorithm synthesis systems such as those described in chapters 16 and 19).

Acknowledgments

My work on the application of term-rewriting techniques for program transformation draws ideas from the work of Nachum Dershowitz (1985), Leo Bachmair (1987), G. Sivakumar (Kapur and Sivakumar 1983) and Wolfgang Kuechlin (1989). I also benefited from the ideas of Valentin Turchin (1986) on the supercompiler system. Finally, I am indebted to Samuel Kamin for introducing me to tree editing.

The implementation of Focus was assisted by Charlene Bloch and Peng Ong. Francois Bronsard and Robert Hasker designed and implemented significant portions of the system.

Notes

1. Many of the program synthesis techniques do use a fair amount of replacement reasoning, but the emphasis appears to be on inferential reasoning.

2. TREEMACS has now been reimplemented as a special mode of EMACS called "TREE-MODE."

References

Bachmair, L. 1987. Proof Methods for Equational Theories. Ph.D. thesis, Univ. of Illinois at Urbana-Champaign.

Balzer, R.; Goldman, N. M.; and Wile, D. S. 1976. On the Transformational Approach to Programming. In Proceedings of the Second International Conference on Software Engineering, 337–344. Washington, D.C.: IEEE Computer Society.

Barstow, D. R. 1979. *Knowledge-Based Program Construction*. New York: Elsevier.

Bibel, W. 1980. Syntax-Directed, Semantics-Supported Program Synthesis. *Artificial Intelligence* 14:243–261.

Bibel, W. 1987. *Automated Theorem Proving*, 2d ed. Braunschweig: Vieweg Verlag.

Bloom, S., and Tindell, R. 1983. Varieties of If-Then-Else. *SIAM Journal on Computing* 12:677–707.

Bronsard, F., and Reddy, U. S. 1990. An Axiomatization of a Functional Logic Language. In *Algebraic and Logic Programming*, eds H. Kirchner and W. Wechler, p. 101-116. Berlin: Springer-Verlag.

Bronsard, F., and Reddy, U. S. 1991. Conditional Rewriting in Focus. In Proceedings of the Second International Workshop on Conditional and Typed Rewriting Systems. Berlin: Springer-Verlag.

Brown, F. M. 1986. An Experimental Logic Based on the Fundamental Deduction Principle. *Artificial Intelligence* 30.

Broy, M., and Pepper, P. 1981. Program Development as a Formal Activity. *IEEE Transactions on Software Engineering* SE-7(1): 14–22.

Burstall, R. M., and Darlington, J. 1977. A Transformation System for Developing Recursive Programs. *Journal of the ACM* 24(1): 44–67.

Burstall, R. M.; MacQueen, D. B.; and Sanella, D. T. 1980. Hope: An Experimental Applicative Language. In Proceedings of the ACM LISP Conference, 136–143. New York: Association of Computing Machinery.

Clocksin , W. F., and Mellish, C. S.1981. *Programming in Prolog*. New York: Springer-Verlag.

Darlington, J. 1981. The Structured Description of Algorithm Derivations. In *Algorithmic Languages*, eds. J. W. de Bakker and J. C. van Vliet, 221–250. Amsterdam: North-Holland.

Darlington, J. 1976. Transforming Specifications into Efficient Programs. Presented at the IFIP Working Group 2.1 Conference on Software Specifications, St. Pierre-de-Chatreuse.

Dershowitz, N. 1985. Synthesis by Completion. In Proceedings of the Ninth International Joint Conference on Artificial Intelligence, 208–214. Menlo Park, Calif.: International Joint Conferences on Artificial Intelligence.

Dershowitz, N. 1982. Orderings for Term-Rewriting Systems. *Theoretical Computer Science* 17(3): 279–301.

Dershowitz, N., and Jouannaud, J.-P. 1989. Rewrite Systems. In *Handbook of Theoretical Computer Science*, volume 2, eds. A. Meyer and J. van Lennwen, 243-320. Amsterdam: North-Holland.

Ershov, A. P. 1982. Mixed Computation: Potential Applications and Problems for Study. *Theoretical Computer Science* 18:41–67.

Fay, M. 1979. First-Order Unification in an Equational Theory. In Proceedings of the Fourth Workshop on Automated Deduction, 161–167.

Feather, M. S. 1982. A System for Assisting Program Transformation. *ACM Transactions on Programming Languages and Systems* 4(1): 1–20.

Feather, M. S. 1979. A System for Developing Programs by Transformation. Ph.D. thesis, Univ. of Edinburgh.

Guessarian, I., and Meseguer, J. 1987. Axiomatization of If-Then-Else. *SIAM Journal on Computing* 16(2): 332–357.

Hammerslag, D. 1988. Treemacs Manual. Technical Report, UIUCDCS-R-88-1427, Univ. Illinois at Urbana-Champaign.

Hammerslag, D. H.; Kamin, S. N.; and Campbell, R. H. 1985. Tree-Oriented Interactive Processing with an Application to Theorem-Proving. In Second Conference on Software Development Tools, Techniques, and Alternatives, 199–206. Washington, D.C.: IEEE Computer Society.

Hsiang, J. 1982. Topics in Automated Theorem Proving and Program Generation. Ph.D. thesis, Univ. of Illinois at Urbana-Champaign.

Huet, G., and Oppen, D. C. 1980. Equations and Rewrite Rules: A Survey. In *Formal Language Theory: Perspectives and Open Problems,* 349–405, ed. R. Book. New York: Academic.

Jones, N. D.; Sestoft, P.; and Sondergaard, H. 1985. An Experiment in Partial Evaluation. In *Rewriting Techniques and Applications,* ed. J.-P. Jouannaud, 124–140 Berlin: Springer-Verlag.

Kapur, D., and Sivakumar, G. 1983. Experiments with and Architecture of RRL, A Rewrite Rule Laboratory. In Proceedings of the NSF Workshop on the Rewrite Rule Laboratory, 33–56. Washington, D.C.: National Science Foundation.

Knuth, D., and Bendix, P. 1970. Simple Word Problems in Universal Algebras. In *Computational Problems in Abstract Algebra,* 263–297, ed. J. Leech. Oxford: Pergamon.

Kuechlin, W. 1989. Inductive Completion by Ground Proof Transformation. In *Resolution of Equations in Algebraic Structures,* eds. H. Ait-Kaci and M. Nivat, 211-245. San Diego: Academic Press.

Manna, Z., and Waldinger, R. 1979. Synthesis: Dreams ⇒ Programs. *IEEE Transactions on Software Engineering* SE-5(4): 294–328.

Milner, R 1984. A Proposal for Standard ML. In ACM Symposium on Lisp and Functional Programming, 184–197. New York: Association of Computing Machinery.

Murray, N. V., and Rosenthal, E. 1988. An Implementation of a Dissolution-Based System Employing Theory Links. In *Conference on Automated Deduction*, eds. E. Lusk and R. Overbeek, 658–674. Berlin: Springer-Verlag.

Paige, R., and Koenig, S. 1982. Finite Differencing of Computable Expressions. *ACM Transactions on Programming Languages and Systems* 4(3): 402–454.

Potter, R. C., and Plaisted, D. A. 1988. Term Rewriting: Some Experimental Results. In *Conference on Automated Deduction*, eds. E. Lusk and R. Overbeek, 435–453. Berlin: Springer-Verlag.

Pottinger, G. 1988. Ulysses: Logical Foundations of the Definition Facility. Technical Report TR 11-9, Ithaca, N.Y.: Odyssey Research Associates.

Reddy, U. S. 1990. Formal Methods in Transformational Derivation of Programs. In *Software Engineering Notices,* 15(4): 104-114.

Reddy, U. S. 1990b. Term Rewriting Induction. In *Conference on Automated Deduction*, ed. M. Stickel, 162–177. Lecture Notes in Artificial Intelligence, volume 449. Springer-Verlag.

Reddy, U. S. 1989. Rewriting Techniques for Program Synthesis. In *Rewriting Techniques and Applications,* ed. N. Dershowitz, 388–403. Lecture Notes in Computer Science, volume 355. Berlin: Springer-Verlag.

Reddy, U. S. 1987. Functional Logic Languages, Part I. In *Graph Reduction*, ed J. H. Fasel and R. M. Keller, 401–425. Lecture Notes in Computer Science, volume 279. Springer-Verlag.

Rich, C., and Waters, R. C. 1986. *Readings in Artificial Intelligence and Software Engineering.* San Mateo, Calif.: Morgan Kaufmann.

Robinson, J. A. 1965. A Machine-Oriented Logic Based on the Resolution Principle. *Journal of the ACM* 12: 23–41.

Scherlis, W. L. 1981. Program Improvement by Internal Specialization. In ACM Symposium on

Principles of Programming Languages, 41–49. New York: ACM.

Sestoft, P. 1985. The Structure of a Self-Applicable Partial Evaluator. In Programs as Data Objects, eds. H. Ganzinger and N. D. Jones, 236–256. Lecture Notes in Computer Science, volume 217. Springer-Verlag.

Smith, D. 1985. Top-Down Synthesis of Divide and Conquer Algorithms. *Artificial Intelligence* 27:43–96.

Turchin, V. F. 1986. The Concept of a Supercompiler. *ACM Transactions on Programming Languages and Systems* 8(3): 292–325.

Turner, D. A. 1985. Miranda: A Non-Strict Functional Language with Polymorphic Types. In *Conference on Functional Programming Languages and Computing Architectures*, 1–16. Springer-Verlag.

Waters, R. 1985. The Programmer's Apprentice: A Session with KBEmacs. *IEEE Transactions on Software Engineering* SE-11(11): 1296–1320.

Wile, D. S. 1983. Program Developments: Formal Explanations of Implementations. *Communications of the ACM* 26(11): 902–911.

Zhang, H., and Kapur, D. 1988. First-Order Theorem Proving Using Conditional Rewrite Rules. In Conference on Automated Deduction, eds. E. Lusk and R. Overbeek, 1–20. Berlin: Springer-Verlag.

KIDS—A Knowledge-Based Software Development System

Douglas R. Smith

The construction of a computer program is based on several kinds of knowledge: knowledge about the particular problem being solved; general knowledge about the application domain; programming knowledge peculiar to the domain; and general programming knowledge about algorithms, data structures, optimization techniques, performance analysis, and so on. I report here on an ongoing effort to formalize and automate various sources of programming knowledge and to integrate them into a highly automated environment for developing formal specifications into correct and efficient programs (Balzer 1983). The system, called KIDS (Kestrel interactive development system), provides tools for performing deductive inference, algorithm design, expression simplification, finite differencing, partial evaluation, data type refinement, and other transformations. The KIDS tools serve to raise the level of language from which the programmer can obtain correct and efficient executable code through the use of automated tools.

A user of KIDS develops a formal specification into a program by interactively applying a sequence of high-level transformations. During develop-

ment, the user views a partially implemented specification annotated with
input assumptions, invariants, and output conditions. A mouse is used to select a transformation from a command menu and to apply it to a subexpression of the specification. In effect, the user makes high-level design decisions, and the system carries them out.

The unique features of KIDS include its algorithm design tactics and its use
of a deductive inference component. Its other operations, such as
simplification and finite differencing, are well known but have not been integrated before in one system. All the KIDS transformations are correctness preserving, and fully automatic (except the algorithm design tactics, which currently require some interaction) and perform significant, meaningful steps
from the user's point of view. Dozens of programs have been derived using
the system, and researchers believe that KIDS could be developed to the point
that it becomes economical to use for routine programming.

After briefly discussing the environment and inference system underlying
KIDS, I move through the derivation of a program for enumerating all solutions to the CostasArray problem, (Costas 1984) which is used to generate
optimal sonar and radar signals. The steps are as follows: First, build a domain theory to state and reason about the problem. Then, a well-structured
but inefficient backtrack algorithm (Smith 1987) is created that works by extending partial solutions. To improve efficiency, I apply simplification and
partial evaluation (Bjorner, Ershov, and Jones 1988; Scherlis 1981) operations. I also perform finite differencing (Paige and Koenig 1982), which results in the introduction of data structures. Next, high-level data types, such
as sets and sequences, are refined into more machine-oriented types, such as
bit vectors and linked lists. Finally, the resulting code is compiled.

The initial algorithm that KIDS designs takes about 50 minutes on a SUN
Sparcstation to enumerate all solutions to the order-9 Costas array problem.
The final optimized version finds the same solutions in 12 seconds. Researchers manually refined the optimized algorithm into C, and this code was
able to enumerate all order-17 solutions in about 6 days, thereby duplicating
all published results (Silverman, Vickers, and Mooney 1988).

Use of KIDS

I present an overview of general characteristics of the KIDS system and how it
is used. Currently, KIDS runs on SUN-4 workstations. It is built on top of RE-
FINE, a commercial knowledge-based programming environment (Abraido-
Fandino 1987). The REFINE environment provides an object-attribute–style
database that is used to represent software-related objects using annotated
abstract syntax trees, grammar-based parser-unparsers that translate between
text and abstract syntax, and a high-level language (also called REFINE) and

compiler. The language supports first-order logic, set-theoretic data types and operations, transformation, and pattern constructs that support the creation of rules. The compiler generates Common Lisp code.

The KIDS system is almost entirely written in REFINE, and all its operations work on the annotated abstract syntax tree representation of specifications in the REFINE database. A key feature of the unparsers (prettyprinters) is the option for *mouse-sensitive syntax:* The prettyprinter lays out the text and sets up active regions on the screen so that by moving the mouse around, the system can compute the nearest subexpression in the text and highlight it.

KIDS is a program-transformation system: One applies a sequence of correctness-preserving transformations to an initial specification and achieves a correct and, hopefully, efficient program. The system emphasizes the application of complex high-level transformations that perform significant and meaningful actions. From the user's point of view, the system allows the user to make high-level design decisions such as "design a divide-and-conquer algorithm for this specification" or "simplify this expression in context." Researchers hope that decisions at this level will be both intuitive to the user and high level enough that useful programs can be derived within a reasonable number of steps.

The user typically goes through the following steps in using KIDS for program development. First is develop a domain theory. The user builds a domain theory by defining appropriate types and functions. The user also provides laws that allow high-level reasoning about the defined functions. Experience has been that distributive and monotonicity laws provide most of the laws that are needed to support design and optimization. Recently, researchers added a theory development component to KIDS that supports the automated derivation of distributive laws. Second is create a specification. The user enters a specification stated in terms of the underlying domain theory. Third is apply a design tactic. The user selects an algorithm design tactic (method) from a menu and applies it to a specification. Currently, KIDS has tactics for simple problem reduction (reducing a specification to a library routine) (Smith 1985), divide-and-conquer (Smith 1985), global search (binary search, backtrack, branch and bound) (Smith 1987), and local search (hill climbing) (Lowry 1987, 1989). Fourth is apply optimizations. The KIDS system allows the application of optimization techniques such as simplification, partial evaluation, finite differencing, and other transformations. The user selects an optimization method from a menu and applies it by pointing at a program expression. Each of the optimization methods is fully automatic and, with the exception of simplification (which is arbitrarily hard), takes only a few seconds. Fifth is apply data type refinements. The user can select implementations for the high-level data types in the program. Data type refinement rules carry out the details of constructing the implementation. Sixth is compile. The resulting code is compiled into executable form. In a sense, KIDS can be regarded as a front end to a conventional compiler.

Actually, the user is free to apply any subset of the KIDS operations in any order; this sequence is typical of the experiments in algorithm design and is followed in this chapter.

Preliminaries

This section summarizes the language, specification format, and style of deductive inference used in this chapter.

Language

A functional specification programming language augmented with set-theoretic data types is used here. The main type constructors and their operations are based on those of the REFINE language. The Boolean type admits the usual operators and quantifiers of the predicate calculus ($\neg$, $\wedge$, $\vee$, $\Rightarrow$, $\forall$, $\exists$) with the exception of equality (=), which is used for logical equivalence.

Finite Sets

$S{:}set(Nat)$	Type declaration
$\{\}$	Empty set
$\{1, 2, 4, 8\}, \{2..5\}$	Literal set former: $\{2..5\} = \{2, 3, 4, 5\}$
$\{f(x) \mid P(x)\}$	General set former
$\in \notin = \neq \subseteq$	Comparison predicates: membership, equality, improper subset
$\cap, \cup,$ union!	Intersection, union, disjoint union
$setdiff(S, R)$	Set difference: $setdiff(\{1, 2, 3\}, \{2, 4\}) = \{1, 3\}$
$reduce(bop, S)$	Reduction of the set S by the associative and commutative operator bop: $reduce(\cup, \{\{1, 2\}, \{2\}, \{3\}\}) = \{1, 2, 3\}$

Finite Sequences

$A{:}seq(integer)$	Type declaration
$[]$	Empty sequence
$[2, 4, 6, 8]$	Literal sequence
$empty(A)$	$A = []$
$length(A)$	The length of A
$A(i)$	The ith element of A: $[4,5,6](2) = 5$
$\in \notin = \neq$	Comparison predicates: membership, equality
$domain(A)$	The set of integers $\{1..length(A)\}$
$range(A)$	Same as $\{A(i) \mid i \in domain(A)\}$
$concat(A, B)$	Concatenate sequences A and B
$append(A, x)$	Same as $concat(A, [x])$

Finite Maps

$M{:}map(integer, integer)$	Type declaration
$\{| |\}$	Empty map
$\{| x \rightarrow f(x) \mid P(x) |\}$	General map former
$domain(M), range(M)$	Domain and range of M
$map\text{-}union(M, N)$	$Map\text{-}union(M, N)(x) =$ if $x \in domain(N)$
	then $N(x)$ else $M(x)$
$dom\text{-}shift(f, m)$	$\{| f(x) \rightarrow M(x) \mid x \in domain(M) |\}$

Specifications

In this chapter, a formal specification serves to define the problem for which an efficient computational solution is desired. A problem is defined by means of functional constraints on input-output behavior. A specification can be presented as a quadruple $F = \langle D, R, I, O \rangle$, where D is the input type restricted to those values satisfying $I{:}D \rightarrow boolean$, the *input condition* (also called *input assumptions*). The output type is R, and the *output condition* $O{:}D \times R \rightarrow boolean$ defines the notion of acceptable or feasible solutions: If $O(x, z)$, then we say z is a *feasible solution* with respect to input x.

Specifications programs are also presented in a more programlike format:

Function F $(x{:}D)$
Where $I(x)$
Returns $\{z{:}R \mid O(x, z)\}$
$= Body$

This program specification for problem F returns the set of all values z of type R that satisfy the output condition O. The expression $Body$ (when present) is code that can be executed to compute F. A specification of this form is *consistent* if for all possible input satisfying the input condition, the body produces the same set as specified in the Returns expression; formally,

$$\forall(x{:}D)(I(x) \Rightarrow F(x) = \{z \mid O(x,z)\}) .$$

Directed Inference

Deductive inference is necessary for applying general knowledge to particular problems. I built a system called RAINBOW II that performs a form of deduction called *directed inference* (Smith 1982). In directed inference, a source term (or formula) is transformed into a target term (or formula) bearing a specified relationship to the first. It can perform first-order theorem-proving and formula simplification as special cases. It also allows the inference of sufficient conditions (antecedents) or necessary conditions (consequents) of a formula. This flexibility allows us to formulate a variety of design and optimization problems as inference tasks. Directed inference can play a constructive role in design rather than simply verifying work done by the user or some system.

Generally, inference tasks in this chapter are specified in the form (which is slightly simplified for the purposes of presentation)

Find some *(Target)* $(A \Rightarrow (Source(x_1, \ldots, mx_m) \rightarrow Target(y_1, \ldots y_m))$,

where A is a conjunction of assumptions; *Source* is the 'source' term; and $\rightarrow$ is a reflexive and transitive ordering relation between terms, called the *inference direction*. For notational simplicity, all free variables are universally quantified. In words, we want to derive some term *Target* expressed over the variables $\{y_1, \ldots, y_m\}$ (a subset of the free variables $\{x_1, \ldots, x_m\}$ of *Source*) such that the relationship $Source(x_1, \ldots, x_m) \rightarrow Target(y_1, \ldots, y_m)$ holds under the given assumptions. Currently, the inference direction can be specified as one of the following:

Forward inference $\Rightarrow$
Backward inference $\Leftarrow$
Simplification $=$
Derivation of a lower bound $\geq$
Derivation of an upper bound $\leq$

The inference process involves applying a sequence of transformations to the source term. The transformations are restricted to those that preserve the specified inference direction.

RAINBOW II relies on a library of theories that comprises over 700 rules for reasoning about REFINE program expressions. The rules have the general form of conditional rewrite rules

$C \Rightarrow (s \rightarrow t)$,

where $\rightarrow$ is an inference direction, C is an applicability condition, s is the source expression, and t is the target expression. The rules are automatically compiled from first-order theorems and are indexed according to, first, the dominant operator symbol in s and, second, the inference direction. For example, when deriving a necessary condition on $P(f(x), g(x, y))$, RAINBOW II retrieves and tries to apply all rules whose dominant symbol is P and whose inference direction is either $\Rightarrow$ or =. RAINBOW II tracks how many inequations it has applied in deriving each target expression and uses this quantity to compute a measure of semantic distance of the source from the target. Semantic distance plus a heuristic measure of computational complexity is used to select an optimal solution from amongst the derived solutions.

Most of the development operations in this chapter invoke RAINBOW II. Some of these tasks could be performed more efficiently by special-purpose inference systems, but I feel that the flexibility and conceptual economy allowed by using a common library of laws and a general-purpose inference system has resulted in a net productivity gain in my research.

RAINBOW II can run in interactive or automatic mode, although in KIDS, it is almost always treated as a subroutine that runs automatically and returns a result. It can be thought of as a transformational search engine that explores alternatives and selects solutions on the basis of a simple complexity measure (which can be user supplied). The traditional problems with using general-purpose inference systems are treated by carefully structuring the deductive tasks that are fed to RAINBOW II so that solutions can be reached without deep search. Also, resource bounds are placed on the execution of RAINBOW II, and it returns the best solution that it can find within the bounds.

A Session with KIDS

KIDS has been used to design and optimize global search algorithms for several dozen problems, some of which are listed in Results and Summary. I use the Costas array problem to illustrate KIDS.

The Costas Array Problem

Costas (1984) introduces a class of permutations that can be used to generate radar and sonar signals with ideal ambiguity functions. Since this time, there has been a flurry of work investigating various combinatorial properties of these permutations, now known as Costas arrays. No general construction was found, and the problem of enumerating Costas arrays was explored by computer search (Silverman, Vickers, and Mooney 1988). A *Costas Array* is a permutation of the set $\{1 \ .. \ n\}$ such that there are no repeated elements in any row of its difference table (figure 1). The first row of the difference table gives the difference of adjacent elements of the permutation, the second row gives the difference of every other element, and so on.

Domain Theory and Specification

Before a specification can be written, the relevant concepts, operations, relationships, and properties of the problem must be defined. Thus, the first and, often, the hardest step in deriving an algorithm for solving a problem is the formalization of its domain theory. KIDS provides rudimentary support for the development of domain theories. A *theory presentation* (or simply a *theory)* comprises a set of imported theories, new type definitions, function specifications with optional operational definitions, laws (axioms and theorems), and rules of inference (Goguen and Winkler 1988; Guttag and Horning 1986). The domain theory for the Costas array problem is summarized later and is presented in full at the end of this chapter. A library of theories is maintained with importation providing hierarchic structure. As of mid-1990, about 30 percent of the KIDS' DOMAIN knowledge was encapsulated in 25 domain theories. The rest of its domain knowledge was represented as an unstructured collection of definitions and rules.

Users can enter definitions of new functions or create new definitions by abstraction on existing expressions. The inference system can be used to verify common properties such as associativity, commutativity, or idempotene.

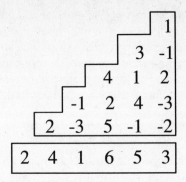

Figure 1. Costas Array of Order 6 and Its Difference Table.

More interestingly, researchers used RAINBOW II to automatically derive theorems from definitions and axioms.

Just as there can be several ways to solve a given problem, there can be several ways to formalize a domain. Some formulations provide a better foundation for subsequent development than others. I tried several formulations of the domain theory for Costas arrays, two of which I discuss below. A useful heuristic in constructing a domain theory is that the laws for reasoning about the domain concepts should be simple. A related notion is that over 80 percent of the laws needed to support design and optimization in KIDS are distributive laws, analogous to the familiar distributive laws of arithmetic:

$a \times (b + c) = (a \times b) + (a \times c)$ (distribute $\times$ over $+$)
$a + (b \times c) = (a + b) \times (a + c)$ (distribute $+$ over $\times$)

Consequently, the working methodology is, whenever possible, to favor domain concepts that have simple distributive laws. In addition, tools were added to KIDS that support the derivation of distributive laws for user-designated functions.

The first attempt at a Costas array theory was based on the notion of the various rows of the difference table. The abstract data type of sequences over $\{1 .. n\}$ was used to represent solutions. I defined $diff(p, i)$ to be the bag of ith differences of the sequence p. The domain theory based on this concept was so complicated that I had a hard time developing its laws. For example, it turned out that *diff* distributes poorly over the operation of sequence concatenation. This result suggested that there must be a simpler formulation.

The second attempt focused on the difference table itself as the basic concept, and this attempt proved successful. The following function builds a difference table for a given sequence:

```
function dt (p:seq(integer)) :map(tuple(integer, integer), integer)
 = {I <i, j> → p(i) – p(i – j) I (i – j) i ∈ domain(p) & j ∈ {1 .. i – 1} I} .
```

As seen in figure 2, *dt* distributes nicely over a concatenation of sequences:

$dt([]) = \{ I \, I \}$

$dt([a]) = \{ I \, I \}$

$dt(concat(p, q)) =$
$\quad map\text{-}union(dt(p), map\text{-}union\ cross\text{-}dt(p, q)\ dom\text{-}shift(\lambda(x)\ x + size(p), dt(q))))$

where

function *cross-dt* $(p:seq(integer), q:seq(integer))$:
$\quad map(tuple(integer, integer), integer)$
$\quad = \{ I <i, j> \rightarrow q(i - n) - p(i - j)\ I\ (i, j, n)$
$\qquad n = size(p)$
$\qquad \&\ i \in image(lambda(k)\ k + n, domain(q))$
$\qquad \&\ j \in \{ i - n \,..\, i - 1 \}\ I \}\ .$

The *dt* function entails the need for other functions: $dtrow(d, i)$ returns the *i*th row of the difference table *d*; $nodups(s)$ holds iff sequence (row) *s* does not contain duplicate occurrences of some element. Distributive laws for these concepts are straightforward. The concept that a sequence is a permutation is expressed by the notion of a bijection (a one-to-one and onto mapping). This concept—and the associated laws for reasoning about it—is imported with the theory called SEQUENCES-AS-MAPS.

function *injective* $(M:seq(integer), S:set(integer)):boolean$
$\quad = range(M) \subseteq S$
$\qquad \&\ \forall\ (i, j)(i \in domain(M)\ \&\ j \in domain(M)\ \&\ i \neq j \Rightarrow M(i) \neq M(j))\ .$

function *bijective* $(M:seq(integer), S:set(integer)):boolean$
$\quad = injective(M, S)\ \&\ range(M) = S\ .$

That is, a sequence *M* is injective into a set *S* if all elements of *M* are in *S*, and no element of *M* occurs twice. A sequence *M* is bijective into a set *S* if it is injective, and each element of *S* occurs in *M*. Distributive laws for the injective predicate are as follows:

$\forall\ (S)(\ injective([], S) = true)$

$\forall\ (W, a, S)\ (\ injective(append(W, a), S)$
$\quad = (injective(W, S)\ \&\ a \in S\ \&\ a \notin range(W)))$

$\forall\ (W1, W2, S)\ (\ injective(concat(W1, W2), S)$
$\quad = (injective(W1, S)\ \&\ injective(W2, S)\ \&\ (range(W1) \cap range(W2) = \{\ \})).$

The complete Costas array theory used in KIDS is listed at the end of this chapter.

We can now formulate a specification for the Costas array problem:

function *costas* $(n:integer)$
$\quad$ where $1 \leq n$
$\quad$ returns $\{ p \mid bijective(p, \{1 \,..\, n\})$
$\qquad \&\ \forall(j)(j \in domain(p) \Rightarrow nodups(dtrow(dt(p), j)))\}\ .$

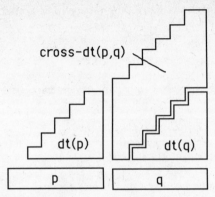

Figure 2. Distributive Law for Difference Tables.

Algorithm Design

The next step is to develop a correct, high-level algorithm for enumerating Costas arrays. We select a global search tactic to design a backtrack algorithm. The basic idea of global search (Smith 1987) is to represent and manipulate sets of candidate solutions. The principal operations are to extract candidate solutions from a set and to split a set into subsets. Derived operations include various *filters* which are used to eliminate sets containing no feasible or optimal solutions. Global search algorithms work as follows: Starting from an initial set that contains all solutions to the given problem instance, the algorithm repeatedly extracts solutions, splits sets, and eliminates sets using filters until no sets remain to be split. The process is often described as a tree search in which a node represents a set of candidates, and an arc represents the split relationship between a set and a subset. The filters serve to prune branches of the tree that cannot lead to solutions.

The sets of candidate solutions are often infinite, and even when finite, they are rarely represented extensionally. Thus, global search algorithms are based on an abstract data type of intensional representations called *space descriptors*. In addition to the extraction and splitting operations previously mentioned, the abstract data type also includes the satisfies predicate that determines when a candidate solution is in the set denoted by a descriptor.

The various operations in the abstract data type of space descriptors, together with problem specifications, can be packaged as a theory. Formally, abstract global search theory (or, simply, gs-theory)

$G = <B, S, J, s_0,$ **Satisfies, Split, Extract**$>$ is presented as follows:

Sorts D, R, S
Operations
    $I : D \rightarrow$ boolean
    $O : D \times R \rightarrow$ boolean

$J : D \times S \rightarrow$ boolean
$s_0 : D \rightarrow S$
Satisfies : $R \times S \rightarrow$ boolean
Split : $D \times S \times S \rightarrow$ boolean
Extract : $R \times S \rightarrow$ boolean

Axioms

GS0. $I(x) \Rightarrow J(x, s_0(x))$
GS1. $I(x)$ & $J(x, s)$ & $Split(x, s, t) \Rightarrow J(x, t)$
GS2. $I(x)$ & $O(x, z) \Rightarrow Satisfies(z, s_0(x))$
GS3. $I(x)$ & $J(x, s) \Rightarrow (Satisfies(z, s) = (\exists t)(Split*(x, s, t)$ & $Extract\,(z, t)))$

where $\mathbf{B} = \mathbf{<D, R, I, O>}$ constitutes a problem specification, $\mathbf{S}$ is the type of space descriptors, $\mathbf{J}$ defines legal space descriptors, $\mathbf{s}$ and $\mathbf{t}$ vary over descriptors, $\mathbf{s_0(x)}$ is the descriptor of the initial set of candidate solutions, **Satisfies(z, s)** means that $\mathbf{z}$ is in the set denoted by descriptor $\mathbf{s}$ or that $\mathbf{z}$ satisfies the constraints that $\mathbf{s}$ represents, **Split(x, s, t)** means that $\mathbf{t}$ is a subspace of $\mathbf{s}$ with respect to input $\mathbf{x}$, and **Extract (z, s)** means that $\mathbf{z}$ is directly extractable from $\mathbf{s}$. Axiom GS0 asserts that the initial descriptor $\mathbf{s_0(x)}$ is a legal descriptor. Axiom GS1 asserts that legal descriptors split into legal descriptors and that **Split** induces a well-founded ordering on spaces. Axiom GS2 constrains the denotation of the initial descriptor—all feasible solutions are contained in the initial space. Axiom GS3 gives the denotation of an arbitrary descriptor $\mathbf{s}$—an output object $\mathbf{z}$ is in the set denoted by $\mathbf{s}$ if and only if $\mathbf{z}$ can be extracted after finitely many applications of **Split** to $\mathbf{s}$, where

$Split*(x, s, t) = \exists\,(k{:}Nat)(Split^k(x, s, t))$

and

$Split^0(x, s\,, r) = (s = r)$

and for all natural numbers $\mathbf{k}$

$Split^{k+1}(x, s, r) = \exists\,(t{:}S)\,(Split(x, s, t)$ & $Split^k(x, t, r))$.

Note that all variables are assumed to be universally quantified unless explicitly specified otherwise.

Example: Enumerating Sequences over a Given Set. Consider the problem of enumerating sequences over a given finite set S. A *space* is a set of sequences with common prefix V and is represented as a sequence V. The descriptor for the initial space is just []. Splitting is performed by appending an element from S onto the end of the common prefix V. The sequence V itself is directly extractable from the space. This global search theory, called *gs_sequences_over_finite_set*, for enumerating sequences can be presented using a correspondence between the components of an abstract gs-theory (Smith and Lowry 1989) and a concrete gs-theory (technically, this correspondence is known as theory interpretation or theory morphism).

D	$\rightarrow set(\alpha) \times integer$
I	$\rightarrow \lambda\ S.\ true$
R	$\rightarrow seq(\alpha)$
O	$\rightarrow \lambda\ S, q.\ range(q) \subseteq S$
S	$\rightarrow seq(\alpha)$
J	$\rightarrow \lambda\ S, V.\ range(V) \subseteq S$
Satisfies	$\rightarrow \lambda\ q, V.\ \exists\ (r)\ (q = concat(V, r))$
s$_0$	$\rightarrow \lambda\ S.\ []$
Split	$\rightarrow \lambda\ S, V, V'.\ \exists\ (i{:}S)\ (V' = append(V, i))$
Extract	$\rightarrow \lambda\ q, V.\ q = V$

In words, the abstract input domain symbol **D** is interpreted here as $set(\alpha)$ $\times$ *integer,* where α is a type variable, allowing the theory to be polymorphic; the input condition **I** is interpreted as the trivial predicate $\lambda\ S.\ true$ that always returns *true;* the **Split** operation of global search theory is interpreted as $\lambda\ S, V, V'.\ \exists\ (i{:}S)\ (V' = append(V, i))$; and so on. This correspondence is used later to instantiate abstract programs (program schemas).

In addition to these components of global search theory, various other operations play a role in producing an efficient algorithm. Filters are crucial to the efficiency of a global search algorithm. Filters correspond to the notion of pruning branches in backtrack algorithms and pruning using lower bounds and dominance relations in branch and bound actions. A *filter* is used to eliminate spaces from further processing. The ideal filter decides the question, "Does a feasible solution exist in space s?" Formally,

$$\exists\ (z{:}R)\ (\textbf{Satisfies}(z, s)\ \&\ O(x, z))\ . \tag{1}$$

However, to directly use formula 1 as a filter would usually be too expensive; instead, we use an approximation to it. A necessary filter Φ satisfies

$$\exists\ (z{:}R)\ (\textbf{Satisfies}\ (z, s)\ \&\ O(x, z)) \Rightarrow \Phi\ (x, s)\ . \tag{2}$$

By the contrapositive of formula 2, if $\Phi(x, s)$ is false for some space s, then no solution exists in s. Thus, necessary filters can be used to eliminate spaces that do not contain solutions. We derive Φ by using directed inference to infer a necessary condition on formula 1 that depends only on the variables x and s.

The design tactic for global search in KIDS is based on two theorems. The proofs can be found in Smith (1987). The first theorem shows how to produce a correct program from a given global search theory. Consequently, the construction of a correct global search program is reduced to the problem of constructing a global search theory. The second theorem tells us how to obtain a global search theory for a given problem by specializing an existing global search theory. This theorem suggests that we set up a library of global search theories for the various data types of our language and simply select and specialize these library theories.

Theorem 1: Let $G = \ <B, S, J, s_0, \textbf{Satisfies}, \textbf{Split}, \textbf{Extract}>$ be a global search theory where $\mathbf{B} = <\mathbf{D, R, I, O}>$. If Φ is a necessary filter, then the following program specification is consistent:

function $\mathbf{F(x:D):set(R)}$
    where $\mathbf{I(x)}$
    returns $\{z \mid O(x, z)\}$
    = If $\Phi(\mathbf{x}, s_0(\mathbf{x}))$
        Then $\mathbf{F\_gs(x}, s_0(\mathbf{x}))$
        Else $\{\}$
function $\mathbf{F\_gs\ (x:D, s:S) : set(R)}$
    where $\mathbf{I\ (x)\ \&\ J(x,s)\ \&\ \Phi(x,s)}$
    returns $\{\mathbf{z \mid Satisfies\ (z, s)\ \&\ O(x\ ,z)}\}$
    = $\{z \mid \mathbf{Extract\ (z, s)\ \&\ O(x,z)}\}$
        $\cup\ \mathbf{reduce}(\cup, \{\ \mathbf{F\_gs(x, t)\ \mid\ Split(x, s, t)\ \&\ \Phi(x, t)}\})$.

In words, the abstract global search program works as follows: On input $\mathbf{x}$, the program F calls F_gs with the initial space $s_0(\mathbf{x})$ if the filter holds; otherwise, there are no feasible solutions. The program F_gs unions two sets: (1) all solutions that can directly be extracted from the space $\mathbf{s}$ and (2) the union of all solutions recursively found in spaces $\mathbf{t}$ that are obtained by splitting $\mathbf{s}$ and that survive the filter. In terms of the search tree model, F_gs unions the solutions found at the current node with the solutions found at the descendants. Note that Φ is an input invariant in F_gs. If we were to apply theorem 1 to gs_sequences_over_finite_set, then we would get a generator of sequences over the input set S.

The following definition gives the conditions under which an algorithm for solving problem B_B can be used to enumerate all solutions to B_A. Specification $B_A= <D_A, R_A, I_A, O_A>$ completely reduces to specification $B_B = <D_B, R_B, I_B, O_B>$ if

$$R_A= R_B\ \&\ \forall\ (x:D_A)\ \exists\ (y:D_B\ )\ \forall\ (z:R_A)(\ I_A(x)\ \&\ O_A(x, z) \Rightarrow O_B\ (y,z)) . \tag{3}$$

B_A completely reduces to B_B with substitution θ if $\theta(y) = t(x)$ and $R_A = R_B\theta$ and

$$\forall\ (x:D_A)\ \forall\ (z:R_A)(\ I_A(x)\ \&\ O_A(x, z) \Rightarrow O_B(t(x), z)) .$$

Theorem 2: Let $G_B = <B_B, \mathbf{S, J}, s_0, \mathbf{Satisfies, Split, Extract}>$ be a global search theory, and let B_A be a specification that completely reduces to B_B with substitution θ, then the structure $G_A = <B_A, \mathbf{S}\theta, \mathbf{J}\theta, \mathbf{Satisfies}\theta, s_0\theta, \mathbf{Split}\theta, \mathbf{Extract}\theta>$ is a global search theory.

A simplified tactic for designing global search algorithms has three steps:

(1) Select a global search theory G_B from a library that solves the problem of enumerating the output type for the given problem A.

(2) Find a substitution θ whereby B_A completely reduces to B_B by verifying formula 3. Apply theorem 2 to create a specialized global search theory G_A.

(3) Derive a necessary filter Φ using formula 2. That is, use directed infer-

ence to derive a necessary condition of formula 2 expressed over the variables $\{x, s\}$. Apply theorem 1 to create a global search program.

The tactic is sound and, thus, only generates correct programs. The interested reader should consult Smith (1987) for the full generality of the global search model and design tactic.

The KIDS library currently contains global search theories for a number of problem domains, such as enumerating sets, sequences, maps, and integers. For the Costas array problem, we select from a library a standard global search theory for enumerating sequences over a finite domain: gs_se-quences_over_finite_set. In accord with step 2, the following inference specification is created by instantiating formula (4):

$set(integer) = set(\alpha)$ &
$\forall\, (n: integer)\, \exists\, (S: set(integer))\, \forall\, (assign: seq(integer))$
  $(bijective(assign, \{1 .. n\})$
    & $\forall(j)(j \in domain(p) \Rightarrow nodups(dtrow(dt(p), j))) \Rightarrow range(assign) \subseteq S)$.

The derivation is simple and proceeds as follows: The types are unified yielding substitution$\{| \alpha \rightarrow integer\ |\}$. By forward inference from $bijective(assign, \{1 .. n\})$, KIDS derives

  $injective(assign, \{1..n\})$ and $range(assign) = \{1 .. n\};$

then

$range(assign) \subseteq S$
=   applying $range(assign) = \{1 .. n\}$
  $\{1..n\} \subseteq S$
=   unifying with the reflexivity law $\forall\ (R)(R \subseteq R)$
  true   with substitution $\{| S \rightarrow \{1 .. n\}\ |\}$.

Thus, altogether the Costas array problem completely reduces to gs_sequences_over_finite_set with substitution $\theta = \{| \alpha \rightarrow integer, S \rightarrow \{1 .. n\}\ |\}$. The construction in theorem 2 yields the following global search theory:

$\mathbf{D} \rightarrow integer$
$\mathbf{I} \rightarrow \lambda\, n.\, 1 \leq n$
$\mathbf{R} \rightarrow seq(integer)$
$\mathbf{O} \rightarrow \lambda n, p.\ bijective(p, \{1 .. n\})$ & $\forall\ (j)(j \in domain(p) \Rightarrow nodups(dtrow(dt(p), j)))$
$\mathbf{S} \rightarrow seq(integer)$
$\mathbf{J} \rightarrow \lambda\, n, V.\ range(V) \subseteq \{1 .. n\}$
$\mathbf{Satisfies} \rightarrow \lambda\, p, V.\ \exists(r)(p, concat(V, r))$
$\mathbf{s_0} \rightarrow [\,]$
$\mathbf{Split} \rightarrow \lambda\, n, V, V'.\ \exists\, (integer)(i \in \{1 .. n\}$ & $V' = append(V, i))$
$\mathbf{Extract} \rightarrow \lambda\, p, V.\ p = V$

This new specialized theory corresponds to the generator shown in figure 3. This generator enumerates a superset of Costas arrays. The next design step is to derive mechanisms for pruning such useless nodes of the search tree. The effect of this step is to incorporate more problem-specific information into the generator to improve efficiency.

To derive a necessary filter for the Costas array problem, the inference system is directed to produce necessary conditions on the existence of an extension of a partial solution V that satisfies all the Costas array constraints; formally,

$$\text{find some } (\Phi) \ (1 \le n \Rightarrow \exists\, (p) \ (\exists\, (r) \ (p = concat(V, r))$$
$$\&\ bijective(p, \{1 .. n\})$$
$$\&\ \forall\, (j)(j \in domain(p) \Rightarrow nodups(dtrow(dt(p), j)))$$
$$\Rightarrow \Phi(n, V))\,.$$

Any such Φ serves as a filter because if Φ does not hold for some partial solution, then by the contrapositive of the implication, an extension does not exist that satisfies the Costas array constraints. The derivations proceed as follows:

$bijective(p, \{1 .. n\})$
$=$ by definition of *bijective*
       $injective(p, \{1 .. n\}) \ \&\ range(p) = \{1 .. n\}$
$\Rightarrow$ applying $p = concat(V, r)$ to the first conjunct
       $injective(concat(V, r), \{1 .. n\})$
$=$ distributing *injective* over *concat*
       $injective(V, \{1 .. n\}) \ \&\ injective(r, \{1 .. n\}) \ \&\ range(V) \cap range(r) = \{\}$
$\Rightarrow$ dropping conjuncts
       $injective(V, \{1 .. n\})\,.$

Also,

$\forall\, (j)(j \in domain(p) \Rightarrow nodups(dtrow(dt(p), j)))$
$=$ applying $p = concat(V, r)$
       $\forall\, (j)(j \in domain(p) \Rightarrow nodups(dtrow(dt(concat(V, r)), j)))$
$=$ distributing *dt* over *concat*
       $\forall\, (j)(j \in domain(p) \Rightarrow nodups(dtrow(map\text{-}union(dt(V),$
       $map\text{-}union(\ cross\text{-}dt(V, r), dom\text{-}shift(\lambda(x)\, x + size(V), dt(r))), j)))$

$=$ distributing *dtrow* over *map-union*
       $\forall\, (j)(j \in domain(p) \Rightarrow nodups(concat(dtrow(dt(V), j),$
            $dtrow(cross\text{-}dt(V, r), j),$
            $dtrow(dom\text{-}shift(\lambda(x)\, x + size(V), dt(r)), j))))$
$=$ distributing *nodups* over *concat*
       $\forall\, (j)(j \in domain(p) \Rightarrow nodups(dtrow(dt(V), j))$
          $\&\ nodups(dtrow(cross\text{-}dt(V, r), j))$
          $\&\ nodups(dom\text{-}shift(\lambda(x)\, x + size(V), dt(r)), j)))$
$\Rightarrow$ dropping conjuncts
       $\forall\, (j)(j \in domain(p) \Rightarrow nodups(dtrow(dt(V), j)))$
$=$ applying $p = concat(V, r)$
       $\forall\, (j)(j \in domain(concat(V, r)) \Rightarrow nodups(dtrow(dt(V), j)))$
$=$ distributing *domain* over *concat*
       $\forall\, (j)(j \in (domain(V) \ union \ j \ in \ domain(r)) \Rightarrow nodups(dtrow(dt(V), j)))$
$\Rightarrow$ distributing and dropping conjuncts
       $\forall\, (j)(j \in domain(V) \Rightarrow nodups(dtrow(dt(V), j)))\,.$

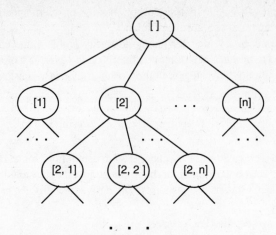

Figure 3. Generator of Sequences over the Set {1 .. n}.

From among the many derived consequents, RAINBOW discards useless ones and presents a menu of possibilities for the user to choose from. The conjunction of any subset results in a correct algorithm. We select the following consequents using dependency analysis (not implemented at the time of this writing).

$$\forall\,(j)(j \in domain(V) \Rightarrow nodups(dtrow(dt(V), j))) \;\&\; injective(V, \{1 \,.\,.\, n\})\,.$$

In words, the partial solution must itself satisfy the constraints that there are no duplicates in the partial solution and that no duplicates exist in any row of its difference table.

Finally the recursive REFINE program in figure 4 is produced by applying theorem 1. That is, the correspondence between the symbols of an abstract gs-theory and concrete expressions is used to instantiate the program scheme in theorem 1. The first set former in COSTAS-GS-AUX simply checks whether the partial solution V is a complete solution and, if so, returns $\{V\}$. The expression *reduce(union!, . . .)* explores all possible extensions to the partial solution V that survive the filter. The program specification COSTAS initializes the backtrack search after checking that the initial partial solution [] survives the filter. Note that the filter is displayed as an input invariant in COSTAS-GS-AUX because it is tested prior to each call to the backtracking function.

Being produced as an instance of a program abstraction, this algorithm obviously has some inefficiencies, even though it is correct. The intent of the design tactics is to produce correct, very-high-level, well-structured algorithms. Subsequent refinement and optimization is necessary to realize the potential of the algorithm.

Simplification

KIDS provides two expression simplifiers. The simplest and fastest, the con-

```
function COSTAS-GS-AUX (var N:integer, var V: seq(integer))
   where 1 ≤ N & range(V) ⊆ {1 .. N}
         & injective(V, {1 .. N})
         & ∀ (J)(J ∈ domain(V) ⇒ nodups(DTROW(DT(V), J)))
   returns {P | extends(P, V)
                  & ∀ (J)(J ∈ domain(P) ⇒ nodups(DTROW(DT(P), J)))
                  & bijective(P, {1 .. N})})
= {P | ∀ (J: integer)(J ∈ domain(P) ⇒ nodups(DTROW(DT(P), J)))
         & bijective(P, {1 .. N})
         & P = V}
   union! reduce(union!,
            {COSTAS-GS-AUX(N, NEW-V) | injective(NEW-V, {1 .. N})
               & ∀ (J)(J ∈ domain(NEW-V) ⇒ nodups(DTROW(DT(NEW-V), J)))
               & ∃ (I: integer)(NEW-V = append(V, I) & I ∈ {1 .. N})})

function COSTAS (var N: integer | 1 ≤ N)
   returns {P | bijective(P, {1 .. N})
                  & ∀ (J)(J ∈ domain(P) ⇒ nodups(DTROW(DT(P), J)))}
= if ∀ (J)(J ∈ domain([]) ⇒ nodups(DTROW(DT([]), J)))
      & injective([], {1 .. N})
   then COSTAS-GS-AUX(N, [])
   else {}
```

Figure 4. Global Search Algorithm for the Costas Array Problem.

text-independent simplifier (CI-SIMPLIFY), is a set of equations treated as left-to-right rewrite rules that are exhaustively fired until none apply. Some typical equations used as rewrite rules are

$length([]) = 0$

and

$(if\ true\ then\ P\ else\ Q) = P$.

The distributive laws in Costas array theory are also treated as rewrite rules; for example,

$injective([], S) = true$

and

$injective(append(W, a), S) = (injective(W, S)\ \&\ a \in S\ \&\ a \notin range(W))$.

We apply CI-Simplify to the body of all newly derived programs. As a result, the conditional in program Costas-Array

$if\ ∀\ (J)(J \in domain([]) ⇒ nodups(dtrow(dt([]), j)))$
    $\&\ injective([], \{1 .. n\})|$
        $then\ COSTAS\text{-}GS\text{-}AUX(n, [])$
        $else\ \{\ \}$

simplifies to $COSTAS\text{-}GS\text{-}AUX(n, [])$.

```
function COSTAS-GS-AUX (var N: integer, var V: seq(integer))
   where 1 ≤ N & range(V) ⊆ {1 .. N}
       & injective(V, {1 .. N})
       & ∀ (J)(J ∈ domain(V) ⇒ nodups(DTROW(DT(V), J)))
   returns ...
   = {V | ∀ (J: integer)(J ∈ domain(V) ⇒ nodups(DTROW(DT(V), J)))
       & bijective(V, {1 .. N})}
     union! reduce(union!,
        {COSTAS-GS-AUX(N, append(V, I)) |
            I ∈ {1 .. N} & I ∉ range(V)
          & injective(V, {1 .. N})
          & ∀ (J)(J ∈ domain(V) ⇒ nodups(DTROW(DT(V), J)))
          & nodups(DTROW(DT(V), 1 + size(V)))
          & ∀ (J)(J ∈ domain(V)
                ⇒ cross-nodups(DTROW(DT(V), J), [I - V(1 + size(V) - J) | J ≤ size(V)]))
          & ∀ (J)(J ∈ domain(V) ⇒ nodups([I - V(1 + size(V) - J)| J ≤ size(V)]))})

function COSTAS (var N: integer | 1 ≤ N)
   returns ...
   = COSTAS-GS-AUX(N, [])
```

Figure 5. Costas-Array Code after Context-Independent Simplification.

Another rule modifies a set former by replacing all occurrences of a local variable that is defined by an equality:

$$\{ C(x) \,|\, x = e \,\&\, P(x) \} = \{ C(e)\,|\,P(e) \} .$$

For example, this rule will replace *new_V* with *append(V, i)* everywhere in COSTAS-GS-AUX. In turn, this replacement triggers the application of the laws for distributing *dt, dtrow, nodups,* and *injective* over *append*.

The result of applying CI-Simplify to the bodies of COSTAS and COSTAS-GS-AUX is shown in figure 5. (For brevity we will sometimes omit or use ellipsis in place of expressions that remain unchanged after a transformation).

There are other simplification opportunities in this code. For example, notice that the predicate *injective*$(v, \{1 .. n\})$ is being tested in COSTAS-GS-AUX, but it is already true because it is an input invariant. The second expression simplifier, Context-Dependent Simplify (CD-Simplify), is designed to simplify a given expression with respect to its context. CD-Simplify gathers all predicates that hold in the context of the expression by walking up the abstract syntax tree gathering the test of encompassing conditionals, sibling conjuncts in the condition of a set former, and so on, until ultimately reaching the input conditions of the encompassing function. The expression is then simplified with respect to this rich assumption set.

In applying CD-Simplify to the predicate of the first set former in

COSTAS-GS-AUX, the following inference task is set up:

find some (simplified_wff)
$$(1 \leq N \ \& \ range(V) \subseteq \{1 .. N\}$$
$$\& \ injective(V, \{1 .. N\})$$
$$\& \ \forall \ (J)(J \in domain(V) \Rightarrow nodups(DTROW(DT(V), J)))$$
$$\Rightarrow (\forall \ (J: integer)(J \in domain(V)$$
$$\Rightarrow nodups(DTROW(DT(V), J))) \ \& \ bijective(V, \{1 .. n\}))$$
$$= simplified\_wff \ (V, n)).$$

The first conjunct of the source expression immediately unifies with an assumption and, thus, simplifies to *true*. For the second conjunct, KIDS infers

bijective(V, {1 .. n})
=   by definition of *bijective*
    injective(V, {1 .. n}) & range(V) = {1 .. n}
=   matching the first conjunct with assumption
    range(V) = {1 .. n}
=   by definition of set equality: $(S = T) = (S \subseteq T \ \& \ T \subseteq S)$
    range(V) ⊆ {1 .. n} & {1 .. n} ⊆ range(V)
=   matching the first conjunct with assumption
    {1 .. n} ⊆ range(V) .

The resulting simplified expression is

    {1 .. n} ⊆ range(V) .

After applying CD-Simplify to the predicates of both set formers in COSTAS-GS-AUX, we obtain the code in figure 6.

Partial Evaluation

Next we notice that the call to *cross-nodups* has an argument of a restricted form—a singleton sequence suggesting the application of partial evaluation (Bjorner, Ershov, and Jones 1988). KIDS has the classic UNFOLD transformation (Burstall and Darlington 1977) that replaces a function call with its definition (with arguments replacing parameters). The definition of *cross-nodups* is part of the domain theory for Costas arrays (presented later in this chapter). Partial evaluation proceeds by first unfolding, then simplifying.

Unfolding *cross_nodups(V, [I])*, we obtain

$$\forall \ (J) \ (J \in domain(V)$$
$$\Rightarrow \forall \ (I1: integer, J1: integer)$$
$$(I1 \in domain(DTROW(DT(V), J)) \ \& \ J1 \in domain([I - V(1 + size(V) - J)])$$
$$\Rightarrow DTROW(DT(V), J)(I1) \neq [I - V(1 + size(V) - J)](J1))) .$$

The following rules in the KIDS rule base

$$domain([x]) = \{1\}$$
$$x \in \{a\} = (x = a)$$
$$\forall \ (x, y)(Q(x) \ \& \ x = e \Rightarrow P(x)) = \forall \ (y)(Q(e) \Rightarrow P(e))$$

and others are used by CI-Simplify, resulting in

```
function COSTAS-GS-AUX (N, V)
   = {V | {1 .. N} ⊆ range(V)}
      union! reduce(union!, {COSTAS-GS-AUX(N, append(V, I)) |
                  I ∈ {1 .. N} & I ∉ range(V)
               & ∀(J)(J ∈ domain(V)
                        ⇒ cross-nodups(DTROW(DT(V), J),[I - V(1 + size(V) - J)]))})
```

Figure 6. COSTAS-GS-AUX after Context-Dependent Simplification.

$$\forall (J) (J \in domain(V) \Rightarrow I - V(1 + size(V) - J) \notin range(DTROW(DT(V), J))) \,.$$

KIDS produces the code in figure 7.

Finite Differencing

Notice that the expression *range(V)* in figure 7 is computed each time COSTAS-GS-AUX is invoked and that the parameter V changes in a regular way: With each recursive call, V has a single element appended to it. This change suggests that we create a new variable whose value is maintained equal to *range(V)* and allows for incremental computation—a significant speedup. This transformation is known as *finite differencing* (Paige and Koenig 1982). I developed and implemented a version of finite differencing for functional programs.

Finite differencing can be decomposed into two more basic operations: abstraction followed by simplification. Abstraction of function $f(x)$ with respect to expression $E(x)$ adds a new parameter c to f's parameter list (now $f(x, c)$) and adds $c = E(x)$ as a new input invariant to f. Any call to f, whether a recursive call within f or an external call, must now be changed to supply the appropriate new argument that satisfies the invariant: Invocation $f(U)$ is changed to $f(U, E(U))$.

It now becomes possible to simplify various expressions within f and calls to f. In the KIDS implementation, CI-Simplify is applied to the new argument in all external calls. Within f we temporarily add the invariant $E(x) = c$ as a rule and apply CI-Simplify to the body of f, replacing all occurrences of $E(x)$ by c. Often, distributive laws apply to $E(U(x))$, yielding an expression of the form $U'(E(x))$ and then $U'(c)$. The real benefit of this optimization comes from the last step because it is at this point that the new value of the expression $E(U(x))$ is computed in terms of the old value $E(x)$.

The evolving algorithm is prepared for finite differencing by subjecting it to conditioning transformations. In this case, they transform two conjuncts

$$I \notin range(V) \,\&\, I \in \{1 .. n\}$$

to

$$I \in setdiff(\{1 .. n\}, range(V)) \,.$$

The rationale is to group information concerning a local variable.

We select the set difference as an expression to incrementally maintain.

```
function COSTAS-GS-AUX (N, V)
  = {V | {1 .. N} ⊆ range(V)}
    union! reduce (union!, {COSTAS-GS-AUX(N, append(V, I)) |
          I ∈ {1 .. N} & I ∉ range(V)
          & ∀ (J) (J ∈ domain(V) ⇒ I – V(1 + size(V) - J) ∉ range(DTROW(DT(V), J)))})
```

Figure 7. COSTAS-GS-AUX after Partial Evaluation / Specialization.


```
function COSTAS-GS-AUX (N, V,POOL)
  where POOL = set-diff({1 .. N}, range(V)) & ..
  = {V | empty(POOL)}
    union! reduce(union!, {COSTAS-GS-AUX(N, append(V, I), POOL less I) |
          I ∈ POOL
          & ∀(J)(J∈domain(V) ⇒ I - V(1 + size(V) - J) ∉ range(DTROW(DT(V), J))) })

function COSTAS (N)
  = COSTAS-GS-AUX(N, [], {1 .. N})
```

Figure 8. Costas-Array Algorithm after One Finite Differencing Step.

The changes include (1) adding a new input parameter, named *pool*, and its invariant to COSTAS-GS-AUX; (2) replacing all occurrences of the term *setdiff*($\{1 . . n\}$, *range*(V)) in COSTAS-GS-AUX with *pool*; and (3) creating and simplifying appropriate arguments for all calls to the function COSTAS-GS-AUX. The initial call to COSTAS-GS-AUX (figure 5) becomes

$COSTAS\text{-}GS\text{-}AUX(n, [], setdiff(\{1 . . n\}, range([])))$,

which CI-Simplifies to $COSTAS\text{-}GS\text{-}AUX(n, [], \{1 . . n\})$.

The recursive call to COSTAS-GS-AUX becomes

$COSTAS\text{-}GS\text{-}AUX(n, append(V, I), setdiff(\{1 . . n\}, range(append(V, I))))$,

which CI-Simplifies to $COSTAS\text{-}GS\text{-}AUX(n, append(V, I), pool - \{I\})$. The resulting code is shown in figure 8.

Notice how finite differencing introduces a meaningful data structure at this point. The concept of which elements of $\{1 . . n\}$ have not yet been added to the partial solution V would naturally occur to many programmers who are developing a Costas array algorithm. Here, it is introduced by a problem-independent transformation technique. Not only is the concept natural in the context of the problem, but its incremental computation dramatically improves the efficiency of the algorithm. Note also the need for a software database; this transformation needs global access to all invocations of a function to consistently modify its interface.

We proceed as previously done by selecting $range(DTROW(DT(V), J))$, then $1 + length(V)$ for incremental maintenance (and naming them *DT-*

```
function COSTAS-GS-AUX (N, V, POOL, DT-RANGE: map(integer, set(integer)),
  VSIZE1 :integer)
  where VSIZE1 = 1 + size(V)
       & DT-RANGE = {I J → DTROW(DT(V), J) I J ∈ domain(V) I}) ..
 = {V I empty(POOL)}
   union! reduce(union!, {COSTAS-GS-AUX(N,
                    append(V, I), POOL less I,
                    map-union({I VSIZE1 → {} I},
                              {I J → {I - V(VSIZE1 - J)} ∪ DT-RANGE (J) I
                               J ∈ domain(V) I}),
                    VSIZE1 + 1) I
                      I ∈ POOL
                      & ∀(J) (J ∈ domain(V) ⇒ I - V(VSIZE1 − J) ∉ DT-RANGE (J))})
```

```
function COSTAS (N)
 = COSTAS-GS-AUX(N, [], {1 .. N}, { }, 1)
```

Figure 9. Costas Array Algorithm after Finite Differencing.

RANGE and *VSIZE*1, respectively), and KIDS produces the code shown in figure 9.

Case Analysis

The COSTAS-GS-AUX algorithm is a union of two set-valued expressions. These two sets treat disjoint cases: When one is non-empty, the other is empty, which suggests the use of case analysis to clarify and simplify the code. The idea of the case analysis transformation in KIDS is simple: An expression *e* is replaced with the expression *if P then e else e,* where *P* is a predicate whose variables are all bound in *e*'s context. The payoff from this transformation rule comes from applying CD-simplification to the branches of the conditional. For COSTAS-GS-AUX, we select the whole body as *e* and select *empty(pool)* as the case analysis predicate. After simplification, we get the code shown in figure 10.

Data Type Refinement

The next step is to choose implementations for the abstract data types in the algorithm. Compilers typically provide a standard implementation for each type in their programming language. However, as the level of the language rises, and as higher-level data types, such as sets, sequences, and mappings, are included in the language, or as users specify their own abstract data types, standard implementations cease being satisfactory. The difficulty is that the higher-level data types can be implemented in many different ways; for example, sets can be implemented as lists, arrays, trees, and so on. De-

```
function COSTAS-GS-AUX (N, V, POOL, DT-RANGE , VSIZE1 )
  = if empty(POOL) then {V}
    else reduce(union!, {COSTAS-GS-AUX(N,
                          append(V, I), POOL less I,
                          map-union({I VSIZE1 → {} I},
                                      {I J → {I - V(VSIZE1 - J)} ∪ DT-RANGE (J) I
                                          J ∈ domain(V) I}),
                        VSIZE1 + 1) I
                        I ∈ POOL
                        & ∀ (J) (J ∈ domain(V)
                              ⇒ I - V(VSIZE1 - J) ∉ DT-RANGE(J))})
```

Figure 10. COSTAS-GS-AUX after Case Analysis

pending on the mix of operations, their relative frequency of invocation, size information, and data flow considerations, one implementation can be much better than another. Thus, no single default implementation gives good performance for all occurrences of an abstract type. Work on data-structure selection and refinement for very high-level languages attempts to deal with these problems (Barstow 1979; Schonberg, Schwartz, and Sharir 1981). Kestrel Institute researchers are currently integrating a data type refinement system (called DTRE and built by Lee Blaine) with KIDS. DTRE allows interactive specification of implementation annotations for data types in programs. It also provides machinery for stating data type refinements (as theory interpretations) and a modified compiler for handling the translation of high-level types to low-level implementations. The following refinements were performed using DTRE but required some manual transformation to deal with special assumptions in the current version. We continue the derivation as if DTRE and KIDS were smoothly integrated, seeing no fundamental impediment to this integration.

Consider the sequence-valued parameter V, which denotes a partial schedule: it is initialized to the empty sequence once; the operation *append* is applied many times; and, occasionally, it is copied to the output. A standard representation for sequences is linked lists; however, this representation is expensive for V because it entails copying V every time the *append* operation is performed. A better representation is to allow alternative versions of V to coexist and share common structure. The data structure V is simply a reversed sequence with a pointer to the last element. In this reversed list representation, initialization and append take constant time, and the assignment operation takes time linear in the length of V (by tracing upward from the element pointed to by V).

Consider next the parameter *DT-RANGE*, which is a map from integers to sets. It is initialized to the empty set once, element membership is often applied to the component sets, and union with a singleton set is often performed on the component sets. If we can deduce bounds on the component sets, then a bit-vector representation would be applicable and efficient; that is, *DT-RANGE* is implemented as an array of bit vectors.

Results and Summary

The Costas array algorithm produced by the global search tactic was optimized, refined, and compiled. It is interesting to note the differences between the initial specification and the final code in figure 10. The code contains no mention of the basic concepts of the domain theory. Instead, it contains derived concepts, such as *DT-RANGE* and *pool,* which combine concepts from the domain theory and global search theory. This observation illustrates the phenomenon that a good descriptive theory of a problem can be different from a good computational theory.

The unoptimized global search algorithm takes just under 50 minutes on a SUN-4/160 to find all 760 Costas arrays of size 9. The final optimized version finds all 760 solutions in about 5 minutes. By manually performing the data type refinements previously discussed, the same 760 solutions were found in 12 seconds. Incorporating a simple isomorph rejection mechanism further cut the time in half. A colleague then hand implemented the resulting algorithm in C and were able to enumerate all 18,276 Costas arrays of size 17 in about 6 days. These results duplicate and confirm the results of Silverman, Vickers, and Mooney (1988) who also enumerate solutions to order 17 (the run time of their code is not described).

The derivation as presented here took place over 1 week, and most of the time was spent developing the domain theory. The actual derivation and variations of it took less than a day. For the Costas array derivation, the user makes a total of 11 high-level decisions, some of which involve subsidiary decisions. It would be easy to significantly cut this number by automatically applying CI-Simplify after every operation (which is not currently done). Each decision involves either selecting from a machine-generated menu, pointing to an expression, or typing a name into a text buffer. The high-level development operators encapsulate the firing of hundreds of low-level transformation rules. Excluding the time spent setting up the Costas array domain theory, the total time for the derivation is about 25 minutes on a SUN -4/160.

There are several opportunities for automating the selection and application of the KIDS operations. The steps of the Costas array derivation are typical of almost all the global search algorithms that KIDS derived. After algorithm design, the program bodies are fully simplified, and partial evaluation is applied followed by finite differencing and data type refinement. It is conceivable that the entire Costas array derivation could automatically be performed.

KIDS has been used to design and optimize algorithms for over 50 problems. Examples include optimal job scheduling (Smith and Pressburger

1988), enumeration of cyclic difference sets (Smith and Lowry 1989), graph colorings search, bin packing, binary search, vertex covers, graph coloring, set covers, knapsack, traveling salesman tours, linear programming (Lowry 1987), maximal segment sum, and sorting (Smith 1985). On several occasions, researchers were able to perform new derivations before an audience.

Related Work

In addition to KIDS, a number of experimental interactive transformational systems have been developed, a few of which I mention here. For a survey of early systems see Partsch (1983). Feather's (1982) ZAP system is built on the basic fold-unfold method (Burstall and Darlington 1977) by introducing *tactics*—metaprograms to control the application of basic transformations. Darlington is currently developing a system that provides a uniform functional and transformational programming environment (Darlington et al. 1989). This project is also exploring the use of functional metaprogramming and high-level transformations such as function inversion and memoizing. The TI (transformational implementation) system at the USC/Information Sciences Institute (Balzer 1981) had a large library of transformations for implementing the GIST specification language. The GLITTER system (Fickas 1985) was built on TI to provide the user with a higher-level of transformational activity. It used a problem-solving model where the user supplies development goals and, occasionally, some formal reasoning steps and manual editing. A library of methods was applied to solve goals, and selection rules were used to prune and order the search. The DRACO system (Neighbors 1984) emphasizes domain-specific modeling and program transformation. LOPS (Bibel 1984) has strategies that are similar in some respects to the KIDS algorithm design tactics. Their intent is to transform logic specifications into a specialized form solvable by known algorithmic methods, such as conditionals and recursion. The NuPrl system (Constable 1986) supports program construction as a byproduct of the interactive development of a constructive mathematical proof. The RAPTS system (Paige and Henglein 1987) emphasizes the optimization of set-theoretic programs. RAPTS achieves a high level of automation by restricting its specification language.

Other automated program development systems are described in Barstow (1988), Lubars and Harandi (1987), McCartney (1987), and Steier (1989) and in this volume. A comparative study of published algorithm derivations is given in Steier and Anderson (1989).

Concluding Remarks

The final Costas array algorithm is apparently not complicated; however, the KIDS derivation reveals it to be an intricate combination of knowledge of the

Costas array problem, the global search algorithm paradigm, various program-optimization techniques, and data-structure refinement. The derivation has left us not only with an efficient, correct program but also assertions that characterize the meaning of all data structures and subprograms. These invariants, together with the derivation itself, serve to explain and justify the structure of the program. The explicit nature of the derivation process allows us to formally capture all design decisions and reuse them for documenting the derivation and helping to evolve the specifications and code as the user's needs change.

KIDS supports a knowledge-based approach to formal program development that is fairly natural to use. The extent to which a KIDS-like system can evolve to the break-even point for routine programming will depend on formalizing enough programming knowledge at an appropriate level of abstraction. Properties of well-formalized programming knowledge include (1) wide applicability, (2) automatic or near-automatic application, and (3) the accomplishment of a significant and readily understandable design step.

KIDS is unique among systems of its kind for having been used to design, optimize, and refine dozens of programs. Application areas include scheduling, combinatorial design, sorting and searching, computational geometry, pattern matching, routing for very large system integration, and linear programming. Researchers have had good success in using KIDS to account for the structure of many well-known algorithms. To demonstrate the practicality of automated knowledge-based support for formal methods, they are working toward the goal of using KIDS for its own development.

Domain Theory for the Costas Array Problem

The Costas Array derivation presented in this chapter depends on the definitions, specifications, and inference rules contained in the Costas Array domain theory. It also depends implicitly on theories for various datatypes, such as sets, sequences, and integers. Building a domain theory is the first—and often the hardest—step in performing a derivation on KIDS. The task involves defining the concepts that can be used to formally specify the problem at hand and giving inference rules for reasoning about those concepts.

The following domain theory is typical of the dozens in the KIDS library. One aspect of the theory is worth pointing out. Most of the inference rules are based on distributive laws and are treated as left-to-right rewrite rules (they fire without provision for backup). Of the roughly 700 rules currently in the KIDS knowledge-base, about 80 percent are based on distributive laws. This fact is encouraging, because by concentrating on deriving distributive laws (and other laws concerned with structure-preservation) before performing a derivation, one has greater confidence that the rule base can allow a derivation to go through. Although deeper laws about the problem are required to derive certain algorithms or perform certain optimizations, I have been able to derive the essential structure of many well-known algorithms using the general techniques described in the chapter and using mainly distributive laws.

The domain theory for the Costas Array problem follows. The compiler directive "rb-compile-simplification-equality" in the THEORY-RULES section tells the compiler to translate a quantified equation as a left-to-right rewrite rule.

THEORY COSTAS-ARRAY-THEORY

THEORY-IMPORTS {SEQUENCES-AS-MAPS}

THEORY-OPERATIONS

function costas (n:integer)
   where $1 \leq n$
   returns { p | bijective(p, {1 .. n})
              & $\forall$ (j)(j $\in$ domain(p) $\Rightarrow$ nodups(dtrow(dt(p),j))) }

function dt (p:seq(integer)) :map(tuple(integer,integer),integer)
  = {| <i,j> $\rightarrow$ p(i) – p(i – j) | (i,j) i$\in$ domain(p) & j$\in$ {1 .. i – 1} | |}

function cross-dt (p:seq(integer),q:seq(integer))
  :map(tuple(integer,integer),integer)
  = {| <i,j> $\rightarrow$ q(i – n) – p(i – j) |
      n = size(p)
      & i $\in$ image(lambda(k) k + n ,domain(q))
      & j$\in$ {i – n .. i – 1} |}

function dtrow (d:map(tuple(integer,integer),integer), j:integer): seq(integer)
  = [d(i,j) | (i) <i,j> $\in$ domain(d)]

function nodups (p:seq(integer)):boolean
  = $\forall$ (i,j)(i$\in$ domain(p) & j$\in$ domain(p) & i $\neq$ j $\Rightarrow$ p(i) $\neq$ p(j))

function cross-nodups (p:seq(integer),q:seq(integer)):boolean
  = $\forall$ (i,j)(i$\in$ domain(p) & j$\in$ domain(q) $\Rightarrow$ p(i) $\neq$ q(j))

THEORY-LAWS

assert distribute-dt-over-emptyseq
  $\forall$ ()(dt([]) = {| |})

assert distribute-dt-over-singleton-seq
  $\forall$ (a)(dt([a]) = {| |})

assert distribute-dt-over-prepend
  $\forall$ (S,a)(dt(prepend(S,a)) = map-union(dt(S), cross-dt(S,[a])))

assert distribute-dt-over-append
  $\forall$ (S,a)(dt(append(S,a)) = map-union(dt(S), cross-dt(S,[a])))

assert distribute-dt-over-concat
  $\forall$ (R,S)(dt(concat(R,S))
        = map-union(dt(R), map-union(cross-dt(R,S), dt(S))))

assert trivial-upper-rows-of-dt
  $\forall$ (l,p)(size(p) $\leq$ l $\Rightarrow$ (dtrow(dt(p),l) = []))

assert trivial-upper-rows-of-cross-dt
  $\forall$ (l,p,q)(size(p) + size(q) $\leq$ l $\Rightarrow$ (dtrow(cross-dt(p,q),l) = []))

assert distribute-dtrow-over-emptymap
  $\forall$ ()(dtrow({| |}, j) = [])

assert distribute-dtrow-over-map-union
  $\forall$ (d,e,j)(dtrow(map-union(d,e),j) = concat(dtrow(d,j), dtrow(e,j)))

assert dtrow-of-incremental-cross-dt
  $\forall$ (p,a,j)(dtrow(cross-dt(p,[a]),j) = [a − p(size(p) + 1 − j) | j $\leq$ size(p)])

assert distribute-nodups-over-emptyseq
  $\forall$ ()(nodups([]) = true)

assert distribute-nodups-over-singleton-seq
  $\forall$ (a)(nodups([a]) = true)

assert distribute-nodups-over-prepend
  $\forall$ (S,a)(nodups(prepend(S,a)) = (nodups(S) & cross-nodups(S,a)))

assert distribute-nodups-over-append
  $\forall$ (S,a)(nodups(append(S,a)) = (nodups(S) & cross-nodups(S,a)))

assert distribute-nodups-over-concat
  $\forall$ (R,S)(nodups(concat(R,S))
        = (nodups(R) & cross-nodups(R,S) & nodups(S)))

assert distribute-cross-nodups-over-emptyseq1
  $\forall$ (S)(cross-nodups([],S) = true)

assert distribute-cross-nodups-over-emptyseq2
  $\forall$ (S)(cross-nodups(S,[]) = true)

THEORY-RULES

function costas-rule-distribute-dt-over-emptyseq ()
  rb-compile-simplification-equality
  distribute-dt-over-emptyseq

function costas-rule-distribute-dt-over-singleton-seq ()
  rb-compile-simplification-equality
  distribute-dt-over-singleton-seq

function costas-rule-distribute-dt-over-prepend ()
  rb-compile-simplification-equality
  distribute-dt-over-prepend

function costas-rule-distribute-dt-over-append ()
  rb-compile-simplification-equality
  distribute-dt-over-append

function costas-rule-distribute-dt-over-concat ()
  rb-compile-simplification-equality
  distribute-dt-over-concat

function costas-rule-trivial-upper-rows-of-dt ()
  rb-compile-equality
  trivial-upper-rows-of-dt

function costas-rule-trivial-upper-rows-of-cross-dt ()
  rb-compile-equality
  trivial-upper-rows-of-cross-dt

function costas-rule-distribute-dtrow-over-emptymap ()
  rb-compile-simplification-equality
  distribute-dtrow-over-emptymap

function costas-rule-distribute-dtrow-over-map-union ()
  rb-compile-simplification-equality
  distribute-dtrow-over-map-union

function costas-rule-dtrow-of-incremental-cross-dt ()
  rb-compile-simplification-equality
  dtrow-of-incremental-cross-dt

function costas-rule-distribute-nodups-over-emptyseq ()
  rb-compile-simplification-equality
  distribute-nodups-over-emptyseq

function costas-rule-distribute-nodups-over-singleton-seq ()
  rb-compile-simplification-equality
  distribute-nodups-over-singleton-seq

function costas-rule-distribute-nodups-over-prepend ()
  rb-compile-simplification-equality
  distribute-nodups-over-prepend

function costas-rule-distribute-nodups-over-append ()
  rb-compile-simplification-equality
  distribute-nodups-over-append

function costas-rule-distribute-nodups-over-concat ()
  rb-compile-simplification-equality
  distribute-nodups-over-concat

```
function costas-rule-distribute-cross-nodups-over-emptyseq1 ()
    rb-compile-simplification-equality
    distribute-cross-nodups-over-emptyseq1
function costas-rule-distribute-cross-nodups-over-emptyseq2 ()
    rb-compile-simplification-equality
    distribute-cross-nodups-over-emptyseq2
```

---

end-theory

Acknowledgments

Marc Lippmann and Ralph Wachter of the Office of Naval Research present-ed the Costas array problem to me as a challenge problem for KIDS. I want to thank Wolfgang Bibel, Mike Lowry, Mitch Lubars, and Tom Pressburger for their comments on drafts of this chapter. Lee Blaine, Li-Mei Gilham, Allen Goldberg, Mike Lowry, Tom Pressburger, Xiaolei Qian, and Stephen West-fold have all contributed to the KIDS system.

References

Abraido-Fandino, L. 1987. An Overview of REFINE 2.0. Presented at *the Second International Symposium on Knowledge Engineering*, 8–10 April, Madrid, Spain.

Balzer, R. M. 1981. Transformational Implementation: An Example. *IEEE Transactions on Software Engineering* SE-7(1): 3–14.

Balzer, R.; Cheatham, T. E.; and Green, C. 1983. Software Technology in the 1990s: Using a New Paradigm. *IEEE Computer* 16(11): 39–45.

Barstow, D. R.1988. Automatic Programming for Streams II: Transformational Implementation. In Proceedings of ICSE-10, 439–447. Washington, D.C.: IEEE Computer Society Press.

Barstow, D. R. 1979. *Knowledge-Based Program Construction*. New York: North-Holland.

Bibel, W., and Hörnig, K. 1984. LOPS—A System Based on a Strategical Approach to Program Synthesis. In *Automatic Program Construction Techniques*, eds. A. Biermann, G. Guiho, and V. Kodratoff. New York: Macmillan.

Bjorner, D.; Ershov, A. P.; and Jones, N. D., eds. 1988. *Partial Evaluation and Mixed Computation*. Amsterdam: North-Holland.

Blaine, L.; Goldberg, A.; Pressburger, T.; Qian, X.; Roberts, T.; and Westfold, S. 1988. Progress on the KBSA Performance Estimation Assistant, Technical Report, KES.U.88.11, Kestrel Institute, Palo Alto, Calif.

Burstall, R. M., and Darlington, J. 1977. A Transformation System for Developing Recursive Programs. *Journal of the ACM* 24(1): 44–67.

Constable, R. L. 1986. *Implementing Mathematics with the NuPrl Proof Development System*. New York: Prentice-Hall.

Costas, J. 1984. A Study of a Class of Detection Waveforms Having Nearly Ideal Range—Doppler Ambiguity Properties. In Proceedings of the 1984 IEEE, 996-1009. Washington, D.C.: IEEE Computer Society.

Darlington, J. D., et al. 1989. A Functional Programming Environment Supporting Execution,

Partial Execution and Transformation. In *PARLE 89: Parallel Architectures and Languages Europe, Volume I: Parallel Architectures*, eds. E. Odijk, M. Rem, and J. Syre, 286–305. Lecture Notes in Computer Science, volume 365. New York: Springer-Verlag.

Feather, M. 1982. A System for Transformationally Deriving Programs. *ACM Transactions on Programming Languages and Systems* 4(1): 1–21.

Fickas, S. F. 1985. Automating the Transformational Development of Software. *IEEE Transactions on Software Engineering* SE-11(11): 1268–1278.

Goguen, J. A., and Winkler, T. 1988. Introducing OBJ3, Technical Report, SRI-CSL-88-09, SRI International, Menlo Park, California.

Goldberg, A. 1989. Reusing Software Developments, Technical Report, Kestrel Institute, Palo Alto, California.

Gordon, M. J.; Milner, A. J.; and Wadsworth, C. P. 1979. *Edinburgh LCF: A Mechanised Logic of Computation*. Lecture Notes in Computer Science, volume 78. Berlin: Springer-Verlag.

Guttag, J., and Horning, J. 1986. Report on the Larch Shared Language. *Science of Computer Programming* 6(2): 103–157.

Lowry, M. R. 1989. *Algorithm Synthesis through Problem Reformulation*. Ph.D. thesis, Computer Science Dept., Stanford Univ.

Lowry, M. R. 1987. Algorithm Synthesis through Problem Reformulation. In Proceedings of the Sixth National Conference on Artificial Intelligence, 432–436. Menlo Park, Calif.: American Association for Artificial Intelligence.

Lubars, M., and Harandi, M. 1987. Knowledge-Based Software Design Using Design Schemas. In Proceedings of the Ninth International Conference on Software Engineering, 253–262. Washington, D.C.: IEEE Computer Society Press.

McCartney, R. D. 1987. Synthesizing Algorithms with Performance Constraints. In Proceedings of the Sixth National Conference on Artificial Intelligence, 149–154. Menlo Park, Calif.: American Association for Artificial Intelligence.

Mostow, J. D. 1983. Machine Transformation of Advice into a Heuristic Search Procedure. In *Machine Learning: An Artificial Intelligence Approach*, eds. R. S.Michalski, J. Carbonell, and T. Mitchell, 367–404. San Mateo, Calif.: Morgan Kaufmann.

Neighbors, J. M. 1984. The DRACO Approach to Constructing Software from Reusable Components. *IEEE Transactions on Software Engineering* SE-10(5): 564–574.

Paige, R., and Henglein, F. 1987. Mechanical Translation of Set-Theoretic Problem Specifications into Efficient RAM Code. *Journal of Symbolic Computation* 4(2): 207–232.

Paige, R., and Koenig, S. 1982. Finite Differencing of Computable Expressions. *ACM Transactions on Programming Languages and Systems* 4(3): 402–454.

Partsch, H. 1983. The CIP Transformation System. In *Program Transformation and Programming Environments*, ed. P. Pepper, 305–322. New York: Springer-Verlag.

Partsch, H., and Steinbrueggen, R. 1983. Program Transformation Systems. *ACM Computing Surveys* 15(3): 199–236.

Scherlis, W. 1981. Program Improvement by Internal Specialization. In Eighth ACM Symposium on Principles of Programming Languages, 41–49. New York: Association of Computing Machinery.

Schonberg, E.; Schwartz, J.; and Sharir, M. 1981. An Automatic Technique for the Selection of Data Representations in SETL Programs. *ACM Transactions on Programming Languages and Systems* 3(2): 126–143.

Silverman, J.; Vickers, V.; and Mooney, J. 1988. On the Number of Costas Arrays as a Function of Array Size. In Proceedings of the 1988 IEEE, 851–853. Washington, D.C.: IEEE Computer Society.

Smith, D. R. 1987. Structure and Design of Global Search Algorithms, Technical Report, KES.U.87.12, Kestrel Institute, Palo Alto, California.

Smith, D. R. 1985. Top-down Synthesis of Divide-and-Conquer Algorithms. *Artificial Intelligence* 27(1): 43-96.

Smith, D. R. 1982. Derived Preconditions and Their Use in Program Synthesis. In *Sixth Conference on Automated Deduction*, ed D. W. Loveland, 172–193. Lecture Notes in Computer Science, volume 138. Berlin: Springer-Verlag.

Smith, D. R., and Lowry, M. R. 1989. Algorithm Theories and Design Tactics. In *Proceedings of the International Conference on Mathematics of Program Construction*, ed. L. van de Snepscheut, 379–398. Lecture Notes in Computer Science, volume 375. Berlin: Springer-Verlag.

Smith, D. R., and Pressburger, T. T. 1988. Knowledge-Based Software Development Tools. In *Software Engineering Environments*, ed. P. Brereton, 79–103. Chichester, England: Ellis Horwood.

Steier, D. 1989. Automatic Algorithm Design within a General Architecture for Intelligence. Ph.D. diss., Dept. of Computer Science, Carnegie-Mellon Univ.

Steier, D. M., and Anderson, A. P. 1989. *Algorithm Synthesis: A Comparative Study.* New York: Springer-Verlag.

Wile, D. S. 1983. Program Developments: Formal Explanations of Implementations. *Communications of the ACM* 26(11): 902–911.

Automating the Design of
Local Search Algorithms

Michael R. Lowry

Software reuse can significantly increase software design productivity, providing a potentially high payoff (Biggerstaff and Perlis 1989). A near-term approach to software reuse is through libraries of standardized programs (Tracz 1988). Software environments can facilitate software reuse by providing shells in which existing programs can easily be patched together. For example, the UNIX operating system enables users to combine programs through standard data flow protocols such as pipes. However, the reuse of library programs often falls short of the flexibility and coverage needed by system designers and the execution efficiency needed by end users. Moreover, it is necessary to find the appropriate program from a library and then design the interface code that matches the library program to the context of its use. The costs of finding the appropriate program and developing the interface code often cancel any savings from reuse.

A longer-term approach, which promises both design flexibility and execution efficiency, is to reuse the knowledge for designing programs rather than the programs themselves. Knowledge reuse enables efficient software to be tailor-made for each new application. Furthermore, knowledge reuse can address the problems of indexing and interfacing as integral parts of software design. The reuse of software design knowledge is currently achieved at enormous human expense by recycling software engineers to design the same kind of software again and again. To automate knowledge reuse, the various sources of software design knowledge need to be formalized and mechanized methods for reasoning with these formalisms developed. Software development environments that facilitate automated knowledge reuse also need to be developed.

Approaches to automating software design span a spectrum from specific to general. In the domain-specific program synthesis approach, transformation rules are developed that combine both domain knowledge and design knowledge. In contrast, the knowledge compilation approach separates the domain knowledge from the design knowledge, so that the two knowledge types can be reused in different combinations. These two sources of knowledge are combined when the knowledge compiler synthesizes a program. The most general approach is pure formal derivation in which programs are directly synthesized from a domain theory and a theory about programming language constructs using just basic transformation or inference rules. Early program synthesis systems, such as presented in Green (1969) that synthesized programs using the clausal resolution rule or in Burstall and Darlington (1977) that transformed specifications into efficient recursive programs through fold/unfold transformations, are examples of this general approach. These systems reuse domain theories and programming language theories, but the design knowledge is essentially rediscovered each time a program is synthesized. Although the pure formal derivation approach is general and theoretically sound, the degree of user interaction or search required can be excessive. For this reason, much current research on formal derivation systems is oriented toward developing tactics that guide the search process.

Tactics are metalevel programs that encapsulate design knowledge for developing software artifacts. For example, Feather's (1982) ZAP system uses tactics as a metalevel control for the application of fold/unfold transformations. Tactics can represent the specific types of design knowledge used in the domain-specific and knowledge compilation approaches for use in a general, formal framework. Design knowledge spans the spectrum from knowledge for developing individual programming language constructs such as loops and conditionals (chapter 21) to knowledge for developing systems for particular application domains (chapter 5). This chapter is concerned with the middle of this spectrum: a tactic for algorithm development.

The next section describes a methodology for developing tactics. The subsequent section describes the relation of this work to problem reformulation. An abstract theory for local search algorithms and an associated functional program schema is presented in Local Search Algorithms. The subsequent section describes natural perturbation neighborhoods and presents an overview of the design tactic. Formalizing Natural Perturbations presents a formalization of natural perturbation neighborhoods using the tools of group theory. An overview of the simplex algorithm is presented in the following section. The formal design tactic is presented in Design Tactic for Local Search Algorithms and is illustrated with the derivation of the simplex algorithm. The chapter closes with a conclusion.

Design Analysis

Design analysis is a methodology for formalizing both the structural properties common to a class of software artifacts and the genetic properties common to their derivations. This formalization is then used to develop a design tactic that automatically designs an artifact in this class given a specification of its behavior. Design analysis formalizes intrinsic structural properties rather than properties specific to a particular programming language or application domain. By abstracting away these particular concerns, the resulting formalization is more broadly applicable. The objective is to find a general mathematical characterization of the structure of a class and, at the same time, capture the features that provide search guidance for designing artifacts in a class. This chapter describes the application of design analysis to the development of a tactic that designs local search algorithms.

The first step of design analysis is to study many examples of a naturally defined class of algorithms. *Local search algorithms*, also referred to as hill-climbing algorithms, are a natural class in which a feasible solution to an optimization problem is iteratively improved by searching a neighborhood of the solution for a better solution, stopping when no neighboring solution is better. Examples of local search algorithms studied during this research include transposition sorting algorithms such as bubble sort, graph algorithms such as traveling salesman and minimum spanning-tree (MST) algorithms, and linear programming algorithms. Linear programming has been particularly important in past theoretical analysis of local search algorithms. A broad class of combinatorial optimization algorithms are equivalent to linear programming (Karp and Papadimitriou 1980) and, thus, can be solved by the simplex algorithm. The automated synthesis of the simplex algorithm validates the generality of this tactic for designing local search algorithms.

The second step of design analysis is to extract the features and structural constraints common to the class of algorithms. These constraints are then formalized to provide a rigorous definition of the class. The computer science literature on algorithms is a good starting point for developing a formal theory of a class of algorithms. However, this literature is usually concerned with the description and performance analysis of algorithms rather than methods for designing algorithms. Therefore, the theoretical descriptions found in the literature typically require modification and extension before they are suitable for automated derivations. The theory of local search algorithms that are guaranteed to return globally optimal solutions is well developed (Luenberger 1984; Papadimitriou and Steiglitz 1982; Savage, Weiner, and Krone 1973) and for combinatorial problems is closely related to the theory of linear programming. Local search is also often used as a heuristic method for generating good but not necessarily optimal solutions. Past work reported in the literature includes probabilistic analysis of heuristic local search algorithms (Lin 1965) and extensions such as simulated annealing (Kirkpatrick, Gelatt, and Vecchi 1983). Whether used as an exact or heuristic method, the key to a local search algorithm is the neighborhood structure imposed on a problem. The derivation of neighborhood structures has not been addressed in past work, although Papidimitriou and Steiglitz (1982) did link neighborhood structures to the intuitive notion of natural perturbations of feasible solutions. One of the key contributions of the research presented in this chapter is the formalization of the notion of natural perturbation such that it is computationally tractable to automatically derive neighborhood structures.

The final steps of design analysis proceed by developing hand derivations of these algorithms, linking the features and structural constraints in the formalization to steps of the derivations. At this point, the initial formalization is likely to be found inadequate to support automated derivation. Extensions of the initial formalization, including specializations and generalizations, should be developed that support computationally tractable derivation steps. The general process is one of iterative and conjugate refinement of the formalization and the derivations. When this process converges, the derivations can be generalized into a design tactic that can be automated.

The initial formalization of neighborhood structures was done in the abstract framework of topology. *Topology* is a branch of mathematics concerned with sets on which a rich structure of nested neighborhoods is defined. Among other uses, topology provides a foundation for analyzing continuous functions in higher-dimensional spaces. It was initially anticipated that the rich structure of nested neighborhoods would provide significant leverage in automatically deriving the neighborhood structures for local search algorithms. However, the axioms of topology are second order. The difficulties of automating the theorem proving for manipulating these second-order axioms became apparent during the course of developing hand derivations of local search algorithms.

At the same time as this research was being pursued, concurrent research was exploring methods for abstracting problems with symmetries. The key idea was that if a problem is invariant under a group of transformations, then it can be abstracted by ignoring those features that change under the transformations and reformulating the problem in terms of features that are invariant under the transformations (Lowry 1988). The mathematical tools for formalizing this idea are part of group theory and can be traced to Felix Klein's

(1893) proposal to classify geometries by their transformation groups and then axiomatize the geometries in terms of their invariant features. This use of invariants can be inverted to derive neighborhood structures for local search algorithms. Here, the invariants are known—these are the constraints for a solution to be a feasible output—and the natural perturbations that transform feasible solution to feasible solution are unknown. This insight provided a tractable framework for derivations of local search algorithms and is formalized in this chapter.

Parameterized Theories

Many different formalisms have been used to represent classes of algorithms. Program schemas and object-oriented representations are popular formalisms discussed in other chapters of this book. Both of these representations are used during the derivation of a local search algorithm, but they are secondary, derivative representations. The primary representation used for both formalizing an algorithm class and deriving a particular algorithm is a parameterized theory. *Parameterized theories* are an extension of mathematical logic originally developed for representing abstract data types (Goguen, Thatcher, and Wagner 1978). Parameterized theories abstract away from the details of programming language and implementation inherent in program schemas and object-oriented representations. The key insight is to represent an algorithm as an interpretation from the abstract theory for an algorithm class to a concrete theory for a particular algorithm, as initially presented in Lowry (1987b). The interpretation is a mapping from the symbols in the abstract theory to definitions in the concrete theory. Part of this mapping is derived simply by parsing the problem specification. The remainder is obtained by extending the problem domain theory with additional components—in the case of a local search algorithm, the additional component is the definition of a neighborhood structure. The axioms of the abstract theory guide the development of these additional components. A mathematical exposition of these ideas is presented in Smith and Lowry (1990).

Related Work

Design analysis and related methodologies have been applied by many researchers to formalize and automate the derivations of different classes of algorithms. In this book, research on formal design analysis of algorithm classes includes Smith's chapter 19, which describes the KIDS system that has design tactics for divide-and-conquer and global search, and Wertheimer's chapter 17, which describes work on formalizing and automating the derivation of rule-based systems. Less formal approaches include Barstow's chapter 6 on automating derivations of device-control algorithms; Braudaway's chapter 12 and Tong's chapter 11 on spatial configuration algorithms; Kant, Daube, MacGregor, and Wald's chapter 8 on finite-difference algorithms;

Mostow's chapter 10 on heuristic search algorithms; and Setliff's chapter 9 on VLSI routing algorithms. Most of the remaining articles on program synthesis also describe various techniques for greatly reducing search during program derivation, including problem decomposition (chapters 11 and 13), replay of derivation histories or generalized derivation histories (chapters 10, 18, 22, and 23), and tactics or strategies (chapters 15, 16, and 21). In general, the research reported in this book and elsewhere has made significant progress toward automating software design knowledge.

Strata

The local search design tactic described in this chapter was implemented as part of the STRATA system (Lowry 1989). STRATA is a research prototype that synthesizes algorithms through problem reformulation. STRATA's overall strategy is to abstract a domain theory with respect to a problem specification, design an abstract algorithm, and then implement this abstract algorithm with efficient data structures and operations. Each of these steps is a different type of problem reformulation with different search characteristics. Abstraction has a convergent search space because it removes structure from a problem domain (Lowry 1987a). However abstraction can require difficult manipulation of the domain theory ontology (signature) and axioms (Lowry 1990). The objective of abstraction is to develop a domain theory tailored to the specified problem in which the essential properties of the problem are made explicit and the non-essential details are suppressed. The objective of design is to develop a high-level operational description of how the problem can be solved. Design has a divergent search space because it inherently adds structure to a problem. Design tactics and parameterized theories guide the search through this combinatorially explosive space (Lowry 1987b). The objective of implementation is to optimize the high-level operational description and develop data structures in which the abstract operations can efficiently be carried out. The implementation search space is also divergent, but considerable guidance is obtained from the abstract algorithm description. STRATA is interfaced to KIDS (chapter 19), which provides a shell for the algorithm design and implementation steps of this strategy. The local search design tactic used by STRATA is described in sufficient detail in this chapter so that other researchers can implement it in their systems.

Local Search Algorithms

Local search is a general technique for solving optimization problems by repeatedly transforming a feasible solution into an improved neighboring feasible solution until a local optimum is reached. (Optimization can either be minimization or maximization, which are interchangeable through a sign change. The standard convention, followed here, is to express the concepts in terms of minimization.) Local search algorithms search a large space by repeated searches over small neighborhoods. The neighborhood structure is the primary factor in determining the properties of a local search algorithm. Small neighborhoods can quickly be searched but can lead to a nearsightedness that causes local dips to appear as global minima. Large neighborhoods can smooth over local dips but take longer to search. The design of the neighborhood structure is the key to deriving a local search algorithm from the specification of an optimization problem.

There are two properties of a neighborhood structure that are important to local search algorithms. The first is the connectivity of the search space. Any feasible solution should be reachable from any other feasible solution by traversing from neighbor to neighbor. The second property is whether local optima are always global optima. When the neighborhood structure is *exact*, which means that all local optima are global optima, then local search provides a precise method for solving optimization problems.

Linear programming and the simplex algorithm play a prominent role in both the theory and the derivation of many exact local search algorithms. Savage used aspects of linear programming theory in developing a model of exact neighborhoods for additive cost subset (ACS) problems (Savage 1972, 1976; Savage, Weiner, and Krone 1973). In an ACS problem, the feasible solutions are subsets of a given finite set, and the cost function is the sum of the weights associated with elements in a feasible solution. This class includes the traveling salesman, minimal spanning tree, and optimal assignment problems. Papadimitriou and Steiglitz (1982) note that exact local search can be considered identical to the simplex algorithm on an appropriately defined linear programming problem. In particular, for ACS problems where no feasible solution contains another, the smallest exact neighborhoods are equivalent to vertex adjacency on a polyhedron corresponding to an equivalent linear programming problem. Various textbooks develop a wide range of combinatorial optimization algorithms, including network flow algorithms, by specializing the simplex algorithm (Luenberger 1984) or the primal-dual simplex algorithm (Papidimitriou and Steiglitz 1982). The simplex algorithm is efficient in practice and can be tailored to specialized classes of problems for even better performance. However, in the worst case, simplex is not polynomial (Klee and Minty 1972). Paradoxically, techniques that treat linear programming as a continuous optimization problem rather than a discrete optimization problem have polynomial performance even in the worst case (Khachian 1979; Karmarkar 1984). Nonetheless, the simplex algorithm and its specializations continue to be preferred methods for solving combinatorial optimization problems.

Local search is also a popular heuristic method for generating near-optimal solutions to optimization problems when exact neighborhood structures are too large to efficiently search. For example, the traveling salesman problem is NP-complete, but a local search algorithm that runs in time N^3 (where N is the number of cities) finds near-optimal solutions (Lin 1965). When used as a heuristic optimization procedure, the trade-off in local search is smaller neighborhoods versus better local optima (Papidimitriou and Steiglitz 1982). Global optimality can always be ensured by enlarging the neighborhood to include the entire feasible space, in which case local search degenerates to enumerating the entire solution space. For the traveling salesman problem, a lower bound on the size of neighborhoods required to ensure that local optimums are global optimums is $(n - 1)!/2$. Thus, a local search algorithm for the traveling salesman that was guaranteed to produce global optima would require exponential time just to search each local neighborhood (Savage 1976). Using smaller neighborhoods results in a heuristic local search algorithm that produces good solutions in polynomial time.

When used as a heuristic method, local search is often enhanced to provide a greater probability of finding a globally optimal solution. One enhancement is multiple randomized starts, choosing the best local optimum that results (Lin 1965). Another enhancement is simulated annealing (Kirkpatrick, Gelatt, Vechi 1983), which imitates the crystallization of a metal as it cools. A simulated annealing algorithm occasionally moves toward worse solutions, thus avoiding being trapped in some local optima. The probability of moving toward worse solutions is proportional to a simulated temperature that is gradually reduced over the course of many iterative steps. At higher temperatures, a simulated annealing algorithm can bounce out of deep local optima, but at lower temperatures, it can only bounce out of shallow local optima. Hence, a simulated annealing algorithm eventually converges on a good locally optimal solution as the temperature is reduced.

Local search algorithms are also used to solve constraint-satisfaction problems by reformulating some of the constraints as optimization criteria. The hill-climbing action of local search incrementally achieves these reformulated constraints, and the remaining constraints define the feasibility conditions. For example, sorting a sequence of elements can be reformulated as minimizing the number of inverted pairs of elements and, thus, solved through a variety of transposition sorting algorithms. This example illustrates reformulating a universally quantified constraint that all pairs be ordered into a cost function measuring the number of pairs satisfying the constraint. Another common example is reformulating a numeric equation as a cost function that is the absolute difference between the left- and right-hand sides of the equation. The optimal value of this cost function is zero.

The development of a suitable neighborhood structure is the primary step in deriving a local search algorithm. Many neighborhood structures can be developed by defining a class of perturbations on feasible solutions; neighboring feasible solutions are perturbations of each other. The notion of a natural perturbation is defined in Natural Perturbations and in Formalizing Natural Perturbations. A design tactic that uses this formalization in developing local search algorithms is described in Design Tactics for Local Search Algorithms.

Formalization of Local Search

A basic problem is specified by defining a set of inputs **D,** a set of outputs **R,** an operation **I** that maps legal inputs to true, and an operation **O** that maps input-output pairs to true when the output is a feasible solution to the input. A basic problem specification is a tuple **B** = ⟨**D,R,I,O**⟩.

An optimization problem is specified by extending a basic problem specification with an ordering relation in which all pairs of feasible solutions are comparable. All such ordering relations can be formulated as a cost function that maps feasible solutions to a totally ordered set. For most problems, the cost function maps feasible solutions to the integers, rationals, or reals. The totally ordered set is denoted ⟨$\Re$, $\leq$⟩, where $\Re$ is the set, and $\leq$ is the total order relation. Thus, an optimization problem is specified through a tuple **Opt** = ⟨**D,R,I,O**,$\Re$,$\leq$,**cost**⟩.

A local search theory **LS** = ⟨**Opt,N**⟩ is specified by an optimization problem and a neighborhood relation. Three axioms, two being optional, constrain the neighborhood relation, which is a ternary relation between an input and two elements of the output domain. First, each feasible solution is in its own neighborhood, so that for any legal input, the neighborhood relation is a reflexive relation on feasible outputs (axiom LS1). If the neighborhood structure is exact, then the local search theory is called exact (axiom LS2). Likewise, if the neighborhood structure is reachable, the local search theory will be called reachable (axiom LS3). A local search theory for a particular optimization problem is defined by a mapping from the components of abstract local search theory to definitions of objects, functions, and relations in the problem domain. More formally, the mapping is a *theory interpretation*, which means that the abstract axioms are true when they are mapped to the problem domain theory. Abstract local search theory is defined as follows:

Sorts **D,R,**$\Re$
Operations
I:D → boolean
O:D × **R** → boolean
cost:D × **R** → $\Re$
$\leq$:$\Re$ × $\Re$ → boolean
N:D × **R** × **R** → boolean
Optimal (x,y) ≡ $\forall(y')$**O**(x,y') ⇒ **cost** (x,y) $\leq$ **cost** (x,y')

Axioms

LS1: Reflexive Neighborhood
$$\forall(x,y)\ \mathbf{I}(x) \wedge \mathbf{O}(x,y) \Rightarrow \mathbf{N}(x,y,y)$$

LS2: Exact Neighborhood
$$\forall(x,y)\ \mathbf{I}(x) \wedge \mathbf{O}(x,y) \wedge [\forall(y')\ \mathbf{O}(x,y') \wedge \mathbf{N}(x,y,y') \Rightarrow \mathbf{cost}\ (x,y) \le \mathbf{cost}\ (x,y')]$$
$$\Rightarrow \text{Optimal}(x,y)$$

LS3: Reachable Neighborhood
$$\forall(x,y,y')\ \mathbf{I}(x) \wedge \mathbf{O}(x,y) \wedge \mathbf{O}(x,y') \Rightarrow \mathbf{N}^*\ (x,y,y')$$
where $\mathbf{N}^*$ is the reflexive and transitive closure of $\mathbf{N}$:
$$\forall\ (x,y)\ \mathbf{N}^0\ (x,y,y) \equiv \mathbf{I}(x) \wedge \mathbf{O}(x,y)$$
$$\forall\ (k \in Nat;\ x,y,y')\ \mathbf{N}^{k+1}\ (x,y,y') \equiv \exists\ (z)\ \mathbf{O}(x,z) \wedge \mathbf{N}^k\ (x,y,z) \wedge \mathbf{N}(x,z,y')$$
$$\forall\ (x,y,y')\ \mathbf{N}^*\ (x,y,y') \equiv \exists(k \in Nat)\ \mathbf{N}^k\ (x,y,y')$$

Exact local search theories form the basis of hill-climbing algorithms, which are guaranteed to terminate in an optimal solution. Reachable local search theories form the basis of heuristic hill-climbing algorithms such as simulated annealing. Reachability ensures that optimal solutions can be reached from an arbitrary starting point, although augmented searches at local optima might be necessary to obtain a globally optimal solution. Reachability is not required for exact neighborhoods because it is theoretically possible for many different global optima, which are isolated from each other, to exist, all with the same cost. As long as all isolated regions contain at least one global optimum, then the neighborhood structure is exact. However, this situation does not appear to arise in practice; thus, the reachable neighborhood axiom can be viewed as a weakening of the exact neighborhood axiom.

To derive a local search algorithm for a particular optimization problem, a partial mapping from abstract local search theory to the components of the optimization problem is first created. Constraints for a suitable neighborhood relation are then derived by instantiating the abstract neighborhood axioms with these components. The main part of the design tactic is to derive the definition of a neighborhood relation from these constraints in terms of the problem domain. Once the neighborhood relation is defined, an initial algorithm can be derived by instantiating a program schema with the components of the derived local search theory. A functional program schema for simple hill-climbing is shown below, which returns a feasible solution that is guaranteed to be locally optimal. To return a globally optimal solution, the derived local search theory must satisfy the exact neighborhood axiom. The function $\mathbf{F}$ is the main program that first calls an auxiliary function $\mathbf{FS}$ that returns an initial feasible solution. The main program then calls a tail-recursive hill climber $\mathbf{F_{LS}}$, which repeatedly calls itself until a local optimum is reached.

```
function F (x:D):R
    where I(x)
    returns (y| O(x,y) ∧ ∀ (y') O(x,y') ∧ N(x,y,y') ⇒ cost(x,y) ≤ cost(x,y'))
    = F_LS (x,FS(x))
```

function $\mathbf{FS}(x:\mathbf{D}):\mathbf{R}$
    where $\mathbf{I}(x)$
    returns $(y|\mathbf{O}(x,y))$

function $\mathbf{F_{LS}}(x:\mathbf{D},z:\mathbf{R}):\mathbf{R}$
    where $\mathbf{I}(x) \land \mathbf{O}(x,z)$
    returns $(y| \mathbf{O}(x,y) \land \forall (y') \mathbf{O}(x,y') \land \mathbf{N}(x,y,y') \Rightarrow \mathbf{cost}(x,y) \leq \mathbf{cost}(x,y'))$
    $= $ If $\forall (y') \mathbf{O}(x,y') \land \mathbf{N}(x,z,y') \Rightarrow \mathbf{cost}(x,z) \leq \mathbf{cost}(x,y')$
    Then z
    Else $\mathbf{F_{LS}}(x,\mathrm{arb}\{y' \mid \mathbf{O}(x,y') \land \mathbf{N}(x,z,y') \land \mathbf{cost}(x,y') < \mathbf{cost}(x,z)\})$

Alternative schemas for variations such as simulated annealing, an imperative programming language, or a parallel architecture could also be defined. Thus, formalizing local search as a theory abstracts away concerns such as programming language but still captures the relevant structural commonalities of local search algorithms.

Natural Perturbations

The key step in deriving a local search algorithm is the "...selection of a neighborhood or a class of neighborhoods, and this is tied to the notion of a 'natural' perturbation of a feasible solution" (Papidimitriou and Steiglitz 1982, p. 469). This section presents the basic concepts of natural perturbation neighborhoods and their role in the design of local search algorithms. The next section presents a formal mathematical description of natural perturbation neighborhoods using permutation group theory and group actions and proves that this formalization satisfies the reachability axiom for neighborhood structures. This formalization is directly incorporated into STRATA's design tactic for local search algorithms. An informal overview of the design tactic is presented at the end of this section, with a formal description presented in Design Tactic for Local Search Algorithms.

Natural perturbations are incremental transformations of feasible solutions. For numeric problems, the transformations are usually delta vectors that incrementally move a feasible solution toward an optimal feasible solution. For combinatorial problems, the transformations are usually based on swapping or substituting components of feasible solutions. A combinatorial problem has a finite set of feasible solutions, each feasible solution being a different combination of a finite set of possible components. Combinatorial local search algorithms are popular, in part because natural perturbations can readily be defined for a wide range of problems. Furthermore, even when a natural perturbation does not lead to an exact local search algorithm, it often does lead to an efficient heuristic algorithm that produces near-optimal solutions.

The insight for the formalization of natural perturbations can be illustrated by considering transposition sorting algorithms. Sorting elements in a sequence can be formulated as an optimization problem where the feasible so-

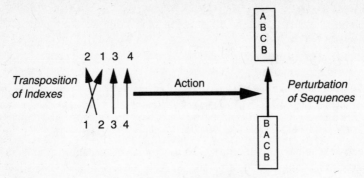

Figure 1. Action Maps Transpositions to Perturbations.

lutions are reorderings of the sequence, and the cost function is the number of inverted pairs of sequence elements. The sequence is a mapping from indexes (of type integer) to elements, with possibly duplicated elements. All feasible solutions have the same bag of elements; this property is invariant under all reorderings. A bag is like a set, but an element can occur more than once. A transposition sorting algorithm generates an optimal reordering by repeatedly swapping inverted elements of the sequence. This swapping is a natural perturbation of feasible solutions.

Formally, a *transposition* is a one-to-one function from a set of objects to the same set such that two objects are exchanged, and the rest are mapped to themselves. In figure 1, a transposition exchanges the first and second index of a sequence. An *action* maps this transposition to a perturbation of the sequence in which the first and second elements of the sequence are swapped. For every sequence, this action maps the transposition that exchanges indexes 1 and 2 into a perturbation of the sequence that swaps the first and second elements. More generally, this action maps any transposition of indexes into perturbations of sequences. The neighborhood structure for transposition sorting algorithms is defined by the set of transpositions on indexes and this action. This neighborhood structure can further be specialized by restricting the transpositions to a subset sufficient for generating the entire set of transpositions. For example, any transposition can be generated by chaining transpositions of adjacent indexes. This specialization defines the neighborhood for the bubble sort algorithm, which sorts a sequence by repeatedly swapping adjacent sequence elements that are out of order.

A basic neighborhood is defined by all the transpositions of some set and an action that maps these transpositions to perturbations of data structures. Basic neighborhoods are a special class of natural perturbation neighborhoods that provide a good starting point for designing combinatorial local search algorithms. Typically, basic neighborhoods are overly general for any particular problem; the design tactic first matches a problem specification to a basic neighborhood and then specializes the basic neighborhood. Currently, STRATA's library of parameterized natural perturbation neighborhood theories consists of six basic neighborhood definitions, which include specifications of their invariants. A basic neighborhood has the following kind of definition as a ternary relation, where y, y' are neighboring feasible solutions with respect to input x:

$$\lambda\, x, y, y', \exists\, (i, j \in S)\ y' = \textbf{Action}\ (x, y, i, j)$$

S is a set derived from the input to an optimization problem. For the transposition sorting example, this set is the indexes of the input sequence. The transpositions on this set are defined by two variables that range over this set, for example, index i and index j. **Action** is a function that takes the input x, current feasible solution y, and transposition variables i, j and produces a neighboring feasible solution y'. In the sorting example, transpositions of indexes are mapped to swapping the corresponding elements of the sequence. The basic neighborhood for transposition sorting has the following definition, where x, y, y' are of type sequence (the domain of a sequence is the set of integer indexes for the sequence):

$$\lambda\, x, y, y'. \exists\, (i, j \in \text{domain}(x))\ y'[i] = y[j] \land y'[j] = y[i]$$
$$\land\ \forall\, (k \in \text{domain}\ (x))\ k \neq i \land k \neq j \Rightarrow y'[k] = y'[k]$$

A local search theory for a basic neighborhood consists of the basic neighborhood definition and definitions for the other components of a local search theory. It is presented as a mapping of the following form from abstract local search theory to a set of definitions:

LS - basic theory
$\textbf{D} \mapsto datatype1\ (\alpha)$
$\textbf{R} \mapsto datatype2\ (\alpha)$
$\textbf{I} \mapsto \lambda x.\textbf{P}(x)$
$\textbf{O} \mapsto \lambda x, y.\ \textbf{Invariant}(x, y)$
$\textbf{N} \mapsto \lambda x, y, y'.\ \exists(i, j \in \textbf{F}(x))\ y' = \textbf{Action}(x, y, i, j)$

The data type for the input and output are parameterized on the type variable α; for sequences, α is the type of element in a sequence. The input predicate is usually the constant true. The input for a specified problem need not be the same as the input to a matched basic neighborhood theory; during matching, the basic neighborhood theory is reformulated so that its input is the same as the problem. The output relation is derived from the invariant properties of the action, as explained in the next section. For the example of mapping transpositions on indexes to perturbations of sequences, the invariant property is the bag of elements in the sequence. The set over which the transpositions are defined is derived from the input by the function $\textbf{F}$; for the example of sequences, $\textbf{F}$ is the domain function that returns the set of indexes of the input sequence. Note that the cost function is not included in the mapping.

The cost function for a particular optimization problem is incorporated into a basic neighborhood theory during specialization of the basic neighborhood theory, as described in Design Tactic for Local Search Algorithms.

The following basic neighborhood theory for sequences is indexed in STRATA's library under the output type *sequence:*

LS - sequence theory
$\mathbf{D} \mapsto seq\,(\alpha)$
$\mathbf{R} \mapsto seq\,(\alpha)$
$\mathbf{I} \mapsto \lambda x.true$
$\mathbf{O} \mapsto \lambda x,y.\text{bag}(x) = \text{bag}(y)$
$\mathbf{N} \mapsto \lambda x,y,y' . \exists (i,j \in \text{domain}(x))\, y'[i] = y[j] \wedge y'[j] = y[i]$
$$\wedge\; \forall\,(k \in \text{domain}(x))\, k \neq i \wedge k \neq j \Rightarrow y'[k] = y[k]$$

Sequences are mappings from integers to elements of type α. The basic neighborhood of a sequence consists of all sequences obtained through single transpositions. The invariant of this basic neighborhood structure is that the bag of elements in a feasible solution is the same as the bag of elements derived from the input. STRATA matches invariants of basic neighborhoods to the feasibility constraints of a problem specification to select an appropriate library theory. This theory for sequences can be matched to a wide range of optimization or constraint-satisfaction problems whose output is a sequence, such as sorting, N-queens, or traveling salesman. Any problem for which the bag of elements in the output sequence is an invariant of feasible solutions will successfully be matched.

In general, a natural perturbation neighborhood can be defined for any data structure. As explained in the next section, a natural perturbation neighborhood structure is defined by a set of permutations and an action mapping these permutations to perturbations of the data structure. A *permutation* is any one-to-one function from a set of objects to the same set; transpositions are a specialized class of permutations. Thus, natural perturbation neighborhoods are a generalization of basic neighborhoods. The closure of this set of permutations under composition defines three interrelated structures: the mutually reachable data structures, a group of permutations, and the invariant properties of mutually reachable data structures.

The power of this approach is that the invariant properties must be equivalent to the feasibility constraints to ensure reachability. If the invariants are stronger than the feasibility constraints, then some feasible solutions would not be reachable from other feasible solutions. If the invariants are weaker than the feasibility constraints, then some feasible solutions would be mapped to infeasible solutions. STRATA'S local search design tactic matches a problem specification to a theory whose invariants are equivalent or weaker than the feasibility constraints and then specializes the theory if the invariants are weaker. Reasoning about invariant properties and feasibility constraints provides a computationally tractable method of matching and then specializing theories in a library to problem specifications. STRATA does not have to directly reason about the second-order reachability axioms, which was already done by the creator of the library theories.

STRATA matches the specification of linear programming described in Simplex Algorithm to a library theory indexed under sets. In this theory, the output type is a subset of a finite set. The input is this finite set and an integer specifying the size of the output subsets. The transpositions range over the finite set. The action of a transposition is to swap an element in the subset with an element outside the subset. The invariant is the size of the subset; if the size of the subset is zero or the size of the finite set, then no transposition has any effect. The following mapping from abstract local search theory defines the basic neighborhood structure for finite subsets:

LS - subset theory
$\mathbf{D} \mapsto set\,(\alpha) \times integer$
$\mathbf{R} \mapsto set\,(\alpha)$
$\mathbf{I} \mapsto \lambda S, m.\ m \le \text{size}(S)$
$\mathbf{O} \mapsto \lambda S, m, y.\ y \subseteq S \wedge \text{size}(y) = m$
$\mathbf{N} \mapsto \lambda S, m, y, y'.\ \exists (i,j) i \in (S-y) \wedge j \in y \wedge y' = (y \cup \{i\}) - \{j\}$

This theory can be matched to a wide range of problems, including the class of ACS problems defined by Savage, Weiner, and Krone (1973). A typical example is the minimal spanning tree (MST) problem, which is to find a minimally weighted subset of edges in a graph that span the nodes of the graph without any cycles. Thus, a spanning tree is a subset of size one less than the number of nodes; this feasibility constraint matches the invariant property of the finite-set library theory. A local search algorithm for MST perturbs a feasible spanning tree by first adding an edge to the tree, thus creating a cycle, and then removing an edge in the cycle, as illustrated in figure 2.

This local search algorithm for MST can be derived by STRATA's local search design tactic. The tactic first matches the specification for MST to the LS-subset theory and then specializes the theory by finding necessary preconditions on transpositions to ensure that feasible solutions are transformed to better feasible solutions. The design tactic involves the following steps:

First, retrieve and match the basic neighborhood theories from the library indexed by the type of feasible solution. For MST, feasible solutions are subsets of edges. A theory matches a problem specification if the invariants of the theory are necessary conditions of the feasibility constraints of the specification. The invariant of LS-subset theory is that the output is a fixed-size subset. This is a necessary condition of the MST feasibility constraints that state that the output is a subset of edges with no cycles whose size is one less than the number of nodes.

Second, determine the necessary preconditions on the transpositions that ensure that a feasible solution is perturbed to a feasible solution. For MST, the

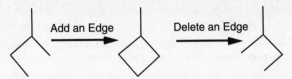

Figure 2. Perturbation of a Spanning Tree in a Minimal Spanning Tree Algorithm.

action of a transposition will be to first add an edge to the spanning tree, thus creating a cycle, and then to remove an edge. The necessary precondition is that the removed edge breaks the cycle.

Third, determine the necessary preconditions on the transpositions that ensure that a feasible solution is perturbed to a better feasible solution. For MST, the precondition is that the added edge has less weight than the deleted edge.

Fourth, determine the necessary conditions for a local optimum to be a global optimum (optional step for deriving exact local search algorithms). For MST, the necessary conditions are trivially true: A locally optimal vertex is always a globally optimal vertex. In fact, MST can be formulated as a special kind of linear programming problem. For linear programming problems, local optima are always global optima.

All these steps of the design tactic call the KIDS' directed inference system RAINBOW II to verify a match and determine the necessary preconditions. The inference system derives this information by manipulating rules in a problem domain theory supplied by the user. The last step of the design tactic is to instantiate a program schema with the components of the derived local search theory. This design tactic is presented in mathematical detail using STRATA's derivation of the simplex algorithm as an example in Design Tactic for Local Search.

Formalizing Natural Perturbations

This formalization entails only two restrictions on the general reachable neighborhood structures axiomatized in the abstract theory of local search: First, neighborhoods are required to be symmetric; that is, if y is in x's neighborhood, then x is in y's neighborhood. Most local search algorithms satisfy this condition. This condition is sufficient to ensure that if z is reachable from w, then w is reachable from z. Second, the neighborhood of each feasible solution is required to have the same intensional description, parameterized on feasible solutions, as any other feasible solution for the same optimization problem. These two restrictions enable the tools of group theory to be used in developing reachable neighborhood structures for a wide variety of optimization problems.

The basic idea is that a neighborhood structure is defined through a set of transformations that map a feasible solution to its neighboring feasible solutions. The reflexive axiom for neighborhoods means that the identity transformation is included in this set of transformations. The additional restriction of symmetric neighborhoods implies that a transformation from a feasible solution to a neighboring feasible solution is invertible. The reachability axiom for neighborhoods means that for every pair of feasible solutions, there is a sequence of transformations that map the first feasible solution to the second. As is shown here, a set of transformations satisfying these criteria also generates a group of transformations.

For any particular optimization problem and any particular input, each transformation could be described extensionally. For example, a transformation could be described as a list of pairs, each consisting of a feasible solution and its perturbed solution. The mathematics of extensionally described transformations is developed first. However, extensional descriptions are inadequate for generalizing to all possible inputs. Thus, the mathematics for intensionally described transformations is developed using group actions.

For combinatorial local search algorithms, the appropriate transformations are permutations that map a finite set to itself. A permutation group satisfies the following definition:

Given a set S, a permutation P is a bijection from S to S.

The set of all permutations on a set S will be denoted π_s and has cardinality $|S|!$ for finite sets.

The identity permutation I_s on a set maps all elements to themselves:
$$\forall\, (y \in S)I_s\,(y) = y$$

The unary operation of inversion is defined for all permutations in π_s, because they are bijections: $\forall\, (P \in \pi_s\,;\, y,y' \in S)P(y) = y' \Leftrightarrow P^{-1}\,(y') = y$

The binary map composition operation $\circ$ is defined for all permutations in π_s:
$$\forall\, (P_1,P_2 \in \pi_s)\,P_1 \circ P_2 \in \pi_s \wedge \forall\, (y \in S)\,P_1 \circ P_2\,(y) = P_1(P_2(y))$$

A permutation group G over set S is a subset of π_s satisfying the following axioms: $I_s \in G$ $\qquad\qquad\qquad$ (identity)

$\qquad$ $\forall\, (P \in G)\,P^{-1} \in G$ $\qquad\quad$ (closure under inversion)

$\qquad$ $\forall\, (P_1, P_2 \in G)\,P_1 \circ P_2 \in G$ $\quad$ (closure under composition)

Given any particular input, we can define various permutation groups on the set of feasible solutions. For all feasible solutions to be mutually reachable, such a permutation group must satisfy the condition that for any pair of feasible solutions, there is a permutation that transforms the first to the second:

Let FS_x be the set of feasible solutions for an optimization problem with a particular input $x1$: $\mathbf{I}(x1) \Rightarrow FS_{x1} = \{y | \mathbf{O}(x1,y)\}$

Let G be a permutation group over the set FS_{x1}. Then all feasible solutions are mutually reachable through G if the following condition is satisfied:

$$\forall(y,y' \in FS_{x1})\,\exists(g \in G)\,g(y) = y'$$

Given such a group of permutations for a particular input, I prove that a neighborhood relation can be defined by a subset of the group that generates the whole group through repeated composition. Formally, a set of generators for a group satisfies the following definition:

Let G be a permutation group over S. Let $H \subseteq G$, such that $h \in H \Rightarrow h^{-1} \in H$. Then H is a set of generators for G iff $H^* = G$, where H^* is inductively defined as follows:

$$H^0 = \{I_s\}$$
$$H^1 = \{h \mid h \in H\}$$
$$H^{k+1} = \{h \circ h' \mid h \in H \wedge h' \in H^k\}$$
$$H^* = \cup \{H^k \mid k \in Nat\}$$

This definition is a minor variation of the usual definition of the generators of a group. Because local search algorithms don't explicitly invert the transformations they apply to feasible solutions, if a permutation is in a generator subset, then so is its inverse.

Note the close relationship between the reachability axiom for a neighborhood and the inductive definition of H^*. The following theorem for any particular input is proved by simple induction; a more general theorem is proved later that extends this theorem to all inputs using intensional descriptions of a neighborhood.

Given an optimization problem and any particular input $x1$, let G be a permutation group over FS_{x1} satisfying the condition:

$$\forall(y,y') \; \mathbf{I}(x) \wedge \mathbf{O}(x1,y) \wedge \mathbf{O}(x1,y') \Rightarrow \exists(g \in G) \; g(y) = y'$$

Let H be a set of generators for G, i.e. $H \subseteq G$ and $H^* = G$.

Let $\mathbf{N}(x1,y,y') \equiv \exists \; (h \in H) \; h(y) = y'$

Theorem 1: $\mathbf{N}(x1,y,y')$ is a reachable neighborhood for input $x1$.

Proof: the inductive definition of the transitive closure of $\mathbf{N}(x1,y,y')$ entails that

$$\mathbf{N}^*(x1,y,y') \Leftrightarrow [\exists(g \in H^*)g(y) = y'] \Leftrightarrow [\exists(g \in G) \; g(y) = y'],$$
which is true by hypothesis.

QED

To give intensional descriptions of a natural perturbation neighborhood that apply to all inputs of an optimization problem, group actions are used. A *group action* maps a group to a subgroup of another permutation group. For example, a group action can map permutations of indexes to permutations over arrays. Thus, no matter what elements are actually in the array given as input, a group action provides an appropriate intensional description. Formally, a group action is a group homomorphism:

An Action of a group G on a set S is a group homomorphism, Action: $G \rightarrow \pi_s$.

Action maps elements of G to permutations of S such that identity, inverse and composition are preserved under the mapping. Given an Action, an orbit of an element $y \in S$ is a subset of S:

$$G_A(y) = \{y' \mid \exists \; (g \in G) \; (\text{Action}(g)) \; (y) = y'\}$$

The orbits either coincide or are disjoint, so they define a partition on S.

Theorem 1 is generalized to all inputs through group actions. A natural perturbation neighborhood is defined by a set of generators and a group action. Basic neighborhoods are a special class where the generators are the transpositions of a set. The following theorem specifies when a natural perturbation neighborhood is a reachable neighborhood:

Given an optimization problem **Opt** = <**D,R,I,O**,$\Re$, ≤ cost>, let FS_x be the set of feasible solutions for a legal input x. Let Action be a group action on **R,** mapping a group G to π_R.

Let H be a set of generators for G, then define a natural perturbation neighborhood: $\mathbf{N}(x,y,y') \equiv \exists(h \in H)\,(\text{Action}(h))(y) = y'$

Theorem 2: If $\forall$ (x,y) $\mathbf{I}(x) \wedge \mathbf{O}(x,y) \Rightarrow G_A(y) = FS_x$, then **N** is a reachable neighborhood.

Proof: by induction, the transitive closure of **N** is defined as follows:
$$\mathbf{N}^*(x,y,y') \equiv \exists(g \in G)\,(\text{Action}(g))(y) = y'$$

By hypothesis, $G_A(y) = \{y' \mid \exists(g \in G)\,(\text{Action}(g))(y) = y'\} = FS_x = \{y' \mid \mathbf{O}(x,y')\}$

Therefore $\forall (x,y,y')\mathbf{I}(x) \wedge \mathbf{O}(x,y) \Rightarrow [\exists(g \in G)(\text{Action}(g))(y) = y'] \Leftrightarrow \mathbf{O}(x,y')$

Therefore $\forall (x,y,y')\mathbf{I}(x) \wedge \mathbf{O}(x,y) \wedge \mathbf{O}(x,y') \Rightarrow [\exists(g \in G)\,(\text{Action}(g))(y) = y']$

Therefore $\forall (x,y,y')\mathbf{I}(x) \wedge \mathbf{O}(x,y) \wedge \mathbf{O}(x,y') \Rightarrow \mathbf{N}^*(x,y,y')$

Q.E.D.

STRATA does not directly reason about the orbits of group actions but, rather, about invariants of group actions. The invariants of group actions are part of the design knowledge STRATA uses in deriving a local search algorithm.

Given Action, a group action on S, an invariant I_A is a function on S such that $\forall(y,y' \in S)\,y' \in G_A(y) \Rightarrow I_A(y) = I_A(y')$

A set of invariants $SI_A = \{I_A^1, I_A^2, \ldots I_A^m\}$ is complete if they define the same partition as the group action:

$\forall(y,y' \in S)\,y' \in G_A(y) \Leftrightarrow [I_A^1(y) = I_A^1(y') \wedge \ldots \wedge I_A^m(y) = I_A^m(y')]$

The invariants of various group actions are manually developed and proven, then put into a library. STRATA derives a local search algorithm by comparing complete sets of invariants to feasibility constraints, retrieving the appropriate group action, and then specializing it to the particular optimization problem. The following theorem justifies STRATA'S method of retrieving the appropriate group action:

Given an optimization problem **Opt** = <**D,R,I,O**,$\Re$, ≤ cost>, let FS_x be the set of feasible solutions for a legal input x. Let Action be a group action on **R,** mapping a group G to π_R. Let H be a set of generators for G. Let $SI_A = \{I_A^1, I_A^2, \ldots I_A^m\}$ be a complete set of invariants for Action.

Theorem 3: If $\forall$ (x,y,y') $\mathbf{I}(x) \wedge \mathbf{O}(x,y) \Rightarrow$
$$[\mathbf{O}(x,y') \Leftrightarrow [I_A^1(y) = I_A^1(y') \wedge \ldots I_A^m(y) = I_A^m(y')]]$$
then $\mathbf{N}(x,y,y') \equiv \exists(h \in H)\,(\text{Action}(h))(y) = y'$ is a reachable neighborhood.

Proof: by definition, the hypothesis is equivalent to:

$\forall (x,y,y')\ \mathbf{I}(x) \wedge \mathbf{O}(x,y) \Rightarrow [\mathbf{O}(x,y') \Leftrightarrow y' \in G_A (y)]$ which is equivalent to theorem 2

$\forall(x,y)\ \mathbf{I}(x) \wedge \mathbf{O}(x,y) \Rightarrow [G_A (y) = FS_x]$

Q.E.D.

By theorem 3, the invariants of a group action can be represented as a predicate of the form **Invariant**(x,y); that is:

$\forall (x,y,y')\ \mathbf{I}(x) \wedge \mathbf{O}(x,y) \Rightarrow [\textbf{Invariant}\ (x,y') \Leftrightarrow \{I_A^l (y) = I_A^l (y') \wedge \ldots \wedge I_A^m(y) = I_A^m(y')]]$

This representation is used in STRATA'S library because it facilitates matching between a library theory and a problem specification.

Simplex Algorithm

Linear programming is the problem of finding the optimum value of a linear cost function given a set of linear constraints. From the abstract viewpoint of Euclidian geometry, the linear constraints describe a convex polyhedron (possibly unbounded or null) in k dimensions, where k is the number of variables. The cost function describes a direction in this k-dimensional space. The desired output is the point(s) on the polyhedron that is furthest along the direction vector, as illustrated in figure 3. The simplex algorithm starts with a vertex of this polyhedron and hill climbs toward an optimal solution by moving from vertex to vertex along the edges of the polyhedron. A fundamental theorem of linear programming proves that if a finite optimal solution exists, then there is always a vertex of the polyhedron that is an optimal solution. Multiple optimal solutions can occur if the direction vector is precisely aligned so that it is perpendicular to a face (or edge) of the polyhedron, in which case all the points on the face (or edge) are also optimal solutions.

The polyhedron is formed by the intersection of half spaces. Each half space splits the k-dimensional space into two halves whose boundary is a $k-1$ dimensional plane called a *hyperplane*. All the points lying in or on one side of the hyperplane are in the half space, and those on the other side are outside the half space. Each face of the polyhedron belongs to one of these hyperplanes. Each vertex of the polyhedron is the intersection of k hyperplanes. Not every intersection of k hyperplanes is a vertex of the polyhedron because most of these intersections lie outside the other half spaces. An edge of the polyhedron is the intersection of $k-1$ hyperplanes, and not every $k-1$ intersection is an edge of the polyhedron.

All variants of the primal simplex algorithm manipulate some representation of the polyhedron as the intersection of half spaces. The current vertex is determined by k hyperplane boundaries, and the movement from vertex to vertex is performed by dropping one of these hyperplanes (the remaining $k-1$ hyperplanes forming an edge) and then adding a different hyperplane, thereby reaching an adjacent vertex. Thus, the basic simplex algorithm is an

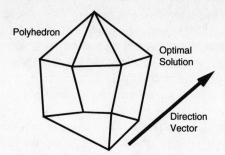

Polyhedron

Optimal
Solution

Direction
Vector

Figure 3. Geometric Interpretation of Linear Programming.

iterative perturbation of a k subset of hyperplanes. However, because not every intersection of k hyperplanes forms a vertex of the polyhedron, this new intersection point needs to be checked to determine if it falls within the other half spaces. This determination can actually be incorporated into the procedure that selects the hyperplanes to add and remove from the k subset.

The local search design tactic is sufficiently general to derive simplex algorithms for different forms of the linear programming problem. The different forms of the linear programming problem lead to different data structures for representing hyperplanes and different implementations of the perturbation operations on k subsets of hyperplanes. The derivation of the simplex algorithm for the standard form of linear programming is presented in the next section. This form is described in textbooks and is pedagogically useful because the implementation of the pivoting operations is somewhat simpler than for other forms. Textbooks (for example, Luenberger [1984]) also describe how other forms of the linear programming problem can be converted into this standard form through various transformations, such as the introduction of slack variables and surplus variables and the elimination of variables whose sign is unconstrained. The standard form of the linear programming problem follows:

minimize dot($\mathbf{c}, \mathbf{x}$)   subject to $\mathbf{Ax} = \mathbf{b}$ and $\forall i \; x_i \geq 0$
Input $\mathbf{A}$ ($m \times n$ matrix), $\mathbf{b}$ (m vector), $\mathbf{c}$ (n vector)
Output: $\mathbf{x}$ (n vector)

In the standard form of linear programming, each vertex is represented as m columns of an m by n matrix $\mathbf{A}$, where the number of rows (m) is less than the number of columns (n). The polyhedron is represented through a combination of the linear system of equations $\mathbf{Ax} = \mathbf{b}$ and the constraint that the coordinates of a feasible solution are all nonnegative. The linear function that is minimized is the dot product of a vector $\mathbf{c}$ given as input and the coordinates of a feasible solution $\mathbf{x}$. For each vertex, the m selected columns correspond to strictly positive coordinates, and the $n-m$ unselected columns correspond to coordinates with the value zero. Let *basis* be the set of indexes to the selected columns and SSM(A, *basis*) be the *m by m* selected submatrix of **A**. The nonzero coordinates of the vertex represented by *basis* can be calculated by solving the linear system of equations SSM(A, *basis*)**x** = **b**, using a procedure such as Gaussian elimination. An adjacent vertex is represented by a new basis in which one of the columns is swapped out and a new column swapped in.

The simplex algorithm for standard form problems hill climbs by perturbing the current basis to obtain a new basis. The constraints that the new basis correspond to a vertex of the polyhedron and, furthermore, that it is an improvement over the old basis can directly be incorporated into the selection of the column to swap out and the new column to swap in. STRATA derives this simplex algorithm from the following specification:

function linear programming(**A**:RMatrix,**b**:Rvector,**c**:Rvector):set(integer)
    where rows(**A**) < columns(**A**)
    returns (y | extremal(y, λ(y1,y2) (dot(**c**,solve(SSM(**A**,y1),**b**))
                                    $\leq$dot(**c**,solve(SSM(**A**,y2),**b**)))),
             {*basis*|*basis* $\subseteq$ {1...colums(**A**)} $\wedge$ size(*basis*) = rows(**A**)
                            $\wedge$ non-neg-coordinates(solve(SSM(**A**,*basis*),**b**))})

The extremal(y. . .) construct designates that its first argument (y) is a minimum in the ordering defined by the second argument (the lambda function) over the set of feasible solutions defined in the third argument (the set former {*basis* | . . .}). The dot function is able to take a second argument that represents only the nonnegative coordinates of a vector. STRATA first derives a general algorithm that perturbs a set of *m* columns to search from vertex to vertex. STRATA then specializes this algorithm by deriving constraints on the columns that are swapped in and out to ensure the new basis is a vertex of the polyhedron. Next, STRATA derives constraints on the columns that are exchanged to ensure that the new vertex is better than the old vertex. In all these steps, STRATA uses the directed inference system RAINBOW II to combine generic knowledge about local search algorithms with domain knowledge about linear algebra.

Many optimizations of this basic simplex algorithm are needed to make the iterative swapping of columns in the basis efficient. For example, because the basis only incrementally changes from vertex to adjacent vertex, the calculation of the coordinates can also incrementally be made. An incremental version of Gaussian elimination can be derived through finite differencing (see Paige and Koenig [1982] for a description of finite-difference optimizations). Furthermore, it is not necessary to explicitly compute the vertex coordinates on each iteration but only to determine whether an optimal solution has been reached and, if not, which hyperplanes should be swapped to obtain a better solution. These optimizations can be achieved through context-dependent simplification and partial evaluation. The result is essentially the pivoting operation described in standard textbook renditions of the simplex algorithm. In fact, the result is better than pivoting for both efficiency and numerical accuracy (Luenberger 1984, section 3.9). These kinds of optimization transformations are not generic to derivations of local search algorithms but, rather, are widely applicable in the final stages of deriving any algorithm and, hence, are done separately through KIDS.

From a pedagogical viewpoint, the details of pivoting often obscure the basic concepts of the simplex algorithm to beginning students. From the viewpoint of automatically deriving local search algorithms, the details of pivoting are too complex to derive from a domain theory through unguided theorem proving. The methodology of design analysis aims to decompose complex derivations into small mechanizable steps, each of which is general enough to be used in the derivations of many different algorithms. The next section describes the mathematical details of STRATA's design tactic and shows how the basic simplex algorithm is derived through a series of small, mechanized steps.

Design Tactic for Local Search Algorithms

A local search algorithm is designed by extending an optimization problem specification with a neighborhood definition to derive a local search theory and then instantiating a program schema with the components of the theory. Syntactically, a local search theory for a particular problem is a correspondence between abstract local search theory and definitions in the problem domain. The design tactic derives these definitions by first matching the feasibility constraints to basic neighborhood theories in the library and then specializing the matched basic neighborhood theory. For example, the design tactic derives a generic transposition sorting algorithm by first matching the LS-sequence theory to the specification of the sorting problem. It then derives a necessary condition for a transposition to improve a feasible solution, namely, that the elements that are exchanged be initially inverted.

In essence, the design tactic is itself a local search algorithm that starts with an overly general basic neighborhood definition and then improves it by incorporating problem constraints to improve efficiency. A basic neighborhood theory matches a problem definition if its invariants are a necessary condition for feasible solutions. Thus, a matched basic neighborhood defines an enlarged neighborhood of each solution: the adjacent basic solutions. Intersecting this neighborhood with the feasible solutions yields the adjacent feasible solutions, as shown in figure 4. This intersection is defined by specializing the basic neighborhood, in particular by deducing necessary preconditions on the transpositions. Finally, the transpositions are again specialized to derive only adjacent feasible solutions that improve the cost of the current

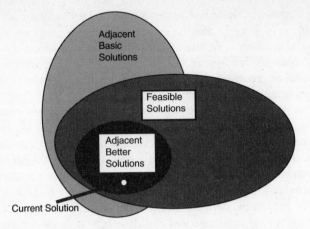

Figure 4. Deriving a Neighborhood Structure.

solution. This step is also done by deducing necessary preconditions on the transpositions. The relationship between basic solutions, feasible solutions, and better solutions is illustrated in figure 4.

Derivation of Basic LS Theory

To ensure that the initial neighborhood is reachable, the feasibility constraints are matched to basic neighborhoods such that every feasible solution can be generated from every other feasible solution through a sequence of transpositions acting on the feasible solutions. The best basic neighborhood match also ensures that no infeasible solutions are generated. For example, the match of the sorting problem to LS-sequence theory has this property because the invariants of the LS-sequence theory are equivalent to the feasibility constraints of the sorting problem. However, given the wide variety of problems to which local search can be applied, it is impossible to provide a large enough set of library theories so that every problem's feasibility constraints will be equivalent to the invariants of some library theory. Therefore, a match is accepted if the invariant properties of the basic neighborhood are a relaxation of the problem's feasibility constraints. A relaxed set of invariant properties admits more solutions. A match is preferable to another match if its invariants are stronger. The following definition formalizes the matching criteria:

> Basic neighborhood $BN = <D_{BN}, R_{BN}, I_{BN}, O_{BN}, N_{BN}>$ matches an optimization problem specification
> $Opt = <D, R, I, O, \Re, \leq, cost>$ if the type R matches the type R_{BN} and the following constraint is satisfied:
> $\forall (x) \exists (z) \forall (y) [I(x) \wedge O(x,y)] \Rightarrow [I_{BN}(z) \wedge O_{BN}(z,y)]$

The basic neighborhood theories in the library are indexed by their parameterized output type. As a result of matching the output type of the problem to the type of the basic neighborhood, the type variables in the basic neighborhood definition are instantiated. For example, matching the specification of sorting a sequence of integers (with output type seq(integer)) to LS-sequence theory (with output type seq(α)) results in type variable α being instantiated to integer. Likewise, as a result of verifying the constraint, the parameters of the input to the basic neighborhood definition are also instantiated. For the simplex algorithm specification, the output is a set of integers representing column indexes; so, the LS-subset theory is retrieved, and the type variable α is instantiated to integer. Matching then requires verifying the following constraint, which is the instantiation of the formal matching definition. This step is set up as a call to the RAINBOW II directed inference system. Note that variables for the input, output, and basic neighborhood input (x,y,z) in the formal definition are replaced by tuples of variables from the problem specification and retrieved basic neighborhood theory in the instantiated definition:

$$\forall\,(\mathbf{A},\mathbf{b},\mathbf{c})\;\exists(S,m)\;\forall\,(basis)\;[\text{rows}(\mathbf{A}) < \text{columns}(\mathbf{A}) \wedge basis \subseteq \{1...\text{columns}(\mathbf{A})\}$$
$$\wedge\;\text{size}(basis) = \text{rows}(\mathbf{A})$$
$$\wedge\;\text{non-neg-coordinates}(\text{solve}(\text{SSM}(\mathbf{A},basis),\mathbf{b}))]$$
$$\Rightarrow [m \leq \text{size}(S) \wedge basis \subseteq S \wedge \text{size}(basis) = m]$$

As a result of successfully verifying this constraint, the basic neighborhood parameters S, m are instantiated to the linear programming problem domain:

$$S \mapsto \{1...\text{columns}(\mathbf{A})\};\; m \mapsto \text{rows}(\mathbf{A}))$$

A basic local search theory for linear programming is obtained by substituting these parameter instantiations into the definition of the basic neighborhood for LS-subset theory. The components corresponding to the basic problem ($\mathbf{B} = \langle \mathbf{D},\mathbf{R},\mathbf{I},\mathbf{O}\rangle$) are directly obtained from the linear programming specification.

LS–basic-linear programming theory
$\mathbf{D} \mapsto$ RMatrix × Rvector × Rvector
$\mathbf{R} \mapsto$ set(integer)
$\mathbf{I} \mapsto \lambda\mathbf{A},\mathbf{b},\mathbf{c}.\; \text{rows}(\mathbf{A}) < \text{columns}(\mathbf{A})$
$\mathbf{O} \mapsto \lambda\mathbf{A},\mathbf{b},\mathbf{c},basis.\; basis \subseteq \{1...\text{columns}(\mathbf{A})\} \wedge \text{size}(basis) = \text{rows}(\mathbf{A})$
$\qquad \wedge\; \text{non-neg-coordinates}(\text{solve}(\text{SSM}(\mathbf{A},basis),\mathbf{b}))$
$\mathbf{N} \mapsto \lambda\mathbf{A},\mathbf{b},\mathbf{c},basis,y'.\; \exists(i,j)\; i \in (\{1...\text{columns}(\mathbf{A})\} - basis) \wedge j \in basis$
$\qquad \wedge\; y' = (basis \cup \{i\}) - \{j\}$

Specializing Basic Neighborhoods to Feasible Solutions

The subsequent steps of the design tactic specialize the basic neighborhood definition derived from this successful match. Necessary conditions are determined on the transpositions for requiring that only feasible solutions are generated, and that feasible solutions are perturbed to better feasible solutions. In the simplex algorithm derivation, STRATA specializes the basic neighborhood to restrict the transpositions so that only bases corresponding to vertexes of the polyhedron are generated. For the standard form of the linear programming problem, this restriction means that the coordinates of each vertex are all nonnegative. This nonnegative constraint is back propagated through the definition of the group action to derive the necessary preconditions on the transpositions. For the simplex algorithm, these derived preconditions are, in fact, both necessary and sufficient, so that through context-dependent simplification, these preconditions replace the explicit check on nonnegative coordinates.

The following definition formalizes the abstract *feasibility constraint* (**FC**), which is a necessary precondition on transpositions that ensures feasible solutions are transformed to feasible solutions by the group action:

$$\forall\ (x,y,y',i,j)\ [\mathbf{I}(x) \wedge \mathbf{O}(x,y) \wedge y' = \mathbf{Action}(x,y,i,j)]$$
$$\Rightarrow \mathbf{O}(x,y') \Rightarrow \mathbf{FC}(x,y,i,j)$$

The design tactic sets up a call to RAINBOW II to derive FC for a particular problem. The conjuncts in the first line of the definition are used as background assumptions by RAINBOW II for deducing the necessary preconditions on the feasibility of the perturbed solution in terms of the variables x, y, i, j. In the simplex algorithm derivation, this definition is instantiated as follows:

$$\forall\ (\mathbf{A},\mathbf{b},\mathbf{c},basis,y',i,j)$$
$$[basis \subseteq \{1\ldots\text{columns}(\mathbf{A})\} \wedge \text{size}(basis) = \text{rows}(\mathbf{A})$$
$$\wedge\ \text{non-neg-coordinates}(\text{solve}(\text{SSM}\ (\mathbf{A},basis),\mathbf{b}))$$
$$\wedge\ y' = basis \cup \{i\} - \{j\}]$$
$$\Rightarrow [y' \subseteq \{1\ldots\text{columns}(\mathbf{A})\} \wedge \text{size}(y') = \text{rows}(\mathbf{A})$$
$$\wedge\ \text{non-neg-coordinates}(\text{solve}(\text{SSM}(\mathbf{A},y'),\mathbf{b}))]$$
$$\Rightarrow \text{FC}(\mathbf{A},\mathbf{b},\mathbf{c},basis,i,j)$$

RAINBOW II uses the domain theory of linear algebra to derive the following definition for FC:

$$\text{FC}(\mathbf{A},\mathbf{b},\mathbf{c},basis,i,j) \equiv 0 \leq \text{solve}\ (\text{SSM}(\mathbf{A},basis),\mathbf{b})[j]\ /\ \text{solve}(\text{SSM}(\mathbf{A},basis),\mathbf{A}[i])[j]$$
$$\wedge\ \text{non-negative-coordinates}(\text{solve}(\text{SSM}(\mathbf{A},basis),\mathbf{b}) -$$
$$\text{solve}(\text{SSM}(\mathbf{A},basis),\mathbf{A}[i]*(\text{solve}(\text{SSM}(\mathbf{A},basis),\mathbf{b})[j]\ /\ \text{solve}(\text{SSM}(\mathbf{A},basis),\mathbf{A}[i])[j]))$$

The first conjunct of FC specifies that the coordinate corresponding to the new column swapped in is nonnegative, and the second conjunct specifies that the coordinates for the columns that remain in the basis remain nonnegative. The notation is mixed Lisp and standard linear algebra; $\mathbf{A}[i]$ denotes the ith column, and solve(. . .)[j] denotes the jth coordinate of the vector returned by solve.

Specializing the Generator to Hill-Climb

The next step of the design tactic again specializes the generator of neighboring solutions by deriving necessary conditions on a solution to be a local optimum. The constraint that an optimal solution has equal or lower cost than any of its neighbors is back propagated through the definition of the group action to derive the necessary preconditions on the transpositions. Because the transpositions generate all the neighbors, these preconditions can be used as a filter for testing whether a solution is a local optimum without actually generating all the neighbors. The negation of these preconditions can also be used to select a transposition to apply to a not locally optimal solution to generate a better solution. When these derived preconditions are both necessary and sufficient, which occurs in the simplex algorithm derivation, then the explicit calculation of the cost of neighboring solutions can be eliminated through context-dependent simplification.

The following definition formalizes this abstract *optimality constraint* (**OC**), which is a necessary precondition for a solution to be locally optimal:

$$\forall\ (x,y,y'i,j)\ [\mathbf{I}(x) \wedge \mathbf{O}(x,y) \wedge \mathbf{O}(x,y') \wedge y' = \mathbf{Action}(x,y,i,j)]$$
$$\Rightarrow \mathbf{cost}(x,y) \le \mathbf{cost}(x,y') \Rightarrow \mathbf{OC}(x,y,i,j)$$

The design tactic sets up a call to RAINBOW II to derive **OC** for a particular problem. The conjuncts in the first line of the definition are used as background assumptions by RAINBOW II for deducing necessary conditions on the unimproved cost of the perturbed solution in terms of the variables x, y, i, j. In the simplex algorithm derivation, the **OC** definition is instantiated as follows:

$$\forall\ (\mathbf{A},\mathbf{b},\mathbf{c},basis,y'i,j)$$
$$[basis \subseteq \{1...\text{columns}(\mathbf{A})\} \wedge \text{size}(basis) = \text{rows}(\mathbf{A})$$
$$\wedge\ \text{non-neg-coordinates}(\text{solve}(\text{SSM}(\mathbf{A},basis),\mathbf{b}))$$
$$\wedge\ y' \subseteq \{1...\text{columns}(\mathbf{A})\} \wedge \text{size}(y') = \text{rows}(\mathbf{A})$$
$$\wedge\ \text{non-neg-coordinates}(\text{solve}(\text{SSM}(\mathbf{A},y'),\mathbf{b}))$$
$$\wedge\ y' = basis \cup \{i\} - \{j\}]$$
$$\Rightarrow \text{dot}(\mathbf{c},\text{solve}(\text{SSM}(\mathbf{A},basis),\mathbf{b})) \le \text{dot}(\mathbf{c},\text{solve}(\text{SSM}(\mathbf{A},y'),\mathbf{b}))$$
$$\Rightarrow \mathbf{OC}(\mathbf{A},\mathbf{b},\mathbf{c},basis,i,j)$$

RAINBOW II uses the domain theory of linear algebra to derive the following definition for **OC**:

$$\mathbf{OC}(\mathbf{A},\mathbf{b},\mathbf{c},basis,i,j) \equiv 0 \le \mathbf{c}[i] - \text{dot}(\mathbf{c},\text{solve}(\text{SSM}(\mathbf{A},basis),\mathbf{A}[i]))$$

In the linear programming literature, the expression on the right of the inequality is called the *relative cost coefficient* for column i. Note that this definition of **OC** depends only on the column i and not the column j. For the linear programming problem, **OC** is both a necessary and sufficient condition for a feasible solution to be optimal, meaning that the test for local optimality is efficient; in fact, it only requires comparing each coordinate i of the vector **c** against an expression over i and the input parameters. Furthermore, if a solution is not optimal, then a better solution can be determined by simply selecting a column (i) that does not satisfy **OC**. Note also that once a column (i) is selected to add to the basis set, then the column (j) to remove from the basis set is determined by the definition of **FC**. Together **OC** and **FC** determine very tight constraints on the transpositions that are mapped to perturbations of the basis set. Furthermore, both these expressions can incrementally be updated as the basis is incrementally perturbed, resulting in further efficiency.

Program Instantiation

The simplex algorithm theory consists of the basic neighborhood definition specialized with **OC** and **FC**. After verifying that local optima are global optima, the final step of the local search design tactic is to instantiate a program schema with the components of the derived simplex algorithm theory. The functional program schema for recursive hill climbing presented in Local Search Algorithms is specialized to the following schema for local search theories derived from basic neighborhoods and definitions **FC** and **OC**:

function $\mathbf{F_{LS}}(x{:}\mathbf{D},z{:}\mathbf{R}){:}\mathbf{R}$
  where $\mathbf{I}(x) \wedge \mathbf{O}(x,z)$
  returns $(y| \mathbf{O}(x,y) \wedge \forall (y')\ \mathbf{O}(x,y') \wedge \mathbf{N}(x,y,y') \Rightarrow \mathbf{cost}(x,y) \leq \mathbf{cost}(x,y'))$
  $= $ If $\forall (y',i,j)\ \mathbf{FC}(x,z,i,j) \wedge \mathbf{O}(x,y') \wedge y' = \mathbf{Action}(x,z,i,j)$
        $\Rightarrow [\mathbf{OC}(x,z,i,j) \wedge \mathbf{cost}(x,z) \leq \mathbf{cost}(x,y')]$
  Then z

  Else $\mathbf{F_{LS}}\ (x,\text{arb}\{ y' \mid \mathbf{FC}(x,z,i,j) \wedge \mathbf{O}(x,y') \wedge y' = \mathbf{Action}(x,z,i,j)$
        $\wedge \neg [\mathbf{OC}(x,z,i,j) \wedge \mathbf{cost}(x,z,) \leq \mathbf{cost}(x,y')]\})$

The program in figure 5 is the instantiation of this program schema with the components of the simplex theory derived by STRATA. The explicit check for improved cost was simplified away, and only the derived cost constraint (OC) remains. Similarly, the explicit check for the feasibility of the new solution was simplified away, and only the derived feasibility constraint (FC) remains. This instantiated schema is a program in REFINE that was successfully tested on example linear programming problems. REFINE is a high-level language that includes logic and set-theoretic constructs; REFINE programs are compiled into Common Lisp by the REFINE compiler. This program is what STRATA actually produced from the specification of linear programming. The notation in this REFINE program differs slightly from that of the definitions derived here because of the Lisplike syntax and because certain conversion functions, such as VECTOR, which converts a single column matrix to a vector, were required in the domain theory to ensure consistent typing.

After further optimizations, this algorithm is equivalent to the one described in Luenberger (1984, section 3.9). For example, finite-differencing optimization transformations produce incremental versions of the solve function in both the FC and OC definitions. Finite differencing and other optimization transformations are separately performed by the KIDS system. One of the strengths of the algorithm design knowledge obtained through design analysis is that it integrates well with other types of knowledge, including domain knowledge and programming knowledge such as knowledge about optimizing algorithms.

```
(defobject HILL-CLIMB-LINEAR-PROGRAMMING-1
    function (A:RMATRIX, B:RVECTOR, C:RVECTOR, BASIS: set(integer)): set(integer) =
  if ∀(J, I, Y')
    (0 ≤ (SOLVE(SSM(A,BASIS),B))(J) / (SOLVE(SSM(A,BASIS),VECTOR(SSM(A,{I}))))(J)
    & NON-NEG-COORDINATES(
      VADD(SOLVE(SSM(A,BASIS), B),
        SCALE-MULTIPLY(SOLVE(SSM(A,BASIS),VECTOR(SSM(A,{I}))),
                     -1.0 *(SOLVE(SSM(A, BASIS), B))(J) /
                           (SOLVE(SSM(A,BASIS),VECTOR (SSM(A,{I})))(J))))
    & (Y' = (BASIS with I less J) & J ∈ BASIS & ¬I ∈ BASIS
      & I ∈ COLUMNS(A) & size(Y') = size(ROWS(A)) & Y' ⊂ COLUMNS(A))
    => 0 ≤ C(I) − DOT(C,SOLVE(SSM(A,BASIS),VECTOR(SSM(A,{I})))))
  then BASIS
  else HILL-CLIMB-LINEAR-PROGRAMMING-1(A,B,C,
    arb({Y' | (J, I, Y')
    ¬(0 ≤ C(I) − DOT(C,SOLVE(SSM(A,BASIS),VECTOR(SSM(A,{I})))))
    & (0 ≤ (SOLVE(SSM(A,BASIS),B))(J) / (SOLVE(SSM(A,BASIS),VECTOR(SSM(A,{I}))))(J)
    & NON-NEG-COORDINATES(
      VADD(SOLVE(SSM(A,BASIS),B),
        SCALE-MULTIPLY(SOLVE(SSM(A,BASIS),VECTOR(SSM(A,{I}))),
                     -1.0 *(SOLVE(SSM(A, BASIS),B))(J) /
                           (SOLVE(SSM(A,BASIS),VECTOR (SSM(A,{I})))(J))))
    & (Y' = (BASIS with I less J) & J ∈ BASIS & ¬I ∈ BASIS
      & I ∈ COLUMNS(A) & size(Y') = size(ROWS(A)) & Y' ⊂ COLUMNS(A))})))
```

Figure 5. Derived simplex Algorithm.

Summary of Design Tactic

Thus, the design tactic decomposes a complex synthesis task, which could
easily lead to a combinatorial search space, into a sequence of steps that can
be handled by current transformational and theorem-proving technology.
This design tactic derives algorithms based on natural perturbation neighborhoods. The design tactic is implemented as a metalevel program in REFINE .
The following are the formal steps of the design tactic:

First, retrieve the basic neighborhood theories from the library indexed by
the type of feasible solution. A theory matches a problem specification if the
invariants of the group action are necessary conditions of the feasibility constraints of the specification, which is verified by calling RAINBOW II with the
following inference specification:

$$\forall (x) \exists (z) \forall (y) [\mathbf{I}(x) \wedge \mathbf{O}(x,y)] \Rightarrow [\mathbf{I_{BN}}(z) \wedge \mathbf{O_{BN}} (z,y)]$$

As a result of matching, the parameters of a basic neighborhood theory
are instantiated to problem-specific definitions. If multiple matches occur,
the instantiated invariants form a partial order under logical implication.
A match with maximally strong invariants is arbitrarily chosen.

Second, determine the necessary preconditions (**FC**) on the transpositions
that ensure that a feasible solution is perturbed to a feasible solution. This

step is done by calling RAINBOW II with the following inference specification:

$$\forall \, (x,y,y',i,j) \, [\mathbf{I}(x) \wedge \mathbf{O}(x,y) \wedge y' = \mathbf{Action}(x,y,i,j)]$$
$$\Rightarrow \mathbf{O}(x,y') \Rightarrow \mathbf{FC}(x,y,i,j)$$

Third, determine the necessary preconditions (**OC**) on the transpositions that ensure that a feasible solution is perturbed to a better feasible solution and that a feasible solution is a local optimum. This task is done by calling RAINBOW II with the following inference specification:

$$\forall \, (x,y,y',i,j) \, [\mathbf{I}(x) \wedge \mathbf{O}(x,y) \wedge \mathbf{O}(x,y') \wedge y' = \mathbf{Action}(x,y,i,j)]$$
$$\Rightarrow \mathbf{cost}(x,y) \leq \mathbf{cost}(x,y') \Rightarrow \mathbf{OC}(x,y,i,j)$$

Fourth, determine the necessary conditions (**GOC**) for a local optimum to be a global optimum (optional step for deriving exact local search algorithms). For the simplex algorithm, these necessary conditions are simply true: A locally optimal vertex is always a globally optimal vertex.

$$\forall \, (x,y,) \, [\mathbf{I}(x) \wedge \mathbf{O}(x,y') \wedge [\forall(y',i,j) \, \mathbf{O}(x,y') \wedge y' = \mathbf{Action}(x,y,i,j)$$
$$\Rightarrow \mathbf{cost}(x,y) \leq \mathbf{cost}(x,y')]]$$
$$\Rightarrow [\forall \, (z) \, \mathbf{O}(x,z) \Rightarrow \mathbf{cost}(x,y) \leq \mathbf{cost}(x,z) \,] \Rightarrow \mathbf{GOC} \, (x,y)$$

Fifth, a program schema is instantiated with the components of the derived local search theory.

Conclusion

Automatic algorithm design is a difficult task. As in any design problem, the search space is combinatorially explosive. Substantial search guidance is needed to enable an automatic programming system such as STRATA to design complicated algorithms such as the simplex algorithm. Design analysis yields the design knowledge needed to guide automatic programming systems. Design analysis is a methodology that begins with an analysis of derivations of a class of algorithms. From this analysis, the structure common to the class of algorithms is formalized as a theory, and the structure common to the derivations is formalized as a design tactic. The design tactic decomposes a complex synthesis task into a sequence of small, mechanizable steps. During program synthesis, the design tactic guides the integration of domain knowledge (in the form of a domain theory) and general knowledge about algorithms (in the form of a theory about a class of algorithms) to automatically design algorithms.

In this article, the structure of local search algorithms was formalized as a theory. A design tactic based on this theory was implemented in STRATA. This tactic derives both heuristic and exact local search algorithms based on the formalization of natural perturbation neighborhoods. The design tactic first matches a problem specification to invariants of natural perturbation neighborhoods stored in a library. It then specializes the initial match to the particular problem specification through a series of inference steps. Finally, it instantiates a program schema to obtain a functional program.

The overall approach to software engineering is one of automated *knowledge reuse* rather than reuse of standardized programs. Reusing the knowledge for deriving programs, rather than the programs themselves, promises both design flexibility and execution efficiency. It also solves the problem of interfacing a program to the context of its use because the interfacing is part of the design process. The knowledge that is reused by STRATA in deriving a local search algorithm includes the domain theory, the theory of local search algorithms, and the library of natural perturbation neighborhoods. To effectively combine all this knowledge, STRATA uses theorem proving and transformational techniques developed by the AI community.

Acknowledgments

Douglas Smith developed the KIDS system that provided a rich environment for implementing the research described in this chapter. I would like to thank Lee Blaine, Laura Jones, Richard Tully, Tom Pressburger, Douglas Smith, and David Zimmerman for their comments on various drafts of this chapter.

Bibliography

Abraido-Fandino, L. 1987. An Overview of REFINE 2.0. In Proceedings of the Second International Symposium on Knowledge Engineering, 8–10 April, Madrid, Spain.

Biggerstaff, T. J., and Perlis, A. J., eds. 1989. *Software Reusability, Volume 1: Concepts and Models.* Reading, Mass.: Addison-Wesley.

Burstall, R. M., and Darlington, J. 1977. A Transformation System for Developing Recursive Programs. *Journal of the ACM* 24(1): 44–67.

Feather, M. 1982. Automating the Transformational Development of Software. *IEEE Transactions on Software Engineering* SE-11(11): 1268–1278.

Goguen, J. A.; Thatcher J. W.; and Wagner, E. G. 1978. An Initial Algebra Approach to the Specification, Correctness, and Implementation of Abstract Data Types. In *Current Trends in Programming Methodology, Volume IV: Data Structuring,* ed. R. T. Yeh, 80–149. Englewood Cliffs, N.J.: Prentice Hall.

Green, C. 1969. Application of Theorem Proving to Problem Solving. In Proceedings of the International Joint Conference on Artificial Intelligence, 219–239. Menlo Park, Calif.: International Joint Conferences on Artificial Intelligence.

Karmarkar, N. 1984. A New Polynomial-Time Algorithm for Linear Programming. *Combinatorica* 4(4): 373–395.

Karp, R. M., and Papidimitriou, C. H. 1980. On Linear Characterizations of Combinatorial Optimization Problems. In Proceedings of the Twenty-First Annual Symposium on Foundations of Computer Science, 1–9. Washington, D.C.: IEEE Computer Society.

Khachian, L. G. 1979. A Polynomial Algorithm for Linear Programming (translation). *Soviet Math. Doklady* 20:191–194.

Kirkpatrick, S.; Gelatt, C. D.; and Vecchi, M. P. 1983. Optimization by Simulated Annealing. *Science* 220(4598): 671–680.

Klee, V., and Minty, G. J. 1972. How Good Is the Simplex Algorithm? In *Inequalities III,* ed. O. Shisha, 159–175. New York: Academic.

Klein, F. 1893. Vergleichende Betrachtungen uber Neuere Geometrische Forschungen. *Bulletin of the New York Mathematical Society* 2:215–249.

Lin, S. 1965. Computer Solutions of the Traveling Salesman Problem. *Bell Systems Technical Journal* 44:2245–2269.

Lowry, M. R. 1990. STRATA: Problem Reformulation and Abstract Data Types. In *Change of Representation and Inductive Bias*, ed. D. P. Benjamin, 41–67. Boston, Mass.: Kluwer Academic.

Lowry, M. R. 1989. Algorithm Synthesis through Problem Reformulation. Ph.D. diss., Dept. of Computer Science, Stanford Univ.

Lowry, M. R. 1988. Invariant Logic: A Calculus for Problem Reformulation. In Proceedings of the Seventh National Conference on Artificial Intelligence, 14–18. Menlo Park, Calif.: American Association for Artificial Intelligence.

Lowry, M. R. 1987a. The Abstraction/Implementation Model of Problem Reformulation. In Proceedings of the Tenth International Joint Conference on Artificial Intelligence, 1004–1010. Menlo Park, Calif.: International Joint Conferences on Artificial Intelligence.

Lowry, M. R. 1987b. Algorithm Synthesis through Problem Reformulation. In Proceedings of the Sixth National Conference on Artificial Intelligence, 432–436. Menlo Park, Calif.: American Association for Artificial Intelligence.

Luenberger, D. G. 1984. *Linear and Nonlinear Programming*, 2d ed. Reading, Mass.: Addison-Wesley.

Paige, R., and Koenig, S. 1982. Finite Differencing of Computable Expressions. *ACM Transactions on Programming Languages and Systems* 4(3): 402–454.

Papadimitriou, C., and Steiglitz, K. 1982. *Combinatorial Optimization: Algorithms and Complexity*. Englewood Cliffs, N.J.: Prentice Hall.

Savage, S. L. 1976. Some Theoretical Implications of Local Search. *Mathematical Programming* 10:345–366.

Savage, S. L. 1972. Toward a Theory of Convergent Local Search. In Proceedings of the Sixth Annual Princeton Conference on Information Sciences and Systems, 375–380. Princeton, N.J.: Princeton University Press.

Savage, S. L.; Weiner, P.; and Krone, M. J. 1973. Convergent Local Search, Research Report, 14, Dept. of Comp. Science, Yale Univ.

Smith, D. R., and Lowry, M. R. 1990. Algorithm Theories and Design Tactics. *Science of Computer Programming* 14:305–321.

Tracz, W., ed. 1988. *Software Reuse: Emerging Technology*. Washington, D.C.: IEEE Computer Society.

21

Formal Software Development
in the KIV System

Maritta Heisel, Wolfgang Reif, and Werner Stephan

The KIV (Karlsruhe interactive verifier) approach is strictly logic based in the sense that during the development process, a correctness proof is generated for the resulting program. From the point of view of logic, development strategies in this sense are essentially formal descriptions of plans that guide the generation of proofs in a given formal system. However, strategies can incorporate any type of knowledge, such as knowledge about programming techniques, problem-solving methods, and special domains. The ultimate aim of the KIV system is to combine logical rigor with strategic considerations.

Several proof-oriented methods for the development of programs are known from the literature. For example, one can use syntax-directed verification rules backward to refine a schematic program step by step. We present such a strategy in A Formalization and Implementation of Gries's Program Development Method. Of course, refinement strategies of this sort do not cover the whole range of formal software development. In Program Construction by Modification, we demonstrate how strategies for classical verification, as well as for the proof of program implications, can be combined with refinement strategies to treat program modifications.

If one is interested in a system that supports many different methods, it is unsatisfactory to develop a special logic for each purpose. Each new formalism would require at least a proof of soundness with respect to some semantic model of the programming language under consideration. Only strict discipline for adding new rules or axioms will prevent such a system from running into inconsistencies. Numerous examples of unsound proof rules that were proposed in the literature show that this task is not a trivial one. Thus, a system consisting of many special-purpose formalisms does not allow the routine development of new rules. Moreover, there is no way to freely combine different strategies.

The KIV system is based on a powerful and general formalism that can serve as a logical foundation for many (development) methods. Because we are also interested in imperative programs, we chose dynamic logic (DL) (Pratt 1976) for this purpose. As our object language, we consider a Pascal-like programming language with a powerful procedure concept. Purely functional programs can be treated as recursive programs satisfying certain syntactical constraints that allow the application of special rules.

As has also been observed in the context of other programming logics, for example, LCF, it is practically impossible to generate large proofs using only the basic rules and axioms. Therefore, we follow the paradigm of tactical theorem proving (Heisel, Reif, and Stephan 1990). An embedding of the deductive machinery into a programming language (metalanguage) allows the programming of sound extensions of the basic formalism. This idea goes back to the Edinburgh LCF system (Gordon, Milner, and Wadsworth 1979).

When we wish to implement a particular development strategy, for example, we start with the definition of suitable new rules that are guaranteed sound by so-called validations attached to them. Because formulas in DL contain complete programs, they exhibit a rich syntactic structure; therefore, derived rules play a central role in our system. In cases where a refinement step cannot be expressed by a single scheme, metalanguage programs called *tactics* generate subgoals by the consecutive application of several rules. On top of derived rules and tactics, we put metalanguage programs called *strategies*, which select the derivation steps according to the given method. Most of the strategies which have been implemented to date are *interactive* in the sense that the user has to supply additional information during the generation of a proof.

The first section gives a brief survey of the KIV system. After introducing the basic syntactic and semantic concepts of DL, we discuss the expressive power of DL and compare it to other languages. We outline our way of axiomatizing programming languages. As an important point, we argue that the standard axiom systems for DL, following the paradigm of so-called interpreted reasoning, are not appropriate for our purposes. We introduce the

HEISEL, REIF, & STEPHAN 549

functional metalanguage PPL (proof programming language) that is designed to program the generation of proofs. This section closes with a description of how to implement proof strategies in the KIV system.

The following section presents the formalization and implementation of Gries's (1981) program development method. The method, as it is given in his book, is reflected in the corresponding DL proof rules and PPL strategies. An example shows how the program and the correctness proof are simultaneously developed.

Program Construction by Modification presents another approach to formal program construction: programming by modification. The basic idea is to modify existing programs to solve related problems by reusing the knowledge about programs that were developed earlier for similar problems. This method was introduced by Dershowitz (1983).

Finally, we give information about other strategies implemented within the KIV environment and compare our system to others well known in this field.

The KIV System

The KIV system combines a special variant of DL and tactical theorem proving to obtain a shell for logic based program verification and program development.

Dynamic Logic

The values of variables occurring in the various syntactic constructs, such as the expression $f(g(x), h(x))$, depend on a valuation or state. In functional programming languages, this state is not changed during the execution of a program. Hence, different occurrences of the same variable stand for the same object. In imperative programming languages, however, this situation is no longer true. Consider, for example, the command $y:= g(x)$; $x:= h(x)$; $x:= f(y, x)$. The assignment $x:= h(x)$ can be looked at as a destructive operation that changes the value of x without generating a copy of this value. This change is, of course, desirable if the value of x is a large data object. Thus, proofs about imperative programs have to account for algebraic properties of data structures as well as the order in which the statements are executed. In this example, if we exchange the first two assignments, the resulting program is not necessarily equivalent to the given one.

Like many other programming logics, dynamic logic uses concepts from modal logic to model the temporal behavior of imperative programs. Instead of using explicit states, transition relations (for each program), and a function that gives the value of a variable in a given state, DL uses a modal operator for each program. These operators are used to refer to properties of (all) states reachable by the associated program. DL can thus be viewed as a multi-modal logic. Using modal logics, we restrict ourselves to certain statements about programs. Apart from some technical points, the main advantage of this approach is that this restriction structures formulas and proofs in a very natural way. For a survey of DL, see, for example, Harel (1984).

DL extends predicate logic (PL) by formulas of the form $[\alpha]\varphi$ ("box $\alpha\ \varphi$"), where α is a program, and φ is an arbitrary DL formula. These formulas have to be read "if α terminates, then φ holds." For example, the formula $x \geq 0 \rightarrow [x := x + 1]x > 0$ asserts that if the content of x is greater than or equal to 0, then after the execution of $x := x + 1$, the content of x is strictly greater than 0. As is common in modal logic, the dual operator leads to formulas $\langle\alpha\rangle\varphi$ ("diamond $\alpha\ \varphi$") that can be regarded as an abbreviation for $\neg [\alpha]\neg \varphi$. The formula $\langle\alpha\rangle\varphi$ has to be read "α terminates, and φ holds afterwards."

Hoare's (1969) logic (HL) considers partial correctness assertions of the form $\psi \{\alpha\}\ \varphi$, where, again, α is a program, and ψ and φ, the so-called precondition and postcondition, respectively, are PL formulas. The term partial refers to the fact that φ holds after the execution of α if ψ holds beforehand, and the execution terminates. The semantic background of HL is much the same as that of DL. Indeed, the language of HL can be regarded as a sublanguage of DL by writing partial correctness assertions as implications $\psi \rightarrow [\alpha]\varphi$. In most axiomatizations of DL, including our system for uninterpreted reasoning presented later, the rules of Hoare-like calculi can be obtained as derived rules. From a DL point of view, HL represents a particular proof strategy. In combination with uninterpreted reasoning, the richer language of DL allows the derivation of proof rules for other strategies. This ability is important if one wants to experiment with various proof rules to synthesize programs. Total correctness assertions, where we also guarantee the termination of the given program, are expressed by using diamond formulas instead of box formulas: $\psi \rightarrow \langle\alpha\rangle\varphi$ (sometimes also written as $\{\psi\}\ \alpha\ \{\varphi\}$).

For deterministic programs, $\langle\alpha\rangle\varphi$ is semantically equivalent to the weakest precondition $wp(\alpha,\ \varphi)$ of α with respect to φ, that is, the weakest condition that must hold before the execution of α to guarantee that α terminates and that φ holds after its execution. The function wp is a predicate transformer. These transformers were invented by Dijkstra (1976) to define the semantics of programming languages. Hence, for deterministic programs, DL can be regarded as a formalization of the concept of weakest precondition.

In contrast to HL, DL is a full logic and, therefore, powerful enough to express properties of programs other than correctness assertions. For example, we are able to treat program equivalence. If x' is a new variable, then $\langle\alpha\rangle x = x' \leftrightarrow \langle\beta\rangle x = x'$ means that the programs α and β are equivalent with respect to the variable x. Even the moderate generalization of (partial and total) correctness assertions, where program formulas are allowed in the preconditions and postconditions has turned out to be useful. In the case of recursive procedures, this sort of formula can be used to prove partial correctness assertions in the presence of procedures as parameters.

HEISEL, REIF, & STEPHAN   551

The Deductive System

To obtain a flexible proof system that allows the formalization of many different strategies, our axiomatization (Reif 1984) is derived from Goldblatt's (1982) system for uninterpreted reasoning. *Uninterpreted reasoning* uses as much programming knowledge as possible in the sense that statements that hold for all interpretations of the symbols occurring in the programs can also be proved without relying on properties of specific data structures.

For assignments, first we have the well-known axiom

$$[x := \tau]\varphi \leftrightarrow \varphi_x^{\tau},$$

where φ is a PL formula and φ_x^{τ} is obtained from φ by substituting the expression τ for all occurrences of x that are free for τ. This axiom allows us to conclude

$$(x \geq 0 \rightarrow [x := x + 1]\, x > 0) \leftrightarrow (x \geq 0 \rightarrow x + 1 > 0).$$

as far as assignments are concerned, this single axiom is sufficient for interpreted reasoning (Harel 1979). To prove

$$(*)\ [x := f(x, y)\,; z := x]\varphi \leftrightarrow [z := f(x, y)\,; x := z]\varphi$$

using the previous axiom, we would have to reduce φ to a PL formula using properties of the data structures involved because the formula following the box operator cannot contain programs. In cases where φ is of the form $[long\_program]\varphi'$, this reduction might be hard to do. Moreover, the proof would obscure the fact that the previous formula is true for all data structures. For uninterpreted reasoning, we need additional axioms, such as

$$[y := \tau][x := \sigma]\varphi \leftrightarrow [x := \sigma_y^{\tau}][y := \tau]\varphi\,, x \notin \text{Var}(y := \tau)\,.$$

In this case, φ is, of course an arbitrary DL formula. Among others, this axiom has to be used to prove the equivalence (*).

To extend uninterpreted reasoning to simple structured programs, we have axioms such as

$$[\alpha\,; \beta]\varphi \leftrightarrow [\alpha][\beta]\varphi$$

for the sequential composition of programs and

$$[\textbf{if } \varepsilon \textbf{ then } \alpha \textbf{ else } \beta \textbf{ fi}]\varphi \leftrightarrow ((\varepsilon \rightarrow [\alpha]) \wedge (\neg \varepsilon \rightarrow [\beta]\varphi))$$

for the conditional composition.

In the case of while loops, Goldblatt uses an infinitary rule, that is, a rule with infinitely many premises. This leads to a nice syntactic characterization of the valid formulas. However, proofs are no longer finite objects in Goldblatt's system. To overcome this difficulty, we introduced a fixed data structure called *counters* with a constant <u>zero</u> and a successor function *next* and additional programming constructs to allow inductive proofs about while loops. As axioms, we have

$$[\textbf{while } \varepsilon \textbf{ do } \alpha \textbf{ od}]\varphi \leftrightarrow \forall i.[(\varepsilon \# \alpha \downarrow i)]\varphi\,, i \notin \text{Var}(\varphi)$$

and

$$[(\varepsilon \# \alpha \downarrow \underline{zero})]\varphi \leftrightarrow (\neg\varepsilon \rightarrow \varphi)$$
$$(\varepsilon \# \alpha \downarrow next(i))]\varphi \leftrightarrow (\varepsilon \rightarrow [\alpha][(\varepsilon \# \alpha \downarrow i)]\varphi) \, .$$

Constructs of the form $(\varepsilon \# \alpha \downarrow \iota)$, where ι is a counter expression, can be regarded as representing approximations of the program **while ε do α od**. The formula $[(\varepsilon \# \alpha \downarrow i)]\varphi$ has to be read "if the loop **while ε do α od** terminates after exactly i iterations, then φ holds." As opposed to the various data structures the programs act on, the auxiliary data structure of counters is regarded as belonging to the basic formalism. For details of our formal system, see Heisel, Reif, and Stephan (1989).

Along the same lines, a rather powerful procedure concept was axiomatized (Stephan 1989). Again, an auxiliary data structure of environments is used to allow inductive proofs about recursive procedures.

As is the case with most of the related systems, deductions are carried out in a sequent calculus. Sequents

$$\varphi_1, \ldots, \varphi_m \vdash \psi_1, \ldots, \psi_n$$

have to be read as implications

$$\varphi_1 \wedge \ldots \wedge \varphi_m \rightarrow \psi_1 \vee \ldots \vee \psi_n \, .$$

As opposed to Hilbert-style systems, sequent calculi use rules instead of logical axioms. For example, on the level of propositional reasoning, we have the rule

$$\frac{\Gamma \vdash \varphi, \Delta \qquad \Gamma \vdash \psi, \Delta}{\Gamma \vdash \varphi \wedge \psi, \Delta},$$

which introduces a conjunction on the right-hand side of $\vdash$. In the previous schema, Γ and Δ stand for lists of formulas. The axioms for the programming language constructs, some of which were previously presented, are added by rules without premises. Given such a formula Ax, we add

$$\frac{}{\vdash Ax}$$

as a basic rule. In terms of proof trees, this sequent can be regarded as a proof tree of height one.

The Metalanguage

The logical system previously described is embedded in a functional programming language (PPL) that allows the programmed generation of proofs. In contrast to ML, which is the metalanguage of Edinburgh LCF, PPL rules are data objects rather than functions. In this aspect, our system is closer to ISABELLE (Paulson 1986). The central data structure of PPL is that of proof trees. The nodes of a proof tree consist of schematic sequents that can contain metavariables of any syntactic category. The basic rule schemes of our

calculus are the elementary proof trees. These trees include the usual introduction rules for logical connectives and quantifiers. The axioms of the programming language are formulated as implications or equivalences. For example, the axiom for sequential composition of programs is expressed as

$\vdash$ [$C1$; $C2$]$F \leftrightarrow$ [$C1$][$C2$]F .

We use the $ sign to mark metavariables in PPL, and we continue to use
Greek letters for arbitrary syntactic objects that might contain metavariables
of PPL. Recall that this scheme is treated as a tree of height one.

Proof trees correspond to partial proofs in that the leaves of a tree need not
be axioms but might as well be open premises. New proof trees are generated
by the operations infer and refine that are generalized forward and backward
proof steps, respectively. The operation $\text{infer}(t_0, [i_1, \ldots, i_n], [t_1, \ldots, t_n])$ performs a forward proof step by using the conclusions of n proof trees $t_1, \ldots, t_n$
as the premises of an instantiation of a proof tree t_0, yielding a proof tree
with a new conclusion. The instantiation of the metavariables of t_0 is formed
in such a way that the instantiation of the i_kth premise of t_0 equals the conclusion of t_k. The operation $\text{refine}(t_1, i, t_2)$ performs a backward proof step by
replacing the ith premise of a proof tree t_1 with an instantiation of proof tree
t_2, yielding a proof tree with the instantiated premises of t_2 as additional subgoals. Both operations use matching rather than unification. In the case of
refine, t_2 can be considered a generalized inference rule whose metavariables
are instantiated to make the conclusion of t_2 equal to the ith premise of t_1.

In addition to the built-in basic rules, the user can define derived rules.
Such derived rules become the logical building blocks for the program-
verification and program development strategies we are going to implement.
To maintain the soundness of the system, the user has to supply a validation
for each derived rule. The validation is either a fixed schematic proof tree (a
proof tree containing metavariables) or a PPL program. In the latter case, the
program is used to generate a proof after the rule scheme is used, and the
metavariables are instantiated. However, this fact does not mean that we have
to execute the validating program immediately after an application of the rule.
If we do program development, in most cases, all the metavariables are not instantiated until the whole proof tree is constructed. At least some of the validations have to be delayed until this point to prevent them from failing.

The simplest derived rules are obtained by turning the basic axioms into
rules. For example, we get the derived rule

$FL1$ $\vdash$ ([$C1$][$C2$]F) $FL2$

$FL1 \vdash$ ([$C1$; $C2$]F) $FL2$

from the axiom for sequential composition, where $FL1$ and $FL2$ are
metavariables for formula lists. Of course, because the axiom is an equivalence, there is also corresponding antecedent rule. In these cases, a schematic

proof exists using only the propositional rules of our basic calculus. Hence, these derived rules can be validated once and for all.

The Implementation of Proof Strategies in the KIV System

A method of program verification, transformation, or development is usually more than just a particular logical system. There are also typical heuristics for how to use it. In PPL, we reflect this distinction between the basic building blocks and the heuristics of a proof method in terms of derived rules, tactics, and strategies. The implementation of a method roughly proceeds as follows: (1) formalize the method in DL, (2) isolate the basic building blocks in terms of derived rules and tactics (at this stage, the system can already be used as a proof checker), and (3) implement the heuristics controlling the application of tactics. At this level, any degree of automation is conceivable.

Tactics are PPL programs implementing the logical building blocks of a proof strategy. Given a goal, a tactic computes a number of subgoals that logically imply this goal, provided all the remaining delayed validations can successfully be executed at some time. A *derived rule* can be regarded as a special case of a tactic where the result can schematically be expressed.

The nonlogical aspects of a method, such as its general structure, bookkeeping facilities, backtracking, and heuristics, are realized by PPL programs that we call *strategies*. The degree of automation incorporated in a strategy can gradually be enlarged. Using heuristics, we can select tactics and detect dead ends of a proof.

In the next section, where we present our implementation of Gries's development method, some of the substrategies are considered in some detail. More information about the implementation of proof strategies is contained in Heisel, Reif, and Stephan (1988).

A Formalization and Implementation of Gries's Program Development Method

In his book *The Science of Programming*, Gries (1981, p. 164) proposes a methodology for program development that is "centered around the concept of a formal proof." It is an elaboration of Dijkstra's (1976) pioneering work. The aim is to make programming a science instead of an art, as it was called by Knuth (1973).

The method is based on a guarded command language with a predicate transformer semantics and an invariant rule for while loops (Gries 1981; Dijkstra 1976). PL is used as the specification language and, occasionally an informal graphic notation. In contrast to many other methods of formal program development that only consist of a calculus, this approach also gives heuristics for developing alternative commands, while loops, and loop invariants. However, if performed by humans without machine support, the method is susceptible to error. It is thus appealing to formalize and implement the method in a proof system: Besides having a guideline for developing a program, the programs developed with the system can be guaranteed correct and terminating with respect to the given specification. Furthermore, the user has the opportunity to experiment with alternative solutions.

In the following discussion, we exemplify Gries's method by describing his formal treatment of loops and the corresponding heuristic. In the subsequent description of the method's implementation within the KIV environment, it is demonstrated that the while rule designed for this purpose exactly reflects the proof obligations arising from the development of a loop. An example shows how a program and its correctness proof are simultaneously built.

The complete strategy and its implementation, together with examples, are given in Heisel (1989). The report also contains validations of various tactics, the complete program text, and the machine output for the examples.

Gries's Program Development Method

The task is to find a program α satisfying the specification $\{\psi\}\ \alpha\ \{\varphi\}$ given ψ and φ as PL formulas. In Gries (1981), α is a program in guarded command notation, but we consider Pascal-like programs. The quotations of Gries in the following discussion are adapted to our notation.

The logical basis of the method consists of proof rules for each programming construct. The corresponding heuristics tell what to do in which order. As an example, we describe the treatment of loops. First, the following theorem relating the predicate transformer semantics of the language to loop invariants is proved:

Theorem about Loops: Let ψ be a formula, τ an integer-valued function, and $t1$ a new identifier:

If   (1) $\psi \wedge \varepsilon \rightarrow wp(\alpha, \psi)$

       (2) $\psi \wedge \varepsilon \rightarrow \tau > 0$

       (3) $\psi \wedge \varepsilon \rightarrow wp(t1 := \tau ; \alpha, \tau < t1)$

then $\psi \rightarrow wp(\textbf{while } \varepsilon \textbf{ do } \alpha \textbf{ od}, \psi \wedge \neg\varepsilon)$.

In a second step, the theorem is transformed into a checklist that gives the proof obligations arising from the development of a loop and brings them into a certain order.

Checklist for Understanding a Loop: To show $\{\psi\}$ **while** ε **do** α **od** $\{\varphi\}$ (with bound function τ):

(1) Show that ψ is true before the execution of the loop.

(2) Show that $\{\psi \wedge \varepsilon\}\ \alpha\ \{\psi\}$; that is, ψ is indeed an invariant of the loop.

(3) Show that $\psi \wedge \neg\varepsilon \rightarrow \varphi$; that is, on termination, the desired result is true.

(4) Show that $\psi \wedge \varepsilon \rightarrow \tau > 0$; that is, τ is bounded from below as long as the loop has not terminated.

(5) Show that $\{\psi \wedge \varepsilon\}\ t1 := \tau ; \alpha\ \{\tau < t1\}$, so that each loop iteration is guaranteed to decrease the bound function.

Suppose we wanted to show

$\{true\}$ $i:= 0$; $x:= 1$ $\{x = fac(i) \wedge 0 \le i \le n\}$ **while** $i \ne$ n **do** $i:= i + 1$; $x:= x*i$ **od**
$\{x = fac(n)\}$

with bound function $n - i$ (the symbol *fac* denotes the factorial function).
There, our proof obligations according to the checklist are

(1) $\{true\}$ $i:= 0$; $x:= 1$ $\{x = fac(i) \wedge 0 \le i \le n\}$,
    which is true because $0 \le 0 \le n$ and $fac(0) = 1$.

(2) $\{x = fac(i) \wedge 0 \le i \le n \wedge i \ne n\}$ $i:= i + 1$; $x:= x * i$ $\{x = fac(i) \wedge 0 \le i \le n\}$,
    which is true because $fac(i + 1) = fac(i) * (i + 1)$ and $0 \le i \le n \wedge \ne n$ implies
    $0 \le i + 1 \le n$.

(3) $x = fac(i) \wedge 0 \le i \le n \wedge i = n \rightarrow x = fac(n)$ (trivial).

(4) $x = fac(i) \wedge 0 \le i \le n \wedge i \ne n \rightarrow n - i > 0$ (trivial).

(5) $\{x = fac(i) \wedge 0 \le i \le n \wedge i \ne n\}$ $t1:= n - i$; $i:= i + 1$; $x:= x * i$ $\{t1 < n - i\}$,
    which is true because $n - (i + 1) < n - i$.

Finally, the third step suggests a heuristic for developing a loop. In this
way, the transition is made from program verification (what the checklist
deals with) to program development: The program has to be developed in
such a way that the proof carries through.

Strategy for Developing a Pascal-like Loop: First, develop the loop con-
dition ε so that $\psi \wedge \neg \varepsilon \rightarrow \varphi$; then develop the body so that it decreases the
bound function and reestablish the loop invariant.

In the next section, we present the implementation of a simple strategy for
developing conditionals. The corresponding heuristic we present is a simplified version of the one given by Gries.

Strategy for Developing a Conditional (simplified version): To invent a
conditional, find a program α whose execution will establish postcondition
φ in at least some cases; find a Boolean ε satisfying $\varepsilon \rightarrow wp(\alpha, \varphi)$, and put
them together to form **if** ε **then** α. To develop the **else** part of the conditional, use the information that $\neg \varepsilon$ holds.

Gries's book also contains several methods for developing invariants. All
these methods are implemented (Heisel 1989) but are not presented here.

Formalization and Implementation of the Method in the KIV System

In the implementation, the operationalized theorems are reflected as tactics.
These tactics create new goals for recursive calls of Gries's strategy reflecting the proof obligations that result from the decision to develop a program
of a certain form. The heuristics that make up the methodology are implemented as PPL strategies. For each programming construct, there is a separate
(sub-)strategy, so that the implementation works like a structural editor.

As for the overall strategy, there is a main function, GRIES_STRAT, offering several possibilities for developing a program. The input specification is a
sequent of the form $\Gamma \vdash \langle \$C \rangle \varphi$, where the formula list Γ denotes the precondi-
tion, the metavariable $\$C$ denotes the program to be developed, and φ is the

t_1:
$$\neg\$B, \Gamma \vdash \langle\$C2\rangle\varphi \qquad \$B, \Gamma \vdash \langle\$C1\rangle\varphi$$

$$\Gamma \vdash \langle \textbf{if } \$B \textbf{ then } \$C1 \textbf{ else } \$C2 \textbf{ fi}\rangle\varphi$$

Figure 1.

postcondition. The user is offered a menu of options for developing the empty program **skip**, assignments, compound, conditional, or while statements. Then, substrategies are called accordingly. The strategies work as follows:

First, use a tactic to create a program scheme fitting the chosen program construct. This step produces a proof tree with the program scheme in its root node. Second, call appropriate (sub-)strategies to prove the leaves of the generated proof tree, using the sequents in the leaves as new specifications. Most of the substrategies are either directly recursive or involve recursive calls of GRIES_STRAT. Third, assemble the results yielded by the recursive calls to form the result of the substrategy, which is also the result of GRIES_STRAT. This method corresponds to top-down program development, where the task is broken into smaller pieces until it is directly solvable.

The strategy terminates when all metavariables and programs are eliminated from the leaves of the proof tree. Thus, the result of GRIES_STRAT is a proof tree whose root contains the developed program and whose leaves contain only PL formulas. These formulas are left as verification conditions to be proven by other PPL programs.

One example of a simple strategy is the following simplified version of the conditional strategy used in the implementation of Gries's method. In this situation, the user decides to develop a conditional for the metavariable *$C* in the specification $\Gamma \vdash \langle\$C\rangle\varphi$. First, the tactic IF_TAC is called and yields the proof tree t_1 shown in figure 1. (Recall that symbols beginning with *$* denote metavariables; other symbols act as placeholders for formulas that can contain metavariables).

The next step is to develop the **then** part of the conditional by recursively calling the overall strategy with the second premise $\$B, \Gamma \vdash \langle\$C1\rangle\varphi$ of t_1 as a specification. The result of this call is the proof tree t_2 given in figure 2 whose conclusion contains a concrete program α_1 instead of *$C1*.

The second premise of t_1 is replaced by this tree to obtain t_3 (figure 3). In the process, *$C1* is instantiated to α_1.

Now the test of the conditional has to be determined. If α_1 contains no loop, this determination is made by computing the weakest precondition of α_1 with respect to φ. Otherwise, it has to be given by the user. The test (say, ε) is inserted into t_3, yielding t_4, which looks exactly like t_3 except that each occurrence of *$B* is replaced by ε. The last step is to call the overall strategy with specification $\neg\varepsilon, \Gamma \vdash \langle\$C2\rangle\varphi$. This call yields a tree t_5 with conclusion $\neg\varepsilon, \Gamma \vdash \langle\alpha_2\rangle\varphi$, which is attached to t_4, yielding

t_2:

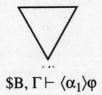

$$\$B, \Gamma \vdash \langle\alpha_1\rangle\varphi$$

Figure 2

t_3:

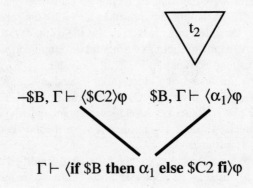

$$-\$B, \Gamma \vdash \langle\$C2\rangle\varphi \qquad \$B, \Gamma \vdash \langle\alpha_1\rangle\varphi$$

$$\Gamma \vdash \langle\textbf{if } \$B \textbf{ then } \alpha_1 \textbf{ else } \$C2 \textbf{ fi}\rangle\varphi$$

Figure 3

t_6:

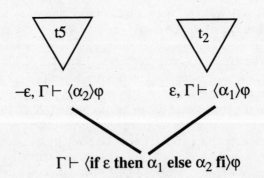

$$-\varepsilon, \Gamma \vdash \langle\alpha_2\rangle\varphi \qquad \varepsilon, \Gamma \vdash \langle\alpha_1\rangle\varphi$$

$$\Gamma \vdash \langle\textbf{if } \varepsilon \textbf{ then } \alpha_1 \textbf{ else } \alpha_2 \textbf{ fi}\rangle\varphi$$

Figure 4

the result t_6 of the conditional strategy shown in figure 4.

This tree is a correctness proof for the program **if** ε **then** α_1 **else** α_2 **fi.** The PPL program implementing this simple strategy looks as follows:

IF_STRAT(seq) = (∗ seq = $\Gamma \vdash \langle \$C1 \rangle \varphi$ ∗)
  let∗   q   = antecedent of seq (∗ = Γ ∗)
    and r   = postcondition of succedent of seq (∗ = φ ∗)
  in let∗ t1   = IF_TAC(q, r)   (∗ scheme for conditional ∗)
    and t2   = GRIES_STRAT(prem(t1, 2))
                           (∗ develop program for then-branch ∗)
    and b   = DEVELOP_TEST_STRAT(conclusion(t2))
    and t'   = mkstree(b, q $\vdash$ succedent(conclusion(t2)))
                           (∗ copy of root of t2, with b instead of $B ∗)
    and t3   = refine(t', 1, t2)   (∗ instantiate developed program with condition ∗)
    and t4   = infer(t1, [2], [t3]) (∗ instantiate scheme to developed program ∗)
    and t5   = GRIES_STRAT(prem(t4, 1))
                           (∗ develop else-branch ∗)
  in infer(t4, [1], [t5])   (∗ instantiate else-branch ∗)

To clarify the correspondence between the method as it is given in Gries's book and its implementation in the KIV system, we explain WHILE_STRAT, the strategy for while loops: First, the user develops an invariant and a bound function. For developing the invariant, the heuristics given in Gries (1981) are at the user's disposal. Then, WHILE_TAC is called to generate a scheme for a loop. This tactic takes the parameters $\Gamma, \varphi, \psi,$ and τ to create the proof tree shown in figure 5.

The formula list Γ is the precondition, φ is the postcondition, ψ is an invariant, and τ is a bound function, that is, a term of sort integer. The variable t is a new variable of sort integer. The first premise of the previous tree corresponds to proof obligation 3 in the checklist for understanding a loop, the second premise corresponds to proof obligation 4, the fourth premise to proof obligation 1, and the third premise to obligations 2 and 5. The third premise is probably the most difficult to establish because we have to show that the loop body decreases the bound function and maintains the invariant.

The next step is to develop the initialization $C1$. For this purpose, GRIES_STRAT is recursively called with the fourth premise, yielding a tree whose root contains a concrete program α' instead of $C1$. The current tree is instantiated with this program.

According to Gries's strategy, the loop condition (say, ε) has to be developed before the loop body. In the implementation, this development is done by user interaction. The condition is then built into the tree. It remains to develop the loop body α'' (to replace C) in such a way that the bound function decreases, and the invariant is maintained. To perform this task, GRIES_STRAT is again recursively called with the third premise. The developed program is α' ; **while** ε **do** α'' **od.**

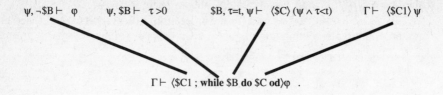

$\psi, \neg \$B \vdash \varphi \qquad \psi, \$B \vdash \tau > 0 \qquad \$B, \tau{=}t, \psi \vdash \langle \$C \rangle (\psi \wedge \tau{<}t) \qquad \Gamma \vdash \langle \$C1 \rangle \psi$

$$\Gamma \vdash \langle \$C1 \,; \textbf{ while } \$B \textbf{ do } \$C \textbf{ od} \rangle \varphi \quad .$$

Figure 5.

Example

In this subsection, we illustrate how to work with our implementation of Gries's strategy. Using the interactive PPL program is much like developing programs by hand with Gries's method. The user only needs to know the commands of the object-programming language and the assertion language. Except for being able to read diamond formulas, no knowledge is required about DL, sequent calculi, or PPL. In the following discussion, we present more information than the user gets in an actual terminal session. For example, intermediate proof trees are not shown on the screen. However, each time GRIES_STRAT is called—and in other situations where the user must make a decision—the current specification and other useful information is provided. The user must make all design decisions: What kind of program should be developed for a given specification? What is the appropriate invariant and bound function? The user does not need to explicitly call any strategies other than the initial call to GRIES_STRAT.

Suppose we want to approximate the quotient q of two real numbers c and d within a given tolerance e. We are given three numbers c, d, and e satisfying the precondition

$$\Gamma \equiv 0 \le c < d, e > 0 ,$$

and we want to establish the postcondition

$$\varphi \equiv |c/_d - q| < e$$

using division by 2 as an elementary operation. Thus, the specification

$$0 \le c < d, e > 0 \vdash \langle \$C \rangle |c/_d - q| < e$$

is given to GRIES_STRAT.

The idea to compute q is as follows: Determine an interval in which c/d is located (from Γ, it follows that $c/d \in [0, 1]$), and develop a loop that halves the possible interval with each iteration. Hence, we choose "loop" when being asked by the system what kind of program we want to develop. The next step is to develop an invariant. For this purpose, we introduce a new variable s for which

$$\psi \equiv q \le c/_d < q + s$$

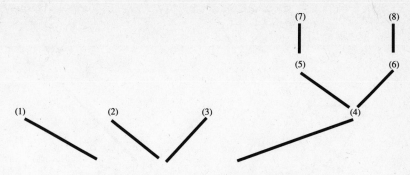

$$0{\leq}c{<}d,\ e{>}0 \vdash\ \langle s{:=}1\ ;\ q{:=}0\ ;\ \textbf{while}\ s{>}e\ \textbf{do}\ \$C\ \textbf{od}\rangle|c/_d{-}q| < e$$

where
(1) $q \leq c/_d < q{+}s,\ e{>}0,\ \neg s{>}e \vdash\ |c/_d{-}q| < e$ (verification condition)
(2) $q \leq c/_d < q{+}s,\ e{>}0,\ s{>}e \vdash\ bf(s,e) > 0$ (verification condition)
(3) $q \leq c/_d < q{+}s,\ e{>}0,\ s{>}e,bf(s,e)=t \vdash\ \langle \$C\rangle(q \leq c/_d < q{+}s\ \wedge\ e{>}0\ \wedge bf(s,e) < t)$
(4) $0 \leq c < d,\ e{>}0 \vdash\ \langle s{:=}1\ ;\ q{:=}0\rangle(q \leq c/_d < q{+}s\ \wedge\ e{>}0)$
(5) $0 \leq c < d,\ e{>}0 \vdash\ \langle s{:=}1\rangle(0 \leq c/_d < s\ \wedge\ e{>}0)$
(6) $0 \leq c/_d < s,\ e{>}0 \vdash\ \langle q{:=}0\rangle(0 \leq c/_d < q{+}s\ \wedge\ e{>}0)$
(7) $0{\leq}c{<}d,\ e{>}0 \vdash\ 0 \leq c/_d < 1\ \wedge\ e{>}0$ (verification condition)
(8) $0 \leq c/_d < s,\ e{>}0 \vdash\ (0 \leq c/_d < q{+}s\ \wedge\ e{>}0)$ (verification condition

Figure 6.

holds. We choose $\psi \wedge e > 0$ as our invariant and hand it to the system. Next, we are asked to give a bound function. Because this function must be of sort integer, we must encode the fact that the size s of our interval will be less than e after finitely many halving operations. Therefore, we type in $bf(s, e) = \lceil s/e \rceil$, where $\lceil x \rceil$ denotes the least integer n with $n \geq x$. This is all information that is needed to call the while tactic. As stated in the previous subsection, the next step is to develop the initialization. We are shown the specification

$$0 \leq c < d, e > 0 \vdash \langle \$C1\rangle(q \leq c/d < q + s \wedge e > 0),$$

and we are asked to choose a programming construct. Because the assignments

$s:= 1 ; q:= 0$

establish the invariant, we choose assignments and enter the previous statements. When subsequently asked to give a loop condition, we type $s > e$.

In the meantime, the proof tree t_1 shown in figure 6 is internally generated by the system.

All metavariables except $\$C$ are instantiated. The root contains the program developed so far. Premise 3 is the specification for the loop body; it is the argument of a recursive call to GRIES_STRAT and, thus, is shown on the screen.

Informally, we have to proceed as follows: First, halve the interval ($s:= s/2$), then decide whether q is located in the lower or upper half (*condition*: $d*(q + s) \leq c$). In this case, increase the lower bound ($q:= q + s$).

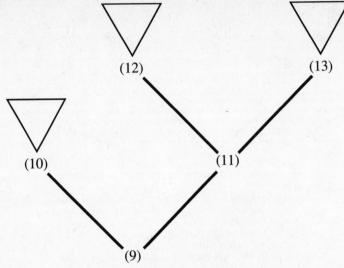

where

(9) $q \le c/_d < q+s, e>0, s>e, bf(s, e) = t$
        $\vdash \langle s:= s/_2 ;$ **if** $d*(q+s) \le c$ **then** $q:= q+s$ **fi**$\rangle(q \le c/_d < q+s \wedge e>0 \wedge bf(s, e) < t)$

(10) $q \le c/_d < q+s, e>0, s>e, bf(s, e) = t$
        $\vdash \langle s:= s/_2\rangle(q \le c/_d < q+2*s \wedge e>0 \wedge 2*s > e \wedge bf(2*s, e) = t)$

(11) $q \le c/_d < q+2*s, e>0, 2*s > e, bf(2*s, e) = t$
        $\vdash \langle$ **if** $d*(q+s) \le c$ **then** $q:= q+s$ **fi**$\rangle(q \le c/_d < q+s \wedge e>0 \wedge bf(s, e) < t)$

(12) $q \le c/_d < q+2*s, e>0, 2*s > e, bf(2*s, e) = t, d*(q+s) \le c$
        $\vdash \langle q:= q+s\rangle(q \le c/_d < q+s \wedge e>0 \wedge bf(s, e) < t)$

(13) $q \le c/_d < q+2*s, e>0, 2*s > e, bf(2*s, e) = t, d*(q+s) > c$
        $\vdash \langle$**skip**$\rangle(q \le c/_d < q+s \wedge e>0 \wedge bf(s, e) < t)$

Figure 7.

Using the system, we develop a compound statement whose first part is the assignment statement s:= s/2, and second part is the conditional **if** $d * (q + s) \le c$ **then** $q:= q + s$ **fi**. This development is made in the same fashion as previously described: A specification is shown to us, and we select the appropriate programming construct, causing the proof tree t_2 for the loop body to be built in the background. This tree is shown in figure 7.

The programs in the sequents (10), (12), and (13) of figure 7 are eliminated by computing the weakest preconditions.

In a final step, t_2 is inserted for premise 3 of t_1, thus instantiating the metavariable C and yielding the proof tree given in figure 8, which is a formal correctness proof for the developed program contained in the conclusion 1. This tree is shown on the screen and now can further be processed, for example, by proving the verification conditions.

Concluding this section, we want to comment on two aspects of the method presented: methodology and implementation. Regarding the methodology, the programming constructs available in the programming language

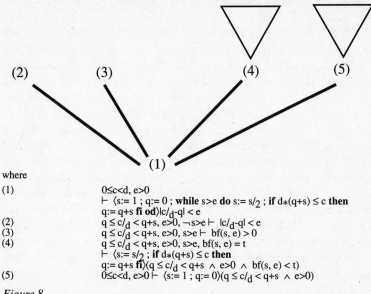

where

(1) $0 \leq c < d,\ e > 0$
             $\vdash\ \langle s := 1\ ;\ q := 0\ ;\ \textbf{while}\ s > e\ \textbf{do}\ s := s/2\ ;\ \textbf{if}\ d_*(q+s) \leq c\ \textbf{then}$
             $q := q+s\ \textbf{fi}\ \textbf{od}\rangle |c/_d - q| < e$

(2) $q \leq c/_d < q+s,\ e > 0,\ \neg s > e \vdash\ |c/_d - q| < e$

(3) $q \leq c/_d < q+s,\ e > 0,\ s > e \vdash\ bf(s, e) > 0$

(4) $q \leq c/_d < q+s,\ e > 0,\ s > e,\ bf(s, e) = t$
             $\vdash\ \langle s := s/2\ ;\ \textbf{if}\ d_*(q+s) \leq c\ \textbf{then}$
             $q := q+s\ \textbf{fi}\rangle(q \leq c/_d < q+s\ \wedge\ e > 0\ \wedge\ bf(s, e) < t)$

(5) $0 \leq c < d,\ e > 0 \vdash\ \langle s := 1\ ;\ q := 0\rangle(q \leq c/_d < q+s\ \wedge\ e > 0)$

Figure 8.

are used as a guide for program development. The syntactic structure of the postcondition is not taken into account. On the one hand, this fact makes the method so general that virtually every programming problem can be tackled with it. On the other hand, this fact also makes it difficult to automate. Nevertheless, the real virtue of the method lies in its heuristics, especially the heuristics for developing loop invariants, and in its aim to make program development a systematic and formal activity. Therefore, an implementation such as the one previously described could be a useful tutoring tool in student education.

Some of the choices left open in the method are committed in the implementation. For example, verification conditions are proved only after program development is finished. One could also decide to prove these conditions as soon as they are generated. In this case, if a verification condition is not provable, it is an immediate indication that there is something wrong with, for example, the loop invariant, and it would be appropriate to backtrack.

Our objective was to show how a method from the literature carries over to our system and how program development steps correspond to proof steps. Other methods from the literature were also adapted to our system in the same way (see Conclusion). Therefore, a user of the KIV system not only has the choice between various proof methods but also the combination and interleaving of several methods. The desirability of such a combination is shown in the next section.

Program Construction by Modification

In his book *The Evolution of Programs*, Dershowitz (1983) presents an appealing approach to program construction, namely, programming by modification. This method reflects the observation that programmers normally devote only a limited amount of their time and effort to create code for a given specification from scratch. Programmers often bring in their knowledge about earlier programs developed for similar problems. Thus, the basic idea is to modify existing programs to solve related problems. In contrast to the methods of transformational programming, the modifications that are used here do not preserve semantics.

We demonstrate how the method can be formalized and implemented in the KIV system. As was the case with Gries's method, our aim here is not to enhance or improve Dershowitz's method but to stress the flexibility of our system to incorporate different methods into a common logical framework.

Furthermore, we point out that programming by modification is a combination of analogy, transformation, synthesis, and classical verification. Thus, Dershowitz's method strikingly illustrates the need for a system that supports all these features.

An Example

Consider the following specification of a square root program: We are given two numbers a and e with

$$\Gamma_2 \equiv a \geq 0, e > 0 \,.$$

The desired result is an approximation r to the square root of a with a precision of e:

$$\varphi_2 \equiv |\sqrt{a} - r| < e \,.$$

We are looking for a program β and a proof of the statement $\Gamma_2 \vdash \langle \beta \rangle \varphi_2$, saying that β terminates with φ_2 whenever the formulas of Γ_2 hold.

In the last section, we developed a division algorithm α for the specification $\Gamma_1 \vdash \langle \alpha \rangle \varphi_1$ together with the corresponding correctness proof, where

$$
\begin{aligned}
\Gamma_1 &\equiv \quad 0 \leq c < d, e > 0 \,, \\
\varphi_1 &\equiv \quad |c/d - q| < e \,, \\
\alpha &\equiv \quad s := 1 \,; q := 0 \,;
\end{aligned}
$$

        while $s > e$ **do**

                $s := s/2$;

                if $d * (q + s) \leq c$ **then** $q := q + s$ **fi**

     od .

To construct β, Dershowitz takes the following approach: Instead of starting from scratch, find a modification *mod* such that $\varphi_2 = mod(\varphi_1)$ and try $mod(\alpha)$ as a first candidate for β. A *modification* is a substitution list (pairs of symbols of the signature or variable-term pairs) that unifies φ_1 and φ_2 when applied to φ_1. It is computed by comparing the postconditions φ_1 and φ_2 and recording their disagreement pairs. In general, this method requires some user-guided reformulation of φ_2 such that the analogy becomes expressible on the symbol or term level.

In the example, there is an obvious analogy: The only disagreement pairs between φ_1 and φ_2 are $(c/d, \sqrt{a})$ and (q, r), which, among others, can be resolved by the substitution $mod = \{c \Leftarrow \sqrt{a}, d \Leftarrow 1, q \Leftarrow r\}$. Hence, $mod(\alpha)$ is

$s := 1 \; ; r := 0 \; ;$
while $s > e$ **do**
    $s := s/2 \; ;$
    if $1 * (r + s) \le \sqrt{a}$ **then** $r := r + s$ **fi**
od .

We are now faced with three problems that are typical of this approach:

First is the transformation problem. One test in $mod(\alpha)$ contains $\sqrt{a}$, which is the function we are going to implement. Thus, we have to apply the transformation $1 * (r + s) \le \sqrt{a} \Leftrightarrow (r + s)^2 \le a$ that preserves the semantics but eliminates $\sqrt{a}$ from the test. Squaring, addition, and comparison are regarded as elementary operations.

Second is the verification problem. From the proof of the division program, we know that $\Gamma_1 \vdash \langle \alpha \rangle \varphi_1$ holds. However, what about $mod(\Gamma_1) \vdash \langle mod(\alpha) \rangle \varphi_2$? This problem has to be proved by classical methods for total correctness.

Third is the synthesis problem. If the second problem is established, we know that $mod(\alpha)$ achieves φ_2 but unfortunately from $mod(\Gamma_1)$ and not from Γ_2, as desired. We have to ask whether there is a program δ (which does not alter the input variables) such that the sequent $\Gamma_2 \vdash \langle \delta \rangle \wedge mod(\Gamma_1)$ holds ($\Gamma_2 \vdash \wedge mod(\Gamma_1)$ is just a special case).

In our example, the verification problem can be solved. However, because $a \ge 0, e > 0 \nvdash \langle \delta \rangle (0 \le \sqrt{a} < 1 \wedge e > 0)$ for any δ that does not alter the input variable a, the synthesis problem has no solution. Thus, $mod(\alpha)$ is not the desired program β. However, $mod(\alpha)$ ends up with the desired output specification, indicating that it is not a completely useless candidate.

There are a few other failure situations, such as the verification problem failing or the transformation producing illegal statements. For all such failure situations, Dershowitz proceeds according to the following overall solution paradigm that exploits the fact that the proof of the given program α contains its specification as well as subspecifications for every code fragment of α. Find all annotated code fragments of α that correctly transform, use these fragments as parts of the desired solution, drop the rest of the transformed program, and create new code to refill the resulting annotated gaps (new synthesis goals).

Of course, in its generality, this paradigm is computationally intractable, but it can be supported by interactive strategies that implement specific heuristic approaches to the problem. One of the simplest strategies is to drop the instructions starting from the front, which remedies situations where the transformation fails because of an unsuitable initialization. This strategy applies to our example, and although restricted to simple situations, it is sufficient for our purposes here. We roughly describe how it can be formalized in the setting of the KIV system.

Formalization in the KIV System

First, Dershowitz's approach is based on annotated programs that record the program as well as its correctness proof. In the KIV system, the knowledge about programs is stored in formal proofs (proof trees) of their total correctness, and the result of the modification is again a formal proof of the correctness of the modified program. Thus, the modified program and its correctness proof are developed hand in hand.

As in the last section, the operations (for example, lookup in the proof tree) used later can be expressed in terms of tactics and strategies (PPL programs) that operate on proof trees. In this subsection, we omit most technical details. The strategy proceeds as follows:

The original program is split into the elementary instructions $(\alpha_1; \ldots; \alpha_n) \equiv \alpha$. From the correctness proof of α, we get an assertion φ_i describing the effect of α_i for every instruction α_i. Given an analogy mod satisfying $\varphi_2 \equiv mod(\varphi_1)$, we have to find a maximal suffix of α such that the diagram shown in figure 9 commutes.

Formally, we have to find a minimal k (and, hence, ψ_k) and a program δ, such that the following sequents hold:

(1) $mod(\psi_k) \vdash \langle mod(\alpha_{k+1}; \ldots; \alpha_n) \rangle \varphi_2$ (verification problem)

(2) $\Gamma_2 \vdash \langle \delta \rangle mod(\psi_k)$ (synthesis problem)

Then $\beta \equiv (\delta; mod(\alpha_{k+1}; \ldots; \alpha_n))$ is the desired solution and the correctness proof easily follows from the proofs of sequents 1 and 2. To determine the value of k, we start with $k = 0$, test these sequents, and increment k if necessary.

In our example α_1, α_2, and α_3 are $s := 1$, $q := 0$, and **while** $s > e$ **do** $s := s/2$; **if** $d * (q + s) \leq c$ **then** $q := q + s$ **fi od**, respectively. To get φ_0, φ_1, φ_2, and φ_3, we scan the proof of the division algorithm (figure 10).

ψ_0 and ψ_3 are the precondition and postcondition in sequent 1 in figure 10. The intermediate formulas ψ_1 and ψ_2 are the postconditions in (6) and (7), respectively.

Applying the modification mod to the formulas yields, for example,

$mod(\psi_0) \equiv 0 \leq \sqrt{a} < 1 \wedge e > 0$

$mod(\psi_1) \equiv 0 \leq \sqrt{a} < s \wedge e > 0$.

For $k = 0$ (which is the situation initially discussed), the synthesis problem

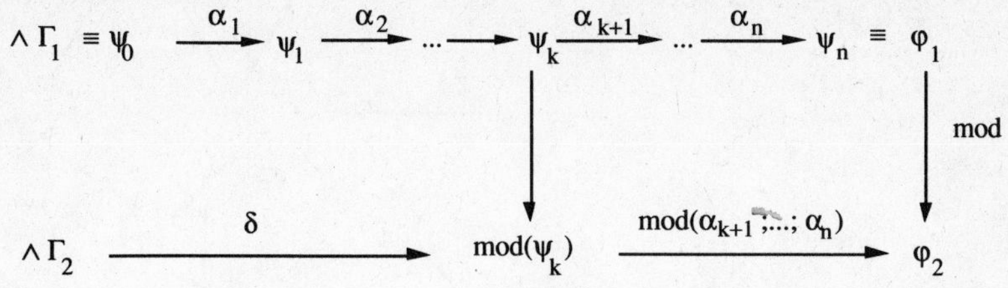

Figure 9.

has no solution. For $k = 1$, we get the following synthesis problem:

$a \geq 0, e > 0 \vdash \langle \delta \rangle (0 \leq \sqrt{a} < s \wedge e > 0).$

This problem can be solved by $\delta \equiv (s := a + 1)$ because the square root of a is bounded from above by $a + 1$. The verification problem for $k = 1$ takes the form

$e > 0, 0 \leq \sqrt{a} < s \vdash \langle mod(\alpha_2 ; \alpha_3) \rangle |\sqrt{a} - r| < e,$

where $mod(\alpha_2 ; \alpha_3)$ is

$r := 0$;
while $s > e$ **do**
    $s := s/2$;
    if $(r + s)^2 \leq a$ **then** $r := r + s$ **fi**
od .

To solve this verification problem, we have to provide an invariant and a bound function for the while loop $mod(\alpha_3)$. The invariant is nothing but the modified invariant of α_3, which can be found in the proof tree for the division algorithm. The same is true for the bound function. Thus, both the synthesis and the verification problem are solved for $k = 1$. Consequently the desired solution β is $(\delta ; mod(\alpha_2 ; \alpha_3))$:

$s := a + 1$;
$r := 0$;
while $s > e$ **do**
    $s := s/2$;
    if $(r + s)^2 \leq a$ **then** $r := r + s$ **fi**
od .

The final result is the proof for $\Gamma_2 \vdash \langle \beta \rangle \varphi_2$ shown in figure 11.

Despite the toy character of the example, the potential virtues of programming by modification become apparent. Once the analogy is found, the user has to develop only those parts of the program that cannot be recycled from the old one, which, hopefully, is much less than to rewrite it as a whole. Furthermore, developing the square root program using GRIES_STRAT, instead of proceeding by analogy, would require the invention of a loop invariant, whereas this approach reuses the (modified) invariant of the quotient program. The reuse of old invariants is a special approach to finding new invariants.

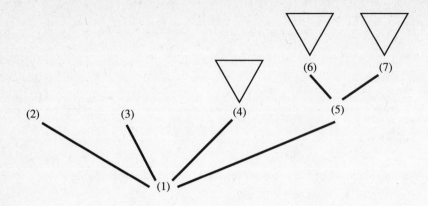

where

(1) $0 \leq c < d,\ e > 0$
    $\vdash \langle s := 1\ ;\ q := 0\ ;\ \textbf{while}\ s > e\ \textbf{do}\ s := s/2\ ;\ \textbf{if}\ d_*(q+s) \leq c\ \textbf{then}\ q := q+s\ \textbf{fi}\ \textbf{od}\rangle |c/_d\text{-}q| < e$
(2) $q \leq c/_d < q+s,\ e > 0,\ \neg s > e \vdash\ |c/_d\text{-}q| < e$
(3) $q \leq c/_d < q+s,\ e > 0,\ s > e \vdash\ bf(s, e) > 0$
(4) $q \leq c/_d < q+s,\ e > 0,\ s > e,\ bf(s, e) = t$
    $\vdash \langle s := s/2\ ;\ \textbf{if}\ d_*(q+s) \leq c\ \textbf{then}\ q := q+s\ \textbf{fi}\rangle (q \leq c/_d < q+s\ \wedge\ e > 0$
    $\wedge\ bf(s, e) < t)$
(5) $0 \leq c < d,\ e > 0 \vdash\ \langle s := 1\ ;\ q := 0\rangle (q \leq c/_d < q+s\ \wedge\ e > 0)$
(6) $0 \leq c < d,\ e > 0 \vdash\ \langle s := 1\rangle (0 \leq c\ /_d < s\ \wedge\ e > 0)$
(7) $0 \leq c/_d < s,\ e > 0 \vdash\ \langle q := 0\rangle (q \leq c/_d < q+s\ \wedge\ e > 0)$

Figure 10.

Although we did not present all the implementational details, Dershowitz's method of programming by modification illustrates two advantages of the KIV system: First, because proofs are data objects, the system supports any strategic reuse of old proofs to guide the search of new ones. Second, because of the uniform logical framework, many different strategies can be combined and easily integrated. Programming by modification required the integration of the verification, transformation, and synthesis strategies.

Conclusion

In the following discussion, we give a list of other proof methods implemented in the KIV system:

First, there are several versions of a prover for PL, for example, with or without equality, complete or terminating.

Second, there is a comfortable interactive implementation of Hoare's (1969) calculus: User guidance and backtracking facilities provided by the system enable the interactive development of proofs. For example, this implementation has the advantage that the user does not need to know all the

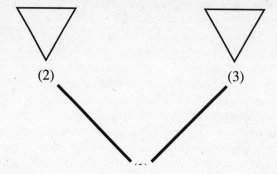

where
(1)   a≥0, e>0
         ⊢ ⟨s:= a+1 ; r:= 0 ; **while** s>e **do** s:= s/$_2$; **if** (r+s)^2 ≤ a **then** r:= r+s **fi od**⟩|√a-r| < e
(2)   a≥0, e>0 ⊢ ⟨s:= a+1⟩(0≤√a<s ∧e>0)
(3)   0≤√a<s, e>0
         ⊢ ⟨r:= 0 ; **while** s>e **do** s:=s/$_2$; **if** (r+s)^2 ≤ a **then** r:= r+s **fi od**⟩|√a-r| < e

Figure 11.

loop invariants in advance and can experiment with several possibilities.

Third, we implemented Bergstra and Klop's (1984) method of proving program inclusion and equivalence. Given a first-order axiomatization Ax of a data structure and two programs α and β, the method proves that α is equivalent to β in every model of Ax by showing

$$Ax' \vdash_{HOARE} \varphi \to [\alpha]\psi \Leftrightarrow Ax' \vdash_{HOARE} \varphi \to [\beta]\psi$$

for all conservative refinements Ax' of Ax and all formulas φ and ψ.

Fourth, an implementation of Burstall's (1974) method (Heisel, Reif, and Stephan 1987) allows the user to verify programs implementing inherently recursive functions by loops. Given the goal $\Gamma \vdash \langle \alpha ; \beta \rangle \varphi$, the strategy eliminates α and computes a new goal of the form $\Gamma' \vdash \langle \beta \rangle \varphi$. However, in contrast to Hoare's calculus, loops are not eliminated by proving an invariance relation but by using structural induction on the data structure involved.

Fifth, to make the program synthesis part of the system more powerful and flexible, we also implemented that part of the method given by Dershowitz (1983) that deals with the problem of deriving programs from specifications. Apart from the fact that this method takes the form of the postcondition into account, it differs from Gries's method by allowing another kind of loop formation.

Sixth, there is an implementation of a strategy (introduced by an example by Dijkstra [1988]) that can generate certain programs completely and automatically.

Seventh, the strategy for developing divide-and-conquer algorithms by deriving antecedents, which was given by Smith (1985) is currently under implementation.

Eighth, most of the existing methods in the literature for the verification and construction of programs are concerned with programming in the small. A module concept for imperative implementations of abstract data types is the first step to also using the KIV system in the development of large verified modular software. A method based on a new logical theory of module correctness was implemented (Reif 1990). Experiments show that realistically sized applications gradually get into the reach of the system. The strategy runs with a high degree of automation, leaving less than 20 percent of the proof decisions to the user. The examples treated so far (efficient imperative implementations of abstract data types, for example, AVL trees) required several 10,000-proof steps (at the level of making a case distinction, applying an induction hypothesis, and so on). Comparative experiments with and without the system showed that none of the examples is tractable (completely formal) without machine support. This statement refers to the time and effort necessary for a complete treatment of all the proof obligations as well as to the correctness of the proofs carried out by hand.

The KIV system was successfully used in a practical course on the verification and formal development of programs. The students were able to manage all the strategies previously given and write a verification condition generator in PPL.

Our experiences with the KIV system are encouraging. The combination of tactical theorem proving with a powerful logic of programs leads to a uniform and flexible system that hosts many different strategies for program verification and construction. On the one hand, the strong emphasis on expressing every method as a derived axiomatization of the basic logic requires a high degree of formalization and demands rigorous correctness proofs for the rules within the logic. On the other hand, this formal rigor increases the trustworthiness of the system and reveals many logical errors in rules that are published in the literature. The reduction to a single logic, which is possible because we use a calculus for uninterpreted reasoning, enables the free combination of different methods. To date, our experiences are based on well-known strategies and heuristics. In the future, we will use the system as a basis for further automation and the design and study of new methods. A first step in this direction is our method of module verification.

It should be noted that in combination with a sufficiently large database of general-purpose rules and tactics, the facilities of the metalanguage made the implementation of strategies easy. However, independent of the implementation of the metalanguage, there is a loss of efficiency compared to systems that directly implement methods. As long as this approach leads to acceptable response times, which is the case with all strategies implemented to date, in our opinion, this price should be paid for a system that is strictly logic based.

As mentioned in the introduction, we call a development system strictly logic based if the development process ends with a correctness proof in a formal system with a fixed syntax and semantics. To this end, one has to use a (programming) logic that is expressive enough to allow the formulation of the desired program properties. Of course, this fact does not mean that a system that is not logic based in this sense necessarily lacks a sound mathematical basis. All the systems mentioned in the following discussion have a distinguished formal background, but only a few totally carry out the development process within an implemented logic.

Classical systems for deductive program synthesis, such as those of Green (1969) and Manna and Waldinger (1980), although based on proof-theoretic methods, do not completely meet the previous requirement because metalogical considerations are necessary to relate the program to the proof from which it was extracted. Only the construction of proofs is carried out in a fixed calculus, namely, a resolution calculus. Strategic considerations can influence the development process only in so far as they lead to special resolution proofs. In the actual implementations of these systems, most of the decisions are left to the user.

A system that was developed more recently in Karlsruhe (Biundo 1988) as part of the INKA system (Biundo, Hummel, Hutter, and Walther 1986) also uses a resolution theorem prover. However, the formulas handed to the prover are generated by a separate part of the system that is directly coded in Lisp and only uses logical rules implicitly. No comprehensive logical formalism covers this part of the system. The development process is guided by certain induction schemata and the special form of function definitions. Heuristics lead to a high degree of automation. If the recursive equations that are generated for the skolem functions are treated as object programs in DL, then, as far as we can see, all rules that are implicitly used by the system can be obtained as derived rules in our system.

Systems such as LOPS (Bibel 1980) and the the KIDS system (chapter 19) do not use implemented logics at all. Bibel derives programs by strategic transformations of the first-order specifications of the problem, and Smith follows the problem-solving paradigm using so-called algorithm theories (Smith and Lowry 1989). In the latter case, the search space is drastically reduced because when selecting a certain program scheme or algorithm theory (for example, divide and conquer or global search), the user has already taken the most important design decision. Therefore, the KIDS system has such a high degree of automation that programs of a more realistic size than is usually the case can be generated with it. The FOCUS system (Reddy 1989) relies on equational logic and is based on a completionlike procedure for program synthesis. Reddy starts with an equational specification and ends with a program that is given by a noetherian set of rewrite rules. In the case of the first two systems, we can see no reason why it should be impossible to formalize the methods in our logic. Indeed, as previously mentioned, work on the problem- solving approach is currently under way. Regarding Reddy's approach, however, it is not clear whether the underlying metalogical considerations can be formalized in our framework.

In the transformational approach (for example Broy [1984] and Burstall and Darlington [1977]), starting with a sufficiently abstract specification, equivalence-preserving transformations are applied to intermediate versions of the program. Especially in Broy's system, a large number of transformation rules for complex imperative programs were implemented. Also, attempts were made to fix a set of basic transformation rules and then derive additional rules within the system itself. Because DL, on the level of uninterpreted reasoning, is well suited to prove program implications, transformations can be proved correct in our system. Currently, an extension of Burstall's method that can be used for the proof of program implications is under development.

Systems of tactical theorem proving combine a fixed powerful logic with a formal metalanguage to implement (proof) strategies. Typically, there is an intermediate layer of derived rules and tactics to provide derived axiomatizations for special purposes. The LCF systems of Edinburgh and Cambridge (Paulson 1987) use a programming logic for (higher-order) functional programs. The KIV system differs from these primarily in the underlying logic and the object language. However, with these systems, there are also differences in important technical points concerning the representation and construction of proofs. For example, there are no metavariables that act as placeholders for unknown or arbitrary syntactic objects. As previously mentioned, our use of metavariables in rules is close to the use of scheme variables in ISABELLE. However, there is no analogous concept for proof trees and validations. ISABELLE has no fixed built-in logic but is intended to support many different logics.

Another system that also uses tactical theorem proving is the NUPRL system (Constable et al. 1986). Its logical basis is a constructive-type theory. Developing programs in this setting is done by proving that certain types are not empty (the type denotes the specification of the program, following the formulas-as-types paradigm). During this proof, an element of the type is constructed that contains the desired program. This approach is not a programming logic in the sense of LCF and DL. Again, as in the case of the LCF systems, the way to construct proofs, as well as define tactics and derived rules, differs much from our approach.

References

Bergstra, J. A., and Klop, J. W. 1984. Proving Program Inclusion Using Hoare's Logic. *Theoretical Computer Science* 30:1–48.

Bibel, W. 1980. Syntax-Directed, Semantics-Supported Program Synthesis. *Artificial Intelligence* 14:243–261.

Biundo, S. 1988. Automated Synthesis of Recursive Algorithms as a Theorem-Proving Tool. In Proceedings of the Eighth European Conference on AI, 553-558.

Biundo, S.; Hummel, B.; Hutter, D.; and Walther, C. 1986. The Karlsruhe Induction Theorem-Proving System. In *Proceedings of the Ninth International Conference on Automated Deduction*, 672-674. Lecture Notes in Computer Science, volume 310. Berlin: Springer Verlag.

Broy, M. 1984. Algebraic Methods for Program Construction: The Project CIP. In *Program Transformations and Programming Environments*, ed. P. Pepper, 199-222 Berlin: Springer Verlag.

Burstall, R. M. 1974. Program Proving as Hand Simulation with a Little Induction. *Information Processing* 74:308-312.

Burstall, R., and Darlington, J. 1977. A Transformation System for Developing Recursive Programs. *Journal of the ACM* 24:44-67.

Constable, R., et al. 1986. *Implementing Mathematics with the NUPRL Proof Development System*. Englewood Cliffs, N.J.: Prentice Hall.

Dershowitz, N. 1983. *The Evolution of Programs*. Boston: Birkhäuser.

Dijkstra, E. W. 1988. Constructive Methods in Computing Science, Lecture, International Summer School, Marktoberdorf.

Dijkstra, E. W. 1976. *A Discipline of Programming*. Englewood Cliffs, N.J.: Prentice-Hall.

Gordon, M.; Milner, R.; and Wadsworth, C. 1979. *Edinburgh LCF*. Lecture Notes in Computer Science, volume 78. Berlin: Springer Verlag.

Goldblatt, R. 1982. *Axiomatising the Logic of Computer Programming*. Lecture Notes in Computer Science, volume 130. Berlin: Springer Verlag.

Green, C. 1969. Application of Theorem Proving to Problem Solving. In Proceedings of the First International Joint Conference on Artificial Intelligence, 219-239. Menlo Park, Calif.: International Joint Conferences on Artificial Intelligence.

Gries, D. 1981. *The Science of Programming*. Berlin: Springer. Verlag

Harel, D. 1984. Dynamic Logic. In *Handbook of Philosophical Logic*, volume 2, eds. D. Gabbay and F. Guenther, 496-604. Dordrecht: Reidel.

Harel, D. 1979. *First-Order Dynamic Logic*. Lecture Notes in Computer Science, volume 68. Berlin: Springer Verlag.

Heisel, M. 1989. A Formalization and Implementation of Gries's Program Development Method within the KIV Environment, Interner Bericht, Fakultät für Informatik, Universität Karlsruhe.

Heisel, M.; Reif, W.; and Stephan, W. 1990. Tactical Theorem Proving in Program Verification. In *Proceedings of the Tenth International Conference on Automated Deduction*, 115-131. Lecture Notes on Artificial Intelligence, volume 449. Berlin: Springer Verlag.

Heisel, M.; Reif, W.; and Stephan, W. 1989. A Dynamic Logic for Program Verification. In *Proceedings of Logic at Botik '89*, 134-145. Lecture Notes in Computer Science, volume 363. Berlin: Springer Verlag.

Heisel, M.; Reif, W.; and Stephan, W. 1988. Implementing Verification Strategies in the KIV System. In *Proceedings of the Ninth International Conference on Automated Deduction*, 131-140. Lecture Notes in Computer Science, volume 310. Berlin: Springer Verlag.

Heisel, M.; Reif, W.; and Stephan, W. 1987. Program Verification by Symbolic Execution and Induction. In *Proceedings of the Eleventh German Workshop on Artificial Intelligence*, 201-210. Informatik Fachberichte 152. Berlin: Springer Verlag.

Hoare, C. A. R. 1969. An Axiomatic Basis for Computer Programming. *Communications of the ACM* 12:576-580.

Knuth, D. E. 1973. *The Art of Computer Programming*. Reading, Mass.: Addison-Wesley.

Manna, Z., and Waldinger, R. 1980. A Deductive Approach to Program Synthesis. *ACM Transactions on Programming Languages and Systems* 2:90–121.

Paulson, L. 1987. *Logic and Computation*. Cambridge: Cambridge University Press.

Paulson, L. 1986. Natural Deduction as Higher-Order Resolution. *The Journal of Logic Programming* 3:237–258.

Pratt, V. R. 1976. Semantical Considerations on Floyd-Hoare Logic. In Proceedings of the Seventeenth Annual IEEE Symposium on Foundations of Computer Science, 109–121. Washington, D.C.: IEEE Computer Society.

Reddy, U. 1989. Rewriting Techniques for Program Synthesis. In *Proceedings of Rewriting Techniques and Applications*, 388–403. Lecture Notes in Computer Science, volume 355. Berlin: Springer Verlag.

Reif, W. 1990. A Logical Theory of Module Correctness. Ph.D. diss., Fakultät fur Informatik, Universität Karlsruhe. Forthcoming.

Reif, W. 1984. Vollständigkeit einer Modifizierten Goldblatt-Logik und Approximation der Omegaregel durch Induktion, Diplomarbeit, Fakultät für Informatik, Universität Karlsruhe.

Smith, D. R. 1985. Top-Down Synthesis of Divide-and-Conquer Algorithms. *Artificial Intelligence* 27:43–96.

Smith, D. R., and Lowry, M. R. 1989. Algorithm Theories and Design Tactics. In *Proceedings of the First Conference on Mathematics of Program Construction*, 379–398. Lecture Notes in Computer Science, volume 375. Berlin: Springer Verlag.

Stephan, W. 1989. Axiomatisierung Rekursiver Prozeduren in der Dynamischen Logik, Habilitationsschrift, Fakultät für Informatik, Universität Karlsruhe.

Cognitive and Planning
Approaches to Software Design

This last section illustrates the fertile relationship between knowledge-based software engineering and other areas of AI research. David Steier's chapter presents an integrated problem-solving and learning architecture for algorithm design that is based on a study of human algorithm designers. This chapter summarizes Steier's recent Ph.D. dissertation at Carnegie Mellon University under the direction of Allen Newell and Elaine Kant. Theodore Linden's chapter shows how recent research in planning can be applied to knowledge-based software engineering and vice versa. Linden is a staff scientist at Advanced Decision Systems, a company that develops knowledge-based application software. He has pioneered the application of transformational techniques to planning.

Steier's chapter describes a series of algorithm design systems implemented in soar, a general-purpose architecture for problem solving and learning. SOAR is based on a model of human cognition that emphasizes reasoning in multiple problem spaces. SOAR learns by chunking the results of problem solving in a subgoal problem space for use in a parent problem space. Essentially, DESIGNER-SOAR designs an algorithm by transferring knowledge from an application-domain problem space to a computational domain problem space. DESIGNER-SOAR gets significant performance speedups through learning. In fact, DESIGNER-SOAR designs algorithms by learning generalized execution procedures through chunking. Acquiring software design knowledge through learning has broad potential.

An interesting aspect of Steier's chapter is the relationship between representation and architecture. SOAR'S architecture includes a small working memory and a large long-term memory accessed through efficient pattern matching. The first two SOAR algorithm design systems Steier developed were reimplementations of other algorithm design systems whose algorithm representations required much processing overhead in SOAR. The processing overhead in SOAR is a result of the complexity of matching rules stored in long-term memory against the contents of working memory. AI research on production systems includes the development of efficient pattern-matching algorithms such as the RETE algorithm (see chapter 17). In contrast to the earlier SOAR systems, DESIGNER-SOAR uses an algorithm representation closely tuned to SOAR's architecture. This representation not only results in low processing overhead but also enables the full power of SOAR's learning mechanism.

Linden's chapter demonstrates the recent convergence between knowledge-based planning and knowledge-based software engineering. Although planning and automatic programming share common roots, research in the past 15 years has tended to diverge. One section of Linden's chapter describes how the transformational paradigm that underlies much research in program synthesis has been applied to planning. Most of his chapter describes how recent ideas in knowledge-based planning can be used to develop software that can satisfy evolving requirements.

The key to extendable software is to represent the knowledge used to develop the software. This knowledge includes domain knowledge; design knowledge; and knowledge about the stable aspects of the requirements, aspects that are unlikely to change as the system evolves. Representing this knowledge allows many partial design decisions to explicitly be recorded without premature commitment to a particular implementation. This approach enables a more flexible and opportunistic process of software development and evolution than is currently achievable. Also, it enables a much higher degree of reuse. The perspective Linden brings from knowledge-based planning to the future possibilities for knowledge-based software engineering complements the perspective of other chapters in this book.

Automating Algorithm Design within a General Architecture for Intelligence

David Steier

Turning the dream of automatic programming into reality will involve, among other things, getting computers to design algorithms. For human algorithm designers, two abilities seem critical for success: (1) making design decisions based on diverse sources of knowledge and (2) improving performance by learning from experience. This chapter describes a line of research focused on incorporating these abilities into automatic algorithm designers, beginning with detailed studies of human designers and leading to a theory of the algorithm design process and a system, DESIGNER-SOAR, that implements much of this theory. DESIGNER-SOAR and two of its predecessor systems, DESIGNER-MEETSSOAR and CYPRESS-SOAR, are based on the SOAR problem-solving and learning architecture (Laird, Newell, and Rosenbloom 1987). In addition to describing the systems and the theory, this chapter includes a comparison of this research to related work in software design and studies in other design domains.

The Software Design Research Context

For the purposes of this chapter, *algorithm design* is defined as going from an understanding of the problem in domain terms to an algorithm description in terms of the target computational model. Algorithm design is a worthwhile task to try to automate for several reasons. Automatic designers would help with the search for new algorithms, especially for new computational models. Optimizations at the algorithm design level often result in exponential speedups; such gains are difficult to achieve later in the software development process. Furthermore, algorithm design plays an important role in computer science: it is a standard part of the undergraduate curriculum, several textbooks for the field exist (Aho, Hopcroft, and Ullman 1974; Sedgewick 1983), and computer science department faculties usually include one or more experts on the subject. Despite this prominent role, the process of algorithm design is not well understood, and it is usually taught by example. As with other complex tasks, building a model of algorithm design precise enough to automate should ultimately contribute to education and practice in the field.

Several researchers have built systems that automate part of the algorithm design task. KIDS (Smith 1988) (which subsumes and updates CYPRESS [Smith 1985]), STRATA (Lowry 1988a), and MEDUSA (McCartney 1987) approached human performance levels for certain classes of domains and design strategies: KIDS in divide-and-conquer and global search (generate-and-test optimizations) algorithms, STRATA in local search algorithms, and MEDUSA, in intersection problems in computational geometry. (These systems are described in other chapters of this book.) This article takes the view that despite the progress demonstrated by such systems, at least two hard problems remain: the overhead for knowledge engineering and an inability to learn from experience. KIDS, STRATA, and MEDUSA all use a single logic-based representation for algorithm and application-domain knowledge. This representation might not be the most natural encoding of the knowledge for human domain experts, leading to substantial overhead for increasing the scope of the systems or even in constructing specifications. Also, none of the systems improve their performance with experience, repeating the same processing even for successive presentations of the same problem (although recent work on KIDS examined the use of history and replay mechanisms). The lack of a learning mechanism leads to both inefficiency and an inability to improve performance by acquiring substantially different knowledge.

The Behavior of Human Algorithm Designers

In general, people are particularly adept at integrating knowledge in diverse forms and learning from experience whether in design or any other intellectual task. Thus, I believe the study of humans, especially with the aid of protocol analysis (Ericsson and Simon 1984), offers useful guidance for the improvement of automated systems. Researchers analyzed audiotape and videotape recordings of computer science undergraduates, graduate students, and faculty (15 people in all) who were instructed to talk aloud while they worked on algorithm design problems. The problems ranged in difficulty from verifying the correctness of a given implementation of binary search to designing algorithms to find the convex hull of a set of points in the plane. The length of the resulting protocols ranged from ten minutes to over an hour. The protocol analysis consisted of hypothesizing that a designer works in particular problem spaces (using certain representations and operators) and studying the protocol, phrase-by-phrase, to refine the hypotheses. In its most detailed form, protocol analysis produces a problem behavior graph (Newell and Simon 1972), which shows how subjects search a given problem space. Problem behavior graphs were drawn for three of the protocols; the remainder were skimmed for evidence to confirm or "disconfirm" the hypothesized model of design. The results of the studies, discussed in detail in Kant and Newell (1982, 1984) and Kant (1985), are summarized here:

Abstract Algorithm Representation: Designers have a representation for algorithms and algorithm fragments that is not tied to a particular programming language (although it can be influenced by languages they know). The key features of this representation are its data flow character, object- (or data-) oriented control, and a small set of primitive steps of general functional character (for example, generate, compare).

Refinement of Schemes: In almost all cases, designers chose a basic scheme, or kernel idea, for the algorithm relatively quickly, and devoted the remainder of the time to refining the initial scheme. Occasionally, a basic scheme is abandoned and a new one selected. An example of a scheme is divide and conquer, and a sample refinement of this scheme is the choice of partitioning a set of numbers about its median to divide a problem into subproblems.

Means-End-Analysis for Control: Means-end analysis is a control strategy in which the desired situation is compared to the current state, and the differences detected are then used to select operations to apply. In algorithm design, this locally driven process often results in differing levels of refinement for different parts of the algorithm. Unless a problem is routine for a designer, there is almost never strict adherence to a top-down refinement strategy.

Execution to Drive Means-End Analysis: Execution of partial algorithms enables means-end analysis by finding differences between the desired properties of the algorithm and the properties present in the current design. The execution works on input at a variety of levels of detail, so that the input might be symbolic, yielding symbolic execution, or actual data items (such as the set $\{2, 5, 7\}$), yielding test-case execution.

Progressive Deepening Behavior: The pattern of execution during design displays much repetition, with the analysis slightly varied or extended on each repetition, in a manner determined by prior knowledge. Evidence of progressive deepening is seen in the problem behavior graphs and is similar to that encountered by de Groot (1965) and Newell and Simon (1972) in protocol analyses of chess players.

Explanation as Another Iteration of Progressive Deepening: When explaining an algorithm to somebody else, designers do not seem to simply be reading off an internal data structure representing the algorithm. Rather, they explain what is happening as they reconstruct the algorithm by execution. The execution process is the same as used for design, so much so that designers often detect bugs during their explanations, interrupting themselves to repair these bugs as if they were still in the design phase.

Learning Pervading the Entire Design Process: Humans continuously learn. In fact, without learning, information only survives a few seconds (the duration of working memory), so that virtually all the knowledge applied in design must somehow have been learned from some previous experience. Learning makes successive executions of algorithms less expensive. Learning is also used in drawing on experience with similar, previously encountered problems and acquiring new terminology and design strategies.

Automating Algorithm Design within SOAR—Background

Because humans have no innate facility for algorithm design, their performance in this domain must arise from the adaptation of general cognitive mechanisms to the algorithm design task. Indeed, the issues raised at the end of The Software Design Research Contract are not unique to automating algorithm design. Such issues were raised for the rest of software development (Barstow 1985) and other complex tasks requiring intelligence, such as engineering design (Rychener et al. 1986) and speech recognition (Erman et al. 1980). Therefore, our research takes the approach that support for knowledge integration and learning is a general need and is amenable to solution by general mechanisms of the sort provided by an architecture for general intelligence. This section briefly describes SOAR,[1] which is intended to be such an architecture, and gives an overview of how two non-SOAR algorithm design systems were partially reimplemented in SOAR, setting the stage for the theory of design embodied in DESIGNER-SOAR.

SOAR

SOAR represents tasks as search in *problem spaces*—sets of states, with operators that move from state to state and have the free ability to search within the space for a desired state that represents task accomplishment. For example, the game of chess can be formulated as a problem space in which the states are board configurations and the operators are the legal moves of the game. Knowledge is used to progress toward a desired state: selecting problem spaces to work in, states to proceed from, and operators to apply. A skilled chess player might use such knowledge to prefer moves that enable a fork or skewer. This knowledge is stored in a long-term recognition memory, implemented as a production system. The conditions of these productions test for the presence or absence of simple patterns in a working memory, and the actions add information to working memory (*working memory* is just a collection of objects with attributes and values). In addition to retrieving information from the recognition memory, productions also implement simple operators by having the appropriate actions in their right-hand sides. Complex operators are treated as tasks, which are accomplished in appropriate problem spaces. Other problem spaces are evoked to handle search control, such as the selection of operators. In this manner, tasks are decomposed into problem spaces in the same way that large conventional programs are broken into modules.

SOAR operates in terms of decision cycles, each consisting of an elaboration phase and a decision procedure. In the elaboration phase, productions fire to retrieve relevant knowledge from long-term memory. The productions augment the problem-solving context and deposit preferences about possible actions to take in working memory. The form of the preferences is domain independent, so the decision procedure can compare preferences against each other to attempt to determine what should be done next. Sample preferences are that it is acceptable to select the chess problem space for the goal of winning a chess game or that the operator that removes a threat to the king is required in a state where a player is in check. If there is a unique choice, then this choice is implemented at the end of the decision cycle. To implement a choice means to change the value of the selected problem space, state, or operator.

Often, the available knowledge is incomplete or inconsistent, so that no conclusion can be reached about an action to perform. In this case, SOAR reaches an impasse and generates a subgoal (and then a problem space) to resolve the impasse. Four types of impasses (no change, rejection, tie, and conflict) arise in SOAR. For example, a common impasse, an operator tie, occurs when several operators are proposed as acceptable for application to a given state, and there is insufficient knowledge to choose between them. An operator-tie impasse is resolved when SOAR has enough preferences to determine a dominant candidate (or set of candidates that are indifferent to each other). SOAR sets up subgoals to resolve such impasses. To work on a subgoal, SOAR applies all its problem-solving machinery, just as it did for the higher-level decisions (selecting a problem space to work in, and so on). Impasses can occur within impasses, leading to the generation of a stack of goal contexts.

When subgoals are terminated, SOAR learns from the experience by building new productions (chunks). The left-hand side of a chunk consists of generalized conditions on the working memory elements used in producing the results of the subgoal. Chunks just augment the knowledge in the space above the subgoal; if the chunk's conditions are satisfied again in the future, the chunk will fire to automatically bring the knowledge from the previous solution to bear. The conditions of the chunk are limited to those aspects of the preimpasse situation that are known to be relevant to result in creation (determined by tracing backward through production firings). Thus, transfer of knowledge occurs because the chunk's conditions abstract away from inessential features of the original situation. That is, the examples provided by SOAR's experience are used to compile the general domain theory accessed in subgoals into operational rules for situations in the original space.

The SOAR architecture is intended to be used both theoretically, as a computational model of intelligence, and practically, as a foundation for building AI systems. Research on SOAR showed how the behavior characteristic of weak methods, for example, means-end-analysis, can be obtained by adding appropriate knowledge increments (Laird and Newell 1983). SOAR also demonstrated that chunking in combination with the appropriate problem-solving behavior has the function of a variety of the classical learning mechanisms, that is, EBG (Rosenbloom and Laird 1986). SOAR systems have solved problems and learned in domains ranging from the traditional AI toy problems, such as the eight puzzle, to more complex knowledge-intensive tasks, such as part of the VAX configuration performed by the R1 expert system (Rosenbloom et al. 1985). A set of mechanisms for perception and motor behavior for SOAR is currently under development, but only the features of central cognition in SOAR are relevant in this chapter.

DESIGNER-MEETS-SOAR

The first algorithm designer built within SOAR was a direct mapping of the structure of the DESIGNER system (Kant and Newell 1983) into the SOAR framework. Important features of DESIGNER include the following:

First is multiple spaces for design. DESIGNER has separate representations for working with partial algorithm descriptions and objects in the application domain. Domain spaces were built for working with sets; sequences; and geometric objects, such as points and figures.

Second is data flow representation for algorithm space. Input specifications, partial designs, and final algorithms are all represented in a single wide-spectrum data flowlike language, similar to the language used to describe algorithms in Newell (1969) and Tappel (1980). The language was used to represent about 10 specifications and algorithms in DESIGNER.

Third is design driven by symbolic and test-case execution: A data flow–driven process was used to execute most of the algorithms represented in DESIGNER (Steier and Kant 1985). Algorithms were executed both on real data (the normal mode for program execution) and symbolic data to derive symbolic expressions for input in terms of output. The symbolic execution process is similar to the symbolic evaluation of plans in the Programmer's Apprentice (Shrobe 1979) and partial evaluation (Komorowski 1982). Additionally, DESIGNER includes rudimentary capabilities within symbolic execution to evaluate algorithm efficiency.

DESIGNER-MEETS-SOAR is a SOAR-based implementation of DESIGNER. It has an algorithm design space at the top level in which the states are partial descriptions of algorithms. Most of the operators in this space edit algorithm descriptions; others add and remove focuses of attention, hence limiting the number of editing operators to be considered as candidates for application to a given state. Ties between candidate operators are resolved in the execution space (covering both symbolic and test-case execution). The states in this space are the descriptions from the algorithm design space augmented with symbolic or actual data to be processed by the algorithm. Operators in this space evaluate the current design, simulating basic processing steps and detecting design-constraint violations.

This framework was tested on five relatively simple problems: finding the largest subset of a given set of integers whose elements are all positive, finding the intersection of two sets, finding the union of two sets, finding the sum of the integers from 1 to 10, and finding the factorial of a given integer. Issues of learning were not investigated in DESIGNER-MEETS-SOAR, and the system does not use examples as a source of knowledge.

DESIGNER-MEETS-SOAR provides several pieces of important data about the prospects for automating algorithm design in SOAR. We achieved what we intended: a demonstration that a designer could search a space of partial algorithm designs, controlled mainly by information derived from executing candidate designs. This result was encouraging but was tempered by a realization that a direct use of DESIGNER's data flow algorithm representation in SOAR is inefficient. Keeping the entire algorithm in working memory as an explicit data structure involves much overhead, both in accessing and updating it. As with all production-based systems, performance deteriorates as the size of working memory increases, so an explicit focus of attention was introduced to reduce the combinatorial explosion in possible matches. However, the resulting increased efficiency was somewhat offset by the problem-solving complexity in deciding where to put the focus of attention.

CYPRESS-SOAR

CYPRESS-SOAR was an experiment in using a different representation for the algorithm space, one that still held the complete algorithm in working memory but without the supporting structure (ports and links) used to connect the steps in the algorithms (indicating data and control flow) in DESIGNER. The extra overhead was avoided by restricting possible algorithms to be instantiations of a specific algorithm scheme (divide-and-conquer), so control and data flow could be left implicit. The scheme for divide and conquer algorithms and the framework for the synthesis were taken from Doug Smith's (1985) CYPRESS system.

Like DESIGNER-MEETS-SOAR, CYPRESS-SOAR searches through a space of candidate algorithm designs to find a solution satisfying the specification. In DESIGNER-MEETS-SOAR, this search is controlled by symbolic execution, but in CYPRESS-SOAR, the search is primarily controlled by the results of a simulation of the RAINBOW deductive engine. CYPRESS itself actually spends most of its time in calls to RAINBOW. However, in developing CYPRESS-SOAR, researchers wanted to focus on the knowledge involved in making design choices rather than deriving antecedents. Thus, as a substitute for a complete reimplementation of RAINBOW, CYPRESS-SOAR includes rules that return the results of calls to RAINBOW on the particular sets of premises and goal formulas needed for the sorting derivations. This approach is clearly inadequate for a fully general design system, but it is sufficient for an investigation of search and learning at the top level, where the method of deduction does not affect the results. These results include the transfer of learned knowledge: CYPRESS-SOAR knows what goal it is working on and caches the result of the goal for future use. Because some goals show up more than once, this learning mechanism reduces problem-solving effort both within the design of a single algorithm and on later designs of different algorithms. RYPRESS does not learn and, consequently, cannot take advantage of repeated subgoals.

A full reimplementation of CYPRESS in CYPRESS-SOAR would have involved a commitment to a propositional representation in which reasoning about algorithms could involve substantial amounts of theorem proving, even in resolving questions that would seem relatively simple to humans. Even with the limited amount of deduction done by CYPRESS-SOAR, manipulating the concrete syntax trees in working memory proved to be expensive. This result furthered the belief that the use of theorem proving as a basic method of inferencing does not efficiently mesh with the SOAR framework, at least not until a substantial store of chunks have been built to directly perform such inferencing.

A Theory of the Algorithm Design Process

One of the lessons learned from DESIGNER-MEETS-SOAR and CYPRESS-SOAR is that automating algorithm design within SOAR (or within any architecture for that matter) requires a representation with low processing overhead. Another lesson is that design systems must carefully be structured to exploit the potential of certain types of knowledge, especially that of the application domain and previous experience. Responding to these concerns and using results on problem solving and learning within the SOAR architecture, researchers developed a theory of the algorithm design process under the conditions normally encountered by human designers. The theory is de-

scribed in this section. The system, DESIGNER-SOAR, that implements much of
the theory is described in the next section.

The theory begins with standard terminology found in algorithm design
texts (Aho, Hopcroft, and Ullman 1974). A *model of computation* specifies
the set of executable primitive operations and their associated costs. An *algorithm* is a procedure that is executable under some model of computation
and that terminates for some class of valid input. A model of computation
defines the space of possible algorithms that could serve as candidate
solutions to an algorithm design problem. Theoretically, one could solve algorithm design problems by searching this space, generating and testing candidate solutions until finding one that satisfies the specifications. The space
of procedures directly defined in terms of primitives at the level of machine
instructions is too large to solve problems in a reasonable amount of time (although it has been tried [Friedberg 1958]). In general, the way to make
search tractable is to apply knowledge to decrease the number of candidate
solutions that need to be tested. In this instance, we know that certain designs
can be considered together because the differences between them do not matter at the functional level at which algorithm design typically takes place.
What is needed is a representation that groups functionally equivalent designs, forming an abstracted version of the original computational model.

The theory incorporates such a representation: Algorithms are procedurally represented in terms of *functional operators* corresponding to the conceptual building blocks of algorithm design. These operators perform such tasks
as repeatedly generating elements of a set, testing a data item for the truth of
some predicate, comparing two data items, selecting a data item from a set,
applying some function to data (perhaps recursively), storing data into memory, and retrieving data from memory. These operators form a natural set in
the sense that people who design algorithms use these terms and that alternatives would not radically vary from these. These operators can be composed
into higher-level operators. For example, in designing divide-and-conquer algorithms, it is often useful to speak of an operation to decompose the problem into subproblems and an operation to compose the solutions to the subproblems to get the answer to the original problem. The level of abstraction
adapts, as appropriate, to the goals of the design process, allowing the designer to focus only on relevant details.

A theory of the algorithm design process must also define how a designer
determines what the desired algorithm is to compute; this information is provided in the problem specification. Researchers assume that at a minimum, a
specification provides (perhaps implicitly) a procedure that exhibits the desired behavior if executed in a model of the application domain. The primitive operations in the application-domain model can be distinct from those
for which the algorithm is being designed. For example, a designer who understands a convex hull problem specification can find the convex hull of a

given set of points, perhaps by using visual operations, without necessarily knowing an algorithm for finding hulls on a conventional computer. Additional constraints might come from performance requirements on the algorithm or from resource limitations on the design process itself. The task of the designer is to find an algorithm for the target computational model that is functionally equivalent to the algorithm for the application-domain model and satisfies the given constraints.

This task formulation requires testing for the equivalent function of two procedures (one for the application-domain model and one for the computational model), which is undecidable in the general case. However, we only desire a mechanism that works for the cases that occur in practice, which are usually simple. A direct match suffices if the relevant functional properties can be represented so that similarities and differences are easily detectable. In a SOAR-based framework, both the domain model and the computational model are mapped into sets of problem spaces and are always executable. Therefore, a possible strategy is to execute both models so that the features of interest can directly be read from the results of the executions. For example, one could check if the behavior of the algorithm designed so far is equivalent to that of the specification for a given class of input by running both the domain model and the computational model on a representative of this class and checking to see if the output match. If the input class includes all valid input to the algorithm, the execution is equivalent to verification if carried out in full generality. Specialized execution procedures have many applications in design, including tests for correctness in specific cases, checks for type clashes, and even efficiency analysis and explanation. These variations arise from changing the input and processing the interpreter doing the execution in accordance with the goals of the designer.

With an execution-based design process, the issue remains of how the process is guided because designs can be executed on many examples and at varying levels of abstraction. The purpose of execution is to make all the information necessary to make the next design decision locally available in the immediate context in which the designer is working. Given the right input and attention to detail, execution can propagate relevant constraints, imposed as a result of previous design decisions, to a single context for inspection. Familiar patterns can then be recognized in the context by a simple match. The next design step can focus on whatever problems or opportunities are found by such recognition. Therefore, execution occurs in the context of means-end analysis: The current state of the design is compared to the desired state, and operators are applied to reduce those discrepancies deemed most critical to the success of the design. The comparison is done by execution and inspection of the results, and recognition of familiar patterns helps to make the decision about the relative importance of problems and the remedies to be applied. The execution takes place as a series of runs, with the partial design executed each time until something unexpected, such as a bug or opportunity for refinement, is noticed, or the algorithm is completely executed and the design considered finished. Much of the algorithm structure is repeatedly traversed, but each run examines a slightly different aspect of the design, resulting in the behavior known as progressive deepening.

Finally, learning from experience plays an important role in the design theory. The algorithm designed is represented as procedural knowledge, which is acquired in the process of learning to execute the algorithm in the computational space. The design terminates when enough such knowledge has been learned so that the algorithm can directly be executed without consulting other sources of knowledge to resolve operator selection and implementation impasses. The learned knowledge constituting the design is stored along with all other knowledge in long-term memory and is evoked when relevant attributes of the problem-solving context have the same values as existed in the situation in which the knowledge was acquired. Thus, learned knowledge can transfer both within a design, as repeated executions, and across designs, as in when the current design problem is appropriately similar to one previously seen.

The theory just proposed can be summarized as follows: First, design takes place in multiple problem spaces. A subset of these spaces embodies the target model of computation, and another set embodies the application-domain model. Second, the task of algorithm design is to use knowledge of the application domain to build a procedure for computing the desired output in the computational spaces. Third, the computational spaces have functional operators corresponding to steps in an algorithm at whatever level of abstraction is necessary for the design. Fourth, means-end analysis on the results of execution drives the design, with the resulting series of execution passes in a design session exhibiting the pattern of progressive deepening. Fifth, any part of the knowledge necessary for accomplishing the design task can be acquired by learning. The algorithm itself is represented as learned knowledge for navigating through the computational spaces.

DESIGNER-SOAR

DESIGNER-SOAR is an algorithm design system that is (approximately) based on our theory of the design process. It can design several simple generate-and-test and divide-and-conquer algorithms in a few domains. It uses multiple levels of abstraction in problem solving in the computational spaces and generalizes from examples in the domain spaces. Furthermore, like CYPRESS-SOAR (but to a much greater degree), it learns from experience, transferring knowledge acquired during the design of one algorithm to aid in the design of others.

The high-level problem space structure of DESIGNER-SOAR is shown in figure 1. Triangles represent problem spaces, and arrows represent transitions

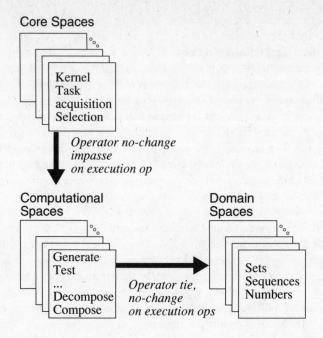

Figure 1. The Spaces in Designer-Soar.

between spaces on impasses. Both the computational and application-domain models of the theory correspond to a set of spaces in DESIGNER-SOAR. The core contains additional operational knowledge about how to work with the two models, acquiring specifications and coordinating executions. The computational spaces consult the domain spaces during execution. DESIGNER-SOAR has problem spaces for three domains: sets, sequences, and numbers. The operators in these spaces are sufficient to perform the set, sequence, and numeric comparison operations needed for domain execution in the subset, intersection, and sorting algorithms.

The computational spaces have functional operators corresponding to the conceptual building blocks for algorithms. For example, one of the computational operators is test, which evaluates a predicate on some input and produces the input with an annotation that the test returned true or false on this item. The first step in implementing the test operator is to create symbolic results to which the annotations will be attached. In the second step, one of the operators test-returns-true or test-returns-false actually attaches the annotation. The test predicate must be known and evaluated to decide which of these operators should apply. If the predicate is known, it is applied in the selection space by the apply-predicate operator, and the result is used to select the tied annotating superoperator. Sometimes the predicate cannot directly be evaluated because it is not expressed in terms that are operational within the model of computation; so, further problem solving, usually involving the domain space, acquires knowledge of how to make the predicate operational.

Algorithm schemes can procedurally be encoded as higher-level operators that are implemented in terms of these building blocks. To represent divide and conquer, DESIGNER-SOAR has operators that decompose problems into subproblems and compose subproblem solutions to get the answer to the original problem. When attempting to apply these compose and decompose operators, an impasse results, with a corresponding subgoal to acquire the knowledge to implement them (that is, apply them to produce new states). DESIGNER-SOAR knows an algorithm when it can select and implement the appropriate functional operators to compute the correct output given any legal input. Thus, DE-SIGNER-SOAR has a uniform procedural representation for abstractions at levels varying from algorithm schemes to computational primitives.

An Example of DESIGNER-SOAR in Action

DESIGNER-SOAR's behavior can be illustrated by its synthesis of an insertion sort of the same form as that created by CYPRESS and CYPRESS-SOAR. The algorithm comprises two divide-and-conquer subalgorithms, one for the top-level sort function and one for the insertion of an element into an ordered sequence (the composition subprocedure). Sort takes a sequence of elements to be sorted as input. If the sequence is empty, it is directly returned as already sorted; otherwise, the sequence is split into its first element and the rest of the sequence. The first element is then inserted into the result achieved by recursively sorting the remainder of the sequence. Insert takes an element and an ordered sequence as input. If the sequence is empty, the function returns a sequence containing only the element; otherwise, a conditional subprogram is called to decompose the input into smaller subproblems. The conditional compares the value of the element parameter to the value of the first element of the sequence parameter. If we assume x_0 corresponds to the smaller element, x_1 to the larger element, and x_2 to the remainder of the sequence, the conditional returns a pair of the form $<x_0, <x_1, x_2>>$. The first parameter is then prefixed to the result of recursively calling the insertion function on the second parameter (the nested pair). In the following subsections, the first few steps of the insertion-sort synthesis are described; for the full synthesis, the reader is referred to Steier (1989).

Acquiring the Specification and a Plan (C1–C2)

DESIGNER-SOAR makes design choices while it repeatedly executes the partially designed algorithm at varying levels of abstraction, using the executions to detect problems and opportunities to guide the design. Because the goal of design is to be able to execute the algorithm without search, DESIGNER-SOAR first attempts to execute the insertion-sort algorithm (which doesn't exist yet) to see what needs to be done.

Execution requires an input for the algorithm, and at first, DESIGNER-SOAR does not even know what the input should be. The knowledge of which domain operator to choose to create the input is part of the specification, which states that when DESIGNER-SOAR is in the sort task in the create-input space, it should choose the create-item operator to create a sequence of integers for use as input to the algorithm it is trying to design. This specification is retrieved when a state no-change impasse occurs in the create-input space, for example, when an initial state is selected, but no operators are proposed as acceptable for this state. To resolve the impasse, a set of task acquisition spaces (generic to SOAR, built by Gregg Yost) interprets the specification and constructs an operator to be proposed as acceptable, allowing the subgoal to be terminated and problem solving to proceed. The chunk built from this subgoal allows DESIGNER-SOAR to bypass the interpretation process (because the chunk prevents the impasse) in future situations where this operator instantiation knowledge is needed.

A symbolic sequence of integers is thereby generated for use as input to the algorithm. Then, an operator-tie impasse results because DESIGNER-SOAR has not yet learned how to select between the computational operators it could apply as a first step. The operator is selected according to the results of a subgoal to evaluate the choice by lookahead, that is, trying out the operator to see if it leads to a final state. *Lookahead* is actually a simple form of planning, in which a plan is adopted if it can be shown to be successful when applied. Because lookahead can be expensive if the entire plan must be formulated and applied before making a decision, DESIGNER-SOAR performs the lookahead in an abstracted version of the computational space, one in which the main function of the operators are implemented, and less important details are ignored. A similar use of abstraction in SOAR is described for a partial reimplementation of R1, the VAX configuration expert system (Unruh, Rosenbloom, and Laird [1987]).

The abstraction in the computational space used for lookahead in DESIGNER-SOAR omits most of the implementation details of the computational operators, checking only the input and output domains for compatibility. In a more sophisticated version of the space, efficiency constraints could be propagated as well. The knowledge used here is that the input to the algorithm is a sequence. Sequences are known to be decomposable into smaller sequences and composable into larger ones, which serves as an indication to DESIGNER-SOAR that a divide-and-conquer algorithm should be considered. The fact that there is a simple way to decompose the input into subproblems does not guarantee that a divide-and-conquer algorithm for the problem is feasible (in fact, nobody knows how to take an arbitrary problem and tell if an efficient divide-and-conquer solution is possible). The decomposability of sequences merely serves as a retrieval cue, so that the possibility of divide and conquer can be considered; other schemes can be considered as well. DESIGN-ER-SOAR evaluates this possibility by applying a sequence of abstract operators: Test an input for decomposability, decompose the input into subproblems if possible, solve the subproblems, and compose the subsolutions. The symbolic result of these operator applications is a sequence, which matches the desired output domain. Thus, the operator selected for (nonabstracted) application is the first step of divide and conquer: a test for the decomposability of the input.

Designing the Top-Level Sort (C3–C6)

To refine the algorithm by applying the nonabstracted operators, the symbolic input is treated as an actual sequence to sort, one that has no elements. Given the decision to execute a divide-and-conquer algorithm, DESIGNER-SOAR attempts to apply the first step, testing for decomposability. DESIGNER-SOAR knows of no way to decompose an empty sequence, so the test is assumed to return an empty sequence annotated with the fact that it is not decomposable. The nondecomposable input can directly be sorted. Because DESIGNER-SOAR knows that the output should be ordered and that empty sequences are already ordered, it conjectures that applying the identity function is sufficient to implement the directly-solve operator. This fact is verified by applying the domain operator known to produce the desired result to the empty sequence and then verifying the equivalence of the output of the domain operation and the execution of the algorithm developed so far.

DESIGNER-SOAR knows that refining a divide-and-conquer algorithm requires consideration of the case where the input is decomposable as well as the case where it is not. The empty sequence was not decomposable. DESIGN-ER-SOAR has the knowledge that the sequence must have at least one element to be decomposable, so DESIGNER-SOAR augments the input with an element to the sequence (yielding a singleton) and begins a new execution pass through the algorithm. To determine the test for decomposability, DESIGNER-SOAR looks ahead for a possible decomposition operator. The system has a preference for selecting the FirstRest operator for decomposition in this case (because the input is a sequence), splitting the first element from the remaining (empty) sequence. The precondition for applying FirstRest, that the sequence has at least one element, is used as the test for decomposability.

FirstRest is then applied to the input, and the resulting subproblems from this decomposition are solved. The first subproblem is an element rather than a sortable sequence and is passed to the composition as is. The remaining subproblem is a sequence, and test-case execution is recursively invoked to sort it. It is decomposed into an element and an empty sequence. The test for decomposability applied to the empty sequence returns false, so it must directly be sorted. Again, the Id function is applied to return the empty sequence.

Choice	Alternatives considered (selected alternatives underlined)	Rationale for Choice
C1. Specification	Sort integer sequence	Domain procedure provided by user
C2. Sort scheme	Divide and conquer Generate and test Other functional operators	Abstract lookahead
C3. Sort decomposability test	Length(*Input*)>0 *true*	Can't decompose empty sequences
C4. Sort directly-solve	Id	Domain op says empty sequence is sorted
C5. Sort DivConq form	Simple decompose Simple compose	Preselected preference
C6. Sort decomposition	FirstRest ListSplit	Preselcted preference
C7. Insertion scheme	Divide and conquer Generate and test Other functional operators	Abstract lookahead
C8. Insertion decomposability test test	Length(*seq-param*)>0 *true*	Can't decompose empty sequences
C9. Insertion DivConq form	Simple compose Simple decompose	Preselected preference
C10. Insertion directly-solve	Cons Second in pair	Cons returns desired result
C11. Insertion decompose scheme	Conditional Nonconditional function	Domain execution shows two possibilities for returning results
C12. Insertion decompose predicate	*int-param* ≥ First *(seq-param)* *int-param* ≤ First *(seq-param)*	Need ordered result for composition
C13. Insertion decompose action	Smallest first in returned result	Ensure smallest element moved to front in example
C13. Insertion composition	Cons Id	Cons returns desired result

Table 1. Insertion-Sort Design in Designer-Soar.

Summary and Experimental Results

The design of insertion sort is summarized in table 1. Column 1 labels the design choice and gives the number of the decision cycle at which the choice occurred. The entire run takes 883 decision cycles, requiring about 35 minutes on a SUN3/260. Column 2 summarizes the effects of design choices, and column 3 gives DESIGNER-SOAR's reasons for making the choice.

To summarize, DESIGNER-SOAR combines knowledge of the domain of sequences with its knowledge about divide-and-conquer algorithms to create an insertion-sort procedure for the target computational model. The knowledge about the domain of sequences, for example, that a sequence can be divided into its first element and a sequence containing the remainder of its elements, is represented as productions fulfilling the appropriate roles in the

Algorithm	Components in design	Decision Cycles
Subset	4	179
Intersection	4	208
Insertion sort	13	883
Merge sort	13	860

Table 2. Statistics for Designer-Soar Designs.

domain problem spaces, for example, operator proposal. The knowledge about divide-and-conquer algorithms is encoded as operator proposal, selection, and implementation knowledge in a space of abstract functional operators, such as decompose and compose. These operators are implemented in the computational space in terms of algorithmic operations that could easily be translated into code in a standard programming language, for example, comparing two integers to see which is greater. The algorithm itself is represented within SOAR as a set of chunks that allow a sequence to directly be sorted in the computational spaces. These chunks encode knowledge, such as the fact that the decomposition of the input into subproblems at the top level should be performed by applying the FirstRest operator. The algorithm design occurs as a result of repeatedly executing different parts of the algorithm until all known execution paths have been explored.

Statistics for the runs of DESIGNER-SOAR on four specifications are shown in table 2. The four algorithms designed are the subset and intersection algorithms designed by DESIGNER-MEETS-SOAR and the insertion- and merge-sort algorithms designed by CYPRESS-SOAR. These runs were made in SOAR 4.4 with learning turned on.

A comparison with figures given in Steier (1989) shows that DESIGNER-SOAR designs the subset algorithm in roughly one-third the time taken by DE-SIGNER-MEETS-SOAR. Furthermore, DESIGNER-SOAR actually accomplishes more during this design because it acquires the specification and uses test-case execution, and DESIGNER-MEETS-SOAR does not. The time it takes DESIGNER-SOAR to design sorting algorithms is larger than it is for CYPRESS-SOAR, but the comparison is misleading because CYPRESS-SOAR synthesizes only part of each sorting algorithm and simulates the necessary deduction, whereas DESIGNER-SOAR designs the complete algorithm and performs all the inferences necessary.

Several experiments were run to test the contributions of learned knowledge over a series of algorithm designs. Learning is so tightly integrated into DESIGNER-SOAR that the boundary between problem solving and learning is fuzzy—designing an algorithm is equivalent to learning to execute it. However, it is possible to turn learning off (so that nothing is ever stored in long-term memory) to isolate the effects of learning. Figure 2 shows the cumulative problem-solving effort needed to design two simple algorithms in sequence, with and without learning. On the left, the two algorithms are subset and intersection; on the right are insertion sort and merge sort. There is a significant savings with learning in both pairs of algorithms: 28 percent for the set algorithms and 69 percent for the sorting algorithms, illustrating that the benefits of learning increase as the designs get more complex (this fact should be true in general for SOAR systems because more complex problems mean that there are more impasses for chunks to avoid). Furthermore, the slope of the learning graph decreases during the design of the second algorithm in each pair, suggesting transfer across, as well as within, the similar designs (both algorithms in each pair are roughly equally complex). We found that without the chunks from the design of insertion sort, the learning run for merge sort takes 860 decision cycles, an increase of 56 percent over the 551 needed with these chunks, verifying substantial transfer. The kinds of knowledge that transfer range from the domain knowledge needed to sort, which is identical for the synthesis of both sorting algorithms, to the fact that divide and conquer is an acceptable algorithm scheme for the sorting problem. In terms of time, a series of 4 algorithms took just under 3 hours to run with all goals learning and 4½ hours with bottom-up learning, factoring out chunking overhead.

Implications for Automatic Algorithm Design

The research described previously has many implications for automatic algorithm design, for futher work in automatic programming, and for design in general.

The Role of Learning

CYPRESS-SOAR and DESIGNER-SOAR both learn from experience using chunking. CYPRESS-SOAR is successful in demonstrating the transfer of knowledge both within and across tasks, but the application of chunking is straightforward, and the problem-solving approach of CYPRESS-SOAR is unaffected by the fact that it was implemented within a learning architecture. Thus, CYPRESS-SOAR can be considered a first-generation application of learning to automatic algorithm design. In contrast, the fact that DESIGNER-SOAR learns from experience permeates almost every facet of its approach to algorithm design, from the way it acquires specifications to how it represents designed algorithms. The distinction between learning and problem solving is blurred in DESIGNER-SOAR because algorithms are designed by learning generalized execution procedures. Researchers expect that second-generation approaches

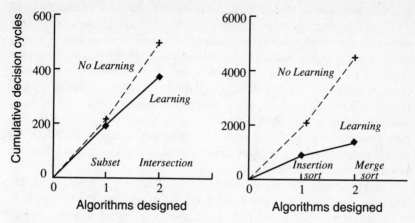

Figure 2. Effects of Learning in DESIGNER-SOAR.

such as that used by DESIGNER-SOAR will become more common as integrated problem-solving and learning architectures gain greater acceptance as foundations for knowledge-based systems. For example, the PLEESE system (Shavlik and Maclin 1988) uses explanation-based learning to generalize an expert's illustrative examples into programs. PLEESE thus incorporates domain knowledge in a way similar to DESIGNER-SOAR, which uses its domain model to constrain search in the computational spaces.

Viewing algorithm design as deliberate learning in which chunking is used to store designed algorithms is not completely new. For example, it was partially articulated at the Workshop on Knowledge Compilation in September 1986 (Bennet, Dietterich, and Mostow 1986). However, the move to take this view seriously, believing that the knowledge embodied in an algorithm should be acquired using a general-purpose learning mechanism, is a radical shift for the field of automatic algorithm design and even for the broader area of automatic programming. The traditional view has algorithms being designed by applying transformations to declarative structures, as in CYPRESS-SOAR, which limits the role of learning to storing these structures. Then, all the problems that prevented the widespread application of derivational analogy to practical problems (Mostow 1986) apply: deciding what to store, difficulty in efficient indexing, and so on.

The key insight obtained from the experience with DESIGNER-SOAR's predecessors is that not all of an algorithm's structure needs to declaratively be represented in working memory at a single time. Algorithms can be viewed as procedures for getting from initial to desired states in computational spaces. Thus, the procedural knowledge can be stored in long-term memory and paged in when needed, resulting in lower overhead because on average, there are fewer items to match against in working memory. Furthermore, algorithms can be designed by applying standard learning techniques in a procedural framework (problem space search). Because an algorithm is exactly the operator selection and implementation knowledge, there is no problem of deciding what to store. The index to the knowledge, represented as the conditions of the chunk, are the generalized attributes of the execution context tested for this knowledge to be relevant. Developing efficient ways to match such conditions against working memory is the focus of research on production systems in general and SOAR in particular (Tambe et al. 1988); the matchers and parallel machines developed in this research work for both learned and nonlearned knowledge.

That all problem solving in DESIGNER-SOAR is subject to chunking has far-reaching implications, not all of which are understood yet. The most obvious effect is that it conserves effort in problem solving, leading to the same kind of transfer effects within trials and across tasks that were seen in CYPRESS-SOAR. The effects of transfer on DESIGNER-SOAR are of a greater magnitude because of the longer (measured in decision cycles) and deeper (measured in subgoals) designs. In turn, the transfer has secondary, less obvious effects. For example, it increases the efficiency of a progressive deepening strategy because chunking makes repeated processing on multiple passes cheap. Chunking also implies that ways must be found to recover from errors that override the effects of incorrect learned knowledge; SOAR can neither directly examine nor excise its chunks. Although such a mechanism was developed (Laird 1988), it has not been incorporated in DESIGNER-SOAR.

Relation to Other Work

Exclusive of learning, DESIGNER-SOAR and the theory it embodies have a number of other aspects relevant to automating software design. Primary among these aspects is the use of executable models in design. The idea of execution that drives the problem solving in a software development system has roots in unpublished work by Newell in 1971 to 1972 but was realized in Brooks's (1975) research. Symbolic execution was studied for several systems as an aid to program testing (King 1976), and a variant of symbolic execution, symbolic interpretation, is used in the Programmer's Apprentice (Shrobe 1979). In emphasizing executable models, the theory characterizes the split between specifications and algorithms differently than the traditional what-how, declarative-procedural dichotomies, which often leave the underlying models implicit. Furthermore, viewing design as a process that maps the behavior of one model to another has the advantage that the framework can naturally be extended to cover other phases of software development. Similar ideas appeared in some of the other research on programming technology, although perhaps not using the terminology of models. The domains in DRACO (Freeman 1987) define different models, and GIST (Balzer 85) and

PAISLEY (Zave and Schell 1986) are examples of executable languages for specifying application domain models.

Another important aspect of DESIGNER-SOAR is its control strategy, means-end analysis. Means-end analysis was used in early systems, such as the HEURISTIC COMPILER (Simon 1972) and HACKER (Sussman 1975). It is less common in more recent systems automatic programming, and for automatic algorithm design in particular: KIDS, STRATA, and MEDUSA have fixed top-down refinement strategies (although the use of antecedent derivation in KIDS can be considered means-end analysis). To my knowledge, *progressive deepening*, the pattern of repeated execution for design displayed by DESIGNER-SOAR, is not used in any software-related design system.

A number of researchers have studied human performance in areas closely related to algorithm design: programming, software design, and other design domains. One can extrapolate from the theory of algorithm design presented here to make conjectures about design in general. In the remainder of this section, I examine a few such conjectures in the context of the following studies: (1) Anderson, Farrel, and Sauers (1984): On Lisp programming, it is a detailed analysis of 3 novice subjects on the reachability, power set, and first-two-elements-of-a-list problems (protocols lasted about 30 hours). (2) Brooks (1975): On Fortran programming, it is a detailed analysis of 1 expert subject on small numeric problems (protocols for the problems averaged 40 minutes). (3) Fisher (1988): On routine software design, it is fairly detailed analysis of 6 subjects on the key database and page indexing problems (protocols lasted about 5 hours). (4) Jeffries, Turner, Polson, and Atwood (1981): On routine software design, it is a rough analysis of 4 experts and 5 novices on the page indexing problem (protocols were 2 hours and more). (5) Adelson and Soloway (1985): On software design, it is a rough analysis of 3 experts and 2 novices on designing electronic mail, library, and interrupt-handling systems (protocols lasted about 2 hours). (6) Ullman, Dietterich, and Stauffer (1988): On mechanical design, it is a rough analysis of 5 semiexpert subjects on the battery contacts and flipper dipper problems (protocols lasted 6 to 10 hours; 46 hours were analyzed). (7) Akin (1986): On architectural design, it is a detailed analysis of 4 expert subjects on a problem to design a single-person dwelling (protocols lasted about 4 hours).

A kernel idea or scheme is first selected and then refined to produce the design: The theory predicts that designers and programmers would have a set of functional operators corresponding to the target design medium and an abstracted version of these operators for selecting a region of design space on which to focus. This finding shows up strongly in the studies of Jeffries et. al, Brooks, Ullman et.al., and Akin as well as in the algorithm design protocols of Kant and Newell.

Design is driven by means-end analysis in the context of examples: The theory predicts that designers would somehow run their solutions to evaluate them in the context of some input to the program or commands to the system. This finding shows up in all seven studies, although not as strongly in the studies of Fisher and Jeffries et. al. Another study of human algorithm designers (Gray, Corbett, and Van Lehn 1988) confirms this finding.

A variety of search strategies are used, determined by the knowledge of the designer: The theory predicts that progressive deepening will characterize the behavior of designers, but the studies surveyed did not analyze the protocols in search of this pattern. Rather, they looked for a search strategy corresponding to one of the classic tree search techniques, such as depth-first or breadth-first search. All the studies found some evidence of top-down refinement but to varying degrees. Jeffries et. al. found evidence of mostly breadth-first search, but Fisher and Ullman et.al. found evidence of mostly depth-first search. Anderson et. al. found depth-first search in novices and breadth-first search in experts, and Adelson and Soloway roughly found the same results, postulating that novices have only low- level plans, and experts work at differing levels of abstraction. This mixture of results is completely consistent with a progressive deepening strategy modulated by differing amounts of task knowledge. In fact, a graph of the progress of one of Akin's subjects in exploring a space of architectural designs shows clear evidence of progressive deepening.

Solving problems by analogy occurs often, particularly when the designer has expertise in the domain: Because the theory assumes that learning continuously occurs while problems are being solved, one would expect that prior experience with similar problems dominates the problem solving of experts. This fact is seen to some extent in the studies of Fisher, Adelson and Soloway, Jeffries et. al, and Ullman et. al. However, the expertise is fairly brittle, and analogy is rarely used in domains that are even moderately unfamiliar, a finding consonant with that of Kant and Newell's subjects working in the new domain of computational geometry. A related finding by Anderson et. al. is that novices often solve problems using analogy with worked-out examples because within the instructional context, the examples are known to be relevant.

Overall, there is strong confirmation from these studies of the generality of the theory. Other findings from the studies either are consequences of the theory or are completely consonant with it. Particularly noteworthy are the cognitive principles established for use in the construction of computer-based tutors (Anderson et al. 1987), for example, provide instruction in the problem-solving context, and facilitate successive approximations to the target skill. The latter is exactly the purpose of progressive deepening.

Theories of Design

A theory of the algorithm design process can embody any of a number of design approaches. Much of the research in automatic algorithm design has been devoted to developing and refining such approaches. For example, Manna and Waldinger (Manna and Waldinger 1979) have long been advocating a deductive approach to design based on the extraction of an algorithm from a constructive proof of the existence of the algorithm's output. More recently, Lowry (Lowry 1988b) casts algorithm design in the framework of the instantiation of parameterized theories.

These approaches guarantee correct algorithms when they can be applied but often assume unlimited design resources and the direct availability of any relevant knowledge in the appropriate form. The view of design as the conversion of knowledge between problem spaces seems more suited to situations where these assumptions do not hold. Algorithm design, like any type of problem solving, is difficult because designers are limited, both in the amount of resources (time, memory, and so on) that can be expended and in the access to relevant knowledge, which can be of a variety of types and come from diverse sources. The existence of such limitations is not dependent on whether the designer is a human being or a computer program; the limitations stem from the need of a finite intelligent agent to cope with the diversity inherent in its environment and the necessity to act in real time.

Under such circumstances, designers must integrate multiple sources of knowledge and learn from their experience; there is no need to do so if knowledge is always directly available, or design resources are unbounded. Algorithms are represented in spaces of abstract functional operators because such spaces are easiest to search for the design task. Specifications are cast in procedures for searching application-domain spaces because the knowledge about the problem is initially available in the environment in this form. Model-based representations are used because purely propositional representations can necessitate large amounts of computation to guarantee correct inferences (if such a guarantee is possible at all). Execution in the context of means-end analysis seems to be a natural way to inspect models so that any potentially relevant knowledge can be brought to bear. With progressive deepening, the entire state of the design does not need to continuously be kept in working memory because the relevant parts can be regenerated on each execution pass. Learning ties all this together by shifting knowledge between spaces, minimizing the expense of repeated execution, and lessening the load on limited working memory by transferring the knowledge to long-term memory. Thus, virtually every important aspect of the theory is affected by these constraints.

The implementation of the theory within DESIGNER-SOAR demonstrates the sufficiency of the theoretical mechanisms, but currently, these results are being obtained at the price of sacrificing depth in any particular application domain. DESIGNER-SOAR does not yet have the algorithm design competence of KIDS, STRATA, or MEDUSA. It is hoped, however, that such progress will be possible using the framework presented in this chapter. This framework is generally consistent with what is known from cognitive psychology about human designers.

The framework is shaped by the necessity to cope with both diversity in knowledge and limitations on problem-solving resources. In the long run, such constraints will have a crucial impact on the structure of future design systems if they are to autonomously operate to solve genuinely new problems.

Acknowledgments

The work described in this chapter was performed while the author was a graduate student at Carnegie Mellon University's School of Computer Science. The guidance of thesis committee members Allen Newell, Elaine Kant, Tom Mitchell and Herbert Simon was invaluable.

Notes

1. The description here is of SOAR 4 (Laird 1986), which differs from the SOAR 5 version used in most research on the architecture (as of this writing).

References

Adelson, B., and Soloway, E. 1885. The Role of Domain Experience in Software Design. *IEEE Transactions on Software Engineering* SE-11(11): 1351-1360.

Aho, A.V.; Hopcroft, J. E.; and Ullman, J. D. 1974. *The Design and Analysis of Computer Algorithms.* Reading, Mass.: Addison-Wesley.

Akin, O. 1986. *The Psychology of Architectural Design.* London: Pion.

Anderson, J. R.; Farrell, R.; and Sauers, R. 1984. Learning to Program in Lisp. *Cognitive Science* 8(2): 87–129.

Anderson, J. R.; Boyle, C. F.; Farrell, R.; and Reiser, B. J. 1987. Cognitive Principles in the Design of Computer Tutors. In *Modelling Cognition.* New York: Wiley.

Balzer, R. 1985. A 15-year Perspective on Automatic Programming. *IEEE Transactions on Software Engineering* SE-11(11): 1257-1268.

Barstow, D. R. 1985. Domain-Specific Automatic Programming. *IEEE Transactions on Software Engineering* SE-11(11): 1321–1336.

Bennet, J.; Dietterich, T.; and Mostow, J. 1986. Preface. In Proceedings of the Workshop on Knowledge Compilation, iii–iv. Corvallis, Ore.: Oregon State University Dept. of Computer Science.

Brooks, R. 1975. A Model of Human Cognitive Behavior in Writing Code for Computer Programs. Ph.D. thesis, Carnegie-Mellon Univ.

de Groot, A. D. 1965. *Thought and Choice in Chess.* The Hague: Mouton.

Ericsson, K. A., and Simon, H. A. 1984. *Protocol Analysis: Verbal Reports as Data.* Cambridge, Mass.: MIT Press.

Erman, D. L.; Hayes-Roth, F.; Lesser, V. R.; and Reddy, D. R. 1980. The HEARSAY-II Speech Understanding System: Integrating Knowledge to Resolve Uncertainty. *ACM Computing Surveys* 12: 213-253

Fisher, C. A. 1988. Advancing the Study of Programming with Computer-Aided Protocol Analysis. In *Experimental Studies of Programmers: 1987 Workshop,* eds. G. Olson, E. Soloway, and S. Sheppard. Norwood, N.J.: Ablex.

Freeman, P. 1987. A Conceptual Analysis of the DRACO Approach to Constructing Software Systems. *IEEE Transactions on Software Engineering* SE-13(7): 830–844.

Friedberg, R. 1958. A Learning Machine: Part 1. *IBM Journal* 2:2-13.

Gray, W. D.; Corbett, A. T.; and Van Lehn, K. 1988. Planning and Implementation Errors in Algorithm Design. Presented at the Cognitive Science Society Conference, Montreal, Canada.

Jeffries, R.; Turner, A. A.; Polson, P. G.; Atwood, M. E. 1981. The Processes Involved in Designing Software. In *Cognitive Skills and Their Acquisition,* eds. J. R. Anderson, 255–283. Hillsdale, N.J.: Lawrence Erlbaum.

Kant, E. 1985. Understanding and Automating Algorithm Design. *IEEE Transactions on Software Engineering* SE-11(11): 1361–1374.

Kant, E., and Newell, A. 1984. Problem-Solving Techniques for the Design of Algorithms. *Information Processing and Management* 20(1–2): 97–118.

Kant, E., and Newell, A. 1983. An Automatic Algorithm Designer: An Initial Implementation. In Proceedings of the Second National Conference on Artificial Intelligence, 177–181. Menlo Park, Calif.: American Association for Artificial Intelligence.

Kant, E., and Newell, A. 1982. Naive Algorithm Design Techniques: A Case Study. Presented at the European Conference on Artificial Intelligence, July, 1982, Orsay, France.

King, J. C. 1976. Symbolic Execution and Program Testing. *Communications of the ACM* 19(7): 385-394.

Komorowski, J. 1982. Partial Evaluation as a Means for Inferencing Data Structures in an Applicative Language: A Theory and Implementation in the Case of Prolog. In Proceedings of the 1982 Principles of Programming Languages Conference, 255–267.

Laird, J. 1988. Recovery from Incorrect Knowledge in SOAR. In Proceedings of the Seventh National Conference on Artificial Intelligence, 618–623. Menlo Park, Calif.: American Association for Artificial Intelligence.

Laird, J. E. 1986. SOAR User's Manual: Version 4.0. Intelligent Systems Laboratory, Xerox Palo Alto Research Center, Palo Alto, California.

Laird, J. E., and Newell, A. 1983. A Universal Weak Method: Summary of Results. In Proceedings of the Eighth International Joint Conference on Artificial Intelligence, 771–773. Menlo Park, Calif.: International Joint Conferences on Artificial Intelligence.

Laird, J. E.; Newell, A.; and Rosenbloom, P. S. 1987. SOAR: An Architecture for General Intelligence. *Artificial Intelligence* 33(1): 1–64.

Lowry, M. R. 1988a. Invariant Logic: A Calculus for Problem Reformulation. In Proceedings of the Seventh National Conference on Artificial Intelligence, 14–18. Menlo Park, Calif.: American Association for Artificial Intelligence.

Lowry, M. R. 1988b. The Structure and Design of Local Search Algorithms. In Proceedings of the Workshop on Automating Software Design, 138–145. Palo Alto, Calif.: Kestrel Institute.

McCartney, R. D. 1987. Synthesizing Algorithms with Performance Constraints. In Proceedings of the Sixth National Conference on Artificial Intelligence, 154–159. Menlo Park, Calif.: American Association for Artificial Intelligence.

Manna, Z., and Waldinger, R. 1979. Synthesis: Dreams R Programs. *IEEE Transactions on Software Engineering* SE-5(4): 294–328.

Mostow, J. 1986. Why Are Design Derivations Hard to Replay? In *Machine Learning: A Guide to Current Research*, eds. T. M. Mitchell, J. G. Carbonell, and R. S. Michalski, 213–218. Boston: Kluwer Academic.

Newell, A. 1969. Heuristic Programming: Ill-Structured Problems. In *Progress in Operations Research,* ed. J. Aronofsky, 360–414. New York: Wiley.

Newell, A., and Simon, H. A. 1972. *Human Problem Solving*. Englewood Cliffs, N.J.: Prentice-Hall.

Rosenbloom, P. S., and Laird, J. E. 1986. Mapping Explanation-Based Generalization onto SOAR. In Proceedings of the Fifth National Conference on Artificial Intelligence, 561–567. Menlo Park, Calif.: American Association for Artificial Intelligence.

Rosenbloom, P. S.; Laird, J. E.; McDermott, J.; Newell, A.; and Orciuch, E. 1985. R1-SOAR: An Experiment in Knowledge-Intensive Programming in a Problem-Solving Architecture. *IEEE Transactions on Pattern Analysis and Machine Intelligence* 7(5): 561–569.

Rychener, M. D.; Farinacci, M. L.; Hulthage, I.; and Fox, M. 1986. Integration of Multiple Knowledge Sources in Aladin, An Alloy Design System. In Proceedings of the Sixth National Conference on Artificial Intelligence, 878–882. Menlo Park, Calif.: American Association for Artificial Intelligence.

Sedgewick, R. 1983. *Algorithms*. Reading, Mass.: Addison-Wesley.

Shavlik, J. , and Maclin, R. 1988. An Approach to Acquiring Algorithms by Observing Expert Behavior. In Proceedings of the Workshop on Automating Software Design. Palo Alto, Calif.: Kestrel Institute.

Shrobe, H. E. 1979. Dependency-Directed Reasoning for Complex Program Understanding, Technical Report, AI-TR 503, Massachusetts Institute of Technology.

Simon, H. A. 1972. The Heuristic Compiler. In *Representation and Meaning: Experiments with Information Processing Systems,* eds. H. A. Simon, and L. Siklossy, 9–43. Englewood Cliffs, N.J.: Prentice-Hall.

Smith, D. R. 1988. KIDS—A Knowledge-Based Software Development System. In Proceedings of the Workshop on Automating Software Design, 129–135. Palo Alto, Calif.: Kestrel Institute.

Smith, D. R. 1985. Top-Down Synthesis of Divide-and-Conquer Algorithms. *Artificial Intelligence* 27(1): 43–96.

Steier, D. M. 1989. Automating Algorithm Design within an Architecture for General Intelligence. Ph.D. thesis, School of Computer Science, Carnegie Mellon Univ.

Steier, D. M., and Kant, E. 1985. The Roles of Execution and Analysis in Algorithm Design. *IEEE Transactions on Software Engineering* SE-11(11): 1375–1386.

Sussman, G. J. 1975. *A Computer Model of Skill Acquisition*. New York: Elsevier.

Tambe, M.; Kalp, D.; Gupta, A.; Forgy, C. L.; Milnes, B. G.; and Newell, A. 1988. SOAR/PSM-E: Investigating Match Parallelism in a Learning Production System. In Proceedings of the ACM/SIGPLAN Symposium on Parallel Programming: Experience with Applications, Languages, and Systems, 146–160. New York: Association of Computing Machinery.

Tappel, S. 1980. Some Algorithm design Methods. In Proceedings of the First National Conference on Artificial Intelligence, 66-64. Menlo Park, Calif.: American Association for Artificial Intelligence

Ullman, D. G.,;Dietterich, T. G.; and Stauffer, L. A. 1988. A Model of the Mechanical Design Process Based on Empirical Data, Technical Report, DPRG-88-1, Design Process Research Group, Oregon State Univ.

Unruh, A.; Rosenbloom, P. S.; and Laird, J. E. 1987. Dynamic Abstraction Problem Solving in SOAR. In Proceedings of the Third Annual Conference on Aerospace Applications of Artificial Intelligence, 245–256. Dayton, Oh.: Dayton Special Interest Group for Artificial Intelligence.

Zave, P., and Schell, W. 1986. Salient Features of an Executable Specification Language and Its Environment. *IEEE Transactions on Software Engineering* SE-12(2): 312–385.

23

Representing Software Designs as Partially Developed Plans

Theodore A. Linden

Programming and planning are analogous activities. I have used transformational synthesis and other ideas from programming research to build several large, real planning applications. Conversely, ideas from planning research apply to the problems of designing extensible software applications and representing the knowledge that exists during the early stages of software design.

Recent planning research addresses the problem of developing partial plans when one has only incomplete information about the goals and the environment in which the plan will execute. A key problem is the knowledge representations needed so that partial plans can be extended as additional knowledge about goals and the environment is obtained. A partial plan needs to capture the plan's goal structures, abstraction levels, dependencies, resource requirements, alternatives, partial decisions, and uncertainties. I propose that similar knowledge-based representations of software designs will allow software systems to deal with evolving requirements.

I begin this chapter by exploring the analogy between planning and extensible programming, and develop the hypothesis that recent results on planning by transformational synthesis can be transferred to the problem of designing software systems that have evolving requirements. Next, I argue that extensible, reusable software is a critical problem that requires knowledge-intensive, opportunistic software development methods, similar to the methods used in recent large planning applications. I summarize recent planning paradigms that are applicable to software design, and characterize them in terms of the kinds of knowledge and knowledge representations they exploit. I cover lessons learned from using transformation synthesis in a series of large planning applications. I argue that the early design of many extensible software applications can be expressed best as a set of transformations acting on a declarative representation of the objects involved in the application's problem space. Finally, I identify the kinds of information about a plan or program that needs to be represented declaratively if the plan or program is to be developed incrementally, extended, and modified for reuse in a different context.

Planning and Programming—A Perspective

At a high level of abstraction, planning and programming are the same: In both, we begin from a set of goals, initial conditions, and primitive operations, and we want to produce a composition of operations that will accomplish the given goals. The goals of a plan correspond to the requirements specification of a program, plans correspond to programs (where a program is a single release of an evolving software system), and the automated planning software corresponds to automated programming tools.

Work on automation of both planning and programming has a common origin in the late 1960s and early 1970s; but, as the two fields moved beyond generic, weak methods and searched for more efficient, knowledge-intensive methods, they explored different approaches. There is now a growing convergence between AI planning technology and that portion of programming technology that deals with programs that have to be extensible over a long life cycle. At some risk of oversimplification, this convergence is illustrated in figure 1. Until recently, most work on knowledge-based planning—together with some work on automatic programming—differed from most work on application programming in two dimensions: problem generality and solution approach.

In the dimension of problem generality, planning systems solve a wide range of problems; for example, a planner for a robot is expected to deal with every situation that the robot might encounter. Large-scale programming methodologies have emphasized narrowly defined requirements specifications where all possible future situations are anticipated.

In the dimension of solution approach, classical planning focused on generic problem-solving methods, and the field moved slowly toward the more knowledge-intensive methods that are computationally tractable for

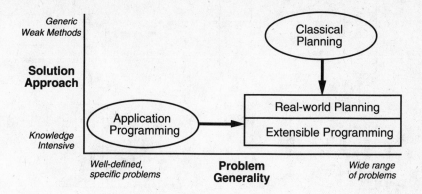

Figure 1. Convergence between Planning and Programming

large problems. Meanwhile, application programming focused on efficient, knowledge-intensive, problem-specific solutions. Unfortunately, when many application-specific details are allowed to permeate the entire solution in an unstructured and uncontrolled manner, generality is lost, and extensibility becomes difficult.

As planning systems move toward solutions that are practical for large-scale problems, they are developing efficient, knowledge-intensive techniques that depend on limited features of the problem space, and they are finding ways to exploit domain-specific knowledge without seriously compromising the generality and extensibility of the planning system. Meanwhile, the design of application programs is driven more and more by generic problems where the key requirements are extensibility and maintainability in the face of unforeseeable needs. Both real-world planning and extensible programming research are now exploring efficient, knowledge-intensive, reusable solutions for general problems, as shown in the lower right corner of figure 1; it will be useful to exploit the insights from both fields as they converge.

Other historical differences between planning systems and extensible software systems are also disappearing:

First is reuse versus regeneration. Until recently, most planning systems have regenerated plans from scratch for each new situation; meanwhile, software systems are extended for each new release. This difference is disappearing as planning research emphasizes replanning and reuse and as transformational implementations of program specifications allow new programs to be generated for each new specification by replaying the transformational derivation history (chapter 5).

Second is partial automation. Classical plan generation is fully automatic, but successive releases of large software systems depend on extensive manual

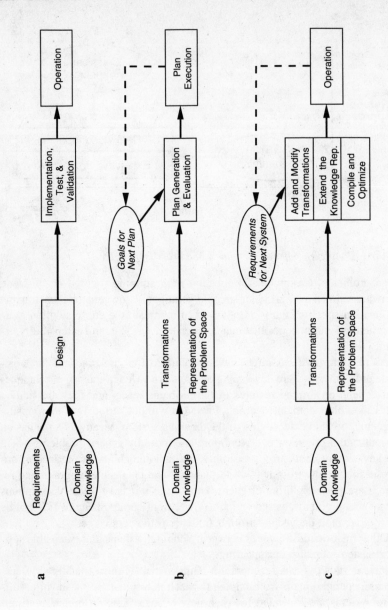

Figure 2a. Simplified Waterfall Model of the Software Life Cycle.

Figure 2b. In Planning Systems, Specific Goals Known Late in the Life Cycle.

Figure 2c. For Extensible Software, Requirements for Future Releases Incrementally Known.

work by programmers. Again, this distinction is rapidly disappearing. Real-world planning applications are often interactive and involve humans in many of the planning decisions, and this book is evidence of the research underway to reduce the amount of manual work that goes into software development.

Third is predictability and uncertainty. Recent planning research has begun to deal with the problem of planning while making limited assumptions about the actions of other agents and the success of one's own operations. For example, a robot trying to lift a box should recover after the box slips from its grasp; and multiple cooperating robots should make limited assumptions about the expected behavior of other robots. These planning results are mildly relevant to programming in the small, but they are very relevant to programming in the large where it is unrealistic to expect that one's own or other software modules will behave predictably and infallibly.

One of the ways that planning systems deal with general problems is by accepting goals and requirements as input parameters. This approach is the same as automatic program synthesis systems but different from application programming where the software engineer is encouraged to begin by defining the software goals, environment, and performance as narrowly as possible in a requirements specification. Figures 2a–c illustrates this difference and the analogy between planning and extensible software life cycles. Figure 2a shows a simplified waterfall model of the software life cycle that does not explicitly deal with iterative releases and enhancements to the software. Figure 2b shows a planning system life cycle, where goals (which correspond to the requirements in the software life cycle) do not arrive until just before a plan is generated. To accommodate the late arrival of the goals, the design of the planning system is shown as transformations on a declarative representation of the problem space (as discussed in a later section on Software Designs as Transformations on a Knowledge Base). Figure 2c shows a simplified version of a proposed software life cycle model that is analogous to figure 2a and deals with incrementally arriving requirements.

Figure 2c oversimplifies the situation by assuming that all the domain knowledge and none of the requirements are known in advance. In practice, additional domain knowledge, requirements, and information about the execution environment are developed throughout the software life cycle, and one needs an opportunistic approach to software development to take advantage of this knowledge as it becomes available.

Knowledge-Intensive, Opportunistic Development of Extensible Software

Solutions for most well-defined, stable software problems were implemented by the computer programmers of the 1960s and 1970s. For the new software design challenges that we face in the 1990s, we should not expect that a requirements specification will be stable over the life cycle of the application. Major extensions and revisions in function should be expected, and the meta-requirement that the system support extensions to vaguely foreseen requirements often drives the design more than any specific functional requirements. Of course, we are also finding that many of the problems that were solved in the past are not as well defined as we had believed, and today, much effort goes into maintaining and extending old programs where most of the critical design information was not captured during its development and must now be reconstructed (chapter 1).

In actual practice, the best software designers spend much of their design time deciding how they can avoid making decisions that would constrain the future extensibility of the software; however, the models of the software development process that we were taught emphasize the development of complete specifications during the early stages of a software project. Often, it is more important to record what has not been decided, deliberately defer making some decisions, and prevent components of the software from becoming dependent on decisions that might change.

Even the *spiral development model* (Boehm 1988), which recognizes the need for rapid prototyping and iterative development, needs to be supplemented by research that specifically deals with the problem of designing and implementing programs that can be reused in future iterations. We have procedural encapsulation, abstraction, information hiding, and other techniques that localize the effect of software changes, but we need even more flexible software design techniques that allow software to evolve and allow us to bind the decisions needed to implement the next release without implicitly committing to these decisions for the entire software life cycle.

When one is designing software to meet evolving requirements, there is a question about how to make progress on the software design before one has well-defined requirements. Experience with planning applications can help answer this question because planning systems have to be designed and implemented before specific goals are known. In practice, there is always knowledge about the application domain, about appropriate planning processes, and about the structure of the problem space that can be captured and formally defined. Much of this knowledge—especially the knowledge structures and the abstractions involved—remains stable over the software life cycle and can be the basis for software design decisions. In the next section, I argue that different planning techniques can be viewed as ways of taking advantage of the different kinds of knowledge that are available in different planning problems.

To the extent that software development is analogous to planning, a software project should focus first on obtaining and defining whatever knowledge will be stable over the application's life cycle. Traditionally, we assumed that a requirements specification is stable, but often, it is not. Alternative knowledge that might be stable includes various forms of knowledge about the application domain (Barstow 1984), the software-execution environments, or appropriate problem-solving strategies. Usually, there is stable knowledge about domain objects and relationships between them that can be captured in a declarative representation. Operations for manipulating these objects are often stable and can be defined using existing object-oriented programming techniques. Often, there is stable knowledge about useful abstractions. In practice, some (but not all) of the requirements are known and can be expected to be stable. Sometimes there is a natural and stable decomposition of the problem space into subproblems that can be used in the design. Domain-independent knowledge about design and programming methods is also a subject of ongoing research (chapter 20; Rich and Waters 1990) and can be exploited during opportunistic design processes.

Experience from planning applications indicates that the kinds of knowledge that are available and stable varies with the application. Thus, the software design process needs to be opportunistic, so the designers can react to, and take advantage of, the knowledge that is available. There is recent recognition in the software-engineering literature that what humans do during software design is to follow an opportunistic methodology: "The generation of opportunistic solutions at different levels of detail accompanied by problem domain modeling had not been observed in previous empirical studies nor had [it] been acknowledged in the software engineering practices" (Guindon and Curtis 1988).

Because each software project needs to follow its own development path in order to take advantage of the knowledge that is available, each project has a planning problem to plan its own development path. This project planning is another point where planning research can support software development. Thoughts about structuring this project planning problem with goals and tasks defined in a four-dimensional space of software definition, formalization, operationalism, and performance is covered in Linden (1990).

An opportunistic approach to the design of extensible software is required because software design is not like designing a fixed artifact. Software can evolve, and it should be designed with future change in mind. I believe that past efforts to introduce more discipline into software development by drawing analogies between software development and the engineering design of bridges, buildings, or electronic circuits will ultimately prove misguided. Software is uniquely able to adapt to changing circumstances, and we should not accept the unnecessary limitation that software is to be designed as a relatively unchangeable object. The early phase of software design is not analogous to most engineering design disciplines (except possibly for genetic engineering); software design is planning for the unforeseeable future. A better analogy for software design is the planning that takes place when founding a new organization or company. One does develop plans, establish goals, and begin the implementation; however, one does not make unchangeable decisions about the management structure of the organization or the future products of the company. Similarly, software designers have to make enough decisions to get the implementation effort underway, but the decisions that are explicitly deferred are often more important than the decisions that are made at the outset.

Useful Paradigms from Planning Research

Recent research in planning is developing general problem solvers that combine generic methods with more efficient methods that depend on features of the problem space and use compiled knowledge to cut lengthy reasoning processes. The knowledge needed to generate plans efficiently can come in many different forms, and it is useful to characterize recently developed planning paradigms in terms of the kinds of knowledge that the paradigms assume is available and the kinds of knowledge representations that they use.

Available planning paradigms that can be used to automate software design are no longer limited to classical methods such as means-ends analysis, goal regression, forward chaining, and refinement of abstractions (Sacerdoti 1977). They include opportunistic island growing, constraint-directed reasoning, case-based reasoning, reactive planning, and automated plan debugging.

As a planning paradigm, *opportunistic island growing* (Hayes-Roth, Rosenschein, and Cammarata 1979) develops the different components of the plan as the knowledge to make the planning decisions becomes available. In the previous section, I argued that this paradigm is appropriate for software design and is characteristic of the way humans do software design. Opportunistic design is often advocated in connection with blackboard systems (Jagannathan, Dodhiawala, and Baum 1989), but it is equally compatible with high-level transformational approaches to planning and design (Planning by Transformational Synthesis; Linden 1989), and the knowledge-based refinement paradigm (chapter 5).

Constraint-directed reasoning is used in a variety of large planning and scheduling applications (Fox 1987; Fox, Sadeh, and Baykan 1989) to take advantage of the structure or texture of specific problem spaces. The constraints capture information about the problem space that is used to direct the search for a solution. Statistics about projected resource availability or other properties of the global situation can also be gathered and used to allow local optimization decisions to be influenced by information about the big picture (Fox and Sycara 1990).

With *case-based reasoning* (Kolodner, Simpson, and Sycara 1985; Hammond 1986; Alterman 1986, 1988), plans used in previous situations (cases) are retrieved and modified for reuse in the current situation. This reuse of plans builds on previous successful experience and enables the planner to reduce the reasoning that would be required to recreate a plan from scratch.

The problem of modifying previous programs and plans to fit a new situation has long been a topic of research in programming (Dershowitz 1983) and, recently, in the planning literature. The question of when it is better to reuse versus regenerate a plan or program is also a topic of ongoing research (Mostow 1989; chapter 5).

Reactive planning is appropriate when plans or programs have to react to external events. In this case, the planning knowledge is often most easily captured in rules about what to do in different situations. These rules can also be generated automatically from higher-level descriptions of the goals and problem domain (Schoppers 1989; Rosenschein 1989).

Work on *automated plan debugging* (Simmons 1988) uses heuristic, associational rules to quickly generate an approximately correct plan and then uses deeper causal models to understand and debug the plan.

Each of these planning techniques takes advantage of certain features of the problem space or the available domain knowledge and is useful for problems or subproblems where knowledge in this form is available.

Planning by Transformational Synthesis

In work to build large planning applications where one needs to integrate different planning techniques for different aspects of the problem, I adopted the transformational approach originally developed during work on automatic programming (Partsch and Steinbruggen 1983; Fickas 1985; Balzer 1985; Smith et al. 85; Rich and Waters 1986; Agresti 1986; Lowry and Duran 1989). My work on these planning applications is an example of transferring results from software research to planning applications (Linden 1989; Linden and Markeosian 1989).

Transformational synthesis is a paradigm for constructing programs, algorithms (chapter 19), software designs (chapter 4), designs of artifacts (chapter 10), plans, and other complex conceptual objects by having them evolve through independent transformations of declarative representations of the problem space. In planning applications, the key property of the transformations is that they are independent of each other and make no implicit assumptions about the content of other transformations or about the order in which the transformations are executed (assumptions can be explicitly recorded in the transformation's preconditions). This independence is key to software generality and reuse. The transformations enable the development of efficient, knowledge-intensive planning systems because they encapsulate large chunks of reusable planning knowledge. From a formal viewpoint, verified transformations are like parameterized lemmas that can be applied at will in a powerful theorem-proving system. They allow much of the reasoning required for plan generation and replanning to be done once and then repeti-

tively reused. By embedding appropriate planning knowledge in transformations, we are able to build planning and scheduling applications that scale up
to large, real-world problems.

Experience using this transformational approach in large planning applications is relevant to the design of extensible software applications in two
ways: First, for some range of software applications that need to be flexible
and extensible, it is appropriate to design and implement the application itself as a set of transformations operating on a knowledge-based representation of the application domain. This range of applications is much broader
than just planning systems, as discussed in Software Designs as Transformations on a Knowledge Base. Second, in the use of transformations to evolve
plans, research shows that the information captured in representations of the
partially developed plans is the key to success. As discussed in Recording
Design Information within Programs, I propose that analogous information
about partially developed software systems needs to be captured in knowledge-based representations if the software is to be evolved opportunistically
and maintained and extended effectively.

When transformational synthesis is applied in planning applications, the
goals and constraints are represented as a partial plan, then planning techniques—implemented as transformations—evolve the plan into a form that
can be executed effectively. The knowledge based representations to which
the planning transformations are applied can be complex. One wants to
embed the application's complexity in the declarative representations. The
representations of the domain objects typically involve abstraction levels, resource aggregations, inheritance hierarchies, constraints, and probabilistic
representations about uncertain information. The representations for partially
developed plans are likely to include abstraction levels, goal-subgoal relationships, task-subtask relationships, task-to-goal relationships, constraints,
dependency information, alternative solution trees, and partial or probabilistic evaluations of alternative partial plans.

Experience with Planning by Transformational Synthesis

Transformational synthesis was used as the design paradigm in several planning applications described in this subsection. Most of these applications involve tens of person-years of effort over several years with the automated planning portion of the application itself requiring 1 to 10 person-years of effort.
An effective evaluation of software design methods requires experience from
large applications; unfortunately, this process is lengthy. Although this planning work on transformational synthesis has been going on for 4 years, only
the first of these applications is complete. In this subsection, I summarize the
experience and the lessons learned thus far from these applications.

The first planning application that used a transformational synthesis approach was the Multivehicle Mission Planner developed under the Defense

Advanced Research Projects Agency (DARPA) Autonomous Land Vehicle (ALV) Program (Linden and Owre 1987; Linden 1989; Linden and Markosian 1989). The plans are synthesized by transformations that evolve goals into plans, where the representation of partially developed plans includes the plan's goal structure, abstraction levels, plan alternatives, uncertainty representations, and probabilistic plan valuations. The transformations themselves elaborate and reformulate the goals, choose abstract operations to achieve the goals through a form of goal regression, search for the most effective refinement of abstract operations, evaluate alternative plans, and make minor modifications to plans to improve their cost effectiveness. These particular transformations were chosen to meet the needs of a real-world reconnaissance planning problem; the planning problem was not tailored to fit the capabilities of the transformational approach.

In other ongoing work transformational synthesis is used in the Advanced Planning System (APS) that will partially automate the daily generation of air tasking orders for Tactical Air Command Centers. This problem is a complex resource-allocation and scheduling problem with many constraints associated with choosing aircraft that are appropriate for each mission, scheduling coordinated tanker refueling and electronic countermeasure support missions, and developing schedules that minimize risks by exploiting opportunities for mutual support between missions. This application is a complex constraint-satisfaction problem, and much of the knowledge about the application is captured in constraints and evaluation functions. In this implementation, each potential resource-allocation and scheduling decision is implemented as a transformation on the state of the schedule. Each of these transformations includes a heuristic look ahead that evaluates the probable effects that this decision would have on other scheduling decisions. This look ahead is supported by statistical computations that identify critical resources in a way that is parallel to recent work by Mark Fox and others at Carnegie-Mellon University (Fox, Sadeh, and Baykan 1989; Fox and Sycara 1990). Metalevel reasoning chooses which transformations are best to apply next. Typically, the metalevel reasoning favors transformations where there is strong evidence for the decision to be made and where the resources to be used are projected as less critical for other missions. Alternatively, the metalevel reasoning can favor transformations that optimize the use of bottleneck resources. For this application, I expect that with a good ordering of the planning and scheduling decisions, it will be possible to generate good schedules without any chronological backtracking. (Chronological backtracking is usually not acceptable when multiple users are cooperating to generate the plan interactively.) The system design does include plan critics that can revise and adjust previous scheduling decisions.

Another feature of this problem is the need for *mixed-initiative planning*, where any planning or scheduling decision can be made by either a human or the automated planner. Because the human planners participate in the planning process, they have to be able to interact with the plan as it evolves during a planning session. The interactive planning has led to a strong emphasis on abstraction in the representation of the intermediate states that occur as a planning session progresses. Mixed-initiative planning requires high-level modeling of the concepts that the humans actually use while they plan.

Another ongoing application of transformational synthesis to a planning problem is for DARPA's Submarine Operational Automation System (SOAS) Program. A key problem in this application is the integration of long-range and reactive planning. In the initial implementation, plans are represented using reactive action packages (RAPs) (Firby 1989), which can be viewed as a language suitable for programming the reactive behaviors of agents operating in complex, dynamic environments. The first phase of this effort produced a reimplementation of RAPs and included transformations that generate a simple RAP at run time. A second phase is now under way and will produce a more complete prototype planning system with transformational synthesis being used to automatically generate reactive plans.

Another application of transformational synthesis, is resource allocation and scheduling of military transportation assets. This research focuses on the reuse and extension of previously developed plans, planning methods, and programs. In all these planning applications, the key to success is in the representation of the problem space and the intermediate states of the plan together with the goal structure, abstractions, dependencies, resources, alternatives, partial decisions, and uncertainties that need to be reasoned about as the plan evolves. Similar representation techniques were used in work on DARPA's AirLand Battle Management (ALBM) Program, where a three-year project to demonstrate the effectiveness of automated planning to assist Army Corps–level staff planners was recently completed (Stachnick and Abram 1988).

Lessons from Planning Research

In these planning applications, the domain information and partially evolved plans are represented in a knowledge base. There are two keys to success in these applications: First, the planning transformations are applied to partial plans that include explicit representations not just for the operations to be performed but also for the goals, subgoals, constraints, abstraction levels, dependencies, resource requirements, alternatives, partial decisions, and uncertainties applicable for each subcomponent of the plan. Second, knowledge obtained from the human expert planners in the domain is used to encode domain-specific planning shortcuts that are implemented as plan transformations. These domain-specific heuristic planning methods are combined with domain-independent methods.

Each of these applications is different in terms of the specific planning techniques that are appropriate for the application and the form of the ex-

perts' knowledge that is available. The ALV and ALBM applications involve plans with complex goals, multiple abstraction levels, and reasoning
about sequences of actions to be performed by multiple agents. A simplifying feature of these applications is that control structures for the planning process can be decided at design time based on knowledge engineering that extracts the planning processes actually followed by expert human
planners in the domain. The planning process control has to be highly
conditional so that it can adapt to the particular planning situation; however, the adaptability that is appropriate does not require much explicit metalevel control reasoning at run time.

In APS, the structure of the plans being developed is much simpler
(the complexity arises from resource allocation and scheduling constraints, not from variability in the structure of the plans), and much of
the domain knowledge is naturally expressed as constraints. Manual
planning processes in the APS domain do adapt to the constraints that
are most critical, and automation of APS uses metalevel reasoning to decide the order in which resource-allocation and scheduling decisions can
best be made.

With the SOAS project, much of the focus is on the selection and execution of reactive plans. Much of the domain knowledge can naturally be expressed as reactive plan fragments (in this situation, a commander would do
such and such), so many of the reactive plans are naturally built in as part of
the system's knowledge base. Some of the reactive plans need to be generated automatically as the system is executing. Route plans are a good example
because they are difficult to express as conjunctions of rules that associate
actions with situations, and RAPs that express route plans for the submarine
are best developed in the run-time situation.

An overall lesson from these applications is that the most effective way to
express the available domain knowledge is different for different applications.
Sometimes it is most effective to directly embed the domain knowledge in
reusable plan fragments, sometimes it is best to use it to drive the processes
that generate plans, and sometimes domain knowledge is best expressed as
constraints that are used at a metalevel to control the planning processes. A
given application can involve domain knowledge that is best expressed in
each of these ways, and transformational synthesis provides a viewpoint that
makes it easy to include domain knowledge in any or all of these forms.

Software Design as Transformations on a Knowledge Base

The applications just discussed are all planning systems, but I propose that
the transformational synthesis paradigm is appropriate for the early design of
many extensible software applications. Recall that using the transformational
paradigm in the actual design of a software application (where the transfor-

mations act on a declarative representation of the application domain) is distinct from using transformations to generate and modify the design (where the transformations act on a representation of the software design). The first case is discussed in this section; design representations needed for the second case are identified in the following section.

I discuss the advantages of designing applications as a set of transformations on a declarative representation by considering the example of text editors. It is relatively easy to program a simple text editor and then extend the editor by incrementally adding functionality. The large-scale life cycle of most text editors does not follow a waterfall model; rather, it involves a series of releases with incremental functionality driven by user feedback about the previous release. In most cases, the previous editor is extended for the new release, although occasional redesign and reimplementation might be necessary—especially when it is necessary to modify the declarative representations. The small-scale life cycle for a single release might follow a waterfall model.

I argue that it is relatively easy to extend text editors because the natural design of a text editor involves a set of independent functions that operate on a well-defined, declarative representation. Because the editing functions can be invoked by users in any order, they must be programmed so that they make no assumptions about the relative order in which they are invoked. As long as one does not need to change the representation of the document, it is relatively easy to add editor functions and modify existing functions. There is some function sharing in editors; for example, both the find and the change commands will share code for searching through the document, but relative to most software, this function sharing is limited. Furthermore, there is a direct, almost one-to-one relationship between requirements and the functions that implement them. All these properties are reasons why text editors are examples of extensible software.

Transformational design is a way to achieve extensibility in other software applications where the application might not directly force a design consisting of a set of representation choices, a set of independent operations that evolve these representations, and an independent source of control decisions for invoking the operations. In these other applications, the representations that are manipulated by transformations can become complex. Sophisticated text editors such as WYSIWYG editors are still extensible even though their document representations are complex. In planning applications, declarative representations capture information about goal hierarchies, task hierarchies, resource hierarchies, task-to-goal relationships, and alternative partial solutions. The representations support information hiding, declarative constraints, and automatic constraint propagation. Similarly complex knowledge representations are needed to support transformational designs for many other kinds of applications. Furthermore, the transformations themselves can have a hierarchical structure with some transformations triggering sets of lower-level transformations.

A key characteristic of transformational design is that it allows deferred binding of control-flow decisions. A simple implementation of a transformational design can use pattern matching to invoke the transformations; however, the control decisions can also be bound during the latter stages of the software design, or they can be bound by metalevel control reasoning to invoke the transformations at run time. Often, much more information is available to make appropriate control-flow decisions during the latter stages of implementing a large software application. As long as the transformations themselves still do not make implicit assumptions about the control flow, then it is usually possible to extend an application by extending the declarative representation, adding or modifying transformations, and then redoing the control-flow bindings. When program changes are limited to extensions of data structures and the addition and modification of transformations, it is relatively easy to control the indirect effects of the changes. See Moriconi and Winkler (1990) for deeper reasoning methods to determine limits on the possible effects of program changes; the conservative approach of extending declarative data structures, adding and modifying transformations, and reoptimizing the control flow is illustrated in figure 2c.

By deferring control-flow decisions, the transformational paradigm is different from the usual box-and-arrow approach to software design that focuses much of the early design effort on the control flow. The transformational paradigm is compatible with data flow design methods. It also builds on object-oriented programming, which can be used for defining the objects that the transformations operate on together with appropriate abstraction levels and information hiding for these objects. A transformational design is also quite similar to a specification written in the UNITY specification language (Chandy and Misra 88) with UNITY statements corresponding to transformations. The logic for reasoning about UNITY specifications could be used to reason about invariants, progress properties, and the termination of transformational designs.

It is hard to characterize precisely the software applications for which a transformational design is appropriate. It is probably not appropriate as the top-level design when there is a natural and stable decomposition of the problem into subproblems or when there is a natural and stable procedural solution to the problem. In both cases, the design should take advantage of this natural task decomposition or procedural solution, but then a transformational design might still be appropriate for each of the component tasks.

Because much of the point to a transformational approach is that it allows control decisions to be deferred, a transformational design is not appropriate when there is a dominating concern to decide whether execution-time performance will be feasible. Early experimentation with control decisions is required here. However, a transformational design need not lead to poor execution-time performance. If control decisions are deferred until the later stages of the design without eliminating control-flow options, then performance can be better than with other design methods that force designers to make many of the control decisions early when less information is available to make them effectively. Many optimization techniques, such as the automated introduction of function sharing (chapter 15), can also be exploited in the context of a transformational design.

Recording Design Information within Programs

In this section, I cover some of the representations for partial plans that are used in planning applications, and I discuss the feasibility of capturing analogous information about software designs. The first two subsections discuss the practicality of explicitly capturing the detailed goal structure of a program (also known as a "requirements trace"). The third subsection uses experience from large planning applications and the analogy between planning and programming to identify other information that would support the incremental development and extension of software designs.

Representing the Goal Structure of a Program or Plan

Goals are specifications about a specific state. *Operations* change state. From a sequence of operations, a lot of information about the intermediate states can be inferred. Despite this redundancy, most practical planning applications are choosing to be explicit in representing goals not only for the final state but also for all intermediate states (see Stachnick and Abram [1988]; Linden [1989]; Schoppers [1989a]; Firby [1989]; and others). Thus, for each intermediate state at each abstraction level in the plan, there is both an operation to be performed and a set of goals to be achieved and maintained.

Several years ago during the early design work on the ALV mission planner for robotic vehicles (Linden 1989), the design team debated whether it was worth increasing the size of the plan representations by explicitly recording goals throughout the entire plan. In many cases, the information seemed redundant; for example, a goal of

$At(Robot\text{-}1, Loc\text{-}5)$

would be associated with the operation

$Move(Robot\text{-}1, Loc\text{-}3, Loc\text{-}5)$.

In some cases, the redundancy seems even worse; for example, in a software application, one might have a local goal of

$y = sin(x)$

associated with the assignment operation

$y := sin(x)$.

Despite these concerns about redundancy, the design team chose a plan representation that had two fundamental kinds of objects—operations (or tasks) and goals—and both typically appeared in pairs throughout the plans that were generated. The reasons for being explicit about representing both the operations and the goals follow:

Designer's Intent: Although the postconditions of an operation can be inferred from knowledge of the prior state and the semantics of the operation, the designer's intent is often only a subset of the postconditions, and it is only the designer's intent that must be preserved during program maintenance.

Explicit Goals of Maintenance: Goals of maintenance (constraints that are to be preserved) are typically not redundant because they are not derivable from the operations within a software module.

Goal-Directed Design: Goals can often be defined before it is appropriate to select specific operations.

Easily Extended Goals: When dealing with goals, extensibility is easy; one can add goals by logical conjunction. Meaningful extensions to a sequence of operations is much more complex.

Understanding and Reuse: The goals help in understanding the plan, and they are needed when extending the plan or reusing parts of it.

When goals are explicitly represented in the plan, then transformations can do more than just restructure the operations, as they typically do in the transformational implementation of compilers. They can also reorganize and decompose goals into separately achievable sets of goals, elaborate goals by instantiating parameters, make partial ordering decisions about the order in which goals can best be achieved, choose operations that are appropriate for achieving goals, and propagate the required preconditions in a form of goal regression.

These reasons for explicitly representing goals apply equally well to software development and argue for recording goals or assertions at many intermediate points in a program. Of course, this approach is not new to programming. The use of assertions about program states goes back to early work on formal verification. The problem is how to make it practical and cost effective to capture and represent all the subgoals and constraints.

The Complexity of Goal Structures

The extra burden involved in making explicit all the subgoals and constraints applicable at different points within a program is intuitively forbidding. Schoppers (1989b) quantifies the size of the goal structure of a typical program relative to the size of the program. He is concerned with control programs that monitor and react to external events, and the goal structure relevant to an operation is all the properties of the state that determine whether this operation is still appropriate. For example, the immediate goals of an operation and all higher-level operations are relevant to the operation (if any of these goals are already true, then it is not necessary to perform the operation). Previously achieved goals that are to be protected during an operation are also part of the goal structure of the operation. Schoppers's result is based on a number of simplifying assumptions, but under these assumptions, his argument is that for a linear program of N operations, the information content of the goal structure grows as $(4 N * ln N)$.

Although an explicit representation of the full goal structure of a program might be large, Schoppers's result indicates that its growth is only slightly worse than linear in the length of the program. The effect of modularity and other programming techniques designed to reduce the conceptual complexity of the program can further reduce this growth. This result agrees with the intuition that the amount of information needed to understand the rationale behind a program is larger than the amount of information recorded in the operations and control flow of a program—but probably not unmanageably larger.

Other evidence about the size and complexity of explicit representations of the goal structures comes from some recent practical planning applications where the goal structure of large plans is explicitly represented. For example, work on the ALBM planner indicates that reasoning about the assumptions and dependencies in an evolving corps-level battle plan—although certainly challenging—can be more computationally tractable than one might expect. The abstract design of a large software system is different from a corps-level battle plan, but both are complex, and the analogy indicates that it might be practical to record and reason about high-level software design decisions and constraints.

Representing Intermediate Stages of a Software Design

Thus far, I have discussed the goal structure of plans and programs. The analogy between planning and programming also suggests ways to capture and formally represent other information that is needed to automate opportunistic approaches to program generation and reuse, as discussed in the following paragraphs.

Explicit Assumptions about the Environment and Resource Requirements: Planning systems often have explicit representations for the assumptions that each part of the plan makes about its execution environment and about the resources it requires. These representations are needed to reuse the plan, and they also allow the agent executing the plan to check these assumptions and adapt as needed. For software, it should be equally useful to capture explicitly the assumptions that a software module makes about its environment and resource requirements. This information can be captured from the instantiated preconditions of the transformations that created the software. A smart run-time environment might use this information to check that the variables, files, and other information required by a module are available and are initialized. Explicit assumptions about required hardware resources could be used when software components are migrating among multiple processors.

Temporal Relations: Within a plan, tasks can be in a specific order because the tasks must be executed in this order, or they can be ordered simply because it was a convenient or even arbitrary ordering choice. This difference is critical when revising a plan. Furthermore, during the incremental development of the plan, it is normally useful to defer ordering choices until an ordering is forced. Thus, plans often include representations for the required temporal relationships between tasks in addition to the planned control flow. Allen's (1984) theory of time is used on the ALBM and other planning projects to represent and make inferences about required temporal relationships. Similar representations would be useful about required temporal relationships between procedures within software systems. This information is important when extending a program, and it might be checked by run-time environments to prevent certain classes of errors.

Failure Detection and Recovery: Planning systems that are to operate in unpredictable and uncertain environments build in checks to validate that planned tasks are successful. For example, a robot's tasks will typically end with a vision task that confirms successful task completion. A plan might include alternative ways to achieve a goal after a failure is detected, or a planner might develop a new plan that starts from the environment that exists after the failure. Analogously, program execution on a small scale is predictable; however, because large programs all contain bugs, the components of large software systems execute in environments that are unpredictable, and the effects of executing large-scale software operations is uncertain. There is a substantial literature on software fault detection and recovery; however, it is often difficult to analyze in advance and develop recovery strategies that are adequate to handle all possible failure combinations. An alternate approach that should be tried is to have a planning system derive a recovery strategy once the specific conditions that exist after the failure are known.

To capture information about high-level software design, one needs to decide on knowledge-based structures for representing the information. The key objects in this knowledge base are modules, goals, and resources, where the software concept of a module corresponds to a task in planning systems. The modules can be implemented using whatever high-level units of modularity are available in the underlying programming language: packages, objects, functions, procedures, modules, processes, or tasks. Here, I focus on structures for representing the early, partial design information about relationships among modules, goals, and resources that are difficult to capture in existing programming languages.

Modules, goals, and resources each have their own hierarchical structures, and interactions between these distinct hierarchies can be complex.

The analogy with planning systems suggests that a software module, when represented as an object in a knowledge base, should have the following kinds of properties and relationships to other objects. This list of properties for software modules extends analogous representations that were used in reactive action packages (Firby 1989), the task representations used on the ALBM project (Stachnick and Abram 1988), and other planning projects previously discussed.

Data and interface declarations define the syntax of the module interface and local data structures. This syntax can be represented in any existing programming language.

Goals to be achieved define the designer's intent at some level of abstraction and are stated as a conjunction of properties about software data structures or external conditions to be achieved.

Preconditions are properties that must be achieved before the module can be invoked.

Constraints and invariants are properties that must be preserved by the module throughout its execution. Unlike preconditions, constraints and invariants automatically propagate to all submodules or subtasks. The preconditions, constraints, and invariants are the primary way of documenting the assumptions that the whole module makes about its environment.

Success criteria are executable tests that can determine whether module operations successfully completed.

The *resources* required define the assumptions that the module makes about the availability of processors, devices, files, supporting software components, execution time, and other resources.

Temporal dependencies define the required temporal relationships with other module executions and can be defined using Allen's theory of time or another approach toward reasoning about temporal relationships.

Semantic specification defines the semantics of the module operation using some high-level specification language such as UNITY (Chandy and Misra 1988).

Implementations are a collection of one or more alternative implementations for each interface function that have preconditions and are either programs expressed in a standard programming language or a collection of submodules (subtasks) with an associated control specification. The control specification could itself be a task that generates the required control decisions at run time.

In most existing programming languages, the information that can formally be represented about a module is typically limited to (1) data and interface definitions, (2) constraints that are usually limited to import-export restrictions, and (3) a single implementation for each of the functions in the interface specification.

The additional attributes previously listed provide opportunities to record design information that is usually left implicit or informal. Some of it can be generated from program text once the implementation is complete; however, the goals, constraints, and other proposed attributes of a module provide an opportunity to record partial decisions before the implementation is complete. They also allow opportunistic reasoning that can develop modules and information about them in different orders depending on the circumstances. For example, one part of a design might proceed by decomposing goals into subgoals and then to module definitions; another part might proceed from goals to high-level modules and then to submodules; and other parts might proceed bottom up, starting from implementations of modules that are expected to prove useful.

Conclusions

Lessons from recent research on knowledge-based planning can be transferred to better understand the kinds of software designs and the knowledge representations that are needed to support the development of extensible software systems. Software designs are complex, and more early design information needs to be captured whether the software design process is manual or partially automated. Furthermore, if software is to be extensible, then the software designs themselves need to be structured to reduce the dependencies between software components. In particular, early design decisions should minimize these dependencies. Control-flow decisions can be deferred by using a transformational design for the early phase of software design. An early design that consists of declarative data representations, together with a set of independent transformations can minimize the dependencies that are built deeply into the software design. Additional dependencies are introduced as control-flow decisions are made, and the software is optimized; however, it is usually best to avoid embedding these kinds of dependencies in the basic software design.

The representation for capturing early software design decisions should allow the designer to record many different kinds of partial design decisions—with the human designers and their automated assistants having the freedom to make design decisions and propagate their effects in an order that is appropriate for the particular application.

Acknowledgments

Karl Levitt helped formulate the idea of planning by transformational synthesis, and Sam Owre developed the first implementation of the idea. For stimulating discussions of ideas covered in this article and comments on early drafts, I am grateful to Cordell Green, Robert Hall, Barry Leiner, Mike Lowry, Larry Markosian, Bob Riemenschneider, Marcel Schoppers, and Douglas Smith. For their cooperative work on the design of one or more of the planning systems described in this chapter, I am indebted to Tom Adams, Ken Allison, David Gaw, Franz Hatfield, Jack Murphy, Roland Payne, and Greg Stachnick.

References

Agresti, W. W. 1986. *New Paradigms for Software Development*. IEEE Computer Society Tutorial, Washington, D.C.: IEEE Computer Society..

Allen, J. F. 1984. Toward a General Theory of Action and Time. *Artificial Intelligence* 23(2): 123–154.

Alterman, R. 1988. Adaptive Planning. *Cognitive Science* 12:393–421.

Alterman, R. 1986. An Adaptive Planner. In Proceedings of the Fifth National Conference on Artificial Intelligence, 65–71. Menlo Park, Calif.: American Association for Artificial Intelligence.

Balzer, R. 1985. A 15-Year Perspective on Automatic Programming." *IEEE Transactions on Software Engineering* SE-11(11): 1257–1268.

Boehm, E. W. 1988. A Spiral Model of Software Development and Enhancement. *IEEE Computer* 21(5): 61–72.

Chandy, K. M., and Misra, J. 1988. *Parallel Program Design, A Foundation*. Reading. Mass.: Addison-Wesley.

Dershowitz, N. 1989. *The Evolution of Programs*. Boston, Mass.: Birhauser.

Fickas, S. F. 1985. Automating the Transformational Development of Software. *IEEE Transactions on Software Engineering* 11(11): 1268–1277.

Firby, R. J. 1989. Adaptive Execution in Complex Dynamic Worlds. Ph.D. thesis, Yale Univ.

Fox, M. S. 1987. *Constraint-Directed Search: A Case Study of Job-Shop Scheduling*. San Mateo, Calif.: Morgan Kaufmann.

Fox, M. S., and Sycara, K. 1990. Knowledge-Based Logistics Planning and Its Application in Manufacturing and Strategic Planning, RADC-TR-89-215, Rome Air Development Center.

Fox, M. S.; Sadeh, N.; Baykan, C. 1989. Constrained Heuristic Search. In Proceedings of the Eleventh International Joint Conference on Artificial Intelligence, 309–315. Menlo Park, Calif.: International Joint Conferences on Artificial Intelligence.

Guindon, R., and Curtis, B. 1988. Control of Cognitive Processes during Software Design: What Tools Are Needed? In Proceedings of CHI'88. New York: Association of Computing Machinery.

Hammond, K. 1986. Case-Based Planning, An Integrated Theory of Planning, Learning, and Memory. Ph.D. thesis, Yale Univ.

Hayes-Roth, B.; Rosenschein, S.; and Cammarata, S. 1979. Modelling Planning as an Incremental, Opportunistic Process. In Proceedings of the Sixth International Joint Conference on Artificial Intelligence, 375–383. Menlo Park, Calif.: International Joint Conferences on Artificial Intelligence.

Jagannathan, V.; Dodhiawala, R.; and Baum, L. S. 1989. *Blackboard Architectures and Applications*. San Diego, Calif.: Academic.

Kolodner, J. L.; Simpson, R. L.; and Sycara, K. 1985. A Process Model of Case-Based Reasoning in Problem Solving. In Proceedings of the Ninth International Joint Conference on Artificial Intelligence, 284–290. Menlo Park, Calif.: International Joint Conferences on Artificial Intelligence.

Linden, T. A. 1990. A Metalevel Software Development Model That Supports V&V for AI Software. In *Expert Systems with Applications*, volume 1, 271-279. Norwood, N.J.: Pergamon.

Linden, T. A. 1989. Planning by Transformational Synthesis *IEEE Expert* 4(2): 46–55.

Linden, T. A., and Markosian, L. Z. 1989. Transformational Synthesis Using Refine. *AI Tools and Techniques*, ed. M. Richer, 261–286. Norwood, N.J.: Ablex.

Linden, T. A., and Owre, S. 1987. Transformational Synthesis Applied to ALV Mission Planning. In Proceedings of the DARPA Knowledge-Based Planning Workshop, 21-1–21-11.

Moriconi, M., and Winkler, T. C. 1990. Approximate Reasoning about the Semantic Effects of Program Changes. *IEEE Transactions on Software Engineering* (Special Issue on Formal Methods) 16(9): 980–992.

Mostow, J. 1989. Design by Derivational Analogy *Artificial Intelligence* 40(1–3):119–184.

Partsch, H., and Steinbruggen, R. 1983. Program Transformation Systems. *ACM Computing Surveys* 15(3): 199–236.

Rich, C., and Waters, R. C. 1990. *The Programmer's Apprentice*. Reading, Mass.: Addison-Wesley. Co.

Rich, C., and Waters, R. C., eds. 1986. *Readings in Artificial Intelligence and Software Engineering*. San Mateo, Calif.: Morgan Kaufmann.

Rosenschein, S. J., 1989. Synthesizing Information-Tracking Automata from Environment Descriptions. In *Proceedings of the First International Conference on Principles of Knowledge Representation and Reasoning*, 386–393. San Mateo, Calif.: Morgan Kaufmann.

Sacerdoti, E. D. 1977. *A Structure for Plans and Behavior*. Amsterdam: North Holland.

Schoppers, M. J. 1989a. Representation and Automatic Synthesis of Reaction Plans, Ph.D. thesis, Dept. of Computer Science, Univ. of Illinois.

Schoppers, M. J. 1989b. Sensory Bandwidth and the Information Content of Goal Structures. *International Journal of Expert Systems* 2(3): 257–292.

Simmons, R. G. 1988. A Theory of Debugging Plans and Interpretations. In Proceedings of the Seventh National Conference on Artificial Intelligence, 94–99. Menlo Park, Calif.: American Association for Artificial Intelligence.

Smith, D. R. 1990. KIDS: A Semi-Automated Program Development System. *IEEE Transactions on Software Engineering* (Special Issue on Formal Methods) 16(9): 1024–1043.

Stachnick, G.L., and Abram, J. M. 1989. Army Maneuver Planning: A Procedural Reasoning Approach. In *The Science of Command and Control: Coping with Uncertainty*, volume 2, eds. S. E. Johnson and A. Levis. Fairfax, Va.: AFCEA International.

24

Software Engineering in the Twenty-First Century

Michael R. Lowry

By the year 2000, there will be a large potential market and a fertile environment for knowledge-based software engineering (KBSE). In the coming decade, hardware improvements will stimulate demand for large and sophisticated application software, while standardization of software interfaces and operating systems will intensify competition among software developers. In this environment, developers who can rapidly create robust and error-free software will flourish. Developers who deliver buggy software years behind schedule, as is typical today, will perish. To meet this challenge, software developers will seek tools and methods to automate software design.

Computer-aided software engineering (CASE) is undergoing tremendous commercial growth. However, the current generation of case tools are limited by shallow representations and shallow reasoning methods. CASE tools will either evolve into or be replaced by tools with deeper representations and more sophisticated reasoning methods. The enabling technology will come from AI, formal methods, programming language theory, and other areas of computer science. This technology will enable much of the knowledge now lost in the software development process to be captured in machine encoded form and automated. KBSE will revolutionize software design, just as computer-aided design has revolutionized hardware design, and desktop publishing has revolutionized publication design.

This conclusion draws on the chapters in this book and other sources to present one vision of the future evolution of KBSE. After an executive summary and a brief history of software engineering, the role of AI technology is examined in mainstream software engineering today. Currently, AI programming environments facilitate rapid prototyping but do not produce efficient, production-quality code. KBSE technology combines the advantages of rapid prototyping and efficient code in a new programming paradigm: transformational programming, described in the subsequent part of the conclusion. In transformational programming, prototyping, validation, and modifications are done at the specification level; automatic program synthesis then translates specifications into efficient code. The following part compares the trade-offs in various approaches to program synthesis. Then several near-term commercial applications of KBSE technology are predicted for the next decade. To scale up from these near-term applications to revolutionizing the entire software lifecycle in the next century, the computational requirements of KBSE technology need to be addressed. An examination of current benchmarks reveals that hardware performance by the year 2000 is not likely to be a limiting factor, but that fundamental issues such as search control require further research. Finally, the future of KBSE in the next century is presented from the viewpoint of different people in the software lifecycle—from end users to the knowledge engineers who encode domain knowledge and design knowledge in software architectures.

Executive Summary

Currently, KBSE is at the same stage of development as early compilers or expert systems. Commercially, a few dozen handcrafted systems are in real use as industrial pilot projects. The first and third sections of this book describe pilot systems for software maintenance and special-purpose program synthesis. In research laboratories, many prototype KBSE systems have been developed that have advanced the science of formalizing and automating software design knowledge. Program synthesis research has matured over the last two decades to the point that sophisticated algorithms can be synthesized with only limited human guidance. Research in intelligent assistance for requirements and specification engineering is less mature but already shows considerable promise.

The Next Decade

Within the next decade, significant commercial use of KBSE technology could occur in software maintenance and special-purpose program synthesis. The influence will be evolutionary and compatible with current software development methods. Some research systems for intelligent assistance in requirements and specification engineering, such as ARIES (chapter 4) and ROSE-2 (chapter 5), incorporate many of the current CASE representations. Thus, as they mature, they could be integrated into the next generation of CASE tools. On the research front, I expect continued progress in representing and reasoning with domain and design knowledge. This research will pay off in more sophisticated tools for requirements and specification engineering as well as better program synthesis systems. Within the decade, the break-even point will be reached in general-purpose program synthesis systems, where given a domain theory, it will be faster to interactively develop a program with one of these systems than by hand. A key to this breakthrough will be continued improvements in search control. Substantial research programs are now under way to scale KBSE technology up from programming in the small to programming in the large.

The Next Century

Software engineering will evolve into a radically changed discipline. Software will become adaptive and self-configuring, enabling end users to specify, modify, and maintain their own software within restricted contexts. Software engineers will deliver knowledge-based application generators rather than unmodifiable application programs. These generators will enable an end user to interactively specify requirements in domain-oriented terms, as is now done by telephony engineers with WATSON (chapter 3), and then automatically generate efficient code that implements these requirements. In essence, software engineers will deliver the knowledge for generating software rather than the software itself.

Although end users will communicate with these software generators in domain-oriented terms, the foundation for the technology will be formal representations. Formal representations can be viewed as the extension of current CASE representations, which only capture structural and syntactic information about a software design, into complete semantic representations that capture the full spectrum of software design knowledge. Formal languages will become the lingua franca, enabling knowledge-based components to be composed into larger systems. Formal specifications will be the interface between interactive problem acquisition components and automatic program synthesis components.

Software development will evolve from an art to a true engineering discipline. Software systems will no longer be developed by handcrafting large bodies of code. Rather, as in other engineering disciplines, components will be combined and specialized through a chain of value-added enhancements. The final specializations will be done by the end user. KBSE will not replace the human software engineer; rather, it will provide the means for leveraging human expertise and knowledge through automated reuse. New subdisciplines, such as domain analysis and design analysis, will emerge to formalize knowledge for use in KBSE components.

Capsule History of Software Engineering

Since the introduction of the electronic digital computer at the end of World War II, hardware performance has increased by an order of magnitude every decade. This rate of improvement has accelerated with the recent introduction of reduced instruction set computer (RISC) architectures, which simplify hardware by pushing complex instructions into software to optimize performance and shorten design times. As hardware has become less expensive, more resources have been devoted to making computers easier to use and program. User interfaces have evolved from punched cards for batch processing to teletypes and cathode ray tubes for time sharing, to graphic user interfaces for networked workstations. In the nineties, new modes of interaction such as handwriting and voice will become common.

Likewise, computers are becoming easier to program. In the fifties and sixties, the first "automatic programming" tools were introduced—assemblers and compilers. Research in cprogramming languages and compiler technology has been a major success for computer science, raising the level of programming from the machine level toward the specification level. In the seventies, interactive programming environments such as Interlisp were created that enabled programs to be developed in small increments and made semantic information about a software system readily available to the programmer (Barstow, Shrobe, and Sandewall 1984). In the eighties, languages designed to facilitate the reuse of software components were introduced, such as Ada and object-oriented extensions of C. Object-oriented programming methodologies encourage a top-down approach in which general object classes are incrementally specialized.

As hardware performance increased, the scope of software projects soon exceeded the capabilities of small teams of programmers. Coordination and communication became dominant management concerns, both horizontally across different teams of programmers and vertically across different phases of software development. Structured methods were introduced to manage and guide software development. In the late sixties and early seventies, structured programming was introduced for incrementally developing correct code from specifications (Dahl, Dijkstra, and Hoare 1972). In *structured programming*, a specification is first developed that states the intended function of a program, and then an implementation is developed through iterative refinement. Structured programming also prescribes methods for making maintenance easier, such as block-structuring programs to simplify control flow.

Although structured programming helped to correct the coding errors of the sixties, it did not address requirements analysis errors and system design errors. These errors are more difficult to detect during testing than coding errors and can be much more expensive to fix. To address this problem, in the late seventies, structured methods were extended to structured analysis and structured design (Bergland and Gordon 1981; Freeman and Wasserman 1983). These methods prescribe step-by-step processes for analyzing requirements and designing a software system. The manual overhead in creating diagrams and documentation was one limitation of structured methods. A more fundamental limitation is that they provide only limited means for validating analysis and designs and, thus, work best for developing familiar types of software, as is common in commercial data processing. For new types of software, exploratory programming techniques developed in the AI community provide better means for incrementally developing and validating analysis and designs.

CASE was introduced in the mid-eighties to provide computer support for structured methods of software development (Chikofsky 1989; Gane 1990). CASE tools include interactive graphic editors for creating annotated structure chart, data flow, and control-flow diagrams. Like CAD, the development of graphically-oriented personal computers and workstations has made CASE economically feasible. The information in these diagrams is stored in a database called a *repository*, which helps to coordinate a software project over the whole development life cycle. In integrated CASE environments, project management tools use the repository to help managers decompose a software project into subtasks, allocate a budget, and monitor the progress of software development.

CASE technology includes limited forms of automatic code generation. Module and data declarations are generated directly from information in a repository. In addition, special-purpose interpreters or compilers called *application generators* have been developed for stereotyped software such as payroll programs and screen generators for video display terminals. Application generators are essentially a user-friendly front-end with a back-end interpreter or sets of macros for code generation. In contrast to knowledge-based program synthesis systems, current application generators have narrow coverage, are difficult to modify, are not composable, and provide limited semantic processing. Nonetheless, they have been successful; it is estimated that over half of current COBOL code is developed by application generators.

The CASE market for just commercial data processing tools totaled several billion dollars in 1988 and is doubling every three to four years (Schindler 1990). The major advantages of using current CASE technology are that it enforces a disciplined, top-down methodology for software design and provides a central repository for information such as module interfaces and data declarations. However, current CASE technology can only represent a small portion of the design decisions necessary to build, maintain, and modify a software system. CASE design tools mainly represent the structural organization of a software design, not the function of the components of a software system. Current CASE tools only provide limited forms of analysis, such as checking the integrity of control and data flow and the consistency of data declarations across modules. CASE technology does not currently provide a means for validating the functional behavior of a software design to ensure that the design satisfies the needs of the customer.

AI and Software Engineering Today

AI has already made a significant impact on software engineering. First, mainstream software engineering has adopted AI programming techniques and environments, including expert system shells, as prototyping tools. A *software prototype* is a system constructed for evaluation purposes that has only limited function and performance. Second, AI components are being integrated into larger systems, particularly where flexibility and ease of modification are needed for rapidly changing requirements. Third, AI inference technology is providing the foundation for more powerful and user-friendly information systems (Barr 1990). Fourth, AI programming paradigms are being adopted in more conventional environments, including graphic user interfaces, object-oriented programming, constraint-based programming, and rule-based programming. In all these applications, the major factor has been the ease of developing, modifying, and maintaining programs written in AI programming environments.

AI technology provides particularly effective exploratory programming tools for poorly understood domains and requirements (Sheil 1986). Exploratory programming converges on well-defined requirements and system specifications by developing a prototype system, testing the prototype with the end user to decide whether it satisfies the customer's needs, and then iteratively modifying the prototype until the end user is satisfied. Exploratory programming identifies errors in requirements and specifications early in the design process, when they are cheap to fix, rather than after the system has been delivered to the customer, when they can cost a hundred to a thousand times as much to fix. This advantage of early feedback with a prototype system is leading to the replacement of linear methods of software development with methods that incorporate one or more passes of prototype development. AI technology is suitable for exploratory programming because its programming constructs, such as objects, rules, and constraints, are much closer to the conceptual level than conventional programming constructs. This approach enables prototype systems to be rapidly constructed and modified.

Prototype systems written in very high-level languages and environments can directly be evolved into working systems when efficient performance is not necessary. For example, many small businesses build their own information and accounting systems on top of standard database and spreadsheet programs. Historically, spreadsheet programs descended from VISICALC, a simple constraint-based reasoning system within a standard accounting paradigm. For scientific applications, Wolfram's MATHEMATICA environment enables scientists and engineers to rapidly develop mathematical models, execute the models, and then graph the results. MATHEMATICA uses a programmable rule-based method for manipulating symbolic mathematics that can also be used for transformational program derivations (chapter 8).

However, when efficient performance is necessary, the current generation of high-level development environments does not provide adequate capabilities because the environments interpret or provide default translations of high-level programs. Although in the future, faster hardware can compensate for constant factor overheads, the most difficult inefficiencies to eliminate are exponential factors that result from applying generic interpretation algorithms to declarative specifications. For example, in the mid-eighties, the New Jersey motor vehicle department developed a new information system using a fourth-generation language, which is essentially an environment for producing database applications. Although the fourth-generation language enabled the system to be developed comparatively fast, the inefficiency of the resulting code caused the system to grind to a halt when it came online and created havoc for several years for the Garden State. As another example, although mathematical models of three-dimensional physical systems can be specified with MATHEMATICA, the execution of large or complex models can be unworkably slow.

When efficient performance is necessary, a prototype system currently can only be used as a specification for a production system; the production system has to be coded manually for efficiency. For example, after a three-dimensional physical system is specified in MATHEMATICA, it still needs to be coded into efficient Fortran code to run simulations (chapter 8). Although both MATHEMATICA and MACSYMA can produce default Fortran code from mathematical specifications, the code is not efficient enough for simulating large three-dimensional systems.

The necessity of recoding a prototype for efficiency incurs additional costs during development but has even more pernicious effects during the maintenance phase of the software life cycle. As the production system is enhanced and modified, the original prototype and documentation are seldom maintained and, therefore, become outdated. Also, because modifications are done at the code level, the system loses its coherency and becomes brittle. Eventually, the system becomes unmaintainable, as described in chapter 1.

Transformational Programming

KBSE seeks to combine the development advantages of high-level environments supporting rapid prototyping, with the efficiency advantages of manually coded software. The objective is to create a new paradigm for software development—transformational programming—in which software is developed, modified, and maintained at the specification level and then automatically transformed into production-quality software (Green et al. 1986). For example, the SINAPSE system described in chapter 8 automates the production of efficient Fortran code from high-level specifications of three-dimensional mathematical models. As another example, the ELF system described in chapter 9 automates the production of efficient, VLSI wire routing software from specifications. Where this automatic translation is achieved, software development, maintenance, and modification can be carried out at the specification level with the aid of knowledge-based tools. Eventually, software engineering will evolve to a higher level and become the discipline of capturing and automating currently undocumented domain and design knowledge.

To understand the impact of automating the translation between the specification level and the implementation level, consider the impact of desktop publishing during the past decade. Before the introduction of computer-based word processing, manually typing or typesetting a report consumed a small fraction of the time and money needed to generate the report. Similarly, manually coding a software system from a detailed specification consumes a small fraction of the resources in the software life cycle. However, in both cases, this manual process is an error-prone bottleneck that prevents modification and reuse. Once a report is typed, seemingly minor modifications, such as inserting a paragraph, can cause a ripple effect requiring a cascade of cutting and repasting. Modifying a software system by patching the code is similar to modifying a report by erasing and typing in changes. After a few rounds of modification, the software system resembles an inner tube that is patched so often that another patch causes it to blow up. When a typewritten report gets to this stage, it is simply retyped. However, when a software system gets to this stage, the original design information is usually lost. Typically, the original programming team has long since departed, and the documentation has not been maintained, making it inadequate and outdated. The only recourse is an expensive re-engineering effort that includes recovering the design of the existing system (chapter 1).

Because maintenance and modification are currently done at the code level, they consume over half the resources in the software life cycle, even though the original coding consumes a small fraction of the life-cycle resources. Most maintenance effort is devoted to understanding the design of the current system (chapter 2) and understanding the impact of proposed modifications. Furthermore, because modification is difficult, so is reuse. It is easy to reuse portions of previous reports when they can easily be modified to fit in a new context. Similarly, it is easy to reuse portions of previous software systems when abstract components can easily be adapted to the context of a new software system. For these reasons, word processing and desktop publishing have had an impact disproportionate to the resources consumed by the manual process they automate. For similar reasons, automating the development of production-quality software from high-level specifications and prototypes will have a revolutionary impact on the software life cycle.

By automating printing, desktop publishing has created a market for computer-based tools to help authors create publications from the initial conceptual stages through the final layout stage. Outlining programs help authors organize and reorganize their ideas. Spelling checkers and grammar checkers help ensure consistency with standards. Page layout programs optimize the visual presentation of the final publication and often integrate several source files into a final product. These tools would be useful even in the absence of automated printing. However, they reach their full potential in environments supporting the complete spectrum of activities for the incremental and iterative development of publications.

Current CASE tools are similar to outliners, grammar checkers, and tools that integrate several source files. CASE tools have not yet reached their full potential because coding is still mostly a labor-intensive manual process. As coding is increasingly automated, more sophisticated tools that support the initial stages of software design will become more useful. Rapidly prototyped systems developed with these tools will be converted with minimal human guidance into production-quality code by program synthesis systems, just as word processing output today is converted almost automatically into publication-quality presentations through page layout programs. CASE representations will move from partial representations of the structure and organization of a software design toward formal specifications. Tools such as WATSON (chapter 3) that interactively elicit requirements from end users and convert them into formal specifications will be one source of formal specifications. Tools such as ARIES (chapter 4) will enable software developers to incrementally develop and modify formal specifications. Tools such as ROSE-2 (chapter 5) will match specifications to existing designs for reuse.

Comparison of Program Synthesis Techniques

The ultimate objective of transformational programming is to enable end users to describe, modify, and maintain a software system in terms natural to their application domain and, at the same time, obtain the efficiency of carefully coded machine-level programs. Great progress has been made toward this objective in the progression from assemblers to compilers to application generators and fourth-generation languages. However, much remains to be done.

Given current technological capabilities, there are trade-offs between several dimensions of automatic translation. The first dimension is the distance spanned between the specification or programming level and the implementation level. The second dimension is the breadth of the domain covered at the specification level. The third dimension is the efficiency of the implemented code. The fourth dimension is the efficiency and degree of automation of the translation process. The fifth dimension is the correctness of the implemented code. The chapters in the sections on domain-specific program synthesis, knowledge compilation, and formal derivation systems show how current KBSE research is expanding our capabilities along each of these dimensions. The following paragraphs compare different approaches to automatic translation.

Compilers for conventional programming languages such as Fortran and COBOL have a wide breadth of coverage and efficient translation and produce fairly efficient code. These accomplishments are achieved with a comparatively short distance between the programming level and the implementation level. Optimizing compilers sometimes have user-supplied pragmas for directing the translation process, thereby getting greater efficiency in the implemented code at the expense of greater user guidance in the translation process. Verifying that a compiler produces correct code is still a major research issue.

Very high-level languages such as logic programming and knowledge interpretation languages also achieve a wide breadth of coverage through a short distance between the programming level and the implementation level. However, the programming level is much closer to the specification level than with conventional programming languages. Programs written in these languages are either interpreted or compiled to remove interpretive overhead such as pattern matching. These languages can be used to write declarative specifications that are generally implemented as generate-and-test algorithms, with correspondingly poor performance. It is also possible to develop efficient logic programs by tuning them to the operation of the interpreter, in effect, declaratively embedding control structure. The code implemented for these programs approaches, within a constant factor, the efficiency of code written for conventional languages, except for the lack of efficient data structures. Efficient logic programs can either be developed manually or can be the target code of a program synthesis system such as PAL (chapter 15) or XPRTS (chapter 16).

Knowledge interpreters such as expert system shells are seldom based on formal semantics, and thus, formally verifying that they produce correct code is impossible. However, some research-oriented languages such as pure Prolog are based on formal semantics. Formal proofs in which abstract compilers for these languages produce correct code for abstract virtual machines have appeared in the research literature (Warren 1977; Despeyroux 1986). These proofs are based on the close relationship between logic programming and theorem proving, for which the soundness and completeness of inference procedures have mathematically been worked out. Proving that real compilers produce correct code for real machines is a much more difficult and detailed undertaking. Success has recently been reported in Hunt (1989), Moore (1989), and Young (1989).

Application generators span a significant distance between the specification level and the implementation level by choosing a narrow domain of coverage. Application generators typically use simple techniques to interpret or produce code in conventional languages, such as filling in parameters of code templates. Thus, the performance of implemented code usually is only fair. The translation process is efficient and automatic. Because application generators are mainly used in commercial data processing, mathematically verifying that an application generator produces correct code has not been a major issue.

Domain-specific program synthesis systems will likely become the next generation of application generators. They also span a significant distance between the specification level and the implementation level by choosing a narrow domain of coverage. They are easier to incrementally develop and modify than conventional application generators because they are based on transformation rules. It is also easier to incorporate more sophisticated problem-solving capabilities. Therefore, compared to conventional application generators, they tend to produce much better code and provide higher-level specifications. In theory, the transformation rules could be derived by composing basic transformation rules that were rigorously based on logic and, therefore, could verifiably be correct. However, in practice, the transformation rules are derived through knowledge engineering. Compared with other program synthesis approaches, the narrow domain enables domain knowledge and search knowledge to be hard wired into the transformation rules; therefore, the translation process is comparatively efficient.

Knowledge compilation research seeks to combine the high-level specification advantages of knowledge interpreters with the efficiency advantages of conventional programs. The goals are broad coverage, a large distance between the specification level and the implementation level, and efficient code. To achieve these goals, the major research issue is search control during program synthesis. Like approaches to domain-specific synthesis, the transformation rules are derived through knowledge engineering and, hence, are not verifiably correct. However, the domain knowledge is usually encoded separately and explicitly; therefore, knowledge compilers can work in different domains given different domain knowledge.

Formal derivation research seeks the same goals as knowledge compilation research but within a framework that is rigorously based on logic and, therefore, is verifiably correct. The formal basis for the extraction of programs from constructive proofs and for basic transformation rules was worked out 20 years ago. As in knowledge compilation, the major research issue is search control during program synthesis. The major approach to search control is to develop metalevel programs called *tactics* and *strategies* that encapsulate search control and design knowledge.

The Next Decade

KBSE will revolutionize the software life cycle, but the path will be evolutionary because its development, as well as its incorporation into software engineering practice, will be incremental. KBSE will adapt itself to current practices before it changes these practices.

In the coming decade, there are several leverage points where KBSE technology could commercially be applied. In each of these potential uses, technology already developed in the research laboratory could be combined with conventional software-engineering tools to provide much better tools. For some of these applications, industrial pilot projects are already under way. First, I review several potential near-term uses, then examine applications in software maintenance and special-purpose program synthesis. The computational requirements of KBSE technology are also discussed.

First, KBSE tools for software understanding will likely be adopted for software maintenance (see section 1). Current AI technology can significantly enhance standard software understanding tools such as data-flow and control flow analyzers. KBSE aims at eventually elevating maintenance from the program level to the specification level. However, because of the enormous investment in the existing stock of software, program maintenance will be the dominant cost in software engineering for decades to come.

Second, AI technology could be used to produce the next generation of application generators (see section 3). Transformational programming provides a flexible and modular basis for a deeper level of semantic processing than is feasible with current application generators. Its use leads to better user interaction and higher-level specifications as input and more optimal code as output. The chapters on domain-specific program synthesis show the near-term potential of this technology.

Third, AI environments for rapid prototyping and exploratory programming could be enhanced and integrated with CASE design tools. Rapid prototyping has recently become a major topic in software engineering. CASE design tools support decomposing a system into a hierarchy of modules. The result is usually a hierarchical graph representation annotated with text commenting on the intended function of the modules. AI programming environments can be used to rapidly prototype the function of these modules and, thus, create an executable prototype of the whole system.

Fourth, the currently small but growing use of formal methods (Wing 1990) for software development could considerably be enhanced through software engineering technology. A method is formal if it has a sound mathematical basis, and, therefore, provides a systematic rather than ad hoc framework for developing software. In Europe, formal languages such as VDM (Jones 1986) and Z (Spivey 1989) have been used in pilot projects to manually develop formal specifications of real software systems. Tools that incorporate automated reasoning could provide substantial assistance in developing formal specifications, as is shown in section 2. Furthermore, within this decade, formal derivation systems will become sufficiently advanced to provide interactive environments for refining formal specifications to code (see section 5).

Finally, a major problem with programming in the large is ensuring that a large software system is consistent: The implementation must be consistent with the system design that, in turn, must be consistent with the requirements; the components of the software system developed by separate teams must be consistent with each other. Current CASE tools use shallow representations and, thus, provide only limited consistency checking. For example, CASE design tools can check that a hierarchy of modules has no dead ends in the flow of control. More complete consistency checking will require deeper representations and more inference capabilities. The research on ROSE-2 (chapter 5) shows that there is an evolutionary path from current CASE consistency checking to consistency checking with deeper representations.

Software Maintenance: The Next Decade

Industry and government have invested hundreds of billions of dollars in existing software systems. Testing, maintaining, modifying, and renovating these systems consumes over half of the software engineering resources and will continue to do so for decades to come. Often, older systems are no longer maintainable because no one understands how they work, preventing these systems from being upgraded or moved to higher-performance hardware platforms. This problem is acute for software written in archaic languages that programmers are no longer trained in.

Intelligent software maintenance assistants are based on AI techniques for software understanding and ramification reasoning. Software understanding is a prerequisite to other maintenance tasks and currently accounts for over half the time spent by maintenance programmers. In the long term, software systems will include built-in self-explanation facilities such as those in LASSIE (chapter 2) and the explainable expert system (Neches, Swartout, and Moore 1985). Today, software understanding is done by *reverse engineering,* analyzing existing code and documentation to derive an abstract description of a software system and recover design information.

Reverse engineering is the first step in *re-engineering* (chapter 1): renovating existing systems, including porting them to newer languages and hardware platforms. Because maintenance is increasingly difficult, re-engineering is especially important for code written long ago in older languages and for older hardware platforms. Many businesses are legally required to be able to access records in databases dating back decades. These databases were written as flat files, making it impossible to integrate them with newer relational databases and requiring the business to keep backward compatibility with old hardware platforms. Reengineering is also needed to port engineering and scientific code written in the sixties and seventies to newer hardware platforms with parallel architectures. Reengineering these older systems occupies many programmers; AI technology can provide significant assistance to this task.

Standard AI techniques such as pattern matching and transformation rules enhance conventional tools for software understanding by enabling higher-level analysis and abstraction (Biggerstaff, Hoskins, and Webster 1989; Hartman 1989; Letovsky 1988; Wills 1989). With these techniques, much of the information needed by current CASE design tools can be recovered semiautomatically, even from archaic assembly language code (chapter 1). One approach is *cliche recognition* (Rich and Waters 1990): Matching stereotyped programming patterns to a program's data and control flow, thereby abstracting the program into a hierarchy of these cliches.

AI techniques for software understanding can also be applied to the testing and integration phases of software development. For example, a major aerospace company used a KBSE system to test two million lines of Fortran code produced by subcontractors for compliance with its coding standards. Hundreds of violations were found, including unstructured do loops, dead code, identifier inconsistency, and incorrectly formatted code. This technique has already saved four person-years of hand checking, yet the system took less than half a person-year to develop. The system was built in REFINE, which is a very high-level programming environment that integrates parsing technology, an object-oriented knowledge base, and AI rule-based technology (Burson, Kotik, and Markosian 1990). Most of the development time was devoted to writing grammar definitions for the three dialects of Fortran used by subcontractors; REFINE automatically generates parsers from the grammar definitions. The core of the system was written as a set of rules and took only a few weeks of development time. Because it was written as a set of rules, it is easily modifiable as coding standards change.

Understanding the existing code is the first step in software modification. The next step is ramification reasoning to determine the impact of proposed modifications to a software system. The objective is to ensure that a modification achieves its goal without causing undesired changes in other software behavior. This is essentially a task for constraint-based reasoning. Ramification reasoning can be done at many levels of abstraction. At the lowest level, it involves tracing through data-flow and control-flow graphs to decide which programs and subroutines could be affected by a proposed modification. Automated ramification reasoning is even more effective when given higher-level design information. For example, it can determine whether proposed modifications violate data-integrity constraints and other invariants. As CASE representations evolve into more complete and formal representations, AI techniques for ramification reasoning will be incorporated into CASE tools.

Special-Purpose Program Synthesis: The Next Decade

Today, application generators are one of the most effective tools for raising programmer productivity. Because they are based on code templates, they provide a more flexible and higher level of software reuse than the reuse of code. The chapters on domain-specific program synthesis show that transformational technology provides the means for higher-performance application generators, which are also potentially easier to develop and modify.

Application generators generally produce code in three phases. The first syntactic analysis phase converts a specification written in an application-oriented language or obtained interactively through menus and forms into a syntactic parse tree. A semantic analysis phase then computes semantic attributes to obtain an augmented semantic tree. The final generation phase traverses the semantic tree and instantiates code templates. The generation phase is similar to macroexpansion in conventional programming languages.

Application generator generators (Cleaveland and Kintala 1988) are tools for building application generators. Parser generators such as YACC take the definition of an application-oriented language as input and produce a parser for the syntactic analysis phase as output. Tools for building the semantic analysis phase are usually based on attribute-grammar manipulation routines. Tools for building the generation phase are similar to macro definition languages.

AI provides technology for much richer semantic processing. In addition, the generation phase can be augmented with program transformations to produce better code. Program transformations enable code templates to be more abstract and, therefore, have wider coverage. For example, code templates can be written with abstract data types, such as sets, that program transformations then refine into concrete data structures. Chapters 8 and 9 describe the use of AI techniques for semantic processing and also program transformations for refining abstract instantiated code templates.

Transformation rules provide a flexible and modular basis for developing and modifying program transformations and semantic analysis routines. Eventually, end users will be able to interactively develop their own transformation rules in restricted contexts (chapter 8). In the near term, transformational technology will enable software engineers to build higher-performance application generators. KBSE environments that include parser-printer generators and support for program-transformation rules, such as REFINE, provide tools for developing knowledge-based application generators.

Intelligent application generators are cost-effective options not only in standard application areas such as business information systems but also in the enhancement of existing software. Automatic code enhancement makes software development and maintenance more efficient and results in fewer bugs. Examples of enhancements include better error handling and better user interfaces.

Making software fault tolerant is particularly important in real-time systems and in transaction systems where the integrity of a database could be affected. Consequently, a significant amount of code in these systems is devoted to error detection and recovery. An informal sampling of large telecommunications programs found that 40 percent to 80 percent of branch points were devoted to error detection. Kelly and McGuiness (1986) developed RIP, a prototype automatic reprogramming system for retrofitting error-handling code into existing software.

User interface code often accounts for 30 percent of an interactive system. Screen generators have long existed for business transaction systems, and graphical user interface generators for workstations have recently been marketed. However, current tools only make it faster to develop precanned displays. Intelligent interfaces are much more flexible. They can adapt to both the semantics of the data they present and the preferences of the user. For example, instead of precanned text, intelligent interfaces use natural language generation techniques that are sensitive to a model of the user's knowledge. Graphics can be optimized to emphasize information important to the user.

However, intelligent interfaces are more difficult to design and program than standard user interfaces, making it costly to incorporate them in each new application. Roth, Mattis, and Mesnard (1990) describe SAGE, a prototype system for application-independent intelligent data presentation. SAGE incorporates design expertise for selecting and synthesizing graphical components in coordination with the generation of natural language descriptions. SAGE combines a declarative representation of data with knowledge representations of users' informational goals to generate graphics and text. An application developer can generate an intelligent presentation system for his(her) application using SAGE.

Program transformation technology can directly be applied to the synthesis of visual presentations. Westfold and Green (1991) describe a transformation system for deriving visual presentations of data relationships. The underlying idea is that designing a visual presentation of data relationships can be viewed as designing a data structure. Starting with a relational description of data, transformations are applied to reformulate the description into equivalent descriptions that have different implementations, that is, different representations on the screen. Many different representations of the same data can be generated, each emphasizing different aspects of the information. For example, an *n*-ary relation can be reformulated so that all the tuples with the same first argument are grouped. Successive applications of this rule gradually transform the *n*-ary relation into a tree. Other rules transform data relationships into display-oriented relationships, which are then rendered graphically.

Computational Requirements

KBSE can be expensive computationally, both in terms of memory and processor cycles. The research systems described in this book often push the performance envelope of current workstations. Hardware capabilities have previously been a limiting factor in the commercial adoption of CAD, CASE, and AI technology. The most limiting factor was the computational requirements of providing a graphical user interface with the hardware available in the late seventies and early eighties. Hardware performance in the nineties will probably not be a major limiting factor in scaling up KBSE technology to industrial applications.

Benchmarks from several industrial pilot projects show that current computer workstations provide sufficient computational power to support KBSE on real problems when appropriate trade-offs are made. A benchmark from domain-specific program synthesis is the SINAPSE system (chapter 8), which synthesizes a 5,000-line Fortran three-dimensional modeling program from a 60-line specification in 10 minutes on a SUN-4 (a SUN-4 is a UNIX workstation running about 12 MIPS with memory from 16 to 64 megabytes). This type of program would take weeks to generate by hand. SINAPSE is specialized to synthesize only finite-difference algorithms, so it can make large-grained decisions without sacrificing automation or the efficiency of the resulting code. SINAPSE also uses knowledge-based techniques to constrain the search space (chapter 7). Another benchmark comes from the testing of Fortran code for adherence to coding standards, which was described earlier. On a SUN-4, 20,000 lines of code were checked each hour.

The computational demands of KBSE technology result from the scope of the knowledge representation, the granularity of automated decision making, and the size and complexity of the software systems produced. Greater breadth or depth of representation requires increased memory, and increased granularity of automated decision making requires increased processor cycles. The critical issue is how computational requirements scale as a function of these variables.

The computational requirements of software-engineering technology can be factored into two groups: those that increase either linearly or within a small polynomial in terms of these variables and those that increase exponentially. The former group includes factors such as the amount of memory needed to represent the history of a derivation, including all the goals and subgoals. As discussed in chapter 23, this amount is probably proportional to $N * log N$, where N is the size of the derivation. The exponential factors include combinatorially explosive search spaces for program derivations. These exponential factors cannot be addressed by any foreseeable increase in hardware performance. Instead, better KBSE technology is required, such as tactics for search control.

Although software engineers will always want more hardware power, increases in hardware performance within the next decade will likely address the computational requirements of KBSE that do not grow exponentially. The benchmarks from industrial pilot projects show that some KBSE technology can already be applied to industrial-scale software systems within the performance limitations of current computer workstations.

Hardware performance within the fiercely competitive workstation market will continue to grow rapidly. Based on technology already in advanced development, an order of magnitude increase is expected by the middle of the decade both in processor speed and memory size. Simpler architectures such as RISC have decreased development time and will facilitate the introduction of faster device technologies such as gallium arsenide and Josephson junctions.

Lucrative, computationally intensive applications, such as real-time digital video processing, will drive hardware performance even higher in the latter part of the decade, with yet another order-of-magnitude increase. Compared with the computational requirements of these applications, scaling up KBSE technology to industrial applications will not be hardware limited if exponential factors can be avoided. The next part of this chapter describes how combinatorially explosive search might be avoided through the reuse of domain and design knowledge.

The Next Century

Within the KBSE community, there is a broad consensus that knowledge-based methods will lead to fundamentally new roles in the software engineering life cycle and a revised view of software as human knowledge that is encapsulated and represented in machine manipulable form. At the beginning of the computer age, this knowledge was represented as the strings of 1's and 0's of machine language. By applying software engineering to itself by developing compilers, the representation level has been raised to data structures and control structures that are closer to the conceptual level. Although this improvement is considerable, most of the domain and design knowledge that is used in developing a modern software system is lost or, at best, is encoded as text in documentation.

The goal of KBSE research is to capture this lost knowledge by developing knowledge representations and automated reasoning tools. As this task is accomplished, software engineering will be elevated to a higher plane that emphasizes formalizing and encoding domain and design knowledge and then automatically replaying and compiling this knowledge to develop working software systems. Below, I envision how future KBSE environments might support different classes of people in the software life cycle, from end users to the knowledge engineers who encode domain knowledge and design knowledge in software architectures.

Maintenance Programmers

In the future, software systems will include built-in, knowledge-based software information systems such as LASSIE (chapter 2). Maintenance programmers will no longer study reams of source code and outdated documentation to understand a software system. Instead, they will query the system itself. Eventually, the information will automatically be updated, so that as a system is modified, the information is kept current. The information in these systems will expand to include the full range of design decisions made in developing the software system. Eventually, these software information systems will be produced as a by-product of software development with KBSE tools.

These software information systems will evolve to become active assistants in software maintenance. They will be able to trace the ramifications of proposed changes at the code, system design, and requirements levels. They will help to ensure that as a software system evolves to meet changing requirements, it remains consistent and bug free. Eventually, maintenance will no longer be done by modifying source code. Instead, desired changes will be specified directly by the end user at the requirements level, and the system will carry them out automatically. Software systems will become self-documenting and self-modifying. The typically junior programmers who are now burdened with maintaining code designed by other programmers will spend their time in more interesting pursuits.

End Users

In the future, end users will interactively customize generic software systems to create applications tailored to their own particular needs. Progress in this direction has already been made. For example, several word processing and spreadsheet programs allow users to customize menus, change keyboard bindings, and create macros. Sometimes, macros are compiled for greater efficiency. KBSE technology will provide much more flexibility in customization, more optimized code, and intelligent assistance in helping an end user develop requirements.

A scenario for future intelligent assistance for end users in scientific computing is presented by Abelson et al. (1989). Below, I examine a simpler domain by considering how a businessperson will develop a custom payroll system in the future (also see chapter 1). Current payroll program generators automate code generation but do not provide substantial help in eliciting and analyzing requirements. An intelligent payroll application generator will include a knowledge base about the payroll domain that defines concepts such as hourly versus salaried employees, various types of bonuses and deductions, tax codes, and different kinds of pay periods. Using this knowledge, a requirement acquisition component will interactively elicit the relevant structure of the buissnessperson's company and the types of output and information desired. During this interaction, the requiremenst acquisition component will check the consistency of evolving requirements with constraints, such as tax codes. It will also guide the businessperson in resolving ambiguities and incompleteness. The result of this requirements elicitation process will be a formal specification of the desired payroll system in the form of declarations and constraints formulated in terms of the concepts and operations of the payroll domain.

To validate the specification, the payroll application generator will then transform these declarations and constraints into a prototype spreadsheet program and try out a few test examples with the businessperson. This step will lead to further refinements of the requirements until the businessperson is satisfied. The payroll program generator will then compile the specification into machine code and generate the proper interfaces for other accounting systems.

The businessperson does not have to be an expert in accounting, tax codes, or business programming, or even be able to develop spreadsheets. The domain knowledge of payrolls would enable the requirements acquisition component to elicit the appropriate information in terms the businessperson can understand.

Many of the capabilities described in this sketch are within range of current KBSE research systems. For example, eliciting payroll requirements involves temporal reasoning that is much less complex than that performed by WATSON (chapter 3) in eliciting requirements for new telephone features. Other recent work on knowledge-based requirements acquisition includes Rubenstein and Waters (1989) and Anderson and Fickas (1989). Similarly, compiling the arithmetic constraints of a payroll specification into efficient code is far less difficult than compiling partial differential equations into efficient finite-difference programs, as done by SINAPSE (chapter 8). What is missing are good tools for acquiring the knowledge of the payroll domain, so that this knowledge can be used by both requirements elicitation components and program synthesis components.

System Developers

The needs of system developers differ from those of end users. End users prefer to interact at the requirements level and be shielded from the complexity of specifications and system design. In contrast, system developers prefer help managing the complexity of specifications and system designs but want to be shielded from the implementation details. Two interrelated ideas currently being developed could meet some of the needs of future system developers: megaprogramming and software architectures.

Megaprogramming is programming at the component level (e.g. user interfaces, databases, device controllers) rather than the code level. To program at the component level, it is necessary to either reuse components or generate components from specifications. Components can more readily be reused or generated if they are defined in the context of a software architecture that identifies major types of components and provides the glue for composing them together. A *software architecture* is a high-level description of a generic type of software system, such as the class of transaction-processing systems.

Software architectures will subsume current CASE design representations. To support software developers, software architectures will include the functional roles of major software components and their interrelationships stated in an application-oriented language; a domain theory that provides precise semantics for the application-oriented language for use in automated reasoning; libraries of prototype components with executable specifications; program synthesis capability to produce optimized code for components after a prototype system has been validated; a constraint system for reasoning about the consistency of a developing software system; and design records that link requirements to design decisions, as in the ROSE-2 system (chapter 5).

In the future, routine system development will be done by small teams of system analysts and domain experts working with KBSE environments that support software architectures. In contrast to the guidance provided for an end user, the KBSE environment will play an assistant role in requirement analysis. The team will start with a set of informal requirements and elaborate them into precise statements in the application-oriented language. As the requirements are made precise, the software-engineering environment will propagate these decisions through the design records to check the feasibility of meeting these requirements. This propagation will also set up default design decisions and record design alternatives to be investigated by the team.

After a subset of the requirements has been made into precise specifications, the KBSE environment will generate executable prototypes to help validate and refine the requirements. Analytic assessments of an evolving design will be provided by having the constraint system determine the ramifications of design decisions. The constraint system will ensure that design decisions are internally consistent and consistent with the software architecture. The team will iteratively refine its requirements, the precise specifications, and the system design using an opportunistic methodology similar to current rapid prototyping methodologies. After the system design is complete, the implementation of the production system will mostly be automatic. The KBSE environment will ask for parameters relevant to performance, such as the size of expected input, and will occasionally ask for guidance on implementation decisions.

System development by a close-knit team with automated support will diminish many communication, coordination, and project management difficulties inherent in managing large numbers of programmers. The feasibility of small teams developing prototype systems has already been shown using an AI programming environment suitable for rapid prototyping, reusable prototype components, and a software architecture (Brown et al. 1988). However, implementing the final production system required a large number of programmers to code efficient versions of the components. In the future, this final production phase will largely be automated.

There is an inherent tension between reusability and performance in component implementations, which is why megaprogramming is currently easier to apply to system prototyping rather than production system implementation. To be maximally reusable, components should make as few assumptions about other components as possible. Reusable components should use abstract data types and late-binding mechanisms common in AI environments. To be maximally efficient, components should take advantage of as much of the context of use as possible, including the implementations of data types in other components and early binding mechanisms. Transformational programming will make it possible to use megaprogramming during system prototyping and then automatically generate efficient production-quality code.

Extensible software (chapter 23) and additive programming (chapter 16) are the foundation for enabling small teams to build large software systems, end users to customize their own applications, and application software to be self-maintaining. A software architecture represents a partial set of decisions about requirements and system design that are generic to a class of software systems. To be reusable, this partial information must be represented so it is extensible. System developers and end users will incrementally add to these decisions to generate a software system. Systems will be modified for changing requirements by retracting decisions and adding new decisions.

Software Architects, Domain Analysts, and Design Analysts

Software architectures will be created through domain analysis and design analysis. *Domain analysis* (Arango 1988) is a form of knowledge acquisition in which the concepts and goals of an application domain are analyzed and then formalized in an application oriented language suitable for expressing software specifications. *Design analysis* is the formalization of transformational implementations for a class of software artifacts. A *domain designer* (Neighbors 1984) is a design analyst who derives implementations for the objects and operations in an application oriented language developed through domain analysis.

System developers will reuse domain analysis by stating requirements, specifications, and system designs in the application oriented language. System developers will also reuse design analysis when they develop an application system through a software architecture. Thus, the cost of domain analysis and design analysis will be spread over many different systems.

Domain knowledge is necessary for intelligent requirement analysis, specification acquisition, and program synthesis. Domain knowledge can implicitly be embedded in special-purpose rules or can be formal and explicit. Formalizing domain knowledge is a difficult task, currently requiring extended collaboration between domain experts and knowledge engineers (Curtis, Krasner, and Iscoe 1988). One advantage of formalizing domain knowledge is that it can then be used in all phases of software development, with the assurance of correctness between implementations and specifications. In other words, if a user validates a specification with a specification assistant, and a program synthesis system derives an implementation for this specification, the program correctly implements the user's intentions. Formalized domain knowledge can also be used with generic automated reasoning tools, thus enabling the reuse of KBSE components.

Domain knowledge is a prerequisite to requirement engineering. Requirements are necessarily described in terms of the application domain in which a software system will be used. Current requirements languages are restricted to expressing system-oriented concepts. Knowledge representation languages will provide the basis for expressing domain knowledge within which domain-oriented requirements can formally be expressed (Borgida, Greenspan, and Mylopoulos 1985). This approach will enable automatic theorem provers to verify whether a set of requirements is consistent with domain knowledge and to fill incompleteness in a partial set of requirements, as is done by WATSON (chapter 3) for the telephone domain. Program synthesis systems use domain knowledge to decompose and implement domain objects and operations. For example, distributive laws in a domain theory are used to decompose and optimize domain operations (chapters 17, 19, and 20).

A future design analyst will first interactively develop transformational derivations for a set of generic programs in an application domain using a general-purpose program synthesis system. These transformational derivations will be recorded as derivation histories (chapter 18). *Derivation histories* can be viewed as the execution trace of an implicit metalevel program that controls the transformational derivation. The objective of design analysis is to make at least part of the information in this metalevel program explicit so that it can be stored in a software architecture and reused by a system developer. A derivation history needs to be generalized so that it can be applied to similar but not necessarily identical specifications. Because of the difficulty of automatically generalizing execution traces to programs, I anticipate that generalizing derivation histories will be a manual process for the foreseeable future, with some computer assistance. In the long-term future, this generalization process might be automated through explanation-based generalization, given a general theory of the teleological structure of transformational derivations. Applications of explanation-based generalization to program synthesis are described in chapters 14 and 22 and also in Shavlik (1990). Fickas (1985) describes GLITTER, a research system that uses teleological structure to partially automate transformational derivations.

The first level of generalizing a derivation history will be done by annotating the derivation history with the dependencies between the individual transformation steps and the overall goal structure of the derivation. Some dependency information will automatically be generated. The annotations will provide information to intelligent replay systems (chapters 10 and 18) to modify a derivation history for use in similar specifications (Mostow 1989). The second level of generalization will be done by creating metalevel tactics (chapters 6, 15, 16, 19, 20, and 21). A third level of generalization will be strategies that encapsulate heuristic knowledge for choosing tactics (chapter 21). These strategies will include methods for decomposing specifications into components to be synthesized by specialized tactics (chapters 11 and 12) and methods for using performance requirements to guide the transformational derivation (chapter 13).

A software architect will integrate the results of domain analysis and design analysis with a constraint system for reasoning about the consistency of a developing software system. The results of domain analysis will be an application-oriented language for a software architecture and a domain theory that defines the semantics of this language. The results of design analysis, that is, annotated derivation histories, tactics, and strategies, will essentially form a set of special-purpose program synthesizers for the components of a software architecture. The software architect will also provide an initial set of design records linking requirements to design decisions for choosing one component over another (chapter 5). These design records will be elaborated by teams of system developers.

In essence, software engineering will become knowledge acquisition followed by redesign. Although creating a software architecture will require more effort than designing any particular software system, it will be paid back over the creation of many software systems. Software architectures will provide the right tools for what is now partially done through copy and edit. Instead of designing a system from scratch, software system developers will extend and redesign the defaults in a software architecture. *Redesign* is the method used for iteratively modifying a rapidly prototyped system. In the future, redesign will be supported with a spectrum of tools, including specification evolution transformations (chapter 4), consistency maintenance systems (chapter 5), and intelligent replay of derivation histories.

KBSE environments that support domain analysis, design analysis, and software architectures are being explored in research laboratories. Domain analysis and design analysis are knowledge-acquisition tasks. A prototype domain analysis environment is DRACO (Neighbors 1984), which includes generators for application-oriented languages. DRACO also provides support for transformation rules within a domain and between domains. KIDS (chapter 19) and WATSON (chapter 3) provide some support for creating and maintaining formal domain theories. In the future, knowledge-acquisition tools will provide sophisticated environments for domain analysis (Marcus 1989).

Design analysis is the acquisition of control knowledge. Representing and acquiring this knowledge is critically dependent on having a good understanding of the structure of transformational derivations. As shown by the chapters in this book, great progress has been made since the early days of program synthesis. For the most part, the program derivations presented here are at a higher level of abstraction than the details of the logical calculi that underlay the individual transformations. Several of the interactive program transformation systems, especially KIDS (chapter 19), provide a natural high-level interface for those schooled in transformational derivations. However, we are just beginning to understand how to encode the rationale for choosing particular paths through the design space. This semantic information is what we need for generalizing derivation histories and developing tactics and strategies. I expect significant progress over the coming decade. For a comparative study of different derivations in the program synthesis literature, see Steier and Anderson (1989), especially the concluding chapter on design space.

Summary

To date, the main use of AI in software engineering has been for rapid prototyping. Rapid prototyping enables requirements and system designs to be iteratively refined with customers before production-quality software is manually coded. However, just as manual typing makes it difficult to modify and reuse publications, manual coding of production-quality software makes it difficult to modify, maintain, and reuse software.

In the next century, transformational programming will create a paradigm shift in software development like that created by desktop publishing. Software development and maintenance will be elevated to the specification level by automating the derivation of efficient code from specifications. Knowledge-based tools for requirement elicitation, specification evolution, and program synthesis will enable end users to specify and modify their own software. Software architectures will enable small teams of system developers to create large software systems. Advances in knowledge representation, knowledge acquisition, and automated reasoning will enable domain experts and design experts to encode their knowledge in software architectures so that it can be reused by system developers and end users. Software engineering will be elevated to the engineering discipline of capturing and automating currently undocumented domain and design knowledge.

The path to this new paradigm will be incremental. In the coming decade,

KBSE will begin to supplant CASE with more powerful knowledge-based tools. This book documents industrial pilot projects in software maintenance and special-purpose program synthesis. Current AI technology can greatly enhance conventional maintenance tools to help maintenance programmers understand a software system and determine the ramifications of changes. Current AI technology can also help re-engineer existing systems. Special-purpose program synthesis systems will likely become the next generation of application generators. Compared to the technology used in existing application generators, transformational technology can produce more optimal code and provide a higher-level user interface. In short, KBSE will revolutionize the practice of software engineering by adapting to and improving current practice.

Acknowledgments

The author thanks the following people for helpful reviews: Lee Blaine, Allen Goldberg, Cordell Green, Laura Jones, Richard Jullig, David Lowry, Larry Markosian, and Stephen Westfold. The ideas in this conclusion were stimulated by the chapters in this book; as well as sources in the literature, numerous conversations with other members of the KBSE community, and various research initiatives sponsored by the U.S. government. The views expressed in this conclusion are the sole responsibility of the author.

References

Abelson, H.; Eisenberg, M.; Halfant, M.; Katzenelson, J.; Sacks, E.; Sussman, G. J.; Wisdom, J.; and Yip, K. 1989. Intelligence in Scientific Computing. *Communications of the ACM* 32(5): 546–562.

Anderson, J. S., and Fickas, S. 1989. A Proposed Perspective Shift: Viewing Specification Design as a Planning Problem. Presented at the Fifth International Workshop on Software Specification and Design, Pittsburgh, May.

Arango, G. 1988. Domain Engineering for Software Reuse. Ph.D. thesis, Dept. of Information and Computer Science, Univ. of California at Irvine.

Barr, A. 1990. The Evolution of Expert Systems. *Heuristics* 3(2): 54–59.

Barstow, D. R.; Shrobe, H. E.; and Sandewall, E., eds. 1984. *Interactive Programming Environments.* New York: McGraw-Hill.

Bergland, G. D., and Gordon, R. D., eds. 1981. *Tutorial: Software Design Strategies.* Washington, D.C.: IEEE Computer Society.

Biggerstaff, T. J.; Hoskins, J.; and Webster, D. 1989. Design Recovery for Reuse and Maintenance, Technical Report STP-378-88, MCC Corp., Austin, Texas.

Boehm, B. W., and Scherlis, W. L. "Software Technology Strategic Planning Material," DARPA supplement to BAA 90-21, *Commerce Business Daily,* 26 September 1990, amended 3 October 1990.

Bordiga, A.; Greenspan, S.; and Mylopoulos, J. 1986. Knowledge Representation as the Basis for Requirements Specifications. In *Readings in Artificial Intelligence and Software Engineering,* eds. C. Rich and R. C. Waters, 561–569. San Mateo, Calif.: Morgan Kaufmann.

Brown, D. W.; Carson, C. D.; Montgomery, W. A.; and Zislis, P. M. 1988. Software Specification and Prototyping Technologies. *AT&T Technical Journal* 67(4): 46–58.

Burson, S.; Kotik, G. B.; and Markosian, L. Z. 1990. A Program Transformation Approach to Automating Software Reengineering. In Proceedings of the Fourteenth International Computer Software and Applications Conference, 314–322. Washington, D.C.: IEEE Computer Society.

Cleaveland, J. C., and Kintala, C. M. R. 1988. Tools for Building Application Generators. *AT&T Technical Journal* 67(4): 46–58.

Chikofsky, E. J. 1989. *Computer-Aided Software Engineering (CASE)*. Washington, D.C.: IEEE Computer Society.

Curtis, B.; Krasner, H.; and Iscoe, N. 1988. A Field Study of the Software Design Process for Large Systems. *Communications of the ACM* 31:1268–1287.

Dahl, O. J.; Dijkstra, E. W.; and Hoare, C. A. R. 1972. Structured Programming. In *A.P.I.C. Studies in Data Processing*, no. 8, eds. F. Duncan and M. J. R. Shave. London: Academic.

Despeyroux, J. 1986. Proof of Translation of Natural Semantics. In Proceedings of the Symposium on Logic in Computer Science. Washington, D.C.: IEEE Computer Society.

Fickas, S. 1985. Automating the Transformational Development of Software. *IEEE Transactions on Software Engineering* SE-11(11): 1268–1277.

Freeman, P., and Wasserman, A.I., eds. 1983. *Tutorial on Software Design Techniques*, 4th ed. Washington, D.C.: IEEE Computer Society.

Gane, C. 1990. *Computer-Aided Software Engineering: The Methodologies, the Products, and the Future*. Englewood Cliffs, N.J.: Prentice Hall.

Green, C; Luckham, D.; Balzer, R.; Cheatham, T.; and Rich, C. 1986. Report on a Knowledge-Based Software Assistant. In *Readings in Artificial Intelligence and Software Engineering*, eds. C. Rich and R. C. Waters, 377–428. San Mateo, Calif.: Morgan Kaufmann.

Hartman, J. 1989. Automatic Control Understanding for Natural Programs. Ph.D. thesis, Dept. of Computer Sciences, Univ. of Texas at Austin.

Hunt, W. A. 1989. Microprocessor Design Verification. *Journal of Automated Reasoning* 5(4): 429–460.

Jones, C. B. 1986. *Systematic Software Development Using VDM*. Englewood Cliffs, N.J.: Prentice Hall.

Lee, K. Proceedings of the Workshop on Domain-Specific Software Architectures. July 9-12 1990, Hidden Valley, Penn.

Letovsky, S. 1988. Plan Analysis of Programs. Ph.D. thesis, Computer Science Dept., Yale Univ.

Marcus, S., ed. 1989. *Machine Learning* (Special Issue on Knowledge Acquisition) 4(3–4).

Moore, J. S. 1989. A Mechanically Verified Language Implementation. *Journal of Automated Reasoning* 5(4): 461–492.

Mostow, J. 1989. Design by Derivational Analogy: Issues in the Automated Replay of Design Plans. *Artificial Intelligence* 40(1–3): 119–184.

Neches, R.; Swartout, W. R.; and Moore, J. D. 1985. Enhanced Maintenance and Explanation of Expert Systems through Explicit Models of Their Development. *IEEE Transactions on Software Engineering* SE-11(11): 1337–1351.

Rich, C., and Waters, R. 1990. *The Programmer's Apprentice*. New York: Association of Computing Machinery.

Roth, S. F.; Mattis, J. A.; and Mesnard, X. A. 1990. Graphics and Natural Language as Components of Automatic Explanation. In *Architectures for Intelligent Interfaces: Elements and Proto-*

types, eds. J. Sullivan and S. Tyler. Reading, Mass.: Addison-Wesley.

Reubenstein, H. B., and Waters, R. C. 1989. The Requirements Apprentice: An Initial Scenario. Presented at the Fifth International Workshop on Software Specification and Design, Pittsburgh, May.

Schindler, M. 1990. *Computer-Aided Software Design*. New York: Wiley.

Shavlik, J. 1990. Acquiring Recursive and Iterative Concepts with Explanation-Based Learning. *Machine Learning* 5(1): 39–70.

Shiel, B. 1986. Power Tools for Programmers. In *Readings in Artificial Intelligence and Software Engineering*, eds. C. Rich and R. C. Waters, 573–580. San Mateo, Calif.: Morgan Kaufmann.

Spivey, J. M. 1989. *The Z Notation: A Reference Manual*. New York: Prentice Hall.

Steier, D. M., and Anderson, A. P. 1989. *Algorithm Synthesis: A Comparative Study*. New York: Springer-Verlag.

Warren, D. H. D. 1977. Implementing Prolog—Compiling Predicate Logic Programs, volumes 1 and 2, D.A.I. Research Reports, 39 and 40, University of Edinburgh.

Westfold, S., and Green, C. 1991. A Theory of Automated Design of Visual Information Presentations. Technical Report KES.U.91.1, Kestrel Institute, Palo Alto, California.

Wills, L. M. 1989. Determining the Limits of Automated Program Recognition, Working Paper, 321, AI Lab., Massachusetts Institute of Technology.

Wing, J. M. 1990. A Specifier's Introduction to Formal Methods. *IEEE Computer* 23(9): 8–26.

Young, W. D. 1989. A Mechanically Verified Code Generator. *Journal of Automated Reasoning* 5(4): 493–518.

Index

Designed by The Live Oak Press

Composed in Times Roman
and output by G&S Typesetters,
Austin, Texas.

Printed by McNaughton-Gunn,
Saline, Michigan